■ THE RESOURCE FOR THE INDEPENDENT TRAVELER

"The guides are aimed not only at young budget travelers but at the indepedent traveler; a sort of streetwise cookbook for traveling alone."

—The New York Times

"Unbeatable; good sight-seeing advice; up-to-date info on restaurants, hotels, and inns; a commitment to money-saving travel; and a wry style that brightens nearly every page."

—The Washington Post

"Lighthearted and sophisticated, informative and fun to read. [Let's Go] helps the novice traveler navigate like a knowledgeable old hand."

—Atlanta Journal-Constitution

"A world-wise traveling companion—always ready with friendly advice and helpful hints, all sprinkled with a bit of wit."

—The Philadelphia Inquirer

■ THE BEST TRAVEL BARGAINS IN YOUR PRICE RANGE

"All the dirt, dirt cheap."

—People

"Anything you need to know about budget traveling is detailed in this book."

—The Chicago Sun-Times

"Let's Go follows the creed that you don't have to toss your life's savings to the wind to travel—unless you want to."

—The Salt Lake Tribune

■ REAL ADVICE FOR REAL EXPERIENCES

"The writers seem to have experienced every rooster-packed bus and lunar-surfaced mattress about which they write."

—The New York Times

"A guide should tell you what to expect from a destination. Here Let's Go shines."

—The Chicago Tribune

"Let's Go's] devoted updaters really walk the walk (and thumb the ride, and trek the trail). Learn how to fish, haggle, find work—anywhere."

—Food & Wine

LET'S GO PUBLICATIONS

TRAVEL GUIDES

Alaska 1st edition **NEW TITLE**
Australia 2004
Austria & Switzerland 2004
Brazil 1st edition **NEW TITLE**
Britain & Ireland 2004
California 2004
Central America 8th edition
Chile 1st edition
China 4th edition
Costa Rica 1st edition
Eastern Europe 2004
Egypt 2nd edition
Europe 2004
France 2004
Germany 2004
Greece 2004
Hawaii 2004
India & Nepal 8th edition
Ireland 2004
Israel 4th edition
Italy 2004
Japan 1st edition **NEW TITLE**
Mexico 20th edition
Middle East 4th edition
New Zealand 6th edition
Pacific Northwest 1st edition **NEW TITLE**
Peru, Ecuador & Bolivia 3rd edition
Puerto Rico 1st edition **NEW TITLE**
South Africa 5th edition
Southeast Asia 8th edition
Southwest USA 3rd edition
Spain & Portugal 2004
Thailand 1st edition
Turkey 5th edition
USA 2004
Western Europe 2004

CITY GUIDES

Amsterdam 3rd edition
Barcelona 3rd edition
Boston 4th edition
London 2004
New York City 2004
Paris 2004
Rome 12th edition
San Francisco 4th edition
Washington, D.C. 13th edition

MAP GUIDES

Amsterdam
Berlin
Boston
Chicago
Dublin
Florence
Hong Kong
London
Los Angeles
Madrid
New Orleans
New York City
Paris
Prague
Rome
San Francisco
Seattle
Sydney
Venice
Washington, D.C.

COMING SOON:
Road Trip USA

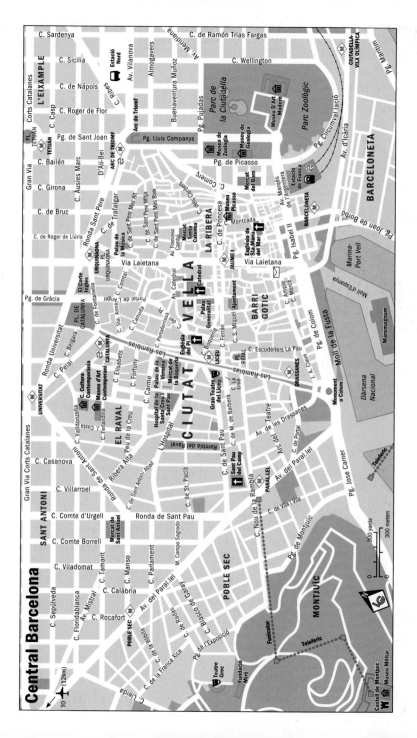

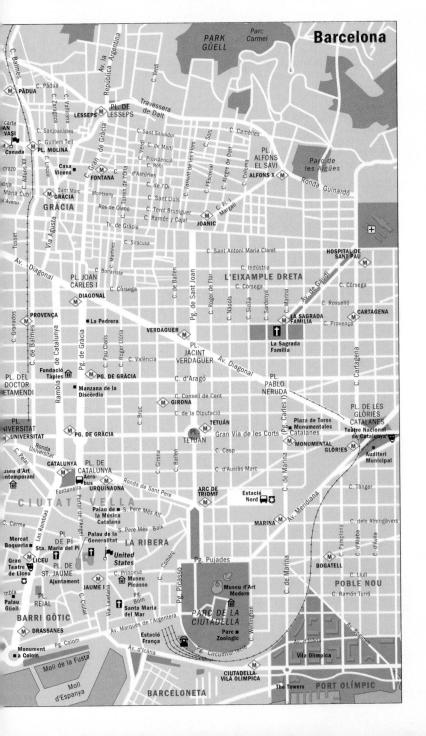

Barcelona Metro

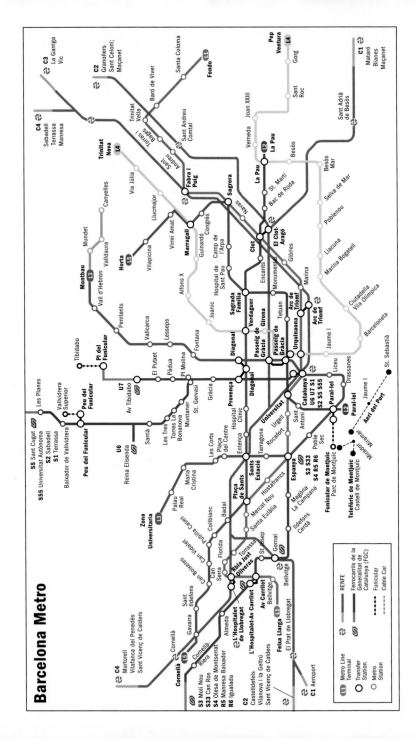

LET'S GO

BARCELONA

STEF LEVNER EDITOR
MEGAN MORAN-GATES ASSOCIATE EDITOR

RESEARCHER-WRITERS
SCOTT MICHAEL COULTER
EMILIE FAURE
MANUELA S. ZONINSEIN

TIM SZETELA MAP EDITOR
SARAH ROBINSON MANAGING EDITOR

ST. MARTIN'S PRESS ✖ NEW YORK

HELPING LET'S GO If you want to share your discoveries, suggestions, or corrections, please drop us a line. We read every piece of correspondence, whether a postcard, a 10-page email, or a coconut. **Address mail to:**

Let's Go: Barcelona
67 Mount Auburn Street
Cambridge, MA 02138
USA

Visit Let's Go at **http://www.letsgo.com,** or send email to:

feedback@letsgo.com
Subject: "Let's Go: Barcelona"

In addition to the invaluable travel advice our readers share with us, many are kind enough to offer their services as researchers or editors. Unfortunately, our charter enables us to employ only currently enrolled Harvard students.

Maps by David Lindroth copyright © 2004 by St. Martin's Press.

Distributed outside the USA and Canada by Macmillan.

① ② ③ ④ ⑤

PRICE RANGES >> BARCELONA

Our researchers list establishments in order of value starting with the best; our favorites are denoted by the Let's Go ✊thumbs-up. Since the best value is not always the cheapest price, we have incorporated a system of price ranges for quick reference. Our ranges are based on a rough expectation of what you will spend. For **accommodations,** we base our price ranges on the cheapest price for a single traveler for one night. For **restaurants** and other dining establishments, we estimate the average amount that you will spend. The table below gives an idea of what one will typically find in Barcelona in the corresponding price range. Numbers are assigned based on actual cost, not value or prices relative to those of similar establishments. Thus, a very expensive ice cream stand will probably still only be marked a ❶.

ACCOMMODATIONS	RANGE	WHAT YOU'RE *LIKELY* TO FIND
❶	€15 and under	Mostly dorm rooms at HI and other hostels. Expect bunk beds and communal bath; you may have to provide or rent towels and sheets. On daytrips, camping is an option.
❷	€16-25	Upper-end hostels, *pensiones,* or small hotels, usually family-run. You may have a small private bath or a sink in your room and a shower in the hall.
❸	€26-40	A small room with a private bath. Should have decent amenities, such as phone, fan, and TV. Breakfast may be included in the price of the room.
❹	€41-50	Similar to ❸, but may have more amenities such as the coveted A/C, or be in a more touristed area.
❺	€51 and up	Large private hotels or upscale chains. If it's a ❺ and it doesn't have the perks you want, you've paid too much.
FOOD	**RANGE**	**WHAT YOU'RE *LIKELY* TO FIND**
❶	€5 and under	Mostly street-corner stands, falafel and pizza places, or fast-food joints. Rarely ever a sit-down meal.
❷	€6-10	*Bocadillos* (sandwiches), tapas, pub food, or low-priced entrees. Three-course lunch menús.
❸	€11-15	Mid-priced entrees, possibly coming with a soup or salad. Three-course dinner menús.
❹	€16-20	A somewhat fancy restaurant; you'll have a special knife. Few restaurants in this range have a dress code, but you may feel underdressed in a t-shirt and jeans.
❺	€21 and up	Undoubtedly a classy joint; you'll probably have more types of forks than you knew existed. Be prepared for painful rejection if you wear your sightseeing gear.

CONTENTS

▪ discover barcelona 1

▪ once in barcelona 21

▪ life & times 37

▣ sights & museums 51

▪ food & drink 113

▪ nightlife 141

♫ entertainment 161

▪ shopping 175

bold denotes a map

♞ accommodations 185

♺ daytripping 203

✈ planning your trip 273

⛷ alternatives to tourism 297

☛ service directory 309

↘ appendix 314

⓲ index 317

☙ map appendix 329

HOW TO USE THIS BOOK

PRICE RANGES AND RANKINGS. Our researchers list establishments in order of value, starting with the best. Our absolute favorites are denoted by the Let's Go thumbs-up. Since the best value does not always mean the cheapest price, we have incorporated a system of price ranges into the guide. The table below lists how prices fall within each bracket.

	❶	❷	❸	❹	❺
ACCOMM.	€15 and under	€16-25	€26-40	€41-50	€51 and up
FOOD	€5 and under	€6-10	€11-15	€16-20	€21 and up

WHEN TO USE IT

TWO MONTHS BEFORE. Our book is filled with practical information to help you before you go. **Planning Your Trip** (p. 273) has advice about passports, plane tickets, insurance, and more. The **Accommodations** chapter (p. 186) can help you with booking a room from home.

ONE MONTH BEFORE. Take care of travel insurance and write down a list of emergency numbers and hotlines to take with you. Make a list of packing essentials and shop for anything you're missing. Make any necessary reservations.

TWO WEEKS BEFORE. Start thinking about your ideal trip. **Discover Barcelona** (see p. 2) lists the city's top 20 sights and also includes suggested itineraries, our new **walking tours** (complete with maps), Let's Go Picks (the best and quirkiest that Barcelona has to offer), and the scoop on each of the city's neighborhoods, including what areas to avoid and what you absolutely should not miss.

ON THE ROAD. Once in Barcelona (see p. 21) will be your best friend after arrival, with all the practical information you'll need, plus tips on acting like a true Barcelonese. This year, *Let's Go: Barcelona* contains features such as in depth coverage of **cuisine** and **festivals,** as well as the scoop on **news** in Barcelona today. When you reach the city, you'll spend most of your time flipping through the following chapters: **Sights & Museums, Food & Drink, Nightlife, Entertainment,** and **Shopping.** When you feel like striking out, the **Daytripping** chapter will help: it provides a list of options for one-day and weekend trips away from Barcelona into the historic or beachy towns of surrounding Catalunya, or the party-hardy Islas Baleares. The **Service Directory** contains a list of local services like laundromats, Internet acess, tourist offices, and emergency numbers. The **Appendix** lists useful Catalan and Spanish phrases to help you navigate almost every situation. The **Map** appendix has area maps of the major neighborhoods in the city, each with plottings of all accommodation, food, and nightlife listings. Finally, remember to put down this guide once in a while and go exploring on your own; you'll be glad you did.

A NOTE TO OUR READERS The information for this book was gathered by *Let's Go* researchers from May through August of 2003. Each listing is based on one researcher's opinion, formed during his or her visit at a particular time. Those traveling at other times may have different experiences since prices, dates, hours, and conditions are always subject to change. You are urged to check the facts presented in this book beforehand to avoid inconvenience and surprises.

RESEARCHER-WRITERS

Scott Michael Coulter   *Las Ramblas & Barri Gòtic, Barceloneta & Port Vell, Costa Dorada, and Inland*

Out of the South and into a Catalan heat wave, this Tennessee native took the city into his own hands, one air-conditioned restaurant at a time. With impeccable maps and hilarious features, Scott proved you can be jail bait *and* know how to write. He developed a love for Spanish fashion, including mullets, and was last seen (surprise, surprise) still in Barcelona.

Emilie Faure   *El Raval, Montjuïc, and Zona Alta*

Raised in France, Emilie went pack for pack and cup for cup with every Barcelonese she encountered. After studying sculpture as an undergraduate, she was equipped to take the Barcelona art scene by storm. Always up to speed on the hottest clubs and best festivals, Emilie and her European *chic* were right at home in the city. She is currently working at a gallery in New York City.

Manuela S. Zoninsein   *La Ribera, l'Eixample, Poble Nou & Port Olímpic, and Costa Brava*

No beach is a match for this Brazilian beauty. A native of Chicago, Manuela stormed the Spanish coast, leaving pristine copy and plenty of broken hearts in her wake. Truly multi-talented, she scoured the city for the best shopping deals and still had time for *fútbol*. Barcelona gave Manuela an addiction to caffeine as well as to travel. She is now studying in Chile.

CONTRIBUTING WRITERS

Thomas N. Bisson is the Lea Professor of Medieval History at Harvard University.

Sarah Jacoby was a *Let's Go* managing editor, a researcher-writer for *Spain and Portugal 1999* and *India & Nepal 2001*, and an associate editor for *Europe 2000*. While living in Barcelona she worked for an Internet consulting company.

Sarah Thomas, Researcher-writer, *Let's Go: Spain & Portugal 2004*, Islas Baleares coverage.

ACKNOWLEDGMENTS

LET'S GO

STEF: To my three researchers, Emilie, Manuela, and Scott: in addition to writing stellar copy, you never once called me from jail. You guys were beyond amazing. Thanks to Scrobins—2-in-1 City Guide/Managing editor—for your excessive patience and even more excessive efficiency; this would not be a book without you. Megan, thank you for churning out paper edits at lightning speed and for the excellent Alts to T chapter. Tim, you are the best mapper with the best taste in music. To the "No Decorations" pod: Magic Wand Crawford, for the helmet and gum (eh?). Magic Stick Mahan, for the sweatshirt and file-cabinet bruises. Sodroski, for being the most politically correct person I know. Miranda, for the rap. Abigail, for putting up with all of it. SPAM, thanks for *las islas*. Prod, I promise, I have no more questions. A shout-out to the Henley crew for the best vacation someone else's money can buy. ATD and MRS, thanks for taking me with a grain of salt. Leigh, I love you like a fat kid love cake. And of course, Mom, Dad, Jack: "thanks" is not enough.

MEGAN: Stef, thanks for making it all come together and never forgetting to have fun along the way. Scrobins, thanks for the unrelenting support, cookies, and laughs. To the rest of the pod: the absurd discussions, constant distractions, and tomfoolery were much appreciated. Special thanks to Chez Renard for good times and a rent-free summer. As always, Mom, Dad, Taylor, Adri, and Rob: thanks for your love and friendship.

TIM: Stef, thanks for the quick corrects and icon praise. To Emilie, Manuela, and Scott, thanks for the great reference maps and the four-way phone call. Maó thanks for SPAM. Thanks of course to Mapland (and Petey) for the support. And thanks always to April, Tony, Rachel, Mom, and Dad.

Editor
Stef Levner
Associate Editor
Megan Moran-Gates
Managing Editor
Sarah Robinson
Map Editor
Tim Szetela
Typesetter
Thomas Bechtold
Phototgrapher
Vanessa Bertozzi

Publishing Director
Julie A. Stephens
Editor-in-Chief
Jeffrey Dubner
Production Manager
Dusty Lewis
Cartography Manager
Nathaniel Brooks
Design Manager
Caleb Beyers
Editorial Managers
Lauren Bonner, Ariel Fox,
Matthew K. Hudson, Emma Nothmann,
Joanna Shawn Brigid O'Leary,
Sarah Robinson
Financial Manager
Suzanne Siu
Marketing & Publicity Managers
Megan Brumagim, Nitin Shah
Personnel Manager
Jesse Reid Andrews
Researcher Manager
Jennifer O'Brien
Web Manager
Jesse Tov
Web Content Director
Abigail Burger
Production Associates
Thomas Bechtold, Jeffrey Hoffman Yip
IT Directors
Travis Good, E. Peyton Sherwood
Financial Assistant
R. Kirkie Maswoswe
Associate Web Manager
Robert Dubbin
Office Coordinators
Abigail Burger, Angelina L. Fryer,
Liz Glynn

Director of Advertising Sales
Daniel Ramsey
Senior Advertising Associates
Sara Barnett, Daniella Boston
Advertising Artwork Editor
Julia Davidson

President
Abhishek Gupta
General Manager
Robert B. Rombauer
Assistant General Manager
Anne E. Chisholm

Discover Barcelona

Barcelona loves to indulge in the fantastic. From the urban carnival that is Las Ramblas to buildings with no straight lines, the city pushes the limits of style in everything it does, and gets away with it. As the center of the whimsical and daring *Modernisme* architectural movement, Barcelona holds fairy-tale creations that are like no others in the world; as home to three of the most well-known Surrealist painters, Salvador Dalí, Pablo Picasso, and Joan Miró, even the most famous art of Barcelona is grounded in a reality alternative to the one that the rest of us know.

The time is now for Barcelona. In the quarter-century since the end of Franco's oppressive regime, Spain has blossomed, with Barcelona at the forefront. It has led the autonomous region of Catalunya in an esoteric and unique resurgence of culture. The city's major makeover of the late 1980s and early 1990s, intended as preparation for the 1992 Olympics, was so successful that the Barcelonese have continued to reinvent their home. The result is a vanguard city squeezed between the mesmerizing blue waters of the Mediterranean and the green Tibidabo hills, flashing with such vibrant colors and intense energy that you'll see Barcelona long after you have closed your eyes.

Take a short siesta, and then stay up as late as you can; you will need every hour available to fully explore this city. Barcelona is a gateway, not only to Catalunya but also to Spain, to the Mediterranean, and to the Pyrenees. Pack your swimsuit and your skis, your art history book and your clubbing shoes, and don't worry if you don't speak Spanish: neither does Barcelona.

BARCELONA BY NUMBER

City population: 1.5 million.

Metropolitan area population: 4.2 million.

White geese in residence: 13 (visit the Cathedral; see p. 57).

White gorillas in residence: 1 (see p. 74).

Average annual rainfall: 23.2 in. (590mm).

Pork consumed per resident annually: 55.78kg.

Percentage of population that chain-smokes: 25%.

Percentage of population that is Roman Catholic: 90%.

Length of longest sausage in Catalunya: 5,200m. (World Record).

Years since the beginning of La Sagrada Família construction: 118.

Density of mimes on Las Ramblas: 4 every 1m.

Density of prostitutes on Las Ramblas: 1 every 4m.

Number of words the English language has drawn from Catalan: 1 (it's yacht).

Number of military strongholds turned into parks: 2.

Number of bars with ancient Roman walls running through them: 7.

Number of absinthes required to knock you out: 3 (at most).

TOP 20 SIGHTS

If you want to catch as many of these sights as possible in one shot, try our **walking tours.**

20. Poble Espanyol, a recreation of all of Spain's greatest hotspots. Hey, if you can't hit the real thing, go for the tacky imitation (see p. 99).

19. Fonts Luminoses, a nighttime show of lights, music, water, and magic (see p. 98).

18. The Aquarium, the largest in Europe, complete with an underwater tunnel that puts visitors face-to-face with the sharks (see p. 94).

17. The Sardana, the traditional Catalan dance, performed in front of the Cathedral on Sunday mornings (see p. 72).

16. Palau Güell, the architectural masterpiece that catapulted Gaudí into the spotlight (see **p. 77**).

15. Museu d'Art Modern, showcasing the best and the brightest of Catalunya's painters from the past century (see p. 73).

14. Museu Nacional d'Art de Catalunya (Palau Nacional), for an almost spiritual tour through medieval masterpieces (see p. 96).

13. The Mediterranean, a fool-proof pleaser. Enjoy swimming, fishing, boating, jet skiing, diving, and, of course, nude tanning (see p. 161).

12. Floquet de Neu, the world's only white gorilla. And isn't he dashing! (see p. 74).

11. El Barça, Barcelona's world-class soccer team, the stars of some killer matches (see p. 166).

10. The Cathedral, the religious center of Barcelona. A cloister, geese, Roman ruins, and mimes out front add to your average Gothic cathedral-going experience (see p. 57).

9. Passeig de Gràcia, the Fifth Avenue of Barcelona: home to Modernist landmarks and designer-store labels (see p. 177).

8. Museu Picasso, one of the best collections of Picasso's works anywhere, from his earliest painting to his late engravings (see p. 68).

7. La Manzana de la Discòrdia, the city block with a Modernist identity crisis, where Modernisme's three most famous sons—Puig i Cadafalch, Domènech i Montaner, and Antoni Gaudí—duke it out to be the tourists' favorite (see p. 86).

6. Fundació Miró, Miró's artistic legacy to his homeland, showcasing his own work and that of up-and-coming Catalan artists (see p. 95).

5. Palau de la Música Catalana, Domènech i Montaner's amazing Modernist architectural tribute to music (see p. 69).

4. Casa Milà (La Pedrera), Gaudí's finished masterpiece and the best look inside his work and his head (see p. 84).

3. Park Güell, Gaudí's unfinished housing project, now the wackiest park in the world. Hikes lead to spectacular views: buns of steel not included (see p. 100).

2. Las Ramblas, the central and most colorful street in Barcelona's oldest district, complete with mimes, flowers, and baby tutles (see p. 52).

1. La Sagrada Família, Gaudí's unfinished masterpiece, and his tomb (see p. 79).

SUGGESTED ITINERARIES

THREE DAYS

DAY 1: MODERNISME 101

Head out to the **La Sagrada Família** (see p. 79) early in the morning to avoid fighting the crowds; grab some *churros y chocolate* at one of the nearby cafes. From there, make your way to the Pl. de Catalunya (M: Catalunya, L1/3) and take the half-day walking tour through **l'Eixample** (which you have now started in reverse; see p. 10), Barcelona's gridded upper neighborhood that is jam-packed with Modernist sights, including **Casa Milà** (see p. 84) and **La Manzana de la Discòrdia** (see p. 86), where you can pick up the Ruta del Modernisme pass that offers discounts on sights all over the city. After pondering the chimneys of Casa Milà, catch the #24 bus from the Pg. de Gràcia up to your last Modernist stop of the day: **Park Güell** in Gràcia (see p. 100). Wander through the colonnades, park it on the longest and most crooked bench in the world, and snap a photo with the drooling lizard. At the end of the day (and the beginning of a long night), head down to one of l'Eixample's many trendy bars and clubs (see p. 148).

DAY 2: OLD TOWN SUPER-TOURIST

Start out at the Pl. de Catalunya (M: Catalunya, L1/3), and head towards the water on **Las Ramblas** (see p. 52) to see the traditional **Boqueria** market, where you can buy pastries or fruit for breakfast (see p. 54). Check out

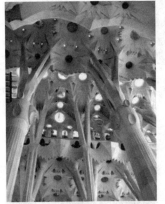
Inside La Sagrada Família

Balcony at Park Güell

Girl with a Birdcage on Las Ramblas

LET'S GO PICKS 📝

🖊 Best place to bond with 120,000 people: **Camp Nou** stadium while **El Barça** plays *fútbol* (p. 166).

🖊 Best place to see the city from above: **La Sagrada Família** (see p. 79).

🖊 Best (and only) white albino gorilla in the whole wide world: **Floquet de Neu** (see p. 74).

🖊 Best place to get an emu (by day) or date (by night): **Las Ramblas** (see **p. 52**).

🖊 Most obscene photo op: the giant phallus in front of the **Museu de l'Eròtica** (see p. 55).

🖊 Best place to take your lover: **Mirador de Vila Paula** (see p. 110).

🖊 Best time of year to hook up with a DJ: June and July when **Sónar** (see p. 105) and the **Festa de la Música** (see p. 74) take the city by storm.

🖊 Best place to see the sun set: **Palau Nacional** (see **p. 96**) in Montjuïc.

🖊 Best bar in which to to hallucinate: **Casa Almirall**, where they'll walk you through your first absinthe.

🖊 Best place to see eggs: it's a tie! The **dancing eggs** during the Corpus Cristi Festival (see p. 18) are pretty cool, but so are the gorgeous egg-shaped details on top of the **Dalí Museum** (see p. 208).

the various offerings of the different sections of Las Ramblas (who on earth buys those baby emus they sell there?), then head into the **Barri Gòtic** via C. Portaferrissa, which will turn into C. dels Boters and ends at the **Cathedral** (see p. 57). Hang out with the resident geese and peruse the Roman walls. Then get your Ruta de Modernisme pass ready for your next stop just off the Via Laietana, the **Palau de la Música Catalana** in La Ribera (see p. 69). Make your way through La Ribera's twisting alleys to the **Museu Picasso** (see p. 68). Check out the galleries in the labyrinth of streets (see p. 76) and stay in the area for tapas (see p. 122). Finish up the night by heading back into the Barri Gòtic for the clubs and bars around the **Plaça Reial** (see p. 116).

DAY 3: ATHLETIC ART

Take a quick ride up to **Montjuïc** from the waterfront on the **Transbordador Aeri cable car** (see p. 93), then head over to the **Fundació Miró** to explore your inner child (see p. 95). Bring a swimsuit and take a dive in the **Olympic pool** (see p. 164). Wander around the other Olympic edifices and then satiate your desire to visit the rest of Spain in the artificial and nostalgic **Poble Espanyol** (see p. 99). Grab lunch here before you trek onwards to the **Museu Nacional d'Art de Catalunya** (see p. 96). On your way out of the museum, try to catch one of the shows of the **Fonts Luminoses** (see p. 98). If you still have energy to party, you can to head back to Poble Espanyol, which transforms from tacky to trendy after dark (see p. 99).

FIVE DAYS

If three days just aren't enough, have another cup of *café* and keep up the pace for another 72 hours.

DAY 4: THE WATERFRONT

Start out your day in the **Parc de la Ciutadella** with a visit to the Barcelona **zoo** and its lovable mascot, **Floquet de Neu** (Snowflake), the world's only albino gorilla (see **p. 74**). If you can tear yourself away from Floquet, stop by the **Museu d'Art Modern** (see p. 73), which houses a good collection of works by Catalan artists. Get lunch at the cafe in the Modernist **Hivernacle** (see **p. 73**) before heading out of the park and down to the **Moll d'Espanya** to Barcelona's **aquarium,** the biggest (and some say best) in Europe (see p. 94). If all this family fun is

4

too much for you, swing up **Las Ramblas** to the nearby, ever-raunchy **Museu de l'Eròtica** (see p. 55). The S&M display will clearly whet your appetite; good thing **Les Quinze Nit's** tasty and affordable paella is around the corner in the **Plaça Reial** (see p. 116). After dinner, bide your time until 3am and then head to the Port Vell and writhe in the cheesy clubs of **Maremàgnum** (see p. 154).

DAY 5: DALÍLAND

Get up early: you've got a train to catch, to nearby **Figueres** (see p. 204). Spend the morning at the surreal **Teatre-Museu Dalí,** the second-most popular museum in Spain, where you can stand on Dalí's tomb (see p. 208), listen to rain inside a Cadillac, or watch a room turn into Mae West. You can make it back to Barcelona before sundown and take a rest, since you haven't lived like a true Spaniard until you've had a *siesta*. Then lose yourself in **Poble Nou's** alternative music and bar scene (see p. 152).

SEVEN DAYS

Still want more? We don't blame you.

DAY 6: EL BARÇA & EL RAVAL

By now you've had plenty of time to get tickets to a **soccer game** (see p. 164), featuring the city's beloved team, **El Barça.** Before you head over to Camp Nou, do some thrift-shopping in El Raval's **Mercat Alternatiu** (see p. 180) and stop by Gaudí's spooky **Palau Güell** (see p. 77). Grab lunch in blue-collar El Raval (see p. 123), then pre-game at the **Museu FCB** (see p. 106), any *fútbol*-lover's heaven. Follow the crowds to the game at **Camp Nou** (see p. 166), and then follow them to the nightlife on the way out.

DAY 7: DAYTRIPPING

What you'll want to do on your last day depends on the weather. If you're traveling in the summer, a daytrip to beachy **Sitges** (see p. 233), with its own wild (and gay-friendly) nightlife, is the way to go. If it's too cold for the beach, the nearby mountains and monastery at **Montserrat** (see p. 242) are one of the wonders of Catalunya. If you're looking for some authentic nightlife for your last night in Barcelona, go to where the locals party; the clubs and pubs around C. Marià Cubí in the **Zona Alta** (see p. 156).

Plaça Espanya at Night

Fundació Miró

View of Sagrada Família from Roof of Casa Milà

Suggested Time: 5hr.

Distance: 3.2km (2 mi.)

When to go: A weekday morning.

Start: M: Liceu, L3.

End: M: Drassanes, L3.

No visit to Barcelona is complete (or even possible) without traversing the famous Las Ramblas. Translated as "The Promenades," Las Ramblas is a series of five individual walkways strung together. Although they are generally referred to as one collective rambla, each has its own distinct character and plenty of built-in entertainment.

1 GRAN TEATRE DEL LICEU. Get off the Metro at Liceu, you can't miss it. Start your morning with the 10am guided tour of Barcelona's premier stage, and bask in the history of one of Europe's greatest opera houses (tours M-F; see p. 55)

2 LA BOQUERIA. Check out the famous market housed in an all-steel Modernist structure. Choose a late-morning snack from this wondrous bounty of fresh food (see p. 54).

3 PALAU DE LA VIRREINA. Wander in the courtyard of this 18th-century Rococo palace and see if any exhibitions are going on. If not, visit the building's Cultural Events Office or admire the upscale souvenirs in the giftshop (see p. 54).

4 PLAÇA CATALUNYA. Now you've come to the city's main hub. Every tourist wanders through at least once; can you tell by the crowds? The busy *plaça* makes a great place to people-watch or just relax. Check out the enormous El Corte Inlgés and do some serious shopping (see p. 181). It is also where the old city meets the new; turn south to catch the rest of this walking tour, but if you continue farther north you begin the l'Eixample walking tour (see p. 10).

5 MUSEU DE L'ERÒTICA. Swing back around the *plaça* and head back down the left side of Las Ramblas. If you dare, check out Spain's only erotica museum. (see p. 55).

6 CAFÉ DE L'OPERA. Enjoy a cup of coffee at the famous cafe (see p. 116). But don't expect to order to go; Europeans like to enjoy their coffee by sipping it leisurely. If you're having trouble ordering a plain cup 'o Joe, see **Can I Get Coffee With That?** (p. 136).

7 MUSEU DE CERA. Peruse over 300 different wax recreations of famous politicians, celebrities, fictional characters, and European royalty. While many of the figures are difficult to recognize, the scenes of death in the horror room are straightforward enough to appreciate (see p. 56).

8 MONUMENT A COLOM. End your tour with a visit to the 60m statue of the man Spanish cities love to claim as their own, Christopher Columbus. Sevilla purports that he is buried in their city (he's not). Barcelona claims that he was born in Catalunya (he wasn't). Christopher Columbus may have been elusive in birth and death, but at least Barcelona has captured the prophet in a moment of inspiration, pointing valiantly, heroically, epically...the wrong way. You can take an elevator to the top of the statue for a stunning view of the city (see p. 56).

NEIGHBORHOODS

CIUTAT VELLA

BARRI GÒTIC AND LAS RAMBLAS

▼ Orientation: *Between Las Ramblas in the west and Via Laietana in the east. The ocean borders the neighborhood to the south and C. Fontanella borders it to the north.* **Sights & Museums:** *see p. 52 and p. 57.* **Food & Drink:** *see p. 116.* **Nightlife:** *see p. 141.* **Accommodations:** *see p. 186.* **Public Transportation:** *M: Catalunya, L1/3; Liceu, L3; Drassanes, L3; and Jaume I, L4. Because of the narrow streets, no buses run through the Barri Gòtic, only on the bordering streets. Buses #14, 38, 59, and 91 traverse Las Ramblas, while buses #17, 19, 40 and 45 drive down Via Laietana.*

see map pp. 334-335

As the oldest sections of Barcelona, the Barri Gòtic and Las Ramblas are the tourist centers of the city. Originally settled by the Romans in the 3rd century BC, the Barri Gòtic is built on top of the original Roman city, Barcino. Subsequent layers of medieval Catholic rule cover Barcino in a maze of narrow, cobbled streets dense with historic and artistic landmarks. The modern tourist industry has added shops, hostels, and bars to the churches and other monuments left over from the Middle Ages. Take a stroll down **C. Avinyò** and you'll see some of Barcelona's most treasured architectural landmarks, just meters away from the area's most popular bars and restaurants. Whether you are drawn in by the new or the old, there is something for everyone in this labyrinth.

DON'T MISS...

Sights & Museums: Relax in the tranquil cloister of **La Catedral de la Santa Creu** (see p. 57).

Food & Drink: Feast on grilled specialties while taking in the live music at **Mi Burrito y Yo** (see p. 117).

Nightlife: The bars in the **Plaça Reial** (see p. 141) are always packed early in the night.

LA RIBERA

▼ Orientation: *La Ribera is separated from the Barri Gòtic by Via Laietana and is bordered on the east by C. Wellington, past the Parc de la Ciutadella. Often lumped together with its northwestern neighbor, Sant Pere, the district extends to Ronda de Sant Pere and southeast to Av. Marqués de l'Argentera and the Estació de França.* **Sights & Museums:** *see p. 68.* **Food & Drink:** *see p. 120.* **Nightlife:** *see p. 144.* **Accommodations:** *see p. 192.* **Public Transportation:** *The most convenient Metro stops are M: Urquinaona, L1/4 and Jaume I, L4. La Ribera is a 15min. walk from Pl. de Catalunya. Buses #17 and 19 drive down Via Laietana.*

see map p. 337

As the stomping ground of Barcelona's many fishermen and merchants, La Ribera has always had a working-class feel. However, its confines were witness to two of the most major events to shape Barcelona's history. In the 18th century, Felipe V demolished much of La Ribera, then the city's commercial hub, to make space for the impressive Ciutadella, the seat of Madrid's oppressive control, and now a park. Angry that Barcelona had sought his opponent, the Archduke Carlos, as its leader, Felipe V stuffed the wealthy, and therefore powerful, citizens of Barcelona into the Ciutadella's chambers. Luckily, his successors were more lenient on their subjects, most victims were freed, and La Ribera was subsequently rejuvenated. Then, when in 1888 the former site of Ciutadella became home to the Universal Exposition, La Ribera served as its launching point, displaying the new flare of Modernisme and the simplicity of old Spanish architecture and values. In recent years, the neighborhood has evolved into Barcelona's bohemian nucleus, attracting a young, artsy crowd of locals and a few expats and tourists in the know.

This walking tour is a trip through both La Ribera, one of the oldest sections of the city, and the Parc de la Ciutadella. Begin your day early with a light breakfast at a restaurant near your room, and stop by your local grocery store for picnic fixings. Take the Metro to Arc de Triomf and get ready to roll.

Time: 5hr.

Distance: 2½km (1½ mi.)

When to go: A weekday without rain

Start: M: Arc de Triomf, L1

End: M: Jaume I, L4

1 ARC DE TRIOMF. This Modernist work was created by Josep Vilaseca to welcome visitors to the 1888 Exposition (see p. 93).

2 MUSEU DE ZOOLOGIA. Follow Pg. Lluís Companys toward Parc de la Ciutadella (four blocks south), one of Barcelona's most beautiful public spaces, great for families with young children and couples on a romantic outing. Domènech i Montaner's Museu de Zoologia (see p. 74) is credited with being one of the first creations that spawned Barcelona's famous architectural movement, Modernisme (see p. 48).

3 CASCADE FOUNTAINS. Across the park from the Museu de Zoologia are the magical Cascade Fountains (see p. 75). Unpack your lunch and relax by the water as children chase pigeons and orange trees sway in the wind. If all the splashing has gotten you in the mood for water sports, rent a boat at the nearby pond.

4 MUSEU D'ART MODERN. Continuing south in the park, follow signs for the Museu D'Art Modern (p. 73). Gaze at one of the finest collections of Noucentiste sculpture in the world, or study some of Dalí's paintings (the only works of his still left in Barcelona).

5 PARC ZOOLÒGIC. You may be thinking to yourself, "I can go to a zoo anywhere. Why should I waste precious time in Barcelona at this one?" There is one simple answer for you: Floquet de Nou, the world's only white gorilla and Barcelona's favorite celebrity (see p. 74).

6 ESGLÉSIA SANTA MARIA DEL MAR. Come see the widest Medieval nave in the world at "Mary of the Sea," a church built in the 14th century to serve the sailors of La Ribera. Another architectural feat of note: if the roof were 2ft. higher it would collapse from structural instability (see p. 70).

DON'T MISS...

Sights & Museums: With a great multimedia English tour explaining its every nuance, the **Palau de la Música Catalana** (see p. 69) will leave even the most jaded tourist in awe of the excessive beauty of Modernisme. The **Picasso Museum** (see p. 68) has a collection of the early and late works by the father of modern art.

Food & Drink: Enjoy tapas and a glass of cava at **Xampanyet** (see p. 122), the most renowned tapas bar in a veritable sea of great tapas bars.

Nightlife: Passieg del Born has some of the hippest, most diverse bars in Barcelona, and a picturesque backdrop for some serious barhopping (see p. 144).

Courtyard in the Barri Gòtic

EL RAVAL

see map p. 336

◪ Orientation: *El Raval is the neighborhood to the west of Las Ramblas. It is bordered on its far sides by Av. Parallel and the Rondas St. Pau, St. Antoni, and Universitat. C. Hospital is the main street that divides the neighborhood into two halves: the quainter northern area and the more run-down southern side.* **Sights & Museums:** *see* **p. 77**. **Food & Drink:** *see p. 123*. **Nightlife:** *see p. 146*. **Public Transportation:** *Metro and bus lines hug the perimeter of El Raval but do not go into the interior of the neighborhood. Metro: M: Liceu, L3; Drassanes, L3; Universitat, L2/3/4; Sant Antoni, L2. Buses: #14, 38, 59, and 91 traverse Las Ramblas.*

Located next to (but so different from) Las Ramblas and the Barri Gòtic, El Raval tends to be a favorite of Barcelona's natives rather than its tourists. This ethnically diverse and culturally rich working-class neighborhood has a special charm, with small, quirky shops and eateries, welcoming bars, and hidden historical attractions. Beginning as a small rural area outside of the city walls, El Raval was enveloped by the new city boundaries in the 14th century and has been squeezing people in ever since. The situation became critical in the late 19th and early 20th centuries, when over-crowding led to an urban nightmare of rampant crime, prostitution, and drug use (see **Big Trouble in Little China**, p. 31). Revitalization efforts, especially since the '92 Olympic games, have worked wonders, however; new museums and cultural centers have paved the way for trendy restaurants and bars, and today El Raval is emerging as one of Barcelona's most dynamic areas.

Entry of the Liceu Opera House

Bull

This tour traverses l'Eixample, the most fashionable neighborhood in Barcelona. The walk will pass upscale shops and the major sights of Modernisme, the intensely visual architectural movement that swept through Barcelona in the late 19th century.

1 PLAÇA DE CATALUNYA. Start at Pl. de Catalunya, the hub of the city. Stop by **El Corte Inglés** (see p. 181) for a free map.

Suggested Time: 5hr.

Distance: 3.2km (2 mi.); about 20 blocks.

When to go: A weekday afternoon, on a clear day.

Start: M: Catalunya, L1/3

End: M: Sagrada Família, L2/5.

2 PASSEIG DE GRÀCIA. Exit El Corte Inglés onto Pg. de Gràcia, and let your wallet do the talking as you pass some of Barcelona's hottest designer shopping (see p. 177). A stop in the free **Museu del Perfum** (see p. 86) will ease your pocketbook and pleasure your nose.

3 LA MANZANA DE LA DISCÒRDIA. Continue on Pg. de Gràcia and just before C. Aragó is the famous **La Manzana de la Discòrdia** (see p. 86). Enter Casa Amatller (no. 41) to buy a **Ruta del Modernisme** (see p. 51), good for discounts at Modernist sights all over the city, including the three houses that make up La Manzana de la Discòrdia: Casa Amatller, Casa Lleó Morera, and Casa Batlló.

4 FUNDACIÓ TÀPIES. Step off the busy Pg. de Gràcia for a Modernisme break. The Fundació Tàipes contains abstract postmodern works; angst at its finest. Check out the über-hip rooftop sculpture (see p. 90).

5 THE EATERIES OF CARRER ARAGÓ. Stop for a late lunch at one of the many, reasonably priced quality restaurants on C. Aragó east of Pg. de Gràcia (see p. 125).

6 CASA MILÀ. Return to Pg. de Gràcia and continue north to Gaudí's Casa Milà, a Modernist masterpiece with an unusual rooftop and an even more unforgettable view (see p. 84).

7 LA SAGRADA FAMÍLIA. Exit onto C. Provença and follow it (without crossing the Pg. de Gràcia again; with your back to the Pl. de Catalunya, follow C. Provença to the right) for 11 blocks to **La Sagrada Família,** the ultimate Gaudí jewel (this one is unfinished—118 years and counting) with infinitely complex views and facades (see p. 79).

DON'T MISS...

Sights & Museums: Gaudí's psychedelic **Palau Güell** (p. 77) is a visual feast, and the **Museu d'Art Contemporani** (p. 77) showcases some of the world's most cutting-edge art.

Food & Drink: Try the creative international dishes served on **Bar Ra's** (p. 124) intimate outdoor patio, or the traditional home-cooked Catalan cuisine at **Restaurante Can Lluís (p. 124)**.

Nightlife: Sip on absinthe at **Casa Almirall** (p. 146).

L'EIXAMPLE

see map pp. 340-341

▶ Orientation: *Bound by C. Ausiàs Marc and Pl. de Catalunya to the south, C. Còrsega to the north, C. Tarragona to the west, and C. del Dos de Maig to the east. L'Eixample is bisected vertically by the Pg. de Gràcia into l'Eixample Esquerra (Left Enlargement) to the west and l'Eixample Dreta (Right Enlargement) to the east.* **Sights & Museums:** *see p. 78.* **Food & Drink:** *see p. 125.* **Nightlife:** *see p. 148.* **Public Transportation:** *Metro lines 3, 4, 5, and the FCG trains run through l'Eixample; about half the city buses pass through this neighborhood, and all Nitbuses originate at Pl. de Catalunya.*

Barcelona's l'Eixample (the Enlargement) is remarkable for the unusual circumstances leading to its development. Right around the time when the oppressive Bourbon walls around the old city were finally demolished in 1854, the Catalan cultural Renaixença was picking up. As the number of wealthy benefactors of industrialization grew, utopian socialist theories spread like wildfire through philosophical circles, including that of l'Eixample designer **Ildefons Cerdà i Sunyer.** Check out the scholarly article **Barcelona Planned** (see p. 195) for more on the expansion

The gridded streets are filled with relatively wealthy residents, designer shops, corporate buildings, and eateries from around the world. Most tourists only see the Pg. de Gràcia and La Sagrada Família areas, but if you have the energy to explore the whole neighborhood, you'll get a great lesson in Modernisme, and a better feel for the Barcelona beyond the tourist attractions.

DON'T MISS...

Sights & Museums: No trip is complete without visiting **La Sagrada Família** (see p. 79), **La Manzana de la Discòrdia** (see p. 86), and **Casa Milà** (see p. 84).

Food & Drink: The Passeig de Gràcia bursts with outdoor cafes and tons of people-watching. Grab a cafe at **Café Torino** (see p. 127), where Gaudí tried his hand at eatery design.

Nightlife: Join the circus at **La Fira** (see p. 149). L'Eixample Esquerra's thumping LGB nightlife (see p. 148) has earned it the nickname, "Gaixample."

POBLE NOU & PORT OLÍMPIC

see map p. 347

▶ Orientation: *Bound by C. de Marina, Av. Diagonal, the Vila Olímpica, and the ocean.* **Sights & Museums:** *see p. 92.* **Food & Drink:** *see p. 131.* **Nightlife:** *see p. 152.* **Public Transportation:** *Central metro stops M: Marina, L1; Bogatell, L4; Llacuna, L4; Ciutadella/Vila Olímpic, L4; Poble Nou, L4. Glories, L1, and Selva de Mar, L4, lie at the outskirts of the neighborhood. Bus lines include #6, 7, 36, 41, 71, and 92.*

While industrial Poble Nou fueled Barcelona's economic growth in the 19th century, it enjoyed little of that era's wealth. Until the last few decades, Poble Nou consisted mainly of factories, warehouses, and low-income housing. Auto shops and commercial supply stores still abound, but the major factories were all removed for the **1992 Olympics.** When Barcelona was granted its Olympic bid in 1986, this privilege presented a two-sided problem: comfortably housing 15,000 athletes while beautifying the city's long-ignored coastline. Oriol Bohigas, Josep Martorall, David Mackay, and Albert Puig Domènech designed the solution: the **Vila Olímpica,** a residential area with wide streets, symmetrical apartment buildings,

Barceloneta Boats

pristine parks, and open-air art pieces. Most social activity in the area takes place in the L-shaped **Port Olímpic,** home to docked sailboats, more than 20 restaurants, a large casino, and a long strip of brash nightclubs.

In the wake of this development, old industrial buildings are slowly being converted into more apartments and nightclubs. With the exception of the Olympic areas, the atmosphere in Poble Nou is village-like compared to most of Barcelona: nondescript corner bars abound, and the tree-lined Rambla de Poble Nou is more likely to be filled with chatting grandmothers, small children, and gossiping teens than street artists and tourists. Besides its Olympic structures, Poble Nou's claims to fame are its sparkling city beaches and a raging alternative/hard rock music scene.

BARCELONETA & PORT VELL

see map p. 348

🛈 Orientation: *Barceloneta and Port Vell lay between Port Olímpic on the waterfront. Pg. Joan de Borbó, running along the port, is the neighborhood's main street, while the Pg. Marítim borders the beach area.* **Sights & Museums:** *see p. 93.* **Food & Drink:** *see p. 132.* **Nightlife:** *see* **p. 154.** **Public Transportation:** *M: Barceloneta, L4, and Drassanes, L3. Buses #59 and 14b run down Las Ramblas to the waterfront area. Also accessible by buses #17, 36, 40, 45, 57, and N8.*

Barri Gòtic

Barceloneta, or "Little Barcelona," was born out of necessity. In 1718, La Ribera was butchered to make room for the enormous **Ciutadella** fortress (see p. 40); the destruction of this historic neighborhood left thousands homeless, and it was not until 30 years later that the city created Barceloneta to house the displaced refugees. This area follows a carefully planned grid pattern, which would later influence the design of l'Eixample. Because of its seaside location, Barceloneta became home to the city's sailors, fishermen, and their families.

Barcelona's drive to refurbish its seafront resulted in the expansion of Port Vell. After moving a congested coastal road underground, the city opened Moll de la Fusta, a wide pedestrian zone that leads to the beaches of Barceloneta and connects the bright **Maremàgnum** (p. 154) and the **Moll d'Espanya.** Today, the rejuvenated Port Vell—the "Old Port"—is as hedonistic and touristy as Barcelona gets.

On the Barceloneta Beach

DON'T MISS...

Sights & Museums: Meet the sea life you keep eating at **L'Aquàrium de Barcelona** (see p. 94). The interactive **Museu Marítim** (see p. 93) is an engrossing experience.

Food & Drink: The **seafood restaurants** along Joan de Borbó are touristy, but they can't be beat for freshness (see p. 132).

Entertainment: Platja San Sebastiá and **Platja Barceloneta** are the neighborhood's biggest draws and Barcelona's best beaches (see p. 161).

Nightlife: Excessively cheesy clubs are always packed at **Maremàgnum** (see p. 154).

MONTJUÏC

A Barceloneta Church

see map p. 346

🛈 Orientation: *Montjuïc lies in the southwest corner of the city, bordering the Poble Sec neighborhood.* **Sights & Museums:** *see p. 95.* **Food & Drink:** *see p. 134.* **Nightlife:** *see p. 154.* **Accommodations:** *see p. 198.* **Public Transportation:** *The Metro has stops on the outskirts of Montjuïc; a few buses run through Montjuïc. M: Espanya is best for reaching the MNAC and Poble Espanyol area, while M: Parallel, L2/3, gives you access to the underground funicular, a convenient way to reach the Fundació Miró, Miramar, and the Castell de Montjuïc; it lets you off on Av. Miramar. The funicular runs 9am-10pm. Take bus #50 from Pl. d'Espanya to reach Poble Espanyol and the more distant Montjuïc sights like the Olympic area.*

Ajuntament

Montjuïc (mon-joo-EEK), the hill at the southwest end of the city, is one of the oldest sections of Barcelona; throughout Barcelona's history, whoever controlled Montjuïc's peak controlled the city. The Laietani collected oysters on Montjuïc before they were subdued by the Romans (see **Life & Times,** p. 38), who erected a temple to Jupiter on its slopes. Since then, dozens of despotic rulers have constructed and modified the **Castell de Montjuïc,** built atop the ancient Jewish cemetery (hence the name "Montjuïc," which means "Jew Hill"). In the 20th century, Franco made the Castell de Montjuïc one of his "interrogation" headquarters; somewhere deep in the recesses of the structure, his *beneméritos* ("honorable ones," a.k.a. the militia) are believed to have shot Catalunya's former president, Lluís Companys, in 1941. The fort was not re-dedicated to the city until 1960.

Since re-acquiring the mountain, Barcelona has given Montjuïc a new identity, transforming it from a military stronghold into a vast park by day and playground by night. Today

Running in a Park by Sant Pau

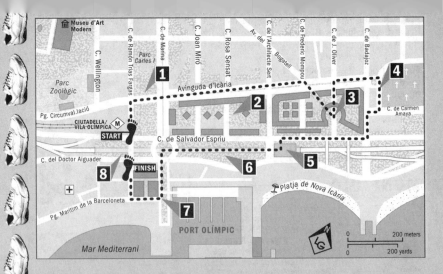

Many of Barcelona's sights will have you indoors pondering the meaning of master-pieces or admiring architectural feats. Try this tour for a breath of fresh air: most of the stops are outside. Feel the breeze of the Mediterranean as you take this easy loop around the parks and *plaças* of Poble Nou and Port Olímpic. Short and sweet, this walk is a great start to any morning.

Time: 2hr.

Distance: 2.8km (1¾ mi.)

When to go: A cool morning.

Start: M: Ciutadella/Vila Olímpica, L4

End: M: Ciutadella/Vila Olímpica, L4.

1 PARC DE CARLES I. Come out of the Metro with the twin sky-scrapers to your right and cross C. Ramon Trias Fargas. Walk up a block and the park is across Av. d'Icària. Check out the **Culo de Urculo** (statue of Hercules's buttocks) before heading back to Av. d'Icària where you can admire the metal constructions in the center of the roadway. Named **Pergolas** by architect Enric Miralles, these sculptures are an ultramodern take on latticed gardens (see p. 93).

2 CENTRE DE LA VILA. Follow Av. d'Icària for a few blocks; the center will be on the right near C. de l'Architecte Sert. This two-story mall is perfect for a mid-morning *café con leche* (see *p.* 93).

3 PL. TIRANT LO BLANC. Past the mall is the center of athlete housing for the 1992 Olympic games; Barcelona style shows through in the wavy sidewalks (see p. 92).

4 CEMENTIRI DE L'EST. Head back to Av. d'Icària and walk to its dead end at this cem-etery which was constructed outside the old city walls in the 1700s (see p. 93).

5 PL. DELS CHAMPIONS. Walk towards the sea, over the highway, and through the Parc dels Ponts to the medal platform of the '92 games. Imagine you are a winner while the names of those who actually are surround you in ground-set plaques (see p. 92).

6 PARC DEL PORT OLÍMPIC. Continue the athletic reverie in this white-spired lined sand walkway which ends at Robert Llimos's Marc statue (see p. 92).

7 PORT OLÍMPIC. Follow the sounds and smells of water. Stop and admire Frank Gehry's **Peix** sculpture (see p. 93) and if you have time, head to the beach for an afternoon in the sun, or simply admire the water from the docks.

8 PARC DE CASCADES. Before getting to the Metro, wander in the shady Parc de Cas-cades and check out Antoni Lelena's **David and Goliath** (see **p.** 93).

the park is one of the city's most visited attractions, with a little bit of something for everyone—world-famous art museums and theater, Olympic history and facilities, walking and biking trails, a healthy/unhealthy dose of nightlife, and an awe-inspiring historical cemetery.

Montjuïc is an immense park, not a neighborhood, and as such is not the easiest area to navigate. Street signs are scant, and building and renovation projects are ongoing. In times of need, a simple map marking particular locations and the curves of major roads is most helpful—check out the map in the **Map index** in the back of this book or pick a map up at the Barcelona tourist office (see **Service Directory,** p. 313) or El Corte Inglés (see **Shopping,** p. 181).

DON'T MISS...

Sights & Museums: The **Castell de Montjuïc** (see p. 97) offers incredible views of the city and the sea. The **Fundació Joan Miró** (see p. 95) will make you a fan of the renowned artist.

Nightlife: The ethereal bar **Tinta Roja** (see **p. 154**) hosts regular live music *espectáculos* while the clubs at Poble Espanyol (see p. 154) are always packed with dancers.

ZONA ALTA

see map p. 342-345

Zona Alta ("Uptown") is the section of Barcelona that lies at the top of most maps: past l'Eixample, in and around the Collserola mountains, and away from the low-lying waterfront districts. The Zona Alta is made of several formerly independent towns. Although all of these have now been incorporated into Barcelona's city limits as residential areas, each neighborhood retains its own character.

GRÀCIA

⊠ Orientation: *Gràcia lies past l'Eixample, above Av. Diagonal and C. de Còrsega, and stretches up to the Park Güell.* **Sights & Museums:** *see* **p. 100.** **Food & Drink:** *see p. 134.* **Nightlife:** *see p. 156.* **Public Transportation:** *M: Lesseps, L3; Fontana, L3; Diagonal, L3/5; Joanic, L4; or FCG: Gràcia. Buses #24, 25, 28, and N4.*

Originally an independent, largely working-class village, Gràcia was incorporated into Barcelona in 1897, much to the protest of its residents. Calls for Gràcian independence continue even today, albeit with less frequency. The area has always had a political streak—a theme that appears in the names of Mercat de Llibertat, Pl. de la Revolució, and others. After incorporation, the area continued to be a center of left-wing activism and resistance, even throughout the oppressive Franco regime.

Gràcia packs a surprising number of Modernist buildings and parks, international cuisine, and chic shops into a relatively small area, making it a good choice for exploring. And because it is relatively untouched by tourism, Gràcia retains a local charm that has been sapped from some of Barcelona's more popular sections.

DON'T MISS...

Sights: Spend an afternoon amid the wonderland of **Park Güell** (see p. 100).

Food & Drink: The eclectic *internacional* restaurants are sure to charm; be sure to sample the egg specialities at **OvUm** (p. 135).

HORTA & VALL D'HEBRON

⊠ Orientation: *Horta and Vall d'Hebron lie past l'Eixample Dreta, in the upper northeastern corner of the city.* **Sights & Museums:** *see p. 105.* **Food & Drink:** *see* **p. 136.** **Public Transportation:** *M: Horta, L5; Vall d'Hebron, L3; Mundet, L3; Montbau, L3.*

Horta did not lose its status as an independent village until 1904, and its abundance of narrow pedestrian streets and old apartment buildings attest to that small town history. It boasts a few farmhouses and fortresses from the Middle

Women at a Catholic Festival

Palau Sant Jordi

Mosaic meets the streets

Ages, as well as aristocratic estates dating from the 19th century, when the base of the Collserola mountains was a popular place to build wealthy country homes. In contrast, the neighboring **Vall d'Hebron** was built up specifically to serve as one of four main Olympic venues in 1992, housing the centers for cycling, tennis, and archery competitions. In general, the area has a nondescript atmosphere perfect for suburbanites but lacking the adventure and excitement sought by many travelers.

PEDRALBES & LES CORTS

🖪 *Orientation: Pedralbes and Les Corts lie above Sants, below the mountains, and west of C. Numància.* **Sights & Museums:** *see p. 106.* **Food & Drink:** *see p. 136.* **Public Transportation:** *M: Palau Reial, L3, or Col-lblanc, L5. Buses #22, 63, 64, 75, and 114 run through the neighborhood.*

Welcome to Pedralbes 90210, home to Barcelona's rich and famous. In the 1950s, the growing University of Barcelona moved most of its academic buildings to the area, but the neighborhood is hardly a "college town," as it remains one of the city's most exclusive residential areas. This part of Zona Alta also has great shopping, particularly along Av. Diagonal.

DON'T MISS...

Sights & Museums: Pedralbes was chosen by Queen Elisenda de Montcada in the 14th century as the site of the **Monestir de Pedralbes** (see p. 106).

Entertainment: Les Corts's most beloved residents are, of course, the *fútbol* superstars on El Barça (see p. 166), whose stadium, Camp Nou, is here.

SANTS

🖪 *Orientation: Sants occupies the western end of the city, between Gran Via de Carles III and C. Tarragona, the area's border with l'Eixample. Montjuïc borders on the ocean side and Les Corts toward the mountains.* **Food & Drink:** *see p. 136.* **Accommodations:** *see p. 199.* **Public Transportation:** *M: Sants-Estació, L3/5, and Pl. de Sant, L1/5. Bus lines include #32, 44, 78, and 109, coming mostly from the outskirts of the city.*

The Sants neighborhood began as a resting spot for travelers heading into historic walled Barcelona (the city gates closed shortly after dark). Today, the area still serves as a point of entry for travelers coming through the city's international train station, **Estació Barcelona-Sants,** but its status as a textile manufacturing zone hardly makes Sants a warm welcome for weary travelers. The busy industrial and commercial area is crammed full of narrow streets, low-level apartment buildings, and *plaças*. Flooded with locals who do much of their household shopping along C. de Sants, the area attracts few tourists besides those passing through the train station. Sants does have an eclectic display of colorful political graffiti, especially in and around the run-down Parc de l'Espanya Industrial.

SARRIÀ

◪ Orientation: *Sarrià lies at the base of the Collserola mountains and is loosely bordered by Av. Pedralbes and Av. Tibidabo on either side. Divided from l'Eixample and Les Corts by Av. Diagonal; Via Augusta separates it from Gràcia.* **Sights & Museums:** *see p. 108.* **Food & Drink:** *see p. 137.* **Public Transportation:** *FGC: Bonanova, Tres Torres, Sarrià, and Reina Elisenda. Bus lines include #66, 30, and 34.*

Sarrià luxuriates both meanings of the name Zona Alta ("Uptown")—economic prosperity and an elevated altitude. The last neighborhood to be incorporated into the city (1921), Sarrià often falls off the edge of Barcelona maps. Despite its geographical fringe, the neighborhood holds many un-touristed sights and residential splendor. Sarrià is home to some of the city's most coveted apartments, mansions, and chic boutiques, yet the neighborhood's center, Pl. Sarrià, still retains an Old World village feel.

COLLSEROLAS & TIBIDABO

◪ Orientation: *The Collserola mountain range, 17km long and 6km wide, marks the western limit of Barcelona, and incorporates the neighborhoods of Tibidabo and Vallvidrera.* **Sights & Museums:** *see p. 109.* **Food & Drink:** *see p. 137.* **Public Transportation:** *The Tibibus runs from Pl. de Catalunya to Pl. Tibidabo (the very top of the mountain) stopping only once en route (every 30-40min., only when the Parc d'Attracions is open; €1.80). FGC (U7) line runs from Pl. de Catalunya to the Tibidabo stop (€1); it stops at the foot of the peak in Pl. JFK, where C. Balmes turns into the Av. Tibidabo.*

The Collserola mountains hovered between wilderness and civilization for centuries. Fossils found in the park from the Neolithic and Bronze Ages suggest it was home to many long before the Romans set up shop in the area. With the fall of the Roman Empire (see **Life & Times,** p. 38), For most of the last 1000 years, the area has been home to agrarian people who built the area's historic chapels and *masias* (traditional Catalan farmhouses). In the last century, the installation of railtracks, trams, and funiculars has made the mountains easily accessible to urban residents wanting to take advantage of the mountains' offerings.

The man most responsible for the development of Tibidabo and surrounding slopes was Dr. Salvador Andreu, who in 1899 founded the Tibidabo Society and invested heavily, installing transportation and building hotels, the amusement park, and an extravagant casino (now in ruins). Soon after, the Barcelona bourgeoisie rushed to outdo one another in country-home construction, and the hillsides are now dotted with outstanding examples of early 20th-century Modernist and Noucentist (defined by a return to classical forms) architecture (see **Life & Times,** p. 48).

DON'T MISS...

Sights & Museums: Gaze down on Barcelona from the heavenly heights of **El Sagrat Cor** (see p. 110). Press their buttons and watch 'em go at the **Museu d'Automats** (see **p. 111**).

Food & Drink: Dine in a medieval setting at **El Asador de Aranda** (see **p. 138**).

Nightlife: Sip cava or cocktails with the glistening lights of Barcelona sprawling before you and your honey at **Mirabé** (see **p. 158**).

Miro Mosaic

View from the Montfuïc Cable Car

Flamenco Dancer at the Museu de Cera

SEASONAL HIGHLIGHTS

While Barcelona is quite different from the rest of Spain, the city shares at least one thing in common with the rest of the country—it knows how to have fun. Festivals abound in this happening city; the trick is to know what will be going on during your visit. For information on all festivals, call the tourist office ☎93 301 77 75 (open M-F 10am-2pm and 4-8pm). Below is a summary of major festivals.

SPRING

With the warm breezes and chirping birds, love is in the air every spring in Barcelona. **Día de Sant Jordi,** celebrated on April 23, is a favorite day for the lovebirds out there and is similar to St. Valentine's Day celebrated in North America. A festival in honor of one of Barcelona's favorite saints, the festivities include men purchasing roses for their girlfriends and women purchasing books for their boyfriends. Check out the flower district on Las Ramblas during this time, as it will be selling both books and flowers for this special occasion (see p. 52). **Setmana Santa** (Catholic Holy week; the week leading up to Easter) is a huge festival complete with grand processions; Barcelona natives pour into the streets to celebrate. On May 10-11, **Fira de Sant Ponç,** a festival dedicated to the patron saint of beekeepers, is celebrated on C. Hospital near Las Ramblas (see p. 52). To satisfy your inner child, head over to Estació de França for the **International Comics Fair,** held every May.

SUMMER

Festivals dubbed **"Festa Major"** are known for their size and popularity. Poble Nou, Sants, Gràcia, and Sitges (see p. 233) host these huge summer festivals. **Focs de Sant Joan** is held in Girona on June 24 (see p. 210). For those on the life-long quest to find a dancing egg, your journey stops in Barcelona. The **Corpus Cristi** festival occurs in June and includes huge parades, huge carnival figures, and of course, the traditional *ou com balla*—the dancing egg. Two music festivals make sure the party never stops, with **Sónar** (mid-June) pumping electronic music and **Festa de la Música** (July 1st) inviting anyone and everyone to perform. Theater, dance, music, and movies flood Barcelona's top venues from late June to the end of July during the city-wide **Grec Festival.**

AUTUMN

Bring your Catalan flag and other favorite Catalan-pride paraphernalia to the **Catalan National Day Festival,** held September 11. You'll find people dressed in traditional costumes and homes decorated with the flag and shield pattern. Wine-makers and *butifarra* (sausage)-makers pile into Barcelona from the surrounding areas to present their goods during the **Feria de Cuina i Vins de Catalunya;** for one entire fall week, you can taste food and wine for only a small price. September 24 brings fireworks and devils to town for the **Festa de la Verge de la Mercè,** when *correfocs* (devils) run through the streets, flashing their pitchforks at the residents. To retaliate, people throw buckets of water at the devils. Human towers (see **I've Got the Tower,** p. 242) are also a common occurrence in the streets around this time of year. Come October, Barceloneses trade their pitchforks and buckets for saxophones as the **Festival Internacional de Jazz** comes to town. Jazz is in the streets, in the clubs, and in the air when some of the world's finest musicians come to town for this event. **The Festival del Sant Çito** begins in November, and is all in all, one of the best city-wide parties.

WINTER

Christmastime proves to be a major time for festivities, but people do tend to spend more time with their families than on the streets, except in early evening when the avenues pack shoppers in like sardines. Rather than have a huge celebration occurring on Christmas Day, Spaniards tend to have a family dinner on *Nochebuena* (Christmas Eve), the most important holiday of the year. Spaniards hold off on exchanging presents until January 5, the **Epiphany,** the day the Three Kings ride their camels into Spain. The night of January 4th, children put their shoes outside to be filled with gifts and candy by the visiting Kings. That night, people gather to devour *roscón,* an oval-shaped sweet bread with a small toy baked into it. If someone finds the special toy, he or she gets to keep it and is dubbed King or Queen for the year. Speaking of special prizes, the caganer ("shitter") become even more popular during this season; just be careful where you step (see p. 132). As residents prepare for the new year, the price of grapes will suddenly skyrocket. Spaniards gather with friends on New Year's Eve, and when the clock strikes midnight, people pop a grape into their mouth for each chime, twelve in all, for good luck during the coming year.

Come February, join natives in celebrating **Festes de Santa Eulàlia,** a holiday dedicated to Barcelona's first patron saint. The Mayor's office organizes events for the city and arranges the special guest appearances by *mulasses* (dragons) in parades; concerts abound during this time. During **Festa de San Medir,** held in Tibidabo, Barcelona's young and old race to the mountain to be showered with candy by men galloping on horses down. At the end of the month, residents celebrate their last week of indulgence before Lent with **Carnaval.** The more daring head over to Sitges (see p. 233) or Vilanova i la Geltrù (see p. 237) for some especially rowdy partying.

Once in Barcelona

Many of Barcelona's avenues correspond to a simple grid layout, especially in the well planned neighborhood l'Eixample. However, the older and more narrow streets of the Ciutat Vella can be particularly confusing, as many are not wide enough for cars and even more are unlabeled. Do not fear; getting lost in Barcelona can be more rewarding than following the map as Roman ruins and striking views await around any number of corners. And if you can't find your way back to a main thoroughfare, simply ask someone on the street; usually the locals will happily redirect.

UPON ARRIVAL

TO AND FROM THE AIRPORT

All flights land at **El Prat de Llobregat** airport (☎ 93 298 38 38; www.aena.es/aeropuertos/barcelona/index.htm), 12km (8 mi.) southwest of Barcelona. From the airport, there are several options for transport into the city. The **Aerobús (A1)** links Terminals A, B, and C to Pl. de Catalunya, the center of town (☎ 934 15 60 20; approx. 40min.; every 15min.; to Pl. de Catalunya M-F 6am-midnight, Sa-Su 6:30am-midnight, to the airport M-F 5:30am-11:15pm, Sa-Su 6am-11:15pm; €3.45).

RENFE (24hr. info ☎ 90 224 02 02; www.renfe.es) trains provide slightly cheaper transportation to and from the airport via *línea mataró* (☎ 90 224 02 02; 17-30min.; every 30min.; 6:13am-11:15pm from airport, 5:43am-11:24pm from Sants; €2.20). The most useful stops are **Estació Barcelona-Sants** and **Plaça de Catalunya.** Tickets are sold at the red automatic machines. In Sants, buy tickets at the "Aeroport" window (open 5am-11pm). After 11pm, get them from the ticket machines or the Recorridos Cercanías window.

The city **bus** offers the only public (and therefore cheapest) late-night transportation. Take bus #106 from Terminal B or C to Pl. de Espanya (airport to Pl. de Espanya 10:15, 11:35pm, 12:50, 2:05am, 3:20am; Pl. de Espanya to airport 10:55pm, 12:10am, 1:25am, 2:40am, and 3:50am; €1.05). The stop in Pl. de Espanya is on the corner of Gran Via de les Corts Catalanes and Av. Reina Maria Cristina. A **taxi** ride between Barcelona and the airport costs €15-27.

Three **national airlines** serve all domestic and major international destinations. **Iberia/Aviaco** has a ticket office in the city at Diputación, 258 (☎93 401 33 81; www.iberia.com). Iberia/Aviaco has the most extensive coverage and usually offers student discounts (except on already reduced fares). Both **Air Europa** (☎90 240 15 01; www.air-europa.com) and **Spanair** (☎90 213 14 15; www.spanair.com) have online reservation options and sometimes offer cheap fares.

Many major international airlines serve Barcelona, including **British Airways** (☎90 211 13 33, airport office ☎93 298 34 55; open 6am-7pm) and **Delta** (☎901 11 69 46; www.delta-air.com). **Easy Jet** (☎90 229 99 92; www.easyjet.com) also offers flights from Barcelona to Amsterdam, Geneva, Liverpool, and London. For more information on international reservations, visit a travel agency in Barcelona (see **Service Directory,** p. 313).

TO AND FROM THE TRAIN STATIONS

Trains are an easy and affordable way to travel within Catalunya and Spain. Barcelona has two main stations, which serve different destinations. When in doubt, go to Estació Barcelona-Sants; while all domestic trains leaving Estació França pass through here, not all trains leaving Barcelona-Sants necessarily pass through Estació França. A taxi between either station and the Pl. de Catalunya will cost approximately €6. For general information about trains and train stations in Barcelona, check with **RENFE,** Spain's main train company (☎90 224 02 02, international ☎93 490 11 22; www.renfe.es).

Estació Barcelona-Sants, in Pl. Països Catalans. M: Sants-Estació, L5, L3. Buses to the station include #30 from Pl. de Espanya, #44 through l'Eixample (stops at La Sagrada Família), and N2. Barcelona-Sants is the main terminal for domestic and international traffic. For late arrivals, the N14 shuttles to Pl. de Catalunya (every 30min. 10:30pm-4:30am, €1). Services include: currency exchange (open daily 8am-10pm), ATMs, pharmacy, tourist office, restaurants, phone center, and touristy shopping. Internet available (€1 per 13min.) in the back of the station in the video-game room. Large lockers €4.50 per 24hr., small €3; storage open daily 5:30am-11:00pm. Station open M-F 4:30am-midnight.

Estació França, Av. Marqués de l'Argentera (☎902 24 02 02). M: Barceloneta, L4. Buses include #17 from Pl. de Catalunya and N6. Open daily 7am-10pm. This recently restored 19th-century station on the edge of the Ciutat Vella serves regional destinations on RENFE, including Girona, Tarragona, and Zaragoza, as well as some international arrivals. Station open daily 6am-11:30pm, ticket office daily 7am-10pm.

TO AND FROM THE BUS STATIONS

Buses are often cheaper and more direct than trains. Most, but not all, buses arrive at the **Barcelona Nord Estació d'Autobuses,** C. Ali-bei, 80 (☎90 230 32 22). The small Nord station features a sandwich shop, restaurant, candy shop, a butcher, money exchange, and luggage storage. The building also houses an office of the **Guardia Urbana,** the local police. (☎93 265 61 32. M: Arc de Triomf, exit to Nàpols.

Info office open daily 7am-9pm.) Buses that go there include #54 along Gran Via (a block from Pl. de Catalunya) and N11. A taxi from Pl. de Catalunya to the station will cost approximately €4. Other buses, particularly **international buses,** arrive at the **Estació d'Autobuses de Sants** station, next to the train station in Pl. Països Catalans (see above). The following companies operate out of Estació Nord:

Eurolines (☎90 240 50 40; www.eurolines.es). Transportation to **London** (25hr., 8:45am and 5:45pm, €92).

Sarfa (☎90 230 20 25; www.sarfa.com). Sarfa buses stop at many beach towns along the Costa Brava, north of Barcelona. Open daily 8am-9pm. To: **Cadaqués** (2½hr., 11:15am and 8:25pm, €15.15); **Palafrugell** (2hr., 13 per day, €11.40); **Tossa del Mar** (1½hr., 10 per day 9am-9pm, €7.50).

Linebús (☎93 265 07 00). Open M-F 8am-8pm, Sa 8:30am-1pm and 5-8pm. To **Paris** (13hr., M-Sa 8pm, €80). Also has daily service to southern France and Morocco. Discounts for travelers under 26 and 60+.

Alsa Enatcar (☎90 242 22 42; www.alsa.es). To: **Alicante** (9hr., 3 per day, €32.50); **Madrid** (8hr., 13 per day, €22); **Valencia** (4hr., 16 per day, €20.50); **Zaragoza** (3½-4½hr., 20 per day, €18); **Naples** (24hr., 5:15pm, €113).

Teleferic Cable Car

TO AND FROM THE FERRY

Barcelona's prime Mediterranean location makes the city an ideal gateway to the **Balearic Islands,** which are renowned for their beaches, raging clubs, and resorts. The main ferry station is **Estació Marítima,** in Port Vell. (M: Drassanes.) Head down Las Ramblas to the **Monument a Colom.** Columbus points straight toward the Estació Marítima. Cross the street and walk right, along the waterfront, until you see the large Trasmediterránea building on your left. Two companies operate out of Estació Marítima. Both offer discounts for students and seniors. Tickets are available at any travel agency or at Estació Marítima.

Bike Tricks at Miró Park

Trasmediterránea (☎90 245 46 45; fax 93 295 91 34), in Estació Marítima-Moll Barcelona, Moll de Sant Bertran. In the summer months only to: **Ibiza** (10-11hr., M-Sa 1 per day, €46); **Palma** (3½hr., 1 per day, €63); **Mahón** (10½hr., 1 per day, €46).

Turbocat (☎90 218 18 88; www.turbocatonline.com), in Estació Marítima-Moll Barcelona, Moll de Sant Bertran. In the summer months only to: **Ciutadella** (3½hr., 1 per day, €65) and **Alcuida** (5hr., 1 per day, €62).

View of Port

GETTING AROUND

METRO AND FGC

Barcelona's public transportation system (info ☎010, claims 93 318 70 74) is quick, cheap, and all-around excellent. The *Guía d'Autobuses Urbans de Barcelona*, free at tourist offices and in Metro stations, maps out the city's bus routes and the five Metro lines; the small book *Guía Facil del Bus per Mour't per Barcelona*, also free, describes the routes in even more detail.

If you plan to use public transportation extensively, consider buying one of the several *abonos* (passes) available, all of which work interchangeably for the Metro, bus, urban lines of the FGC commuter trains, bus routes, and the Nitbus. The **T-10 pass** (€5.80) is valid for 10 rides and saves you nearly 50% off the cost of single tickets. The **T-Día pass** (€4.40) is good for a full day of unlimited travel, while the **T-Mes** (€37.65) and the **T-Trisemestre** (€103.60) offer the same for one month and 90 days respectively. The **T-50/30** (€24.30) buys 50 trips in a 30-day period. Finally, for short stays, the **3 Dies** (€11.30) gets you three days of unlimited travel; the **5 Dies** (€17.30) is good for five days. Both save you money if you use public transport more than three times per day.

Metro (☎93 298 70 00; www.tmb.net). Automatic vending machines and ticket windows sell Metro passes. Stations are indicated by red diamonds with the letter "M" inside of them. Hold on to your ticket until you exit—an official with a white-and-red pin-striped shirt may ask to see it. Riding without a ticket carries a hefty fine of €40. Most trains run M-Th 5am-midnight, F-Sa 5am-2am, Su and holidays 6am-midnight. €1.05 per *sencillo* (single ride).

Ferrocarrils de la Generalitat de Catalunya: FGC (☎93 205 15 15; www.fgc.es). Commuter trains with main stations at Pl. de Catalunya and Pl. de Espanya. Service to **Montserrat** (from Pl. de Espanya). Blue symbols resembling two interlocking "V"s mark connections with the Metro. The commuter line charges the same as the Metro (€1.05) until Tibidabo. After that, rates go up by zone: zone 2 destinations €1.55, zone 3 destinations €2.20. Metro passes are valid on FGC trains. Information office at the Pl. de Catalunya station open M-F 7am-9pm.

BUS

Barcelona has a comprehensive bus system, with more than 80 lines connecting different parts of the city; the passes that work on the Metro and FGC trains are also good on buses. Bus stops have red signs and brown benches under a small roof; the numbers of bus lines that use the stop will be posted there. Always respect the line at the bus stop. Try to buy a ticket before you get on the bus, as the drivers tend to be cranky about cash and may even refuse to make change. When you get on the bus, you'll see two machines at the front; if you have a Metro pass, insert your ticket into it, printed side facing up, arrow pointing down, and the machine will stamp your ticket. To signal the driver to stop, press one of the small red buttons on the railing inside the bus. Most major lines are partially wheelchair-accessible, meaning that at least some, though not all, of the buses on the line have wheelchair lifts. Buses keep the same hours and charge the same fees as the Metro (see above). See the *Guía d'Autobuses Urbans* or *Guía Facil del Bus*, free at tourist offices or Metro stations, for more details. Some of the most useful lines include the following:

#10: Bisects the city from top to bottom, passing by the Parc de la Vall d'Hebron, La Sagrada Família, Teatre Nacional, Parc de la Ciutadella, Museu d'Art Modern, and Parc de las Cascades on the way to its final stop on Pg. Marítim, right in front of Platja Barceloneta.

#14: Begins above l'Eixample Dreta and runs down Las Ramblas, stopping near the Mercat de la Boqueria, Palau de la Música Catalana, Catedral, and Gran Teatre de Liceu. Continues from there to the Museu Marítim and Port Vell and then takes Pg. Colom past the Estació de França, Parc de la Ciutadella, Estació de Autobuses Barcelona Nord, and Vila Olímpica.

#19: Starts in Port Vell and passes near the Museu Picasso, Palau de la Música Catalana, the Arc de Triomf, and La Sagrada Família.

#24: Runs from Pl. de Catalunya up Pg. de Gràcia to Park Güell, along the way passing by La Manzana de la Discòrdia, Casa Milà, and the Palau Robert.

#50: The most useful part of this line connects Montjuïc to La Sagrada Família, passing by the Palau Nacional, Estadi Olímpic, and Poble Espanyol.

Bus Turístic: Departing from the Pl. de Catalunya, this bus is one of the easiest ways to get to all the tourist attractions in the city. Tickets €15 for one day, €19 for 2 consecutive days. See p. 52 for more details.

NITBUS

When the regular bus system and Metro close, the Nitbus begins. Sixteen different lines, twelve of which stop at PL. de Catalunya, run 10:30pm-4:30am, every 30min. A Metro pass is valid on the Nitbus; you can also buy a single ride on the bus for €1.05, or 10 rides for €5. The buses stop in front of most club complexes and work their way through the Ciutat Vella and the Zona Alta. Some Nitbuses go to the airport. Maps are available at *estancos* (tobacco shops) and marked by signs in Metro stations (☎901 51 11 51).

TAXI

Taxis are everywhere in Barcelona. On weekend nights, however, you may wait up to 30min. in some locations; long lines form at popular club spots like the Port Olímpic. A *lliure* or *libre* sign in the windshield or a lit green light on the roof means they are vacant; yellow means they are occupied. To summon a cab by phone, try the companies in the **Service Directory,** p. 312. Disabled travelers should call ☎93 420 80 88. Taxi prices are set: Daily 6am-10pm €1.80 plus €0.66 per km. After 10pm and on Saturday, Sunday, and fiesta days, €1.95 plus €0.84. per km (www.bcntaxi.com).

BICYCLE AND MOPED

As you make your way through the streets of the city, be wary of speeding businessmen and grandmothers on *motos*. It seems as if everyone in Barcelona owns a moped. To change your status from the hunted to the hunter, visit one of Barcelona's many rental shops. Bicycles are not widely used in the city.

Vanguard Rent a Car, C. Viladomat, 297, between Londres and Paris (☎93 439 38 80). Min. age 21 to rent (ID required). Mopeds start at €38 per day for 3 days or less, €32 per day for more than 3 days. More expensive, 2-person *motos* also available. Insurance, helmet, and IVA included. Open M-F 8am-2pm and 4-8pm, Sa-Su, and holidays 9am-1pm.

CARS

Public transportation is by far the easiest way to get around the city; cars are more of a hassle than they are useful. Spanish drivers are notoriously aggressive, gas is expensive, and parking in Barcelona is an adventure in itself. If you plan to drive in the hazardously tight Ciutat Vella, you had better have nerves of steel and above-average dexterity. To drive a car while in Spain, you must be over 18; an **International Driving Permit** (IDP; see **Planning Your Trip,** p. 289) is highly recommended.

RENTING

Except for reaching small towns in the Pyrenees with infrequent bus service, traveling in Spain and living in Barcelona do not necessitate the use of a car, which will only triple the cost of a trip. For those who desire that get-up-and-go convenience, you can generally make reservations before you leave by calling major international offices in your home country (see **Planning your Trip,** p. 289). To rent a car from most of these establishments, you need to be at least 23 years old; very few let 18-year-olds slip by. Some agencies require renters to be 25, and most charge those under 25 an additional insurance fee (around US$5-6 per day). Policies and prices vary from agency to agency. Small local operations occasionally rent to people under 21, but be sure to ask about the insurance coverage and deductible, and always check the fine print. Try to get a policy that includes **roadside assistance.**

DRIVING PRECAUTIONS. When traveling in the summer, bring substantial amounts of water (a suggested 5 liters of **water** per person per day) for drinking and for the radiator. For long drives to unpopulated areas, such as the Pyrenees, register with police or contact a friend before beginning the trip and again upon arrival at the destination. When traveling long distances, make sure your tires are in good repair and have enough air, and get good maps. A **compass** and a **car manual** can also be very useful. You should always carry a **spare tire** and **jack, jumper cables, extra oil, flares, a torch (flashlight),** and **heavy blankets** (in case your car breaks down at night or in the winter). If you don't know how to **change a tire,** learn before heading out, especially if you are planning on traveling in less populated areas. Blowouts in the mountains are common. If you do have a breakdown, **stay with your car;** if you wander off, there's less of a likelihood that the police will find you.

COSTS AND INSURANCE. Including basic insurance and taxes, rental car prices start at around US$90 per day from national companies. Expect to pay more for larger cars and for 4WD. Cars with **automatic transmission** can cost twice as much as standard manuals (stick shift), and in some places, automatic transmission is hard to find in the first place. It is virtually impossible, no matter where you are, to find an automatic 4WD.

Many rental packages offer unlimited km, while others offer a set number of km per day with a per-km surcharge after that. Be sure to ask whether the price includes **insurance** against theft and collision. Remember that if you are driving a conventional vehicle on an **unpaved road** in a rental car, you are almost never covered by insurance; ask about this before leaving the rental agency. Be aware that cars rented on **American Express** or **Visa/Mastercard Gold** or **Platinum** credit cards in Spain might *not* carry the automatic insurance that they would in some other countries; check with your credit card company. Insurance plans almost always come with a **deductible** (or excess) for conventional vehicles which can often be reduced or waived entirely if you pay an additional charge.

ON THE ROAD. In Spain cars drive on the right side of the road. Within the city there are specific lanes for taxis and buses which you cannot drive in unless you are turning off of the main roadway. Outside of the city limits and within the rest of Catalunya **speeders beware:** police can "photograph" the speed and license plate of your car, and issue a ticket without pulling you over. Purchase **gas** in super (97-octane), normal (92-octane), diesel, and unleaded. Prices are astronomical by North American standards: about €1.40-1.50 per liter.

MONEY MATTERS

Banking hours in Barcelona from June through September are generally Monday through Friday 9am-2pm; from October to May, banks are also open Saturday 9am-1pm. Some banks are also open in the afternoon. **Santander Central Hispano** often provides good exchange rates. Most ATMs in Barcelona and Catalunya accept Visa, Mastercard, Cirrus, and Plus; Discover, American Express, and Star are not as prevalent for ATMs but are accepted for cash advances at all major banks.

Spain has a 7% **Value Added Tax,** known as IVA, on money spent at all restaurants and accommodations. The prices listed in *Let's Go* include IVA unless otherwise indicated. Retail goods bear a much higher 16% IVA, although listed prices are usually inclusive. Non-EU citizens who have stayed in the EU for fewer than 180 days can claim back the tax paid on purchases at the airport. Ask the shop where you have made the purchase to supply you with a tax return form.

If you run out of money while traveling, the easiest and cheapest solution is to have someone back home make a deposit to your credit card or cash (ATM) card. Failing that, consider one of the following options.

WIRING MONEY. It is possible to arrange a bank money transfer, which means asking a bank back home to wire money to a bank in Spain. This is the cheapest way to transfer cash, but it's also the slowest, usually taking several days or more. Note that some banks may only release your funds in local currency, potentially sticking you with a poor exchange rate. Money transfer services like **Western Union** are faster and more convenient than bank transfers—but also much pricier. Western Union has many locations worldwide. Visit www.westernunion.com, or call: in Australia ☎ 800 501 500, in Canada ☎ 800-235-0000, in New Zealand ☎ 800 27 0000, in South Africa ☎ 0860 100031, in Spain ☎ 900 633 633, in the UK ☎ 0800 83 38 33, in the US ☎ 800-325-6000. There are Western Union representatives all over Barcelona, including one at Admon Manuel Martín, Las Ramblas, 41. (Open daily 9:30am-midnight.)

US STATE DEPARTMENT (US CITIZENS ONLY). In dire emergencies only, the US State Department will forward money within hours to the nearest consular office, which will then disburse it according to instructions for a US$15 fee. If you wish to use this service, you must contact the Overseas Citizens Service division of the US State Department (☎ 202-647-5225; nights, Sundays, and holidays ☎ 202-647-4000).

SAFETY AND SECURITY

MEDICAL CARE

Should you require a house call for a condition not requiring hospitalization, any hospital (see **Service Directory**, p. 315) should be able to refer you to a dentist, optometrist, or ophthalmologist. Request documentation (including diagnoses) and receipts to submit to your home insurance company for reimbursement.

Estacio França

View of the Street

Façade of the Cathedral

Olympic Track

Plaça del Pi

Walking over the Miro Mosaic

EU citizens can get reciprocal health benefits, entitling them to a practitioner registered with the state system, by filling out a E111 or E112 form before departure; this is available at most major post offices. They will generally treat your maladies whether or not you can pay in advance. EU citizens studying in Spain also qualify for long-term care. Other travelers should ensure they have adequate medical insurance before leaving; if your regular insurance policy does not cover travel abroad, you may wish to purchase additional coverage (see **Planning Your Trip**, p. 283). With the exception of Medicare, most health insurance plans cover members' medical emergencies during trips abroad; check with your insurance carrier to be sure.

If you need a **doctor** (*un metge/un médico*), call the nearest hospital for a list of local practitioners. If you are receiving reciprocal health care, make sure you call a doctor who is linked to the state health care system. Note that the same medicines may have different names in Spain than in your home country; check with your doctor before you leave. A single visit to a clinic in Spain can cost anywhere from US$40 to US$100, depending on the service.

Farmacias (pharmacies) in Spain are also very helpful. By government regulation at least one *farmacia* in each town is open and there are a plethora of 24hr. pharmacies in Barcelona; look for a green cross. Spanish pharmacies are not the places to find your cheap flip-flops or greeting cards: they sell contraceptives, common medications, and many prescription drugs. They can also answer simple medical questions and help you find a doctor.

PERSONAL SAFETY

Spain has a low crime rate, but visitors can always fall victim to tourist-related crimes. Tourists should take particular care in and around Las Ramblas and in crowded tourist sights such as La Sagrada Família. If you're visiting the Costa del Sol in a car, be aware of the fact that this area has seen increased car theft in recent years. For those travelers using public transportation, it is essential to be on the lookout for potential muggings and pickpockets.

TERRORISM

Basque terrorism concerns all travelers in Spain and is a highly controversial issue both domestically and internationally. ETA, or Euskadi Ta

Askatasuna (meaning Basque Homeland and Freedom), is the militant wing of the Basque separatist movement. It was founded in 1959 to fight for Basque self-determination, concentrating on establishing the Basque region as its own independent country, distinct from Spain and France. ETA attacks have resulted in more than 800 deaths since 1968. While Barcelona and Catalunya are not high risk areas for Basque terrorism, travelers should be aware of the ETA's activities.

MEDITERRANEAN MANNERS

CHURCH ETIQUETTE. Catalunya's religious buildings are open to the public at various hours; be aware that a visit to them requires a certain dress code and respectful attitude. Shorts and tank tops are considered inappropriate; keep your arms and legs covered if you don't want to be ushered out by a clergy member. Some chapels are reserved for devotional purposes only. Camera regulations vary from site to site, but use of a flash is almost never permitted. Noise above a whisper is inappropriate, unless you are participating in a mass.

EUROPEANS WHO DISAPPEAR IN AUGUST. The European summer schedule is quite pleasant for those who work in Europe and quite bizarre for those who come to visit. Many employees have a month off in the summer, which they usually take in August. Barcelona's native residents clear out of the city during this month and head to the nearby beach towns. The city is noticeably deflated at this time of year, although the tourists keep coming; be prepared for some small businesses, such as hostels and restaurants, to close down for a few weeks in the summer.

PUBLIC BEHAVIOR. Spaniards are formally polite in mannerisms and social behavior. To blend in, it's a good idea to be as formal as possible during a first meeting. Introduce yourself in detail, giving more than just your name. You'll be welcomed openly and made to feel at home if you say who you are, where you're from, and what you are doing in Spain. Be sure to address Spaniards as *Señor* (Mr.), *Señora* (Mrs.), or *Señorita* (Ms.), and don't be surprised if you receive kisses on both cheeks instead of a handshake.

HOURS. Spaniards observe the siesta, which can be a nap, but also serves to describe an even grander tradition. Excluding larger companies and needed services, all of Spain shuts down in the afternoon so the family can eat their midday meal—the largest meal of the day—together. Businesses generally open around 9 or 10 am, close from 2-5pm, and open again until after 9pm. Many tourist sights stay open all day; be sure to check sight and museum hours before visiting.

SMOKING. Spaniards smoke a lot. They also smoke virtually everywhere, even where it is clearly prohibited, such as on Metro platforms. Restaurants, bars, and clubs accommodate a smoking clientele.

DRUGS AND ALCOHOL. Recreational drugs are illegal in Spain. Possession of small amounts of marijuana sometimes goes unpunished, but any attempt to buy or sell will definitely land you in jail or with a heavy fine. In terms of drinking, alcohol and wine accompany many meals; however, there is little public drunkenness on the part of city natives.

TIPPING & BARGAINING. Both are rare. At most restaurants prices for food differs depending on whether you sit at the bar, at a table, or outside. People sometimes leave change after a meal or coffee, but tipping is not expected. Light bargaining is only acceptable with non-licensed street vendors and in flea markets.

KEEPING IN TOUCH

BY TELEPHONE

How much a given phone call will cost is dependent upon what sort of a call it is; this edition of *Let's Go* has formatted telephone numbers to reflect those price differences. The city code for Barcelona is 93; a number that begins with 93 is on a land-line within the city and will be charged at a local rate. You must dial this city code, even within the city; it is not charged as a long distance call. Other areas in Catalunya use the code 97.

> **PLACING INTERNATIONAL CALLS.** To call Barcelona from home or to call home from Barcelona dial (see the back cover for more helpful numbers):
>
> **1.** The **international dialing prefix.** To call out of out of **Spain,** the **Republic of Ireland, New Zealand,** or the **UK,** dial 00; **Australia,** 0011; **Canada** or the **US,** 011; **South Africa,** 09.
>
> **2.** The **country code** of the country you want to call. To call **Australia,** dial 61; **Canada** or the **US,** 1; the **Republic of Ireland,** 353; **New Zealand,** 64; **South Africa,** 27; the **UK,** 44; **Spain,** 34.
>
> **3.** The **city/area code.** The city code for Barcelona is 93 and for Catalunya is 97. If the first digit of an area code is a zero (e.g., 020 for London), omit the zero when calling from abroad (e.g., dial 20 from Barcelona to reach London).
>
> **4.** The **local number.**

Spain is currently ensnared in a phone number format dilemma. Regional phone numbers can be listed either in the 2-3-2-2 format or the 3-3-3 format; that is, a number in Barcelona may appear either as 93 555 55 55 or 935 555 555. *Let's Go Barcelona* uses the 2-3-2-2 format to visually separate local or regional calls from other sorts of calls, which begin with a three-digit prefix. A number that begins with the three-digit prefix 900 is a toll-free number; other three digit-prefixes that do not begin with 9 are toll numbers. Most mobile phone numbers begin with 6; calling these phones from a land line costs more than a local call.

CALLING CARDS

Pay phones in Spain always accept coins, but this is not the best way to make a local or international call. Opt for prepaid **calling cards,** issued in denominations of €6 and €12 and sold at *estancos* (tobacco shops; identifiable by brown signs with yellow lettering and tobacco leaf icons) and most post offices. Some *kioscos* (newsstands) and many tourist shops along Las Ramblas also sell calling cards. Choose your phone card based on who you want to call. For **local calls** or calls from **payphones,** the cards that you insert into the payphone are best; for **international calls** or calls made from **private phones,** the telephone cards with a Personal Identification Number (PIN) and a toll-free access number have the cheapest rates; try the *Eurocity* cards to call North America (110min. for €6). These cards can be used to make international as well as domestic calls; different brands offer discount rates on calls to certain countries; shop owners have detailed rate lists behind the counter.

LOCAL CALLS

The one and only Spanish phone company is **Telefónica.** Phone booths are marked by signs that say *teléfono público.* Local calls cost €0.15 to dial and then €0.05 per min. from 8am to 6pm and €0.02 per min. from 6pm to 8am. Be aware that it is almost five times as expensive to call mobile phones (€0.24 per min. 8am-6pm; €0.12 per min. 6pm-8am; minimum charge €0.66). For directory assistance or information, dial ☎003.

Fax service is available at **Easy Everything, Las Ramblas, 31**. (Open daily 8am-1am; local numbers first page €1.28, additional pages €0.81; first page to Europe €2.90, additional pages €1.97.) Private phone and fax service is also available at **Estació Barcelona-Sants**, and at local post offices.

INTERNATIONAL CALLS

There are two sets of rates for international calls: *normal* and *reducida*. *Normal* rates apply 8am-8pm, and *reducida* rates apply 8pm-8am. The minimum charge for making an international call is €1.80. The following are the *normal-reducida* rates for calls from Barcelona, using change or a *Telefónica* phone card. To the US and Canada, €0.54-0.50 per min.; to England or Ireland €0.48-0.44 per min.; to Australia or New Zealand €1.41-1.20 per min.; to South Africa €1.65-1.50 per min. You can also buy competing phone company cards (see **Calling Cards**).

It is possible to bring an international calling card from home, issued by your phone company. Calls are billed collect or to your account. These usually have rates far higher than the cards that you can find in Barcelona, but the convenience of billing and the security that they provide may make them worth having in case of an emergency. You can frequently call collect without even possessing a company's calling card by calling their access number and following the instructions. **To obtain a calling card,** contact your national telecommunications service before leaving home (see **Planning your Trip,** p. 284).

For an international **Telefónica** operator, call ☎ 11840. Placing a **collect call** through an international operator is more expensive, but may be necessary in case of an emergency. For **Directory Assistance,** call ☎ 11818 for numbers within Spain, and ☎ 11825 for international numbers.

MOBILE PHONES

For a longer stay in the city, a mobile phone might be a good investment and a great convenience, but be sure to do comparative shopping between the major companies before purchasing (*Telefónica, Movistar,* and *Airtel* offer the best service) All three companies offer pay-as-you-go plans through which one can buy minutes as they need them. Look on bulletin boards for people selling old phones. For shorter stays, you can rent a Nokia phone from **Rent-A-Phone,** C. Numància, 212. Pay the up-front deposit of €150.25 with a credit card (AmEx/MC/V); the company will charge the same credit card €29.45 per month, in addition to €0.02 per sec.

in recent news

Big Trouble in Little China

El Raval has long been considered Barcelona's dirty little secret, the side of the city the image-conscious urban planners don't want visitors to see. In the 19th century, industrialization hit the neighborhood hard. Workers and their families crammed into the low-rent housing, making El Raval one of the most densely populated urban areas in Europe. Pollution, crime, and prostitution followed. The southern half of the neighborhood was given the nickname *El Barri Xino* (Chinatown), as it reminded some of the red-light districts of Chinatowns in other cities, with its brothels and debaucherous atmosphere.

In the early 1990s, with the Olympics coming to Barcelona, city leaders made an effort to revitalize the neighborhood. Investment poured in, the brothels were closed, and, as social and economic conditions improved, crime rates dropped. El Raval's problems are far from over. Still, in the last 10 years it has undergone a metamorphosis, and its community—the most ethnically diverse of the city's *zonas*—is coming together with a new energy and vision, leaving the label "El Barri Xino" in the area's long and colorful past.

for calls in Spain, and €2.10 per min. for international calls (minimum charge of €7.20 per day). The phones work from anywhere in Europe and Rent-A-Phone will retrieve these phones for free from any European country. (☎93 280 21 31. M: Maria Christina. Walk down Diagonal with El Corte Inglés on your right, then go left on C. Numància. Open M-F 9:30am-2pm and 4-7:30pm.) There is another **branch** at Moll d'Espanya. (☎93 225 81 06. Open daily 11am-10:30pm.)

TIME DIFFERENCES

Barcelona is 1hr. ahead of Greenwich Mean Time (GMT), and 2hr. ahead during Daylight Savings Time (DST). Barcelona is 6hr. ahead of New York, 9hr. ahead of Vancouver and San Francisco. Spain observes DST, and since fall and spring switch-over times vary between countries; during winter, Spain is 1hr. behind Johannesburg, 10hr. behind Sydney, and 12hr. behind Auckland; in Spain's summer, Spain is on the same time as Johannesburg, 8hr. behind Sydney, and 10hr. behind Auckland.

BY MAIL

SENDING MAIL HOME FROM BARCELONA

Airmail takes five to eight business days to reach the US or Canada; service is faster to the UK and Ireland and slower to Australia and New Zealand. Standard postage is €0.76 to North America. Surface mail, while considerably less expensive than air mail, can take over a month, and packages will take two to three months. Registered or express mail (*registrado* or *certificado*) is the most reliable way to send a letter or parcel home, and takes 4-7 business days. An express letter to North America is €2.91. Spain's overnight mail is not worth the added expense, since it is not exactly "overnight." For better service, try private companies such as DHL, UPS, or the Spanish company SEUR (www.seur.es); look under *mensajerías* in the yellow pages. Their reliability does, however, come at a high cost. Stamps (*sellos*) are sold at post offices and tobacconists (*estancos* or *tabacos*). Mail letters and postcards from the yellow mailboxes scattered throughout the city, or from the post office.

RECEIVING MAIL IN BARCELONA

Receiving airmail in Barcelona from the US requires 4-7 days. Letters from Europe are a few days faster, while mail from Australia, New Zealand, or South Africa, can take up to 2 weeks. Mail will take even longer if picking up mail in towns outside of the city. Envelopes should be marked "air mail" or *"par avion."* The best way to arrange to pick up letters while abroad is by way of *Poste Restante*, the international term for "General Delivery." The mail will go to a special desk in the central post office, unless you specify a post office by street address or postal code. As a rule, it is best to use the largest post office in the area as mail may be sent there regardless of what is written on the envelope. It is usually safer and quicker to send mail express or registered. When picking up your mail, bring a form of photo ID, preferably a passport. There is generally no surcharge; if there is a charge, it should not exceed the cost of postage. If the clerks insist there is nothing for you, have them check under your first name as well. *Let's Go* lists post offices in the **Service Directory** (see p. 309) for Barcelona and the **Practical Information** section for other towns in the **Daytripping** chapter (see p. 203). Letters should be addressed in the format below:

LASTNAME, First name
Poste Restante
Lista de Correos
08070, Barcelona
SPAIN

BY EMAIL & INTERNET

Internet addicts won't have to worry about withdrawal symptoms, thanks to Barcelona's plethora of Internet cafes. You can surf the Web in almost any electronics store, or try more posh locales where you can surf with a drink and bocadillo at your side. Internet access costs about €1.50-5 per hr.; if you'll be going to the same establishment several times, buying an *abono*, that is, a voucher for a certain number of access hours paid up front, is the most economical option. The website www.tangaworld.com lists nearly 200 cybercafes across Spain by location and name. **Internet cafes** are available all over the city; check the **Service Directory,** p. 311.

TOURIST OFFICES

Tourist office representatives dot the Barri Gòtic from July to September (daily 10am-8pm). Look for officials wearing red vests.

Informació Turística Plaça Catalunya, Pl. de Catalunya, 17S, below Pl. de Catalunya. M: Catalunya. The motherlode of Barcelona information. Provides multilingual advice, maps, pamphlets, transportation passes, hotel information and reservations, currency exchange, telephone cards, email kiosks, and souvenirs for purchase. Updates Barcelona Visitor's Info Line (☎90 730 12 82 in Spain; ☎93 368 97 31 30 abroad). Open daily 9am-9pm.

Informació Turística Plaça Sant Jaume, Pl. Sant Jaume, 1, off C. Ciutat. M: Jaume I. (☎90 630 12 82; www.bcn.es). Fewer services and more personal attention than its big mama in Pl. de Catalunya. Open M-Sa 10am-8pm, Su 10am-2pm.

Aeroport El Prat de Llobregat (☎93 478 05 65), in terminal B at the airport outside the baggage claim area. English-speaking agents offer information on Catalunya and Barcelona, maps, transit passes, and hotel and tour reservations. Both in-person and phone services are available daily 9am-9pm.

LOCAL MEDIA

TELEVISION

Sadly, for English-language viewing, the small screen is not your best option. Most Spanish television consists of poorly dubbed American programming—*The Simpsons* are all the rage—and some original Spanish fare, including a hefty dose of *telenovelas* (soap operas). Check the *Guía del Ocio* for weekly listings and TV highlights. Daily newspapers (see below) also carry the goods.

TVE1: Features dubbed American series and a good selection of late-night movies.

TVE2: News and some documentaries along with made-for-TV movies, Spanish style.

TV3 and Canal 33: All Catalan programming, all the time.

Tele 5: Dubbed American programming from *Club Disney* to *The Simpsons* to *Melrose Place.*

Antena 3: Regional news, game shows, and dubbed and original series. Heavy on family programming.

BTV: City station with local news and some offbeat programming.

Canal Plus: A paid channel, much like the US's HBO, with original television programs, music specials, and movies. Programming is almost entirely in Spanish.

Flaix TV (Channel 9): Catalunya's version of MTV, with plenty of British and American videos in heavy rotation.

Guide to Party

If you speak any Spanish, your first purchase in Barcelona should be the **Guía del Ocio,** or, Guide to Leisure—which should be re-named "Guide to Party." The *Guía* is a booklet that lists anything and everything happening in Barcelona in the coming week: concerts, restaurant events, temporary exhibits, nightlife, galleries, games, free events, theater and dance performances, movie listings, and more. The guide comes out on Thursday or Friday, so be sure you're picking up the current one. Though the *Guía is* published in Spanish, even those who don't speak the language can benefit from the easy-to-understand listings and advertisements. The *Guía del Ocio* is available at newsstands all over the city for the economical price of €0.90.

For English speakers, the **Barcelona Metropolitan** is the best option. The self-proclaimed "city's magazine in English" is published monthly and can be obtained at any tourist office for free. While it consists mostly of cultural articles (rather than listings of actual events), it provides information on a variety of topics, such as Catalan cuisine and fashion. The magazine also includes pages of listings and advertisements specifically for English speakers, ranging from English-friendly dentists to English-style hair salons. The Metropolitan is truly invaluable for the Spanish-deficient tourist.

RADIO

When you turn on the radio in Barcelona, expect to hear lots of Catalan—nearly all the DJs prefer to speak in the mother tongue rather than in Spanish. Many also have the irritating habit of jabbering over at least half of the song being played. Categorizing stations is a challenge, since most change genre according to the time of day.

91.0 News, sports, debates. Visit the station's website www.comradio.com/programacio for list of programs.

92.3 An eclectic mix of reggae, folk, salsa, flamenco, and classical music, topped with the occasional catalan poetry reading in the evening.

95.5 The dependable "Radio Club 25" can always be counted on not to stray too far from top-40 pop. The station where you'll hear the song-of-the-moment at least hourly.

96.6 Independent radio; can shift from house to jazz to metal in a matter of moments.

100.8 Dance, you fool, dance! *Con el ritmo latino.*

101.5 Música Catalunya; soothing classical and opera sounds.

102.8 Catalunya Radio; all the latest news—in Catalan, but they'll throw some Spanish in there, too.

105.0 Soft rock, except for when it's rocking out with dance pop.

105.7 The most popular choice of the young set—house, dance, and techno music, all the time. Afternoon dance party, anyone?

106.6 Oldies ranging from the 50s to the 80s, depending on their mood.

NEWSPAPERS & MAGAZINES

Two Catalunya-published papers dominate shelf space in the bourgeois l'Eixample: **El Periódico,** a left-leaning publication available in Catalan and Spanish, and **La VanGuardia,** a more conservative paper published in Spanish. For the more radical Catalanists, there's the **Abui,** a nationalist paper produced in Catalan only, and for the left there's **El País,** and **El Mundo,** based in Madrid, are popular among Barcelona's immigrant and working class population. Also from Madrid are the arch-conservative **ABC** and the more mildly rightist **La Razón.** Not surprisingly, none of the Madrid papers make it into Catalunya without a special section dedicated to affairs of the fair northeastern province.

Of course, Spain would not be Spain (and Barcelona has to count itself in here) without a thriving *prensa rosa*, or tabloid press. By far the most popular magazines are **Hola!**, a sensationalist gossip magazine splashed with up-close pictures and details on the lives of the rich and famous, and **Lecturas**, an equally sensationalist but less picture-heavy review that's ever-so-slightly more in touch with the non-jet-set crowd. For movie buffs, there's **Fotogramas**, and for science, ecology, and technology nerds, **Muy Interesante** keeps up to date on all of the latest breakthroughs. **Quo**, meanwhile, has a better-rounded selection of writing on health, nature, and news. For **English-speaking** expats, the English monthly **Barcelona Metropolitan** is full of personal stories, advice, and news about the city, while the **Broadsheet** covers Spain as a whole with more long feature articles on history, culture, and news.

And of course, last but far from least, there's the indispensable **Guía del Ocio** (see p. 34), Barcelona's comprehensive guide on how to have fun every single weekend; it includes restaurant, nightlife, and theater listings, as well as info on the week's cultural events and performances. The guide is in Spanish, but listings are easy enough to understand even for the non-speaker (what about "*Harry Potter* 9pm" isn't clear?). Directions to venues are often lacking, but may be available in the **Entertainment** chapter (see p. 167) of this guide.

Life & Times

Barcelona is a thriving Spanish city, but to equate Barcelona with Spain is not entirely accurate. Spain is a recent creation, a combination of many older, formerly independent cultures and nations. Consequently, when Barceloneses express patriotism, it is often to an alternate homeland: **Catalunya** (Catalonia or *Cataluña* in Spanish), which was its own nation in medieval times. Barcelona was (and still is) Catalunya's capital and has always celebrated these unique roots, even when they've been at odds with Spanish identity.

During the Middle Ages, the city was an important port on the Mediterranean trade route. In the 16th century, as Spanish trade with the Americas flourished—monopolized by Sevilla—commercial routes shifted away from the Mediterranean, leaving Barcelona in decline. Not until the 19th century, when the Industrial Revolution's textile mills propelled a financial boom, was Barcelona able to regain economic prestige. The aristocracy grew in status and power, and as the 20th century approached, Josep Batlló, Eusebi Güell, and their compatriots commissioned architects like Domènech i Montaner, Puig i Cadafalch, and the legendary Antoni Gaudí to build private residences in l'Eixample, resulting in the artistic movement **Modernisme.** Even the suffocating years of Francisco Franco's Fascist regime could not dampen Barcelona's stature as the world's premier showcase of avant-garde architecture.

Today Barcelona continues to show its distinctive character through political sensibility, a living language, novel approaches to art, and a healthy secession movement. To appreciate the diversity of Spain, one has to visit Barcelona; to appreciate Barcelona, one has to consider it separate from Spain.

HISTORY

ROMAN TIMES

In an effort to subdue the North African powers in Carthage, the Romans ripped through the Iberian peninsula with a vengeance in the 3rd century BC. They subjugated Barcelona's ancient residents, the **Laietani,** and settled next to Montjuïc in 210 BC. In honor of Augustine's rule in 15 BC, the Romans gave the small town the unwieldy name of Colonia Julia Augusta Faventia Paterna Barcino. **Barcino**—Roman Barcelona—lies mostly underneath the modern day Barri Gòtic. As an unimportant provincial town Barcino, was dwarfed in importance by her southern neighbor **Tarragona,** now home to better beaches and ruins (see p. 237). Over the course of almost seven centuries, the Romans drastically altered the region, introducing Rome's language, architecture, roads, irrigation techniques, grapes, olives, and wheat. Constantine declared **Christianity** the official religion of the region in AD 312. As in the rest of the Roman Empire, Roman power in Catalunya declined after Constantine's rule.

VISIGOTHS, MOORS & FRANKS

A slew of Germanic tribes swept over Iberia in the early 5th century; the **Visigoths** were the lucky winners of the peninsula, establishing their court at Barcelona in 415 and laying the foundations of the Catalan feudal society of later centuries. Though the Visigoths effectively ruled Spain for the next 300 years, the empire was more a collection of politically fragmented tribes than a unified whole, paving the way for the next wave of invaders, this time from the south. Following Muslim unification, a small force of Arabs, Berbers, and Syrians, the **Moors,** invaded Spain in 711. Encountering little resistance from the divided Visigoths, Iberia quickly fell under the control of the caliphate of Damascus.

The Moorish presence in Catalunya was short-lived. Charlemagne undermined Moorish power in the late 700s, and his son, Louis the Pious, defeated the Moors in Catalunya in 801. The government Louis the Pious left behind dominated the Catalan Middle Ages, promptly reinstating Christian power under the **Franks,** while most of Spain spent centuries under Islamic rule.

THE MIDDLE & GOLDEN AGES

The common Christianity of the Frankish counts and the Catalans they ruled made the Middle Ages a relatively cooperative time. The Frankish king, **Charles the Bald,** installed **Guifré el Pilós,** or Wilfred the Hairy (oh, the irony), as count of the region in 874. Guifré spent his life defending his monarch, endowing religious institutions, moving power and importance from Tarragona to Barcelona, unifying various parts of Catalunya, and growing more hair every day.

The Moorish attempt to return to Barcelona in 985 marked the beginning of Catalan independence. Guifré's descendant, **Count Borrell,** a man with unknown quantities of bodily hair, asked the Frankish king for military aid to defend against Moorish invasion. When the king ignored this request, Catalunya ceased to acknowledge his sovereignty and went on to defeat the Moors on their own in 989.

Independent from Frankish rule, Barcelona grew wealthy at the start of the new millennium under the successive power of four counts by the same name of **Ramon Berenguer,** all of whom expanded the geographical boundaries of Catalunya. Ramon Berenguer III married Princess Dolça of Provence and so extended Catalan power into modern-day France. **Ramon Berenguer IV's** 1137 marriage to Petronella of Aragón, the daughter of the king of Aragón (a neighboring province), gave even more power to Catalunya.

Using the profits from lucrative iron and wool exports, **Jaume I** (1213-76) expanded the region's waterfront by conquering Valencia and the Balearic Islands; he also created the infrastructures of **Les Corts** and the **Generalitat,** which are the basis for the modern government in the region. With so much seafront property, Barcelona was one of the wealthiest ports in the Mediterranean and therefore also very desirable to its neighbors on the peninsula. Two main factors left the region open to takeover: first, the **Black Death** killed a substantial portion of the population in the 1340s, and second, the last of Guifré's ruling descendants, Martí I, died childless in 1410.

CASTILIANIZATION

CATHOLIC MONARCHS

Plaça Reial

In 1469, the marriage of **Los Reyes Católicos** (the Catholic Monarchs), **Fernando de Aragón** and **Isabel de Castilla,** joined Iberia's two mightiest Christian kingdoms, Castilla and Aragón. Since Aragón was already loosely united with Catalunya, Fernando inherited Catalunya in 1479. By 1492, the dynamic duo had captured Granada (the last Moorish stronghold) and shuttled **Columbus** off across the Atlantic. The Catholic Monarchs introduced the **Inquisition** in 1478, executing and then burning heretics, principally Jews. With Spanish unification as one of its main goals, the Inquisition hit the independent-minded Catalans and the region's significant Jewish population with destructive force.

Barcelona now took orders from the court at Segovia, in the distant region of Castilla y Leon. The Mediterranean was no longer the trade center; Spanish attention shifted to the Americas, and officially banned Catalunya from trading directly with the New World. Over their approximately 50 years of rule, Fernando and Isabel heightened Spain's position as a world economic, political, and cultural power. Yet this prosperity for a newly united Spain did not mean prosperity for Catalunya, which lost its autonomy and faced a crippling economic recession.

The Steps to the Palau d'Art Catalana

THE HAPSBURG DYNASTY

The daughter of Fernando and Isabel, **Juana la Loca** (the Mad), married **Felipe el Hermoso** (the Fair) of the powerful Hapsburg dynasty. Their son, **Carlos I** (1516-1556), reigned over an immense empire comprised of modern-day Holland, Belgium, Austria, Spain, parts of Germany, and Italy, and the American colonies. Spain was arguably the most powerful empire in the world under the Hapsburgs, leading to a **Golden Age** of painting and literature for the peninsula.

Fundació Tàpies

However, as most of Spain enjoyed the Golden Age, Catalunya was marginalized, both economically and culturally. While central Spain produced painters like Velázquez and El Greco, Catalunya mainly produced rebellion. Barcelona had lost her importance as a trade city, and the region was inconveniently in the midst of numerous battles between the French and Spanish, beginning in 1635 and resulting in the **Guerra dels Segadors** (Reapers' War) in 1640.

The Guerra dels Segadors—a name which later became the title of the Catalan national anthem—was an attempt at independence originating from within the oppressed masses. The 12 years of war began with civil disobedience and escalated to Catalunya siding with France, hoping to use the tense Franco-Iberian relations to her advantage. It worked, and **Louis XIII** of France even went so far as to send troops to help the Catalans defend themselves in their fight for independence. However, the war was administrated badly on the Catalan side, and the French eventually betrayed Catalunya, creating an alliance with Spain. When the war ended in 1652, these two nations divided the spoils: a treaty returned Catalunya to Hapsburg control, with the exception of the northeastern corner, which was ceded to France.

WAR OF SPANISH SUCCESSION

When Hapsburg king **Carlos II** died before producing an heir, Europe was presented with the opportunity to install some lucky heir on the Spanish throne. There were two main candidates for the position of Spanish monarch: the **Archduke Carlos,** from Austria, and **Felipe V,** a Bourbon from France and grandson of Louis XIV. Still bitter with France about their betrayal in the Guerra dels Segadors, Catalunya chose to support the Austrian candidate in the ensuing War of Spanish Succession. Spain and France chose the French contender and it was soon clear that Catalunya had backed the wrong horse; in 1713 the **Treaty of Utrecht** made Felipe V the new monarch.

BOURBON ON THE ROCKS

Felipe V (1713-1746) came down with an iron fist on Catalunya, punishing the region for not backing him in the War of Spanish Succession. In an attempt to Castilianize the region and break its spirit, Felipe V restricted the use of the Catalan language. He also built the infamous **Ciutadella** (now a park; see p. 72) in 1718 which left a visible military presence, an oppressive reminder to Barcelona not to cross Felipe again.

Luckily for Catalunya, the Bourbons who followed Felipe lightened restrictions and improved the region's infrastructure. New canals, roads, organized settlements, agricultural reforms, and industrial expansion encouraged Barcelona's natural inclination to trade. **Carlos III** (1759-1788) lifted the ban on Catalan trade with the Americas in 1778, which led Barcelona to another economic boom.

These good times didn't last. **Napoleon** invaded Spain in 1808 as part of his quest for world domination and he tempted Catalunya with promises of independence. Catalunya's decision to side with Madrid in an effort to oust the French is one of the rare times that the region showed total solidarity with Spain. The cooperation worked: the French were expelled in 1814. Industry and trade picked up again as a result. However, soon after, under **Fernando VII** (1814-1833), Spain started losing her empire. Inspired by liberal ideas in the brand-spanking-new Spanish **constitution** (1812) most of the Latin American empire soon attained independence. Domestically, parliamentary liberalism was restored in 1833 upon Fernando VII's death and survived the conservative challenge of the **Carlist Wars** (1833-1840) and dominated Spanish politics until the 1920s.

EXPANSION, THE RENAIXENÇA & ANARCHY

Rapid industrialization and prosperity marked 19th-century Spain, including Catalunya, and as Barcelona's population quickly grew, it was necessary to tear down the **old walls** (1854). This monumental bit of urban planning led to the city's expansion in the form of **l'Eixample** (the Enlargement). For more on the planning of l'Eixample, see p. 195.

The late 19th and early 20th centuries yielded Catalunya's industrial-inspired **Renaixença** (Renaissance), one of the most creative artistic periods in Catalan and Spanish history. The gridded blocks of l'Eixample were slowly filled in with bourgeois and buildings from Barcelona's **Modernisme** movement in architecture and design (see p. 48). The Renaixença also saw the return of regional nationalism as the Catalan language was standardized and reaffirmed.

The liberal mayor **Francesc de Paula Rius i Taulet** was a defining force in Barcelona at this time. In 1888, Rius i Taulet hosted the **Universal Exposition** in Barcelona, an event which introduced Catalan Modernisme to the world and transformed the face of the city. In a master stroke of symbolism, Rius i Taulet held the exposition in a formerly hated location: the site of Felipe V's oppressive Ciutadella. The event was an excuse to revamp and develop the city, rejuvenating Barcelona while showcasing it's artistic developments to the world.

Communications Tower on Montjuïc

The last half of the 19th century also saw the rise of **anarchy** in Barcelona, primarily among the impoverished working class. The 1890s saw a series of bombings, the most notable being the 1893 bombing of the Liceu opera house (now restored; see p. 55), designed to attack the wealthy and the system of centralized authority. True anarchy hit the city in 1909 with the **Setmana Trágica (Tragic Week).** Protests against an unpopular imperialist war with Morocco drew support from Socialists and anarchists. Protests turned into organized strikes, which in turn morphed into unorganized revolts and riots. The week ended in the destruction of almost 100 buildings and in over 100 dead citizens.

Statue of Columbus

DICTATORSHIPS & DRAMA

THE FIRST DICTATOR & THE SECOND REPUBLIC

Despite abstention, Spain was deeply affected by **World War I.** Europe's wartime economy brought waves of impoverished rural workers to Spain's cities, including Barcelona. The influx of people looking for work rocked labor standards, invited chaos, allowing Castilian Captain General **Miguel Primo de Rivera** to shut down Parliament and ascend to dictatorship in 1923, with the permission of **King Alfonso XIII** (1902-1931).

Primo de Rivera's years in power are often quickly passed over in history books because they pale in comparison to the dictatorship

Park Güell Structures

that would follow; however, the dictatorship was no walk in the park. Once again, Catalunya's language and culture were repressed. In 1929, Primo de Rivera attempted to demonstrate that Barcelona was still thriving with an **International Exhibition** that resulted in the tourist-trap **Poble Espanyol;** whether he achieved this goal is debatable (see p. 99).

In the 1920s, Spain had both a dictator and a monarch; by 1931, it had neither. Primo de Rivera retired in 1930, and King Alfonso XIII, disgraced by his support for Primo de Rivera, fled Spain. His departure gave rise to the **Second Republic** (1931-1936), beloved by liberals and intellectuals everywhere. During this short time, Republican liberals and Socialists established safeguards for farmers and industrial workers, granted women suffrage, assured religious tolerance, and chipped away at traditional military dominance.

National euphoria faded quickly. The 1933 elections split the Republican-Socialist coalition, in the process increasing the power of right wing and Catholic parties. Military dissatisfaction led to a heightened profile of the Fascist party **Falange,** which further polarized national politics. By 1936, radicals, anarchists, Socialists, and Republicans had formed a loose, federated alliance to win the next elections. The Republic was weak, victory was short-lived, and once **Generalísimo Francisco Franco** took control of the Spanish army, the military rebelled, and the nation dove into war.

THE CIVIL WAR

The three-year **Civil War** (1936-1939) ignited worldwide ideological passions; the causes and effects of the Civil War touch every aspect of 20th-century Spain. Germany and Italy dropped troops, supplies, and munitions into Franco's lap, while the stubbornly isolationist US and the liberal European states were slow to aid the Republicans. Although Franco and the Nationalists enjoyed support in Andalucía, Galicia, Navarra, and parts of Castilla, the Republicans controlled most population and industrial centers. Barcelona was actually the Republican capital from 1937 until Franco finally won the Civil War in 1939. The Soviet Union, somewhat indirectly, called for a **Popular Front** of Communists, Socialists, and other leftist sympathizers to battle Franco's Fascism. But soon after, the West abandoned the coalition, and aid from the Soviet Union waned as Stalin began to see the benefits of an alliance with Hitler. Without international aid, Republican forces found themselves cut off from supplies and food, and began to surrender. All told, bombings, executions, combat, starvation, and disease took nearly 600,000 lives nationwide.

FRANCO

By the time the Civil War ended, **World War II** was already in full swing. With so many dead and such overwhelming debt in the wake of their own war, it was impossible for Spain to participate. The first decades of Franco's rule were marked by braindrain (as leading intellectuals emigrated or were assassinated), worker dissatisfaction, student unrest, regional discontent, and international isolation. However, his one positive contribution was helping Jews out of France during World War II. Nevertheless, Barcelona lost virtually all of her innovative painters, artists, and writers to intimidation and exile (with the exception of Dalí, who suddenly became very controversial in the international art realm by ceasing to produce any art of consequence). With intellectual and artistic growth thus stunted, Franco moved on to old-fashioned oppression: the Catalan language was again outlawed. Money was constantly drained out of Catalunya to be redistributed where Franco saw fit; as a result, Barcelona constantly protested. Close to the French border and far from Madrid's watchful eye, the city was able to rebel against Franco more than other cities in Spain. In 1960, **Jordi Pujol,** the future leader of Catalunya, even went so far as to sing the decidedly illegal Catalan national anthem in front of Franco at a concert on one of the dictator's visits, for which he spent three years in jail.

In his old age, Franco tried to smooth international relations by joining NATO and encouraging tourism, but the "national tragedy" (as the war and dictatorship were later called) did not officially end until Franco's death in 1975. Shortly before his

I f it is true that "Barcelona radiates style," (see **Barcelona Planned**, p. 195) it is equally true that Barcelona radiates history. By "history" I mean not the grand expansion after 1850, which endowed the city with a distinctively Modernist space and habitat—from my perspective, that is current events, not the history that explains why the clearing and paving of farmlands failed to obliterate much deeper pasts that remain for all to see.

What happened in the 19th century was that a Roman military settlement called *Barcino* lost its historic character as the focal—and therefore "modern"—space of an ancient city. People got tired of renovating it, they had been doing that for 1500 years. The villagers north of the little rectangle the Romans lived in were quite willing to be bought out. So the Roman space survives today because the latest modernizers failed to complete the destruction visited on it by invaders, settlers, and builders who lived in the Middle Ages.

The great age of ancient Barcelona, and the earliest we know much about, was the 2nd century, when a temple stood on a little hill between streams emptying into the sea. A civic center (forum) stood nearby; an aqueduct brought water to a north portal, to the west of which a civic cemetery was laid out. These things are still visible, together with the ruins of a ponderous wall, which dates from a 4th-century Germanic invasion. A bishop's church near the old temple was built at the same time.

All these features figure in what is today called the Barri Gòtic, or "Gothic Quarter." But this usage confuses Barcelona's pasts, for it refers to the Roman space as it looked after about 1250. Even then, nearly a millennium after the Romans, the ponderous turrets looked "Roman," but they were in ruins, salvaged only by great lords and merchants who had them made over as castles. Of new Gothic buildings, the spaciously arched Catalan Gothic is visible famously in Santa Maria del Mar, the merchants' church east of the old city, and also in the Count's palace, with the adjoining chapel of Santa Agatha, the Cathedral of Santa Creu and Santa Eulàlia, and the Palau de la Generalitat.

But to speak of the old Roman city adorned with late medieval Gothic structures as the "Gothic Quarter" is to overlook the least known of Barcelona's pasts, that of an ancient city under Visigoths, conquered by Muslims, then conquered by the Franks, who appointed a deputy called "count" to govern in the (Frankish) king's name. Barcelona suffered a devastating attack by Muslims in 985, then recovered in a burgeoning mercantile expansion, so that its population burst outside the walls by the 12th century. One or two medieval houses in the Jewish quarter just west of the cathedral can still be seen; while the chapel of the businessman Bernat Marcuç just east of the eastern wall evokes the new suburban life of that age. Count Ramon Berenguer IV (1131-1162) married the heiress to the kingdom of Aragón, and their descendants ruled a cluster of principalities in which Barcelona remained central. One of the ways in which Barcelona radiates history today is in the architectural reminders of centrality in a territorial Catalan culture: the *Llotja*, or merchants' hall, evoking the Mediterranean trade of the Crown of Aragón; the Palau de la Generalitat, the organ of a precocious parliamentary life in Catalunya.

Because the Romans built better and some of their successors built much later, not very much of what may be called the "heroic age" of Barcelona is visible today. Evidence in writing as well as in stone disappeared. Masses of documents were burned in 985. The Romanesque cathedral of 1058 became the Gothic cathedral (begun in 1298) we see today. So it is a deep past, lasting some seven centuries, that separates the Roman and late medieval cities of Barcelona that are triumphantly visible to the citizens and visitors of today. Yet even this murky history is accessible in Barcelona, if one knows where to look for it. The Catalan religious culture that tended to progress stylistically in Barcelona as a city remained insistently traditional in the countrysides. The cathedral of La Seu d'Urgell, adjoining Andorra in the Pyrenees Mountains, stands today as it was built around 1120; a jewel of Romanesque architecture. Many hundreds of rural churches were built and rebuilt in the old style. And the religious painting in those churches from the 10th to the 13th century, visible in the Museum of the Art of Catalunya, is the record of an old way of life and imagination, deeply influenced by late Roman art (still visible everywhere in the 11th century). Catalan Gothic, a brave new style, never drove it out. Barcelona is as modern in the 21st century as it was in the 12th, a crossroads of its own deep pasts.

Thomas N. Bisson is the Lea Professor of Medieval History at Harvard University.

Barceloneta

Bullfighting Arena

Arxiu Courtyard

own death, Franco reinstated **King Juan Carlos I** (1975-), grandson of Alfonso XIII. Juan Carlos I carefully set out to undo Franco's damage, reinstituting Spanish democracy when he could conceivably have continued the cycle of political oppression. In 1978, under premier **Adolfo Suárez,** Spain adopted a new constitution in a national referendum that led to the restoration of parliamentary government. This assured a comfortable degree of regional autonomy for Catalunya.

DEMOCRACY AND AUTONOMY

The post-Franco years have been marked by progressive social change. In 1978 the Catalan Generalitat, a regional semi-autonomous government, was created. **Jordi Pujol** became president in 1980, and continues to lead the region today. Catalunya still has a secession movement, but it is not violent. The region is generally comfortable with the degree of autonomy it has, which celebrates the Catalan language in public schools and allows Catalan control over the region's major resources.

Charismatic **Felipe González** led the PSOE (Spanish Socialist Worker's Party) to victory in the 1982 national elections. In 1986, González opened the Spanish economy and championed consensus policies, overseeing Spain's integration into what was then the European Community (EC), now the **European Union (EU).** Despite unpopular economic stands, González was reelected in 1986 and continued a program of massive public investment. The years 1986 to 1990 were outstanding for Spain's economy, but by the end of 1993, recession set in. In 1993, González and the PSOE barely maintained a majority in Parliament over the conservative **Partido Popular (PP). José Maria Aznar** led the PP into power after González's support eroded and has maintained a delicately balanced coalition with the support of the Catalan regional party.

TODAY

The last decade has seen mixed progress in one of Spain's most pressing areas of concern— Basque nationalism and terrorism, carried out by the Basque separatist group, **ETA.** This issue concerns the whole country; while Basque hostility is traditionally directed at Madrid, there has been hostility toward Catalunya. Basque violence generally occurs in the form of assassinations of political figures and terrorist bombings. Between September and December of 2000, two politicians and one police officer were shot within Barcelona's city limits; two bomb attacks during the same months injured others. The most recent attack in Catalunya occurred in March 2001, when a police officer was killed in Rosas, north of Barcelona; in the same month, a car bomb was successfully diffused in Valencia.

On a brighter national note, Barcelona is one of the wealthiest cities in Spain, the Spanish economy is currently stable and growing with the EU's success. Aznar describes visions of "a new Spain" and plans to reduce unemployment even further, draw more women into the workforce, and improve the faltering birthrate by restructuring family and work arrangements. Though the work reforms implemented have reduced the unemployment rate, they are not without controversy (see **Workers of the World,** p. 88). Catalan regional politics is also in good shape. Catalan hero Jordi Pujol maintains control of the regional government, the **Generalitat;** the current mayor of the city, the **Ajuntament,** is Socialist **Joan Clos.**

LANGUAGE

Catalunya, like many other regions of Spain, is bilingual. **Castellano** (Castilian or *Castellà* in Catalan), a.k.a. **Spanish,** spoken by almost everyone with varying degrees of ease, is Spain's official language. **Català (Catalan)** is spoken in all of Catalunya and has given rise through permutations to *Valencià*, the language of Valencia, *Mallorquín* of Mallorica, *Menorquín* of Menorca, and *Evissinc* of Ibiza. Catalan is not a dialect of Spanish but rather a full-fledged Romance language in an of itself. Catalans will get insulted if a tourist—or a Spaniard—refers to their language as a dialect. Catalan and Castilian have separate standardized grammars and their own oral and written literary traditions. Regional television broadcasts, strong political associations, the use of Catalan as vernacular and in church, and extensive schooling have served not only to save the language Catalan from extinction, but also to reinforce patriotism for Catalan culture.

ART

PAINTING & SCULPTURE

Over its long history, Catalan painting has seen a series of luminaries separated by several lulls. Flemish, French, and Italian techniques influenced the Middle Ages and the Renaissance; in recent history the Surrealists have forged a dazzling, distinctive, and influential body of work.

EARLY, GOTHIC & RENAISSANCE

The **Spanish Golden Age** and the **Catalan Golden Age** occurred at two different times. The 16th century produced such giants as El Greco and Velásquez in central Spain, but the most productive time for Catalan painting came earlier. In the 11th and 12th centuries, through the Renaissance (not to be confused with the 19th-century Renaixença; see p. 40), the most significant paintings were frescoes that decorated churches and libraries. Fourteenth-century **Ferrer Bassa** is the most renowned Catalan painter; his frescoes can be seen in the Monestir de Pedralbes (see p. 106). The works of famous painters from this period, such as 15th-century **Jaume Huguet** and Flemish-influenced **Bartolomé Bermejo,** are on display in the MNAC (see p. 96); Huguet also has an important work in the Museu d'Història de Catalunya (see p. 94).

BIRTH OF MODERNISM

Catalan painting experienced a lull under the Hapsburgs until the 1800s, when Impressionist-inspired **Marià Fortuny** started to gain recognition; his paintings can be seen in the Museu d'Art Modern (see p. 73). His appearance reenergized Catalan art and began a long line of talented painters that would emerge in the 19th and 20th centuries.

MODERNISME

Although Catalan Modernist painting, which mostly just followed the latest trends in Paris, is not as internationally recognized as Catalan Modernist architecture (see p. 48), it still produced some memorable characters and admirable works. One such fellow is **Ramon Casas** (1866-1932), illustrator of the popular literary magazine **Pel i Plom,** owner of the first car in Barcelona, hot commodity in the advertising industry, and painter extraordinaire. His contemporary, **Santiago Rusinyol** (1861-1931), was another significant figure on the Modernist scene. Despite his addiction to morphine and his literary aspirations, his novel use of color in his representations of nature produced a number of memorable works. Both artists are represented in the Museu d'Art Modern (see p. 73).

SURREALISM

Surrealism explores the experience of the subconscious through various approaches: the world of childhood, the world of dreams, the world of madness. While this movement was started in France by André Breton, Catalunya produced some of the most innovative artists of the movement. Painter and sculptor **Joan Miró** (1893-1983) approached the subconscious from the perspective of childhood (see p. 95). His cryptic and symbolic squiggles became a statement against the authoritarian society of the post-Civil War years; indeed, his works are so closely tied to the events of 20th-century Spain that one can date them simply by observing the colors and images used. By contrast, fellow Catalan **Salvador Dalí** (1904-1989) scandalized high society and leftist intellectuals in France and Spain by reportedly supporting the Fascists; in reality, Dalí knew nothing about politics and he probably only encouraged such rumors to keep the spotlight on himself. **Picasso** also dabbled in Surrealism, but his main contribution to the artistic world came in quite another form.

CUBISM

It is hard to imagine an artist who has had as profound an effect upon 20th-century painting as Andalucian-born **Pablo Ruíz Picasso** (1881-1973). As a child prodigy, Picasso headed for Barcelona, a hothouse for Modernist architecture and political activism. Bouncing back and forth between Barcelona and Paris, Picasso in 1900 inaugurated his Blue Period, characterized by somber depictions of society's outcasts. His permanent move to Paris in 1904 initiated his Rose Period, during which he probed into the curiously engrossing lives of clowns and acrobats. This thematic and stylistic evolution led Picasso through his own revolutionary style.

With his French colleague Georges Braque, Picasso founded Cubism, a method of painting objects simultaneously from multiple perspectives. Cubism evolved slowly, but the first Cubist painting is commonly recognized as **Las Señoritas de Avignon** (**The Ladies of Avignon;** 1907). His most famous Cubist work, the gigantic 1937 mural *Guernica*, portrays the bombing of that Basque city by Nazi planes in cahoots with Fascist forces during the Spanish Civil War. A vehement protest against violence and fascism, *Guernica* now resides in the Centro de Arte Reina Sofía in Madrid. Barcelona's Museu Picasso has a commendable chronological spread of Picasso's work, from his earliest paintings to his Cubist engravings (see p. 68).

ABSTRACT

Since Franco's death in 1975, a new generation of artists has thrived. Catalan **Antoni Tàpies** constructs definition-defying works out of unusual and unorthodox materials most would refer to as trash. Tàpies is a founding member of the self-proclaimed "Abstract Generation," which sponsored the magazine **Dau al Set.** Tàpies work is commonly interpreted as an expression of urban alienation and decay in the wake of Franco's oppression. The Fundació Tàpies showcases his postmodern angst (see p. 90).

ARCHITECTURE

As a reflection of its distinct political and social history, Barcelona lacks the "typically" Spanish, Moor-influenced style. Instead, the city boasts some of the most innovative and exciting architecture in the world as a result of the **Modernisme** movement.

ENTER THE ROMANS

The numerous **Roman ruins** that sprinkle the Spanish countryside testify to six centuries of colonization. While Barcelona holds a few remnants of the Romans' inhabitation (in the form of columns, walls, and sewers), the ruins in **Tarragona** are much more extensive (see p. 237).

Gay Pride Parade

ROMANESQUE

Little architecture remains from the Visigoths, who inhabited the area from 415 AD until the eighth century. Until the 12th century, the **Romanesque** style prevailed in Iberia. The Romanesque style is characterized by its extreme simplicity. North of the city, in Ripoll, **Santa Maria de Ripoll** is a striking example of Romanesque architecture (see p. 246).

GOTHIC STYLE

The **Spanish Gothic** style, like Gothic elsewhere in Europe, brought experimentation with pointed arches, flying buttresses, slender walls, airy spaces, and stained-glass windows. In keeping with their patriotic love of deviation, the Catalan developed their own style by employing internal wall supports rather than external buttresses. The **Catalan Gothic** movement, dominant from the 13th to the 15th century, differs in that it is not as ornate and flamboyant as the rest of the world's take on the Gothic style, but is more plain and simple in decoration and style. Rather than high pointy towers, the Catalans created hexagonal towers. Instead of trying to surpass other buildings in vertical height, the Barcelona architects tested the use of horizontal planes in their surprisingly flat Gothic buildings. Using materials such as iron and stone, they created huge facades protecting beautiful gardens inside. **Santa Maria del Mar** and **Santa Maria del Pi** are two churches that exemplify this style (see p. 70 and p. 64). Barcelona's main Cathedral, **Església Catedral de la Santa Creu,** is the city's most traditional building from this period (see p. 57).

Palau Güell

Paintings for Sale in Plaça Pi

I Dream of Dalí

As an adult, Salvador Dalí always appeared to be confident in his artistic talents, but he was not so confident in every aspect of his life. The artist was extremely introverted and socially awkward. From an early age, Dalí was plagued by nightmares and insecurities. Sexually inexperienced until a late age, Dalí was sexually ambiguous and had a fear of sexual contact and impotence.

But the nightmares, it seems, had positive effects on his work: Dalí was able to recreate them on canvas. His dreamlike landscapes blend reality and fantasy to form a picture of what our subconscious might look like. Often, the artist would set a canvas beside his bed, so as to capture subconscious imagery directly upon waking. Later in his career, he would come to describe his work as "hand painted dream photographs." His insecurities and fears, from both dreams and human interaction, became one of his central subjects.

Inspired by Freud's work *The Interpretation of Dreams*, as well as by the French surrealist poet Andre Breton, Dalí created his own brand of surrealism. While in Madrid, he developed friendships with such artist giants as Federico Garcia Lorca, Pablo Neruda, and Luis Bunuel. Bunuel and Dalí collaborated on the film *Un Chien Andalou*, a masterpiece of surrealist cinema, as hallucinatory as the painter's work on canvas.

RENAISSANCE & BAROQUE

New World riches inspired the **Plateresque** ("in the manner of a silversmith") style, a flashy extreme of Gothic that transformed wealthy Andalucia. Intricate stonework and extravagant use of gold and silver splashed 15th- and 16th-century buildings. In the late 16th century, **Italian Renaissance** innovations in perspective and symmetry arrived in Spain to sober up the Plateresque style. In the 17th and 18th centuries **Baroque** came to Spain, in the form of Gothic renovations. The movement is responsible for the the **Palau Dalmases** (see p. 145).

MODERNISME

The Modernisme movement was born out of a growing sense of Catalan pride and nationalism; it became a symbolic and creative outlet for the province's increasing political autonomy. While Modernisme was not limited to Barcelona (known as *art nouveau* in France and *Jugendstil* in Germany), **Catalan Modernisme** has a unique flavor. The movement exploded onto the architecture scene at the **1888 Universal Exposition** and remained at its height through the first decade of the 20th century.

Modernisme rebelled against the conventional rigidity of 19th century realism. Instead, Modernisme combined Nordic Gothic architecture with natural influences to create imaginative shapes and designs. While some critics have dismissed the Modernisme movement as pretentious, the popularity of Barcelona's **Ruta del Modernisme** and support from the Surrealist movement is evidence for its overwhelming intrigue (see p. 51).

Antoni Gaudí i Comet, the most famous of the Modernisme architects, constructed the two most touristed sites in Barcelona, **La Casa Milà** (Milà House) and **La Sagrada Família** (The Sacred Family). Gaudí's genius comes in the form of his understanding of space and this effect on his personal vision of the finished project. Combining Gothic influences with inspiration from nature and innovative materials, Gaudí created such marvels as **Casa Batlló** and **Park Güell** (see p. 87 and p. 100). The colorful infusion of history and nature, in every detail, are his defining characteristics. Gaudí's ideas were so unprecedented that he worked alongside the craftsmen in order to fully execute his vision.

While Gaudí is the most famous of the Modernisme architects, two others, Lluís Domènech i Montaner and Josep Puig i Cadafalch, deserve mention. As the director of Barcelona's School of Architecture, **Domènech i Montaner** was in the position to influence not only Barcelona's architecture, but also its future architects. At the Universal Exposition of 1888 he presented his **Castell de Tres Dragones** (Castle of Three Dragons), designed as a restaurant for the Exposition. It was a huge success and marked the official beginning of the Modernisme movement. Domènech was especially innovative in his choice of building materials. He used stucco to imitate stone and also ignored the contemporary disdain for brick, as he was drawn to its organic quality and its connection to the earth. He alone allowed Moorish influences to creep into his work. His most renowned works are the **Hospital de la Santa Creu i Sant Pau** and the **Palau de la Música Catalana** (see p. 81 and p. 69).

Josep Puig i Cadafalch is the youngest of the main Modernisme architects of Barcelona. He resented the label "Modernisme," as he felt that his and his peers' works exhibited more local flare than the beginnings of an international architectural movement. His use of spatial effects and attention to surface are especially notable. Puig was more of a planner than Gaudí or Domènech i Montaner, and his works are clearly influenced by Gothic architecture; his most well-known building is **Casa Amatller** (see p. 88).

NOUCENTISME

Noucentisme—a movement which covered all spheres of visual arts—is often overshadowed by other movements; indeed the movement pales in comparison to its Modernist architectural counterpart. A reaction to the disorder brought by Modernisme and World War I, Noucentisme is a Neoclassical revival that focused on order and simplicity. Puig i Cadafalch, reborn as a Noucentisme architect, was responsible for the redesign of Pl. de Catalunya. For examples of this movement, check out the area surrounding the **plaça**, the **Estació França**, and the **Museu Arqueològic**. The latter two were both built for the 1929 International Exhibition (see p. 41).

THE 20TH CENTURY TO THE PRESENT

After the Civil War destroyed Spain's economy and Franco entered the scene, growth and development of Barcelona's once prospering architectural innovations came to a halt. Few noteworthy architectural developments occurred during this era. Franco did sponsor the building of the university, although construction stopped a few years later due to a lack of funding. The building of **Camp Nou,** the soccer stadium, was funded by the people of Barcelona.

Today the city is going through rapid urban development. Since Franco's death, there has been a movement toward eliminating the changes he had made to Barcelona, as well as a focus on beautifying the city. Mayor **Pasqual Maragall** was the key player in this endeavor; after managing to secure the **1992 Summer Olympics** for the city, he brought modern high rises to Barcelona's beachfront property and turned the waterfront into Nightlife Central.

Sights & Museums

TOURS

RUTA DEL MODERNISME

For those with a few days in the city and an interest in seeing some of the most popular sights, the Ruta del Modernisme is the cheapest and most flexible option. The Ruta del Modernisme is not a tour, precisely, in the sense that it doesn't offer a guide or organized transportation; it's a ticket which provides discount admission to dozens of Modernist buildings throughout the city. Passes (€3.60; students, over 65, and groups over 10 people €2.60) are good for 30 days and give holders a 25-30% discount on entrance to Palau de la Música Catalana (see p. 69), Fundació Antoni Tàpies (see p. 85), the Museu d'Art Modern (see p. 73), the Museu de Zoologia (see p. 75), tours of El Hospital de la Santa Creu i Sant Pau (see p. 81) and the facades of La Manzana de la Discòrdia (Casas Amatller, Lleó Morera, and Batlló; see p. 86), and map tours of Gaudí, Domènech i Montaner, and Puig i Cadafalch, among other attractions. The pass comes with a map and a pamphlet that gives a history of the different sites that is helpful in prioritizing visits. Purchase passes at **Casa Amatller,** Pg. Gràcia, 41 (M: Pg. de Gràcia, L2/3/4; ☎93 488 01 39; www.rutamodernisme.com; see

NO WORK ALL PLAY

The Melting Pot

Watch out, world! Barcelona, the Spanish Government, and UNESCO are uniting to stamp out racism, ignorance, and poverty! Or so says the mission for the first **Universal Forum of Cultures,** a huge summer-long festival set to bloom for the first time in 2004. The event, which runs from May 9th to Sept. 26th, seeks to promote a "renewal of thought and attitudes" toward cultural diversity, development, and conditions for peace.

Plans include six film festivals, over 60 international congresses, and more than 300 "gastronomic experiences." With 2004 marking the Forum's inaugural event, sponsors are envisioning a global communal experience akin to a cultural Olympics, with a particularly important message of peace. What does this mean for Barcelona? Tons of new parks (140,000sq.m to be exact) in addition to renewed seashore and beaches. Some are even drawing comparisons to the make-overs preceding the **1888 Universal Exposition** and the **1992 Olympics**. But while this means fun and games for Barcelona in the summer, winter, and spring tourists should watch out for unexpected construction as the city beautifies for the Forum.

p. 88) near the intersection with C. Aragó. Many of these sights have tour time and length restrictions; visiting all of them on the same day is virtually impossible.

BUS TURÍSTIC

Sit back and let the sights come to you. The Bus Turístic stops at 26 points of interest along two different elliptical routes (red for the northbound buses, blue for the south-bound). Tickets come with a comprehensive eight-language brochure with information about each sight. A full ride on both routes takes 3-3½ hours depending on traffic, but feel free to get on and off as often as you want. You can buy tickets once on board, or ahead of time at **Turisme de Catalunya**, 17 Pl. de Catalunya (☎906 30 12 82), in front of El Corte Inglés (see **Shopping,** p. 181). Many of the museums and sights covered by the bus offer discounts with the bus ticket; keep in mind that some are closed on Mondays. Overall, the bus is a good idea if you want to see the whole city quickly, as it cuts transportation time, but it's not necessary if you have the time to explore the city at a more leisurely pace. (Buses run daily except Dec. 25 and Jan. 1, every 10-30min. 9am-9:30pm; 1-day pass €15, ages 4-12 €9, 2-day pass €19.)

LAS RAMBLAS

see map pp. 334-335

⚐ M: Catalunya, L1/3; Liceu, L3; Drassanes, L3. Lower numbered addresses begin at the port, while higher numbers are toward the top of Las Ramblas, Pl. de Catalunya.

Las Ramblas, a pedestrian-only median strip, is a cosmopolitan cornucopia of street performers, fortune-tellers, human statues, vendors, and artists, all for the benefit of the visiting droves of tourists. A stroll along this bustling avenue can be an adventure at almost any hour, day or night. The wide, tree-lined thoroughfare dubbed Las Ramblas is actually composed of five (six if you count the small Rambla de Mar) distinct ramblas (promenades) that together form one boulevard, about 1km long; what follows is a description of the different segments of Las Ramblas and the sights and museums along the way, beginning with Pl. de Catalunya in the north and heading towards the port in the south. Locals almost always refer to the streets as one entity, Las Ramblas, and not by their individual names. Check out the **Walking Tour** (p. 8) for help on approaching Las Ramblas.

LA RAMBLA DE LES CANALETES

The port-ward journey along las Ramblas begins at the **Font de les Canaletes,** the glorified water pump for which la Rambla de les Canaletes is named; it's recognizable by the four faucets and the Catalan crests (red crosses next to red and yellow stripes) that adorn it. Legend has it that visitors who sample the water will fall in love with the city (if they haven't already) and are bound to return to Barcelona someday. Stationed around here are the first of many living statues that line Las Ramblas during the day. Because of its symbolically important position at the top of Las Ramblas on the Pl. de Catalunya, La Rambla de les Canaletes also sees a fair number of political demonstrations.

Living Statue on Las Ramblas

LA RAMBLA DELS ESTUDIS

You'll hear the squawking of the caged residents of the next section of Las Ramblas before you see them. The next stretch of Las Ramblas, which extends to C. Carme and C. Portaferrissa, is often referred to as "La Rambla dels Ocells" ("Promenade of the Birds"). A number of stalls here sell birds of nearly every kind: roosters, parrots, ducks, and even baby emus. Guinea pigs, prairie dogs, fish, caimans, and pretty much every other kind of caged creature is also available. The official name of this stretch of rambla comes from the university that used to be located here; *estudis* is Catalan for "studies."

Park Güell Serpentine Bench

LA RAMBLA DE SANT JOSEP

If the noise of the previous rambla wasn't enough to put you into sensory overload, perhaps the wonderful fragrance of La Rambla de Sant Josep will be. The screeching birds give way to the sunflowers, roses, and tulips on this segment of Las Ramblas, commonly known as "La Rambla de les Flors" ("Promenade of the Flowers"). Vendors here have offered a good variety of bouquets since the mid-1800s. In April, the flower stands are joined by book vendors in preparation for the **Día de Sant Jordi,** a Catalan

La Boqueria

The Local LEGEND

Sant Jordi

Some English speakers know the legend of Saint George and the Dragon from British religious and folkloric tradition; Saint George is, after all, the patron saint of Britain, renowned for battling a dragon and saving many a Christian. However, the English are not the only Christians, nor the only people, with a claim to Saint George, known in Barcelona by his Catalan name, Sant Jordi. In the 13th century, King Jaume I had a vision of Sant Jordi aiding him in battle against Mallorca. Another myth tells the story of a small town held hostage by a fierce dragon which was placated periodically with a sacrificial virgin, chosen via lottery. Eventually, the King's daughter "won" the lottery. As the princess went to the dragon, Sant Jordi arrived and slew the beast, freeing the princess. The entire town subsequently converted to Christianity and Catalans have been enamored with him ever since.

In 1456, April 23 was declared Sant Jordi's day in Barcelona. By the end of the 19th century Sant Jordi was a symbol of Catalan nationalism and the Sant Jordi cross is the highest honor awarded by the Generalitat. Also the Sant Jordi prayer is a plea to God to guard the Catalan culture and language.

variance on Valentine's Day. On April 23, couples exchange gifts; females of all ages receive flowers while males receive books.

The hulking stone building at the corner of C. Carme is the Església de Betlem, a Baroque church whose interior never recovered from an anarchist torching during the Spanish Civil War. A bit farther down is the famous traditional Catalan market, **Mercat de la Boqueria** (see below), officially named **El Mercat de Sant Josep**, the oldest of the city's some 40 markets. At Pl. Boqueria, just before the Metro station Liceu, you'll walk across Joan Miró's circular pavement mosaic, created for the city in 1976 and now a popular meeting point. Last but certainly not least, this part of Las Ramblas is home to the infamous **Museu de l'Eròtica** (see p. 55).

LA BOQUERIA (MERCAT DE SANT JOSEP)

🖪 *Las Ramblas, 95. M: Liceu, L3 outside the Mercat exit. Open M-Sa 8am-8pm.*

Besides being one of the cheapest and best places to get food in the city, La Boqueria is a sight in itself: a traditional (and very clean) Catalan market located right on Las Ramblas in a giant, all-steel Modernist structure. Specialized vendors sell delicious produce, fish, and meat from one of a seemingly infinite number of independent stands inside. This wonderland offers wholesale prices for all kinds of fruit, cheese, meat, bread, wine, and more. There are even a couple of bars, like **Barcentral La Boqueria,** where you can sit down and treat yourself to a lunch of fresh fish (€5.50-16.80) or meat (€4-10.50).

PALAU DE LA VIRREINA

🖪 *Las Ramblas, 99, at C. Carme. M: Liceu, L3. ☎93 316 10 00. Open Tu-Sa 11am-8:30pm; Su 11am-3pm. Free.*

Once the residence of a Peruvian viceroy, this 18th-century palace houses temporary photography, music, and graphics exhibits. Also on display are the latest incarnations of the 10-15 foot tall dolls which have taken part in the city's Carnival celebrations since 1399. The imposing couple Jaume and Violant, dressed in long, regal robes, are the undisputed king and queen of the Carnival parade. The cultural institute here serves as information headquarters for Barcelona's cultural festivals. Be sure to check out the famous rainbow stained-glass facade of the **Casa Beethoven** next door at Las Ramblas 97, now a well-stocked music store (see **Shopping,** p. 182).

MUSEU DE L'ERÒTICA

🔲 *Las Ramblas, 96, on the left as you face the port. M: Cat-alunya, L1/3. ☎ 93 318 98 65. www.erotica-museum.com. Open June-Sept. 10am-midnight; Oct.-May 11am-9pm. €7.50, students €6.50.*

This unique museum examines the history of eroticism, from ancient Greece, Asia, and Africa to the sadomasochism of the eighteenth century to the modern era. As Spain's only erotica museum, the exhibits attract many of Barcelona's most intrepid tourists. The random assortment, part of one person's private collection, spans human history (somewhat unevenly) and depicts a variety of seemingly impossible sexual acrobatics that push the limits of human flexibility. Check out a porn flick commissioned by Spain's very own King Alfonso XIII and listen to dirty talk in English, German, Spanish, or French. The seven-foot wooden phallus overlooking the Boqueria market (see p. 54) is an irresistible photo op. Many of the works on display are for sale. In the end, the museum's greatest historical revelation may be that, indeed, little has changed.

LA RAMBLA DELS CAPUTXINS

Miró's street mosaic marks the beginning of La Rambla dels Caputxins, the most user-friendly of the five Ramblas and the first of Las Ramblas to be converted into an actual promenade. The pedestrian area widens, and the majestic trees provide a bit more shade. Across from the recently renovated opera house (the **Liceu;** see below), a strip of restaurants with outdoor seating vie for tourist euros, offering unremarkable and fairly expensive food; perhaps the prime people-watching perches these restaurants offer make the extra cost worth it.

GRAN TEATRE DEL LICEU

🔲 *Las Ramblas, 51-59, on the corner of C. Sant Pau. M: Liceu, L3. Box Office ☎ 93 485 99 11, Information 93 485 99 13, Tour Reservation 93 485 99 14; www.liceubarce-lona.com. Information office open M-F 2-8:30pm and 1hr. before performances. Tours 10am M-F. €5.*

The Gran Teatre del Liceu has been Barcelona's opera house for over a century. It was once one of Europe's leading stages, playing host to the likes of José Carreras in his early years. Ravaged by a fire in January 1994, it reopened for performances in 1999. It is adorned with palatial ornamentation, gold facades, sculptures, grand circular side rooms, and a hall of mirrors.

It's All Greek to Me

What could be better than a summer of endless dance, theatre, and music performances, all in one of the most contemporary cities in the world? The annual **Grec Festival** lasts from the end of June until the end of August, and includes over a hundred different artistic spectacles, ranging from Greek theatre to independent film. People pour into Barcelona to catch as many events as they can, so try to make reservations for accommodations at least a month in advance. The festival doesn't have a general admittance ticket and therefore can get pretty pricey; shows each charge their own admission and generally range in price from €10-25. However, most of the events are well worth the cost, especially the cinema screenings. They are generally very engaging and somewhat less expensive than the other more traditional performance genres (like opera).

Get tickets at Tel-Entrada (☎ 90 210 12 12; www.telen-trada.com), Palau de la Virre-ina, La Rambla 99 (☎ 93 316 11 11; M-Sa 10am-7pm), Pl. Catalunya, Portal de l'Angel (Daily 10am-8pm), or at any Caixa Catalunya offices (M-F 8am-2:30pm).

■ LA RAMBLA DE SANTA MONICA

Following the tradition of nicknaming the parts of Las Ramblas after the goods sold there, this stretch would most likely be nicknamed La Rambla de las Prostitutas. At night, women of the oldest profession patrol this wide area leading up to the port, beckoning passers-by with loud kissing noises and lots of cleavage. During the day, however, the street distinguishes itself with skilled practitioners of a different fine art. These prodigies can whip up dead-on caricatures in just five minutes, and if you pay them a bit more money they'll invest more time in creating startlingly life-like portraits. La Rambla de Santa Monica is also home to the **Centre d'Art de Santa Monica** and the **Museu de Cera** (see below). Usually on weekends vendors also set up small stands and sell crafts. Although the area's nighttime reputation is somewhat notorious, La Rambla de Santa Monica is not particularly unsafe; as always, however, group travel is a good idea. Las Ramblas ends at La Rambla de Mar, a completely barren gangway serving the sole purpose of connecting Las Ramblas to Port Vell. Before you get there, though, you'll notice one very visible statue.

■ CENTRE D'ART DE SANTA MONICA

🏛 *Las Ramblas, 7, on the right as you approach the port. M: Drassanes, L3. ☎ 93 316 27 27. Cultural center open M-F 9:30am-2pm and 3:30-7:30pm, Sa 10am-2pm, holidays 11am-3pm. Gallery open M-F 11am-2pm and 5-8pm. Call for info on exhibitions. Free.*

One can only imagine what the nuns of this former convent would have thought of the edgy art installations (recently "How Difficult it is to Sleep Alone" and "Transsexual Express") that rotate through this free gallery, which is definitely worth a visit for modern art fans. The site also houses a cultural information center, with info on museums and festivals throughout the city.

MONUMENT A COLOM

🏛 *Portal de la Pau. M: Drassanes, L3. Elevator open June-Sept. daily 9am-8:30pm; Oct.-Mar. M-F 10am-1:30pm and 3:30-6:30pm, Sa-Su 10am-6:30pm; Apr.-May M-F 10am-1:30pm and 3:30-7:30pm, Sa-Su 10am-7:30pm. €2, ages 4-12 and over 65 €1.30, groups of more than 15 €1.70 per person, ages 4 and under free. Groups should make reservations.*

At the port end of Las Ramblas, Ruis i Taulet's Monument a Colom towers 60m above the city. During the late 19th-century Renaixenca movement in Barcelona, Catalan enthusiasts went a little overboard in their regional pride and decided to adopt Columbus as one of their own. Columbus, they claimed, was in fact from a northern town near Girona, and so in 1887-88 they built this statue in his honor. The fact that the statue points proudly toward Libya, not the Americas, doesn't help their claim; historians now agree that Columbus was actually from Genoa, Italy. At night, spotlights turn the statue, renovated in 1982, into a firebrand. Take the elevator up to the top and get a stunning, albeit somewhat obstructed, view of Barcelona.

MUSEU DE CERA (WAX MUSEUM)

🏛 *Las Ramblas, 4, on the left as you face the port. M: Drassanes, L3. ☎ 93 317 26 49. Open Oct.-June, M-F 10am-1:30pm and 4-7:30pm, Sa-Su and holidays 11am-2pm and 4:30-8:30pm; July-Sept. daily 10am-8pm. €6.65, ages 5-11 €3.75.*

While somewhat entertaining, this museum is more of a tourist trap than anything. Some 300 wax figures are crowded into a multilevel building, forming an endless parade of celebrities, fictional characters, and European historical figures you've probably never heard of. Try guessing their identities before looking at the nameplates; it may be more difficult than the museum would hope. The most recognizable figures are generally ones with distinctive facial hair, like Adolf Hitler, Fidel Castro, and Chewbacca from Star Wars.

BARRI GÒTIC

see map pp. 334-335

🚩 *Walking tours of the Barri Gòtic offered by the tourist office in Pl. Catalunya (M: Catalunya, L3) Sa-Su 10am in English; noon in Catalan and Spanish. Visit www.bgb.es or www.barcelonaturisme.com. Spaces are limited; buy tickets at the office or the Ajuntament (see p. 62) in advance. €7, ages 4-12 €3.*

Entertainer on Las Ramblas

The Barri Gòtic is the oldest part of Barcelona; it came into existence well before the inception of the grid layout found in the rest of the city. The Barri Gòtic took form during Roman times and continued to develop during medieval Romanesque and Gothic periods. As a result, the Barri Gòtic is somewhat less navigable than neighborhoods like l'Eixample. Its narrow, serpentine streets are not the products of careful planning and rapid execution, but rather the results of an urban evolution spanning centuries.

Be sure to set a day aside to wander around the Barri Gòtic: while the ancient cathedrals and palaces can give the impression that this neighborhood's time has passed, the area is still very much alive, evident in the ever-crowded streets.

📷 ESGLÉSIA CATEDRAL DE LA SANTA CREU

🚩 *M: Jaume I, L4. In Pl. Seu, up C. Bisbe from Pl. St. Jaume. Cathedral open daily 8am-1:30pm and 4-7:30pm. Cloister open 9am-1:15pm and 4-7pm. Elevator to the roof open M-Sa 10:30am-12:30pm and 4:30-6pm; €1.35. Choir area open M-F 9am-1pm and 4-7pm, Sa-Su 9am-1pm; €0.90. History recording (English) €1.*

Erotic Museum

La Catedral de la Santa Creu (the Cathedral of the Holy Cross) is one of Barcelona's most popular historical monuments. More than 3 million people visit it every year, and it still serves as the active center of Barcelona's Catholic community, recently playing host to Pope John Paul II's one hundredth archbishopric visit. Three separate buildings have actually existed on the site: a 4th-century basilica, an 11th-century Romanesque church, and finally the present Gothic Cathedral, begun in 1298. The much-photographed main facade comes from yet another era (1882), when it was added to the main structure by architect Josep Mestres. Mestres worked from a plan drawn up by Frenchman Carles Galtés de Ruán in 1408, however, so the cathedral maintains a genuinely Gothic appearance.

La Rambla del Mar

THE GUILD-ED AGE

Worker guilds were the labor unions of medieval times. Guilds were organizations of workers of one particular trade that came together to protect members by fixing goods and services prices. However, guilds were not the quaint, mildly cooperative operations that history sometimes paints them to be. A member was not allowed to practice a trade without guild approval, and once a member, economic and social survival was utterly dependent upon obeying all price fixings, quality controls, and production rules.

The guilds had close connections to both the government and the Church (most maintained by their own chapels, many of which are still exist in the Cathedral cloister), and when war broke out, they were often the first source of organized fighters. Naturally, the guilds tended to set up shop near one another for the purpose of sharing resources, and it is from their geographic concentrations that many of the streets in the Barri Gòtic get their names: needle-makers worked in C. Agullers, rope-weavers in C. Corders, cotton-sewers in C. Cotoners, shield-makers in C. Escudellers, glass-makers in C. Vidre, knife-molders in C. Dagueria, and so on.

In the cathedral's *plaça*, seven stylized letters crafted by Joan Brossa spell out "Barcino," commemorating the original Roman city settled on what is now Barcelona. The Romans first ripped through Spain in the 3rd century BC in an effort to subdue North African powers in Carthage. They subjugated the resident Laietani and settled next to Montjuïc in 210 BC. In 15 BC, in honor of Augustus's rule, the Romans gave the small town the unwieldy name of Colonia Julia Augusta Faventia Paterna Barcino.

As you enter the church, the cathedral **choir** is directly in front of you. The backs of the stalls are painted with 46 coats of arms commemorating the Chapter of the Order of the Golden Fleece, an early United Nations meeting of sorts, held in Barcelona in 1519. Walk around the choir, passing several of the Cathedral's small chapels (on the left and the right), and you will find the most important liturgical elements of the Cathedral, including the marble **cathedra** (bishop's throne; the origin of the word "cathedral"), the altar with the bronze **cross** designed by Frederic Marès in 1976, and most famous of all, the sunken **Crypt of Santa Eulalia,** one of Barcelona's patron saints. The crypt holds a white marble sarcophagus that depicts scenes from the saint's martyrdom at age 13. Discovered in the Santa Maria del Mar in 877, Santa Eulalia's remains were not transported here until 1339.

Behind the altar, the Chapel of St. Joan Baptista i St. Josep features one of the most famous pieces of artwork in the Cathedral, the *Transfiguration of the Lord* altarpiece created by Bernat Martorell in 1450. The elevator to the roof is to the left of the altar, through the **Capella de les Animes del Purgatori;** it will give you a close-up view of the Cathedral's spires, as well as a bird's-eye view of Barcelona. The Cathedral treasury, to the right behind the sacristy door, holds the famous monstrance (the receptacle used for holding the Host, the holy bread of the Catholic religion), made of gold and silver and dripping with precious jewels. Legend has it that the monstrance was given to the cathedral by the last Catalan king, Martí, before he died childless in 1410. Outside of the sacristy is the tomb or Ramon Berenguer I, who founded the Romanesque Cathedral that occupied this site in 4th century.

Just to the right of the tomb is the exit into the peaceful ▨**cloister,** home to the **Fountain of St. Jordi,** which is located directly across from the votive candle vending machines (€1 for a small votive, €2 for a large one). Thirteen white geese occupy the cloister, serving as a reminder of St. Eulalia's age at the time of her death. They are joined by a less aesthetically pleasing group of uninvited pigeons. The chapels in the cloister were once dedicated to the various guilds of Barcelona, and a few of them are still maintained today (including the shoe-makers' and electricians'; see **The Guilded Age,** p. 58). If you look back toward the Cathedral interior, you can see the only remaining piece of the Romanesque structure, the large, arched doorway leading back inside. The earlier 4th-century building was almost entirely destroyed by Muslim invaders in 985; what little is left is visible underground in the **Museu d'Història de la Ciutat** (see p. 64). Coming from the Cathedral, you will find at the near right corner of the cloister the **Cathedral museum,** whose most notable holding is Bartolomé Bermejo's renowned oil painting *Pietà*, the image of Christ dying in the arms of his mother (in the Sala Capitular, to the left upon entrance).

Palau Güell Façade

The front of the Cathedral is also the place to catch an impromptu performance of the **sardana,** the traditional Catalan dance (see p. 72). Performances generally occur Sunday mornings and afternoons after mass. (Services begin at noon and 6:30pm.)

PLAÇA DE L'ANGEL

7 *M: Jaume I, L4.*

The Jaume I Metro stop lets out at the Plaça de l'Angel, where the main Roman gate into Barcelona (Barcino during those times) was once located. The *plaça* gets its name from the legend surrounding the moving of St. Eulalia's remains from Santa Maria del Mar to the cathedral: supposedly the martyred saint's body suddenly became too heavy to carry, and an angel appeared in the *plaça* pointing a finger at one of the church officials, who, it turned out, had secretly broken off and stolen one of Eulalia's toes. The angel statue placed in the *plaça* in the 17th century to commemorate the event is now in the **Museu d'Història de la Ciutat** (see p. 64).

Cheese at La Boqueria

ROMAN WALLS

7 *M: Jaume I, L4.*

Several sections of the northeastern walls of Roman Barcino are still standing near the cathedral. C. Tapineria, which runs from Pl. de l'Angel (to the left when you are facing Via Laietana) to **Pl. Ramon Berenguer,** serves both as parking space for mopeds and a viewing area from which you can see a large stretch of a 4th-century barricade under the Palau Reial Major. Continuing along C. Tapineria and making a left onto Av. de la Catedral lands you in Pl. Seu (in front of the

Barri Gotic

in recent news

Women Strike for Peace

Barcelona has seen its fair share of strikes over the past century. One of the more memorable strikes of the last decade took place during the Spring of 2003 at Plaça Sant Jaume, where women of all ages and all nationalities united to speak out against the war on Iraq. The demonstration included a full day of festivities that made use of not only speech but also music and dance. Banners decorating the main stage declared "Global Women's Strike—Stop the World and Change It" in six languages: Spanish, Catalan, Arabic, Urdu, Basque, and English.

The diverse selection of speakers also served to further the global unity behind the movement, with words from pop star Amparanoia and one Venezuelan woman who read a declaration of the Venezuelan government in support of the strike. Perhaps the most profound moment of the demonstration came after a three-day old video of Barcelona police violently evicting anti-war squatters; the subsequent silence was eerily deafening.

For more information about Women Strike, visit http://womenstrike8m. server101.com.

Cathedral), where you can see the only intact octagonal corner tower left today (part of the **Museu Diocesà,** see p. 67). To the right of the cathedral are several more Roman towers and a reconstruction of one of the two aqueducts which supplied water to Barcino.

CARRER DEL BISBE

🚇 *M: Jaume I, L4. Make a sharp left when you exit the main door of the Cathedral. Walk to the end of C. de Santa Llúcia, and you will intersect Carrer del Bisbe.*

In Roman times, C. del Bisbe served as the city's main north-south thoroughfare. Today it is lined with various official buildings. As you walk from the Cathedral to C. del Bisbe, on the right is the entrance to the medieval **Casa de l'Ardiaca,** once home to the archdeacon and now the location of Barcelona's newspaper archives. Stop and check out the mail slot designed by Domènech i Montaner in 1902, next to a sculpted tortoise with several swallows—according to one popular theory, an expression of his opinion of the postal service (supposedly as quick as a bird but actually as slow as a turtle).

Directly across from the Casa de l'Ardiaca is the **Capella de Santa Llúcia;** it is not well labeled, but you can enter through one of two small metal doors. The chapel was built in 1268 and is one of only a few remaining Romanesque churches in the entire city. Every December 13, the Day of Santa Llúcia, locals pay their respects to the saint and the Fair of Sant Llúcia begins around the Cathedral.

Once you exit the chapel, make a left onto C. Bisbe. Walking down the street will take you past the **Palau de la Generalitat** on the right (see p. 4) and the **Casa de los Canónigos** on the left, once home to the religious canons and now the office of the Catalan president. The two are connected by an elaborate neo-Gothic bridge built in 1929 as part of the restoration of the Barri Gòtic.

ROMAN TOMBS

🚇 *M: Liceu or Catalunya, L3. From M: Liceu, walk up Las Ramblas (away from the port) and turn right onto C. Portaferrissa. Take the first left onto C. d'En Bot; it will lead directly to the Pl. de la Vila de Madrid. From M: Catalunya, walk down Las Ramblas and turn left onto C. la Canuda. Make sure not to confuse C. la Canuda with C. Santa Anna; C. la Canuda slopes downward. Walk about thirty yards and Pl. de la Vila de Madrid is on the right.*

Located in the Upper Barri Gòtic, the **Plaça de la Vila de Madrid** contains one final Roman site worth visiting: a row of 2nd- to 4th-century Roman tombs, lined up just as they originally were along a road leading out of Barcino.

(Roman law forbade burial within the city walls.) Look for the tombs underneath the walkways over the tomb pits; the recently restored tombs are significantly lower than the rest of the *plaça*, proof of how much the physical terrain of Barcelona has changed over the past 2000 years.

PLAÇA DE SANT JAUME

◪ M: Jaume I, L4. From the Metro, walk down either C. Jaume I or C. Llibreteria to the plaça.

When Roman colonizers constructed new outpost towns, they always followed the same basic plan, laying down two main streets that intersected in the shape of a short Latin cross (in Barcino, the longer C. Bisbe ran north-south and the shorter C. Llibreteria east-west). At the central intersection they would build their forum, the center of civic and political life. (Under Augustus's rule, the forum also had to include a temple to the emperor.) The site of Barcino's original forum has ever since served as the seat of power in Barcelona; today the city government and provincial government face off across the broad square, with the **Ajuntament** on the C. Jaume I side, and the **Generalitat** on the C. Llibreteria side. *Sardanas* are frequently danced here (see **May I Have This Dance,** p. 72), and the *plaça* always fills with merrymaking crowds on Catalan holidays. Just off the *plaça*, the Gothic **Església de Sants Just i Pastor** (1342) occupies a small square just off C. Ciutat. This is the only remaining church in the city that honors living wills: someone about to die can make a will to a friend, who can then repeat his last words at this altar, whereupon they become legally binding.

PALAU DE LA GENERALITAT

◪ Pl. St. Jaume. Enter to the right on C. Bisbe. M: Jaume I, L4. ☎ 93 402 46 16; www.gencat.es. Open the 2nd and 4th Su of every month 10:30am-1:30pm. Closed Aug. Mandatory tours in Catalan, Spanish, or English every 30min. starting at 10:30am (in English usually 11 or 11:30am, but call to be sure). Tours are limited in size, so come early, and bring ID. Free. Limited wheelchair accessibility. The first Su of every month the Palace hosts a free bell concert at noon.

The Palace of the Generalitat is the center of Catalunya's regional government and has served as the seat of power for 115 presidents of Catalunya, from Berenguer de Cruïlles in 1359 to current president Jordi Pujol. The oldest part of the building is the Gothic facade in C. Bisbe, site of the original entrance; the government officials who commissioned it in 1416 were so happy with the St. Jordi medallion designed by Marc Safont that they paid him

Dancing the *Sardana*

Sant Jordi

Feeding Pigeons in Plaça Catalunya

CATALAN JEWS

Spain has not always treated its minorities as Spanish equals. The Catalan treatment of Jews is no exception; though perhaps the most persecuted people in the land, Jews still make up a substantial percentage of the country's, and Catalunya's, most culturally accomplished, financially successful, and intellectually renowned individuals.

The paradox inherent in this situation loomed particularly large during Christopher Columbus's voyages to the New World. The sailor's first trip was financed mainly by King Fernando's treasurer Lluís Santagel, a converted Jew from Valencia, and the news of Columbus's shocking discoveries was spread throughout Europe by another converted Jew, publisher Leandre de Coscó. Meanwhile, Fernando and Isabel were busy recapturing Granada from the Muslims, and Santagel financed Columbus's second trip predominantly with confiscated goods...from all of the Jews expelled from Spain in 1492.

Today, there are still Jews in parts of the Middle East who speak a form a Catalan and cook decidedly Catalan food. These men and women are descendants of the Jews expelled from Barcelona in the 1400s. However, within city limits the Hebrew population never rebuilt itself, and today there are fewer than 6000 Jewish inhabitants on record.

double what they had originally promised. Most of the center of the palace was added in the 16th and 17th centuries, including the beautiful **Pati dels Tarongers** (Patio of Oranges) and the **Salón Dorado** (Gold Room), a hall with an ornate gold ceiling and tapestries inspired by Petrarch depicting the triumph of honor over death and time over honor. Also notable is the **Salón de Sant Jordi,** whose cupola is visible from the Pl. St. Jaume. Part of the 17th-century additions, this extravagant room features a St. Jordi statue by Frederic Marès and is covered in allegorical paintings delineating the history of Catalunya. Be sure to stay with the tour group; if you wander off, you may find yourself having to explain yourself to one of the friendly security guards.

AJUNTAMENT

🚩 *Pl. St. Jaume. M: Jaume 1, L4. Open Su 10am-1:45pm. Tours at 10:30, 11:30am, and 12:30pm or as needed by large groups, usually in Catalan or Spanish. For English or French call ☎ 93 268 24 44. Self-guided tours also allowed; pamphlet guides are available in Catalan, Spanish, English, and French. Free.*

The Ajuntament is Barcelona's city hall and office of Socialist Mayor Joan Clos. In the late 14th century, Barcelona's elite Consell de Cent (Council of One Hundred) decided that the site of the original Roman forum would be the perfect place to construct their power-house. The most impressive room in the building, the **Saló de Cent,** was completed in 1369; King Pere III had his first meeting with the Consell de Cent there in 1373. With red-and-gold-brocaded walls, high arches, and a profusion of crystal chandeliers, it oozes with Catalan pride. Smaller but equally stunning is the **Saló de la Reina Regente,** designed in 1860 for plenary meetings and containing a half-dome stained glass skylight. The **Saló de las Crónicas** wall decorations, created by Josep Marià Sert, depict episodes from Roger de Flor's 14th century expedition to the Far East. The entrance **courtyard,** meanwhile, further facilitates the glorifying of Catalan culture by displaying sculptures by some of Barcelona's most famous artists, including Josep Llimona, Josep Subirachs, and Joan Miró.

TEMPLE OF AUGUSTUS

🚩 *M: Jaume I, L4. Inside the Centre Excursionista de Catalunya building. Enter Pl. St. Jaume from C. Bisbe and take a hairpin left turn into tiny C. Paradís. Follow this street around the corner and to the end. The gate opens Su and Tu-Sa 10am-2pm, but the remains are visible through the gate.*

At the end of C. Paradís a plaque marks **Mont Tàber,** the highest point of Roman Barcino, all of 16.9m above sea level. Right behind the plaque, inside the protective walls of the **Centre Excursionista Catalunya,** a local outdoors club, are the four columns from the original Roman **Temple of Augustus.** The columns are larger than pretty much every other Roman column in the Barri Gòtic; one might be tempted to interpret the superior size of the columns as an attempt on Augustus's part to assert his dominance over the citizens of Barcino. Built on the formerly towering summit of Mont Tàber over 2000 years ago, the now eye-level columns have not moved from their original position.

SOUTHERN ROMAN WALLS

🚏 *C. Regomir, 3. M: Jaume I, L4. From Pl. St. Jaume, take C. Ciutat; just as the street turns into C. Regomir, the Centre Pati Llimona will be on your left. ☎ 93 268 21 70. Centre Pati Llimona open M-F 9am-10pm and Sa-Su 10am-2pm. Free.*

In case you haven't had your fill of ancient walls yet, the second concentrated stretch of Roman walls is located in what was the southeastern corner of the original city, near present-day Pl. Regomir and Pl. Traginers. This civic center hosts free art exhibitions in its front room (usually photography) and also showcases a substantial piece of first-century Roman wall. The wall is visible from the street through a glass window but is also accessible for free via a ramp inside the building.

Soon after passing the civic center, turn left on C. Correu Vell. A tiny alley, C. de Groch, branches off to the left into a space where you can see a stretch of 4th-century wall and two square towers. If you then go back and take C. Correu Vell to its end, you will find yourself in the quiet **Plaça Traginers,** which hosts yet another substantial segment of 4th-century walls. Check out the tower on the corner of C. Correu Vell and Baixada de Viladecols, right off Pl. Traginers. It was one of 78 towers that made up the second enclosing wall of Barcino in the 4th century, and unlike other Roman sites in the city, it has not yet been tainted by modern construction.

EL CALL (JEWISH QUARTER)

🚏 *M: Liceu, L3.*

Records indicate that Jewish families started moving to Roman Barcino as early as the 2nd century. The Jewish quarter sprang to life near the center of town, between present-day Pl. St. Jaume, C. Ferran, C. Banys Nous, and the Església Santa Maria del Pi. Although today there is little indicating the Jewish heritage of this area, for centuries El Call was the most vibrant center of intellectual and financial activity in all of Barcelona; Jews even received a certain amount of governmental support and protection in return for their substantial economic and cultural contributions to the city.

Anti-Semitism spread throughout Europe in the thirteenth century, however, and Spain was no exception. In 1243, Jaume I ordered the complete isolation of the Jewish quarter from the rest of the city, and he forced all Jews to wear identifying red-and-yellow buttons. Anti-Semitism increased even more as citizens looked for scapegoats for the growing plagues and poverty of the 14th century, and in 1348, hundreds of Jews were blamed for the Black Death and tortured mercilessly until they "confessed" to their crimes. In 1391, as harassment of Jews spread throughout Spain, a riot ended in the murder of nearly 1000 Jews in Barcelona's Call. By 1401, every single synagogue and Jewish cemetery was demolished, making the forced conversion law of 1492 an easy next step (see **Catalan Jews,** p. 62).

One Jewish synagogue was turned into a church, the **Església de Sant Jaume** (C. Ferran, 28) which is still in use today. However, the only remaining tangible evidence of Jewish inhabitants in El Call is the ancient **Hebrew plaque** in tiny C. Marlet. To see it, from Pl. St. Jaume take C. Call and turn right onto C. Sant Domènech de Call and then left onto C. Marlet; it will be at the end on the right.

One of the best-known alleys in El Call has nothing to do with Jewish history: to the left off the end of C. Sant Domènech de Call (coming from C. Call) is the **Baixada de Sta. Eulalia,** said to be the place where the city's patron saint was tortured to death

Born Again

The old Born market which sits at the head of Pg. del Born in La Ribera has a long and sordid past. In the 14th century, jousting tournaments were held in the Pl. del Born underneath the current market site. In fact, the word "born" originates from the name of the tips of the jousting spears used in these tournaments, which continued through the 17th century. Carrying on its violent tradition, the *plaça* was briefly used as a site for the *autos-da-fé* during the Inquisition later that century. From the late 19th century, however, the *plaça's* bloody legacy was present only in the meat stalls in the Mercat del Born.

Josep Fontseré was commissioned to design the market along with his work in the nearby Parc de la Ciutadella (see p. 72). His creation, a marvel of steel and glass that allowed for plenty of natural light, served as the city's major wholesale market for almost 100 years. When the market was moved out of the city in 1976, the building stood unused for many years. Finally, a joint project between the Ajuntament, the Ministry of Education and Culture, and the Generalitat was launched to convert the old market into a provincial library for Barcelona, slated to be open in 2005 with as much of Fontseré's original design preserved as possible. Meanwhile, a team of archaeologists from the Museu d'Història de la Ciutat (see p. 64) is working hard to uncover any medieval relics.

and joined the ranks of Christian martyrdom (see **Església Catedral de la Santa Creu**, p. 63). On the wall at the start of the street is a plaque written by Catalan poet Jacint Verdaguer, commemorating the legend.

SANTA MARIA DEL PI

*M: Liceu, L3. Take C. Cardenal Casañas from Las Ramblas. Open M-F 8:30am-1pm and 4:30-8:30pm, Sa 8:30am-1pm and 4-9pm, Su 9am-2pm and 5-9pm. Be sure to observe proper church etiquette (see **Once in Barcelona**, p. 29). Free.*

As far as religious buildings go, the Catedral de la Santa Creu tends to usurp tourist attention in the Barri Gòtic. However, the most popular among locals is the Església de Santa Maria del Pi, a small 14th-century church with exquisite Gothic stained-glass windows. The three *plaças* surrounding the church (Pl. del Pi, Placeta del Pi, and Pl. de St. Oriol) are pleasant places for relaxing in the shade.

PLAÇA REIAL

M: Liceu or Drassanes, L3.

The most crowded, happening *plaça* in the entire Barri Gòtic is the **Pl. Reial,** where tourists and locals alike congregate to eat and drink at night, and to buy and sell at the Sunday morning flea market. Francesc Daniel Milona designed the *plaça* in one of Barcelona's first spurts of constructive (rather than oppressive) urban planning, replacing decrepit Barri Gòtic streets with a large, architecturally cohesive *plaça* in the 1850s. Near the fountain in the center of the square there are two street lamps designed by Antoni Gaudí at the very beginning of his architectural career. The *plaça* is a great place to grab a drink or meal, as some of the Barri Gòtic's happening restaurants and bars reside here. Don't let the *plaça's* somewhat questionable reputation for pick-pockets deter you; the ever-present police patrols make the Pl. Reial one of the safest places to hang out in Barcelona, day or night.

MUSEU D'HISTÒRIA DE LA CIUTAT

In Pl. del Rei. M: Jaume I, L4. Walk up C. Jaume I and take the first right. Enter on C. Verguer. ☎ 93 315 11 11; www.bcn.es/cultura. Open June-Sept. Su 10am-3pm, Tu-Sa 10am-8pm; Oct.-May Su 10am-3pm, Tu-Sa 10am-2pm and 4-8pm. Closed Jan. 1, May 1, June 24, and Dec. 25-26. Museum €4, students €2.50; exhibition €3.50, students €2; combined museum and exhibition €6, students €4. Free admission first Sa afternoon of every month, first W afternoon for groups. Your ticket can be used again if you ask them to issue you another access card on the way out. Most displays are in Spanish and Catalan, but pamphlets are available in English.

There are two components to the Museu d'Història de la Ciutat (Museum of the History of Barcelona): the Palau Reial Major and the subterranean excavations of the Roman city Barcino. Built on top of the fourth-century city walls, the **Palau Reial Major** served as the residence of the Catalan-Aragonese monarchs from the end of the 10th century through the 15th century. After the last Catalan king died in 1410, it began to deteriorate and was eventually abandoned by royalty in the 16th century, becoming a headquarters for royal scribes and the Inquisition. In 1718, the palace was given to the Sisters of Santa Clara as a convent when Felipe's construction of the Ciutadella (see p. 72) forced them out of their original location. The nuns left the Palau Reial Major at the start of the Spanish Civil War. Later, as restoration on the building began, the **Saló de Tinell** (Throne Room) was discovered wholly intact under a baroque chapel. Finished in 1370, the huge Gothic room is believed to be the place where Fernando and Isabel received Columbus after his journey to America. Today, it houses year-long temporary exhibitions. The museum itself is an interesting look at the history of ancient Barcelona.

Next to the Saló de Tinell you will find the **Capella de Santa Agata,** begun in 1302 during the reign of Jaume II and now considered one of the most beautiful works of medieval architecture in Barcelona. Its star attraction is the *Epiphany* altarpiece done by Jaume Huguet in 1465; resplendent in gold, with highly realistic portrayals of the most significant scenes of the life of Jesus, this *retablo* is considered by some to be one of the best examples of Catalan Gothic painting. From the chapel you can access the **Mirador del Rei Martí,** a watchtower built in 1557 but named for the last Catalan king; from here you can see the **Pl. del Rei,** the *plaça* formed by the Palau Reial Major; the Chapel of St. Agatha; and the **Palau de Lloctinent,** a 16th-century modification of the royal palace that until 1994 housed the archives of the Crown of Aragó.

The second part of the museum lies underground, in an area discovered under Pl. del Rei when space was being cleared for the Via Laietana. The largest underground excavation of any ancient city in Europe, this 4000m^2 **archeological exhibit** was excavated from 1930 to 1960 and now allows visitors to walk through the incredibly intact 1st- to 6th-century remains of a corner of the Roman city of Barcino. You can see the

Santa Maria del Mar

Sant Pau in El Raval

Palau Güell Roof Terrace

Parc de la Ciutadella

Penguin at the Zoo

Casacada Fountain

original city boundary wall and walking paths, a dye-shop, and laundry shop which still has faintly visible soap residues, a *garum* fermentation facility (see **Rotting Fish Entrails,** p. 122), and a wine production area with intact ceramic wine containers. You can also walk through a large portion of the sprawling Episcopal palace and see a mosaic floor from the home of a wealthy second-century Roman.

MUSEU FREDERIC MARÈS

🔢 *Pl. Sant Lu, 5-6, in the Palau Reial. From M: Jaume I, L4, walk down C. Llibreteria and turn right on C. Freneria, which leads to the museum. ☎ 93 310 58 00; www.museu-mares.bcn.es. Open Tu-Sa 10am-7pm, Su and holidays 10am-3pm. Free guided tours in Catalan and Spanish every Su 11:30am; for private tours or tours in English, call ahead. Museum cafe open Apr.-Sept. 10am-10pm. €3, groups of ten or more €1.80, students under 25 €1.50, under 16 free. Free W afternoons and first Su of the month. Wheelchair accessible. Cash only.*

This museum is the answer to the question, "What happens when you give an eccentric collector with a keen interest in art a lot of money and tons of travel time?" Marès (1893-1991) was one of Spain's better-known sculptors, and an avid collector of just about everything. In 1946, in a classic example of the individualized bourgeois patronage of the arts so common in Catalunya, he founded this museum and donated his entire private collection, as well as some of his own sculptures. The building itself was originally part of the Palau Reial Major, home to the monarchs of the Aragonese dynasty from the end of the 10th century through the 15th century. The Renaissance-style door to the museum still has the original 16th-century royal sign above it, and the courtyard dates from the 13th century (ground floor) and 15th century (upper galleries).

Inside the museum, the lower floors house a huge collection of Spanish and Hispanic sculpture, from pre-Roman times (including tiny Iberian religious figurines) through the 20th century. The seemingly endless collection of wooden Christ figures and Mary-with-Jesus carvings on the ground floor becomes repetitive. But of particular note is the collection of Marés's own sculptures in his private library on the second floor. The upper floors contain Marès's "Sentimental Museum;" an overwhelming collection of middle-class daily life objects from the Romantic era including fans, jewelry, combs, purses, watches, canes, pipes, and eyeglasses. In addition to Marès's collection, the entrance floor has a small temporary exhibition space to the left of the reception. The museum can be overwhelming and repetitive to even the most dedicated of art history students, but any average tourist will enjoy a quick look at the bizarre and unique collection.

MUSEU DIOCESÀ

🚩 *Av. de la Catedral, 4, next to the cathedral. M: Jaume 1, L4. ☎ 93 315 22 13. Open Su 11am-2pm, Tu-Sa 10am-2pm and 5-8pm. Descriptions and free pamphlet guide are in Catalan, but the staff is extremely friendly and speaks Spanish. €2, students €1.50. Wheelchair accessible.*

This small museum tends to be overshadowed by the cathedral next door (both literally and figuratively), but it is a treasure trove for history buffs, as it contains the city's only intact octagonal defense tower from Roman Barcino. A journey through the Museu Diocesà begins with a long, monotonous video/slideshow about the life of Gaudí; narration available in Spanish and English. Then, continue up the floors of the museum; a wire with flags indicates the age of each part of the tower. The round base at the bottom was built by the Romans during the first century AD, the octagonal base on top of that during the 4th century, the next section during medieval times (look for uniform windows), and the fourth during the Gothic period (14th and 15th centuries; look for the higher, more delicate row of windows). From the top floor gallery, you can even see blackened stones from fires started by invading Muslim armies in the Middle Ages. The entrance to the museum leads through the original Roman wall and into a Gothic building that was the city's oldest homeless shelter/soup kitchen, the **Pia Almoina.** During the 18th century, under the dreaded Felipe V, the building was converted into a prison—you can see wall etchings by prisoners at the top of the stairs leading to the top floor. Most believe that the old graffiti includes a camping/outdoors scene and a long line of tally marks counting the passing days.

The museum's collection of religious artifacts covers two main periods, the Romanesque (12th and 13th centuries), and the Gothic (14th and 15th centuries). Highlights include an almost entirely intact church fresco from 1122 AD, varied wood and marble Virgin sculptures, and a beautifully handwritten Latin document by Felipe II. The museum's crown jewel, however, is the stunning, gold, diamond-adorned **Custodià del Pi,** made in 1587 and originally used in the nearby Santa Maria del Pi church. In the Catholic religion, the *custodià* is used to store the Host, or holy bread, before and after the rite of communion. Still in perfect condition today, it drips with ornate detail and delicate religious symbolism. Equally breathtaking is the view of the cathedral from the museum's top-floor gallery. The museum also hosts a series of rotating historical exhibits.

MUSEU DEL CALÇAT (SHOE MUSEUM)

🚩 *Pl. Sant Felip Neri, 5. M: Jaume I, L4. ☎ 93 301 45 33. Open Su and Tu-Sa 11am-2pm. €2. Only 1½ rooms, but you can call for guided tours. Pamphlet on the history of the museum €2.*

This bizarre collection of footwear is a tribute to the ancient guilds of Barcelona, tracing the existence of master shoemakers to an official document signed by the Bishop of Barcelona in 1203 (even today a few faithful members tend to the guild's chapel in the Cathedral de la Sant Creu; see **The Guilded Age,** p. 58). The tiny and unremarkable museum will probably interest only the most dedicated of shoe fans. The exhibit, tucked obscurely away in the Pl. Sant Felip Neri, includes reproductions of shoes from as far back as the 1st century. The majority of the collection comes from the past three centuries and includes everything from eighteenth-century men's sandals to track spikes from the 1940s to the boots which Carles Vallés wore to the top of Mt. Everest to plant the Catalan flag. The museum also includes a few antique shoe-making tools. Modern-day men can leave their twentieth century machismo at the door and admire some of the pointed-toe, high-heeled men's boots of years past, while women can take relief in the fact that pricey, silver-plated dress shoes aren't quite the rage they once were.

in an hour

The Picasso Museum

Though some students of art history spend their entire lives analyzing the style and innovations of the man who some have called the father of modern art, an hour in the Múseu Picasso can easily leave you with enough knowledge to impress your friends. To help create the image of an artistic scholar, be sure to tilt your head and put on a look of extreme concentration at these key works.

La Primera Comunió (*The First Communion,* 1896) was the young master's first major work, which he submitted at the Third Exposition of Fine Arts and Artistic Industries in Barcelona. At only 15 years of age, Picasso was presented alongside prestigious professionals.

Retrat de la Tía Pepa (*Portrait of my Aunt Pepa,* 1896) was the artist's first attempt at portraiture. Here he shows an ability to capture a personality in a painting.

Caballo Corneado (*Gored Horse,* 1917) depicts a horse falling on a knife or bull's horn. The charcoal drawing recalls Picasso's obsession with horses and bullfights that inspired his painting *Guernica.*

cont'd on next page

68

OTHER PLAÇAS IN THE BARRI GÒTIC

🚇 M: Liceu, L3 or Jaume I, L4.

Farther toward the water, off C. Ample, the much newer **Pl. Mercé** is a popular spot for weddings, as well as for Barcelona's soccer team: the **Església de la Mercé** on one side holds the image of the mother of God to which FCB players dedicate all of their successful games. One last *plaça* worth seeing is the **Pl. de Sant Felip Neri,** a right off C. Bisbe when you are coming from the Cathedral. It is peaceful and pretty today, but it has a rather morbid past: it was once the site of a Jewish cemetery, and in January of 1938 a Civil War bomb ripped through the area, killing 20 children. Shrapnel marks are still slightly visible on the facade of the Església de Sant Felip Neri.

LA RIBERA

see map p. 337

🖼 MUSEU PICASSO

When I was a child, my mother said to me, "If you become a soldier, you'll be a general. If you become a monk, you'll end up as the Pope." Instead, I became a painter and wound up as Picasso.
—Pablo Picasso

🚇 C. Montcada, 15-23. Go down C. Princesa from the Metro, and turn right on C. Montcada. ☎ 93 319 63 10; www.museupicasso.bcn.es. M: Jaume I, L4. Open Su 10am-3pm, Tu-Sa 10am-8pm. €5, students and seniors €2.50, under 16 free. Special exhibits €5, students and seniors €2.50. First Su of each month free. Wheelchair accessible.

This incredible museum traces the development of Picasso as an artist with a chronologically organized exhibit of his early works. The large collection weaves through five connected mansions, once occupied by Barcelona's nobility. Although the museum offers little from Picasso's more well known middle years, it boasts the world's best collection of works from his formative period in Barcelona. The museum showcases each of Picasso's re-inventions of himself, from his deeply personal, tormented Blue Period, to his form-fascinated Rose Period, to his reign as master of Cubism. Like the Fundació Miró (see p. 95), the museum is practically an autobiography of the artist's life, depicting his many (many) lovers, emotional ups and downs, obsessions with the bull and the taurine, as well as the political atmosphere in Spain. The collection was started in 1963 with a donation from Picasso's friend Jaume Sabartés; it was later expanded by Picasso himself, and then by relatives after his death.

Most impressive of all the work in the museum is the display of the artist's 58 Cubist interpretations of Velásquez's original *Las Meninas* (translated as *Ladies in Waiting*, hanging in the Museu del Prado in Madrid). The original *Las Meninas* is a breathtaking, 7ft. masterpiece depicting a familial royal scene. Rather than the typical posed painting, Velásquez's captured an instantaneous moment on canvas. Hailed as the finest Spanish painting, *Las Meninas* is often re-interpreted by Spanish painters as a sort of rite of passage into greatness. Francisco Goya considered himself the inheritor of Velásquez's position as the best Spanish painter and himself etched the master's famous painting. This pattern continued with Picasso, who considered himself the next in line for the title. What is remarkable about Picasso is that instead of recreating the painting in its original grandeur as Goya did, he chose to apply his own, unique styles to Velásquez's mysterious work. Picasso reinvents the many vantage points of the original in his Cubist reinterpretation, with its multiple angles and lines of vision, all on his own terms.

Other exhibits of the museum showcase his early award-winning paintings and his later ceramic work. Special temporary exhibitions are generally related to Picasso's work or artists from the same time period as his own. As Barcelona's most popular museum, the Museu Picasso often has lines snaking a good way down C. Montcada; the best times to avoid the museum-going masses are mornings and early evenings

🖼 PALAU DE LA MÚSICA CATALANA

🚩 *C. Sant Francese de Paula, 2. M: Urquinaona, L1. Exit Pl. Urquinaona, walk down Via Laietana to Pl. Luis Millet; at the intersection of C. Jonqueres. ☎ 93 295 72 00; www.palaumusica.org. Open daily Aug. 10am-6pm, Sept.-July 10am-3:30pm. Box office open M-Sa 10am-9pm, Su from 1hr. prior to the concert. Entrance only with tour; in English on the hr., in Spanish on the half-hour. June-Aug. reserve 1 day in advance. Purchase tickets inside the Palau. No concerts in Aug.; check the Guía del Ocio for listings. €7, students and seniors €6; with Ruta del Modernisme pass €2.50. Concert tickets €6-150. Wheelchair accessible. MC/V.*

Flowers, flowers, and more flowers sprout and bloom in every crevice of this masterpiece of a music hall. In 1905 the massively popular Orfeó Catalan, a society organized to promote

cont'd from previous page

Ciencia y Caridad (*Science and Charity,* 1897) adhered to guidelines of then-popular social realism, gaining him second prize at the General Fine Arts Exhibition in Madrid.

Las Meninas (*Ladies in waiting)* in Sala 11 are 58 pieces based on Velásquez's celebrated 1656 work; don't miss **Las Meninas (conjunto)** (1957), where, rather than focusing on isolated parts of the original, Picasso reinterprets the entire work.

Desamparados (*Abandoned ones,* 1903) is one of the museum's few pieces from the **Blue Period** (1901-1904; brought on by the suicide of the artist's friend Casagemas, whose lover Picasso had wooed away), during which Picasso used blue tones to express melancholy in his subject matter.

El Retrato de la Señora Canals is from Picasso's brief **Rose Period** (1904-5), during which he sent the blues (hues and otherwise) packing and embraced bright colors and more optimistic subjects.

LGB ▼
BARCELONA

Gay for a Day

The municipality of Barcelona has finally decided to pay more attention to its lesbian, gay, and transsexual community. The Catalan Comissio Unitaria, organizes a series of events throughout the year, which culminate in the June 28th Día del Orgullo Gay, Lesbico, y Transexual (Day of Gay, Lesbian, and Transexual Pride). Although other cities in the world celebrate this day, its causes are often diluted in a citywide reason to party. In Barcelona this also holds true—just later in the night. Until the music starts taking the scene, participants march across the city to "rehabilitate the gay, lesbian, and transsexual victims of franquismo," and listen to a chosen author read a manifesto, underlining the march's goal of pressurizing the government to grant the community marriage and adoption rights, among other freedoms. After June 28th, the 6 day-long Muestra Internacional de Cine Gay y Lesbico de Barcelona in July presents over 40 films revolving around gay and lesbian issues, some of which focus on the new homosexual family model.

To learn more on gay pride activities in Barcelona visit www.28juny.org/28J-Comissio.htm, and www.lambdaweb.org.

musical culture, commissioned Modernist master Luis Domènech i Montaner. The result is nature colorfully harmonized with acoustics and architecture in this must-see concert venue. In 1997, UNESCO declared this magical palace a World Heritage Site. Debate continues over the political message of the inverted dome (weighing in, incidentally, at one ton of glass and iron), which is painted with 40 women dressed as angels. Some believe that Montaner was implying that women sing like angels and should have been allowed in the choir (at that time it was exclusively male). Others argue he was depicting women's fickleness by painting them with 40 different faces. The 2073-seat concert hall is also home to a 4000-pipe tubed organ which has been broken since 1970 but is slated to be tooting away again sometime in 2004.

🖼 MUSEU DE LA XOCOLATA (CHOCOLATE MUSEUM)

⚑ *Pl. Pons i Clerch, corner of C. Comerç. M: Jaume I, L4. Follow C. Princesa and turn left on C. Comerç. ☎ 93 268 78 78; www.museudexocolata.com. Open M and W-Sa 10am-7pm, Su 10am-3pm. €3.80, students and seniors €3.30. Workshops start at €6, guided tours €5. Wheelchair accessible.*

Arguably the most delectable museum in Spain. If you can halt the inevitable salivation for a few moments, the multilingual signs spew gobs of information about the history, production, and ingestion of this sensuous treat. Perhaps more interesting are the exquisite chocolate sculptures, particularly the edible versions of La Sagrada Família and the Arc de Triomf. Still not satisfied? Do some hands-on training at the small cafe and indulge in a workshop on cake baking, the history of chocolate, or chocolate tasting; call for class schedule and general information. Reservations required.

SANTA MARIA DEL MAR

⚑ *Pl. Santa Maria, 1. M: Jaume 1, L4. From the Metro, walk down C. de la Argentina to Pl. Santa Maria. ☎ 93 310 23 90, concert information 93 319 05 16. Open daily 9am-1:30pm and 4:30-8pm. Mass held Su 11am-1pm and 7:30pm, M-Sa 9:30am and 7:30pm. Free.*

La Ribera's streets come together—in prayer, it could be said—at the foot of the Església Santa Maria del Mar's octagonal towers. The 14th-century structure, built over the course of 55 years with stone extracted from Montjuïc, owes its name (Mary of the Sea) partially to the many sailors that then populated La Ribera, and the commonly held 14th-century belief that before the port was built up, the sea came to the church's door. Statues of Saint Peter and Saint Paul, flanking the austere front portal, beckon visitors into the surprisingly tall and quite breathtaking space. The sparse interior is a result of numerous fires that have passed through the church, most recently and destructively in 1936, when the church was set ablaze and burned for 11 days, destroying the altar, tombs, and images. Only the walls and columns you now see remained to create this hall of somber majesty (with great acoustics). At 12m apart, the supporting columns are spaced further apart than any other medieval building in the world—This church is also a fascinating example of the limits of Gothic architecture—if it were 2 ft. higher it would collapse from structural instability. Check with the information desk near the back entrance for a detailed pamphlet on the church's history.

EL FOSSAR DE LES MORERES

🚩 *Off C. de Santa Maria and next to the church's back entrance.*

Even without knowledge of the significance of this site, the brick-covered depression in the ground flagged with a red metal curved sculpture would catch your eye. Topped with an eternal flame, the Fossar de les Moreres (Mulberry Cemetery) memorial is a significant reminder of the Catalan struggle for cultural autonomy, which in many ways is still ongoing. The Catalans who resisted Felipe V's conquering troops in 1714 (see p. 38) were buried here in a mass grave, commemorated by mulberry trees *(les moreres)* and a plaque with a verse by the poet Sefari Pitarra: "In the Mulberry Cemetery no traitors are buried. Even though we lose our flags, this will be the urn of honor." The monument is sunken to recall the sinking of the grave as the bodies decomposed, and an eternal flame burns so that the light of their memory will never be extinguished. Demonstrators and patriots converge on Catalan National Day, September 11th, to commemorate the siege of Barcelona and the subsequent ban on displays of Catalan nationalism.

MUSEU TÉXTIL I D'INDUMENTÀRIA

🚩 *C. Montcada, 12-14. M: Jaume I, L4. ☎ 93 319 76 03; museutextil@mail.bcn.es. Open Su 10am-3pm, Tu-Sa 10am-6pm. Combined admission with Museu Barbier-Mueller; buy tickets there (see below). One ticket gets you into this museum, the Museu de les Arts Decoratives (see p. 108), and the Museu de Ceràmica (see p. 108) up to one month after purchase. €3.50, students and seniors €2. 1st Sa of the month after 3pm free. Wheelchair accessible.*

Still trying to figure out what Spanish lace is? The Museu Téxtil I D'Indumentària offers not only a lesson in lace, but also a quick tour of the history of European fashion, from bustles and sadistic-looking corsets to V-necks and miniskirts. While the visual history of clothing can be titillating to the true fashionista, all signs are in Catalan. Ask for an information packet in English from the front desk. For those who lack a sense of style, the swank cafe and "gift shop" (more of a chic clothing shop than a tourist trove) can add a touch of class to almost anyone who thinks a fanny pack is an "accessory."

MUSEU BARBIER-MUELLER

🚩 *C. Montcada, 12-14. M: Jaume I, L4. ☎ 93 310 45 16; www.barbier-mueller.ch. Open Su 10am-3pm, Tu-Sa 10am-6pm. Combined admission with Museu Téxtil i d'Indumentària next door; see above. €3, students and seniors €1.50. Free 1st Su of the month. Wheelchair accessible.*

Eerily illuminated relics from the pre-Columbian Americas line darkened rooms in this small museum devoted to the conquistadors' booty: tapestries, carvings, ornaments, vases, sculptures, and jewelry dating from 200 BC and taken from Olmec, Maya, Aztec, Cocle, Mochica, and Inca sites. You may want to pass up this meager museum (only 3 rooms), which does not even discuss Spain or Catalunya, in favor of the larger museums that abound in the area.

MAY I HAVE THIS DANCE?

Those expecting to see flowing dresses and castanets will be disappointed: Catalunya does not have a tradition of flamenco dance. Instead, Catalans hold the **sardana** dear to their heart. The *sardana* is a dance in which Catalans of all ages and genders join hands in a circle and perform a variety of complicated skips and jumps in unison. Unlike flamenco, the *sardana* is not preformed in concert style, but rather outside. All participants wear white shoes and the dance is dependent upon the cooperation of the entire group, symbolizing the unity of the village.

A band keeps tempo during the dance, which can last for several hours. The *sardana* is a somber tradition that is taken seriously by both its dancers and viewers; while the rest of Spain, and some ignorant foreign viewers, have been known to mock the *sardana* for its nearly comatose pace, the Catalan people take pride in their traditional dance and consider it an integral part of their culture. Their methodical and perfectly synchronized movements make it seem as if they were born knowing the dance. A good place to catch the *sardana* is in front of **la Catedral de Santa Creu** in the Pl. de la Seu (see p. 57) after mass on Sunday morning.

PARC DE LA CIUTADELLA & ITS SIGHTS

🛈 Orientation and Transportation: *M: Ciutadella-Vila Olímpica for zoo and rear entrance; M: Arc de Triomf for main entrance and the walking tour (see p. 8). Bus #14 runs from Pl. de Catalunya and stops at the Pg. Picasso/Av. Marqués de l'Argentera entrance. ☎ 62 900 39 96. The park is bordered by Pg. Pujades to the west, Pg. Cicumvallació to the east, C. Wellington to the north, and Pg. Picasso to the south. The* **Museu de Zoologia, Hivernacle, Museu de Geologia,** *and* **Umbracle** *all line the Pg. Picasso side, while the* **Museu d'Art Modern,** *and the* **Pl. D'Armes** *are on the side of the park closer to C. Wellington. The* **Cascada fountain** *is at the corner of C. Wellington and Pg. Pujades and faces the small lake. The* **zoo** *has an entrance on C. Wellington.* **Bike rental** *is available from Los Paticletos, (☎ 93 319 78 85) Pg. Picasso, 44 (from €2.40 per hr.). Park gates open daily from 7:30am-10pm.*

Sandwiched between La Ribera and Poble Nou, and a quick walk from Barceloneta and Barri Gòtic, Parc de la Ciutadella can be described as a touristic all-in-one gem: a cool, refreshing break from the speed of the city while still culturally valuable and educational. Take a nap, take a stroll, take a lover—as the Barcelonese do—or take advantage of the sea of sights in the 30-acre-plus park.

Barcelona's military resistance to the Bourbon monarchy in the early 18th century convinced Felipe V to quarantine the city's influential citizens in the Ciutadella, a large citadel on the site of what is now Pg. Picasso. An entire neighborhood was razed and its citizens evacuated to make room for the citadel, which lorded threateningly over Barcelona. In a popular move, the city demolished the fortress in 1878, under the direction of **General Joan Prim** (honored with a statue at the end of Av. dels Tillers), and replaced it with the peaceful promenades of Parc de la Ciutadella. Architect Josep Fontseré designed the new park, and brought with him newcomers Domènech i Montaner (of Palau de la Música Catalana fame, see p. 69) and **Antoni Gaudí.** Several Modernist buildings went up years later when Ciutadella hosted the **Universal Exposition** in 1888 (see **Life & Times,** p. 40), including Montaner's stately **Castell dels Tres Dragons** (now the **Museu de Zoologia**). Expo '88 also inspired the **Arc de Triomf,** just across Pg. Pujades and Pg. Lluís Companys from the park. Rather than commemorating a military triumph, the Arc de Triomf was designed as the entrance to Expo '88. A stylistic nod to the Spanish Moors, the red bricks surround green and yellow ceramic tiles and sculpted bats, angels, and lions. The main facade is a friendly face smiling down at you, dear tourist—it represents the welcoming of foreign visitors to Barcelona.

🖼 HIVERNACLE

🔢 *On Pg. Picasso, behind the Museu de Zoologia. M: Arc de Triomf, L1. ☎ 93 295 40 17. Cafe menú €12, entrees €6-17. Open Su noon-5pm, M-Sa 9am-midnight. Wheelchair accessible. MC/V.*

Originally built to showcase unusual tropical plants not sturdy enough for the climate of Barcelona, Josep Amergós's iron and glass Hivernacle (greenhouse) now houses white-clothed tables and bow-tied waiters alongside a room of exotic fauna for a tropical afternoon meal or drink. The park's **public restrooms** also lurk amongst the greenery. On Wednesday evenings from May through July, the Hivernacle holds jazz concerts (10:30pm, €4 if not dining), and Thursday nights in July free classical music concerts begin at 10:15pm. Farther down the Pg. Picasso on the other side of the Museu Geologia, the iron-tiered **Umbracle,** built in 1883 and renovated in 2001, offers a cooler, shadier escape than its brother greenhouse, as well as a few more plants.

Floquet

🖼 MUSEU D'ART MODERN

🔢 *In Pl. D'Armes. M: Arc de Triomf, L1. Follow Pg. Tilles to the statue of General Prim at the roundabout and turn left toward Pl. D'Armes; signs point the way to the museum. ☎ 93 319 57 28; www.mnac.es. Open Su 10am-2:30pm, Tu-Sa 10am-7pm. €3, students and children €2.10. Free entrance first Th of every month. Wheelchair accessible.*

Modernism is Barcelona's claim to fame, and this is the place to learn all about the movement's multifaceted, quirky character. Easily manageable in about an hour, the museum simultaneously offers a quick lesson in Catalan art and a glimpse into the city as it was at the turn of the century. Check out noteworthy works like Francesc Lacoma's *La Família del Pintor* (see his mom looking over his shoulder?), Ramon Casas's *Plein Air*, Josep Llimona's *Desconsol* (the original of the sculpture in the Plaça d'Armes), Maria Fortuny's *La Vicaria*, Homar's surprisingly Japanese-like works, and Isidre Nonell's paintings of Gypsy women. Don't miss the room of Josep Clará's *Noucentist* sculptures, reminiscent of French sculptor Rodin. (Noucentism, which was a derivative of Modernism, sought to reinsert classical beauty into art by adding motion and emotion without adhering to formal techniques.) The museum also displays furniture designed by

Parc d'Attracions

Detail on la Palau de Música

73

NO **WORK** ALL **PLAY**

Dancing in the Streets

Initiated in 1998, the Festa de la Música has become one of the main cultural events of the summer in Barcelona, with an ever-increasing audience (28,000 in 1998 and 60,000 in 2003). The Festa attracts international musicians, in addition to the hundreds of European artists that participate. Celebrated every July 1st, the Festa marks the beginning of the summer. Unlike traditional music festivals, this celebration is a free-for-all, literally. Anybody can perform and there are no ticket costs; performances are both planned and impromptu. The event has music for all audiences—in the streets, in parks, in museums, in *plaças*, in bars, and in clubs. You'll no doubt find music to your liking, and probably a lot of stuff you can't stand.

In addition to providing opportunities for small bands, large institutions like orchestras use the Festa to go beyond their usual bounds and explore less mainstream types of music. With Sónar (see p. 105) taking place a few weeks before the Festa, Barcelona is now at the vanguard of music.

For more info visit www.bcn.es/festadelamusica.

Antoni Gaudí for Casa Batlló (see p. 87), as well as several fixtures from Puig i Cadalfach's Casa Amatller (see p. 88). Don't get too excited for the two Dalí paintings in the collection; they are from his formative stages and, therefore, differ greatly from the surrealist puzzles for which he is known.

■ PARC ZOOLÒGIC

🚊 *M: Ciutadella/Vila Olímpica, L4. Follow C. Wellington out of the Metro. The zoo is accessible from a separate entrance on C. Wellington. From inside the park, the zoo entrance is next to the Museu d'Art Modern/Parliament building.* ☎ *93 225 67 80; www.zoobarcelona.com. Open daily May-Aug. 9:30am-7:30pm; Apr. and Sept. 10am-7pm; Mar. and Oct. 10am-6pm; Nov.-Feb. 10am-5pm. Two-person motorcarts (€11 per hr.) are available near the park-side entrance. The zoo has its own restaurants and snack bars. €11.50, ages 3-12 €7.50, 65+ €6.60; May-Sept. after 5pm entrance €6.50, children €4, and seniors €3.60. Map of zoo €1. Wheelchair accessible. AmEx/D/MC/V.*

Animal rights activists be prepared: the cages may be smaller and less well-kept in Spain than those in other countries. Quarters are cramped for the animals, however the zoo's current focus is improving its residents' living standards. Perhaps the only reason for high attendance is the charismatic. **▣Floquet de Neu** (Snowflake), the world's only albino gorilla. Don't hover around Floquet the whole day, though; check out the aquarium, petting zoo, and the famous **Senyoreta del Paraigua** sculpture, located in the south of the park by the aquarium. Enduring symbols of the 1888 Exposition, the sculpture and fountain have become emblems of Barcelona. *Senyoreta del Paraigua* (*Lady with the Umbrella*; 1885) was designed by the sculptor Joan Roig i Solé, a founder of the Sitges school. The *senyoreta*, who shoots water from the top of her umbrella, was modeled after the Catalan painter Pepita Teixidor and is known informally to many Barceloneses simply as "Pepita."

MUSEU DE ZOOLOGIA (CASTELL DELS TRES DRAGONS)

🚊 *Entrances on Pg. Pujades/Pg. de Lluís Companys and Pg. Picasso/C. Princesa. M: Arc de Triomf, L1.* ☎ *93 319 69 12; museuzoologia@mail.bcn.es. Open Su, Tu-W, and F-Sa 10am-2pm; Th 10am-6:30pm. €3.90, students and seniors €1.80, first Su of each month free. Combined entrance with Museu de Geologia (see below). Wheelchair accessible.*

Designed as a restaurant for Expo '88, it was later used by Domènech i Montaner as a Modernist workshop. Taking its name from a then-popular Frederic Soler play, Montaner's Castell dels Tres Dragons (Castle of Three Dragons), the building's outside showcases intricate tile work and brick turrets. Inside, besides an impressively large whale skeleton on the first floor, an unremarkable collection of taxidermy and fauna samples fills the majority of the museum. However, the fact that most informational placards are in English may be enough to attract Catalan-weary visitors.

MUSEU DE GEOLOGIA

🔏 *On Pg. Picasso, 2 buildings behind the Museu Zoologia. M: Arc de Triomf, L1. Entrance faces inside of park. ☎ 93 319 68 95. Open Su, Tu-W, and F-Sa 10am-2pm; Th 10am-6:30pm. €3.90, students and seniors €1.80, first Su of each month free. Combined entrance with Museu de Zoologia (see above). Wheelchair accessible.*

A park structure designed by Fontseré (with the help of Antoni Rovira i Trias), the Museu de Geologia opened in 1882 as the first public museum in the city…perhaps a geological craze had swept through Catalunya in that era. But in more modern times, the basic rock museum, lacking much explanation in any language other than the scientific names and places of origin, may be a bit tedious for the average tourist.

PLAÇA D'ARMES

🔏 *In front of the Museu d'Art Modern and the Parliament of Catalunya. Enter through the gate at Pg. Picasso/Av. Marqués de L'Argentera, and continue straight past the statue of General Prim.*

Despite its militant name, this *plaça*, laid out by French landscape artist Jean Forestier, is less about military power and more about contemplative tranquility. The tall, squared hedges of the *plaça's* inner boundaries enclose a copy of Josep Llimona's sculpture **Desconsol** (1907), a woman collapsed in despair, centered in a glass-like pond. This is a perfect place for a quiet break before or after attacking the modern marvels of the nearby Museu d'Art Modern.

CASCADA FOUNTAIN & LAKE

🔏 *In the northeast corner of the park, directly accessible from the Pg. Pujades/C. Wellington entrance. Open M-F noon-7pm, Sa-Su 11am-8:30pm. The lake rents paddle boats, €2 per 30min.*

The grandiose, often excessive details of Ciutadella's Cascada Fountain are, not surprisingly, the work of Fontseré's young assistant Antoni Gaudí. The eye-catching structure is adorned with grecian statues, dragons, and a Venus on the half shell. The front of the fountain faces a small snack bar (bocadillos €3-4, water €1) and a full-scale statue of a Mammoth, the large beasts whose remains have been discovered near Les Corts.

OTHER SIGHTS IN LA RIBERA

Across from the elaborate Palacio de Justicia, off Pg. Lluís Companys, **Mercat de Santa Caterine** is a traditional market and a great, cheap place to pick up sightseeing snacks or ingredients for dinner. Dozens of vendors sell produce, flowers, meats, and fish. The **Carrer de Montcada,** beginning behind Santa Maria del Mar, validates Barcelona's reputation as *"la ciudad del diseño"* (the city of design). Museums, art galleries, workshops, and Baroque palaces that once housed Barcelona's 16th-century bureaucrats are packed into just two blocks. The **Museu Picasso** (see p. 68) inhabits several such mansions, and the **Galería Maeght** (see p. 76) was once an equally prestigious medieval aristocrat's manor. Off the Placeta de Montcada at the Pg. del Born end is the city's narrowest street, **C. de les Mosques** (Street of Flies), which was finally closed off in 1991 after residents complained that the narrow alley was being used far too frequently as a public urinal. Also worth a look is Antoni Tàpies's **Homenatge a Picasso,** a glass-enclosed sculpture on Pg. Picasso in front of the Museu Geologia. Installed in 1983, the jumble of wood furniture and steel beams was inspired by Picasso's

Façade of La Sagrada Família

Spiral Staircase at La Sagrada Família

Gaudí's Casa Batlló

comment that "A picture is not something to decorate a sitting room, but a weapon of attack and of defense against the enemy."

GALLERIES IN LA RIBERA

One of the capitals of cutting-edge art, Barcelona showcases many of the latest trends. Many private collections display the works of both budding artists and renowned masters, but don't expect cheap finds on either count. Most of Barcelona's galleries are located around **C. Montcada.** The following galleries all welcome visitors and carry museum-quality works.

Galería Maeght, C. Montcada, 25 (☎93 310 42 45; www.maeght.com). M: Jaume I, L4. Two floors of displays including pieces from Miró, Tàpies, Calder, and Giacometti. Shop carries a wide selection of art books (€22+), prints, posters, and postcards, as well as temporary exhibitions. Open Tu-Sa 10am-2pm and 4-8pm.

ARTquitect, C. Comerç, 31 (☎93 844 40 71; fax 93 844 40 71). M: Barceloneta, L4. Finding beauty in the art of bathroom design, a quirky gallery for those tired of traditional art. Eccentricity and function combine in the well-lighted displays of bowls, baths, showers, and tiles. Open M-F 10am-2pm and 4-8pm, Sa 11am-8pm.

Círculo del Arte, C. Princesa, 52 (☎93 268 88 20; www.circulodelarte.com). M: Jaume I, L4. Spacious modern gallery with seasonal exhibits rotating every 3 months. This bookstore/publishing house sells original prints and lithographs (illustrations by Borges, Paz, and Kafka for example). Showcases mainly Spanish artists. Regular offerings of Miró, Calder, Keith Haring, and Claes Oldenburg. Open M-F 11am-8pm, Sa 11am-2pm and 3:30-8pm. MC/V.

Metronom, C. Fusina, 9 (☎93 268 42 98; info@metronom-bcn.org). A recently opened experimental and contemporary art presentation space of the Fundació Rafael Tous d'Art Contemporani. Attracts lots of young viewers. Pieces often sold. Open Tu-Sa 11am-2pm and 5-8pm. Wheelchair accessible.

Villa de Arte, M: Jaume 1, L4. A Dutch-owned gallery on the east side of the Museu Diocesà, houses contemporary art by both international and Spanish artists. Open daily 10am-11pm in the summer, 10am-8pm the rest of the year.

Galería Surrealista, C. Montcada, 19 (☎93 310 33 11; fax 93 310 68 15). M: Jaume I, L4. Next to the Museu Picasso and just as well-stocked. Specializes entirely in the work of Dalí, Miró, and Picasso, featuring limited editions, lithographs, and ceramics. Picasso's *Guernica* sketches are a steal starting at €100. Open M-Sa 10am-7pm.

Galería Montcada, C. Montcada, 20 (☎93 268 00 14; www.galeriamontcada.com). M: Jaume I, L4. A small gallery in the historic Palau Dalmases. Its rotating, month-long exhibits generally spotlight Catalan artists. Best bet for (possibly) affordable art. Open Su and Tu-Sa 11am-2pm and 4-8pm.

EL RAVAL

◪ PALAU GÜELL

◪ *C. Nou de La Rambla, 3-5. M: Liceu, L3. 2 blocks from the Opera Liceu, off Las Ramblas.* ☎*93 317 39 74; fax 93 317 37 79. Open Mar.-Oct. Su 10am-2pm, M-Sa 10am-8pm, last tour at 6:15pm; Nov.-Dec. M-Sa 10am-6pm. €3, students €1.50. Visits by guided tour only, departing every 15min. Often sells out for the day in the afternoon; get your tickets early.*

see map p. 336

Modernist and Modern

Antoni Gaudí's Palau Güell (1886-90) has one of Barcelona's most spectacular interiors. A dark, haunting Modernist residence built for patron Eusebi Güell (of Park Güell fame), the mansion was declared a UN World Heritage Site in 1999. Güell and Gaudí spared no expense in the construction of this sumptuous, dream-like home, with which some say Gaudí truly came into his own as a premier architect. Note the brilliant equation of function and design, as well as the various psychedelic ceilings; legend has it that Güell was able to spy on his guests through the ceiling in the Visitor's Room. The 20 unique rooftop chimneys display Gaudí's first use of the *trencadis*—the covering of surfaces with irregular shards of ceramic or glass—a technique often seen in his later work.

Façade of Casa Mila

◪ MUSEU D'ART CONTEMPORANI (MACBA)

◪ *Pl. dels Angels, 1. M: Universitat or Catalunya. From Pl. de Catalunya, take a right onto C. Elisabets and follow it to Pl. dels Angels.* ☎*93 412 08 10; www.macba.es. Open July-Sept. Su 10am-3pm., M-F 11am-8pm, Sa 10am-8pm; Oct.-June Su 10am-3pm, M-F 11am-7:30pm, Sa 10am-8pm. €7, students €3; W €3 for all, 16 and under free.*

The gleaming white MACBA building, designed by American architect Richard Meier in 1995, was the final product of a collaboration between Barcelona's mayor and the Catalan government to restore El Raval by turning the neighborhood into a regional artistic and cultural focal point. The museum's modernity and scale, as well as sheer brightness, are a startling contrast with the narrow alleys and aging cobblestone streets of the neighborhood where it sits. The building's

Casa Lleo Morera

sparse decor was designed to allow the art to speak for itself, which it has—the MACBA has received worldwide acclaim for its focus on avant-garde art between the two world wars. While the permanent collection provides a general overview of Western contemporary art, it is particularly successful in introducing the public to the works of some acclaimed artists from Barcelona. The temporary exhibits are often interactive. Past ones included "Sonic Process: A New Geography of Sounds," an impressive exploration of the hybridization of music and the visual arts, and "Genius Without Talent," an exhibit on the witty French artist Robert Filiou.

CENTRE DE CULTURA CONTEMPORÀNIA DE BARCELONA (CCCB)

🖪 *Casa de Caritat. C. Montalegre, 5. M: Catalunya L1/3, or Universitat, L1/2, next to the MACBA (see above).* ☎ *93 306 41 00; www.cccb.org. Open Tu, Th, and F 11am-2pm and 4-8pm; W and Sa 11am-8pm; Su and holidays 11am-7pm. €4, students €3; W €3 for all, children free.*

At first glance, the center stands out for its jarring mixture of architectural styles, consisting of an unassuming early 20th-century theater and its 1994 addition, an enormous and very sleek wing constructed of black glass. The institution itself stands out as well, with a wonderful variety of temporary art exhibits, including film screenings, music, and dance performances. In 2003 exhibits included: "Trash Culture: the Potholes of Taste," an excessive display of bad taste, the kind no one will admit loving. Check the *Guía del Ocio* for scheduled events.

ESGLÉSIA DE SANT PAU DEL CAMP

🖪 *M: Parallel L2/3, at the intersection of C. Sant Pau and C. Carretes, 2 blocks off Av. Parallel. Open Su-M and W-Sa 5-8pm.*

Although this small, ancient stone church may not impress at first glance, art and design students will note the decorated columns, vaulted ceilings, and tiny, intricately detailed stained-glass windows that together make this medieval marvel one of the most important examples of Romanesque architecture in the city of Barcelona. When first founded in AD 912, the church stood in the country, well outside the city walls. However, the current church building, constructed in the 12th century, is very much a part of the city. Guifré Borrell, the church's founder and the son of Wilfred the Hairy (see **Life & Times,** p. 38), was buried here in AD 911.

UNIVERSITAT DE BARCELONA

🖪 *Pl. Universitat. M: Universitat, L1/2/3. Open M-F 9am-10pm.*

Overlooking Gran Vía, this palatial 19th-century building housed the University of Barcelona until much of its campus moved north to Pedralbes in the 1950s. Today, the philosophy, religion, mathematics, and language departments remain in the regal hallways. The grounds include several beautiful, shady courtyards lined by arches and columns and filled with trees, ponds, and fountains. The library is open to the public for consultation; bring a picture ID. For those looking to sublet a room in a nearby apartment, check the bulletin boards scattered around on the ground floor.

see map pp. 340-341

L'EIXAMPLE

As Barcelona's bourgeoisie have increasingly moved uptown, the earlier residential districts of l'Eixample, around Pg. de Gràcia, have filled with offices, services, and shops. But despite the gentrification, the original Modernist architecture that draws visitors remains intact. The buildings on Pg. de Gràcia (such as Casa Milà, p. 84, and La Manzana de la Discòrdia, p. 86), Gaudí's Sagrada Família (p. 79), and Domènech i Montaner's Hospital de la Santa Creu i Sant Pau (p. 81) are the landmark attractions. Dedicated architecture lovers should wander the streets of the so-called *Quadrant d'Or*, the area bounded by Av. Diagonal, C. Aribau, Pg. St. Joan, and the lower Rondas (Rda. Universitat and Rda. St. Pere). This neighborhood cradles the majority of expensive homes first built when the walls of the old city were torn down. If you plan on seeing a lot of the sights in l'Eixample, be sure to get a **Ruta del Modernisme** pass (see p. 51) and allow more than just an afternoon as two days can easily be consumed with sightseeing and architecture-admiring here. This sights and museums in this neighborhood are grouped by area: l'Eixample Dreta, Pg. de Gràcia, and l'Eixample Esquerra.

L'EIXAMPLE DRETA

⬛ LA SAGRADA FAMÍLIA

🔺 *C. Mallorca, 401; main entrance on C. Sardenya between C. Provença and C. Mallorca. M: Sagrada Família, L2/5. ☎ 93 207 30 31 or 93 208 04 14. Open Oct.-Mar. daily 9am-6pm, elevator open 9:30am-5:45pm; Apr.-Sept. daily 9am-8pm, elevator open 9:30am-7:45pm.* ⬛ *Guided tours Apr.-Sept. daily every hour 11am-5pm; Oct. 11am-3pm; Nov.-Mar. F-M 11am-1pm. €3 (buy tickets right inside the Sardenya entrance.) Elevator €2. Audio guides available in English, €3. Combined ticket for the Sagrada Família and Casa-Museu Gaudí (in Parc Güell, see p. 103) €9. Just La Sagrada Família and its museum €8, students, €5. Cash only. Wheelchair accessible.*

Although Gaudí's unfinished masterpiece is barely a shell of the intended finished product, La Sagrada Família is without a doubt the world's most visited construction site. Despite the completion of only eight of the 18 planned towers (and those the shortest, at that) and the church still doesn't have an "interior," millions of people make the touristic pilgrimage to witness the work-in-progress. Its construction is entirely funded by popular donations (as opposed to the state or the Vatican); in the past, the Church told donors their patronage guaranteed them a place in heaven. Luckily, visitors' entrance fees are considered just such "popular donations." But while it is questionable whether the price of admission will get you through the pearly gates, it will get you into an awe-inspiring world of nature, spirituality, and art. Finished or not, La Sagrada Família has become tightly intertwined with the image of Barcelona.

La Sagrada Família was commissioned not by the Roman Catholic Church, but by an extremely pious right-wing organization called the Spiritual

GET sm**art**

I Get By With a Little Help from my Friends

The name of Antoni Gaudí has gained such international fame that he tends to be unilaterally associated with his greatest works. In reality, though, Gaudí usually operated more as a loose coordinator of a host of extremely skilled sculptors, iron-workers, and painters, to some of whom he gave huge creative leeway.

This was particularly true of his collaborative relationship with a man named **Josep Marià Jujol.** Some critics actually consider Jujol to be directly responsible for Gaudí's artistic shift, between 1904 and 1908; Gaudí left his earlier, heavier designs for the much more fluid, almost magical (and more famous) ones of his later years. Jujol designed the furniture for Casa Batlló and had complete control over the construction of the Casa Mila- roof while Gaudí was away on other projects. Jujol even created the famous ceramic-clad, winding bench at the Park Güell. With such an intense relationship, why didn't Jujol gain control of La Sagrada Família after Gaudí's untimely death? Many are upset about this oversight, but it remains a mystery of architectural intrigue.

GET sm**art**

Far-out Facade

Gaudí was a religious man, and his plans for La Sagrada Família called for elaborate and deliberate symbolism in almost every decorative element of the church. The cypress tree on the **Nativity Facade,** according to one theory, symbolizes the stairway to heaven: cypress trees do not put down deeper roots with time but only grow increasingly taller. The tree is crowned with the word *Tau,* the Greek for God. Similarly, the top of each of the eight finished towers carries the first letter of one of the names of the apostles, and the words "Hosanna" and "Excelsis" are written in a spiral up the sides of the towers. Inside, on the **Portal of the Rosary,** overt references to modern life lurk amongst more traditional religious imagery: the Temptation of Man is represented by the devil handing a bomb to a terrorist and by his waving a purse at a prostitute.

Josep María Subirachs, Gaudí's successor, continued religious symbolism in his **Passion Facade.** To the left, snake lurks behind Judas, symbolizing the disciple's betrayal of Jesus. The 4x4 box of numbers beside him contains 310 combinations of four numbers, each of which adds up to 33, Christ's age at when he died.

Association for Devotion to St. Joseph, or the Josephines. Founded in 1866 in reaction to the liberal ideas spreading throughout Europe, the group was determined to build an Expiatory Temple for Barcelona, where the city could reaffirm its faith to the Holy Family of Jesus, Mary, and Joseph, hence the building's full name, **Templo Expiatori de la Sagrada Família.** The first architect they chose quit almost immediately when his ideas for the church swayed from those of the project's commissar, and they replaced him with Gaudí in 1884, when he was only 31 years old. For the first 15 or 20 years, private contributions kept the building process going, but as the mood and culture of the city changed with the onset of the modern age, construction slowed drastically, and the Civil War (see p. 42) brought it to a complete halt. The years of the war proved tragic for the temple. First Gaudí died after being hit by a tram just outside the church's walls in 1926, having overseen the completion of only the **Nativity Facade.** To make matters worse, in 1936, arsonists on the revolutionary side of the Civil War broke into the crypt, opened Gaudí's tomb, smashed his plaster models, and burned every single document in the workshop in a display of anti-establishment fury.

Today, the building remains under the auspices of the Josephines; architect Jordi Bonet, whose father worked directly with Gaudí, is heading up the project with sculptor Josep Marià Subirachs, who finished the Passion Facade in 1998. Hampered by the lack of Gaudí's exact calculations, they are working from ongoing reconstructions of his original plaster models. The computer models that engineers are using to recreate his underlying mathematical logic are so complicated that only three people in the world know how to use them. As today's workers slowly put into form what they think Gaudí had in mind, they are doing things, architecturally, that have literally never been done before. Until now, it was nearly impossible to set a completion date because of the intricacies of the reconstructed models, new building, and the unsteady flow of donations. However, in 2001 Bonet announced that La Sagrada Família is expected to be finished by 2022.

The continuation of Gaudí's greatest obsession has been fraught with fierce controversy. Some, like Salvador Dalí, have argued that the church should have been left incomplete as a monument to the architect. Others believe that La Sagrada Família should be finished, but in a more "authentic" manner than has thus been the case. Critics usually attack most vehemently Subirachs's Passion Facade. The abstract, Cubist design contrasts starkly with the more traditional Nativity Facade, which depicts Christ's birth and faces the Pl. de Gaudí. The controversial **Passion Facade,** which faces the Pl. de la Sagrada Família, portrays Christ's Passion—Catholic lingo for his crucifixion, death, and resurrection. When completed, the front of the temple—the Glory Facade—will feature four more bell towers like those that already exist; together the 12 towers will represent the 12 apostles. Above the center of the church will rise a massive 170m Tower of Jesus, with a shorter spire just behind dedicated to Mary. The Jesus tower will in turn be surrounded by four more towers symbolizing the four Evangelists (the authors of the four gospels). As finishing touches, Gaudí envisioned an extravagant spouting fountain in front of the main Glory Facade and a tall purifying flame at the back. Gaudí's dedication to religious themes in his work on La Sagrada Família (see **Far-Out Facade,** p. 80) has even earned the attention of the Vatican.

Casa Amatller Detail

Visitors today can see detailed paintings of the projected church in the Museu Gaudí. Also on display are numerous pictures from the early years of the project, sketches by Gaudí, the glass-walled workshop where his models are still being restored, and various sculptures and decorative pieces from the temple. For a more somber experience, you can gaze down on Gaudí's crypt, where roses and tea lights line the grave as a statue of Mary watches over the man that lived (and arguably died) for this church.

Courtyard of Casa Mila

HOSPITAL DE LA SANTA CREU I SANT PAU

🏛 *Sant Antoni M. Claret, 167. Entrance at intersection with C. Cartagena. M: Hospital de St. Pau, L5. ☎ 93 488 20 78; www.santpau.es. Hospital grounds open 24hr. 50min. guided tours Sa-Su 10am-2pm every 30min., in Catalan, Spanish, or English. Last tour leaves 1:30pm. €4.25, students and 65+ €3. Cash only. Free information pamphlet and map of grounds in foyer.*

Designated a UNESCO monument in 1997, the brilliant Modernist Hospital de la Santa Creu i Sant Pau was Domènech i Montaner's lifetime masterpiece. The entire complex covers nine full l'Eixample blocks (320 acres) and the pavilions are whimsically decorated, resembling gingerbread houses. The outdoor spaces are often compared to an oasis in a desert of monotonous urban gridding; they once

Looking down from La Sagrada Família

Fiesta with Fire

When you're in Barcelona, don't be frightened when kids start lighting firecrackers and home-made explosives in the streets: it is only the Fiesta de Sant Joan, or St. John's day, when all of Catalunya joins in a traditional celebration of the shortest night of the year.

Though initially a pagan holiday celebrating the summer solstice, the ancient traditions have come to symbolize, for many, an important element of Catalan identity. Originally, fires were lit in the main squares of small villages, and townspeople gathered to burn old belongings and furniture. Today the holiday is celebrated by gathering with family to eat (especially sweet things such as cakes with dried fruits and/or pine nuts, called *coca*), drink, or go to *revetlles* (revels) and *verbenas* (parties). Fires sometimes are still lit in the streets, especially by students: as the holiday coincides with the end of the school year, many take the opportunity to burn their books. Starting at sun-down June 23rd, and going straight through to dawn of the 24th, make some noise and join the Catalans as they come out to clelebrate.

For more information visit: www.santjoan.org or www.bcn.es/santjoan/.

included a small forest and still boast more than 300 different types of plants, as well as plenty of wide, shaded paths.

Begun in 1905, this unusual hospital owes its existence to a wealthy Catalan banker named Pau Gil who spent his entire adult life in Paris. While there, he was influenced by new French theories on proper hygiene and therapeutic hospital designs. He endowed the construction of a new type of city hospital: not only sanitary, but also aesthetically pleasing (for a more complete healing experience). A design by architect Domènech i Estapa was originally chosen for the building, but he was soon dropped in favor of Domènech i Montaner, whose plan more skillfully incorporated medical and sanitary concerns. Montaner designed 12 pavilions, each of which would be no more than one or two stories and would serve only 28 patients. The interior of each pavilion was painted in various shades of green, and each room had plenty of natural light. He even took note of wind patterns and put the most infectious wards at the back of the hospital, at the "end" of the current.

The money for Montaner's design ran out in 1910 and construction halted until 1915, when the hospital gained further financial backing by merging with the city's ancient Hospital de la Santa Creu (founded 1401). Montaner's son undertook the expansion of his father's work, though in a completely different style. (Modernism fell out of fashion as soon as he began working.) The completed joint complex, with 48 pavilions, was officially opened in 1930 by King Alfonso XIII. Even with the vast additions to Montaner's pavilions, the Hospital de la Santa Creu i Sant Pau still has one of the highest space-to-patient ratios in all of Europe, with 140sq. m for each of the 600 patients.

The hospital's most interesting feature is the main administrative building, which is steeped in decorative symbolism. The letters P and G, a tribute to Pau Gil, repeat in various motifs. The four sculpted figures on the front facade represent faith, hope, charity, and work; the multi-domed ceiling of the entrance foyer is covered with the symbols of Catalunya, Barcelona, St. Jordi, the city of Paris, the bankers' association (a nod to P.G. again), and the years in which the Modernist portion of the building was begun and finished.

The hospital is actually slated to close in the year 2004, when the medical services will be relocated to more modern facilities nearby. The future fate of the complex has not yet been decided, but rumor has it that it may become a stunning university.

MUSEU DEL CÒMIC I DE LA ILLUSTRACIÓ

◪ *C. Santa Carolina, 25. M: Alfons X, L4. Walk down Trav. de Gràcia and take a right on C. Padilla; C. Santa Carolina is on the left 2 blocks down. Knock on the metal door for entrance. ☎ 93 348 15 13; www.interars.com. Open M-Sa 10am-2pm and 5-8pm. €3, under 14 and 65+ €2.10.*

Comic strip artists in Spain have not had an easy time between the Civil War, postwar economic difficulties, Franco's censorship, and overwhelming competition from Japanese animation. This small private collection was carefully put together as a sampling of some of the best comics drawn in Spain between 1915 and the 1970s. For the politically minded, the Franco propaganda aimed directly at children is particularly interesting; look for the January 30, 1938 and July 18, 1939 editions of *Flecha*, the *"semanario nacional infantil"* (children's national weekly) of the time, in order to see proud soldiers grasping the Spanish flag and cheering, "Franco! Franco! Franco!" While the avid comic enthusiast may be drooling at the displays, the one-room collection may be a bit small and disappointing for those not cartoon-obsessed. Bear in mind, also, that the majority of work is in Spanish or Catalan.

ESGLÉSIA DE LES SALESES

◪ *Pg. de St. Joan. M: Verdaguer, L4/5.*

The Església de les Saleses stands out as one of the most striking churches in the entire city. Built in 1885 by Joan Martorell i Montells, one of Gaudí's mentors, it originally served as a convent, but was severely damaged during the 1909 **Setmana Tràgica** (Tragic Week; see **Life & Times**, p. 40). After it was repaired in 1945, it became a school, and finally, a Catholic parish. It is generally considered a direct precursor to the works of the Modernist movement, with its detailed brick, stone, and glass exterior decorations. Renovations are ongoing; check with the school on C. Roger de Flor for hours of operation.

PLAÇA GLÒRIES

◪ *M: Glòries, L1.*

The Pl. Glòries is by far the biggest *plaça* in l'Eixample. Located at the intersection of Av. Meridiana and Av. Diagonal, its small central park is entirely encircled by a wide roadway packed with fast-moving cars. The bizarre Monument to the Metre crosses the length of the park in a bronze cross section of the earth that is disturbingly reminiscent of a jagged razor. Donated by the Dunkirk (Ireland) City Council in 1992, it commemorates the 200th anniversary of the measuring of the Prime Meridian between Barcelona and Dunkirk, marking where the master of all longitudinal lines slices through the city. The black plaques around the *plaça* use famous quotations to memorialize 12 "glorious" elements of Catalan history, including Romanesque art, Gothic architecture, industrialization, scientific advancement, Catalan law, and more. But biggest doesn't necessarily mean best; the space is more dustbowl than "park," and its lack of proximity to other sights may make it an area to leave off a tight itinerary.

MUSEU TAURÍ

◪ *Gran Via de les Corts Catalanes, 749. ☎ 93 245 58 04. M: Monumental, L2. Open M-Sa 11am-2pm and 4-8pm, Su 11am-2pm, fight days 10:30am-1pm. Admission includes entrance to the museum, bullring, and bull pens. Museum descriptions in English, Spanish, German, and Italian. €4, children €3.*

This dense, two-room collection proudly commemorates the tradition of bullfighting with pictures of major fights and fighters, old posters, and stamps. The exhibit includes a colorful display of the evolution of the bullfighter's costume and a number of stuffed bulls' heads (minus, of course, the ears their human opponents claimed upon completing the kill). You can also see a picture display of one much luckier beast, the first bull to be spared in the Plaza Monumental by unanimous public request—a remarkable feat after more than 50 years of fights in the ring ending with bulls' deaths. For tickets to a bullfight (which is a less common form of entertainment in Barcelona than it is in the rest of Spain), see **Entertainment**, p. 167; for some perspective on the sport, see **Bye-Bye Bully**, p. 166. While a bullfight can be off-putting for even the most sturdy stomach, a trip to this museum will satisfy curiosity without having to bear witness to the violence.

PLAÇA TETUÁN

⚐ *M: Tetuán, L2.*

The centerpiece of the Pl. Tetuán is a hefty monument to **Bartomeu Robert**, created by Josep Llimona in 1910 in honor of the former city mayor. Torn down under Franco because of its "excessive" nationalistic symbolism, it was finally replaced in 1985 by King Juan Carlos and Queen Sofia. The curving base supports the bust of a man, presumably Robert, surrounded by a talking crowd.

OTHER SIGHTS IN L'EIXAMPLE DRETA

A good number of Barcelona's more than 400 monuments adorn l'Eixample, where wide streets and open corners lend them plenty of visibility. Some of the better-known include the submarine sculpture in honor of inventor **Narcís Monturiol** (C. Girona and Av. Diagonal; M: Verdaguer, L4/5), the monument to **Anton Clavé**, founder of many popular choral societies (Pg. de St. Joan and Trav. de Gràcia; M: Joanic, L4), and the monument to Catalan poet **Jacint Verdaguer** (Pg. St. Joan and Av. Diagonal; M: Verdaguer, L4/5).

One of the most famous Modernist houses in the city sits near the intersection of Av. Diagonal and C. Roger de Llúria, at Av. Diagonal, 416-420 (M: Joanic, L4). Designed by Puig i Cadafalch in 1905, it is called the **Casa de las Punxes (House of Spikes)**, or La Casa Terrades, for the distinctive medieval turrets that lend it a castle-like appearance. One block up, Salvador Valeri's **Casa Comalat** (Av. Diagonal 442) has two facades; the one facing Av. Diagonal is symmetrical and well decorated with subtle stone textures. Across the street, Puig i Cadafalch's **Palau del Baló de Quadras**, (Av. Diagonal, 373) has an even more ornate facade—it's almost entirely capped in sculptures.

PG. DE GRÀCIA

▨ CASA MILÀ (LA PEDRERA)

⚐ *Pg. de Gràcia, 92. M: Pg. de Gràcia, L2/3/4. Enter around the corner on C. Provença. ☎ 93 484 59 95; ticket info 93 484 59 00. Open daily 10am-8pm; last entry 7:30pm. Free guided tours M-F 4pm (English) and 6pm (Spanish and Catalan). Tour times change frequently with the season; call ahead to check the current schedule. €7, students and 65+ €3.50. Wheelchair accessible.*

Although innovative, Gaudí's unusual designs for Casa Milà were not all admired 100 years ago, and the name, La Pedrera (which means stone quarry in Spanish), came about as a result of popular jokes, critiques, and caricatures. The building's namesake, wealthy businessman Pere Milà, hired Gaudí because he liked his work on neighboring Casa Batlló (see p. 87). But as the project progressed between 1906 and 1910, Milà's wife, Roger Segimon, became increasingly unhappy with the appearance and refused to pay the excessive costs of the building. Gaudí eventually filed a lawsuit against the couple over his fees (he won and promptly gave all of the money to the poor), and the Casa Milà ended up being the only residence he designed for which he did not also craft the furniture. Gaudí also originally intended to place a massive sculpture of the Virgin and Child in the most prominent corner of the rooftop, as the edifice purported to be a tribute to the Immaculate Conception. The Milàs either didn't like the idea or they were afraid to boast such a display of faith after the horrific violence of the Setmana

Trágica in 1909 (see p. 40). In any case, Gaudí was denied this final touch on this last residential building he constructed.

Today, visitors have access to the main and top floors of the building. The rest of Casa Milà is inhabited by the lucky yet patient (and wealthy) people who sat on the twenty-year waiting list for an apartment. The top floor is filled with displays in four different languages (English, Castellano, Catalan, French) about the construction of this and other Gaudí works. Casa Milà in particular is built around two central courtyards, with an underground park in the basement and not a single flat wall in the entire space. For a great photo-op, climb to the roof of Casa Milà to take a picture of **La Sagrada Família** (see p. 79) framed by an arch.

Casa Mila

FUNDACIÓ FRANCISCO GODIA

🛈 *C. Valencia, 284. M: Pg. de Gràcia, L2/3/4. ☎ 93 272 31 80; www.fundacionfgodia.org. Open Su-M and W-Sa 10am-8pm. Free guided tours Sa-Su noon in Spanish and Catalan; otherwise call ahead for a guided tour, €6. Wall descriptions and printed guides are in English, Spanish, and Catalan. €4.50; students, 65+, and disabled €2.10. Joint ticket with the Museu Egipci (see below) €8.50; students, 65+, and disabled €6.50. Wheelchair accessible. MC/V.*

The Fundació Francisco Godia was created in 1998 by the Godia's daughter in order to open his private art collection for public viewing. Francisco Godia (1921-1990) was a bizarre combination of astute businessman, accomplished Formula One race car driver, and passionate supporter of the arts. His collection runs from the 12th to the 20th century, with a heavy emphasis on medieval sculpture and painting, Spanish ceramics of the last 500 years, and modern Spanish paintings. Highlights include Solana's bold, dark-lined *Bullfight at Ronda* (1927), Isidre Nonell's dark *Gypsy Woman* (1905), Francesc Gimeno's life-like *Mother and Daughter* (1898), and the popular piece *At the Racecourse* (1905), by Ramon Casas. The Fundació also organizes exhibitions featuring private collections from throughout Spain. Be sure to check out the front room filled with Godia's racing trophies, proof that NASCAR and art are not mutually exclusive.

Casa de las Punxes

MUSEU EGIPCI

🛈 *C. Valencia, 284, just to the left of Pg. de Gràcia when you're facing Pl. de Catalunya. M: Pg. de Gràcia, L2/3/4. ☎ 93 488 01 88; www.fundclos.com. Open M-Sa 10am-*

Inside the Museu del Perfum

Festival time in Barceloneta

Stone Fox Architctural Detail

View of the Pier

8pm, Su 10am-2pm. Closed Dec. 25-26 and Jan. 1. Descriptions in Spanish and Catalan. Free tours in Spanish and Catalan Sa 11am and 5pm; call ahead to hire an English guide (€8.50). €5.50; students, 65+, and disabled €4.50. Joint admission with the Fundació Godia (next door; see above) €8.50; students, 65+, and disabled €6.50. Wheelchair accessible. MC/V.

In 1993, the wealthy Jordi Clos decided to turn a private passion into Spain's only museum dedicated entirely to Pharaonic Egypt. More than 500 Egyptian artifacts and several displays focused on tombs, mummies, and the beliefs surrounding death in ancient Egypt pack two floors as tightly as a Pharaoh's tomb. The museum is extremely well organized (displays are arranged by theme); ask for an English guide and receive a 30-page booklet with detailed descriptions of each artifact. Catch the dramatic reenactment of Egyptian legends Friday nights 9:30-11pm, complete with a tour and a cup of *cava*. (€12, students €10.50; reservations required.)

MUSEU DEL PERFUM

🚩 *Pg. de Gràcia, 39. M: Pg. de Gràcia, L2/3/4. ☎93 216 01 46; www.museodelperfume.com; Open M-F 10:30am-1:30pm and 5-8pm, Sa 11am-1:30pm. Wheelchair accessible. Free.*

Located in the back of a perfectly ordinary-looking perfume store, the Museu del Perfum is easy to miss. The collection inside, however, should not be overlooked, with nearly a thousand perfume containers, from 2nd-century BC Roman vials to 14th-century Arab pieces to miniatures from pre-Columbian Ecuador. Some of the original designs include a mouse, a lightbulb, the Eiffel Tower, and a suicidal bottle with a knife-shaped throat applicator. Even Salvador Dalí took a crack at this little-known art form, with a huge bottle he called "The Sun King."

🖼 LA MANZANA DE LA DISCÒRDIA

According to Greek myth, a piece of fruit was responsible for the Trojan War: the goddess of Discord created a golden apple as a prize for the most beautiful, and divine disharmony ensued. Barcelona has its own competition for the golden apple on the block of Pg. de Gràcia between C. Consell de Cent and C. Aragó, where trademark houses by the three most important architects of Modernism stand side-by-side in proud competition: the Casa Lleó Morera by Domènech i Montaner, the Casa Amatller by Puig i Cadafalch, and the

Casa Batlló by Gaudí. Even the strongest Catalanists haven't wanted to give up the pun in the old name *"la manzana,"* which in Castilian means both "block" and "apple." The name "Block of Discord" is especially indicative of the contrast (and clash) between the styles and aesthetics of the three houses. All of these creations are renovations of older, pre-existing edifices. To see the architectural contrast most clearly, take a look from across the street.

CASA BATLLÓ

◪ *Pg. de Gràcia, 43 (☎ 93 216 03 06; www.casabatllo.es). Open M-Sa 9am-2pm, Su 9am-8pm. €8, students €6.*

As the most fantastical member of the Block of Discord, Gaudí's Casa Batlló sees the most visitors. Gaudí was 52 when he re-constructed this house—often considered one of his first works which was clearly and completely "Gaudian" in style—after years of developing it. Shimmering and curving in shades of blue and green, the house looks slightly different at every hour of the day. Many see the building as a depiction of the legend of St. Jordi and the dragon. This interpretation incorporates all the major facets of the building: the tall pinnacle on the left symbolizes the knight's lance after it has pierced the dragon's scaly back (represented by the warped, multi-colored, ceramic roof). The stairway supposedly represents the winding of the dragon's tail or the curves of his vertebrae, the outside balconies skulls, and the molded columns the bones of his unfortunate victims. Others see the house as having an underwater theme, correlating to the new excitement over exploration and developments in technology at the time of building. The house is like something out of the *Little Mermaid;* walls and stained-glass windows are fluid and wavelike, and many of the ceilings in the building spiral as if in a whirlpool.

Like the other two houses on the block, Casa Batlló was the result of a remodeling job on an older, ordinary building, this one requested in 1905 by Josep Batlló, a wealthy beneficiary of the Industrial Revolution's textile boom. Gaudí did away with straight lines altogether, even in the furniture. Particularly interesting is the way he tiled the central inner patio, dark blue on the top and lighter on the bottom, in order to distribute the light from above as evenly as possible.

Apparently, candy manufacturers have a taste for Modernism: the ChupaChups lollipop company now owns the Casa Batlló, and it is closed to the public other than for daily tours. Fortunately, the Espai Gaudí in Casa Milà has a good video presentation showing throughout the day which allows you to see the tiled walls, colorful mosaics, and sensuous curves of the inside of the house, as well as some interesting details on the exterior.

CASA LLEÓ MORERA

In 1902, textile tycoon Albert Lleó Morera hired Domènech i Montaner to add some pizzazz to his boring 1864 home on the corner of Pg. de Gràcia and C. Consell de Cent. Montaner responded by creating one of the most lavish examples of decorative architecture in Barcelona, for which he won the Ajuntament's annual prize for Best Building of the Year in 1905. Much of the street-level exterior was destroyed by the Loewe leather shop that now occupies the entry, but if you look up at the second-floor balconies on either side of the corner tribune, you can see two nymphs on each balcony, holding (from left to right) a gramophone, an electric lightbulb, a telephone, and a camera: symbols of the new leisure technology available to the bourgeoisie of the early 1900s. On the wall of the balcony above the tribune itself you can see carved lions. Mulberry leaves lace around the tops of the tribune's vertical columns. Together these refer to the family name: *lleó* in Catalan means "lion," and *morera* means "mulberry tree."

The mezzanine level of the interior, unfortunately closed to the public, boasts a stunning dining room with glimmering stained-glass windows and detailed ceramic mosaics of the Lleó Morera family picnicking outdoors. The famous

in recent news

Workers of the World

European workers spend less time working per week than the laborers of almost every other continent (save Africa). Worker strikes in Europe, however, take place surprisingly frequently and Barcelona is no exception. Ever since the notorious Barcelona labor strike of 1931, strikes have become a particularly powerful way of affecting change in labor practices. On June 20, 2002, the *Confederación General del Trabajo* (CGT; General Confederation of Labor) organized a strike that paralyzed Barcelona, shutting down all major businesses, buses, and metro services, effectively bringing the city to a standstill.

The thousands of workers, united under the CGT, mobilized and paraded through the streets in an effort to address the plight of workers in Spain. The CGT accused the Spanish government of favoring big business at the cost of the plebeian worker. Today, the CGT still claims that workers suffer from the lowest purchasing power and the highest unemployment rate of the entire European Union.

For more information, visit the CGT website: www.cgt.es.

furniture that Gaspar Homar originally designed for this room is permanently on display at the Museu d'Art Modern (see p. 73), and the Ruta del Modernisme booklet guide has a decent picture of the gorgeous stained-glass wall, as do most coffee-table books on Barcelona's architecture.

CASA AMATLLER

Chocolate mogul Antoni Amatller planted the first seed for La Manzana de la Discòrdia in 1898, when he commissioned Puig i Cadafalch to redo the facade of his prominent home. Cadafalch turned out a mix of Catalan, neo-Gothic, Islamic, and Dutch architecture best known for its stylized, geometric, pink, blue, and cream upper facade. It is the combination of foreign and native elements that people note about Cadafalch's creation. The lower exterior of the house also has character; look carefully and you can see various facets of the owner's personality and background inscribed in sculpture. Above the main door, the prominent carving of Catalan hero St. Jordi battling the dragon demonstrates Amatller's Catalan nationalism and the four figures engaged in painting, sculpture, architecture, and music represent Amatller's broad cultural interests. On either side of the main second-floor windows, there are caricatures of Amatller's favorite pastimes. On the left, small monkeys and rabbits busily mold iron (the main Catalan industry of Amatller's time), and a donkey with glasses reads a book while another plays with a camera; on the right side, frogs and pigs hold glass vases and pottery, a reference to Amatller's passion for vase-collecting. A huge "A" for Amatller adorns the outside of the entrance, intertwined with almond leaves (*amatller* means "almond" in Catalan). The long, single balcony with many doorways leading onto it were also elements of traditional Catalan architecture.

The building's facade resembles Flemish architecture, which some argue is a reference to the fact that Amatller traded chocolate in Flanders, a Spanish colony. Notice the green wood lattice windows, which allow one to look out onto the street without being seen. Others suggest that the resemblance to this style was a political statement by Puig i Cadafalch, a protest against Catalunya's own near-colonial relationship with the central government in Madrid. Still others believe that it was simply the best shape to cover the photography studio on the top floor.

Inside, the entrance foyer still has fascinating iron-and-glass lamps, bright decorative tiles, and a stained-glass skylight just to the right off the main hallway. The small temporary art exhibit in the back room features various explorations relevant to Modernist architecture—for example, mini architectural models, stained-glass exhibitions, and mirrors. Buy some Amatller chocolate to see for yourself whether he deserved his fortune. The apartment where the millionaire lived with his daughter is now home to the **Institut Amatller d'Art Hispànic,** open to students of the institute.

The **Joieria Bagués,** which holds a well-known collection of Modernist pieces from the Masriera tradition, occupies the right side of the entrance level. They offer a tour of the store's sparkling dragonflies, nymphs, and flowers. (Open M-F 10am-8:30pm, Sa 10am-12:30pm and 5-8:30pm.)

OTHER SIGHTS ON PG. DE GRÀCIA

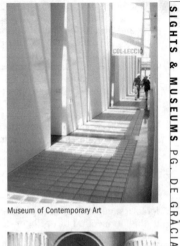
Museum of Contemporary Art

If you want to prolong the magical mystery tour of Modernisme, a jaunt down the Pg. de Gràcia will acquaint you with equally interesting though less famous Modernist facades. Start at M: Catalunya and make your way up the Pg. de Gràcia. On the right at no. 18, you will see the **Joieria Roca,** a boxy building with glass-block exterior matched with pink. Though today it is reminiscent of retro-cool Art Deco, this curving building was way ahead of its time in 1934, when architect Josep Lluís Sert sparked a serious conservative backlash with his unconventional design for the facade. **Casa Olano,** at no. 60, was used as headquarters for the Basque government during the Spanish Civil War; a plaque to this effect still hangs above the doorway. The building earned its nickname "Pirate House" from the rendition of sailor Juan Sebastian Elcano from the front wall that glares menacingly down at passersby. Up a little farther, at no. 66, is one of the most attractive corner facades on the Pg. de Gràcia, part of the **Casa Vidua Marfà,** built by Manual Comas Thos in 1905. Today it houses Barcelona's School of Tourism, and though you can't walk through the entire building, you can still walk into the entrance foyer and look up at the multi-colored skylight.

Art School, Plaça Veronica

A few blocks away, at no. 96, is **Casa Casas,** less well-known than its neighbor Casa Milà, but still worth a visit. Notable mainly for its previous inhabitant, the Catalan painter Ramon Casas, the first two floors now house the **Vinçon** furniture and knick-knack stores (see **Shopping,** p. 182). Walk inside to view the original stone entry, stairwell, and an imposing carved fireplace, or outside to the back patio, where you can see the reddish-colored back side of La Pedrera.

Barceloneta Clock Tower

One block over, at the intersection of Diagonal and Rambla de Catalunya (no. 126), the literally two-faced **Can Serra** is worth a look as well. The original turreted pink-and-peach stone building, constructed in French Gothic style, was completed by Puig i Cadafalch in 1908 and is adorned with a sculpture by Eusebi Arnau of St. Jordi, the dragon, the princess, and some strangely entangled centaurs. The bulk of the house was razed in 1981, and now the old Gothic facade wraps around a smooth, black, glossy structure home to the Diputació of Barcelona.

Still want more? Then go back to Pl. de Catalunya and walk up the Pg. de Gràcia only one block to C. Casp, where you will turn right and continue for a few blocks to no. 48, **Casa Calvet** (☎93 412 40 12). This house was Gaudí's first apartment building. It was also, in fact, the only thing he ever won an award for during his lifetime: the Ajuntament's first annual prize for Best Building of the Year, given out in 1900. Now the building houses an upscale restaurant with a gorgeous interior colored by stained glass. From Casa Calvet, backtrack half a block to C. Roger de Llúria, turn right, and walk down 2½ blocks. On your right, at no. 56, will be a small passageway leading to the **Torre de les Aigües,** the water tower built by Josep Oriol Mestres in 1879 to supply water to the first houses of l'Eixample. Today it overlooks a small summertime pool for neighborhood children. A half-block farther up, at the intersection of C. Roger de Llúria and C. Consell de Cent, you will see the pink-and-peach painted exterior of the oldest house in l'Eixample, built in 1864. Four houses were actually built here at once, one on each corner, for landowner Josep Cerdà, but only this one remains today.

L'EIXAMPLE ESQUERRA

FUNDACIÓ ANTONI TÀPIES

🚩 *C. Aragó, 255. M: Pg. de Gràcia, L2/3/4. Around the corner from the Manzana de la Discòrdia and between Pg. de Gràcia and La Rambla de Catalunya. ☎93 487 03 15; www.fundaciotapies.org. Museum open Tu-Su 10am-8pm. Upstairs library open by appointment only, Tu-F 11am-8pm. €4.20, students and seniors €2.10. Wheelchair accessible.*

Antoni Tàpies's massive and bizarre wire sculpture *(Cloud with Chair)* atop Domènech i Montaner's red brick building announces this collection of contemporary abstract art. The top floor of the foundation is dedicated to famous Catalans, particularly Tàpies, while the other two floors feature temporary exhibits of other modern artists' work.

Tàpies is one of Catalunya's best-known artists; his works often defy definition, springing from Surrealism and Magicism, and drawing inspiration from Picasso and Miró. Most of his pieces mix painting and sculpture, and are generally referred to as collage, although he also creates abstract sculptures. Most of his paintings include a "T" in some form, a symbol that has been variously interpreted (or misinterpreted) as a religious cross, sexual penetration, and the artist's own signature. In truth, no one knows the real meaning, if there is one. Tàpies's use of unorthodox materials—including objects found in the trash—and his dark, dirty colors are often construed as a protest against the dictatorship and the subsequent urban alienation pervading Spain's cities. Everyday materials, like sand, glue, wood, marble powder, dirt, and wire show the eloquence inherent in simplicity.

The Fundació Tàpies is known for showcasing avant garde contemporary art, both kinetic sculptures and performance art, from famous masters to relative unknowns. An exhibit focusing on Contemporary Arabic Exhibitions is slated for the beginning of 2004, Steve McQueen will be featured December 2003-February 2004, and a study entitled "Tourisms," is scheduled to coincide with the Universal Culture Forum, May 9-September 26, 2004.

MEDITATION

⚑ M: Catalunya, L3. From Pl. de Catalunya, walk up La Rambla de Catalunya one block to Gran Via; the statue is in the middle of La Rambla, across from Comme-Bio.

Officially entitled *Meditation*, the bull's thoughtful pose mimics that of Rodin's *The Thinker*. Easy to miss, but impossible to forget, his brooding countenance will be forever emblazoned on your memory. At the opposite end of the avenue, his cousin scupture, *Coquette*, a flirtatious giraffe of questionable virtue, seduces passersby on Av. Diagonal.

MUSEU DE L'ESPORT

⚑ C. Buenos Aires, 56-8. M: Hospital Clìnic, L5. Walk north on C. Villarroel and turn left onto C. Buenos Aires. ☎ 93 419 22 32. Open M-F 10am-2pm and 4-8pm. Free.

Yup, there are more sports in Spain than soccer, and this museum sets out to prove it; whether they succeed is debatale. The architecture of the building, however, is worth a look. Puig i Cadafalch's **Casa Company** houses the Museu de l'Esport collection.

OTHER SIGHTS IN L'EIXAMPLE ESQUERRA

L'Eixample Esquerra is home to several Modernist masterpieces. **Casa Golferichs,** Gran Via, 491, at the intersection with C. Viladomat (M: Urgell, L1), is a brown brick structure with Moorish influences that was designed by one of Gaudí's collaborators, Joan Rubió, in 1901. Concerts are often held in the courtyard during the summer, and the interior hosts art exhibitions and conferences. (☎ 93 323 77 90. Open M-F 10am-2pm and 4-10pm, Sa 10am-2pm and 5-9pm. Wheelchair accessible. Free.) Further down at Gran Via, 475, Pere Falques and Antoni de Flaguerra's **Casa de Lactància** (M: Urgell, L1) is now a nursing home. Stone carvings by Eusebi Arnau and a mosaic flag of Barcelona can be viewed from outside, but step inside the foyer to see the equally impressive wrought iron interior balcony and delicate stained glass windows.

At the other end of l'Eixample, **Casa Company,** C. Buenos Aires, 56-58, at the intersection with C. Casanova (M: Hosptial Clìnic, L5), was constructed for a local family by Puig i Cadafalch in 1911. The creamy white Art Deco building with painted decorations was converted into Dr. Melcior Colet's gynecology practice in 1940, and later donated to the government of Catalunya. Today, it houses the **Museu de l'Esport** (see p. 91).

Circular Shark Tank at the Aquarium

Architecture in Poble Espanyol

Cannon on Montjuïc

Sardana Statue

see map p. 347

POBLE NOU & PORT OLÍMPIC

OLYMPIC SIGHTS

From 1982 to 1997, the industrious Socialist **Pasqual Maragall** was the mayor of Barcelona. It was thanks to his efforts that Barcelona was able to secure the **1992 Summer Olympic** bid. Maragall then used the pressure of the international spotlight as an opportunity to completely revamp the city. New athletic arenas and apartment complexes were built, the beaches were cleaned up, the waterfront was remodeled into party central, and the prostitutes were (very temporarily) shuffled into less visible neighborhoods.

Meditation Bull

At the intersection with Av. Bogatell and C. Frederic Mompau, a red-brick ramp on the right leads upward to the **Pl. Tirant lo Blanc,** the center of the athlete housing, and the perfect place to sit and imagine what it must have been like to live in the Vila Olímpica in 1992. A statue of an athlete staring wistfully into a stream commemorates the site. In classic Barcelona style, even the curbs of the sidewalks curve in long wavy lines. The Parc dels Ponts, on the other side of the highway and waterway, houses the **Pl. dels Champions,** site of the tiered platform used to honor gold, silver, and bronze medal-winners. Names of the Olympic winners are set in plaques in the ground. Continuing onward brings you to the **Parc del Port Olímpic,** a long, triumphant sand walkway lined by tall white spires and culminating in Robert Llimos's Marc statue, an apt symbol for a city known for muscling past both physical boundaries and architectural norms; you can walk between the spires, or on the shaded pathway next to them. Across the fountain lies the **Parc de Cascades,** home to Antoni Llena's Dalí-esque **David and Goliath.** To reach Frank Gehry's copper **Peix (Fish)** and the **Port Olímpic,** return to the fountain, turn right toward the water, and go left at the beach.

MUSEU DE CARROSSES FÚNEBRES (HEARSE MUSEUM)

🛈 *C. Sancho de Ávila, 2. M: Marina, L1. From the Metro, follow Av. Meridiana away from C. Marina until its intersection with C. Sancho de Ávila. Enter the gray office building right on the corner labeled Serveis Funeraris de Barcelona, S.A., and ask at the information desk inside for the Museu*

Lizard at Park Güell

de Carrosses. ☎93 484 17 00; www.funerariabarcelona.com. Open M-F 10am-1pm and 4-6pm, Sa-Su 10am-1pm. Wheelchair accessible. Free; really excited guides available to lead tours.

This small collection of 22 plush 19th- and early 20th-century horse-drawn hearses may be morbid, especially since the building also deals with funeral arrangements of the recently deceased. However, the museum is full of surprisingly intriguing facts on Spanish funerals, like only virgins could ride to their graves in white carriages.

CEMENTIRI DE L'EST

🚩 *At the dead-end of Av. Icària. M: Llacuna, L4. From the Metro, walk down C. Ciutat de Granada toward the waterfront towers; at the T-intersection with C. Taulat, turn right and follow the white walls of the cemetery to the gated opening. Open daily 8am-6pm.*

Pre-l'Eixample Barcelona desperately needed every inch inside city walls for living space, so in 1773 this cemetery was built outside the walls to safely house some of Barcelona's deceased elite. Crumbling monuments and miniature churches crowd the back of the plot; towards the front of the cemetery, in the center aisle, there is also a statue erected in memory of the thousands of people in Barcelona who died during the Yellow Fever epidemic of 1821.

OTHER SIGHTS IN POBLE NOU

The neighborhood is best viewed in an easy loop (see **Walking Tour**, p. 14) at M: Ciutadella/Villa Olímpica, L4. Come out of the Metro with the twin skyscrapers to your right and cross C. Ramon Trias Fargos to get to the intersection of C. de Marina and Avinguda d'Icària. To your left lies the **Parc de Carles I** with its tall, infamous **Culo de Urculo** statue (of Hercules's, um, posterior). On Av. Icària huge metal sculptures run down the center of the street and resemble something like a mix of thatched roofs and telephone poles. Named **Pergolas** by architect Enric Miralles; they are an ultra-modern take on the original latticed rooftop gardens with climbing plants common in ancient Egypt. To the right on the second block of Av. Icària is the **Centre de la Vila,** a two-story shopping mall, lacking most of the major store names scattered throughout the rest of Barcelona but boasting, nonetheless, a 15-screen cinema, several decent restaurants, and any basic last-minute beach essentials you might need.

BARCELONETA & PORT VELL

🏛 TORRE SAN SEBASTIÀ

🚩 *Pg. Joan de Borbó. M: Barceloneta, L4. Walk all the way down Joan de Borbó until you see the beach, then bear right and head to the imposing tower with the cable cars coming out of it. ☎93 441 48 20. Open daily June-Sept. 11am-8pm, Oct.-Mar. 10:15am-6pm, Apr.-May 10:45am-*
see map p. 348
*7:15pm. To Jaume I one-way or round-trip €7.50, to Montjuïc €7.50/€9.50, or to the top for the view €3.50. The torre is also accessible from Montjuïc (see the **Jardins Verdaguer,** p. 99).*

One of the easiest and best ways to view the city is on these cable cars, which connect beachy Barceloneta and the Port Vell area with Montjuïc. The full ride takes about 10min. each way, and there's an intermediate stop near Monument a Colom at Jaume 1 if you're ready to explore Las Ramblas from the South. Bring your camera to get some postcard-perfect shots of Barcelona. If you're looking to splurge, there's also a fancy restaurant at the top of the San Sebastià tower.

🏛 MUSEU MARÍTIM

🚩 *Av. Drassanes, off the rotary around the Monument a Colom. M: Drassanes, L3. ☎93 342 99 20; www.diba.es/mmaritim. Open daily 10am-7pm. Closed Jan. 1 and 6, Dec. 25-26. Wheelchair accessible. €5.40; under 16, students, and seniors €2.70. **Pailebot Santa Eulália:** In the port, when you're facing the water it's to the left of Rambla del Mar. Same hours as museum. €2.40; under 16, students and seniors €1.20.*

The *Drassanes Reiales de Barcelona* (Royal Shipyards of Barcelona) began constructing ships for the Catalan-Aragonese empire in the 13th century. Still amazingly well preserved, the shipyards are considered the world's greatest standing example of Civil (i.e., non-religious) Gothic architecture and are currently awaiting nomination as a UNESCO World Heritage Site. The complex consists of a series of huge indoor bays with slender pillars, in which entire ships could be constructed and stored over the winter. Since 1941, the building has housed the Maritime Museum, which traces the evolution of shipbuilding and life on the high seas. Surprisingly high-tech and modern, the museum provides detailed and sleekly produced audio guides to the exhibits in English, Spanish, German, and French. Model ships, medieval maps, and detailed dioramas illuminate maritime history from the raft to the submarine. The highlight of the museum is undoubtedly the 16th-century war galley of Juan de Austria; watch a projection of slaves rowing the ship. As an extension of your visit, venture to the water and check out the **Pailebot Santa Eulàlia.** This three-mast schooner was first launched in 1918, and in 85 years has undergone a series of transformations. In 1997 the Museu Marítim purchased the ship at an auction, and subsequently undertook the difficult and costly task of restoring it to its original condition. Having been completely renovated, the Santa Eulália is now considered to be not only the flagship of the museum, but also the city's ambassador to the seas.

■ L'AQUÀRIUM DE BARCELONA

⌖ *On the Moll d'Espanya, next to Maremàgnum and the cinema. M: Drassanes, L3, or Barceloneta, L4. ☎93 221 74 74. Open daily July-Aug. 9:30am-11pm; Sept.-June 9:30am-9pm. Last entrance 1hr. before closing. €13, under 12 and 65+ €9, students €12. Wheelchair accessible.*

Barcelona's aquarium—the largest in Europe—is a state-of-the-art aquatic wonder. The museum features over 20 tanks that focus on Mediterranean sealife, although you'll find plenty of other international creatures, including a plethora of penguins from the polar regions and a cornucopia of coral from the Great Barrier Reef. The museum's layout facilitates a scuba diver's view of some of the most elusive marine life while sparing the hassle of oxygen tanks and decompression. Take a ride on the moving walkway through the 70m long glass tunnel that takes you into the heart of an enormous tank filled with sting rays, flounders, and a wide variety of sharks; just four inches of glass separate the crowds from thousands of fish and over a million gallons of water from the Mediterranean Sea. The tour ends with a series of 50 interactive exhibits about the ocean and its inhabitants, which kids (and playful adults) will adore. Make sure to size yourself up to the reproduction of the man-sized fossilized jaw of a *carcharodon megalodon*, an ancient shark giant that grew to over 50 feet in length and undoubtedly could have consumed a Smart car.

MUSEU D'HISTÓRIA DE CATALUNYA

⌖ *Palau de Mar, Pl. Pau Vila, 3, on the waterfront. M: Barceloneta, L4. ☎93 225 47 00; www.cultura.gencat.es/museus/mhc. Open Tu-Sa 10am-7pm, Su 10am-2:30pm. Ask at the front desk to borrow an English or Spanish text guide for free. €3; students, seniors, and children €2.10. Groups €2.40 per person. Mandatory bag check €0.50. There is a cafe located on the 4th fl.*

This museum sits in the recently renovated Palau de Mar (Palace of the Sea). While the building's style deliberately implies the grandeur of the Catalan palaces of past eras, Palau de Mar was in fact originally constructed in 1900 as a decidedly un-palatial port warehouse. Nowadays the former storage facility has aesthetic supremacy over the rest of the Port Vell area. The two floors of the museum take you on an interactive tour through the history of the Catalan people, from their prehistoric origins to the glory of the 20th century. The first floor houses temporary exhibits, most of which go in-depth into a certain aspect of Catalan history. Major displays are in Catalan, English, and Spanish; most secondary displays are in fairly basic Catalan. One interactive exhibit allows you to try on a full suit of medieval armor while another facilitates a more relaxed perception of Catalan history with a replica of a 1950s Barcelona soda shop.

OTHER SIGHTS AROUND PORT VELL

⓴ M: Drassanes, L3, or Barceloneta, L4.

Since hosting the 1992 Olympic games, Barcelona has slowly but surely established itself as one of the greatest ports on the Mediterranean. The newest addition to the waterfront is the **World Trade Center,** built in 1999 and designed by the renowned architect I. M. Pei (who also built the glass pyramid in front of Paris's Louvre Museum). The design reminds many of a cruise ship, only fitting considering the building's proximity to the cruise ship docks of the port. The ultra-modern complex includes the luxurious Grand Marina Hotel (completed in 2002), office space, restaurants and cafes, and a convention center. At the other end of Pg. Colom in front of the post office (a postal palace created for the 1929 International Exhibition and a sight in and of itself) is **Cap de Barcelona,** also known as Barcelona Head. This must-see sculpture—a bright, cartoonish woman's face—was created by the late American pop artist Roy Lichtenstein for the 1992 Olympics.

MONTJUÏC

⧉ FUNDACIÓ JOAN MIRÓ

see map p. 346

⓴ Av. Miramar, 71-75. Take the funicular from M: Parallel, L2/ L3. Turn left out of the funicular station; 5min. walk. ☎93 443 94 70; www.bcn.fjmiro.es. Open Su 10am-2:30pm, Tu-W and F-Sa 10am-7pm (until 8pm July-Sept.), Th 10am-9:30pm. €7.20, students and seniors €3.90. Temporary exhibit only €3.60, students and seniors €1.80. Wheelchair accessible.

Miró's pieces are a personal and poignant tour through 20th-century Spanish history; the fundamental optimism of his later works, and the generosity he demonstrated throughout his life have made him one of Spain's—not just Catalunya's—most beloved artists. More than a museum, the Fundació Miró is a rotating collection of 11,000 of Miró's works, pieces by other artists inspired by Miró's unique style, and a foundation to support contemporary art and young Catalan artists.

GET sm**art**

Miró's Obsessions

Tormented and anxious for years, Miró used humor and exuberance in painting to fight depression. While living in Normandy during WWII, he developed what he later referred to as his "obsessions:" a repertoire of pictorial symbols used in both his paintings and sculptures to convey his way of seeing the world. He most frequently painted women and birds. Other obsessions include a net (the earth) and stars (the unattainable heavens). His symbols are not all so lofty; don't confuse the stars with Miró's infamous asterisk, a symbol for the anus.

In addition to his works illustrating an emotional state, they also serve as a measurement of the politics of his time. From the Civil War and the ensuing dictatorship came dark-toned paintings and depictions of fearsome creatures. Conversely, democracy gave birth to paintings bursting with color and optimism, reflecting Miró's improved health and the hope he placed in the future of his country. He is celebrated today as the man who aimed, as he put it, "to express precisely all the golden sparks of our soul" and so elegantly marked Spain's cultural heritage.

in recent
news

Where have all the
motos gone?

The *moto* (motorcycle) is a ubiquitous presence in Barcelona, not to mention the rest of Spain. However, the Spanish motorcycle market has decreased 66% in recent years, from 335,000 bikes sold in 1999 to only 114,000 in 2002, according to Anesdor, patron of the motorcycle sector.

Insurance prices seem to be the main challenge for *moto* drivers. While it is possible to get insurance directly from the government (at €340), private insurance groups charge up to €1200 for those under 25, the largest population of *moto* owners in Barcelona.

The Spanish government is also being charged with making motorcycle use more difficult, as it embarks on a plan, "Anticipation and Renovation," which supports use of safer and more environmentally friendly vehicles. In response, *moto* drivers organized under the platform *Por la Moto* (For the Moto) with a collection of motorist associations, sports federations, businesses and workers in this sector. They argue that the *moto* is a solution and not a problem, claiming that bikes create business and decrease congestion within cities.

Designed by Miró's friend Josep Luís Sert, the Fundació links interior and exterior spaces with massive windows and outdoor patios. Skylights illuminate an extensive collection of statues, paintings, and *sobreteixims* (paintings on tapestry) from Miró's career. The Fundació also sponsors music recitals in the summer months, and occasionally hosts film festivals (check the website for listings).

The first room of the permanent collection features the *Tapestry of the Foundation*, a colorful and wall-sized depiction of a woman. Outside, between rooms 11 and 12, *The Mercury Fountain* created by Miró's good friend Alexander Calder commemorates the civil war-torn town of Almaden. Room 16 displays Miro's *Dream Paintings* (1925-1927), an eerie depiction of a world where "the pull of gravity" no longer exists. *The Constellation Series*, the more poetic of Miro's works, are on display in room 17. Pick up a free headphone set from the ticket desk to guide you to some of the most famous pieces in the foundation.

▧ MUSEU NACIONAL D'ART DE CATALUNYA (PALAU NACIONAL)

🔁 *From M: Espanya, L1/L3/FGC, walk up Av. Reina María Cristina, away from the twin brick towers, and take the escalators to the top. ☎ 93 622 03 60; www.mnac.es. Open Su 10am-2:30pm, Tu–Sa 10am-7pm. €4.80, with temporary exhibits €6, temporary exhibit only €4.20; 30% discount for students and seniors. Free first Th of every month. Wheelchair accessible.*

Designed by Enric Catá and Pedro Cendoya, for the 1929 International Exposition (see **Life & Times,** p. 41), the beautiful Palau Nacional has housed the Museu Nacional d'Art de Catalunya (MNAC) since 1934. Its main hall is a public event space, while the wings are home to the world's finest collection of Catalan Romanesque art and a wide variety of Gothic pieces. The Romanesque frescoes, now integrated as murals into dummy chapels, were salvaged in the 1920s from their original, less protected locations in northern Catalunya's churches. Their restoration creates a surprisingly spiritual tour through the medieval masterpieces. The museum's Gothic art corridor displays paintings on wood, the medium of choice during that period. The chronological tour of the galleries underlines the growing influence of Italy over Catalunya's artistic development, and ends with a breathtaking series of paintings by Gothic master Bernat Martorell. The museum also hosts temporary exhibits; 2003 featured *The Fascination of the Orient*, a comprehensive showcase of objects from the Far East imported by the Spanish monarchy from the 16th century onward.

In the midst of these displays, the MNAC is constructing and renovating separate areas of the building to house a collection of Renaissance and Baroque art, the Museu d'Art Modern collection, as well as a second space for temporary exhibits, which will open in early 2004.

▨ CASTELL DE MONTJUÏC

🛈 *From M: Parallel, L2/L3, take the funicular (every 10min.) to Av. Miramar and then the Teleféric de Montjuïc cable car to the castle. Teleféric open daily 11:15am-9pm. One-way €3.40, round-trip €4.80. Alternatively, walk up the steep slope on C. Foc, next to the funicular station. Open Tu-Su Mar. 15-Nov. 15 9:30am-8pm; Nov. 16-Mar. 14 9:30-5pm. Castle and mirador €1, with ticket to Museu Militar €2.50.*

The first section of this massive castle was built in 1640 in just 30 days. Fifty-four years later the main castle was constructed. It continued to expand until 1799, when it could accommodate over 3000 people. In 1960, the castle was given to the city, which eventually converted it into a military museum. A visit to this historic fortress and its **Museu Militar** (see below) is a great way to get an overview of the city—both its layout and its history. The castle's exterior mirador offers spectacular views of the bay and the city. Enjoy a sandwich and coffee in the shade at the outdoor **cafe** while cannons from the early 19th-century stare you down.

MUSEU MILITAR

🛈 *Inside the **Castell de Montjuïc** (see above). ☎ 93 329 86 13. Open Tu-Su Mar. 15-Nov. 15 9:30am-8pm; Nov. 16-Mar. 14 9:30-5pm. €2.50, includes castle entrance.*

The Museu Militar displays just about every kind of weapon you could imagine a soldier might have carried over the last millennium, as well as countless other Montjuïc relics. The impressive miniature models of the fortresses of Catalunya are accompanied by the second-largest collection of miniature soldiers in Spain. Keep an eye out for Barcelona's only remaining statue of Franco, and a series of oil paintings depicting Catalan leaders beginning with Charlemagne.

CEMENTIRI DEL SUD-OEST

🛈 *Fossar de la Perdera. Bus #38 from Pl. de Catalunya will drop you off across from the main entrance. Or, from inside Montjuïc, follow Av. del Castell to the left with your back to the Castle. The back entrance to the cemetery is a 20min. walk downhill and will be on your left. To get to Fossar de la Pedrera, turn left on Via Santa Eulalia by the cemetery's main entrance, and then take the 2nd right onto Sant Josep. Follow this paved path and look for Fossor signs. A helpful cemetery map is available from the administration offices at the main entrance, across from the bus stop. ☎ 93 223 14 55. Open daily 8am-6pm. Free.*

This gigantic Modernist cemetery, dating from 1883, is an amazing complex of stone, brick, sculpture, and stained glass. Of special note are the **Amatller family tomb** designed by Puig i Cadafalch (who also designed their house in l'Eixample; see p. 88) and the statuary-topped Batlló family resting place (of Casa Batlló fame; see p. 87). In the cemetery's northeast corner, the **Fossar de la Pedrera** commemorates the site where many Republican heroes of the Civil War were rounded up and shot immediately following the war. Stone pillars are engraved with the names of the victims, and an arched statue set in a small pond honors Catalan President Lluís Companys, who was assassinated by Franco on this very spot in 1940.

MUSEU ETNOLÒGIC

🚩 *Pg. Santa Madrona, uphill from Museu Arqueològic (see below).* ☎ *93 424 64 02; www.museuetnologic.bcn.es. Open Su and Tu-Sa 10am-2pm. €3, students and seniors €1.50. Free 1st Su of every month 10-3pm.*

Rotating exhibits focus on aspects of specific cultures through displays of documentary photographs, crafts, and artifacts. Recent exhibits have included *Japan: Tradition and the Future*, an exploration of the ways in which tradition has adapted to societal change in Japan, and *Daily life in the 1940s*.

MUSEU ARQUEOLÒGIC DE CATALUNYA

🚩 *Pg. Santa Madrona, 39-41. From M: Espanya, L1/L3, take bus #55 up the hill to the Palau Nacional. When you are facing the Palau Nacional, the museum is to the left.* ☎ *93 423 21 49; www.mac.es. Open Su 10am-2:30pm, Tu-Sa 9:30am-7pm. €2.40, students and seniors €1.80.*

Founded in 1932, the Museu Arqueològic is located in the beautiful Palau de Artes Graficas, constructed in 1929 for the *Exposición Universal*. A tour of the galleries' jewelry, earthenware, sculptures, mosaics, and countless other artifacts will take you from prehistoric times to the Medieval Ages in Catalunya and the Balearic Islands. Unfortunately, much is left to the imagination, as the historical context and explanations are somewhat sparse. Several rooms feature a collection of Carthaginian art from Ibiza, fascinating models of huge megalithic funeral monuments, and excavated relics from the Greco-Roman city of Empúries in surrounding Catalunya.

FONTS LUMINOSES

🚩 *On Av. Reina María Cristina. M: Espanya, L1/L3. Shows June-Sept. Su and Th-Sa every 30min. 9:30pm-12:30am; Oct.-May F-Sa 7-8:30pm. Free.*

The Fonts Luminoses (Illuminated Fountains) run alongside Av. Reina Maria Cristina and are dominated by the huge central **La Font Mágica** (Magic Fountain). The fountains are visible from Pl. d'Espanya, in front of the **Palau Nacional** (see p. 96). During the weekends, colored lights and dramatic music bring the fountains to life in a spectacular display that is not to be missed.

JARDINS MOSSÉN JACINT VERDAGUER

🚩 *Av. Miramar. Between the Fundació Miró and the Castell de Montjuïc. From M: Parallel, L2/L3, take the funicular to Av. Miramar. Turn right out of the funicular and walk along Av. Miramar, then uphill on C. Montjuïc.* ☎ *90 030 20 30. Open daily May-Aug. 10am-9pm; Apr. and Sept. 10am-8pm; Mar. and Oct. 10am-7pm; Nov.-Feb. 10am-6pm. Free.*

Named after the Catalan poet Mossén Jacint Verdaguer, these expansive gardens merit a visit on a leisurely day. Walk to the top of the hill where a pond feeds water to geometric pools below—the view from here is spectacular. On C. Montjuïc, the smaller Jardins de Joan Brossa holds the **Carmen Amaya** statue crafted by Josep Cañas i Cañas in 1966, in commemoration of the traditional Catalan *sardana* dance.

PAVELLÓ MIES VAN DER ROHE

🚩 *From M: Espanya, L1/L3, follow Av. Reina Maria Cristina until the Font Mágica. Face the Palau Nacional and the Font Mágica; the Pavelló is to the right.* ☎ *93 423 40 16; www.miesbcn.com. Open daily 10am-8pm. €3, students €1.50, under 18 free.*

Renowned as one of the most original works of the famous German architect Mies van der Rohe, this aesthetically provocative pavilion, also known as the **Pavelló Barcelona,** is an example of spatial serenity that is far ahead of its time.

Van der Rohe built a pavilion for the 1929 International Exhibition, but his contribution—a minimalist marvel of glass, stone, marble, and steel—was demolished in 1930 when no one bought it. The pavilion standing in its place today is a replica commissioned by the city government; the reconstruction was led by architects Critstian Circi, Fernando Ramos, and Ignasi de Sola Morales. The open-air courtyards are home to Georg Kolbe's graceful statue, ⬛*Morning*, and several copies of van der Rohe's famous *Barcelona Chair*, one of the first tubular steel chairs ever designed.

POBLE ESPANYOL

🚩 *On Av. Marqués de Comillas, to the right when you are facing the Palau Nacional. From M: Espanya, L1/L3, go up the outdoor escalators or catch bus #50 at Pl. d'Espanya and ask to be let off at Poble Espanyol.☎ 93 508 63 30; www.poble-espanyol.com. Open Su 9am-midnight, M 9am-8pm, Tu-Th 9am-2am, F-Sa 9am-4am. Ticket booth closes one hr. before the park. €7, students and seniors €5, ages 7-12 €4. Guided tours in English daily 10am-7pm; ask for ticket "con guía" at the door; €2 plus admission. MC/V.*

Created for the 1929 International Exhibition (see **Life & Times,** p. 41), this "town" features replicas of famous buildings and sights from every region of Spain, complete with swarms of school children and tourists. Shops and artists' workshops sell everything from tacky souvenirs to gallery pieces, and the large open-air courtyard occasionally serves as a performance venue. The Fran Darell Contemporary Art Foundation lies in the center of this souvenir bazaar and offers a welcome break from the crammed outdoor shopping mall. Overall, it's a better place to visit at night, when the crowds will give you a taste of what Spain does best: party.

PARC JOAN MIRÓ

🚩 *C. Tarragona. M: Espanya, L1/L3, or Tarragona, L3. A 5min. walk down C. Tarragona from Pl. de Espanya.*

Miró's giant ⬛*Dona i Ocell* (*Woman and Bird*, 1982) holds court in the center of a park dedicated to the artist. This colorful sculpture rises 22m (72 ft.) into the air, a mosaic of glazed greens, yellows, reds, and blues in homage to Gaudí. Miró changed the name from *Le Coq* after city planners objected.

ANELLA OLÍMPICA

🚩 *The easiest way to get to the Olympic Area is to take the funicular from inside M: Parallel L2/L3 at Av. Parallel and Nou de la Rambla. Turn left out of the funicular station on to Av. Miramar and follow it past the Fundació Miró. The road turns into Av. de l'Estadi; the stadium is on your left. Alternatively, take bus #50 from la Plaça d'Espanya and ask to be let off when you see the stadium on your right. Wheelchair accessible.*

In 1929, Barcelona inaugurated the Estadi Olímpic de Montjuïc (Olympic Stadium) in its unsuccessful bid for the 1932 Olympic games. Over 50 years later, Catalan architects Federic Correa and Alfons Milà, designers of the *Anella Olímpica* (Olympic Ring) esplanade, completed the facilities in time for the '92 Games with the help of Italian architect Vittorio Gregotti. Nearby, the **Torre de Telefónica,** designed by Valencian Santiago Calatrava, commands the Olympic skyline at 106m (348ft). Today, Montjuïc's Olympic area is still a major tourist draw. The well-equipped *Anella Olímpica* lives on, serving the sporting needs of professionals and amateurs alike. Come here to catch a soccer game at the **Estadi Olímpic** (see **Entertainment,** p. 164) or swim in the **Piscines Bernat Picornell** (see p. 164).

Gràcia Markets

Park Güell Structures

see map p. 342-345

Casa de las Punxes

GALERÍA OLÍMPICA

7 *At the far end of the Estadi Olímpic, toward Palau Sant Jordi. ☎93 426 06 60. Open Apr.-Sept. 10am-2pm and 4-7pm; Jan.-Mar. and Oct.-Dec. M-F 10am-1pm and 4-6pm. €2.50, students €2.20, seniors and under 12 €1.20.*

Video segments, colorful costumes, sports equipment, plenty of merchandise, and giant photos displayed everywhere try to tell (and sell) the story of the 25th Olympic Games at this small permanent exhibition. If you're pressed for time and can't visit, don't worry about missing anything substantial.

ZONA ALTA

GRÀCIA

▓ PARK GÜELL

7 *Main entrance faces C. Olot. Other entrances on Av. Sant Josep de la Muntanya, Carretera del Carmel, and Av. del Coll del Portell. Buses #24, 25, 31, 32, 74 have stops near the park. Bus #25 connects the park to the Sagrada Família. From M: Vallarca, walk down Av. l'Hospital Militar for 4 blocks, turn left onto Baixada de la Gloria, and take the outdoor escalators to the back entrance. ☎93 219 38 11. Open daily May-Sept. 10am-9pm; Mar.-Apr. and Oct. 10am-7pm; Nov.-Feb. 10am-6pm. Free.*

On a hill at the northern edge of Gràcia lies Barcelona's most enchanting public park, designed entirely by Gaudí, and—in typical Gaudí fashion—not completed until after his death. After the pleasing results of his collaboration with Gaudí on Güell's Palau, Eusebi Güell, a Catalan industrialist and arts patron, commissioned the renowned architect to fashion a garden city in the tradition of Hampstead Heath and other parks in England, where Güell had spent many years. Güell was fascinated with rank and power (he longed to be granted a title by the king), and he envisioned a utopic community devoid of the lower classes (the turn-of-the century take on the gated community), with 60 houses. Started in 1900, construction slowed to a halt in 1914 due to financial difficulties, and only three houses were completed. Barceloneses at the turn of the century were put off both by Gaudí's shockingly bold designs and the park's then great distance from the city. As a result, only two aristocrats signed on and as a housing development it was a complete failure.

As a park, Park Güell is fantastic. In 1918, the Barcelona City Council bought Park Güell, and in 1923 the council opened the multicolored dwarfish buildings and sparkling ceramic-mosaic stairways to the public. The park has since been honored by being named a UNESCO World Heritage Site. Combining natural influences, Catalan themes, and religious symbolism, Gaudí's Park Güell is a symphony of color and form. The most eye-catching elements of the park—the surreal mosaics and fairy tale fountains—are clustered around the main entrance on C. Olot. The entrance's **Palmetto Gate,** a replica of the iron work on Gaudí's Casa Vicens, is flanked by two dwarfish buildings originally meant to house the community's administration offices and the porter. Visitors today can stop by the **LAIE** book and gift shop in the house on the left as you face the park. (☎ 93 284 62 00. Open during park hours.) These other-wordly houses were inspired by a Catalan production of *Hansel and Gretel;* the spire-topped construction belongs to the children, and the other, crowned with a bright red poisonous mushroom, belongs to the witch. Lavishly decorated with fan-shaped mosaics, the roofs resemble edible gingerbread and cream frosting. Behind Hansel and Gretel's house, you will find the park's restrooms and a popular cafe. (Coffee €1.50; tapas €1-3; bocadillos €3-6. Open during park hours.)

Little Girl in Poble Espanyol

Facing the majestic double staircase, a cavernous stone area to the right was originally meant to house the carriages of park residents. The structure, reminiscent of an elephant, now serves as a shaded rest area for visitors. The staircase itself is divided into three sections, each with its own mosaic fountain. Tourists jostle to take pictures of their loved ones with the gaping, multicolored **■salamander fountain** as it drools into the basin below. The animal's sleek body is covered with a tightly woven mosaic of green, orange, and blue. Some believe it is a reference to the coat of arms of the French city of Nîmes, the northern boundary of Old Catalunya. At the next level, a curvaceous red mosaic fountain holds a stone interpreted to be either an oracle or the philosopher's stone. The mouth-like bench behind it is supposedly entirely protected from the wind, and remains in the shade for three seasons (winter is the sunny one).

Monastery of Pedralbes

Stairs lead up to the **Hall of One Hundred Columns (Teatro Griego),** a Modernist masterpiece of 86 Doric columns (but who's counting?). A spectacular open space meant for the community's market, the hall's columns support a ceiling constructed of white-tiled domes. Toward the center, where musicians often play classical

Tomb at Monastery of Pedralbes

Montjuïc Steps

El Indio

Inside Fundació Miró

102

music, multicolored medallions are interspersed among the ceiling domes. Josep Maria Jujol, Gaudí's right-hand man, created every medallion, using bits scraps discarded of mirrors, plates, glasses, and even porcelain dolls.

Stairs on either side of the hall lead up to the **Pl. de la Naturalesa,** a barren open area partly supported by the columned hall below and surrounded by the **serpentine bench.** The shape of the bench is not only aesthetically pleasing, but also structurally necessary given the position of the columns below. It is also designed to cradle visitors' buttocks and is consequently incredibly comfortable. It's all thanks to the rumored "creative methods" of Jujol. He is said to have made one of the workers sit bare-assed in the wet cement to add that extra, anatomically correct touch. Pieced together from broken ceramic remnants from local pottery workshops, Gaudí and Jujol's multicolored bench is covered with brightly colored flowers, geometric patterns, and the odd religious image or two. During the park's restoration in 1995, workers discovered that the 21 distinct tones of white are cast-offs from the Casa Milà (see p. 84) that had been cemented in the bench. The bench's abstract collage later became a great inspiration for Joan Miró's Surrealist work.

From here, sweeping paths supported by columns (meant to resemble palm trees) swerve through hedges and ascend to the park's summit, which commands tremendous views of the city. A pleasant walk through the grounds begins at the path directly to right when facing the salamander fountain. Follow the wide path past the sunny flower beds and open grassy area and veer right toward the shaded benches. As the path twists uphill, the turreted, pink **Casa-Museu Gaudí** (see below) appears on your left. Farther ahead, the **Pont dels Enamorats** offers views of the city all the way to the sea, and Gaudí's **stone trees**—tall columns topped with agave plants—are interspersed with curved benches. Around the next curve, **Casa Trías** (1905), the park's third house, purchased by the lawyer Trías Domènech and still owned by his family, is surrounded by less scenic walking paths that loop around to the left along Av. del Coll del Portell. Farther along the wide, main path, past a grassy area with a small playground and plenty of benches, an upward slope spirals to **El Turo de Les Tres Creus.** Originally destined to be the park residents' church, the small tower is topped only with three crosses (one resembles an arrow) which appear to form one when you look toward the east. This peak is the park's highest point, and it offers a dazzling 360° view of the city below. To head back down, follow the twisting path that slopes down toward the sea. Check out the views of the Hansel and Gretel houses and other park structures. At the Av. Sant Josep de la Muntanya entrance, follow a narrow path to the right until it becomes **El Viaducte de la Bugadera** as it passes Güell's house (now a school) on the right. The irregularly shaped stone columns that support the covered passageway are each composed of fascinating, unusual shapes and configurations. You'll find the statue of **La Bugadera** (the washerwoman) on one of the last columns in the passageway. Stairs ahead lead back to the Pl. de la Naturalesa.

CASA-MUSEU GAUDÍ

◪ *Inside Park Güell (see above), to the right of the Hall of One Hundred Columns when you are facing away from the sea. Closest direct park entrance is Carretera del Carmel.* ☎ *93 219 38 11. Open daily Oct.-Mar. 10am-6pm; Apr.-Sept. 10am-8pm. Last entrance 15min. before closing. €4, €3 for students with ISIC, €9 for admittance to museum and La Sagrada Família.*

Designed not by Gaudí but by his friend and colleague, Fransesc Berenguer, the Casa-Museu Gaudí was the celebrated architect's home from 1906 to 1926 until he moved into the Sagrada Família several months before his death. Gaudí's leftover fence work from other projects was used to create the garden of metallic plant sculptures in front of the museum. The three-story house is a great place to examine close-up Gaudí's anatomical furniture designs from the Casa Batlló, paintings of several of his works by notable artists, and the master's own austere bedroom, where the bronze cast of his death mask keeps an eye on visitors. The ceilings, different in every room, highlight the otherwise sober rooms with touches of color and eye-catching patterns. Before leaving, peek into the Modernist bathroom where the toilet seat curves in Gaudí's trademark saddle-shape.

OTHER CASAS IN GRÀCIA

◪ *M: Diagonal L3/5 or Fontana L3.*

Aside from the Park Güell, the narrow, peaceful streets of Gràcia are home to several of Modernisme's lesser known, but no less grand, architectural masterpieces. Since these buildings truly are *casas* (private houses), their interiors are closed to the public; however, the captivating external designs and details are incentives to visit. Get ready to walk, however, as the mountains which surround the city begin in the hills of Gràcia.

Gaudí's first major project, **◪Casa Vicens,** C. Carolines 24-26, was designed between 1883 and 1888 for a local tile manufacturer, and is fittingly decorated with blocks of cheerful white, green, and yellow ceramic tiles accented with red-painted brick. Gaudí studied Arabic design to come up with the colorful rigid angles that characterize this *casa.* The graceful, fluid ironwork that spills out of the windows as balconies and creeps up the facade as a palm-fronted gate foreshadows the architect's anti-angle ideals evident in later projects.

Several blocks up the Gran de Gràcia, **Casa Ramos,** Pl. de Lesseps, 32, was completed by Jaume Torres in 1906 and is in fact three separate buildings which share a facade. Although the building is partially blocked by storefronts and a ramp, its Modernist floral motif and insect-patterned grilles still manage to stand out. Back toward Av. Diagonal, **Casa Cama,** Gran de Gràcia, 15, is one of Berenguer's designs, with delicately curved stained-glass windows. Across the street, at Pg. de Gràcia, 132, **Casa Fuster** marks the transition between Gran de Gràcia and the Pg. de Gràcia. Lluís Domènech i Montaner fashioned this impressive asymmetrical neo-Gothic building from 1908 to 1911, putting heavy emphasis on the cylindrical corner tower. Get up close to see the nesting birds sculpted at the top of the corner columns. **Casa Bonaventura Ferrer,** Pg. de Gràcia, 113, was completed in 1906 by Pere Falqués. One of the few Modernist baroque buildings in Barcelona, its stone facade finds beauty in simple lines and understated grandeur.

Museum Fun

Flags

Walking in Poble Nou

PLAÇAS IN GRÀCIA

⑦ *M: Diagonal L3/5 or Fontana L3.*

Gràcia has several notable *plaças* where locals gather over long meals at outdoor tables, day and night; a quick stroll through them is a great way to get acquainted with the neighborhood. **▒Pl. Ruis i Taulet,** two blocks below Trav. de Gràcia near the Gran de Gràcia, is home to the **Torre del Reloj** (Clock Tower), an emblem of the Revolution of 1868. Facing the *plaça* is Gràcia's sky blue town hall, a Modernist work designed by local architect Francesc Berenguer and adorned with Gràcia's coat of arms. Several blocks down C. Puigmartí, at the intersection of C. Quevado, is **Pl. de John Lennon,** which honors the rock legend with a record-shaped plaque engraved with "Give Peace a Chance" in Catalan. This is a favorite playground for local children and their parents. While the **Pl. del Poble Romaní,** one block down C. Siracusa, is not the loveliest of the group, it is the former site of the Puigmartí textile factory and now commemorates the local Gypsy community, as well as Gràcia's working-class roots, with a large brick tower. **Pl. del Diamante,** farther uphill on C. Astúries, was made famous by Catalan author Mercè Rodoreda's 1962 novel of the same title. The novel is commemorated by *La Colometa*, a dramatic bronze statue of Rodoreda's heroine, who deals with the trials of everyday living during and following the Spanish Civil War. Farther along C. Astúries, **Pl. Virreina** is bordered by tapas bars, pastel painted houses, and the grand Church of Sant Joan de Gràcia. Across C. L'Or, the pink and cream **Casa Rubina** at no. 44 is one of Berenguer's most decorative works. Tiny but tantalizing, **Pl. del Sol,** one block above Trav. de Gràcia off C. Canó, is skirted by a fantastic selection of cafes and bars teeming with young locals at night.

MARKETS

Gràcia's markets embody the multifaceted soul of this eclectic community, as older residents shop alongside hip young things. Two major markets offer inexpensive food options and great people-watching. Vegetarians beware: the meat and fish stands are not for the faint of heart. **Mercat de la Llibertat,** in the Pl. de la Llibertat, one block off Via Augusta from FGC: Gràcia, was originally designed as an open-air market by Berenguer in 1875 but was covered years later. The wrought iron gates and floral details are particularly impressive, as is the drinking fountain at the front of the market, which bears Gràcia's shield. Vendors offer everything from fresh eggs to dried fruit. (☎93 415 90 93. Open M 5-8pm, Tu-Th 8am-2pm and 5-8pm, F 8am-8pm, Sa 7am-3pm). **Mercat Central** is conveniently located in the heart of Gràcia at the intersection of Trav. de Gràcia and C. Torrijos. The produce stalls are inside, while outside vendors sell flowers, clothing, and trinkets. (M: Joanic, L4. Open M-Th 7am-2:30pm and 5:30-8:30pm, F-Sa 6am-3pm and 5-8:30pm.)

HORTA & VALL D'HEBRON

Horta is less a sightseeing mecca than a great place to plunk down for the afternoon in a park somewhere, or work up a sweat at one of the sports facilities.

JARDINS DEL LABERINT D'HORTA

🚩 *C. dels Germans Desvalts. M: Mundet, L3. Exit on the right and follow Pg. de Vall d'Hebron, turning left before the Velodróm cycling facility. Jardins are directly behind the Velodróm, up the steep steps.* ☎ *93 428 39 34. Guided tours in Spanish and Catalan available every day until 2pm. Open daily May-Aug. 10am-9pm, Apr. and Sept. 10am-8pm, Mar. and Oct. 10am-7pm, Nov.-Feb. 10am-6pm. Entrance €1.85, under 6 and 60+ free. Su and W free for all.*

Once the private grounds of a wealthy marquis, this neoclassical 17-acre garden—complete with sculptures of Greek heroes, manicured walkways, a love canal, a cascade, and, of course, the labyrinth—warrants the trip from town. A hot summer afternoon can instantly become a cool, refreshing bit of paradise when enjoying the shade of this fairy-tale park.

PARC DE LA CREUTA DEL COLL

🚩 *Pg. Mare de Déu del Coll, 93. M: Vallcarca, L3 or bus #25, 28, or 87. Exit metro onto Av. L'Hospital Militar and walk down C. La Argentina to a left turn onto C. Cambrils, which turns into C. Gustavo Bécquer. Take a sharp right turn up a ramp and at the head of the bridge, take a left onto Pg. Mare de Déu del Coll, and follow uphill for about 15min.; the park entrance lies above a set of sandstone steps. ☎93 459 24 27. Pool open late June-Aug. M-F 10am-4pm, Sa-Su 10am-7pm. Park gates open daily May-Aug. 10am-9pm; Apr. and Sept. 10am-8pm; Mar. and Oct. 10am-7pm; Nov.-Feb. 10am-6pm. Beach chairs €2.50. Swimming M-F €2.70, Sa-Su and holidays €3. Wheelchair-accessible, but the entrance is steep, and there is a lot of sand inside.*

NO **WORK** ALL **PLAY**

Symphonic and Electronic

If you are into electronic music and multimedia, or just want to enjoy a 3-day citywide party, you'll want to be in Barcelona for **Sónar Festival.** In Dedicated to electronic music, the festival attracts up to 90,000 people every summer. Since its origin a decade ago, Sónar has been a precursor of trends in electronic music, bringing in artists such as Björk, Aphex Twin, and Carl Cox, as well as lesser known musicians and DJs whom Sónar has provided with the opportunity to reach a wide audience. The concerts occur at all hours for three consecutive days in Montjuic Park and the MAGBA Museum of Art.

If you can't purchase a ticket (they sell rapidly), you can still participate in the nighttime activities which explode during the festival. Although Sónar takes the foreground with its worldwide notoriety, smaller venues take advantage of this period to offer other concerts or DJ sets on the fringe of the festival. After-hours beach parties are a perfect (and cheap) way to make the most of the music and meet those who come to hear it.

Festival is in mid-June. Visit www.sonar.es for details.

This park is like a small, arid, man-made valley basin, carved out of a steep hill-side and complete with a long, shallow pool. The pool, tennis tables, and play-ground make this a good place to bring young children on a hot day.

PEDRALBES & LES CORTS

MUSEU DEL FÚTBOL CLUB BARCELONA

C. Aristides Maillol, next to the stadium. M: Collblanc, L5. Enter through access gates 7 or 9. ☎ 93 496 36 08. Open M-Sa 10am-6:30pm, Su 10am-2pm. English and Spanish tours every 15min. Museum entrance €5, children under 13 €3.50; with 45min. stadium tour €9. Tickets sold until 15min. before museum closes. Cash only.

Busloads of tour groups from all over the world pour into this museum, making it one of Barcelona's most visited. The museum merits all the attention it gets, as it has created a fitting homage to one of soccer's greatest clubs. Any sports fan will appreciate the storied history of the team, which began in 1899 when a Swiss soccer star, Hans Gamper, moved to Barcelona and gathered a group interested in playing soccer. Recent greats on the team include Maradona, Ronaldo, Luis Figo, and Rivaldo. Room after room displays countless cups the team has won, including the coveted European Cup which the team won in 1992. The museum includes soccer-related art and photos of past teams. Check out some of the funky uniform variations on the familiar blue and burgundy team colors. The high point, especially if you can't get to an actual match, is the chance to enter the **Camp Nou** (see p. 166) stadium itself. In addition, the tour shows you the dressing rooms, a tunnel to the playing field, players' benches, the press rooms, the chapel, and the presidential box. In the same complex, a gift shop sells all varieties of official FCB merchandise.

MONESTIR DE PEDRALBES

Baixada del Monestir, 9. M: Palau Reial, L3. Go north on Av. Pedralbes from Pl. Pius XII (street is not well labeled, but it is the major roadway) and follow road signs to the monastery. Also accessible by buses #22, 63, 64, 75, 78. ☎ 93 203 92 82 or 93 203 91 16. Ticket to Museum and art collection €4.50. First Su. of every month free. Open Su and Tu-Sa 10am-2pm. Church open Su 11am-12:30pm, M-Sa 11am-1pm.

The devout Queen Elisenda founded this monastery in 1327 to atone for her earthly sins, and it has housed the Poor Clares order ever since. Today, visitors can peek into the lives these women led centuries ago: the courtyard, infirmary, kitchen, and dining hall are all open to the public. Set amidst the low-rise apartments of Zona Alta, the monastery makes a refreshing and historically interesting break for those with the time to leave the chaos of downtown Barcelona. The monastery also has a large collection of furniture and manuscripts from the Middle Ages. The artistic highlight of the cloister is the Capella St. Miguel, where a set of frescoes by the Italian artist Ferrer Bassa depict the Seven Joys of the Blessed Virgin on the bottom level, and scenes from the Passion of Christ on the top level. Part of the **Thyssen-Bornemisza** (see below) collection from Madrid is also on view at the monastery.

COLLECIÓ THYSSEN-BORNEMISZA

Baixada del Monestir, 9, in the Monestir de Pedralbes (see above). M: Palau Reial, L3. ☎ 93 481 10 41; www.museotissen.org. Same hours as the monastery. €3, students and over 65 €1.80, under 16 free. Combined ticket with monastery €4.50, students €3, children free.

The former dormitory of the St. Clare nuns houses a small but impressive collection of Italian Renaissance, nothern European and late Venetian Baroque art, consisting almost entirely of religious paintings from the larger collection in Madrid. Highlights include works by Velásquez's, Rubens, and Fra Angelico. This museum is a must-see for art history buffs.

PALAU REIAL DE PEDRALBES

🮕 *Av. Diagonal, 686, recognizable by its distinctive pale orange entrance. M: Palau Reial, L3. For an audio tour of the park and its points of interest, cell phone users can call ☎ 629 003 998 to hear descriptions in English, Spanish, or Catalan; simply press the number corresponding to the area to hear a short history and explanation. At the far end of the park is the Palau Reial de Pedralbes.*

Located around the corner from the University of Barcelona, the Palau Reial de Pedralbes and its quiet park provide a secluded getaway from the rest of the city. Only real Gaudí enthusiasts will want to check out the drinking fountain. The architect constructed it in his early years and it pales in comparison to his more grandiose works. The fountain lies off to the left of the main path to the palace, in a small forest of bamboo shoots. The simple design is a rather small twisting iron dragon that spouts water over a Catalan shield. Above, a bust of Hercules surveys the proceedings. "Rediscovered" in 1983 after decades of neglect, the fountain was restored. It now provides perfectly drinkable water to the numerous students picnicking in the park. The Palau itself, commissioned by the Güell family for the King of Spain for making their father **Eusebi Güell** a count, was given to Spain at the International Exposition of 1929. The pale orange mansion is tastefully designed and houses the **Museu de les Arts Decoratives** and the **Museu de Ceràmica** (see below).

El Sagrat Col

MUSEU DE LES ARTS DECORATIVES

Parc d'Attracions

🮕 *Av. Diagonal, 686. M: Palau Reial, L3 on the 2nd floor of the Palau Reial (see above) opposite the Museu de Ceràmica. ☎ 93 280 50 24; www.museuartsdecoratives.bcn.es. Ticket will also get you into the Museu de Ceràmica (see below) and the Museu Téxtil (see p. 71). Open Tu-Sa 10am-6pm, Su and holidays 10am-3pm. €3.50, students under 25 €2.50, under 16 free.*

Recognizing the artistic value of items often taken for granted in daily life, the Museum of Decorative Arts displays European home furnishings from as far back as the Middle Ages. A large collection of 19th-century furniture shows how the Catalan bourgeoisie lived. The eclectic collection also contains an extensive display of industrial furniture from the 20th century. A broad range of temporary exhibitions are held throughout the year.

Family Fun

SIESTA STORIES

In Barcelona, as everywhere in Spain, the siesta is sacred. If you're not into afternoon naps, you'll need a few good novels to delve into while you wait for the city to wake up. The following are books and films set in Barcelona that depict what the neighborhoods might be like behind closed doors.

Alicia Gimenez-Bartlett's *Día de Perros*: A novel about two policemen's involvement with Barcelona's underground dog fight circles.

Carmen Laforet's *Nada*: The coming of age of a young girl in an eccentric Barcelona family. Won the Premio Nadal, one of the highest literary honors Iberia has to offer.

Whit Stillman's *Barcelona*: An uptight American working in Barcelona only discovers the pleasures the city has to offer when her free-spirited brother pays her a visit.

Pedro Almodovar's *All About My Mother*: This Oscar winning film about a single mother and the transvestite father of her son took the world by storm.

Cedric Klapish's *Casa de Locos (L'aubergue Espagnol)*: A film about a student from Paris who decides to study in Barcelona and moves in with a group of international students. The story of their year together will make you roam the city in search of the places they visited.

MUSEU DE CERÀMICA

🏛 *Av. Diagonal, 686, 2nd and 3rd floors of the Palau Reial. M: Palau Reial, L3. ☎ 93 280 16 21; www.museuceramica.bcn.es. Open Tu-Sa 10am-6pm, Su and holidays 10am. Shared ticket with the Museu de les Arts Decoratives (see above).*

The display in the Museu de Ceràmica traces the evolution of Spanish ceramic sculpture from the 11th century to the present. The exhibits showcase skillfully crafted plates, tiles, jars, and bowls gathered from all regions of Spain. The five rooms of 20th-century ceramics display abstract works by Picasso and Miró; imagine drinking sangria out of a pitcher designed by the master of Cubism. This highlight hardly redeems the rest of the collection, but if you're visiting the Museu de Les Arts Decoratives it's worth a look.

FINCA GÜELL

🏛 *Av. Pedralbes, 7. M: Palau Reial, L3. A 5min. walk from Av. Diagonal, on the left. Private residence, closed to the public.*

Those disappointed with the relatively unimposing Gaudí iron dragon in the Parc del Palau Reial should head up Av. Pedralbes to see the beast Gaudí created for this estate's gate. Meticulously welded, the animal spreads its wings across the front fence of the *finca* (farm), flashing fearsome fangs to the curious who might be tempted to cross the gate.

SARRIÀ

A visit to Sarrià is a pleasant way to see the traditional home of the Catalan bourgeois and a more suburban side of Barcelona. The upper part of Sarrià, closer to the Collserola hills, is the place to stroll and gawk at the lavish gated mansions and private schools. Gaudí's Casa Bellesguard and Collegi de les Teresianes are worth the walk uphill. The lower, older area of Sarrià is concentrated around the **Pl. Sarrià,** notable for the Neoclassical **Sant Vicenç de Sarrià Church** (1816). The front entrance of the church faces **C. Major de Sarrià,** the area's main street, which is full of restaurants and cafes. Pl. Sarrià also has an antique flea market during the summer on Tuesdays (9am-8pm) and a small used-book flea market on Fridays (9am-8pm). Once a year, on May 11, the small shady **Pl. Sant Vicenç** off of C. Major de Sarrià, hosts **La Fira de Sant Ponç,** a festival honoring the patron saint of herbalists and beekeepers; various medicinal plants, honey products, and cheeses are put out for the occasion.

CASA BELLESGUARD

⚑ *C. Bellesguard, 16-20. FCG: Sarrià or Av. Tibidabo. Take bus #14, 30, 66, 70, or 72 to Pg. Bonanova, then take C. Escoles Pies up the steep hill to where it dead-ends at C. Immaculada, and make a right. Walk for several long blocks until C. Immaculada dead-ends at C. Bellesguard and make a left up the hill; Casa Bellesguard is on your right.*

Casa Bellesguard's striking design merits a look, even if Sarrià's steep incline makes your thighs burn. The building, now a private home, is closed to the public, but for true Gaudí fanatics even a peek from the street is worth the walk. Built by Gaudí in 1902, Casa Bellesguard is one of the architect's neo-Gothic designs and resembles something out of a medieval fairy tale. Tall and fairly compact, with one sculpture-topped spire, Casa Bellesguard is adorned with metal grillwork, tiled benches resplendent with blue and red fish, and three Rapunzel-esque balconies. A stone staircase and landing to the left of the entrance gate provide a picturesque view of the building and the surrounding hills.

COLLEGI DE LES TERESIANES

⚑ *C. Ganduxer, 85-105. FGC: Bonanova. Bus #14, 16, 72, or 74.* ☎ *93 212 33 54. Must call in advance to schedule a tour, offered Sept.-June Sa 11am-1pm. Free.*

The construction of this stately neo-Gothic building, started by an unknown architect in 1888, was taken over by Gaudí the following year. The building now serves as a Catholic school. Gaudí designed a wing (to the right as you enter the gate), and though constrained by a low budget, he managed to create some innovative features. On the building's facade, a row of repeating letters—JSH, for *Jesú Salvate Hombres* (Jesus Saves Men)—adorns the space between two rows of windows. The arcs of the lower windows recall the shape of hands in prayer, and the pineapple shape which tops a tower on the left symbolizes strength. Though Gaudí was content to supervise most of the wing's construction, he fashioned the iron gate himself, repeating symbols of Saint Teresa. While these details can be appreciated from outside, it is the school's main internal hallways and two skylights which are admired by architects worldwide for their perfect parabolic arches.

JARDINS DE LAS VILLA CECILIA Y AMÈLIA

⚑ *FGC: Sarrià Walk down C. Cardenal Sentmenat, turn right on C. Dels Vergòs, and cross the Pl. d'Artos onto C. de Santa Amèlia. The parks are 4 blocks down. Open daily May-Aug. 10am-9pm; Mar. and Oct. 10am-7pm; Apr. and Sept. 10am-8pm; Dec.-Feb. 10am-6pm.*

Sarrià boasts some of the most relaxing and well-manicured public spaces in the city. The **Jardins de la Villa Amèlia** provide families with children and mid-afternoon loungers with plenty of playgrounds and bench space. Palm tree- and eucalyptus-lined paths radiate out from a central fountain, a few feet away from an unobtrusive cafe. Across the street, the **Jardins Villa Cecilia,** with its basketball court and ping-pong tables, attracts a crowd of teenage locals.

TIBIDABO

Tibidabo is named for the phrase the Devil used to tempt Job: *Haec omnia tibidabo si cadens adoraveris me.* (All of this I will give to you if you worship me.) "All of this" is a gloriously high view of Barcelona spilling into the seemingly endless aquamarine Mediterranean. Besides enjoying the view, pleasure-seekers and those seeking God can both be satisfied with the rather incongruous duo of the adjacent amusement park and church. On the way up the mountain, the colorful **La Rotonda** in Pl. JFK and **Casa Roviralta** (Av. Tibidabo, 31, on the way up to Pl. Dr. Andreu), a stunning Modernist edifice and a National Historic and Artistic monument, both evoke the aristocracy's penchant for beautiful buildings. At the base of the Tibidabo mountain lies the distinctive silver-domed **Observatori Fabra,** built in 1904. Piercing the skyline next to **El Sagrat Cor** is the **Torre de Collserola** communications tower, built for the 1992 Olympics. Tibidabo is also home to several museums, though in truth, none compare to the grandiose view.

PARC D'ATTRACIONS

🔁 *Pl. Tibidabo. ☎ 93 211 79 42. Open June Sa-Su noon-8pm; July M-Th noon-8pm, F noon-9pm, Sa-Su noon-10pm; Aug.–Sept. M-Th noon-10pm, F–Su noon-11pm; Oct. Sa-Su noon-7pm; Nov.-Dec. Sa-Su and holidays noon-6pm; Jan.-Feb. Sa-Su noon-6pm; Mar.-May Sa-Su noon-7pm; closed Dec. 25. €20 for unlimited ride access, 60+ or under 110cm tall €8, disabled visitors €5; €10 for the 6 most popular rides only. Most attractions wheelchair-accessible.*

This colorful amusement park may be more weekend carnival than Disney World, but the rides use the mountain to its full advantage. The park also has marionette and haunted house shows, miradors with pay-per-use binoculars (€0.50), the **Museu de Autòmats** (see p. 111), and three restaurants.

EL SAGRAT COR

🔁 *Pl. Tibidabo. ☎ 93 417 56 86. Lower stairs, which offer decent views, open 10am-7pm. Elevator to the top open daily 10am-2pm and 3-7pm; €1.50. Wheelchair-accessible at the lower levels.*

This neo-Gothic church of the Sacred Heart overlooks the city from the top of Tibidabo. After St. John Bosco founded the church in 1886, several additions were made resulting in the eclectic testimony to different architectural styles. At its peak, 575.07m high, the church affords visitors a spectacular view.

TORRE DE COLLSEROLA

🔁 *Bus #211 from Pl. Tibidabo or a short walk from Vallvidrera or Tibidabo (when facing the funicular station, follow path to the right). ☎ 93 406 93 54. Open Su and W-Sa 11:30am-2:30pm and 3:30-6pm. €4.40, groups of 15+ €3.10 per person, under 7 free. MC/V.*

Barcelona's sparkling white communication tower, soaring 560m above sea level, hardly blends in with the area's architectural style, and remains quite controversial amongst locals. Built to transmit TV and radio signals for the 1992 Olympics, the tower now has external glass elevator that visitors take to the 10th platform where captioned pictures of the city help explain the seemingly endless views. While the Torre is interesting, the view from Sagrat Cor is higher, more majestic, and free (not to mention closer to the funicular station).

PARC DE COLLSEROLA

🔁 *Take the FGC train to Baixador de Vallvidrera and follow the steps above the exit for 10min. Information center at C. Carretera de l'Església, 92. ☎ 93 280 35 52; http://parccollserola.amb.es. Open daily 9:30am-3pm except Dec. 25-26 and Jan. 1 and 6.*

Created as part of Barcelona's 1976 General Metropolitan Plan, the Parc de Collserola encompasses 16,000 acres of greenery easily accessible from the city center. People come here to hike, bike, horseback ride, and drive on designated routes through the forest. There are more than two dozen restaurants, snack bars, and picnic places scattered throughout the hills. Before exploring the park, stop at the extremely useful **Centre d'Informació.** There is a permanent exhibit in the center, on birds and the park itself, and the helpful staff sells numerous guides and maps in addition to providing free pamphlets. Those planning to make extended or repeat visits should invest in the hefty trilingual Parc de Collserola Guide Book (€18); it comes with color photos and a keyed map locating every picture in the book (as well as suggesting a hiking/biking route you can use to get there). The smaller, cheaper Peu Per Collserola (€11.40) also has pictures and locator maps but is only available in Catalan. The main map (€6; available in English) is by far the most useful, as it plots every major road and service in the park. The center also has bathrooms, a snack bar, a public telephone, and a brief informational video about the park, available on request.

Parc de Collserola is full of enough natural and man-made sights to pack a long afternoon escape from the city. Most hiking and biking routes offer good views of the city and surrounding hills, especially the Passeig Mirador de las Aigues, a 9km route easily accessible from the Information Center. Also inside the park are more than 50 notable archaeological finds and ruins. Walk across the viaduct in Can Ribes for a view of the Arrabassada torrent, or enjoy a rest in the shady **Font d'Arrabassada,** a colorful Modernist fountain built around a spring in 1908. The water from the spring was said to have medicinal properties—today it is perhaps wiser to bring your own bottled water. **Castellciuró,** a castle built in the 14th century over 12th-century remains, serves as a particularly good lookout point. Interesting remains from the last two centuries include the Modernist turreted washing and disinfection pavilion "El Castell," begun as a tuberculosis hospital on Tibidabo but never completed, and the remains of Dr. Salvador Andreu's **Arrabassada Casino.** Opened in 1911 with a proud exterior staircase reminiscent of that of the Paris Opera, the building was closed down by municipal authorities in 1912 and is now in an advanced state of ruin. Rumor has it that its closing was related to its popularity as a place to play roulette—Russian roulette, with suicide room included.

MUSEU D'AUTÒMATS

🚩 Located inside the Parc d'Attracions. Same hours as the park (see above). Free with park admission.

An entertaining collection of 19th- and 20th-century automated displays, from models of ski hills and the park itself to full-fledged jazz bands, dancers in ballrooms, and a winking gypsy. Just press the green buttons and watch 'em go. Be sure to catch the morbid, and of course automated, re-creation of a beheading and hanging, all in miniature dimensions.

MUSEU-CASA VERDAGUER

🚩 Carretera de les Planes. FGC: Baixador de Vallvidrera. Follow signs from the train station. ☎93 204 78 05; call ☎93 315 11 11 for a guided tour. Open Sa-Su 10am-2pm. Free.

Jacint Verdaguer, the most celebrated poet of the Catalan literary renaissance, lived in this 18th-century house before his death in 1902. Verdaguer is known for winning the Catalan poetry contest with his epic poem *L'Atlantida*. The rooms have been preserved as they were before his death, and detailed explanations of the artist's life and works fill the house; unfortunately for many visitors, all the explanations are in Catalan. The path up to the museum is peppered with his poetry, also in Catalan.

MUSEU DE LA CIENCIA

🚩 C. Teodor Roviralta, 55. FGC: Tibidabo. Buses #17, 22, 58, 77 stop at Pl. JFK and bus #60 at N. de Collserola. ☎93 212 60 50. Open Tu-Su 10am-8pm. Closed M except public holidays. Closed Dec. 26 and Jan. 1-6.

Located at the halfway stop on the bus or tram from Pl. JFK to Pl. Dr. Andreu, the recently renovated science museum offers extremely well organized, hands-on exhibits that are great for kids.

Food & Drink

Barcelona offers every kind of food you could possibly desire. Whether it be Basque, Chinese, Indian, American, or Spanish, chances are you'll find an establishment that will meet and exceed your culinary expectations. While it's tempting to stick to types of food you're familiar with, be sure to sample the local flavors. Catalan cuisine is definitely worth your while. Below are listings of restaurants organized by neighborhood; for a table of **restaurants by type,** see below. For a Spanish-language **menu reader,** see p. 121. For a summary of some of the region's specialties check out **Catalan cuisine,** p. 128.

The following chart shows *Let's Go's* price ranges and their corresponding icons:

ICON	❶	❷	❸	❹	❺
PRICE	€5 and under	€6-10	€11-15	€16-20	€21 and up

FOOD BY TYPE

AMERICAN		BASQUE	
The Bagel Shop (119)	BG ❶	Euskal Etxea (122)	RB ❸
Hard Rock Café (139)	EIX ❷	Irati (118)	BG ❷
Sandwich & Friends (123)	LR ❶	Txapela (Euskal Taberna) (126)	EIX ❷
Vips (139)	EIX ❷	Txirimiri (123)	RB ❶

BRAZILIAN
El Rodizio Grill (129) — EIX ❷

BRUNCH
The Bagel Shop (119) — BG ❶
▨ Bar Ra (124) — ER ❷

BUFFETS
A-Tipic (129) — EIX ❷
FresCo (138) — EIX ❷
▨ Laie Llibreria Café (128) — EIX ❷
La Pérgola (134) — M ❸
Restaurante Biocenter (125) — ER ❷
El Rodizio Grill (129) — EIX ❷
Terrablava (119) — BG ❷

CAFÉS
L'Ancora (136) — LC ❷
Arc Café (118) — BG ❷
Buenas Migas (124) — ER ❶
Café del Born (123) — RB ❷
Café L'Imma (133) — BAR ❸
Café Miranda (126) — EIX ❹
▨ Café de l'Opera (116) — LR ❷
Café Torino (127) — EIX ❶
Caffe San Marco (137) — SA ❶
Can Cortada (136) — H ❹
Can Travi Nou (136) — H ❹
Escribà (116) — LR ❶
Forn de la Vila (137) — SA ❶
FresCo (138) — EIX ❷
Fresh & Ready (138) — CH ❶
▨ Laie Llibreria Café (128) — EIX ❷
Mamacafé (124) — ER ❷
El Raconet (130) — EIX ❷
Restaurante Bar Marcelino (134) — M ❷
▨ Tèxtil Café (123) — RB ❶
Xavi Petit (135) — G ❷
Zahara (133) — BAR ❷

CATALAN
▨ Agua (131) — PN ❸
▨ El Asador de Aranda (138) — T ❺
A'Rogueira (137) — SA ❷
Bar Restaurante Romesco (125) — ER ❶
Bodega La Tinaja (121) — RB ❷
Buenas Migas (124) — ER ❶
Café del Born (123) — RB ❷
Café L'Imma (133) — BAR ❸
Campechano (129) — EIX ❷
Can Cargol (128) — EIX ❷
Carmelitas (124) — ER ❸
Los Caracoles (118) — BG ❸
El Cargolet Picant (136) — LC ❷
Casa Joana (137) — SA ❸
El Club dels Aventurers (138) — T ❸
▨ Colibri (120) — ER ❺
DosTrece (124) — ER ❸
La Flauta (130) — EIX ❷
La Font de Prades (134) — M ❸
FresCo (138) — EIX ❷

CATALAN, CONT'D
Hostal de Rita (126) — EIX ❷
▨ Laie Llibreria Café (128) — EIX ❷
Madrid-Barcelona (126) — EIX ❷
Mandongo (132) — BAR ❷
▨ OvUm (135) — G ❸
La Parra (136) — ST ❷
El Pebre Blau (120) — LR ❷
La Pérgola (134) — M ❸
La Provença (130) — EIX ❹
▨ Les Quinze Nits (118) — BG ❶
Els Quatre Gats (119) — BG ❸
El Raconet (130) — EIX ❷
Restaurante Can Lluís (124) — ER ❸
Restaurante Terrani (130) — EIX ❹
El Rodizio Grill (129) — EIX ❷
Suborn (123) — RB ❷
El Tastavins (135) — G ❷
La Taverna d'en Pep (133) — BAR ❸
Txirimiri (123) — RB ❶
La Venta (138) — T ❹
Via Veneto (137) — SA ❺

CHINESE, JAPANESE & THAI
Elj apo nes (126) — EIX ❸
Ginza (130) — EIX ❸
Mandalay Café (128) — EIX ❸
Mandongo (132) — BAR ❷
Taira (121) — RB ❹
▨ Thai Gardens (126) — EIX ❸
Wok & Bol (128) — EIX ❸

CUBAN
La Habana Vieja (121) — RB ❷

DESSERT
La Colmena (119) — BG ❶
Escribà (116) — LR ❶
Foix de Sarrià (137) — SA ❶
Forn de la Vila (137) — SA ❶
Fratello (133) — EIX ❶
Italiano's (117) — LR ❶
Mauri (127) — EIX ❶
Xavi Petit (135) — G ❷

FONDUE
Gades (122) — RB ❸
Wok & Bol (128) — EIX ❸

FRENCH
Via Veneto (137) — SA ❺

INDIAN
Govinda (120) — BG ❷
Shalimar (125) — ER ❷

INDONESIAN
Betawi (120) — BG ❷

INTERNATIONAL
52 (126) — EIX ❷
▨ Bar Ra (124) — ER ❷

NEIGHBORHOOD ABBREVIATIONS: LR Las Ramblas **BG** Barri Gòtic **RB** La Ribera **ER** El Raval **EIX** l'Eixample **BAR** Barceloneta & Port Vell **PN** Poble Nou & Port Olímpic **M** Montjuïc **G** Gràcia **LC** Les Corts **ST** Sants **SA** Sarrià **T** Tibidabo **CH** Chains

INTERNATIONAL, CONT'D

La Cocotte (121)	RB ❷
Gades (122)	RB ❸
Mamacafé (124)	ER ❷
Oolong (119)	BG ❷
🍴 El Pebre Blau (120)	RB ❷
🍴 Pla dels Angels (124)	ER ❷
🍴 El Racó d'en Baltá (129)	EIX ❹
Silenus (124)	ER ❹

ITALIAN

Buenas Migas (124)	ER ❶
Cuitat Comtal (137)	ST ❷
🍴 La Gavina (135)	G ❸
🍴 Il Mercante di Venezia (117)	BG ❷
PastaFiore (139)	CH ❶
El Salón (118)	BG ❷

MIDDLE EASTERN & AFRICAN

dahabi (130)	EIX ❸
NUT (135)	G ❷
Thiossan (119)	BG ❶

PERUVIAN

El Criollo (130)	EIX ❷

SANDWICH SHOPS

L'Ancora (136)	LC ❷
The Bagel Shop (119)	BG ❶
La Baguetina Catalana (138)	CH ❶
Bocatta (139)	CH ❶
Cerveceria Catalana (131)	EIX ❶
La Flauta (130)	EIX ❷
Forn de la Vila (137)	SA ❶
Fresh & Ready (138)	CH ❶
Mauri (127)	EIX ❶
Pans & Co. (138)	CH ❶
Restaurante Bar Marcelino (134)	M ❷
Sandwich & Friends (123)	RB ❶
🍴 Tèxtil Café (123)	RB ❶
Venus Delicatessen (119)	BG ❷
🍴 Xaloc (119)	BG ❶

SEAFOOD

🍴 Agua (131)	PN ❸
Café L'Imma (133)	BAR ❸
El Cargolet Picant (136)	LC ❷
Cerveceria Catalana (131)	EIX ❶
Hostal de Rita (126)	EIX ❸
La Mar Salada (133)	BAR ❸
La Muscleria (128)	EIX ❷
La Oca Mar (132)	PN ❸
La Provença (130)	EIX ❹
Restaurant 7 Portes (121)	RB ❸
La Taverna d'en Pep (133)	BAR ❸

SPANISH

🍴 L'Antic Bocoi del Gòtic (117)	BG ❷
Bar Restaurante Los Toreros (125)	ER ❷
🍴 Café de l'Opera (116)	LR ❷
Casa Regina (El 19 De La Riera) (135)	G ❸
Cullera de Boix (129)	EIX ❷
Frankfurt D'Or (131)	EIX ❶
🍴 Mi Burrito y Yo (117)	BG ❹
Restaurant Font de Les Planes (138)	T ❸
Via Veneto (137)	SA ❺
Vips (139)	EIX ❷

TAPAS BARS

A'Rogueira (137)	SA ❷
ba-ba-reeba (127)	EIX ❷
Barcelónia (122)	RB ❷
Bar Restaurante Los Toreros (125)	ER ❷
🍴 Café de l'Opera (116)	LR ❷
Cal Pep (122)	RB ❷
El Cargolet Picant (136)	LC ❷
Cerveceria Catalana (131)	EIX ❶
Euskal Etxea (122)	RB ❸
TapasBar (138)	CH ❸
Txapela (Euskal Taberna) (126)	EIX ❷
Txirimiri (123)	RB ❶
🍴 Va de Vi (122)	RB ❷
🍴 Xampanyet (122)	RB ❶

VEGETARIAN/VEGAN

A-Tipic (129)	EIX ❷
🍴 Agua (131)	PN ❸
🍴 Bar Ra (124)	ER ❷
Café del Born (123)	RB ❷
Carmelitas (124)	ER ❸
Casa Regina (El 19 De La Riera) (135)	G ❸
La Cocotte (121)	RB ❷
🍴 Comme-Bio (127)	EIX ❷
La Flauta (130)	EIX ❷
Govinda (120)	BG ❷
Juicy Jones (119)	BG ❷
Kamasawa (119)	BG ❷
L'Hortet (124)	ER ❷
🍴 Laie Llibreria Café (128)	EIX ❷
Mamacafé (124)	ER ❷
🍴 OvUm (135)	G ❸
El Raconet (130)	EIX ❷
Restaurante Biocenter (125)	ER ❷
🍴 Restaurante Illa de Gràcia (135)	G ❶
Restaurante Maravillas (137)	SA ❸
Restaurante Self Naturista (120)	BG ❶
Suborn (123)	RB ❷
Terrablava (119)	BG ❷
Tomate (121)	RB ❶
Venus Delicatessen (119)	BG ❷

TAPAS 101

Hopping from one tapas bar to another is a fun and cheap way to pass the evening. When you arrive, don't wait to be seated and don't look for a waiter to serve you; most tapas bars are self-serve and standing (or crowding) room only. Ask for a *plato* (plate) and help yourself to the toothpick-skewered goodies that line the bars. Keep your toothpicks—they'll be tallied up on your way out to determine your bill. If you're tired of standing at the bar, most places offer more expensive sit-down menus as well. Barcelona's many tapas (sometimes called *pintxos*) bars, concentrated in La Ribera and Gràcia, often serve *montaditos*, thick slices of bread topped with all sorts of delectables from sausage to tortillas to anchovies. Vegetarian tapas are rare—be forewarned, for example, that slender white strands on some *montaditos* are actually eels masquerading as noodles. Generally served around lunchtime and dinnertime, *montaditos* are presented on platters at the bar. *Montaditos* go well with a glass of cava (see p. 135) or a cup of *sidra*, a Basque alcoholic cider generally poured from several feet above your glass.

FOOD BY NEIGHBORHOOD

BARRI GÒTIC & LAS RAMBLAS

see map pp. 334-335

As the oldest part of the city, the Barri Gòtic sets the bar when it comes to cuisine; it's a world-class culinary cornucopia that not only excites the most discerning gourmet but also caters to the most penny-pinching of budget travelers. Most food spots are unpretentious and intimate by default, on the account of the lack of space in these old Spanish buildings. For late-night munchies or to keep to a super-tight budget, head to the popular falafel and schwarma stands; tasty options with good prices are **Maoz Falafel,** C. Ferran 13 (Falafel €2.95. Open Su-Th 11am-2am, F-Sa 11am-3am), and **Buen Bocado,** C. Escudellers 3. (Falafel €2.20, schwarma €3.20. Open Su-Th 11am-2am, F-Sa 11am-3am.)

LAS RAMBLAS

Food on Las Ramblas is everywhere and generally unremarkable; people here eat at the restaurants, which are mostly carbon copies of one another, more for people-watching and convenience, rather than the delicacies which are few and far between.

🍽 **Café de l'Opera,** Las Ramblas, 74 (☎93 317 75 85). M: Liceu, L3. A drink at this Barcelona institution used to be a post-opera bourgeois tradition and still attracts a large crowd after concerts. Today, the cafe retains the same upscale ambience while offering well-priced drinks and tapas to an eclectic crowd of all ages. Outdoor seating is available. Hot chocolate €1.70, churros €1.20, drinks €2-16, tapas €2-4, salads €2-8, cheeses €3-6. Open Su 10am-2:30am, M-Th 9am-2:30am, F-Sa 9am-2:45am. ❷

Escribà, Las Ramblas, 83 (☎93 301 60 27). M: Liceu, L3. Delight in one of their delicious pastries while watching the world go by on La Rambla de les Flores. This small, classy cafe is still as much of an aesthetic gem as it was in 1906, when it was founded. There's no menu; just choose a pastry from the case at the front counter and they'll bring it to your table. Outside seating is available. Coffee €1.50, pastries €2-3. Open daily 8:30am-9pm. ❶

Italiano's, Las Ramblas, 78. M: Liceu, L3. Nothing goes better with ice cream on a hot summer day than a half-liter of beer, right? Test it out for yourself at this popular heladería/cervecería. Try the *gofres* (Belgian waffles; €1.75). Single scoop of ice cream €1.70, triple €3. Beer €3.20. Coffee, tea, or horchata €0.80-1.60. Open Su-Th 10am-2am, F-Sa 10am-2:30am. ❶

LOWER BARRI GÒTIC

🔏 **Il Mercante di Venezia,** C. Jose Anselmo Clavé, 11 (☎93 317 18 28). M: Drassanes, L3. Curtain-adorned fresco archways, sheet music lampshade, and an overall attention to detail (not to mention an extensive menu of Italian food) make this perfect for a romantic meal. Gnocchi is their specialty, and they offer a wide range of smaller-portioned creative dishes, with starters €6-8, pasta €6-10, pizza €7-9, meat and fish dishes €7-15. Reservations recommended, necessary F-Sa (people are reserved for one of two seatings, either at 8:30 or 11pm; 11pm seating is less rushed). Open Su 8:30pm-midnight, Tu-Sa 11am-2:45pm and 8:30pm-midnight (a bit later on F and Sa). MC/V. Just a few minutes further down C. Clavé, in Pl. Duc de Medinaceli, sister restaurant **Le Tre Venezie** (☎93 342 42 52) serves similar food in a sharper, cooler atmosphere, better for larger parties. Open Su 1:30-3:30pm, W-Sa 1:30-4pm and 8:30pm-midnight. MC/V. ❷

Café de l'Opera

🔏 **Mi Burrito y Yo,** C. del Pas de l'Ensenyanca, 2 (☎93 318 27 42). M: Jaume I, L4, in the Barri Gòtic. To the left off C. Ferran immediately after Pl. St. Jaume. Not a touristy Mexican joint (burrito here means "little donkey"), but rather one of the most inviting, lively grill-restaurant/*bodegas* in the city. Live music in the basement starting at 9:30pm. Upstairs, the supremely decorated interior drips with red wine bottles, dark wood, paintings, and wall-size murals. It can be a little expensive; try going during the day and ordering the delicious daily menú €9.50. Specialties include grilled meat dishes *(carne a la brasa)*. Starters €6-19. Most entrees €12-20. Wines €12-20. Open daily 1pm-midnight. AmEx/MC/V. ❸

Les Quinze Nits

🔏 **L'Antic Bocoi del Gòtic,** Baixada de Viladecols, 3 (☎93 310 50 67). M: Jaume I, L4. At the end of the street that starts as C. Dagueria, a left off C. Jaume I coming from Pl. del Angel (it changes names 3 times en route). For the most part, the only tourists who come to this small, intimate restaurant/*bodega* are those invited by local friends; formed in part by an ancient first-century Roman wall, it's precisely the kind of tiny, romantic, and hard-to-find place one imagines stumbling upon in the "Gothic Quarter." With excellent salads (€4.25-7.60), pâtés (€8-12), sausages (€12-15), cheeses (€10-12), and wines (€6.50-20), this is undoubtedly one of the best places in the area. Reservations recommended. Open M-Sa 8:30pm-midnight. AmEx/MC/V. ❷

Pouring Sidra at Irati

Ham-ing It Up

Jamón. The word pervades every menu, butcher shop, and household not only in Barcelona but in all of Spain. On tapas, on the plate, and in your mouth, avoiding this porcine obsession proves almost as difficult as successfully ordering tap water at a Barcelona restaurant. Frito-Lay even makes *Jamón! Jamón!* flavored chips. To say that Spaniards worship ham is not that far off the mark—the infamous obsequiousness of the meat has religious origins. During the Spanish Inquisition, thousands of Jews and Muslims were being persecuted as heretics; Spaniards of all religious backgrounds ate pork products as a way of showing their Christian allegiance and avoiding the wrath of the Church. The reasoning was, the more ham you ingested, the less likely you were to fall under suspicion.

Though the Inquisition eventually ended, the cult of *jamón* had caught on. Ham consumption transformed into a show of nationalism rather than religious affiliation. Nowadays, most Spaniards would probably not describe their ham as either pious or patriotic. To them, it's just plain yummy.

Les Quinze Nits, Pl. Reial, 6 (☎ 93 317 30 75). M: Liceu, L3. In the back left corner of the Pl. Reial coming from Las Ramblas. Without a doubt, one of the most popular restaurants in Barcelona, with nightly lines of up to 50 people waiting to get in (don't be afraid—they move relatively quickly). Stylish white-linen decor with minimalist, ambient lighting. Pleasant interior with earth-toned walls covered with potted plants on racks. Delicious Catalan entrees at unbelievable prices (€3-8). Come at lunch time to avoid the crowds and take advantage of the daily lunch menú (€7). No reservations. Open daily 1-3:45pm and 8:30-11:30pm. AmEx/MC/V. ❶

Los Caracoles, C. Escudellers, 14 (☎93 301 20 41). M: Drassanes, L3. What started as a snail shop in 1835 has now evolved into one of the most delicious Catalan restaurants in the Barri Gòtic, with chickens roasting over open flames, walls and ceilings covered with oversized veggies and utensils, and food sizzling in front of you in the walk-through kitchen. Dishes taste as good as they look; specialties include, of course, the *caracoles* (snails; €7.20), half of a rabbit (€10.50), and chicken (€9). Expect a wait for dinner. Open daily 1pm-midnight. AmEx/MC/V. ❸

El Salón, C. l'Hostal d'en Sol, 6-8 (☎93 315 21 59). M: Jaume I, L4. Follow Via Laietana toward the water, turn right on C. d'Angel Baixeras and then right on tiny C. l'Hostal d'en Sol; it's on the left. This mellow bar-bistro is perfect for unwinding after a day spent jostling fellow tourists. Sit in the terrace, nestled against a large section of first-century Roman wall, and feast on plates of bruschetta, gnocchi, chicken, pork, or fish (€7.80-15). Menú €9.50. Wine €2-6, cocktails €4.50. Open M-Sa 1:30pm-2:30am. AmEx/MC/V. ❷

Arc Café, C. Carabassa, 19 (☎93 302 52 04). M: Drassanes, L3. Turn onto C. Clavé (turns into C. Ample) from Las Ramblas and make the fifth left; restaurant will be on your right. If you're looking to get away from the crowded areas of Barri Gòtic, this gay-friendly cafe and bar serves creative soups and salads in a cozy, out-of-the-way niche. The high ceilings and exposed brick make for an open, airy ambience. Breakfast served until 1pm, €1.35-6.50. Entrees €5.50-8, lunch menú €7.50. Open M-Th 9am-1am, F 9am-3am, Sa 11am-3am, Su 11am-1am. ❷

Irati, C. Cardenal Casañas, 17 (☎93 302 30 84). M: Liceu, L3. An excellent Basque restaurant that attracts droves of hungry tapas-seekers. Ask for a plate, fill it with one of the somewhat limited variety of *montaditos* (tapa-like snacks on bread, see p. 116) from the long bar covered in serving platters, and they'll count the toothpicks at the end to figure out your bill (€1.10 apiece). Bartenders also pour Basque *sidra* (cider) with the bottle high above your glass. Starters around €8-16. Entrees €13-20. Open daily noon-1am. AmEx/MC/V. ❷

Juicy Jones, C. Cardenal Casañas, 7 (☎93 302 43 30; group dinner reservations 60 620 49 06). M: Liceu, L3. A unique vegan haven, Juicy Jones is a refreshing touch of psychedelic flower-power, with wildly decorated walls and a long bar spilling over with fresh fruit. The creative vegan menú (€7) features rice, veggies, soups, and salad (after 1pm only). They offer a full juice bar with any conceivable mixture of fresh juices and soy milkshakes €2-3. Dining room in the back with low ceiling and limited seating. Open daily 10am-midnight. Cash only. ❷

Venus Delicatessen, C. Avinyó, 25 (☎93 301 15 85). M: Liceu, L3. Take a right off C. Ferran coming from Las Ramblas. With a black-and-white tiled floor and monthly local art shows on the stucco walls, this Mediterranean cafe fits in well with the funky scene on C. Avinyó right by Pl. Trippy; it's very popular with the locals. Try the *ensalada erótica* with lasagna, hummus, or an omelette and a glass of wine while you watch the street that inspired Picasso's *Mademoiselles d'Avignon*. Coffee, wine, pastries (€3.50-3.80), and a large selection of vegetarian dishes (€6-8.50). Salads €4.50-6. Menú €8. Open M-Sa noon-midnight. Cash only. ❷

Oolong, C. Gignàs, 25 (☎93 315 12 59). M: Jaume I, L4, a right off Via Laietana coming from the Metro. A tiny but terrific hole-in-the-wall that serves self-described *comida mundial divertida* (fun international food). The menu includes everything from duck breast, tortellini, and chicken fajitas to veggies with mango sauce and Caribbean salad. Salads €5-8. Hot dishes €5-12. Drinks €2-4. Open M-Sa 8pm-2am, Su 8pm-1am. Cash only. ❷

Kamasawa, C. Escudellers, 39 (☎65 833 30 30). M: Liceu or Drassanes, L3. An alternative and decidedly romantic experience in every sense of the word, with mood lighting, matrimonial decor (including faux-marble columns and draped white veils), and exotic twists on health food utilizing fruits, vegetables, rice, noodles, and tofu. Salads €5.50-9. Menús €12-15. Open daily 7:30pm-midnight. Cash only. ❷

Thiossan, C. del Vidre, 3 (☎93 3317 10 31). M: Liceu, L3. Just off Pl. Reial, in the left corner near the waterfront. A small funky Senegalese restaurant/bar, with decent reggae music, colorful wall hangings, friendly staff, and a limited but unique menu: beer, ginger, or *bissap* €2. Daily African plate €6. Open Su and Tu-Th 8:30pm-2am, F-Sa 8:30pm-3am. Cash only. ❶

UPPER BARRI GÒTIC

🖾 **Xaloc,** C. de la Palla, 13-17 (☎93 301 19 90). M: Liceu, L3. From Las Ramblas, turn onto C. Casañas, walk straight through Pl. del Pi and bear left onto C. la Palla; the restaurant is on your left. Tucked away from the chaos on a small side street, this classy delicatessen is centered around a butcher/cheese counter with pig legs hanging from the high ceiling. Specialties include salads (€3.40-9.30), meat and poultry sandwiches on tasty baguettes (€3-7), a selection of *carpaccios*, and an extensive wine list. Tapas €1-6.50. Open daily 9am-midnight. AmEx/MC/V. ❶

Terrablava, Via Laietana, 55 (☎93 322 15 85). An all-you-can-eat buffet of veggies, pasta, pizza, meat dishes, fruit, coffee, and probably one of the most extensive salad bars in the area. Lunchtime brings a circus of famished locals. Food also available *à la carte* to go. Buffet €8.40 (includes tax and a drink). Open daily 12:30pm-1am. Cash only. ❷

La Colmena, Pl. de l'Angel, 12 (☎93 315 13 56). M: Jaume I, L4. After more than 120 years in the Pl. de l'Angel, this divine pastry and candy shop has more than earned its prime location. Don't walk in unless you're prepared to buy, because you *will*—no one's strong enough to resist. Pastries €1-4. Open daily 9am-9pm. AmEx/MC/V. ❶

The Bagel Shop, C. Canuda, 25 (☎93 302 41 61). M: Catalunya, L3. Walk down Las Ramblas and take the 1st left and then bear right onto C. Canuda; it's on the left in Pl. Vila de Madrid. Barcelona meets New York City. Diverse bagel selection (€0.60 each, toasted extra €0.15), bagel sandwiches (€3-5), and varied spreads, from cream cheese to caramel (€3-6). Try a speciality Catalan bagel (€1.50-3). A good place to go for a tasty, inexpensive lunch. Sept.-June they serve a Su pancake- and eggs-brunch 11am-4pm (€5). Open M-Sa 9:30am-9:30pm, Su (Sept.-June only) 11am-4pm. Cash only. **Branch** at Pl. Rius i Taulet, 8 (☎93 217 61 01). Open M and W-F 8am-10pm, Sa-Su 10am-10pm. Closed Tu. Cash Only. ❶

Els Quatre Gats, C. Montsió, 3 (☎93 302 41 40). M: Catalunya, L3. Take the 2nd left off Av. Portal de l'Angel. Usually translated as "the four cats," *Els Quatre Gats* is actually a figurative Catalan expression meaning "just a few guys," an ironically diminutive name considering the cafe's presti-

the BIG $plurge

From Fresh to First-Class

Early each morning, the chef at **Colibri** goes to the Boqueria market to buy the freshest ingredients available. By evening, as if by magic, they have been combined to become some of the tastiest meals to be had in all of Barcelona, perhaps even some of the most divinely flavored dishes you have ever tasted. An amiable English-speaking staff complements the elegant but unpretentious atmosphere. The dishes are worth every euro: try the roasted pigeon (€18) for starters, and the pistachio vinaigrette sea bass filet (€31) as an entree. If you have any extra room, try the fresh cheese with raspberry ice cream and tomato jam, a unique twist on the traditional Spanish dessert.

*C. Riera Alta, 33-35 (☎93 443 23 06). M: Sant Antoni, L2, in **El Raval**. From the Metro, head down C. Riera Alta; it will be on your right at the intersection with C. Sant Vincenç.Call ahead for reservations. Open M-Sa 1:30-3:30pm and 8:30-11:30pm. AmEx/MC/V.* ❺

gious clientele. An old Modernist hangout of Picasso's with lots of Bohemian character; he loved it so much he designed a personalized menu (on display at Museu Picasso; see p. 68). Ramon Casas left his artistic mark as well, in the form of a self-portrait of himself and a fellow artist on a bicycle built for two (on display in the Museu d'Art Modern; see p. 73). Reproductions of these works and more adorn the walls. The restaurant tends to attract more tourists than locals, but it is probably worth having one nice meal here. Food is expensive (entrees around €12-18), making tapas the best way to go (about €2-4). Live piano and violin 9pm-1am. Open daily 1pm-1am. Closed Aug. AmEx/MC/V. ❸

Betawi, C. Montsió, 6 (☎93 412 62 64). M: Catalunya, L3. Take the 2nd left off Portal de l'Angel coming from the Metro, across the street from Els Quatre Gats. A peaceful, delicately decorated Indonesian restaurant serving high quality food in small portions. Menú €10, entrees €7-13. Open M 1-4pm, Tu-Sa 1-4pm and 8-11pm. AmEx/MC/V. ❷

Govinda, Pl. Vila de Madrid, 4 (☎93 318 77 29). M: Catalunya, L3. Just to the right off Las Ramblas on C. Canuda. A flute-playing mural of Krishna greets happy vegetarian and vegan customers. A true product of globalization: vegetarian Indian food served just a few feet away from a row of 2000-year-old Roman tombs in one of the world's most pork-crazed countries. Serves *thali* (traditional Indian "sampler" meals with a variety of dishes on one platter; €15-20), as well as spring rolls, crepes, rice, Indian bread, fruit *lassis* (yogurt shakes), and more. International salad bar €4-6. M-F menú €8. Most entrees around €7. Open daily 1-4pm, for dinner Tu-Th 8-11pm and F-Sa 8-11:45pm. AmEx/MC/V. ❷

Restaurante Self Naturista, C. Santa Anna, 11-17 (☎93 318 26 84). M: Catalunya, L4, on the left on C. Santa Anna off Las Ramblas. A self-service vegetarian cafeteria with enormous selection and enough dessert options to fill a bakery. Entrees under €3. Lunch menú €7. Open M-Sa 11:30am-10pm. Cash only. ❶

LA RIBERA

see map p. 337

East of Via Laietana, La Ribera is home to numerous bars and small restaurants. The neighborhood's narrow alleys and old-fashioned street lamps make for romantic dinners. From Catalan to creative concoctions—you will not be disappointed here.

RESTAURANTS

☒ **El Pebre Blau,** C. Banys Vells, 21 (☎93 319 13 08). M: Jaume I, L4. Ring the bell and cross your fingers for entrance into the younger sister restaurant of

L'Oucomballa (a 25-year-old fail-safe), serving delicate gourmet dishes that creatively fuse Mediterranean, Oriental, and Sephardic flavors. The most difficult part will be choosing. The specialties—foie gras with apricots and honeyed sauce, and seared duck with forest berries—are to die for. Dessert will never be the same after trying the balsamic vinegar ice cream. Kitchen open daily 8:30pm-midnight, reservations highly recommended on weekends. Wheelchair accessible. MC/V. ❹

Bodega La Tinaja, C. Esparteria, 9 (☎93 310 22 50). M: Jaume I, L4. The wine selection is excellent (€1.50-5 per glass), and the dishes that accompany the wine are even tastier. The cheese, pate, fish, and meat accompaniments for bread are mouth-watering. Mix and match new tastes in this wood-beamed restaurant. Open Su and Tu-Sa 6pm-2am. MC/V. ❷

Taira, C. Comerç, 7 (☎93 310 24 97). From M: Jaume I, L4, follow C. Princesa, then turn left on C. Comerç. Paper lanterns surround the "in" crowd. Chill on floor-level futons and funky chairs at this swank sushi hot spot. Splurge on the moriawase (€17), and finish up with a sorbete de sake (€4). Menú €8. Cafeteria open M-F 8am-4pm, restaurant and bar open Su 8:30pm-1am, Tu-Sa 1pm-4pm and 9pm-midnight. Wheelchair accessible. AmEx/MC/V. ❹

La Cocotte, Pg. del Born, 16 (☎93 319 17 34). M: Jaume I, L4. Mostly vegetarian international dishes served in a cozy, green-and-white checkered interior. Culinary offerings range from moussaka (€7.50) to vegetarian burritos (€6.50) to chicken curry (€8.50). Eat in or take out. Entrees €4.50-9. Open Su and Tu-Sa 9pm-midnight. Wheelchair accessible. ❷

La Habana Vieja, C. Banys Vells, 2 (☎93 268 25 04). M: Jaume I, L4. Banys Vells is parallel to C. Montcada. Pulsing Cuban music sets the mood in this family-style place. Large portions great for sharing. Cuban rice €3.50-6, meat dishes €10-12. Interesting cocktails €3.50-5. Open daily 1:30-3:30pm, 5:30-11pm, F-Sa until midnight. AmEx/MC/V. ❷

Tomate, C. Sombrerers, 17 (☎93 315 10 48). M: Jaume I, L4. This vegetarian hole-in-the-wall serves up healthy burritos (€3.35-4.50), soups (€3-5), and lasagna (€6.25) using seitan, veggies, and soy products to satisfy both the palate and the wallet. Menú €7. Fresh-squeezed juice €2. Open Tu-Sa 1:30-11:30pm, Su 1:30-5pm. Cash only. ❶

Restaurant 7 Portes, Pg. Isabel II, 14 (☎93 319 30 33; www.7puertas.com). M: Barceloneta, L4. This classy seafood restaurant is known city-wide for its paella (starting at €15.50). Dark wood beamed ceiling, blue-tiled walls, and elegant lighting; it's the right place if you want to impress. Reservations highly recommended. Entrees €11-48. Open daily 1pm-1am. Wheelchair accessible. AmEx/MC/V. ❸

MENU READER

Before traveling to Barcelona, you will want to consider any specific dietary needs you require to make sure they can be met during your visit. Below is a glossary of common Spanish words that you will encounter on menus during your stay. ¡Buen provecho!

aceitunas: olives.

aceite y vinagre: olive oil and vinegar; typically used as a salad dressing.

agua: water; sin gas is still water and con gas is carbonated water.

arroz: rice.

batido: milk shake.

bocadillo: baguette sandwich.

calamares: calamari (squid).

chipirones: baby squids, usually fried and eaten whole.

chorizo: Spanish-style sausage; often spicy, it can be eaten in a sandwich or as a tapa.

churros: sticks of fried dough dipped in sugar or chocalate; usually eaten for breakfast.

cerveza: beer.

cocido: stew; varieties include cocido madrileño and cocido gallego, both of which are meat- and bean-heavy.

cordero asado: roasted lamb with garlic.

embutidos: high-quality cold cuts.

ensalada: salad.

fideua: like paella, but uses noodles instead of rice.

fruta: fruit.

galletas: cookies or crackers.

gambas: prawns.

infusión: herbal tea.

jamón serrano: serrano ham.

lomo: cured ham.

(Continued on p. 123.)

Rotting Fish Entrails

"There's nothing more appetizing and sexually stimulating than the freshly spilled blood of a still squirming Mackerel. Better yet, let's mix the blood with the fish's gastrointestinal tract, add a dash of salt, and let it all ferment under the sun. Perfect. We'll call it *garum*."

This is what some ancient Roman culinary genius may have been thinking when he invented *garum*, a Mediterranean delicacy that, thankfully, has changed quite a bit over the last millennium. While these fermented fish guts were used in kinky sexual practices in ancient Rome, modern *garum* has been adopted by Catalan restaurants in a strictly plutonic sense. Nowadays, it is a surprisingly tasty puree of a variety of fresh herbs, spices, capers, olives, eggs, and anchovy filets. Usually served as an appetizer, it should be spread on toast, like a pâté. While *garum* hasn't exactly worked its way into mainstream Catalan cuisine, you can find it at a few restaurants in Barcelona including **Hotel Ampurdan**, Antigua Carretera a Franci; (☎97 250 05 62; menú €30), **Merlot**, C. Caballers 6, Tarragona (☎97 722 10 76; full meal €35), and occasionally at **Vinissim**, C. Sant Domenec de Dall 12 (☎93 301 45 75; tapa portion €3.50).

Gades, C. L'Esparteria, 10 (☎93 310 44 55; www.gadesfondues.com). M: Jaume I, L4. Enter C. Vidreira across from C. Montcada off Pg. del Born, and take the first left onto C. L'Esparteria. Get your "dip" on in this romantic fondue heaven. A wide range of cheese and meat fondues (€11-17). Interesting salads (€6-7.50) for those with a fondue phobia. Open M-Th 10:30pm-12:30am, F-Sa 10:30pm-1:30am. Wheelchair accessible. MC/V. ❸

TAPAS BARS

☒ **Xampanyet,** C. Montcada, 22 (☎93 319 70 03). M: Jaume I, L4. Next to the Museu Picasso and packed with people. Juan Carlos, the 3rd-generation proprietor, treats everyone like family. The house special—cava (choose from 17 varieties)—is served with anchovies and, of course, bread with tomato (€1.10). Glasses €0.85 and up, bottles €6.50 and up. Open Su noon-4pm, Tu-Sa noon-4pm and 7-11:30pm. Closed in Aug. ❶

☒ **Va de Vi,** C. Banys Vells, 16 (☎93 319 29 00). From M: Jaume I, L4, walk down C. Princesa, turn right on C. Montcada, right again on C. Barra de Ferro, and finally left on C. Banys Vells. Possibly the most romantic restaurant in La Ribera. Cavernous, medieval wine bar in a 16th-century stone building, softly illumined by candles and delicate lamps. Choose from over 170 varieties of wine and cava (glasses €1.60-4), a wide selection of cheeses (€4-15.50) and tapas (€1.80-13). Open Su-W 6pm-1am, Th 6pm-2am, F-Sa 6pm-3am. Wheelchair accessible. ❷

Cal Pep, Pl. de les Olles, 8 (☎93 310 79 61; www.calpep.net). From M: Barceloneta, L4, follow Pg. Joan de Borbó, then turn right on Av. Marqués de l'Argentera, and left on C. Palau. It can be difficult to find even standing room at the small bar, but the fresh, unusual tapas—like sauteed spinach with garbanzo beans and smoked ham (€4)—make it all worthwhile. Country-style sit-down restaurant in rear (entrees €4-9); they bring food until you say stop. Beer €1.50, drinks €3-6. Open Tu-Sa 1-4:30pm and 8pm-midnight. Closed in Aug. ❷

Euskal Etxea, Pl. Montcada, 1-3 (☎93 310 21 85). M: Jaume I, L4, at the end of C. Montcada by Pg. del Born. Locals cram into the standing-room only bar to greet the endless trays of delectable tapas. Sit-down restaurant in back serves Basque cuisine (entrees €8-16). Tapas begin at €1.25. Beer €1.50, mixed drinks €1-4. Open M-Sa 11:30am-midnight. ❸

Barcelónia, Pl. Comercial, 11 (☎93 268 70 21). From M: Jaume I, L4, follow C. Princesa almost to its end and turn right on C. Comerç; the *plaça* is ahead on the right. Neighborhood trendoids gather to feast on a traditional selection of tapas (€1-2). Innovative menu includes dishes like *foie* terine with pistachios and forest fruit reduction. Entrees €5-11. Lunch menú €8. Beer and wine from €1. Open daily 1-4:30pm and 7:30pm-midnight. Wheelchair accessible. ❷

Txirimiri, C. Princesa, 11 (☎93 310 18 05). Jaume I, L4. Walk straight down C. Princesa away from the metro station. Enough tapas to feed a small village (€1 each). Sit at the long wooden bar and try *la gula*, a seafood and veggie specialty from the Basque region. Tapas outshine the small lunch and dinner menu. Beer €1.50, cava and wine €1.80. Open Su and Tu-Sa noon-midnight. MC/V. ❶

CAFES

▓ **Tèxtil Café,** C. Montcada, 12-14 (☎93 268 25 98). M: Jaume I, L4. Set in the picturesque courtyard of the Museu Tèxtil i d'Indumentària (see **Sights & Museums,** p. 71) Elegant but relaxed cafe great for a post-museum coffee or meal. Breakfast €4.75, weekday lunch menú €9. Wine and cava €1.60-3. Hot and cold sandwiches €3-6. Tapas €5. Open Su and Tu-Sa 10am-midnight. Wheelchair accessible. ❶

Suborn, Pg. Picasso, 42 (☎93 310 11 10). M: Barceloneta, L4, across from Parc de la Ciutadella. Eclectic restaurant with plenty of vegetarian options by day; popular, bass-thumping bar by night. Entrees like tuna tartare with couscous, mango, avocado and cucumber from €6-14. Lunch menú €9. Beer €2, drinks €5. Open Su and Tu-Th 12:30-4:30pm and 9pm-2:30am, F-Sa 12:30-4:30pm and 9pm-3am. ❷

Sandwich & Friends, Pg. del Born, 27 (☎93 310 07 86; www.sandwichandfriends.com). From M: Jaume I, L4, follow C. Princesa, and turn right on C. Comerç and right again on Pg. del Born. Sleek and super-trendy sandwich bar serves veggie- or meat-filled goodies (€3.40-7) and salads (€4-5). Try the *Bim*—eggplant, gouda, zucchini, tomato, and onion on a baguette (€4.40), or the *Elena*—white rice, corn, pears, lettuce, and soy dressing (€3.75). Open Su-W noon-12:30am, Th-Sa noon-1am. ❶

Café del Born, Pl. Comercial, 10 (☎93 268 32 72). M: Jaume I, L4. Bistro-style cafe with more leg room than its neighbors. Vegetarian selections like four-cheese spaghetti with asparagus (€7), as well as traditional meat-filled Catalan dishes (€4-13). Tasty lunch menú €6. Bocadillos €1.50-4.20. Open Su-W 9am-1am, Th-Sa 9am-3am.❷

EL RAVAL

The area west of Las Ramblas is filled with more than its share of good restaurants. Numerous tiny local places reflect the ethnic diversity of the neighborhood, but as the government continues its efforts

see map p. 336

to clean up and revitalize El Raval, trendier gourmet places have started to move into the

---

MENU READER

(continued from p. 121)

mantequilla: butter.

mazapán: marzipan.

mejillones: mussels.

menú: A daily set menu, served at lunch or dinner. Generally two courses, bread, dessert, and a drink.

horchata: tiger-nut milk (often referred to as rice water); tastes like almond.

paella: a family-size rice dish typically filled with seafood or meat.

pan: bread; Spaniards typically eat the baguette kind. *Pan integral* is wheat bread; *pan de molde* is sliced bread.

pasteles: pastries.

patatas: potatoes. *Patatas bravas* are a popular tapa consisting of potatoes in a spicy sauce.

pavo: turkey.

pescado: fish. Varieties include *salmon* (salmon), *trucha* (trout), *bacalao* (cod), *atún* (tuna), *ángilas* (eel), and more.

pollo: chicken.

polvorones: a holiday sweet made from crushed almonds and sugar.

postre: dessert.

puerco: pork.

queso: cheese; varieties include *Manchego* (hard sheep's cheese) and *fresco* (soft).

Raciones: larger portions of tapas.

sopa: soup.

tarta: cake.

ternera: beef.

tortilla española: a potato omelette.

turrón: a nougat or toffee-like sweet. The harder, white *turrón* is like nougat with almonds.

area as well. Because of the enormous range of clientele to which these restaurants cater—students, tourists, blue-collar workers, yuppies, recent immigrants, and businessmen—great food comes for fairly inexpensive prices.

▨ Pla dels Angels, C. Ferlandina, 23 (☎93 443 31 03). M: Universitat, L1/2/3. Directly in front of the MACBA (see **Sights & Museums,** p. 77). The funky decor of this colorful, inexpensive eatery is fitting for its proximity to the contemporary art museum. Indulge in *gnocchi* with curry sauce and raisins (€3.20) or leg of duck in asparagus and caramelized cava sauce (€5.75). Pastas €3.20, entrees €5.55-5.75. Open M-Th 1-4pm and 9-11:30pm, F-Sa 9pm-midnight. Cash Only. ❷

▨ Bar Ra, Pl. de la Garduña (☎93 301 41 63, reservations 61 595 98 72). M: Liceu, L3, just behind Las Ramblas's Boqueria market. Everything about Ra exudes cool, from its erotic Hindu mural to the individually painted tablecloths to the waiters themselves. The artfully prepared international offerings use fresh ingredients from the nearby Boqueria market. Try the excellent vegetarian lasagna (€7.50) and duck magret with mango sauce (€9.50), or come for Sunday brunch in the sun. Entrees €6.50-13. Open M-Sa 9am-midnight. Su brunch noon-6pm. Dinner by reservation only. AmEx/MC/V. ❷

Buenas Migas, Pl. Bonsuccés, 6 (☎93 318 37 08). M: Catalunya, L1/3, off Las Ramblas. This *focacceria* on the Pl. Bonsuccés offers one of the neighborhood's most pleasant outdoor eating experiences. Enjoy coffee or tea (€1-1.30) at one of the shaded outside tables, or stay in the rustic-feeling interior with your *focaccia* (thick Italian bread; €2-4) topped with everything from vegetables to bacon and brie. The quiches (€4) and homemade cakes (€3) are hearty and delicious. Open Su-W 10am-10pm, Th-Sa 10am-midnight. Cash only. ❶

DosTrece, C. Carme 40, (☎93 301 73 06; www.dostrece.net). From M: Catalunya, L1/3, take a right off C. Carme. This restaurant, quiet during the day, turns into one of the hottest spots to eat at night. Crowds of young locals dine in the fine decor of stained glass and candles, while listening to live music (jazz Tu, flamenco W, hip-hop Th, soul F, and house Sa). Try one of the bar's numerous fruity cocktails out on the terrace (€6-7). Lunch menú €9. Appetizers €5.80-7. Entrees €7.50-15. Open M-Sa 1:30-4pm and 9-midnight. Terrace open until 3am. AmEx/MC/V. ❸

Restaurante Can Lluís, C. Cera, 49 (☎93 441 11 87). M: Sant Antoni, L2. From the Metro, head down Ronda S. Pau and take the 2nd left on C. Cera. For over 100 years, Can Lluís has been a defining force in Barcelona's cuisine. Eschewing trendiness, the menu is filled with traditional Catalan favorites prepared home-style and always bursting with flavor, including succulent lamb ribs (€9.80), grilled squid (€10), and fresh-grilled asparagus (€5.40). Lunch menú €7. Dinner menús (€20-35) include wine. Entrees €6-20. Open M-Sa 1:30-4pm and 8:30-11:30pm. V. ❸

Silenus, C. Angels, 8 (☎93 302 26 80). From M: Catalunya, L1/3, a right off C. Carme. As much art gallery as restaurant, the softly elegant Silenus is the place for good meals and quiet conversation. The menu, unforgettably titled "A Short Treatise on the Passions of Flavors," includes duck and tuna (€12-20), as well as the exotic *filete de kangoo* in raspberry sauce: yep, kangaroo (€16.20). Lunch menú changes daily (€6-14). Open M-Th 11am-11:30pm, F 11am-midnight, Sa 1pm-midnight. AmEx/MC/V. ❹

Mamacafé, C. Doctor Dou, 10 (☎93 301 29 40), M: Catalunya, L1/3, a right off C. Pintor Fortuny. A great place to find healthy, fresh vegetarian options with an exotic twist. The ambience is casual without being shabby, and artsy without being pretentious. Lunch menú €8. Try the green noodles with tuna and Chinese onions (€12). Open M-Sa 1pm-1am. MC/V. ❷

Carmelitas, C. Carme, 42 (☎93 412 46 84), From M: Catalunya, L1/3, right on C. Carme. Sunshine brightens the simple and stylish interior of this new, airy restaurant during the day; a red light illuminates it at night. For lunch, entrees of fresh fish straight from the nearby Boqueria market (rotating appetizers and entrees €4-14). At night, try the excellent *calamares a la plancha* (€8.50). Vegetarian options. Reservations recommended Th-Sa. Open daily 1:30-4pm; Su-W 9pm-midnight; Th-Sa 9pm-1am. AmEx/MC/V. ❸

L'Hortet, C. del Pintor Fortuny, 32 (☎93 317 61 89). M: Catalunya, L1/3. Off Las Ramblas. Gorgeous landscape paintings complement freshly prepared vegetarian options. Lunch menú €7.75, dinner menú €10. Light entrees feature pastas, pizzas, and couscous. Open daily 1:15-4pm and 8:30-11pm. Cash only. ❷

Bar Restaurante Los Toreros, C. d'En Xuclá, 3-5 (☎93 318 23 25). M: Catalunya. L1/3. Walk down Las Ramblas and turn right on C. Carme; C. d'En Xuclá will be the first street on your right. Decorated with a bull's head and bullfighting pictures, the popular Los Toreros specializes in group meals—come with friends and order from one of the many *menús para grupos,* which feed at least 6 people (€14-21 per person). The tasty menú (€7.50), paellas (€9-11) and tapas (€2-8.25) are favorites among locals. Open daily 1pm-midnight. Cash only. ❷

Restaurante Biocenter, C. del Pintor Fortuny, 25 (☎93 301 45 83). From M: Catalunya, L1/3, right on C. del Pintor Fortuny. Wholesome vegetarian foods served under the soothing glow of the restaurant's large orange lamps. The lunch menú comes with an all-you-can-eat buffet option (M-F €7.50, Sa €10.50). Open M-Sa 1-5pm. Cash only. ❷

Thai Garden

Shalimar, C. Carme, 71 (☎93 329 34 96). From M: Catalunya, L1/3, right on C. Carme. To add some spice, look to the tasty and relatively inexpensive Pakistani and Indian favorites offered at this small restaurant. Chicken, lamb, and seafood curries €6.50-9. Chicken tandoori €6.50. Open W-M 1-4pm and 8-11:30pm, Tu 8-11:30pm. MC/V. ❷

Bar Restaurante Romesco, C. Sant Pau, 28 (☎93 318 93 81). M: Liceu, L3. Turn onto C. Sant Pau from Las Ramblas. Take the 1st right; Romesco is immediately on the left. This small diner serves simple, dirt-cheap food. *Frijoles negros* (black beans; €4) and *crema catalana* (€2) are their specialties. Fries are among the best in Barcelona. Fish, chicken, and meat dishes €3-6. Open M-Sa 1pm-midnight. Cash only. ❶

Platter of Tapas

L'EIXAMPLE

With sidewalk cafes serving everything from multi-ethnic to super traditional, wandering in l'Eixample can easily induce rumbling tummies, especially during a long day of shopping. These upper neighborhoods are full of good places to spend a long dinner (especially l'Eixample Esquerra), but they are spread out widely and interspersed with plenty of nondescript corner bars serving the endless apartment buildings in the area. If you want to sample one of l'Eixample's trendy, high-quality restaurants, pick one ahead of time and walk with blinders on past all the tempting but, in truth, carbon-copied eateries. Expect to make reservations on weekends and be prepared to pay well for the food and atmosphere.

see map pp. 340-341

Sangría at ba-ba-reeba

WHAT A DRAG

It's lavishly furnished with faux leopard fur and palm trees, but **Café Miranda** has more to please the eye than merely a flashy decor. Ladies and gentlemen, Café Miranda presents, for your dining enjoyment, male and female drag performers. As a diner here, you'll be serenaded by these talented men and women at regular half-hour intervals from 10:30pm until close.

On a less important note: the seasonal menu has a seafood focus and includes Mediterranean delicacies like marinated calamari salad in black vinegar and spring rolls stuffed with goat cheese and spinach. The friendly, and ultra-trendy waitstaff serve a mixed crowd. Miranda is an extremely popular place; reservations are recommended during the week and are absolutely necessary on the weekends. Don't leave without taking a peek at the hotpink and electric-blue (gender designated) bathrooms.

C. Casanova, 30 (☎93 453 52 49; cafemir-anda@hotmail.com). M: Universitat, L1/2, in l'Eixample. Three-course menú €20; entrees €5-20. Wine from €6 per bottle. Open daily 9pm-1am. MC/V. ❹

AROUND PG. DE GRÀCIA

Pg. de Gràcia is lined with nearly as many tapas bars and cafes as shops and Modernist structures. Most are tourist-oriented, have sidewalk tables, and are on the expensive side, especially to eat outside (many charge up to 15% extra for this privilege). Perhaps the best way to find the quality food at low prices during the day is to follow those in the know: the businessmen and women who day-in and day-out eat their lunches here and who know the best values. On the weekends this area is also a good choice for late-night food, as many places stay open until 2am.

❖ **Thai Gardens,** C. Diputació, 273 (☎93 487 98 98). M: Catalunya, L1/3/5. Extravagant decor, complete with a wooden bridge entrance, lush greenery, and colorful silk pillows give Thai Gardens the aroma of *amor* (along with the sweetly spiced incense). Call ahead to reserve a traditional *kantok* table (cushions on the ground) for you and a date. Vegetarian options. Pad thai €6.50, entrees €11-14.20. Weekday lunch menú €11; dinner menú €25. Open Su-Th 1-4pm and 8pm-midnight, F-Sa 1:30-4pm and 8pm-1am. Wheelchair accessible. ❸

Txapela (Euskal Taberna), Pg. de Gràcia, 8-10 (☎93 412 02 89). M: Catalunya, L1/3/5. This Basque restaurant serves unique tapas: delicate combinations of meats, cheeses, fish, and sauces. The placemats have pictures with the name and description of each tapa, which you order by number. Be forewarned: you will get that exact, single tapa, and nothing more. But it will be delicious. Tapas €1.30-2. Open M-Th 8am-1:30am, F-Su 10am-2am. Wheelchair accessible. ❷

Hostal de Rita, C. Aragó, 279 (☎93 487 23 76). M: Pg. de Gràcia, L2/3/4. To the right of Pg. de Gràcia, coming from Pl. de Catalunya. Lines of up to 20 locals waiting to eat lunch here are not uncommon; the food is just as tasty and elegant as it is cheap. A fish- and chicken-based menu section is dedicated to low-calorie dishes. Weekday lunch menú €7. Entrees €4-9.50. Open daily 1-4:30pm and 8:30-11:30pm. Wheelchair accessible. AmEx/MC/V. ❷

Elj apo nes, Passatge de la Concepcio, 2 (☎93 487 25 92). M: Pg. de Gràcia, L2/3/4. Just off of Pg. de Gràcia. Serving all the Japanese cooking you could want: from tempura to skewers and noodles to sushi. The yummy food, the reasonable bill, and the streamlined, stylish red interior will leave you feeling as chic as the rest of Barcelona. Entrees €2.65-12, sushi plate €16.50. Open Su-W 1:30-4pm and 8:30pm-midnight, Th-Sa 1:30-4pm and 8:30pm-1am. Wheelchair accessible. AmEx/MC/V. ❸

52, Valldonzella, 52. M: Universitat, L1/2. Take Ronda Sant Antoni away from Pl. Universitat and take the second left onto Valldonzella. Learn directly from the students: eat at this funky new-age eatery with cool, minimalist lighting and the newest healthy-Asian-Mexican-Catalan fusion concoctions you never imagined. The ambiance is young and creative and the price is right. Nibble away. Bocadillos €3.65, entrees €2.50-6.50. Open M-W 5pm-1am, Th-Sa 8pm-1am. Wheelchair accessible. Cash only. ❷

Madrid-Barcelona (Pa Amb Tomàquet), C. Aragó, 282 (☎93 215 70 27). M: Pg. de Gràcia, L2/3/4. On the corner with Pg. de Gràcia. Named for the railroad line that used to run here, this classy but cheap lunchtime hotspot attracts hordes of native businessmen and shoppers. Waiters ladle soup and rice at your table, straight from the stove, and the classic Catalan dishes are worthwhile. Entrees €4-14.10. Open M-Sa 1-4pm and 8:30pm-midnight. Wheelchair accessible. AmEx/MC/V. ❷

ba-ba-reeba, Pg. de Gràcia, 28 (☎93 301 43 02). M: Pg. de Gràcia, L2/3/4. One of the most obvious spots on the Passeig, the tapas here—bigger and glossier than usual—have definitely been Americanized, but if size is what you want, they taste pretty good, especially the *pa amb tomaquet*. Entrees €3.50-15. Tapas €2.30-12.50. Sidewalk seating 15% extra. Take-out available. Open M-Th 7:30am-1:30am, F 7:30am-2am, Sa 8am-2am, Su 8am-1:30am. Wheelchair accessible. AmEx/MC/V. ❷

Café Torino, Pg. de Gràcia, 59 (☎93 487 71 75). M: Pg. de Gràcia, L2/3/4. Originally designed by the likes of Gaudí, Puig i Cadafalch, and Falqués as a spot for sampling vermouth, at that time a drink novelty, this popular Modernist coffee spot has ceilings that seem to ooze and melt at the sides. A veritable landmark, Torino celebrated its 100th anniversary in 2002. The outdoor tables are blissfully cool and shaded in the morning. Coffee and tea €1-2.15. Hot cocoa €2. Open Su-Th 8am-10:30pm, F-Sa 9am-1am. Wheelchair accessible. Cash only. ❶

Mauri, Rambla de Catalunya, 102 (☎93 215 10 20). M: Diagonal, L3/5. This *pastisseria* (pastry and sweet shop) has been turning out delicate sweets, mouth-watering bonbons, and gourmet sandwiches since 1929. Come to buy delectable gifts, to have lunch in the delicatessen-style restaurant (lunch menú €10), or simply to admire the cake decorations and drool. A second location across the street, at no. 103, specializes in candy and gift baskets (☎93 215 81 46). Open M-F 8am-9pm, Sa 9am-9pm, Su and holidays 9am-3pm. ❶

L'EIXAMPLE DRETA

🗷 **Comme-Bio,** Av. Gran Via, 603 (☎93 301 03 76; www.commebio.es), on the corner of Gran Via and Rambla de Catalunya. M: Catalunya, L1/3, or Universitat, L1/2. If you're starting to miss dishes with that

Bakery

Sampling Tapas

Gazpacho at La Provenca

CATALAN CUISINE

Pa amb tomaquet/Pan con tomate: toasted bread served with tomato and garlic. Sometimes comes prepared, but more authentic places let you do it yourself. Cut the tomato in half and rub it generously over the toast. Then cut the garlic in half and rub it on the toast. Easy on the garlic, or you'll be reeking of it for days to come.

Crema catalana: The definitive Catalan dessert. A light custard with a caramelized top, very similar to *crème brulée*. So popular that ice cream stores sell *crema catalana* ice cream and Dunkin' Donuts offers a *crema catalana*-filled donut. Especially delicious is the *crema catalana* liqueur, with the consistency of Kahlua or Bailey's and a nutmeg flavor similar to egg nog.

Espinacs a la catalana: spinach sautéed with pine nuts, raisins, and sometimes anchovies.

Romesco de peix: a seafood medley in a *romesco* sauce of tomatoes, garlic, peppers, and nuts.

Fideus: like a *paella*, but prepared with thin noodles instead of rice.

Esqueixada: a shredded cod, olive, vinegar, tomato, bean, and red pepper salad.

Mel i Mató: a dessert of honey and curd cheese.

personal touch, or you're getting tired of meat, come here for fresh salad, hummus, tofu, yogurt, or juice. Restaurant, take-out, and small grocery store all in one. Pasta, rice, and veggie pizzas around €9; salads €6-8. Open daily 9am-11:30pm; dinner service starts at 8pm. Another **branch** a few blocks away, Via Laietana, 28 (☎93 319 89 68). ❷

🔲 **Laie Llibreria Café,** C. Pau Claris, 85 (☎93 302 63 10; www.laie.es). M: Urquinaona, L1/4. An ultra-cool lunch spot for more than just bookworms. This urban oasis offers a cheap, fresh, and plentiful all-you-can-eat Catalan-style buffet lunch (€8.25) in an open, bamboo-draped lunch room that's well lit via the glass ceiling. Grab a praline cappuccino (€2.30) at the bar on the way out. Vegetarian options. Internet access €1 per 15min. Open M-F 9am-1am, Sa 10am-1am. AmEx/MC/V. ❷

Mandalay Café, C. Provença, 330 (☎93 458 60 17; www.mandalaycafe.net), between C. Roger de Llúria and C. Bruc. M: Verdaguer, L4/5. Exotic pan-Asian cuisine, including gourmet dim sum, Vietnamese noodles, seared fish, delicate meat, and elegant salads, served in a room so draped in color and sultanesque luxury (you can eat on a bed!) it's been featured in books on interior decorating. F-Sa night trapeze artist around 11pm; variable extra cover charge for show (around €2.50). Entrees €9-13. English-speaking host. Open Tu-Sa 8:30pm-midnight. Wheelchair accessible. AmEx/MC/V. ❸

Wok & Bol, C. Diputació, 294 (☎ 93 302 76 75), between C. Roger de Llúria and C. Bruc. M: Girona, L4. An elegantly designed, stand-out Chinese restaurant serving dim sum (€4.50-6.60 per small dish), whole Peking ducks (€16.20 per person), and Chinese fondue (€18), in addition to more common dishes like chow mein and veggie stir-fry (€5). Reservations recommended. Open M-F 1:30-3:30pm and 9:15-11:30pm, Sa 2-11:30pm. ❸

La Muscleria, C. Mallorca, 290 (☎93 458 98 44; www.accua.com/musleria), on the corner with C. Bruc. M: Verdaguer, L4/5. Mussels of every size, shape, and flavor, culled from Catalunya, France, Galicia, and The Netherlands, and served in a bustling basement. Main plates begin at €7.75 and come with fries. Salads €5.25-5.75, *cocas* (like pizzas) €6-6.25. Make reservations F-Sa. Open M-Th 1-4pm and 8:30pm-midnight, F-Sa 1-4pm and 8:30pm-1am. No Sa lunch July-Aug. Wheelchair accessible. MC/V. ❷

Can Cargol, C. València, 324 (☎93 458 96 31), on the corner with C. Bruc. M: Girona, L4. Extremely popular—and thus noisy—Catalan restaurant with make-your-own *pan con tomate* and lots of snail options. Snails €7.25. Fish and meat dishes €4-5.75, some €10-14.25. Make reservations on weekends. Open 1:30-4pm and 8:30pm-midnight. ❷

El Rodizio Grill, C. Consell de Cent, 403 (☎93 265 51 12), right next to M: Girona, L4. All-you-can-eat Brazilian and Mediterranean buffet *a la churrascaria:* grilled shish kebab-style meats featuring chicken, salmon, and cod. Cold dishes include sushi, pasta, and salads. Lunch €9, dinner €13.50. Includes 1 drink and coffee. Rich and gooey desserts €2.60. Open M-Th 1-4pm and 9pm-midnight, F-Sa 1-4pm and 9pm-1am, Su 1-4pm. ❷

A-Tipic, C. Bruc, 79 (☎93 215 51 06), between C. Aragó and C. Consell de Cent. M: Girona, L4. A lunchtime gem for vegetarians. A simple buffet (€8) that tastes more like home than like a cafeteria, served in a relaxing blue-and-yellow dining room. Excellent choice of salad, rice, pasta, and veggie calzones. Open Sept.-July M-F 1-4pm. MC/V. ❷

Cullera de Boix, C. Ronda de St. Pere, 24 (☎93 268 13 36), between C. Bruc and Pl. Urquinaona. M: Urquinaona, L1/4. With metal chairs, light wood tables, and sleek hanging lamps, this upscale restaurant could easily be in Manhattan. Specializes in rice (€6-10). Entrees €5-12, lunch menú €9. Weekend reservations recommended. Open daily 7:30am-midnight. Wheelchair accessible. AmEx/MC/V. ❷

Churros con Chocolate

Campechano, C. València, 286 (☎/fax 93 215 62 33), just to the right of Pg. de Gràcia when you're coming from Pl. de Catalunya. M: Catalunya, L1/3. This restaurant goes all out to recreate the atmosphere of a 1940s *merendero* (BBQ/picnic area) on the Barcelona mountainside, from a few live trees and a painted forest wall to train stop signs marking your progress "toward the mountain." Picnic tables make it perfect for large groups. Choose your favorite meat or poultry from their huge list and they'll grill it; french fries, salad, and a few other dishes serve as sides. Menú €7, salads €1.50-2, grilled entrees €5-14.50. Open daily 1:30-4pm and 8:30-midnight. Su-M open in the afternoon only. ❷

Horse Meat

L'EIXAMPLE ESQUERRA

▨ **El Racó d'en Baltá,** C. Aribau, 125 (☎93 453 10 44), at the intersection with C. Rosselló. M: Diagonal, L3/5. This eccentric restaurant features an incredibly creative and flavorful Mediterranean-style menu, which they update 3 times per year to keep it interesting. Dishes inspired by ingredients from all over the world, like the mouth-watering duck breast with mustard, forest fruits sauce, and pear wine (€13), and the unique cold soup of white chocolate sauce and coconut mousse (€3). F-Sa nights the funky top floor is opened up for your dining pleasure. Fish and meat entrees €11.50-17. Bottles of wine and cava €4-16. Open Su 9-10:45pm, Tu-Sa 1-3:30pm and 9-10:45pm, F-Sa until 11pm. Wheelchair accessible. AmEx/D/MC/V. ❹

Granizado

the BIG $plurge

Cooking with the Hottest Chef

Agustin Comobella is one of the hottest chefs in Barcelona—not only is he a stud in the kitchen, he is a stud period. And now you can enjoy both aspects of Comobella's hotness at once: learn how to cook with him.

One of the best things about Barcelona is the food. Postcards and pictures won't do when it comes to taste. Head to **Arrel del Born** where Comobella serves unbelievable seafood *and* teaches you how to make it. After cooking for the rich and famous in Miami, Comobella is now settled in a small space of the old quarter of El Born. He attracts crowds of seafood lovers with seafood as fresh as it gets since his uncle catches fish for the restaurant every morning.

The classes are small (4 people on average), and will turn even the most careless cook into a master of crustacean cuisine. The best part of the lesson comes in the end, when you sit down for a meal served with fine local wine and a taste of how you are soon to impress your own dinner-party guests.

Fusina 5. ☎ *93 319 92 99; www.arreldelborn.com. Lesson and meal: €175 per person.*

El Criollo, C. Aribau, 85 (☎93 454 23 28). M: Hospital Clìnic, L5. A Peruvian oasis in l'Eixample. Choose from hearty dishes like *ají de gallina*—shredded chicken in a thick, spicy nut sauce (€7). Weekday lunch menú €7.50. Entrees €5.70-9. Open M 9pm-midnight, Tu-Sa 1-4pm and 9pm-midnight. Wheelchair accessible. AmEx/MC/V. ❷

Restaurante Terrani, C. Londres, 89 (☎93 321 15 22). M: Hospital Clìnic, L5. Take the Villarroel exit, walk 3 blocks up Villarroel, and turn right on Londres; it's 1½ blocks down on your left. Asian-styled wooden frames separate tables from each other, and a light, jazzy mix complements the chef's delicious takes on Catalan cuisine (€10-13). Lunch menú €12, dinner menú €20 and up. Reservations suggested for dinner. Open daily 1-4pm and 9pm-midnight. Wheelchair accessible. AmEx/D/MC/V. ❹

Ginza, C. Provença, 205 (☎93 451 71 93), between Balmes and Enric Granados. M: Diagonal, L3. Sleek, bamboo- and wood-filled restaurant serves delectable but affordable Japanese food. Eat in or take out. Sushi €5-13.25. Weekday four-course lunch menú €7.20. Dinner menú M-Th €9.35, F-Su €11. Open M-Sa 1-4pm and 8pm-midnight, Su 1-4pm. Wheelchair accessible. D/MC/V. ❸

La Provença, C. Provença, 242 (☎93 323 23 67; www.laprovenza.com). M: Diagonal, L3. Enter through a classically designed hall with wood floors and dim lamps, into a quiet banquet room with chandeliers and pastel tablecloths. Dishes have a slight Mediterranean influence. Specialties include carpaccio, fresh fish, and vegetables. Entrees €6-11. Dress well, this place is a bit formal. Reservations recommended, especially on weekends. Open daily 1:30-3:30pm and 9pm-11:30pm. AmEx/D/MC/V. ❹

El Raconet, C. Enrique Granados, 95 (☎93 218 10 57). M: Diagonal, L3. Family-run corner eatery with sidewalk tables. Plenty of Catalan mainstays, including a wide selection of *bacalao* (cod), and vegetarian options. Small offering of bagels topped with cheeses or meats (€5.10), in addition to bocadillos (starting at €2.30). Meat and fish entrees €7.50-14. M-F 7am-10pm, Sa 8am-2am. AmEx/MC/V. ❷

dahabi, Pl. Universitat, 1 (☎93 451 43 39). M: Universitat, L1. A trendy spiritual aura hangs amidst the waiters in long black robes, the gold crushed-velvet benches, and the elegantly presented Syrian-Lebanese cuisine. Huge 3-course sampler comes with dessert (starting at €19 per person). Vegetarian options. Entrees €8.50-15. Open M-Th 1pm-1am, F-Sa 1pm-1:30am. AmEx/MC/V. ❸

La Flauta, C. Aribau, 23 (☎93 323 70 38). M: Pg. de Gràcia, L2/3/4. The house specialties are hot or cold *flautas*—skinny, crusty bread sandwiches stuffed with veggies, cheeses, and meats (half €2.50-6, whole €3-8). Plenty of vegetarian options and a large selection of *tapas del día*. Weekday lunch menú €9. Dishes €3-15. Open M-F 7am-12:30am, Sa 7am-1am, Su noon-1am. MC/V. **Branch** at C. Balmes, 164-166 (☎93 415 51 86). ❷

Cerveceria Catalana, C. Mallorca, 236 (☎93 216 03 63). M: Pg. de Gràcia, L2/3/4. This is basically your all-in-one Catalan bar: they've got *flautas* (€3-7), tapas (€3-12), seafood, salads, burgers, and beers (€2). Cheap, noisy, friendly; you'll feel as at home as the locals who fill this place. Open daily 7:30am-1:30am. Wheelchair accessible. AmEx/MC/V. ❶

Frankfurt D'Or, Rambla de Catalunya, 44 (☎93 215 64 39). M: Pg. de Gràcia, L2/3/4. Since 1974, this little corner spot with prime people-watching outdoor seating has been the perfect, cheap break from a hard day of shopping. Served straight off the grill and into your tummy. Frankfurters €1.80, bratwurst €2.10, and hamburgers €2.25. Open 10:30am-1am. Wheelchair accessible. AmEx/MC/V. ❶

Brains

POBLE NOU & PORT OLÍMPIC

Cheap food is readily available in Poble Nou, although you'll stick out as a tourist if you eat in the neighborhood watering holes. After a long day at the beach, wander inland through Poble Nou and you'll find endless out-

see map p. 347

door bars and restaurants serving Catalan cuisine, bocadillos, and seafood, especially along La Rambla de Poble Nou, where families and friends gather later in the evening for a few drinks.

Juicy Jones

Food in the Port Olímpic area, however, is not cheap, even in the fast-food restaurants that are starting to move in. For a budget day at the beach or for walking the Olympic parks, pack a picnic lunch from one of the **supermarkets** listed on p. 312 and bring it with you. Or do as locals often do and buy a *flauta* or bocadillo at a cheaper location and snack on it at the beach. If you want to eat in the port itself, there are more than 20 restaurants, mostly seafood-based, to choose from. In most, a full three-course dinner meal will cost €30-50. The following listings are standouts among the waterfront restaurants, which are always best in good weather, when you can sit outside and enjoy the seaside view.

Agua, Pg. Marítim de la Barceloneta, 30 (☎93 225 12 72; www.grupotragaluz.com), the farthest establishment to the right of the copper fish. This

Interesting Seafood

131

Waste with taste

Shit happens. Indeed, we are all too familiar with the unfortunate and unique sensation of freeing our foot from the grips of a mound of feces. Rather than dreading the experience, however, Catalans have adopted a somewhat different attitude. They have embraced the omnipresence of poop, deciding to assign luck and religious merit to the fruits of defecation. Around Christmas, things get even more "fecetious:" *Caganers,* or "shitters," are permanent fixtures in nativity scenes: next to Mary, the Three Kings, and baby Jesus, a little ceramic guy watches with his little ceramic business underneath. The opposite of offensive, the *caganer* is a Catalan symbol of fertility. During the Christmas season pastry shops also decorate their windows with edible feces called *tifas.* Made from marzipan, these sweets dangle in bakery displays, tempting the appetites of Catalan children and adults alike.

The shitstorm continues when Catalan families place the *Caga Tío,* or "Shitting Log," under the Christmas tree. Covered with a blanket, the box contains sweets and gifts hidden inside. Children force the *Caga Tío* to give up its treasure when they beat the shit out of it (pun intended) with a stick. The ritual begins with the Catalan chant: "Shit log shit! Sweets and nougat, and if you don't shit good, I'll bash you with my stick!" Putting the Mexican piñata to shame, the beating of the *Caga Tío* is undoubtedly the shittiest religious practice ever.

upscale restaurant, another member of the Grupo Tragaluz restaurant empire, and which appeared in *Town and Country* in 2002 and attracts large numbers of tourists, trendy Barcelonese, and GQ-business-types. Don't be scared off by the fancy Art Deco interior; the prices are actually quite reasonable. Stare at the Picasso wannabes that dot the walls as you enjoy Agua's specialties: delicate seafood and rice dishes. Vegetarian options. Getting a table on the terrace is difficult, but worth the trouble. Tapas €1.50-14, starters €4.50-7.50, pastas €6.50-8.50, entrees €5.50-27. Wheelchair accessible. Open daily 1:30-4pm and 8:30pm-midnight. Reservations recommended. AmEx/MC/V. ❸

La Oca Mar (☎ 93 225 01 00; www.restaurantelaoca.com), on Platja Nova Marbella. A 20min. walk up the beach from the Port Olímpic (keeping the water on your right), next to the Platja Mar Bella. A hike without a car, but it may be unusual enough to be worth it: the entire restaurant is built like a large ship, with a long "bow" (terrace) extending far into the ocean for sunset-gazing. Best for large groups since small parties are seated inside, away from windows with the panoramic views. Specializes in seafood. Entrees €5-30. Open daily 1pm-1am. Wheelchair accessible. AmEx/MC/V. ❸

BARCELONETA & PORT VELL

see map p. 348

Restaurants tend to group around two central areas: in the vicinities of the Palau de Mar and around Maremàgnum. The **Port Vell** side of the Palau de Mar, or "Palace of the Sea," (on Port Vell at the far end of Pg. Colom) houses several fancy harborside restaurants, where well-dressed waiters serve lunch to tourists in baseball caps and flip-flops. (Dinners, however, are considerably more formal.) **Maremàgnum,** Barcelona's glitzy leisure center, has a number of unsurprisingly seafood- and tourist-oriented restaurants. Fast food joints, ice-cream shops and pricey tapas places are in abundant supply. One somewhat exceptional (though slightly indulgent) choice is **Mandongo** ❸, on the second floor. The decor evokes a beach-side bungalow, and the cuisine is a fusion of Asian and Mediterranean. Dishes include an outstanding salmon in banana leaves (€12), mouth-watering steaks (€11-25), and a specialty *paella* (€12.20). The sushi (€9), however, leaves a bit to be desired. (☎ 93 225 81 43. Open M-F 1-4pm and 8pm-midnight, Sa-Su 1pm-midnight. AmEx/MC/V.)

Given **Barceloneta's** proximity to the more popular beaches, it's only fitting that it offers some of the better seafood cuisine of the city. Moreover, the vast majority of the restaurants in the area serve the same quality fish as the more upscale Waterfront and Port Olímpic areas, but for lower prices. The only thing as abundant as seafood in Barceloneta is ice cream. You can't walk more than a hundred feet down Pg. Joan de Borbó without seeing a street stand or gelatería.

Bite to Eat in the Sun

Zahara, Pg. Joan de Borbó, 69 (☎93 221 37 65; www.zahara.com). Toward the end of Joan de Borbó, on the left. This hip cocktail bar is a diamond in the rough of mainstream Barceloneta cafes. The extensive drink menu makes use of color-codes and icons to inform on the content and the potency of each cocktail. Tasty salads €8-9, sandwiches €4-5, cocktails €6-9, beer €2.50. Open daily 10am-3am. MC/V. ❷

La Mar Salada, Pg. Joan de Borbó, 58 (☎93 221 21 27). M: Barceloneta, L4. Toward the end of Joan de Borbó on the left, near the beach. The friendly staff makes this bright and open restaurant all the more pleasant. Penny pinchers should try the mussels (€7.50), while bigger spenders can opt for the huge 2-person shellfish platter, which includes a Lobster Velvet crab, oysters, clams, small Norwegian lobsters, and large prawns (€46). Seating for large groups available upstairs. Menú €8. Open Su-M and W-Sa 1-4pm and 8pm-midnight. AmEx/MC/V. ❸

Els Quatre Gats

Café L'Imma, Pg. Joan de Borbó, 30 (☎93 221 40 03). M: Barceloneta, L4. This portside restaurant, nestled among the many eateries catering to tourists, separates itself from the rest with its wide selection of fresh fish. Chill under an umbrella outside, or on hot summer days enjoy the well air-conditioned interior. Menú €9, fish dishes €10.50-26, meat dishes €5.90-14.60. Open daily noon-4:30pm and 8pm-midnight. AmEx/MC/V. ❸

La Taverna d'en Pep, C. de La Manquista, 8 (☎93 331 89 12). M: Barceloneta, L4. If you're looking to get away from the crowds head a block inland to this friendly restaurant. Enjoy the extensive wine list, in addition to the excellent meat and seafood options. Definitely worth the few extra euros. Menú €9, sizable fish and meat dishes €8-16. Open M-Sa 1-3:30pm and 9-11:30pm for meals, 9pm-midnight for drinks and appetizers. ❸

Fratello, Pg. Joan de Borbó, 15 (☎93 221 48 39). M: Barceloneta, L4. One of the better gelato joints, Fratello offers dozens of fresh flavors and generous portions. The tastefully decorated interior includes a bar and widescreen television with DVD. Gelato €1.50-3. Open Su 9am-1am, M-Sa 11am-1am. AmEx/MC/V. ❶

Granizado

CAVA

You see it on every wine list, and everyone says it is Champagne. But then you also notice Champagne on the menu—what's the deal? Cava is Catalunya's sparkling white wine created through the same method as Champagne.

Cava is the Catalan word for cellar, referring to the underground rooms in which the wine is aged. Its history begins in the mid-1800s, when local families who enjoyed Champagne decided to begin producing their own version with local grapes. Josep Raventós produced the first 3000 bottles in 1872 in the Sant Sadurni d'Anoia region in Catalunya. Today, around 200 million bottles are exported yearly.

The *methode traditionelle champagnois* is different from other wine-making techniques because of a second fermentation. The first fermentation comes after the grape pressing, then the different grape varieties are blended in different proportions to create the "cuvée." This mixture is then sealed with yeast and sugar to ferment again, this time for at least 9 months. The bottles are kept on their sides until maturity, when they are racked neck down to gather the sediment, which is released before packaging, corking, and shipping.

MONTJUÏC

Food options are not as plentiful in Montjuïc as in the rest of the city. The Fundació Miró, MNAC, Castell de Montjuïc, and Teatre Grec all have pleasant cafes, but to find more than drinks and sand- see map p. 346 wiches, enter the depths of Poble Espanyol, where menús including food from all over Spain run €10-15 or try one of the listings below. Some restaurants, bars, and grocery stores also line **Av. Parallel** in Poble Sec.

La Font de Prades, (☎93 426 75 19) at the Plaça de la Font in Poble Espanyol. M: Espanya, L1/3. Set back in a quiet, less-trafficked area of Poble Espanyol, is this surprisingly elegant restaurant. Slightly more tranquil than neighboring restaurants. Menú €13. Open Tu-Sa 1-4pm. ❸

La Pérgola, (☎93 325 20 08) at the corner of Av. Reina María Cristina and Av. del Marques de Comillas. M: Espanya, L1/3. 2 different restaurants at the same location. One offers a tasty buffet-style menú (€10) popular with both international businessmen and tourists. Open daily 9:30am-9pm. Kitchen closes at 4pm. After 4pm, drinks only. Closed M-Tu the first 2 weeks of Aug. The other offers a classic full-service dining room in which the tuxedoed staff will serve you such carefully prepared favorites as Perigord duck marinated in ginger (€13). Menú €42. Open daily 1-4pm. Closed Aug. ❸

Restaurante Bar Marcelino, (☎93 441 10 79) on Av. Miramar outside the funicular station. Refresh yourself at the bar or enjoy a meal from the selection of combination plates, sandwiches, and pizzas (around €6) on the outdoor patio. Open Su-W and F-Sa 8am-9:30pm. ❷

ZONA ALTA

GRÀCIA

Without a doubt, Gràcia is the best place in Barcelona to find authentic cuisine from anywhere around the globe. Traditional markets see map p. 342-345 (see **Sights and Museums,** p. 104) and Catalan menus abound, but the side streets of Gràcia are really the place to find varied and reasonably priced vegetarian cuisine (yes, Spain does have vegetables). Tapas bars dominate Pl. del Sol and Pl. Virreina.

OvUm, C. Encarnacio, 56. M: Joanic, L4. Follow C. Escorial for 2 blocks and turn left on C. Encarnacio. True to its name, this charming low-lit restaurant features egg specialties and vegetarian options with a Catalan twist. Meat lovers won't be disappointed by the Nius (€5), round bread filled with ham, pork, and egg and cooked in an oven. Try the sweet omelette (€4) for dessert. Reservations recommended F-Sa. Open Su and Tu-Sa noon-1pm and 8:30-midnight. Closed 1st week of Aug. AmEx/MC/V. ❷

La Gavina, C. Ros de Olano, 17 (☎93 415 74 50). M: Fontana, L3. Walk down C. Gran de Gràcia and turn left on C. Ros de Olano. Enjoy delicious Italian food in this unassuming pizzeria, complete with a life-size patron saint and confessional candles. Pizzas serving several people €7.50-10; try the *Catalana*—tomato, mozzarella, chorizo sausage, garlic, and artichokes (€16). Open Su and Tu-Th 6pm-1am, F-Sa 6pm-2am. Wheelchair accessible. ❸

Ice Cream for the Escalator

Restaurant Illa de Gràcia, C. Sant Domenec, 19 (☎93 238 02 29). M: Diagonal, L3/5. Follow Gran de Gràcia for 5 blocks and make a right onto C. Sant Domenec. Choose from a wide variety of cheap vegetarian options in this stylish restaurant full of young and beautiful people. Try the *Crep Illa de Gràcia*, a crêpe filled with mushrooms and peppers. Delicious homemade desserts and an excellent selection of fresh juices. Salads €3.50-4.50. Entrees €2.55-5.25. Open Su and Tu-Sa 2-4pm and 9pm-midnight. Closed last two weeks in Aug. and from Th-Su during Semana Santa. D/MC/V. ❶

Restaurante Casa Regina (El 19 De La Riera), C. Riera De Sant Miquel, 19 (☎93 237 86 01). M: Diagonal, L3/5. Turn left on Diagonal, and C. Riera de Sant Miquel is the 1st right. Serves only organic food, including grilled meats and many vegetarian options. Plenty of magazines to browse through while eating. Fixed menú €9.50, entrees €5-42. Open M-Sa 1-4pm and 9-11:30pm. MC/V. ❸

Ordering at Els Quatre Gats

El Tastavins, C. Ramón y Cajal, 12 (☎93 213 60 31), near Pl. Sol. M: Joanic, L4. A small offering of satisfying Catalan mainstays. No English menu (or speakers), but waiters have become masters of charades by impersonating the dishes they wish to explain. Entrees €9.50-15. Open Su 1:30-4pm, Tu-Sa 1:30-4pm and 9pm-midnight. ❷

NUT, C. Verdi, 2 (☎93 210 86 40), at Pl. Revolució Setembre de 1868. M: Fontana, L3. Cuisine from the land of the Pharaohs, like *kuchari* (rice with lentils and spices; €6.25) and Egypt's traditional drink *carcade* (€3.50) in a stone-walled dining room bedecked by hieroglyphic tapestries. Entrees €6.25-10.50. Open daily 12:30-5pm and 8:30pm-1am. ❷

Xavi Petit, C. Bonavista, 2 (☎93 237 88 26). M: Diagonal, L3/5, off Gran de Gràcia. Cheese-, meat-, and chocolate-filled crêpes. Enjoy a hearty meal or

Lunch at Bar Ra

Can I get Coffee with that?

Spanish coffee is known for being tasty and strong. Don't expect a water-downed version of a cup of Joe, because you're about to get the real thing. Also don't expect to find coffees to go (except at some chain stores), as European custom demands drinking leisurely on the spot.

Azucar: sugar.

Café: coffee usually served with milk and sugar on the side.

Café con leche: half coffee and half milk with sugar on the side. You can request to have it in a mug or a glass; generally consumed only at breakfast.

Café americano: a shot of espresso lengthened with hot water.

Café sólo: black coffee (no milk or sugar).

Café con hielo: iced coffee served in a tall glass; sugar on the side.

Cortado: an espresso-like coffee served in a smaller mug. It is mostly coffee with a bit of milk; sugar is provided on the side.

Leche: milk.

Other options: You can also request to have a **doble de café** which means that the *camarero* will double the amount of coffee in your drink (and add some milk) and serve it in a tall glass.

just dessert at this friendly neighborhood cafe. Crêpes €4. Crêpe-less afternoon menú €8, tapas €2.50. Open M-Sa 8am-11:30pm. AmEx/V. ❷

HORTA

Can Cortada, Av. de l'Estatut de Catalunya (☎93 427 23 15; www.barcelonarestaurant.com). M: Mundet, L3. Visible from Pg. de Vall d'Hebron. This impressive 11th-century building, originally a feudal defense tower, was converted into a farmhouse in the 15th century. On the way to the downstairs dining room you can still see the old underground dungeon tunnels and the horse-feeding corner. Feast on hearty Catalan staples like the *filete a la piedra*—meat cooked on a hot stone in front of you. Entrees around €10, three-course meal €18-27. Open daily 1-4pm and 8pm-1am. Reservations recommended. Wheelchair accessible. AmEx/MC/V. ❹

Can Travi Nou, C. Jorge Manrique (☎93 428 03 01). M: Mundet, L3. Exit to the left and turn right onto Pg. de Vall d'Hebron. Take a right at C. Jorge Manrique; it's at the end of the street. Nestled in the shade, Can Travi Nou has a cozy dinner atmosphere. Three-course meal €24-30. Open M-Sa 1:30-4pm and 8:30-11pm, Su 1:30-6pm. Reservations recommended. Wheelchair accessible. AmEx/MC/V. ❹

LES CORTS

Dining in Les Corts doesn't get too fancy. The neighborhood's small bars and cafes feed hordes of soccer fans on game days, but the area is not known for its cuisine.

El Cargolet Picant, Riera Blanca, 7 (☎93 334 04 54), at the corner of Trav. de Les Corts and C. Aristides Maillol. M: Collblanc, L5. Busy even on non-game days, "The Spicy Snail" specializes in, of course, 7 snail dishes (about €5 each). Less adventurous visitors can choose from a number of delicious tapas on display at the bar (€2-9 per plate). Open daily 7am-1:30am. Cash only. ❷

L'Ancora, Passatge Costa, 6 (☎93 440 00 07), off C. de Collblanc. M: Collblanc, L5. A convenient *cervecería* (beer cafe) that also sells ice cream and sandwiches. Start a debate over the latest Barça controversy while munching on bocadillos (€3) or Catalan entrees (€6). Open M-Sa 7am-8pm. Cash only. ❷

SANTS

La Parra, C. Joanot Martorall, 3 (☎93 332 51 34), a steep alley right of C. Sants, 2 blocks from M: Hostafrancs, L1. An authentic experience if ever there was one. This hidden gem has been serving fresh Mediterranean fare in the same house for two centuries. Huge appetizers €10-15, entrees €6-19. Open Tu-F 8:30pm-midnight, Sa-Su noon-4pm. MC/V. ❷

Cuitat Comtal, C. Galileo, 1 (☎93 411 04 13), off of Pl. de Sants. M: Pl. de Sants, L1/5. An Italian haven for pizza and pasta lovers (€5-6). Takeout available. Open daily 1-4pm and 7pm-midnight. Wheelchair accessible. MC/V. ❷

SARRIÀ

Sarrià is an excellent area for no-frills Catalan fare; most restaurants are on or very near C. Major de Sarrià. Come armed with your Catalan dictionary or just a sense of culinary adventure—most menus and waiters do not provide English translations. All restaurants are near M: Sarrià. Exit the FGC station at the "Sortida Mare de Déu de Núria," then make a right. Make the first left (down a very short street), and then a left onto C. Mare de Déu de Núria. Then make a right onto C. Canet and follow Canet to the end and turn onto C. Major Sarrià.

Casa Joana, C. Major de Sarrià, 59 (☎93 203 10 36; fax 93 203 23 06). Traditional, tasty Catalan dishes are served in big portions at reasonable prices in this fourth-generation restaurant. Menú (€11.50) includes an appetizer, entree, drink, and dessert. Open M-Sa 1-4pm and 9-11pm. D/MC/V. ❸

Caffe San Marco, C. Pedro de la Creu, 15, on the corner of C. Major de Sarrià (☎93 280 29 73). A little taste of Venice right here in Barcelona, complete with elaborate glass chandeliers. Coffee €0.85, teas €1.90. Open daily 8am-9:30pm. ❶

Foix de Sarrià, C. Major de Sarrià, 57 (☎93 203 07 14; fax 93 280 65 56). Elegant local pastry institution founded in 1886 and named after Catalan poet J. V. Foix. Peruse the irresistible selection of homemade tarts and cream-filled delights (around €2). Just try to defy temptation. Also stocks gelato (around €2), wine, cheeses, chocolates, and meats. Open daily 8am-9pm. Another **branch** right up the street in Pl. de Sarrià, 12-13 (☎ 93 203 04 73) open daily 8am-9pm. ❶

Restaurante Maravillas, C. Cornet i Mas, 38. From C. Major de Sarrià, turn onto C. Rocaberti and walk 1 short block. Three tasteful and romantic rooms with soft lighting and pastel walls. Vegetarian options. Entrees €6-16. Open M-Sa 1:30-4pm and 9-11:30pm. MC/V. ❸

Via Veneto, C. Ganduxer, 10-12. FGC: Bonanova. Just past Pl. Francesco Macia. C. Ganduxer on Av. Diagonal; the restaurant is 1 block up on the right. Surrounded by the upscale shops and modern high-rise apartment buildings of lower Sarrià, Via Veneto is right at home. Famous for having been one of Dalí's favorite spots (he is said to have once ordered raw sausage to hang around his companion's neck), this swanky and pricey restaurant serves Spanish, Catalan, and French dishes. Appetizers €11-39, entrees €23-46. Open M-F 1:30-4pm and 8:45-11:30pm, Sa 8:45-11:30pm. MC/V. ❺

A'Rogueira, Pl. d'Artos, 6. A popular bar and restaurant with plenty of outside tables on the busy Pl. d'Artos, at the bottom of C. Major de Sarrià. More affordable than most options in Sarrià. Pick from a choice of typically Catalan tapas listed on a chalkboard outside. Menú €6.60. Open daily 6:45am-2am. Cash only. ❷

Forn de la Vila, Consell de la Vila, 9 (☎93 204 79 58). Just off of C. Major de Sarrià. Pick from a choice of pastries (around €1.50), ice cream (€1), sandwiches, and cold and hot drinks to enjoy on the terrace in the shady and quiet Pl. del Ajuntament. Open daily 7am-9:30pm. ❶

TIBIDABO

Tibidabo has several options for food, but most of them require stretching your budget; thirty- and forty-something professionals dominate the crowds here. Inside the Parc de Collserola, mediocre food options abound; check with the info office for a location guide. For a cheaper meal, look out for *merenderos*, open-air spaces with picnic tables, grills, and any utensils you need available for rent. Try the one at **Font de les Planes,** FGC: Les Planes, across the highway bridge. (Tables €4 each; grills €3, plus €10 deposit; bag of charcoal €3.80; *paella* pans €3 plus €3 deposit. Open M and W-Sa 9am-7pm.)

El Asador de Aranda, Av. de Tibidabo, 31 (☎93 417 01 15; www.asadoraranda.com). FGC: Av. Tibidabo. Halfway up the hill from Pl. JFK. The Casa Roviralta, a stunning Modernist building designed by Rubio, houses this traditional restaurant. A meal on the luxurious terrace overlooking the city while enjoying *lechazo asado* (pork roasted in a large stone oven) is well worth the cost. Menús start at €31. Open M-Sa 1-4pm and 9pm-midnight, Su 1-4pm. AmEx/MC/V. ❺

Restaurant Font de Les Planes, (☎93 280 59 49). FGC: Les Planes. Walk across the bridge to the left of the station exit and continue through the large parking lot. Restaurant is right behind the *merendero.* Make-your-own *pan con tomate* complements the succulent *paella* and grilled meats in this shady retreat from the bustle of the urban landscape. Great for a mid-hike meal. Entrees €12-18. Reservations recommended Sa-Su. Open daily June-Sept. 9am-midnight, Sept.-June closed Tu. MC/V. ❸

La Venta, Pl. Dr. Andreu (☎93 212 64 55; www.restaurantelaventa.com), at the end of Av. de Tibidabo. An upscale restaurant where you can enjoy Catalan specialities. Entrees €10-40. Open M-Sa 1:30-3:15pm and 9-11:15pm. AmEx/MC/V. ❹

El Club dels Aventurers, Pl. del Tibidabo (☎93 417 63 50). In front of Parc d'Attracions. Tourist families venture into this self-dubbed "magic restaurant" for a large—but pricey—meal. Appetizers €7-14, entrees €11-18, fixed menú for children €14. Seating available on outside terrace in the summer. Same hours as the Parc d'Attracions (see p. 110). MC/V. ❸

CHAINS

RESTAURANT CHAINS

Pans & Company. Perhaps the most visible franchise in Spain, this fast-food bocadillo chain started up in 1991 right here in Barcelona, as its Catalan name attests. Since then, it has spread like a tasty virus. Hot and cold bocadillos of ham, chicken, tuna, or other fillings €2.40-4.40. Pre-prepared vegetable and pasta salads €2.30-2.70. Learn to love Pans (and all the other chains they own)—it's inescapable. ❶

TapasBar (☎93 225 81 80), Moll d'Espanya. In spite of its tacky name, TapasBar is a card-carrying member of the elite club of Grade A restaurant chains; their bright yellow logo is a stamp of quality of atmosphere as well as of food. They have nearly 30 locations in Spain and Portugal (6 of them in Barcelona) and specialize in, you guessed it, tapas! (Two popular locations include the Moll d'Espanya and near the Hotel Arts on Av. Litoral Mar.) For adventurous diners, they offer 2-person meals of 8 kinds of tapas (€30). Most tapas €3-5. Coffee, desserts, full meals available. Hours vary by store, but most open around M-F 11am-1am, Sa-Su 11am-2am. AmEx/MC/V. ❸

FresCo, Ronda Universitat, 29 (☎93 301 68 37) off Pl. de Catalunya. M: Catalunya. A hugely popular all-you-can-eat buffet extravaganza. Three l'Eixample locations attract everyone from tiny female Spaniards picking delicately at their salads to packs of ravenous families gorging themselves on a good deal. Either way, the endlessly varied salad bar, pasta, pizza, frozen yogurt, coffee, and fruit are the perfect escape from meat and oil-heavy Catalan staples. Lunch buffet €6.60, dinner buffet (starting 6pm) €8.80; both include 1 drink. Also at Av. Diagonal, 449 and C. València, 263. Open daily 12:30pm-1am. MC/V. ❷

Fresh & Ready. This 7-store chain has rapidly become a crutch for busy Catalan career-minded types. They serve coffee, juice, and pastries like any cafe, but also offer a huge array of refrigerated, prepackaged salads, sandwiches, and yogurts to-go, ranging from Thai chicken and smoked salmon to simple *tortilla española.* The food is indeed fresh, though a little pricey for the small portions. Sandwiches and salads €2.55-3.75, half-sandwiches €1.50. Open Su-Th 8am-11pm, F-Sa 8am-midnight. Cash only. ❶

La Baguetina Catalana (☎93 539 52 08). With more than 24 stores in Barcelona, La Baguetina is almost as ubiquitous as Pans & Co. Its main offerings include bocadillos, *palmeras,* croissants, and *cocas* (bread with sugar and pine nuts), but it is best known for its late hours in tourist-heavy areas like Las Ramblas, where stumbling revelers line up for bready snacks until 3am. Bocadillos €3.90. *Cocas* €2.50. Opening hours range from 6-8am, depending on location, and closing hours from midnight to 3am. Cash only. ❶

Pastafiore. Owned by the same company as Pans & Co., Pastafiore serves up quick Italian food, including spaghetti, lasagna, ravioli, and tortellini. The hot dishes aren't half bad. Pasta menú €6.90, pizza menú €9—both come with a small salad and drink. Pasta dishes €4.75-5.40. Salads €3, pizzas €4.90-6. Open Su-Th noon-midnight, F-Sa noon-1am. Cash only. ❶

Bocatta. Virtually indistinguishable from the yellow Pans & Co. (which recently bought it out), save the green decor, and a selection of vegetable bocadillos (€2.50-4). Hot and cold bocadillos, heavy on the ham. Buy any sandwich, and fries and a drink come for €2.90. Salad selection a bit more varied (€1.50-3). Cash only. ❶

Vips, Ramgla de Catalunya, 7-9 (93 317 48 05). M: Catalunya, L1/3. An international farnchise, perfect for homesick Americans. Spanish and American food served in the restaurant, including grilled chicken salads, veggie sandwiches, quesadillas, and hamburgers (most around €6). The store sells books, road maps, and magazines, as well as CDs, videos, , snakcs, drinks, gifts, and cards. 4 computers for pricey Internet use, but check for frequently offered "specials." Open daily 9am-6am. Wheelchair accessible. AmEx/MC/V. ❷

Hard Rock Café, Pl. de Catalunya, 21 (☎93 270 23 50). M: Catalunya, L1/3. You might find that the 2hr. wait on most nights is worth the good burgers. Or you might want to head down Las Ramblas for a more relaxing and less touristy way to spend the evening. But the burers *are* super tasty. Burgers €6.75-9.25 (including veggie burgers), "Really Big Sandwiches" €8-9.25. Open M-Th 12:30pm-2am; F-Sa until 3am. T-shirt seekers, the gift shop opens at 10am and closes half an hour before the restaurant. AmEx/MC/V.

COFFEE CHAINS

All coffeehouse chains in Barcelona are roughly similar in prices and design; all serve a range of coffees and a small selection of ice cream, pastries, teas, and bocadillos,and generally offer breakfast specials for €1.50-3. **Jamaica** and **Il Caffe di Roma** are nearly indistinguishable. **Aroma** is the classiest of the lot, with warmly lit, dark wood interiors that almost conceal its chain staus. But for all those homesick for a good ol' styrofoam cup of Joe, **Dunkin' Donuts** pops up seemingly everywhere, and so does the recently implanted **Starbucks**.

Nightlife

The nightlife in Barcelona needs no introduction: whether you're looking for psyche-delic absinthe shots, a great place for grunge rock, a sunrise foam party, or just someplace quiet to sit back and enjoy a drink (surrounded by fake gnomes), this city has it all. Things don't get going until late (don't bother showing up at a club before 1am) and keep going for as long as you can handle it. Check the *Guía del Ocio*, available at newsstands, for even more up-to-date listings of nighttime fun.

BARRI GÒTIC & LAS RAMBLAS

Nightfall is the only thing that really distinguishes the upper from the lower Barri Gòtic. The area above C. Ferran, dominated by shops, res-taurants, and hostels, virtually shuts down by midnight, while C. Fer-ran and below starts to look like a human river, with tourists and locals weaving their way from bar to bar. There are a few clubs and several hybrid bar/clubs in and around Pl. Reial, but overall the Barri Gòtic is the place for drinking and hanging out rather than for wild and crazy dance parties of the type found at **Maremàgnum** (p. 154) or **Montjuic** (p. 154). Also, be advised that while the Pl. Reial has some great nightlife, it is favorite tourist spot and therefore attracts such practices as drug dealing, pick-pocket-ing, and prostitution. While such activities do exist in the area (and you will see dozens

see map pp. 334-335

of prostitutes on Las Ramblas), they are not as common as rumors would have you believe. The area is generally well-policed and whispers of "hashish" are probably the only indications of lawlessness that you'll encounter.

In **Plaça "Trippy"** on the other hand, things are not quite as tame. Located at the end of C. Escudellers from Las Ramblas, this is the kind of place your mom prays you'll never set foot. Officially named **Plaça George Orwell,** this is a popular hangout for Barcelona's alternative crowd. It is rumored that the government removed all of the benches here to discourage loitering and drug dealing; how successful they were is highly debatable. Two popular bar-restaurants in the *plaça* have outside seating: **La Verònica** (see p. 143) and the grungier **Bar Ovisos,** which stays open until 1am and offers simple Catalan food and cheap beer (€1.20 during the day, €1.80 at night).

BARS

Barcelona Pipa Club, Pl. Reial, 3 (☎93 302 47 32). M: Liceu, L3. Decidedly unmarked; look for the small name plaque on the door to the left of Glacier bar (on your left as you enter the square from Las Ramblas) and ring the doorbell to be let in. Don't let the pseudo-secrecy deter you though, this is a very welcoming place that's wonderful for late-night cocktails. The decor is 100% Sherlock Holmes, the music is mostly jazz and fusion, and the people are a mix of local bartenders, artists, and tourists in the know. One small (but free to use) pool table. Occasional activities like tango classes and poetry readings. Gets crowded after 2am, no entrance allowed after 4am. Cocktails €5.50, beer €3.50. Open daily 11pm-5am. Cash only.

Molly's Fair City, C. Ferran, 7 (☎93 342 40 26). M: Liceu, L3. With blaring music, fast-flowing imported beer, and a prime location next to the Pl. Reial, Molly's is the place to go if you're looking to meet English-speaking tourists in the Barri Gòtic, guzzling pricey but strong mixed drinks. Molly's is a favorite of the spectator sport enthusiast, staying open as late as necessary to catch the end of the game. Guinness on tap €5.20, bottled beer €3.50, mixed drinks €7. Open Su-Th 8pm-2:30am, F-Sa 7pm-3am. Cash only.

Fonfone, C. Escudellers, 24 (☎93 317 14 24). M: Liceu, L3 or Drassanes, L3. A wall of muted rectangular block lights flashing behind the bar, atmospheric lighting, and decidedly cool sounds draw 1-3am crowds to Fonfone, another futuristic bar/club hybrid with plenty of green velveteen couches and a good-sized dance area. Different DJs every night from all over the world. Music range includes lounge, house, free style, and garage. Beer €3.20, mixed drinks €6. Open Su-Th 9:30pm-2:30am, F-Sa 9:30pm-3am. Cash only.

Schilling, C. Ferran, 23 (☎93 317 67 87). M: Liceu, L3. On the left as you go down C. Ferran from Las Ramblas. Don't let the relatively fancy exterior or interior fool you. Schilling is surprisingly diverse and is one of the more chill bars in the area, with a lot more breathing space than most bars in the Barri Gòtic. Mixed gay and straight crowd. Excellent sangría (pitcher €13.40), mixed drinks €5, wine and beer €2. Open daily 10am-2:30am. Cash only.

Vildsvin, C. Ferran, 38 (☎93 317 94 07). M: Liceu, L3. On your right as you go down C. Ferran from Las Ramblas. Oysters are the speciality of the house at this Norwegian bar; get them on their own (half dozen €7.20; one dozen €13.20), with beer, or with cava (two oysters and a beer or a glass of cava €4.50). Large selection of international beers (€4-7.50). Mixed crowd of tourists and locals. Full restaurant downstairs. Outside seating is available. Tapas €3-5, desserts €3.50-5, entrees €8-14. Open M-Th 9am-2am, F-Sa 9am-3am. AmEx/MC/V.

El Bosq de les Fades, (☎93 317 26 49). M: Drassanes, L3. Walk down the alley to the Wax Museum and then make a right. From the maniacal geniuses who brought you the wax museum, El Bosq de les Fades (the Forest of Fables) is a mystical place, complete with gnarly trees, waterfalls, gnomes, a small bridge, and plush side rooms. Always a crowd pleaser, it's a good place for couples and groups to hang out before hitting up a club. Open M-Th 10am-1:30am, F-Sa 10am-2:30am. Cash only.

Glaciar Bar, Pl. Reial, 3. M: Liceu, L3. In the near left corner coming from Las Ramblas. A hidden treasure in a sea of indistinguishable tourist bars. Glacier has a rather small but nicely decorated interior; most people sit outside in the Pl. Reial. Go here to start your night off with some excellent tapas (€2-4) or bocadillos (€3-5). Plenty of outside tables, and free winter photo exhibits upstairs combine to make Glaciar a very chill place. Beer €1.50-2, mixed drinks €4, liter of sangría €10. Open Su 8am-2:30am, M-Sa 4pm-2:30am. Cash only.

Margarita Blue, C. J. A. Clavé, 6 (☎93 317 71 76). M: Drassanes, L3. Walk past the wax museum and take a left. It's off Las Ramblas, about 1 block from the port. With small blue margaritas, a strangely arranged wall of mirrors behind the bar, and retro-80s pop tunes, this Mexican-themed bar draws a 20- and 30-something crowd. Creative Mexican food (entrees €3.50-8) accompanies the tequila. Blue margaritas €3, beer €3.30, mixed drinks €5.10. Tu night magic shows, W night drag queen performances (around 11:30pm-midnight). Open Su-W 7pm-2am, Th 7pm-2:30am, F-Sa 7pm-3am (kitchen closes Su-Th at 1am, F-Sa at 1:30am).

Dot Light Club, C. Nou de Sant Francesc, 7 (☎93 302 70 26). M: Drassanes, L3. Take the second right off C. Escudellers; it's on your left about 100 feet down. It's easy to miss, so watch for the sign that reads "DOT" above the door. The chic atmosphere in this futuristic 2-room bar/club is all about funky lighting and cutting edge DJ action every night, with a different theme for each night of the week: W "Deep Beats," Th "Phat Beats," F "Spacefunk," etc. Nightly indy films at 10:30pm. Beer €3, drinks €5.40. Open Su-Th 11pm-1:30am, F-Sa 11pm-3am. Cash only.

La Verònica, C. Avinyò, 30 (☎93 412 12 22). M: Liceu, L3. Also has an entrance and outside tables on Plaça George Orwell. This funky bar fits in well with its location, serving cheap beer (€2) to an alternative crowd on Plaça "Trippy." The friendly staff will make you feel more welcome than the Plaça would otherwise. Salads and pizza served on weekend afternoons, with lots of vegetarian options. Predominantly gay crowd. Mixed drinks €3-5. Open daily 7pm-2am.

Café Royale, C. Nou de Zurbano, 3 (☎93 412 14 33). M: Liceu, L3. On the tiny street leading out of the corner of Pl. Reial occupied by Jamboree (it's the street on the right if you walk into the plaça from Las Ramblas). The self-proclaimed "only" place in the city to chill out to soul and funk. Arrive by midnight if you want one of the velveteen or leather seats; after that, chances are you'll have to wait up to 1hr to get in. Attracts crowd of local 20- and 30-somethings. Beer €4, mixed drinks €5-8. Open Su-Th 8:30pm-2:30am, F-Sa 8:30pm-3am. V, min. charge €2.

Harlem Jazz Club, C. Comtesa de Sobradiel, 8 (☎93 310 07 55). M: Liceu, L3. Between Pl. Reial and Via Laietana. Live music alternating between blues, jazz, reggae, flamenco, and acoustic rock attracts international musicians from as far away as Senegal, Kenya, Brazil, and Cuba. Two sessions per night: Tu-Th and Su 10:30pm and midnight, F-Sa 11:30pm and 1am. The second session is always

DRINKING LIKE A SPANIARD

Anís: anisette; a licorice flavored liquor.

Bosca: vodka and a citrus carbonated beverage.

Calimocho: cheap red wine and coke.

Cacique: rum with coke and lemon or orange soda.

Cava: Catalunya's versions of champagne. Tasty, and cheaper than the real stuff.

Cerveza: Beer! *Caña de cerveza* means draught beer. For more on beer, see p. 148.

Chupito: a shot, generally taken after dinner or at a club.

Clara: beer with lemonade.

Creme Catalana: a sweet liquor, similar to Bailey's.

Cuba Libre: generally a rum and coke, although if you specify *con ginebra,* it's with gin.

Mini: a liter of beer

Mosto: sweet white wine.

Sangría: a changing recipe that depends on the taste of the maker. Generally, *sangría* is made up of very cheap wine, spiced up with hard liquor, fruit, fruit juice, and some form of carbonated citrus beverage. The wooden spoon is to keep the ice and the fruit *out* of your glass; don't dump it all in.

Sidra: Basque cider, poured from a height to aerate the cider.

Sol y Sombra: cognac and anisette.

Ponché: also known as the "silver bullet." A sweet liqueur.

Rioja: a region in Spain famous for its red wine.

into: red wine.

Don Simón: the cheapest way to get drunk. Boxed wine; typically mixed with Casera.

LGB ▼
BARCELONA

Nights of Delight

Barcelona (and the surrounding beach towns, like Sitges) have some of the best nightlife in all of Europe, and the Mediterranean coast as a whole is (in)famous for its LGB scene. With everything from raging clubs to low-key bars, Barcelona nights certainly hold a little something for everyone. Check out these establishments, and find one that suits your tastes. In particular, the part of the l'Eixample Esquerra between C. Urgell, C. Aragó, the Gran Via, and C. Aribau is considered a mecca for gay partying. You can't go wrong with:

Aire (Sala Diana; p. 152)

Arena (p. 152)

Bahía (p. 157)

Caligula (p. 150)

D_Mer (p. 158)

Dietrich (p. 149)

Divina's (p. 151)

Fuse (p. 149)

Illusion (p. 152)

La Verònica (p. 143)

Moog (p. 148)

Punto BCN (p. 152)

Salvation (p. 151)

Schilling (p. 142)

Topxi (p. 150)

much more crowded, especially on weekends. Advance tickets and current play schedules available at tourist offices and www.atrapalo.com. F-Sa cover €6; occasionally weekday shows charge cover as well. Open daily 10pm-4am. Closes once a week, either on M or Tu. Get a schedule for the month at the front door. Cash only.

Casa El Agüelo, C. Avinyò, 37 (☎93 310 23 25). M: Liceu, L3. Take a right off C. Ferran, coming from Las Ramblas. A relatively cozy tavern whose decor is somewhere between medieval Catalunya and the American West. When the place fills, it can get overcrowded. Brick walls, fireplaces, long wooden tables, and a cavernous, dungeon-like basement. A good place for cheap beer with a big group of friends. Beer €3-4; pitcher of sangría €9.20. Open M-F 7pm-2am, Sa-Su 7pm-3am. Cash only.

CLUBS

Jamboree, Pl. Reial, 17 (☎93 319 17 89). M: Liceu, L3. On the corner immediately to your right coming from Las Ramblas. What was once a convent now serves as one of the city's most popular live music venues. At 1:30am, the brick basement area turns into a packed hip-hop dance club (open until 5am; cover €3, beer €9). M-F €6 cover includes one drink, Sa-Su €12-15; €1.20 discount if you buy ahead of time at a ServiCaixa machine. Open daily 11pm-1am. Upstairs, the attached club Tarantos hosts flamenco shows for the tourist set. (€25; open M-Sa 9:30pm-midnight.)

New York, C. Escudellers, 5 (☎93 318 87 30). M: Drassanes, L3. Right off Las Ramblas. Once a strip joint, New York is now the biggest club in the Barri Gòtic, with plenty of drink tables overlooking the red and black, strobe-lit dance floor for your voyeuristic pleasure. Crowds don't arrive until after 3am; music includes reggae and British pop. Cover 11:30pm-2am €6 (includes 1 beer); 2-5am €13 (includes any drink). Open Th-Sa midnight-5am. Cash only.

LA RIBERA

see map p. 337

El Copetin, Pg. del Born, 19. M: Jaume I, L4. Cuban rhythm infuses everything in this casual yet peppy nightspot. Grab a *mojito* (€5), the mint and rum sugary concoction that is the *copetin* (cocktail) of the house, and enjoy the live Cuban music that fills the air with tropical spirit. Su 11pm live bolero performance. Open Su-Th 7pm-2:30am, F-Sa 7pm-3am.

El Born, Pg. del Born, 26 (☎93 319 53 33). M: Jaume I, L4. Sit at the marble counter over the basins where fish were once sold. Follow the tiny spiral staircase upstairs for a meal. Fondues €12-15. Excellent cocktails (€4-5.25). Open Su-Th 6pm-2am, F-Sa 6pm-3am. Wheelchair accessible.

Palau Dalmases, C. Montcada, 20 (☎93 310 06 73). M: Jaume I, L4. A self-labeled "Baroque space" in a 17th-century palace fittingly decorated with lavish oil paintings and statues. Romantic candle-lit tables complete the atmosphere. Live opera performances Th at 11pm (€18, includes one drink). Beer and mixed drinks €6-10, fresh juice €8. Open Su 6-10pm, Tu-Sa 10pm-2am.

Pitin Bar, Pg. del Born, 34 (☎93 319 50 87). M: Barceloneta, L4. Chill beneath a starry sky of tiny blue lights, or people-watch from one of the intimate upstairs tables. Trippy lounge music will put you in the mood for absinthe (€2.70). Mixed drinks €4.50-8. Open daily 6pm-3am.

La Vinya del Senyor, Pl. Santa Maria, 5 (☎93 310 33 79). M: Jaume I, L4. Across from Santa Maria del Mar. Cluster around the tiny tables inside the cozy bar or sit outside and watch the church visitors over a glass of wine and plate of cheese (€4). Every 15 days the wine list changes (€1.25-8.20 per glass). Open Tu-Th noon-1am, F-Sa noon-2am, Su noon-midnight. Wheelchair accessible.

Mudanzas, C. Vidreira, 15 (☎98 319 11 37; www.dominios.net/LaRibera). M: Jaume I, L4. Everything is black and white and serious. The only color comes from hundreds of illuminated bottles lining the wall behind the bar. A hip, young, professional crowd. Wide selection of rum, whiskey, and wine €2-6; beer €2. Open Su-F 9:30pm-3am, Sa 10pm-2am.

Plàstic Café, Pg. del Born, 19 (☎93 310 25 96; www.plastic-bcn.com). M: Jaume I, L4. Follow C. Princesa, turn right on C. Comerç, and right again on Pg. del Born. "Café" is a misnomer for this jam-packed, hyper-trendy bar, with a funky mix of international, house, and 80s pop. Watch friendly bartenders do fancy tricks with bottles, or hit the small dance floor reserved for those who just can't help shaking their booty to the head-bobbing tunes. Beer €3. Mixed drinks €5-6. Open Su and Tu-Sa 10pm-3am.

Upiaywasi, C. Allada-Vermell, 11 (☎93 268 01 54). M: Jaume I, L4. Away from the metro station across Via Laietana down C. Princesa, make a left on Allada-Vermell. This *cocteleria*, whose *Quechua* name literally means "house for drinking" offers live music, including Brazilian and jazz every night to accompany its inventive drinks. Drinks €5, beer €2. Open Su and Tu-Sa 6pm-3am.

in recent
news

Inside Voices

Pumping house beats might be the nighttime prowler's idea of a good time, but one man's pleasure is another man's pain. The people of **La Ribera**—or at least those whose clubbin' days belong to yesteryear—have decided they have had enough of being kept up by the vocal pyrotechnics of drunken tourists belting out their national anthems or the latest moanings of Britney Spears. So they're creating some noise of their own—by making their dissatisfaction known to the city government. Frustrated that their complaints have been ignored because the nightlife industry brings so much revenue to the city, the locals organized themselves into an association, **El Fórum Veïnal de la Ribera** (**FVR,**The Local Ribera Forum), and have demanded a reduction in the late-night noise.

The forum managed to get outdoor terraces closed one hour earlier than last year, so patios in La Ribera must now close at 1am instead of 2am. The forum continues to fight for quieter streets and restrictions on noise levels, but the nightlife in the neighborhood is still alive and thumping.

For more information on the neighborhood's efforts see the Forum's website: www.khamen.net/forum/index.html.

Absinthe Minded

Inside the old-fashioned bars of El Raval you are likely to find *absenta* (absinthe), the golden firewater banned everywhere except in Spain and the Czech Republic. This licorice-flavored alcohol derived from the ajenjo plant is said to have hallucinogenic affects similar to those of peyote. Once France's national drink, 150-proof absinthe was all the rage among Impressionist painters and the Parisian bourgeoisie. Supposedly, the death of artist Paul Gauguin (and the discovery of more than 200 bottles under his bed) prompted the call for absinthe abstinence.

Spain chose not to follow suit, however, and the drink is still available—though in a safer 110-proof version (a more potent 140-proof version is also sometimes available). It's served with a bottle of water, a sugar cube, and a spoon. There is a certain method to its madness: first, soak the sugar cube in the flammable alcohol. Then, holding the cube in the spoon, light the sugar on fire, repeating as necessary, until the sugar has melted and can be stirred into the drink. The water serves to dilute, or as a chaser if you choose to take it straight up.

Though hardly hallucinogenic, this bewitching drink can still create a detached, spaced-out feeling and cause memory loss. Sage bartenders warn that even two absinthes may end your night early.

EL RAVAL

see map p. 336

BARS

If glamorous clubs and all-night dancing are your scene, El Raval is not for you. The streets are densely packed with a bar for every variety of bar-hopper—Irish pubbers, American backpackers, absinthe abusers, social drinkers, lounge lizards, and foosball maniacs will find themselves at home in El Raval.

🖼 **Casa Almirall,** C. Joaquim Costa, 33 (☎93 318 99 17). M: Universitat, L1/2/3. Take the C. Pelai Metro exit, turn left at the end of the block, and turn again at the 2nd left. The bar is down a few blocks at the corner of C. Ferlandina. A cavernous space with weathered couches and a dark, warm ambience, Casa Almirall is Barcelona's oldest bar, founded in 1860. The staff will walk you through your first glass of *absenta* (€4.50)—and cut you off after your second (see **Absinthe Minded**, p. 146). Beer €1.90, mixed drinks €5. Open Su-Th 6:30pm-2:30am, F-Sa 6:30pm-3am.

🖼 **Muebles Navarro (El Café que pone),** C. la Riera Alta, 4-6 (☎93 442 39 66). M: Catalunya, L1/3. It's a right off C. Carme. Eclectic art decorates the walls of this unpretentiously stylish bar. Enjoy the mellow ambience and watch friends get friendlier as they sink into the comfy couches together. Beer €2.10 before midnight, €2.30 after; wine €2, mixed drinks €4.50-7. Snacks (€1-5) served until 11:30pm. Open Su 6pm-1am, Tu-Th 6pm-2am, F-Sa 6pm-3am.

London Bar, C. Nou de la Rambla, 34 (☎93 318 52 61). M: Liceu, L3. Off Las Ramblas. Locals and unruly expats rub shoulders at this smoky, and always crowded, Modernist tavern. Live music in the back room starts nightly at 12:30am, usually rock or blues. Beer €2.50-3, wine €2.50, mixed drinks €5.50-7, absinthe €3. Open Su and Tu-Th 7:30pm-4:30am, F-Sa 7:30pm-5am. AmEx/MC/V.

Sant Pau 68, C. de Sant Pau, 68 (☎93 441 31 15). M: Liceu, L3. 4 blocks from Las Ramblas. Popular among locals, Sant Pau 68 is one of the most hip bars in El Raval. The main dimly lit ground floor has a club-like feel to it, although you won't see anyone dancing. For a more intimate setting, bring your drink upstairs. Beer €2, mixed drinks €4.30-5. Open Tu-Th 8pm-2:30am, F-Sa 8pm-3am. Cash only.

Marsella Bar, C. de Sant Pau, 65 (☎93 442 72 63). M: Liceu, L3. Follow C. Sant Pau off Las Ramblas to the corner of Sant Ramon. Religious figurines grace the dark wood-paneled walls of this weathered watering hole; perhaps they're praying for the adventurous absinthe drinkers (€3.40) who frequent the place. Beer €2.10, mixed drinks €4.50-5.75. Open M-Th 10pm-2:30am, F-Sa 10pm-3:30am. Cash only.

Lupino, C. Carme, 33 (☎93 412 36 97). From M: Catalunya, L1/3, take a right on C. Carme. Ultra-chic restaurant and lounge right out of L.A. combines atmospheric lighting and sophisticated furnishing into a stylish haven for fashionable people. Restaurant offers such delights as lamb confit with peach medley sauce (€10.20). Cocktails €5.50. Restaurant open daily 1:30pm-4pm, Su-W 9pm-1am, Th-Sa 9pm-2am. Bar open Su-Th 9pm-2:30am, F-Sa 9pm-3am. AmEx/MC/V.

Rita Blue, Pl. Sant Agustí, 3 (☎93 342 40 86). M: Liceu, L3. On C. Hospital off Las Ramblas. It's not clear why Rita is blue, considering the excellent live music at her hip, colorful restaurant/bar/club. Live house music plays downstairs W-Su 11pm. DJs, poetry slams, and other musical performances are scheduled regularly. Call ahead for dinner reservations. Beer €2.20, mixed drinks €5.40-8. Open Su-W 7pm-2am, Th-Sa 7pm-3am.

The Quiet Man, Marqués Barbera, 11 (☎93 412 12 19). M: Liceu, L3. Take C. Unió off Las Ramblas; after 2 blocks it becomes Marqués Barbera. As authentic an Irish pub as you'll find in Barcelona, with a homey decor, a good collection of Beleek (fine Irish china), and a friendly Irish staff. Live music (pop or rock F-Sa midnight, Su 8:30pm). Pints of imported drafts €4.40, mixed drinks €5.60. Open Su-W 6pm-2:30am, Th-Sa 6pm-3am. Cash only.

La Oveja Negra, C. Sitges, 5 (☎93 317 10 87). M: Catalunya, L1/3. From Pl. de Catalunya, go down Las Ramblas and take the 1st right onto C. Tallers; C. Sitges is the 1st left. Young English-speaking tourists crowd this tavern for cheap beer and sangría and a turn on the foosball tables. Huge pitchers of beer or sangría €7.30. Open Su 5pm-3am, M-Th 9am-3am, F-Sa 9am-2:30am. Cash Only.

Pastis, Santa Mónica, 4 (☎93 318 79 80), M: Drassanes, L3. Walk one block up Las Ramblas, and turn left on Santa Monica. An older crowd of absinthe and pastis drinkers come to enjoy live music shows in this small, over 50-year-old tavern. Every square inch is covered with something of interest: portraits, pictures, a false woman suspended from the ceiling, etc. Absinthe and pastis €3.50, beer €2, mixed drinks €6. Live tango Tu. Open Su-Th 7:30pm-2am, F-Sa 7:30pm-3:30am. MC/V.

La Confitería, C. de Sant Pau, 128 (☎93 443 04 58). M: Parallel, L2/3. At the corner of Rda. Sant Pau. Happily chatting customers from all over the world have replaced the sweets and candy formerly on display in the ex-candy store's large windows. Wood panels and soft frescoes decorate the front room, while the back room has a more

Lesbian Tango

Absinthe

Waiting at a Bar

147

ON THE MENU

¡Una cerveza más, por favor!

Barcelona beer-drinkers have been "dammed" to an eternity of mediocre beers, thanks to a near monopoly by the Damm brewing company. Barcelona's biggest brewery produces **Estrella Damm** (www.estrellad-amm.es), the default beer at nearly every bar in the city and often the only choice on tap. If you want to drink cheaply, get used to this average at best pilsner. Other less common variants include Voll-Damm, a 7.2% alcohol beast of a beer, and just plain Damm.

Of local beers, **San Miguel** (www.sanmiguel.es) is perhaps the best option, a bit smoother than its Damm counterparts. One can occasionally order southern Spanish beers such as **Cruzcampo** (www.cruz-campo.es), which does little more than assure Barcelona drinkers that they're not missing much. **Heineken**, which has a brewery in Sevilla, is by far the most common import, with the Mexican **Coronita** (Corona to the rest of us) also a favorite. Perhaps spurred on by the uninspiring Spanish beer selection, the city has a surprising number of Irish pubs, where one can always find a good pint of **Guinness**.

modern feel. Beer €1.50, wine €1.60, mixed drinks €5. Tapas (€3.10-8.45) served until midnight. Open Su 7pm-2am, M-Sa 7pm-3am. Cash only.

Muy Buenas, C. Carme, 63 (☎93 442 50 53). M: Catalunya, L1/3/4. The bar area suggests a time-warp back to the early days of the last century. Serves Middle Eastern and Cuban food daily 1-5pm and 8pm-12:30am. Come after 1am for *mojitos, caipirinhas,* and late-night freshly cooked pizzas. Beer €2.10-3, mixed drinks €4.80-7. Poetry readings Su and W 9pm. Open Su 6pm-3am, M-Sa 7am-3am. MC/V.

Raval-Bar, C. Doctor Dou, 19 (☎93 302 41 33). M: Catalunya, L1/3/4. No matter how tired or stressed they may be, 30-something locals come here to sit with friends, listen to music, and waste their night away on huge U-shaped couches, while staring up at a 6m tall woman with a beer. Beer €2.40, wine €1.80, mixed drinks €4.80-5.40. Open Su-Th 8pm-2:30am, F-Sa 8pm-3am. Cash only.

CLUBS

La Paloma, C. Tigre, 27 (☎93 301 68 97). M: Universitat, L1/2. Take the C. Pelai Metro exit, turn left at the end of the block, and walk down Rda. Sant Antoni until you reach C. Tigre on your left. The club is a block down. One would never guess that this dance hall, with its ornate, theater-like interior and balcony seating was a factory until 1903. Live salsa and popular Spanish music keep a mature clientele dancing throughout the night, but a younger crowd storms the place on the weekend. Th the club turns into "Bongo Lounge," a raging dance scene (midnight-4am); F-Sa live DJs take control of things. Drinks approx €7. Cover €7. Open Th-Su 6-9:30pm, F 11:30pm-4am, Sa 11:30pm-5am.

Moog, Arc del Teatre, 3 (☎93 301 72 82). M: Drassanes, L3. Off Las Ramblas, down the alley next to the Easy Everything Internet center. Serious fans pack this small club for a late-night dose of hard electronica. Regular appearances by major international DJs. Upstairs, on a smaller dance floor, a gay-straight mixed crowd grooves to 70s and 80s disco music (open 2-5am). Cover and drink €12, €4 discount on W, F, and Sa before 2am with flyer given out on Las Ramblas. Beer €4, mixed drinks €9. Open daily 11:30pm-5am or later.

L'EIXAMPLE

see map pp. 340-341

The wide variety of nightlife options in l'Eixample reflects the area's ideal of openness; there is a place for everyone here. Most of the biggest and best *discotecas* rock it here outside the tourist-heavy Ramblas area—this is where many natives do their dancing. Most of the places worth trekking to are located in l'Eixample Esquerra. The part of l'Eixample Esquerra (west of Pg. de Gràcia) between C. Urgell, C. Aragó, the Gran Via, and C. Aribau is dense with gay nightlife, hence its apropos nickname, "Gay-xiample." Be forewarned that most bars in this neighborhood close at 3am.

BARS

⚑ Dietrich, C. Consell de Cent, 255 (☎93 451 77 07). M: Pg. de Gràcia, L2/3/4. A rather unflattering painting of Marlene Dietrich in the semi-nude greets a mostly gay crowd. Bartenders are scantily clad, and at 1:30am you can see even more flesh and some incredible feats of flexibility when the nightly drag/strip/dance show begins. Beer €4, drinks €5-8. Open Su-Th 10:30pm-2:30am, F-Sa 10:30pm-3am. Wheelchair accessible.

⚑ La Fira, C. Provença, 171 (☎617 77 65 89). M: Hospital Clìnic, L5. Open later than other bars in the area, La Fira is a hodgepodge collection of fun house and circus castaways. Bartenders pour drinks under the big top for a hip crowd reclining in red pleather booths or dangling from carousel swings. Creepy fun-house mirrors and laughing clowns complete the picture. DJs spin a mix of commercial electronic music. Cover charge after 2am €8; beers from €3, drinks €8 and up. Open Su 6pm-1am, M-Th 10pm-3am, F-Sa 10pm-4:30am. Wheelchair accessible.

Fuse, C. Roger de Llúria, 40 (☎93 301 74 99), between C. Gran Via and C. Diputació. M: Tetuán, L2, or Pg. de Gràcia, L2/3/4. A cutting-edge Japanese-Mediterranean restaurant, cocktail bar, dance club, and Internet cafe all in one. Techno and electronic dance floor with riser seating for people-watching. Mixed gay and straight crowd in their 20s. Beer €2.40, mixed drinks €6. Restaurant open M-Sa 8:30pm-1am (3 courses with wine €26-35). Bar/club open Th-Sa 1-3am. MC/V.

Les Gens que J'Aime, C. València, 286 (☎93 215 68 79), just off Pg. de Gràcia. M: Pg. de Gràcia, L2/3/4. Travel back to Gaudí's time in this intimate bar dripping with chandeliers, mirrors, old paintings, plush corner sofas, and arm chairs. Background soul, funk, and jazz soothes those looking for something a bit more chill. Beer €3, mixed drinks €5.50, half-bottles of wine €9. Open daily 6pm-3am, open at 7pm June-Aug. Cash only.

The Michael Collins Irish Pub, Pl. Sagrada Família, 4 (☎93 459 19 64). M: Sagrada Família, blue and purple lines. Directly across the *plaça* from the church. Popular among locals in their late 20s and

Damm Beer

Beautiful Drag

Maremàgnum

149

TOP TEN THINGS TO DO AT 3AM

1. Try not to hallucinate as you stumble out of **Casa Almirall** (see p. 146) post absinthe-sampling.

2. Stop in at **Vips** (see p. 139) for a late night snack and catch up on tabloid news with the trashy English magazines.

3. Rub shoulders with travelers from all over the world in the always packed **Plaça Reial**. Follow the crowds to that night's party.

4. Surf the net at the 24hr. **Easy Everything** (see p. 311) on Las Ramblas.

5. Learn how to keep 3/2 time at the **Buenavista Salsoteca** (see p. 151).

6. Go to bed.

7. Go to someone else's bed.

8. Chain-smoke and pretend you are super-sophisticated while listening to poetry or jazz at **Barcelona Pipa Club** (see p. 142).

9. Be at one with the bass until the wee hours as you groove to tehno at the trendy **Otto Zutz** (see p. 158).

10. Sprawl on the sandy beaches of Barceloneta or Poble Nou and wait for the sun to come up.

30s. 100% Irish, from the waitstaff to the smoky, wooden decor. American and European sports on the TV. Bacon and cheese bocadillos are the only food served (€3). Live music Th-Su after 11pm (Irish, local guitarists, covers of American rock). Pint of Guinness and all draft beer €4, bottled beer €2.50-3.50, mixed drinks €5. Open daily 2pm-3am, and will open earlier for televised games. Cash only.

Berlin, C. Muntaner, 240 (☎93 200 65 42). M: Diagonal, L3/5. A slice of streamlined German style in Barcelona. Corner bar with marble accents and huge, naked light bulbs attracts area hipsters, and hordes of l'Eixample yuppies, and Barcelona's most beautiful people. Beer €2 during the day, €3 at night, €3.50 on weekends; cocktails €9. Open M-W 9:30pm-2am, Th-Sa 9:30pm-3am.

domèstic, C. Diputació, 215 (☎93 453 16 61). M: Urgell, L1. Multifaceted *bar-musical* with frequent poetry readings, art expositions, and live music. If all that seems too ambitious, it's also a fine place to just sit and have a drink. Artsy, too-cool-for-capital-letters crowd takes in funk, acid jazz, and soul rhythms on domèstic's overstuffed chairs. Small offering of eclectic Mediterranean food until midnight €5.90-11.30; sushi Th-F. Beer €3, mixed drinks €5. Open Su and Tu-Th 7pm-2:30am, F-Sa 8pm-3am.

Topxi, C. València, 358 (☎93 207 01 20), just off Pg. St. Joan. M: Verdaguer, L4/5. A small, unpretentious bar/club that just happens to put on some of the most flamboyant drag queen shows in the city—in intimate quarters. Daily shows at 2am, plus a sit-down show Su at 8pm. Mostly gay crowd, but some women and straight couples as well. Cover €6 for men, €9 for women (includes 1 drink). Open Su 7pm-5am, W-Th 11pm-5am, F-Sa 11pm-6am. Cash only.

Caligula, C. Consell de Cent, 257 (☎93 451 48 92). M: Pg. de Gràcia, L2/3/4. Bar designed in a pan-Asian style invokes a romantic atmosphere with draped fabrics, tea lights, Oriental music, Buddha statues, and massive floral arrangements. A chill crowd gathers around the bar and sidewalk tables. After 10pm there are transvestite spectacles. Beer €4.20, mixed drinks €6-9. Open daily 8pm-3am. Wheelchair accessible.Cash only.

The Pop Bar, C. Aribau, 103 (☎93 451 29 58). M: Hospital Clìnic, L5. Groovy baby, yeah! Join a hip 30-something crowd and travel back in time to the early 60s, when orange and brown was a cool color combination and people thought they looked good in paisley. DJs spin house, techno, and pop, as well as the requisite 60s-80s tunes. Beer €3-3.60, mixed drinks €4.80. Open W-Th 10pm-3am, F-Su 10pm-3:30am.

Aloha, C. Provença, 159 (☎93 451 79 62). M: Hospital Clìnic, L5. Barcelona's Hawaiian paradise—complete with exotic caged birds, leis, and plenty of bamboo. 2 pool tables and a wide liquor selection. All sorts of people find their haven in Hawaii here. Cross the bridge by the waterfall to find the darkened, intimate tiki huts perfect for private parties of 2 to 20; call ahead to reserve a table. Try the *coco loco,* coconut milk and rum (€6). Open Su-Th 6pm-3am and F-Sa 6pm-4am.

La Philharmonica, C. Mallorca, 204 (☎93 451 11 53; www.lafilharmonica.com). M: Hospital Clìnic, L5. English pub hosts live music (jazz, tango, blues, country) almost every night, and is a popular place for both young and old. Don't miss the country line dance classes Su and Tu nights, or quiz night (in English) on Th. Daily menú €7.60. Sunday's special is roast beef and potatoes. Pint of Guinness is €3.50 until 8pm. Live music cover €3.75-6. Open Su 10am-3am, M-Th 9am-3am, F 9am-3:30am, Sa 11am-3:30am.

Mas i Mas

Divina's, Av. Diagonal, 337 (☎93 458 21 60; http://divina's.tc7.net), next to Pg. St. Joan. M: Verdaguer, L4/5. A small, personally decorated lesbian bar: notice the necklaces hanging on the walls for sale and sketches above the bar. Good rock and roll, Spanish music, and female artists. Beer €2, cocktails up to €8. Open Tu-W 6pm-1am, Th 6pm-2am, F-Sa 6pm-3am. Wheelchair accessible. Cash only.

CLUBS

🕮 **Buenavista Salsoteca,** C. Rosselló, 217 (☎93 237 65 28; www.salsabuenavista.com). FGC: Provença. Appropriately, this over-the-top salsa club manages to attract a laid-back, mixed crowd. The Latin music is irresistible and the dancers are not shy, and encourage all novices. Free salsa, bachata, and merengue lessons W-Th 11:30pm. Su-Th free; F-Sa cover €10 (includes 1 drink). Open Su 8pm-2am, W-Th 11pm-4am, F-Sa 11pm-5am.

Pool at La Oveja

Luz de Gas, C. Muntaner, 246 (☎93 209 77 11). M: Diagonal, L3/5. Chandeliers, gilded mirrors, and deep red walls set the mood in this hip, uptown club. Live music every night including the occasional big-name jazz, blues, or soul performer like Branford Marsalis or Monica Green. In the 7 years since opening 4000 performances have taken place here. After 1am, the chairs are folded up and the luxurious club becomes a high-class disco playing pop music. For a more personal, quiet space, head to the glassed-in balcony. Beer €6, mixed drinks €9. Live music concerts €15; check the *Guía del Ocio* for listings and times. Open daily 11pm-5am; July-Aug. closed Su. Wheelchair accessible.

Salvation, Ronda de St. Pere, 19-21, between C. Bruc and Pl. Urquinaona. M: Urquinaona. The place to come if you've sinned...and want to keep on sin-

Beer in Plaça Pi

ning. A popular gay club with 2 huge dance floors and pounding house music. Su is a mixed crowd. Beer €5; mixed drinks €8. Cover €11 (includes 1 drink). Open F-Su midnight-6am. Wheelchair accessible.

La Boîte, Av. Diagonal, 477 (☎93 419 92 98). M: Hospital Clínic, L5. Big names, such as Lenny Kravitz and the Cindy Blackman Group, sometimes come to perform in this intimate disco setting. Live jazz, funk, and blues nightly midnight-2am. A smaller dance floor and plenty of bar room makes this a great place for people that shun the gyrating masses of larger venues. Drinks €4.20-7.20. Music cover Su-Th €7, F-Sa €10. Disco no cover Su-Th after 2am, cover €9 F-Sa after 2am (includes one drink). Open M-Th 11:30pm-4am, F-Sa 11:30pm-6am.

Illusion, C. Lepanto, 408 (☎93 247 36 00), right below M: Alfons X, L4. A favorite destination for students and local kids in their 20s, this club is more happening in winter than in summer. Two dance rooms: house music in the main and salsa in the smaller. Go-go shows tease the audience every 15min. or so, starting around 3am. Beer €4, mixed drinks €6. Hosts a gay session ("T Dance") Su 7pm-midnight. 18+. Cover Su €8, F €7, Sa €9. Open F midnight-5am, Sa 6-10pm (for 16+) and 12:30-5:30am. Closed Aug. Cash only.

Arena (Sala Diana), C. València, 236. M: Pg. de Gràcia, L2/3/4. One of Barcelona's biggest and most popular lesbian clubs. Throngs of women crowd the multicolored dance floor, grooving to pop, house, and 80s classics. Women-only strip show from 6-10pm first Su of every month. Cover Su-F €5, Sa €6 (includes one drink). Open Su-F 11pm-3am. Check out the Arena family's other **gay discos,** some of the most popular in the area: **Arena (Sala Classic)** at C. Diputació, 233 plays 80s tunes; **Arena (Sala Dandy)** at Gran Via, 593 pumps techno beats. The popular **Arena (Sala Madre)** at C. Balmes, 32 is mostly for men, as is the more relaxed **Punto BCN** bar at C. Muntaner, 63.

Sol, C. Villarroel, 216 (☎93 237 86 58). M: Hospital Clínic, L5, or Diagonal, L3/5. Barcelona's beautiful, uptown set hits the wooden, elegantly lighted dance floor or mingles upstairs on the couches. Downstairs disco plays pop and house; upstairs is smaller, more laid-back, and plays less intense disco. Mixed drinks €5-7.50. Cover €10 (includes one drink). Open Th-Sa midnight-5:30am.

POBLE NOU & PORT OLÍMPIC

If you want to party in **Poble Nou,** trade in your skimpy clubbing outfit for something a little more grunge, brush up on your foosball skills, and be prepared to indulge in some heavy metal with rebellious Spanish teens or some classic rock with the 30-somethings. This neighborhood is the place to be for hard rock and alternative music. Locals have put abandoned see map p. 347 warehouses to good use in the blocks around M: Marina, L1, and more than 20 bars and discos coexist within a few minutes of each one another. The drinking here is remarkably cheap, and as the patrons are locals, not tourists, the crowd flow is the reverse of the rest of the city: packed during the school year and slower in the summer.

L'Ovella Negra (Megataverna del Poble Nou), C. Zamora, 78 (☎93 309 59 38; http://personal.redestb.es/ovella_negra/on.htm). From M: Marina, walk 2 blocks along C. Almogàvers and turn right on C. Zamora. This cavernous warehouse-turned-medieval tavern is the brother of La Oveja Negra in El Raval and given the wallet-friendly prices, is *the* place to come for the first few beers of the night: €2 for large beer; cocktails start at €2. As the night progresses, the massive space fills up. Foosball games on the 2nd floor are nearly as intense as the real-life FCB/Real Madrid rivalry. Filling bocadillos €2-3. Open F-Sa 5pm-3am, Su 5-10:30pm; kitchen open until 12:30am. Wheelchair accessible.

Razzmatazz, C. Pamplona, 88 (☎93 320 82 00; www.razzmatazz.com), 2½ blocks from M: Marina; follow C. Almogàvers. Another huge warehouse-turned-entertainment complex, with strobe-lit dance floors and concert space for indy-rock. A 2-in-1 club: choose either the front entrance for 3 rooms or the back entrance for 2; the entrances are not connected. Cover €9, includes 1 drink. Concert prices vary, call ahead for listings. Beer €3, cocktails begin at €5. Open F-Sa, and holidays midnight-4am. MC/V.

Boveda, C. Pallars, 97 (☎93 412 62 15; www.bovedagroup.com). A consistently popular club with loud, pounding pop and dance beats. Beer €3, cocktails €5 and up. Open Su 6pm-11:30pm, Th-Sa midnight-5:30am, and F-Sa 6-10pm. Part of the same complex with a more relaxed environment, **DIXI 724,** boasts cheap beer, a bizarre shark-turned-airplane hanging from the ceiling, independent music (especially rock), and tons of space for college crowds. Beer €1.90, cocktails €4-5. Open F-Su 6pm-3am.

Bar Coyote & Co., C. Pere IV, 68. An American-Western twist on the typical Spanish bar, complete with a poster of the cast of *Coyote Ugly* on the wall. Music is mostly heavy metal and rock. Open Th 9pm-3am, F-Su 7pm-3am. Wheelchair accessible.

The Other Place Biker Bar, C. Pujades, 226 (☎93 309 87 15; www.theotherplace.es), kitty-corner from M: Poble Nou. Hell's Angels memorabilia, biker videos playing on the televisions, and even its very own biker clothing line make this place more than just your average bar. Open Th-Su 10pm-3am.

Plaça del Sol

PASSEIG MARÍTIM

Cinderella and the **Port Olímpic** have one thing in common: after midnight they become entirely different creatures. In contrast to the rest of Poble Nou, the Passeig Marítim caters to tourists with money to burn. A long strip of single-room, side-by-side glitzy clubs fling open their doors, and the once-peaceful walkway becomes a packed carnival of wild, skimpily-dressed dance fiends and late-night eaters and drinkers (food options include McDonald's, Haägen-Dazs, hotdog stands, and fish restaurants). Mixed drinks are expensive (€6-8), but people seem to get enough to start table-dancing almost as soon as the doors open. **Pachito** is the place to go for swanky clubbers; the **Kennedy Irish Sailing Club** (beer €4.50) is a popular haven for pubbers. There is no cover anywhere. If you don't like the music in one club, just shove your way outside and choose another; the range includes salsa, techno, hip-hop, and plenty of American pop. All the clubs on the block are open 5pm-6am.

Club Danzatoria, C. Ramon Trias Fargas, 24 (☎93 206 49 50; www.gruposalsitos.com), on the corner with Pg. Marítim. The sleek interior decorating and strut-your-stuff entryway make this place one of the hottest places in town, if not to get a date then at least to people-watch. House music will keep the pressure on. Cover €15, one drink included. Open Th-Su midnight until empty.

Casa Almirall

Jamboree

Baja Beach Club, Pg. Marítim, 34 (☎93 225 91 00; www.bajabeach.es). If Baywatch were a club, this would be it. When not platform-dancing, bikini-clad waitresses and shirtless muscle men serve drinks as patrons get their groove on amidst fake palm trees and a decorative speedboat. The indoor/outdoor restaurant serves seafood, and American-fast-food-inspired fare is served until 1am; entrees €7-18.50. Menú €12. Beer €3.50, mixed drinks €7. Cover Th-Sa €14, Su €12; Su free for ladies, and free if you eat dinner. Opens daily 1pm on the terrace for the day; to dance, Th-F 9pm-4:30am, Sa-Su 9pm-5am. Wheelchair accessible. AmEx/MC/V.

El Gran Casino, C. Marina, 19 (☎93 225 78 78; www.casino-barcelona.com), under the fish. Minimum bets are quite low, starting at €2, despite the glam atmosphere. An older crowd, mostly over 40 (must be 18 to play). Entrance fee €4.50. Blackjack, American roulette, French roulette, slots, and *punto banco* are the main options. No sneakers or beach clothes; jacket recommended for men. Passport required. Open daily 1pm-5am. Wheelchair accessible. MC/V.

BARCELONETA & PORT VELL

Like Dr. Jekyll, Barcelona's biggest mall has more than one personality. By night, the waterfront shopping center transforms into an overwhelming tri-level maze of cheesy, tourist-packed dance clubs. Each club plays its own music, from pop to salsa to house, for crowds of international students, tourists, and the occasional Spaniard. **Maremàgnum** is not an "authentic" Barcelona experience in any way; unless you're desperate to get your groove on during the week or after bars close at 3am, look elsewhere for a good time. While no one charges cover, clubs make their money by charging way too much money for drinks. Catching a cab home can be a nightmare for bleary-eyed revelers. All clubs are accessible by M: Drassanes, L3 and can be reached by walking to the ocean end of Las Ramblas and continuing over the ocean on La Rambla del Mar footbridge.

see map p. 348

Nayandei (☎93 225 81 37), top floor. Actually 2 clubs side by side: **Disco**, with scantily-clad go-go dancers and an open-door policy, and **Boite**, which is slightly more exclusive, with a dress code. Whatever the outfit, both clubs attempt at being the Pied Piper of English-speaking tourists, playing energetic dance-pop with a somewhat disingenuous Latin flavor. Beer €5, mixed drinks €8-10. Open Su-Th 9pm-4:30am, F-Sa 9pm-5am.

Star Winds, top floor. Pumping bass and non-stop house make this the choice of clubbers unable to stomach the cheesy pop or golden oldies playing elsewhere. Beer €5, mixed drinks €8-10. Open Su-Th 10:30pm-4:30am, F-Sa 10:30pm-5am.

Mojito Bar (☎93 225 80 14), first floor. The windows of this *salsoteca* are often as crowded as the dance floor itself, as admirers gawk at the cliché moves of dancers inside. The salsa and merengue music attracts both talented dancers and drunk novices who do their best to keep up. In the summer, salsa dance lessons every night at 9pm—call ahead to sign up. Beer €5, mixed drinks €6. Open Su-Th 9pm-4:30am, F-Sa 9pm-5am.

Central Golf, top floor. The clubs upstairs surround this mini-golf course, a favorite drunken leisure activity. If you're seeing multiple holes, aim for the middle one. €5 per round. Open Su-Th noon-3am, F-Sa noon-4am.

MONTJUÏC

BARS

▨ **Tinta Roja,** C. Creu dels Molers, 17 (☎93 443 32 43). From M: Poble Sec, L3, walk down Av. Parallel and turn right on C. Creu dels Molers; it will be on your left. An old factory that has been lovingly converted into a spectacle of Argentinian delights by owners (and tango gurus) Hugo and Carmen. Eclectically furnished with mirrors, deep red walls, and thrift-store leftovers, Tinta Roja is a multifaceted art space featuring

see map p. 346

tango dance and music (see **It takes two to Tango,** p. 156). Spike your *tinta roja* (red wine and lemonade) with a shot of the Argentinian liquor Caña Legui, the bar's specialty, served in exquisite gold-rimmed glasses. Candlelit bar and tables. Shows Th-Sa 10pm, €9-12 with drink; call ahead for reservations. Tango lessons W 9pm-1:30am, €50 per month. Open July-Aug. Tu-Th 7pm-1:30am, F-Sa 8pm-3am; Sept.-June Su and Tu-Th 7pm-1:30am, F-Sa 8pm-3am. Cash only.

Mau Mau, C. d'En Fontrodona, 33 (☎60 686 06 17). M: Parallel, L2/L3. Follow C. d'En Fontrodona as it bends right, past C. Blai. Look for a gray door on the left as you walk up the street and ring the bell. This hideout has an incredibly warm feel to it with young locals on couches spread across the lounge. Films screened Su 8:30, 10:30pm. Residents from Barcelona buy yearlong "membership" (€5), but out-of-towners need only sign in at the door. Drinks €3 and up. Open Su 7-11pm, Th 11pm-2:30am, F-Sa 11pm-3am. Cash Only.

Fake Moustaches

Rouge, C. Poeta Cabanyes, 21 (☎93 442 49 85). M: Parallel, L2/L3. From Av. Parallel, turn onto C. Peeta Cabanyes. Look for the door on your left and ring the bell. Bathed in warm red light, Rouge is a hip bar and lounge with a clientele and a cocktail menu to match. Test the strong and tasty Rouge Punch—rum, cane sugar, and lime (€6.50)—while the DJ/owner spins hip-hop, electronica, jazz, and pop. Drinks €3-8. Open Th-Sa 11pm-5am. Cash only.

CLUBS

Club Apolo/Nitsaclub, C. Nou de la Rambla, 113 (☎93 301 00 90; www.sala-apolo.com). M: Parallel, L2/L3. Old 1950s dance hall hosts live music shows, usually reggae, rock, or funk. Th nights *Power Room*—a blend of funk, soul, jazz—is arguably the best way to celebrate the upcoming weekend. Cover €6 includes one drink; pick up a flyer at Mau Mau bar (see bar listings) for free entrance. F-Sa nights **Nitsaclub,** a hip-hop/pop/soul extravaganza, features a slew of international guest DJs. Smaller dance floor upstairs gets it going to house. Cover €12, includes 1 drink. Open daily 12:30-6:30am.

Cava at Xampanyet

La Terrazza/Discothèque (☎93 423 12 85), on Av. Marqués de Comillas. M: Espanya, L1/3. Enter to the right of the front gates of Poble Espanyol. Crowds decked out in everything from fancy club wear to leather and chains groove until dawn. Mostly house beats and the sounds of an occasional guest DJ on La Terazza's outdoor plaza. Same deal when the club heads inside Oct.-May and becomes **Discothèque.** Drinks €4-8. Cover €20, includes 1 drink. Open Th-Sa midnight-6am.

Torres de Ávila (☎93 424 93 09), next to the main entrance of Poble Espanyol. M: Espanya, L1/3. A million-peseta construction that was at the height of

Poble Espanyol at Night

the local story

It takes two to Tango

*Carmen Cubero, from Spain, runs a dance bar with her Argentinian partner Hugo Zubillaga. **Tinta Roja**, in Poble Sec at the foot of Montjuïc, both hosts performances and offers tango lessons (see listing p. 154).*

LG: Why did you choose this area to open a bar?

A: Poble Sec has always had a vibrant nightlife; there are a lot of theatre and concert venues... The area is very art-oriented; Hugo and I feel it has a good future ahead of it. It made sense to open a bar/performance space in such an environment.

LG: How do you orchestrate the artistic side of the enterprise?

A: Hugo's background is in theater, and mine is in dance and painting... People hear of Tinta Roja by word of mouth, and then they come to us with proposals for performances.

LG: What types of performances are generally put on?

A: Everything ranging from theater to dance or music. We offer a lot of concerts of Argentinian music. Ethnic music is also a big part of the schedule. And tango. "Tinta Roja" is the name of a tango.

LG: What about Tinta Roja do you most enjoy?

A: That there is passion within it. In all corners, you can find passion.

club chic when it was built in the '80s. Torres is still going strong as one of the city's hottest night spots, complete with glass elevators, 7 bars, and a summertime rooftop terrace with gorgeous views of the city. DJs spin house and techno. Drinks €5-10. Dress to impress. Cover €18, includes 1 drink. Open Th-Sa midnight-6:30am.

Candela, C. Mexic 7-9, parallel to Av. Reina María Cristina and close to Poble Espanyol. M: Espanya, L1/3. New warehouse-style club is an un-touristed find featuring merengue and salsa rhythms that will make you sweat. Occasionally has live music. Gets started late. Drinks €4-9. No sneakers. Cover €6. Open F-Su 11:30pm-5am.

ZONA ALTA

GRÀCIA

see map p. 342-345

After dark, local hipsters are drawn to Gràcia like bees to honey. The scene is on the mellow side—groups and young couples converge on the area's many bars and crowd the *plaças* until well into the night, often accompanied by an amateur guitarist or two. **Pl. Virreina** and **Pl. de Rius i Taulet** have a variety of tapas bars and relaxed crowds. 🔲**Pl. del Sol** is the busiest place to party—try **Sol Soler** (☎689 384 524), **Sol de Nit** (☎93 237 39 37), and **Cafe del Sol** (☎93 415 56 63). All three are open daily until 2 or 3am. If the bars are as packed, feel free to bring your drink or even a bottle of wine out to the *plaça*.

BARS

🔲 **Gasterea,** C. Verdi, 39 (☎93 237 23 43). M: Fontana, L3. Follow C. Astúries for several blocks and make a right on C. Verdi. Yellow walls cast a warm glow in this table-less bar. Grab a seat at one of the counters and dig in to Gasterea's selection of excellent, fresh tapas (€1.05). Mixed drinks €5. Su-Tu and Th 7pm-1am, F-Sa 7pm-2am. Cash only.

St. Germain, C. Torrent de l'Olla, 113 (☎932180413). M: Fontana, L3. Turn left on C. d'Asturies, and right on C. Torrent de l'Olla. Walk three blocks. Bring your artwork to show the manager--St. Germain might well put it up on its walls for a few weeks. Not an aspiring artist? Then just come to enjoy the paintings and a slideshow of photographs in the back while you sip your drink (beer €1.60 or ½L €4, mixed drinks €4). Serves food as well. Try the leek, bacon, and goat cheese quiche (€2.10). Open Su-Tu and Th 6pm-2:30am, F-Sa 6pm-3am. Cash only.

Buda, C. Torrent de L'Olla, 134 (☎65 804 567). M: Fontana, L3. Follow C. Astúries and turn right on C. Torrent de L'Olla. Exposed stone walls illuminate funky wall lamps at this chill bar with pool table. Oh-so-good for relaxing. Beer €2.40-3, mixed drinks €4.70-9.50. Open M-Th 9:30pm-2:30am, F-Sa 9pm-3:30am.

Ikastola, C. La Perla, 22 (☎647719198), off C. Verdi. M: Fontana, L3. Does being a grown-up have you down? Then head back to Ikastola (the Basque word for "nursery school") without letting go of the perks of adulthood (like alcohol). Chalkboard-covered walls beckon would-be Picassos and Verdaguers to leave their mark. Beer and red wine only (€3). Open M-Th 6pm-midnight, Sa-Su 6pm-2am. Cash only.

Flann O'Brien's, C. Casanova, 264 (☎93 201 16 06). M: Diagonal, L3/5. Authentic Irish pub with barrels for tables and rugby shirts hanging from the ceiling. Popular with Barcelona's English-speaking expats. Top off your evening with a Guinness or a mixed drink (€3.80-5.20). Open daily 6pm-3am.

Casablanca, C. Bonavista, 6 (☎93 237 63 99). M: Diagonal, L3/5. In this plush, black marble and mirror bar, images of Rick and Ilsa beckon you to try one of Casablanca's cava (Catalan champagne) specialties, like the *jalisco* with tequila and lemon juice (€6). Sophisticated crowd at night. Also open during the day. Appetizers €3.80-7.80, entrees €3-13.50. Open M-Th 8am-5pm and 6pm-2:30am, F-Sa 8am-5pm and 6pm-3:30am. MC/V.

I que? C. Topazi, 8. (☎93 416 07 33) M: Fontana, L3. Turn left on C. d'Asturies and walk three blocks to Pl. del Diamant; C. Topazi will be on your left. Young locals crowd this brightly lit bar to enjoy cheap drinks and an upbeat atmosphere. Sit at the one of the bar's many tables to drink your *clara* while conversing with your neighbor. Also serves tapas, pizzas, and pasta. Open Su-Th 6pm-1:30am, F 6pm-3am, Sa 8pm-3am. Cash only.

Blues Café, C. La Perla, 37 (☎93 416 09 65). M: Fontana, L3. Follow C. Astúries to C. Verdi and turn right, walk 2 blocks to C. Perla, and turn left. Plastered with photos of blues legends. Plenty of cheap beer to go around (€2). Mixed drinks €4.50. Open Su-Th 6:30pm-2:30am, F-Sa 6:30pm-3am. Cash only.

Bahía, C. Sèneca, 12. (☎63 646 68 20). From M: Diagonal, L3/5, walk uphill on Pg. de Gràcia and turn left on C. Seneca. Popular and funky lesbian bar. All are welcome. Beer €3, mixed drinks €5-6. Open Tu-Th 10pm-3am, F-Sa 10pm-3am, Su 6am-10am.

Bamboleo, C. Topazi, 24 (☎93 217 32 60). M: Fontana, L3. Above Pl. del Diamante. Cuban bar hosts salsa, techno, and rock DJs, and friendly, informal turns on the foosball table. Calimocho, mojitos, and piña coladas €4 each. An unbelievably long list of *chupitos* (€2.50 each). A good place to end the night. Open M-Th 7pm-2:30am, F-Sa 7pm-3am.

CLUBS

Nick Havanna, C. Rosello, 208 (☎60 749 79 81; www.nickhavanna.com). FGC: Provenca. Trendy Spaniards and tourists converge to grind to pop hits. Check out the rotating slide projections. Dress to impress (no sneakers). Drinks €6-8. Cover €10. Open W-Sa, 11:30pm-5am. AmEx/MC/V.

KGB, C. Alegre de Dalt, 55 (☎93 210 59 06). M: Joanic, L4. Walk along C. Pi i Maragall and take the 1st left; to get a cab home, come back to Pi i Maragall. Loud rock, and techno play to a mixed crowd of students and Soviet secret agents. Occasional live concerts 9pm. Beer €3-4, mixed drinks €6. Cover €10, includes 1 drink. Open Su and F-Sa 1-8am. Cash only.

TIBIDABO

Although pricey and hard to access, the few bars in Tibidabo offer fabulous, shimmering night views of Barcelona from on high. Unless you have really good shoes and willpower, getting there by taxi is the only option. Ask the driver for the number of the taxi company to call on the way back.

Trying Absinthe

Torres de Ávila

Dancing

BARS

Mirabé, Manuel Arnus, 2 (☎934 340 035; www.mirabe.com). Pl. Dr. Andreu. A large elegant bar overlooks the Mediterranean shore. The club on the lower floor is open Th-Sa. Walk from the crowded dance floor onto an outside patio to sip your drink on a beach chair under the stars. Beers €4, cocktails €8. Open daily 7pm-5am. AmEx/MC/V.

Mirablau, Pl. Dr. Andreu (☎93 418 58 79). Next to Mirabé (see above). The bar's organic architecture, dim lighting, impressive cocktail menu, and discreet staff attract well-dressed couples and young professionals. The nightclub downstairs offers the same spectacular view as the bar, but is only worth going to on weekends. Drinks €6-11. Open M-Th 11pm-4:30am, F and Sa 11pm-5:45am. MC/V.

Meybeyé, Pl. Dr. Andreu (☎93 417 92 79). Set slightly back from the cliff, this is a good choice for those afraid of heights. A swank and sultry interior greets loungers for tapas and cocktails, while the outside glass canopy provides an intimate setting for couples and small groups of friends. Beer €3.60, drinks €6. Open daily noon-2am.

CLUBS

Partycular, Av. Tibidabo, 61 (☎93 211 62 61; www.partycular.com), halfway up the hill from Pl. JFK. This sophisticated old mansion brims with a young crowd gyrating to pop, dance, and house hits. Drinks €7-8. Open daily 9pm-4am.

🎷 BETWEEN SARRIÀ AND GRÀCIA

Sick of expats and backpackers guzzling Guinness? Want to meet someone down the with local scene? The eclectic mix of late-night cafes, bars, and clubs around Pl. Molina is packed with established hot spots and savvy Barcelonese who know better than to join the tourists on Las Ramblas at night.

🎷 **Otto Zutz,** C. Lincoln, 15 (☎93 238 07 22; www.ottozutz.com) FGC: Pl. Molina. Walk downhill on Via Augusta and take C. Lincoln when it splits off to the right. One of the larger nightlife spots in the area, Otto Zutz is the place to see and be seen. Well-heeled Spaniards groove to house, hip-hop, funk, and rap on 2 floors, with a floor for private parties and a lounge soaked in red light. Occasionally has live music. Beer €5, mixed drinks €8. Cover €15 (includes 1 drink), but look for discount cards at bars and upscale hotels all over the city, or email to get on the guest list for a discount. Open Tu-Sa midnight-6:30am.

🎷 **D_Mer,** C. Plató, 13 (☎93 201 62 07). FCG: Muntaner. Walk uphill on C. Muntaner for 2 blocks and turn right on C. Plató. A blue-hued heaven for lesbians of all ages to chat it up by the orchids that decorate the bar, or boogie on the dance floor to fun pop tunes. A touch of class, a dash of whimsy, and a ton of fun. Women and gay men only. F-Sa cover €7. Beer €3.50, mixed drinks €6. Open Th-Sa 11pm-3:30am.

Bar Marcel, C. Santaló, 42 (☎93 209 89 48), at C. de Marià Cubí. Before midnight, this enormously popular bar masquerades as a quiet, unassuming cafe. But when the clock strikes 12, locals pack the place in search of cheap booze. Certainly not the fanciest bar in the neighborhood, but possibly the most loved. Coffee €1, beer €1.60, mixed drinks €5. Prices vary outdoors/indoors, day/night. Open daily 8pm-3am.

Bubblic Bar, C. Marià Cubí, 183 (☎93 414 54 01; www.bubblicbar.com). FCG: Muntaner. Walk down C. Muntaner and turn right on C. Marià Cubí. With 2 dance floors downstairs, 1 upstairs, and outdoor drinking amidst the yellow glow of tiki torches, this bar/club manages to cater to almost every taste, miraculously leaving enough room for bargoers to breathe. DJs spin English and Spanish pop and house. Beer €3, mixed drinks €5. No cover. Open Th-Sa 11:30pm-3:30am. MC/V.

Mas i Mas, C. Marià Cubí, 199 (☎93 209 45 02). FGC: Muntaner. Walk down C. Muntaner and turn right on C. Marià Cubí. Walk three blocks. This small, simply decorated bar gets cramped, but that just adds to the fun. DJ spins hip-hop and pop. Beer €3, mixed drinks €5. Open Su-Th 7pm-2:30am, F-Sa 7pm-3am.

Eternity Cafe, C. Amigo 22-24 (☎93 534 12 25). FGC: Muntaner. Walk two blocks up Via Augusta and turn left on C. Amigo. This recently opened bar fits the neighborhood's penchant for unpretentious style. The sidewalk terrace attracts young locals with its cheap beer (€1.50) in the late afternoon and chill music at night. Mixed drinks €4.50-5. Open Su-Th 5:30pm-2am, F-Sa until 3am.

Entertainment

Barcelona offers a wide range of entertainment, from outdoor activities, sports, and bullfights to shopping, cinema, festivals, and performances of all sorts. Consult the invaluable **Guía del Ocio,** €0.90 at newsstands, for info on movies (*Cine*), live concerts (*Música*), nightlife (*Tarde/Noche*), and cultural events. While Barcelona proper is full of great parks, those truly interested in outdoor activities should be sure to peruse the **Daytrips** chapter (see p. 203) for information on nearby beaches, mountain hikes, ski resorts, and other outdoor sports.

BEACHES

POBLE NOU

🏴 *Beach info* ☎ *93 481 00 53. Dogs, camping tents, motorcycles, soap, music, and trash are not allowed on the beaches. Police, the Red Cross, various restaurants and bars, and information are available on the promenade between Nova Icària and Bogatell, and at Nova Mar Bella, May 15-Sept.15 daily 10am-7pm. Lockers at police stations. Mar Bella and Nova Mar Bella are fully wheelchair-accessible.*

The beaches to the north of Port Olímpic (left, facing the water) include Platja Nova Icària, Platja del Bogatell, Platja Mar Bella, and Platja Nova Mar Bella (from the port to Nova Mar Bella is about a 20min. walk). Each of them has a lifeguard, shower stations, a restaurant on the walkway above the sand, and a refreshment stand on the

the BIG $plurge

Full of Hot Air

If the Barcelona summer heat is getting to you, look no further than Baló Tour for escape from the confines of a terrestrial existence. Baló is a Barcelona-based hot air balloon company that specializes in passenger trips for both tourists and business groups. Every precaution is taken to assure a safe journey and all meteorological factors are carefully considered before each flight. To read a detailed profile of each balloon and pilot visit www.balotour.com.

Baló offers three types of rides, all complete with your very own flight diploma and meal in air: The "complete flight" option takes about 90 minutes and costs €135 per person, ages 6-12 €80. The "flight with change of passengers" offers a 45 minute trip to a group of no fewer than 10 people, stopping midway through the trip to change passengers. (€90, ages 6-12 €50.) If you're really looking to splurge, try the "Two Reservoir Traverse." The trip gets to altitudes of 2000-3000m and surveys such places as Plaça de l'Estany, Garroxta, Selva and Empordá. (€900 per group, maximum of five people.)

C. Montecassino, 2. ☎93 414 47 74. Reservations required. Flights take off at 7am in summer, 9am in winter and last all morning. AmEx/MC/V.

beach. There is usually someone renting sunbathing chairs (€3 per day) on Nova Icària, and people often bring volleyball nets and balls to the shore. The beaches are clean and safe for public use.

BARCELONETA

🚏 *M: Barceloneta, L4, or any "Pg. Marítim" bus route. For daily information on the city's beaches, call ☎93 48 100 53. Police, Red Cross, and information services are all available in a booth behind the outdoor showers; open all day.*

Barceloneta's two main beaches, Platja San Sebastià and Platja Barceloneta (adjacent to one another), are the neighborhood's biggest draws, having been re-vamped for the Olympics. The beaches are cleaned every night by large sifting tractors, but depending on what time of day you come you may encounter a few cigarette butts and beer cans lying around. In the summer, natives and tourists alike flock to the area for a daily dose of sun and swim. One of the city's longest stretches of sand, San Sebastià is the beach at the end of Pg. Joan de Borbó, farthest from Port Vell. On weekends in particular, the center area near the entrance is the most crowded of all. Venture farther afield for a less congested area. Open space does have its price—be prepared for some hardcore nudity. Topless-tanning is common on all the city beaches, but people begin to lose their bottoms as well toward the nether regions of San Sebastià. The exposed beach bums of San Sebastià prefer sunbathing to leisure sports, so take your volleyball elsewhere.

The central beach on the Barceloneta peninsula is Platja Barceloneta, which leads up to Port Olímpic and Frank Gehry's famous copper **Peix** (Fish) sculpture. Another public sculpture is **Homage to Barceloneta** by Rebecca Horn, which resembles a teetering stack of children's blocks. The proximity to the park makes the beach popular with tourists.

WATERFRONT ACTIVITIES

For those who would rather be active than lie in the sun, there are several options in the Vila Olímpica area, both on water and land. Boating and beach sports abound, and the coastal bike path runs about 4km in total length. Below is a list of beach clubs with different waterfront options, including plenty of nighttime beach-front fun.

BOAT TOURS

Las Golondrinas (☎93 442 31 06), on Portal de la Pau. M: Drassanes, L3. At the foot of the Monument a Colom, in **Port Vell**. 2-decker ferries chug around the entire Port Vell, as far as Montjuïc and back. (35min.; July-Aug. daily every 40min. 11:45am-9pm, Sept.-June every hr. M-F noon-6pm, Sa-Su noon-7:30pm; €3.50, children €1.75) A longer excursion includes a **tour of Port Olímpic**. (1½hr.; July-Aug. daily every hr. 11:30am-7:30pm; Sept.-June 3 per day 11am-5:30pm; round-trip €8.50, seniors and students €6.10, ages 4-10 €3.70. MC/V.)

Catamarán Orsom (☎93 441 05 37, fax 93 441 21 14; www.barcelona-orsom.com), right next to Las Golondrinas on Portal de la Pau in Port Vell. M: Drassanes, L3. This 75ft catamaran will take you on a more upscale, relaxing sail around the Barcelona coast at up to 16 knots. Feel free to sunbathe in the back while snacking on delicious hors d'oeuvres. 1hr 20min. cruises at 1, 4, and 6pm: round-trip €12, ages 11-18 and seniors €9, 4-10 €6. MC/V.

WATERSPORT RENTALS

Base Náutica de Mar Bella, Av. Littoral (☎93 221 04 32; www.basenautica.org), on Platja de la Mar Bella. The Mar Bella nautical base offers classes in windsurfing (€120 for 10hr.), catamaran sailing (€150 for 16hr.), sailboat sailing (€187 for 16hr.), kayaking (€79 for 10hr.), and diving and navigation. Membership (€145 per year) brings a 10-30% discount off all courses. The base also rents kayaks (€11 per hr.), windsurfing boards (€16 per hr.), and catamarans (€21 per hr.) and leads group trips. Open daily May-Sept. 10am-8pm; Oct.-Apr. 10am-4:30pm.

Centre Municipal de Vela (☎93 225 79 40; cmv@fcv.es), Moll de Gregal Port Olímpic. In the left corner of the port as you walk toward the water, lower level. Like the nautical base, the municipal sailing center offers lessons in windsurfing, sailing, and navigation for varying time periods, as well as member services including saunas and massages. This posh workout palace is a more expensive, elite option than the nautical base, with a plethora of offerings; check the website or pick up an informational newsletter at the front desk. Membership 21+ is €160 annually, ages 15-20 €124, 14 and under €98. Family prices available. Open daily 10am-8pm.

Spanish Guitar

GUíA DEL oCIO

Grec Festival Advertisement

the BIG $plurge

¡GOOOOAL!

Be a Barça fan for a day and go all out. First, slather on red-and-blue face paint. buy an authentic red-and-blue striped jersey. Then grab a 6-pack of San Miguel and get ready to scream...a lot.

You might be able to watch the game on television, but never will you be able replicate the hype, the energy, the camaraderie, the cheers and chants ("Olé...olé, olé, olé....), the sweat, the love, the victory and loss, or the announcer's sweet, rewarding, almost never-ending "Gooooooool!". All of these elements help to make up the culture of the Spanish soccer game, and attending one of these in Barcelona will never be forgotten, granting you a glimpse into a sacred aspect of Spanish life.

For information on upcoming games, check with the the El Barca office (☎ 93 496 36 00; www.fcbarcelona.com). Tickets can only be purchased in person; open Sept.-June M-F (and the day before matches) 9:30am-1:30pm and 3:30-6pm; July-Aug. 8am-2:30pm. Tickets vary in price, but lowest will generally €30 for normal games. Bigger games can go up to €90. See Spectator Sports, p. 175, for directions.

OLYMPIC FACILITIES

MONTJUÏC

SOCCER

Estadi Olímpic de Montjuïc, Pg. Olímpic, 17-19 (☎93 426 20 89, 24hr. 90 210 12 12). The stadium hosts free soccer games for Barcelona's second beloved team, R.C. Deportivo Espanyol, a.k.a. los periquitos (parakeets). Open daily 10am-8pm. Obtain R.C. Deportivo Espanyol tickets from Banco Catalana.

SWIMMING

Piscines Bernat Picornell, Av. Estadi, 30-40 (☎93 423 40 41; www.picornell.com), to the right when you're facing the stadium. Test your swimming skills in the Olympic pools, two gorgeous facilities surrounded by stadium seating. A favorite for families and sunbathers. There is also a small cafe inside the complex. €4.40 for outdoor pool, €8 for pool and workout facilities including sauna, massage parlor, and gym. Outdoor pool open Su 9am-8pm, M-Sa 9am-9pm. Workout facilities open Su 7:30am-8pm, M-F 7am-midnight, Sa 7am-9pm.

THE GREAT OUTDOORS

The Collserola mountains at Barcelona's back door definitely compensate for the metropolitan area's lack of greenery. Hiking, biking, picnicking, and horseback riding opportunities abound in their moderate peaks. For other outdoor activities, such as skiing in the Pyrenees or hiking Montserrat, see **Daytrips,** p. 203.

PARC DE COLLSEROLA

The **Centro d'Informació,** Carretera de l'Església, 92, has all the information you'll need on activities in the park. (See p. 110; ☎93 280 35 52. http://ParcCollserola.amb.es. FGC: Baixador de Vallvidrera, then follow signs to center. Open daily 9:30am-3pm; closed Dec. 25-26 and Jan. 1 and 6.) The main **map** (€6; available in English) plots major roads and services in the park. The staff can advise you on various facilities and options in and around the park.

HIKING

The information center provides numerous useful guides to hiking paths in the park. For those who want to stay close to home, there are six hikes, marked with red, yellow, orange, blue, green, or purple, which start and end near the center itself. The red path to the **Font de la Budellera** (Budellera Spring), is an easy hike to the Torre de Collserola, Tibidabo, or the town of Vallvidrera. The leaflet "Walks Around," available for free at the center, gives a detailed description of each color-coded itinerary, which range from 15min. (green path) to 2¼hr. (purple path). For info on more in-depth hiking, the *Parc de Collserola Guide Book* (€18) lists five hikes which traverse large portions of the park and begin and end at public transportation. Separate guided tours can be arranged for €81 per group of 20. The tours are available every morning all year except in August and last about three hours. Call in advance for tours in English (☎93 280 35 52). The park has few extremely challenging hikes and can be as rewarding for beginners as for the more experienced.

BIKING

Biking in the park is limited to paths which are at least 3m wide, but there are plenty of them. The problem is locating them; the info office stopped publishing its bike guide. However, the main map (€6) notes road conditions, and most roads are marked with signs indicating whether they are bicycle-friendly. In another twist of bad luck for bikers, there is no bike rental shop near the park; you will have to rent one downtown and bring it up on an FGC train (see **Bike Rentals,** p. 309). Most FGC stations are equipped with escalators and ramps along the stairwells. One of the most popular paths, though not very far into the park, is the **Passeig Mirador de las Aigues,** which offers bikers and hikers a view of Barcelona along a 9km trail. To get there, take the FGC from Pl. de Catalunya to the Peu del Funicular stop, catch the funicular, and press the request button to get out halfway up, at C. de Aigües.

HORSEBACK RIDING

There are six stables in the park, but most of them are far from public transportation. One exception is the **Hípica Severino,** Pg. Calado, 12, near the town of Sant Cugat. Guides here lead 1hr. trips every hour on the hour. Call ahead to reserve a space. (☎93 674 11 40. From M: Lesseps catch the A6 bus to Sant Cugat; get off at the Vasconcell stop, before reaching the Sant Cugat monastery. Open daily 10am-2pm and 4-7pm. €14 per hr.)

More Than a Rivalry

When Franco came to power, he attempted to destroy regionalism and create a centralized Spain, controlled by Madrid and dominated by Castilian culture. The Catalan flag and language were subsequently banned and the **Fútbol Club Barcelona** (also known as Barça) became the only outlet for Catalan nationalism. The team's logo bears the Catalan coat of arms, with a red cross and red and gold stripes above the blue and burgundy stripes of Barça.

Because Catalan nationalism was so oppressed, **Real Madrid,** Franco's team, became a hated rival, both for its excellence on the field and the fascism it represented. In 1941, the FCB was told they had to lose a cup match against Madrid. The team protested the fix by allowing a blowout, letting Madrid win 11-1; Barça's goalie was suspended for life for his flagrant nonchalance. When Barça became a powerhouse in the 1950s, Franco forced the team to give up one of its star players to Madrid. In protest, the entire Barça board of directors resigned. Franco used Real in the 1950s and 1960s to legitimize his government to the rest of Europe, winning the European Cup 6 times.

Though the rivalry no longer holds the same political implications, it remains every bit as intense. The two teams, both with enormous financial resources and fiercely loyal fans, regularly battle for the championship of the Spanish First Division.

Bye-Bye Bully

Though the bullfight has been one of the defining characteristics of the Spanish culture for centuries, over the past 50 years enthusiasm for the tradition has waned. In 1950, Barcelona was home to 3 rings which housed over 120 fights yearly. Today, only the Plaza Monumental remains and fights per year has dwindled to 30.

Some believe that this trend hasn't gone far enough. The Asociación para la Defensa de los Derechos de los Animales (Association for the Defense of Animal Rights) has recently joined forces with the World Society for the Protection of Animals in an attempt to end the animal-unfriendly practice. The coalition's first target is Barcelona, a city known for its willingness to dissent from the rest of Spain. Barcelona was the first city in Spain to issue an Animal Rights Declaration and to prohibit euthanasia in the municipal dog pound. One of the coalition's goals is to ban bullfighting in Barcelona before May 2004, when the city will host the Universal Forum of Cultures (see **The Melting Pot,** p. 52). An event designed to spread peace through the promotion of cultural diversity, they argue bullfighting must be illegal before a convention claiming to be peaceful can be legitimate. While over 65% of Barcelona supports the ban, it will no doubt be met with considerable opposition, as businessmen make millions every year off of the industry, and many diehard traditionalists take pride in what they consider their nation's national art form.

SPECTATOR SPORTS

EL BARÇA

🏷 *The team plays at Camp Nou, on C. Aristides Maillol. M: Collblanc. Head down C. Francese Layret and take the 2nd right onto Trav. de les Corts. A block later, turn left onto C. Aristides Maillol, which leads to the ticket office and museum entrance (see Sights & Museums, p. 106). ☎ 93 496 36 00; www.fcbarcelona.com. Tickets available for all club sport events. Ticket office open Sept.-June M-F (and the day before matches) 9:30am-1:30pm and 3:30-6pm; July-Aug. 8am-2:30pm.*

FÚTBOL CLUB BARCELONA

The term *Fútbol Club Barcelona*, FCB for short, refers to Barcelona's soccer team and their fervently devoted fan club. A visit to Camp Nou, home of FCB, can be compared to a religious experience for many fans. The team, commonly referred to as El Barça, has the motto of *"més que un club"* (more than a club), and it's easy to see why. El Barça is a symbol of Catalunya and its proud people, and the team carries the political agendas of the entire region (see **More than a Rivalry,** p. 165). The club has a devoted worldwide following, and boasts more than 100,000 members. Even the Pope, while visiting Barcelona in 1982, signed the membership book and became an honorary member.

The FCB also has teams in several other sports, including basketball, rugby, and roller hockey, who play in other buildings in the Camp Nou complex, which includes basketball courts, a mini-stadium and the Palau Blaugrana (Blue-Burgundy Palace).

GETTING TICKETS

Inaugurated in 1957, **Camp Nou** stadium was expanded in 1982 to hold 120,000 for the World Cup, and is today Europe's largest fútbol ground. However, getting tickets to a Barça match is not always easy; hardcore FCB fans already have tickets, leaving slim pickings for visitors. Matches usually take place on Sunday evenings at 9pm, and the bigger the match, the harder it is to get in. *Entradas* (tickets) are available at the ticket office and usually go on sale to the public the Thursday before the match. A number of scalpers also try to unload tickets for copious amounts of cash in the days before the match. At the ticket office, expect to pay €30-60, and bring your binoculars, as most available seats are on the third level. The seats may be in the nosebleed section, but even at that height, any Barça match is an incredible experience. The cheap seats offer a bird's eye view of the action and gorgeous views of the mountains of Tibidabo and Montjuïc. Even if you can't tell which player scored the goal, you'll have just as much fun celebrating it with 70,000 newfound friends.

BULLFIGHTING

Catalunya is not the stronghold of bullfighting in Spain; bullfights will typically not sell out and will be dominated by tourists. For more on the sport, see **Museu Taurí** (p. 83) and **Bye-Bye Bully** (p. 166).

Plaça de Toros Monumental, Gran Via de les Corts Catalans, 743 (☎93 245 58 02; www.torosbarcelona.com). M: Monumental. Built in 1915 by Ignasi i Morell, the bullring is one of the few prominent buildings in the city that draws overtly from Arabic architectural influences; it is a rare touch of Andalucia in Catalunya. The *corrida* (bullfighting) season runs Apr.-Sept., with fights every Su at 7pm. Tickets (€18-95) may be purchased at the bullring; ticket window open M-Sa 11am-2pm and 4-8pm; Su 11am-1pm. Tourist visits to the bull ring are also permitted during those hours; adults €4, children €3. Tickets may also be purchased at C. Muntaner, 24 (☎93 453 38 21; fax 93 451 69 98). Cash only.

THEATER, MUSIC & DANCE

VENUES

Barcelona affords theater aficionados many options, although most performances are in Catalan (*Guía del Ocio* lists the language of the performance). Reserve tickets through **Tel Entrada** (☎90 210 12 12, 24hr.; www.telentrada.com) or any branch of **Caixa Catalunya** bank. (Open M-F 8am-2:30pm.)

The **Grec** summer festival (see p. 55) turns Barcelona into an international theater, music, and dance extravaganza from late June to the end of July (www.grec.bcn.com). For information about the festival, which takes place in venues across the city, ask at the tourist office, stop by the booth that's located at the bottom of Pl. de Catalunya for the duration of the festival (Portal de l'Angel, open daily 10am-8pm), or swing by the **Institut de Cultura de Barcelona (ICUB),** Palau de la Virreina, Ramblas, 99. (☎93 316 11 11. Open for info year-round M-F 10am-2pm and 4-8pm. Grec ticket sales M-Sa 10am-9pm. Tickets €10-25.)

Barceloneta Beach from above

Plaça de Toros Monumental

Liceu Opera House

kids

IN THE CITY

PLAY TIME

Not all sights in Barcelona require standing around ooo-hing and aaahing artistic masterpieces. If you are traveling with children, or simply want to release your inner kid, take some time out of museum hopping with these activities.

Park Güell: With its smurf-like houses and mosaic fountains, this park, designed by Gaudí, will enchant children and adults alike (see p. 100).

Aquarium: Over 60 tanks with fish from all parts of the world. The highlight of the visit is the shark tank: walk through the plexiglas tunnel while the fins circle around (see p. 94).

Zoo: Visit the house of Floquet de Neu, the world's one and only albino gorilla (see p. 74).

Markets: Any market in the city is a festival of colors and smells. Walk children through the alleys of stalls, and ask for samples from the stacks of mouthwatering foods.

Bowling: Lace up the really cool shoes and hit the lanes. Maybe not typical of Barcelona, but definitely fun (see p. 172).

Amusement Park: Tibidabo's park offers stunning views of the city from its hilltop rides (see p. 110).

Palau de la Música Catalana, C. Sant Francesc de Paula, 2 (☎93 295 72 00; www.palaumusica.org). M: Jaume I, L4, in **La Ribera.** Off Via Laietana near Pl. Urquinaona. Head up Via Laietana to the intersection of C. Ionqueres. Box office open M-Sa 10am-9pm, Su from 1hr. prior to the concert. No concerts in Aug.; check the *Guía del Ocio* for listings. Concert tickets €6-150. MC/V.

Centre Artesá Tradicionàrius, C. Trav. de Sant Antoni, 6-8 (☎93 218 44 85; www.personal4.iddeo.es/tramcat), M: Fontana, L3 in **Gràcia.** Catalan folk music concerts Sept.-June F, 10pm. Building has a small cafe/bar and informational display on Catalan music. Tickets €10. Classes in traditional Catalan music (€84) and dance (€60) offered each trimester; call for information. Open M-F 11am-2pm and 5-9pm. Closed Aug. Wheelchair accessible.

Gran Teatre del Liceu, Las Ramblas, 51-59, on the corner of C. Sant Pau. (Box Office ☎93 485 99 11, info 93 485 99 13, tour reservations 93 485 99 14; www.liceubarcelona.com.) M: Liceu, L3. Information office open M-F 2-8:30pm and 1hr. before performances. Tours M-F 10am. €5. Founded in 1847, the Liceu was one of the world's leading opera stages until its interior was destroyed by a fire in 1994. It recently reopened after extensive repairs and has regained its status as the city's finest concert hall. Tickets begin at €7 and rise fast; be sure to reserve tickets well in advance.

Teatre Lliure, C. Montseny, 47 (☎93 218 92 51; www.teatrelliure.com), in **Gràcia.** M: Fontana. Showcases contemporary theater productions from summer festivals to Shakespeare. Call or check website for information. Tickets may be purchased at the theater or by calling Tel Entrada. Shows May-Oct. Tu-Sa 9pm, Su 7pm; Nov.-Apr. Tu-Sa 9pm, Su 6pm. Closed in Aug. Tickets M-W balcony €11.70, orchestra €15.60; Th-Su balcony €14.10, orchestra €18.80. 20% discount for students. Wheelchair accessible.

Teatre Grec, Pg. Santa Madron, 38 (Tel-Entrada ☎902 10 12 12; www.grec.bcn.es), across from the Museu d'Arqueològia. From M: Espanya, L1/L3 take bus #55 to **Montjuïc.** Located in the picturesque Jardins Amargós, the Teatre Grec was carved out of an old stone quarry in 1929 under the direction of Ramon Reventós. The open-air Grecian-style amphitheater is the namesake and occasional host of the Grec Barcelona Summer Theater Festival (see p. 55). Most theater performances tend are in Spanish or Catalan, but there are plenty of music and dance shows. Outdoor cafe open July daily 8pm-3am.

Mercat de Les Flors, C. Lleida, 59 (☎93 426 18 75; www.bcn.es/icub/mflorsteatre). From M: Espanya, L1/L3, take bus #55 to **Montjuïc.** A converted flower market, now one of the city's major theater venues and a stage for the Grec festival. The

Mercat de Les Flors and Teatre Grec will soon be incorporated into the *Ciutat del Teatre* (City of Theater)—a home for theater performance and training in Barcelona. For tickets, call Tel Entrada or stop by the Palau de la Virreina at Las Ramblas, 99.

Teatre Nacional de Catalunya, Pl. de les Arts, 1 (☎93 306 57 00; ticket sales 93 306 07 06; www.tnc.es), near the intersection of Av. Diagonal and Av. Meridiana. M: Glòries, L1, in **l'Eixample.** This national theater hosts classical theater and ballet in its main room (usually 1-2 months per show) and varied contemporary music, dance, circus, and textual performances in accompanying spaces. Tickets for the main room €20-24, students and seniors 20% discount. Available over the phone, through ServiCaixa (www.servicaixa.com), or at ticket windows (open M noon-3pm and 4-9pm, Tu-Sa noon-9pm, Su noon-6pm, shorter hours in winter).

Picornell Olympic Pool

L'Auditori, C. Lepanto, 150 (☎93 247 93 00; www.auditori.com), between M: Marina, L1, and Glòries, L1, next to the Teatre Nacional, in **l'Eixample.** Soon to be the new home of the city's Museu de la Música (currently closed to move), the Auditori is the dedicated performance space of the city orchestra (www.obc.es), although it occasionally hosts other concerts as well. Symphony season is Sept. to mid-May, with performances F-Sa either at 7 or 9pm, Su at 11am. Tickets €10-43, depending on the day and seating zone (Su is cheapest). Available by phone, through ServiCaixa, or at ticket windows (open M-Sa noon-9pm, Su 1 hr. before show starts).

L'Espai de Dansa i Música de la Generalitat de Catalunya, Trav. de Gràcia, 65 (☎93 414 31 33; cultura.gencat.es/espai), just above the intersection of Av. Diagonal and C. Aribau. M: Diagonal or FCG: **Gràcia.** Contemporary dance and musical performances, mostly from Catalunya but drawing from other regions in Spain and France as well. Tickets usually €10-14. Available at the ticket window or through ServiCaixa. Performances M-Sa 10pm, and Su 7pm. Ticket window open M-Sa 7-9:30pm, Su 5-7pm.

Dancing in the Dark

Palau d'Esports Sant Jordi (☎93 426 20 89) on **Montjuïc.** This huge venue hosts big-name musicians. For concert information, check www.agendabcn.com or the *Guía del Ocio.*

Palau de la Generalitat (☎93 402 46 16; www.gencat.es), at Pl. Sant Jaume. M: Jaume I, L4, in the **Barri Gòtic.** The Palau hosts a free bell concert on the first Sunday of every month at noon.

FLAMENCO

Although Catalunya does not have a tradition of flamenco, a dance which originated with the gypsies in southern Spain's Andalucia, the tourist industry has fed the demand for fla-

Camp Nou

the BIG splurge

Flamenco, flamenco

Originally from Andalucia, flamenco has nonetheless carved itself a niche in Barcelona's nightlife. The restaurant **El Tablao de Carmen** combines Andalusian cuisine and flamenco for an evening of good food and great dancing. With paper lanterns and Picasso-esque paintings, the restaurant is on the site where the great Carmen Amaya danced for King Alfonso XIII at the opening of Poble Espanyol (see p. 99) in 1929. Enjoy a night of sexy, energetic dancing and lyrical guitar rhythms. All performances cover a variety of types of flamenco, providing an example of each dance. The evening includes a complete three-course meal with wine. For a cheaper option, eat beforehand and watch the show with a drink. *Av. Marquesde Comillas, inside Poble Espanyol. M: Espanya, L1/L3. ☎ 93 325 68 95; www.tablaodecarmen.com. Shows Su and Tu-Sa 9:30, 11:30pm. Call ahead for reservations. Dinner and show €53; drink and show €28. Both options include entrance to Poble Espanyol.*

menco venues. Though shows are geared toward tourists, in no way does that reflect poorly on their quality; some of the best flamenco musicians and dancers in Spain pass through these establishments.

El Patio Andaluz, C. Aribau, 242 (☎ 93 209 33 78), in **Gràcia.** M: Diagonal. From the Metro, take a left on Diagonal and turn right on C. Aribau. Lively Andalusian-themed restaurant showcases traditional Spanish flamenco dancing. Show and 1 drink €29.96; show and menú from €53.50. Daily shows at 9:30pm and midnight. Call 9am-7pm for reservations. El Patio's red-paneled bar, Las Sevillanas del Patio, stays open until 3am for drinks and dancing.

Guasch Teatre, C. Aragó, 140 (☎ 93 323 39 50 or 93 451 34 62). M: Urgell, L1, in **l'Eixample.** Presents both children's theater, like *Cinderella* and *Gulliver's Travel's,* and adult theater. Children's theater generally shown Su 5:30pm, Th 6pm, F-Sa 12:30pm; adult theater Su 7:30pm, Th 9pm, F-Sa 10pm. Ticket office opens 1hr. prior to performance. Tickets €6-18. Often showcases flamenco; call for schedules.

CINEMA

MOVIE THEATERS

Movies in Spain come in two varieties and are marked accordingly in listings. The first is **vose** or **V.O. subtítulo** (original version with subtitles); this indicates that the film will show in the original language with Catalan or Spanish subtitles. The second variety is **doblado** (dubbed), with the original language lines dubbed over into Spanish or Catalan; most major movies and theaters show movies this way and only indicate if they are shown otherwise. Movies in Spain are generally not shown until 4 or 5pm and continue playing well after midnight on weekends (with night showings listed as *madrugada* showings). To find movie times and listings, check the *Guía del Ocio* (see p. 34; available at newsstands).

Icària-Yelmo Cineplex, C. Salvador Espriu, 61 (☎ 93 221 75 85; tickets ☎ 90 212 41 34; www.yelmocineplex.es), in the **Vila Olímpica** mall. M: Ciutat-Vila Olímpica, L4. 15 screens show a wide range of Spanish and international films, both in the subtitled original version and the ever-entertaining dubbed version. Weekend late-night showings usually feature American films in *V.O. subtítulo.* Tu-Su €5.75, M and matinees €4.30. Open 11am-11pm; most shows begin after 3pm. Wheelchair accessible.

Verdi, C. Verdi, 32 (☎ 93 238 79 90; www.cinemesverdi.com). M: Fontana, in **Gràcia.** Follow C. Astúries for several blocks and turn right on C. Verdi. Movie theater with plenty of subtitled films. International selection leans toward recent European artsy releases. Tickets Tu-Su €5.50, M €4. Matinees M-Sa 4-7:30pm €4. Generally screens post-midnight shows F-Sa. Wheelchair accessible.

Cinesa Maremàgnum (☎902 33 32 31), Moll d'Espanya. M: Drassanes, L3 or Barceloneta, L4. In the **Port Vell,** between the mall and the aquarium. 8 screens of dubbed Hollywood hits and a few Spanish-language originals. No English subtitles. M-Tu and Th-Su €5.30, W €4.20, F night €5.60.

IMAX Port Vell (☎93 225 11 11; www.imaxintegral.com), Moll d'Espanya, in the **Port Vell,** next to the aquarium and Maremàgnum. M: Drassanes, L3 or Barceloneta, L4. One 600m^2 IMAX screen, an 900m^2 Omnimax screen, and 3-D projection. Unfortunately for some, all features are in either Spanish or Catalan. Get tickets at the door, through ServiCaixa automatic machines, or by phone through Tel Entrada (☎90 210 12 12; www.telentrada.com). Tickets €10, matinee €7. Show times 10:30am-12:30am.

IMAX in Port Vell

Filmoteca: Cine Aquitania, Av. Sarrià, 33 (☎93 410 75 90). M: Hospital Clínic, L5, in **l'Eixample.** Screens classic, cult, and otherwise exceptional films. Program changes daily. €3.

Méliès Cinemas, Villarroel, 102 (☎93 451 00 51). M: Urgell, L1, in **l'Eixample.** 2 screens show classic films, generally spotlighting a particular director or actor. Su and Tu-Sa €4, M €2.70.

Casablanca, Pg. de Gràcia, 115 (☎93 218 43 45). M: Diagonal, L3, in **l'Eixample.** Features recently released indie films in 2 theaters. Su and Tu-Sa €5.80, M €4.

Cine Malda, C. del Pi, 5 (☎93 317 85 29), just inside the Malda Galería, a shopping center. M: Liceu, L3, in the **Barri Gòtic.** This is the only theatre in the city that lets you see two movies with one ticket. Two V.O. movies are screened in back-to-back pairs each week, including American and other international films. Check the weekly schedule flyers outside the ticket window. Tickets M €4.20, Tu-F €5.30, Sa-Su €5.50. Cash only.

Live Band at London Bar

Renoir-Les Corts, Eugeni d'Ors, 12 (☎93 490 43 05). M: Les Corts, L3, in **Les Corts.** From Trav. de Les Corts, take C. Les Corts, then the first left. Popular with the student population in the area. Independent international films in V.O. €5.50. M-F (except holidays) matinees, 65+, and students €4.

MOVIE RENTALS

Void, C. Santa Creu, 1 (☎93 44 34 203). M: Fontana. Above Pl. Virreina. If you're lucky enough to have access to a VCR in Barcelona, Void is the place to go for off-beat, interesting video rentals. If not, call ahead to reserve Void's big hot pink room and screen

Beach near Port Olímpic

Devil in the Pride Parade

your favorite film on-site (€2 per person). Pick up a video catalogue for Void's cinematic offerings from Scorsese to Rossellini. Open Su and W-Sa 6pm-midnight. Wheelchair accessible.

Blockbuster, Balmes, 129 (☎93 454 44 90), at C. Rossello. FGC: Provença. Even Barcelona has been invaded by the global master of the video rental, so "Make it a Blockbuster Night." Lots of DVDs in multiple languages. Overseas cardholders need to register in Barcelona with passport, phone number, and proof of address. Open daily 11am-11pm.

OTHER ACTIVITIES

Not only are these establishments great for families, but they also draw decent crowds looking for an alternative to clubby nightlife.

BOWLING

Bowling Pedralbes, Av. Dr. Mariñón, 11 (☎93 333 03 52). M: Collblanc. 14 lanes and a bar just a block from the Camp Nou stadium make for a welcome late-night change of pace. (One game M-Th afternoons €1.50, M-Th evenings €2.50, F-Su €3.70; shoe rental €1.) Pool tables (€1.50 per game) and foosball also available. Fixed lunch menú €7.20. Open daily 10am-2am.

ICE SKATING

Skating Pista de Gel, C. Roger de Flor, 168 (☎93 245 28 00; www.skatingbcn.com), between C. Aragó and C. Consell de Cent, in **l'Eixample.** M: Pg. de Gràcia, L2/3/4. 1 of only 2 ice-skating rinks in the city, and the only one open year-round and at night. €9.50 for entrance and skates; if you rent skates, you can bring 1 non-skate renter guest to the upstairs bar for free. Day sessions Tu-F 10:30am-1:30pm, Sa-Su 10:30am-2pm. Night sessions with colored lights and music M-Th 5-10pm, F-Sa 5pm-midnight. Cash only.

Matador

GYMS

Club Natació Atlètic-Barceloneta (☎93 221 00 10; www.cnab.org). On Plaça del Mar, Pg. Joan de Borbó, across the street from the Torre San Sebastià cable car tower. This athletic club, on Platje San Sebastià offers outdoor and indoor pools in addition to beach access, a sauna, a jacuzzi, and a full weight room. Memberships start at €27 a month. Joining fee €56. Non-members €7 per day. Open M-F 6:30am-11pm, Sa 7am-11pm, Su and holidays 8am-5pm. AmEx/MC/V.

Nova-Icària Sports Club, Av. Icària, 167 (☎93 221 25 80; atenciousuari@novaicaria.com), on the corner of C. Arquitecte Sert. M: Ciutadella/Port

Lifeguard on Barceloneta's Beaches

Olímpic, L4. A full-service sports club, with weight lifting, aerobics, a pool, tennis courts, basketball courts, and more. Membership €33 per month, €67.50 start-up fee. Non-members €6.65 per visit. Open Su 8am-4pm, M-F 7am-11pm, Sa 8am-11pm. Closed holidays.

Club Sant Jordi, C. Paris, 114 (☎93 410 92 61). M: Hospital Clìnic, L5. Passes available for facilities, including a sauna, weights, and a stairmaster. Bring your passport and your flip flops and swim cap—they are mandatory, but the pool does not provide any. Pool €3.60. Open daily 6am-5pm. Children over 3 admitted with adult supervision daily 1-5pm only.

Centre Muncipal de Tennis, Pg. Vall d'Hebron, 178 (☎93 427 55 00) and **Centre Muncipal d'Esports,** Pg. Vall d'Hebron, 166 (☎93 428 39 52). M: Montbau, L3. Exit metro opposite Jardins de Pedro Muñoz Seca. Turn right down Pg. de Vall D'Hebron; the tennis center will be directly in front of you. The centers offer tennis and raquetball courts, a pool, yoga, and more. Monthly pool membership €52. Non-members pay per visit. Single visit €6 before 4pm, €3.35 after 4pm; under 12 €3.75 before 4pm, €2.10 after 4pm. Open M-Th 10am-8pm, F-Su and holidays 8am-9pm. Wheelchair accessible. MC/V accepted for membership payments only.

Shopping

Barcelona is cosmopolitan, trendy, and outrageous; shopping options reflect all these personalities. L'Eixample is full of designer stores, while other areas, like La Ribera and El Raval, have more unique, out-of-the-way shops. Below is an alphabetical list of categories of stores with listings beneath each category. If you're in the city during the first weeks of January or July, take advantage of the government-regulated sales (see **Talking Shop(ping)**, p. 178). For European clothing or shoe sizes, check the **sizing chart** (see p. 316).

ARTS AND CRAFTS

Arlequí Máscares, C. Princesa, 7 (☎93 268 27 52). M: Jaume I, L4, in **La Ribera.** Masks, marionettes, and puppets playfully greet customers from the crammed walls and shelves of this 19th-century Modernist building. Most goods on the premises, such as the *papier mâché* finger puppets, start at €4. Masks €17-244. Open Su 10am-4pm, M-Sa 10:30am-8:30pm.

Art Escudellers, C. Escudellers, 23-25 (☎93 412 68 01; www.escudellers-art.com). M: Drassanes or Liceu. C. Escudellers is a left off **Las Ramblas** between M: Liceu and Drassanes. Popular among the cruise-ship crowd, this warehouse-like tourist store sells local crafts from every part of Spain, including pottery, glassware, tea sets, and handmade jewelry. You probably won't find any locals perusing this place. The goods are sorted by region and labeled clearly with highlighted maps. The basement level holds an art gallery/wine cellar. Open daily 11am-11pm. AmEx/MC/V.

Giving Italy the Boot

It seems that Spain is no longer Italy's second in the footwear department. Innovative designs and good quality have propelled Spanish brands like Camper, New Rock, Panama Jack, and Havana Joe to levels of international renown. Barcelona's penchant for avant-garde fashion design makes it a particularly good spot for shoe fanatics. Leave your Nikes behind and walk the streets of Barcelona in pumps that are easy on your feet as well as your wallet.

Spain, historically known for leather products, is expanding into the shoe market, completing outfits for shoppers around the world. Italian brands have ceased to monopolize the European market as these Spanish labels continue to rise in popularity. Try metal heels (Havana Joe) for late night dancing and tire soles (Camper) for urban hiking. In addition to internationally known brnads, windows around the Ciutat Vella and along the Pg. de Gràcia are stacked with cool pairs at relatively cheap prices. Try **La Manual Alpargatera** at C. D'Avinyo, 7 (☎93 301 01 72), M: Liceu, L3, for sandals, or the **Camper** store at C. de Pelai, 38 (☎93 302 4124), M: Catalunya, L1/3, for walking shoes. If you're more into looking than buying, go see the shoes on display at Barcelona's **Museu Têxtil i d'Indumentària** (see p. 71) or the **Museu del Calçat** (see p. 67) .

2Bis, C. Bisbe, 2 (☎93 315 09 54). M: Jaume I, L4. Just off Pl. St. Jaume, in the **Barri Gòtic.** This bright, colorful store is smaller than Art Escudellers but compensates by filling itself to the brim with arts and crafts from Catalan artists, including varied figurines, ceramics, jewelry, painted masks, and an eclectic selection of glass creations. Open M-Sa 10am-8:30pm. AmEx/MC/V.

GRÀCIA

Gràcia has escaped conquest by chain stores and small, mom-and-pop establishments thrive among the crevices they call streets. **Trav. de Gràcia** hosts specialty shops carrying everything from traditional Catalan pottery and lamps to kitchen wares and used books.

🛍 **Locura Cotidiana,** Pl. Rius i Taulet, 12 (☎93 415 97 54). M: Fontana or Diagonal, FGC: Gràcia. Reasonably priced, unusual jewelry and crafts (many items €10-20). Most are made in the rear of the store in the workshop. Open M-Sa 10am-2pm and 4:30-8:30pm. D/MC/V.

do.bella, C. Astúries, 43 (☎93 237 33 88). M: Fontana. Stylish handmade beaded jewelry, bags, and silk scarves at affordable prices. All work done on the premises. Open M 5-8:30pm, Tu-Sa 11am–2pm and 5-8:30pm. AmEx/MC/V.

BOOKSTORES

Llibreria del Raval, C. Elisabets, 6 (☎93 317 02 93), off Las Ramblas. M: Catalunya, in **El Raval.** Literature and nonfiction in 4 languages (Catalan, Spanish, English, and French) fill the shelves of this spacious bookstore, born in 1693 as the Gothic-style Church of la Misericòrdia. Pocket Catalan/Spanish and Catalan/English dictionaries (€11) are useful for travelers. Open M-Sa 10am-9pm.

LAIE, Av. Pau Claris, 85 (☎93 318 17 39; www.laie.es). M: Urquinaona, L1, in **La Ribera.** Small but adequate English book section with a selection of travel guides and a cafe upstairs. Bookstore open M-F 10am-9pm, Sa 10:30am-9pm. Cafe open M-F 9am-1am, Sa 10am-1am.

Bell Books, C. Sant Salvador, 41 (☎67 889 15 81). M: Lesseps, L3 in **Gràcia.** Follow Trav. del Dalt and make a right on C. Verdi and a left on Sant Salvador. Best used bookstore around, run by an eccentric British expat and her cat, Arnold Schwarzenegger. Trade-ins accepted. Video club includes English films. Open M-F 1-8pm, Sa 10am-8pm.

Come In, C. Provença, 203 (☎93 453 12 04). M: Diagonal, L3, in **l'Eixample.** Primarily designed for people learning English, Barcelona's biggest English bookstore holds a slightly random collection of literature, travel guides, board games, and language books. Peruse the message boards outside for apartment listings and postings for Spanish classes and conversation partners. Open M-Sa 10am-2pm and 4:30-8pm. Wheelchair accessible. AmEx/MC/V.

Crisol Libros y Más, La Rambla de Catalunya, 81 (☎93 215 27 20; www.crisol.es). M: Pg. de Gràcia, L2/3/4, in **l'Eixample.** This Madrid transplant stocks a wide range of music (lots of international titles), books (fiction, plays, self-help, cooking, travel guides, road maps), magazines, videos, DVDs, small gifts, and stationery. There is also a large children's section, some English novels, and original English-version videos. Open M-Sa 9am-10pm. Wheelchair accessible. AmEx/MC/V.

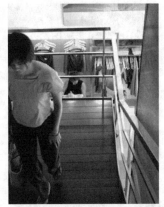
Shopping on Pg. de Gràcia

CLOTHING & ACCESSORIES

The **Barri Gòtic** bursts with both trendy and alternative clothing and accessories. If you're on the prowl for typical European women's clothing, check out C. Portaferrissa and Av. Portal de l'Angel. If you're more into the alternative scene of Pl. Trippy, take a stroll down C. Avinyó and its smaller side streets. You can find all sorts of less expensive jewelry, accessories, and other cool knick-knacks perfect for gift-giving on C. Boqueria. If you're looking for more legitimate jewelry, meander into one of the gems on C. Call. If you have extra cash or just want to go drool on the windows of European designers, check out Pg. de Gràcia in **l'Eixample.**

Couvenir Shop

Blanco, Diagonal, 572 (☎93 200 15 29; www.blancoint.com), at corner of C. d'Aribau. M: Diagonal, L3/5, in **l'Eixample.** Of-the-minute styles at mid-range, reasonable prices, with lots of mix-and-match options for big nights out. Cheap leather goods among the many clothes to be found by those who look carefully. Shirts begin at €6, pants at €20. MC/V.

QKbcn, Trav. de Gràcia, 176-78 (☎93 210 40 00), near C. Torrent de l'Olla. M: Joanic, L4, in **Gràcia.** A women's clothing boutique that carries innovative and colorful designs by Basque and Catalan designers. Open M-Sa 10am-2pm and 5-9pm.

El Corte Inglés

Zara, Pg. de Gràcia, 16 (☎93 318 76 75). M: Pg de Gràcia, L2/3/4, in **l'Eixample.** With 12 locations in Barcelona alone (grab a directory brochure at the counter), more than 200 stores in Spain, and almost that many abroad, Zara has hit paydirt: snazzy, very European styles, but in much cheaper materials (and prices) than you'll get from designers. Anything you buy may not last through next year, but by that time you'll want to come back for the newest look,

Talking Shop(ping)

When new retail shops start popping up in the city, competition can't be far behind. That isn't necessarily true when it comes to Barcelona, however. There are already laws in place preventing the proliferation of huge chains that would put smaller, private shops out of business, and the government has also chosen to regulate sales. By law, stores in Barcelona may only have sales (in Catalan *rebaixes* and in Spanish *rebajas*) twice a year, in January and July, during which they may only discount their current merchandise up to 30%. Not only can they not bring in special goods for the sales, but neither can they restock or change the type of merchandise on sale. As the sales progress, they may raise the discount. If the store jumps the gun and puts its stuff on sale before the officially designated start day, the fashion police crack down with hefty fines.

What does all this mean for the die-hard shopper visiting Barcelona? Hit the sales early even though the discounts increase because the quantity and quality of merchandise goes fast. And if you happen to miss the fashion feeding frenzies, don't worry; even though shops cannot have storewide sales at other times of the year, prices on some items can be discounted. Also, there are still plenty of cheap and discount boutiques and chains waiting to be picked and pawed (see **Discount Clothing,** p. 178).

anyway. Expect to wait in line both to try on and to pay. Most skirts, pants, and shirts €12-30. Open M-Sa 10am-9pm. Wheelchair accessible. MC/V.

Mango, Pg. de Gràcia, 8-10 (☎ 93 412 15 99; main operator 93 860 22 22). M: Pg. de Gràcia, L2/3/4, in **l'Eixample.** Has 12 other locations in the city (and an outlet, see p. 180); ask for a directory. The same idea and prices as Zara but with fewer staples. Try on funky dresses, sleek nighttime wear, and shiny accessories. Clubbing shirts €15. Open M-Sa 10:15am-9pm. Wheelchair accessible. MC/V.

Casa Ciutad, Av. Portal de l'Angel, 14 (☎93 317 04 33). M: Catalunya, L3, in the **Barri Gòtic.** Founded in 1892, this elegant, old-fashioned accessories store caters mostly to women. They sell quality hair clips, brushes, nylons, underwear, toiletry kits, and nail care sets at reasonable prices. Open M-F 10am-8:30pm, Sa 10:30am-9pm. AmEx/MC/V.

0,925 Argenters, C. Montcada, 25 (☎93 319 43 18). M: Jaume I, L4, in **La Ribera.** Fashionable jewelry boutique nestled in one of C. Montcada's gothic residences. Mainly silver designs by Spanish artists, starting at €20 (and going up to €2000). Friendly staff welcomes browsers. Open Su 11:30am-3:30pm, M-F 10:30am-8:30pm, Sa 11am-8pm.

Schindia, C. València, 167 (☎93 451 28 16). M: Hospital Clìnic, L5, in **l'Eixample.** Hippie-chic clothing and accessories imported from India and China, low-priced silver jewelry, and funky yet comfy skirts with wild patterns; prices begin around €20. Open M-F 10:30am-9pm, Sa 11am-2pm and 5-8:30pm. Closed Sa in Aug. AmEx/MC/V.

DISCOUNT CLOTHING

You won't find any true discount shopping within the city proper. If you're looking for that action, you'll probably have to travel out to the suburbs. If you're content to stay inside the city, however, check out the reasonably priced merchandise at these stores.

Taxi Moda, Pg. de Gràcia, 81 (☎ 93 215 03 80). M: Diagonal, L3, in **l'Eixample.** A fabulous find for budget-traveling label whores: high-class brands from last year at 20-50% discounts, some up to 60%. Men's and women's suits, pants, skirts, dresses, and shirts from Versace, D&G, Hugo Boss, Alberta Ferreti, Guess?, and more. In general, the older the style, the greater the discount. Be prepared to sift through the many offerings for the best deals. Open M-Sa 10:30am-2pm and 4:30-8:30pm. MC/V.

Factory Store, Pg. de Gràcia, 26 (☎93 318 20 70), down a small passageway off the main street. M: Pg. de Gràcia, L2/3/4, in **l'Eixample.** The same business model as **Taxi Moda** but a wider selection, wilder and more contemporary styles (therefore smaller discounts, up to 50% only), and a few different brands. Small shoe and purse selection. Open M-Sa 10:30am-8:30pm. Wheelchair accessible. MC/V.

Contribuciones, C. Riera San Miquel, 30 (☎93 218 74 36). M: Diagonal, L3/5, in **Gràcia.** High-end Spanish and Italian labels are half-off at this designer discount store, though prices are still quite steep. Check out the top floor for better bargains. Open M-Sa 11am-2pm and 5-9pm. AmEx/D/MC/V.

H&M, C. Portaferrissa, 16 (☎ 93 343 50 60). M: Catalunya, L1/3/4, in the **Barri Gòtic.** A left off Las Ramblas. The mecca of throw-away club clothes. With its worldwide slogan of "fashion and quality at the best price," H&M is not unique to Barcelona and probably doesn't need an introduction; cheap and stylish, it is wildly popular in most of the 14 countries in which it has opened. Shirts €6-20. Skirts and pants €15-40. Open M-Sa 10am-9pm. Closed Su. AmEx/MC/V.

Revolver Records

La Tienda de los Milagros, C. Rera Palau, 7 (☎93 319 67 30). Off Pl. de les Olles, in **La Ribera.** M: Jaume I, L4. Praise the clothing gods for these funky, retro finds at decent prices. The "shop of miracles" stocks unique accessories and outfits from casual to club wear. Open M-Sa 10:30am-3pm and 4-9pm. Wheelchair accessible.

don bolso, C. València, 247 (☎93 488 33 63), just to the right of Pg. de Gràcia when you're facing the Pl. de Catalunya. M: Pg. de Gràcia, L2/3/4, in **l'Eixample.** If you must have lots of bags and purses, but don't want to splurge Kate Spade-style, come here; most handbags are under €20. No promise the bags will last long, but they've got a colorful variety. Open M-Sa 10am-8:30pm. Wheelchair accessible. MC/V.

L.O.G.O. Designer Fashion Outlet, Rambla Catalunya, 48 (☎93 272 11 75) in **l'Eixample.** One of the many stores sprinkled throughout Barcelona and the Pg. de Gràcia area that features big name clothing at major discounts—often half off the original price. Label fiends will adore it. Open M-Sa 10am-9pm. Wheelchair accessible. MC/V.

Zara

Outlet del Born, C. L'Esparteria, 12 (☎93 268 72 49), in **La Ribera.** Recently opened discount label store, with Armani, Calvin Klein, and Miu Miu, among other styles. Last years trends at prices reduced by up to 50%. Open M-Sa 11am-9:30pm. Wheelchair accessible. AmEx/MC/V.

CALLE GIRONA

One place to try for bargains is **Calle Girona,** between C. Casp and Gran Via, in **l'Eixample,** where you'll find a small line of discount shops offering girls' and women's clothing, and men's dress clothes, shoes, bags, and accessories. (M: Tetuán, L2. Walk two blocks down Gran Via and take a left on C. Girona.) **Calle**

Antique Store

the hidden deal

IT'S A STEAL

Sick of waiting for *rebaixes* (sales) to come around in July or January, only to find that the main-stream stores have only marked down 20%? And the chic and original boutiques have reduced the price of that dress from a whopping €300 to a mere, what? €200? Thinking of resorting to a five-finger discount just to get some new pants?

Do not fear. This shop has some ready-made steals for you. Ludicrously cheap but absolutely stylish **Las 40 Ladronas** (The 40 Thieves) has innovative style for preppies and punks alike. Recently opened, the store is a shopper's dream, with everything from African threads to funky party styles and hippy wear. If you imagine it, the *Ladronas* (feminine, of course) have probably got it. The cozy and welcoming shop will lure you in with its €3 deals—same price as a bocadillo! So skip lunch (as many Spanish women already do) and buy yourself some new threads.

C. L'Esparteria, 17. M: Jaume I, L4, in **La Ribera**. ☎93 315 00 44. Open Su 6-9pm, M-Th 11am-3pm and 5-9pm, F-Sa 11am-3pm and 5-10pm. Cash only.

180

Bruc, one street over, offers more retail delights for bargain-hunters. Be aware that stores marked "Venta al Mejor" are wholesale sellers who aren't happy with only windowshopping

Mango Outlet, C. Girona, 37 (☎93 412 29 35), between C. Casp and Gran Via. M: Girona, L4, or Tetuán, L2, in **l'Eixample**. Last season's Mango clothes and accessories at 20-40% discounts, during clearance sales up to 50%. A great place to buy random shirts and nightclub tanks you'll never use again (sometimes for as little as €3). Find the tight pants you see every Spanish woman wearing. Open M-Sa 10:15am-9pm. Wheelchair accessible. MC/V.

MERCAT ALTERNATIU

Another area to try for discounts is the **Mercat Alternatiu (Alternative Market)** on C. Riera Baixa in **El Raval**. (M: Liceu. Take C. Hospital—a right off Las Ramblas if you're facing the ocean—and follow it to C. Riera Baixa, the 7th right, shortly after the stone hospital building.) This street is crammed with secondhand and thrift stores covering everything from music to clothes.

Mies & Felj, C. Riera Baixa, 5 (☎93 442 07 55). M: Liceu, L3, in **El Raval**. This small store has a great selection of secondhand clothes, in good shape and at reasonable prices. The Adidas shirt and leather jacket collections are both worth a close look. Open M-Sa 11am-2pm and 5-9pm.

G.I. Joe Surplus, C. Hospital, 82 (☎93 329 96 52). M: Liceu, L3. Off Las Ramblas, at the corner of Riera Baixa's Mercat Alternatiu, in **El Raval**. Offers a variety of army/navy-type alternative clothing, at low prices. Now you know. And knowing is half the battle. Open M-Sa 10:30am-2pm and 4:30-8pm.

Discos Edison's, C. Riera Baixa, 9-10 (☎93 441 96 74). M: Liceu, L3, in **El Raval**. All used, all the time. Buy or sell used CDs, records, cassettes, and DVDs, most in the €3-12 range. This is the place to unload that Ace of Base album. Open M-Sa 10:30am-2pm and 4:30-8:30pm.

Zeus, C. Riera Alta, 20 (☎93 442 97 95). M: Sant Antoni, L2, in **El Raval**. Specializes in gay videos (no lesbian action here), with an extensive collection in the front room. Venture into the back room for toys. Ask for the *plano gay*, a map of Barcelona and Sitges's main gay attractions. Open M-Sa 10am-9pm.

DEPARTMENT STORES & MALLS

Spain has a series of laws against franchises in order to protect the economic prosperity of small businesses. The theory is that if franchises

are allowed to be open all the time, small business, whose limited staff must take off Sundays and for *siesta*, will have no way to compete. Americans will be shocked to see that these monstrous department stores are only open six days a week; commercial law prevents them from being open on Sundays, except for the first Sunday of each month.

El Corte Inglés, Pl. de Catalunya, 14 (☎93 306 38 00; www.elcorteingles.es). M: Catalunya, L1/3, in **Pl. de Catalunya.** This behemoth department store has practically everything you could ever need or want. **Free map** of Barcelona available from the information desk. Also has English books, hair salon, rooftop cafeteria, supermarket, the *oportunidades* discount department, currency exchange, and telephones. Open M-Sa and first Su of every month 10am-10pm. Other **branches:** across the street from the tourist office, Portal de L'Angel, 19-20 (M: Catalunya, L1/3); Av. Diagonal, 471-473 (M: Hospital Clínic, L5); Av. Diagonal, 617 (M: Maria Cristina, L3).

Shopping

Triangle, Pl. de Catalunya, 4 (☎93 318 01 08; www.triangle.es). M: Catalunya, L1/3, in **Pl. de Catalunya.** Since its opening in 1999, architecture buffs have bemoaned this shopping center's utter lack of imagination and style. Shopaholics, however, are more enthusiastic. The upper floor **FNAC** electronics store/bookstore and the first floor of clothing and sunglasses shops are favorites. Triangle's branch of **Sephora** is the largest cosmetics store in the world in square footage. Open M-Sa 10am-10pm. On the corner near Las Ramblas sits the always crowded **Café Zurich,** a re-creation of the classic cafe that once occupied this site but was torn down to accommodate the new mall.

Looking for Books

Maremàgnum, Moll d'Espanya (☎93 225 81 00; www.maremagnum.es). M: Drassanes, L3, in **Port Vell.** Small stores fill the first 2 floors of this mall and all-around leisure super-stop that dominates the waterfront skyline. A must-see for *fútbol* (soccer) fans is the **Botiga del Barça,** a smaller version of the official F.C. Barcelona souvenir shop at the Camp Nou stadium (see p. 166), featuring posters, jerseys, and all varieties of memorabilia pertaining to the beloved Catalan team. Stores open daily, most 11am-11pm. (At night, the bars and clubs open as Maremàgnum transforms itself into a nightlife playground.)

HOUSEWARES

The area around C. Banys Nou (M: Jaume I), in **La Ribera,** is a great place to look for antiques and cheap homegoods.

Boutique Shopping

1748, C. Montcada, 2 (☎93 319 54 13) M: Jaume I, L4, in **La Ribera.** Ceramics, delicate housewares, and other special Spanish memorabilia. Open M-Sa 10:30am-5:30pm, Su 10:30am-3pm. MC/V.

Vinçon, Pg. de Gràcia, 96 (☎93 215 60 50; www.vincon.com). M: Diagonal, L3/5, in **l'Eixample.** More of an experience than a store, Vinçon has been setting the house decor standard in Barcelona since 1941. Cutting-edge bedroom sets and rows of funky lamps and knick-knacks entertain wandering shoppers. Modernisme fans will want to see the original interior of the **Casa Casas** (see **Sights & Museums,** p. 84) on display here. Open M-Sa 10am-8:30pm. AmEx/MC/V.

Next, C. Consell de Cent, 248 (☎93 451 40 32). M: Pg. de Gràcia, L2/3/4, in **l'Eixample.** Funky home and bath accessories with colorful, sleek designs. *The* place for ladybug toilet seat covers, toilet paper with euros on it, and enough inflatable furniture to allow for an entire apartment furnished with your own hot air. Open M 4:30-8:30pm, Tu-Th 10:30am-1:30pm and 4:30-8:30pm, F-Sa 10:30am-2pm and 4:30-8:30pm. AmEx/MC/V.

LSD, Gran de Gràcia, 56. M: Diagonal, L3/5 or Fontana, L3, in **l'Eixample.** Though you won't find any drugs (as far as we know), the plastic grass-covered walls psychedelically illuminated by black and colored lights will have you thinking you are definitely on something. Take a trip here to pick up incense, candles, and wild home decor accents in countless varieties, along with kitschy trinkets that make perfect gifts. Open M-Sa 10am-9pm.

MARKETS, FAIRS & FLEA MARKETS

Barcelona has a number of good weekly outdoor markets, as well as some more seasonal fairs and sales. Local **painters** display their work in the **Plaça St. Josep Oriol** (M: Jaume I, L4, in **La Ribera**) every Saturday 11am-7pm and Sunday 11am-2pm, while the **Plaça del Pi** (M: Liceu, L3, in **Barri Gòtic**) hosts a small **food market** on the first and third weekend of each month (F-Su 11am-2pm and 5-9pm). **Plaça Reial** (M: Liceu, L3, in **Barri Gòtic**) is famous for its huge Sunday morning stamp and coin flea market (9am-2pm); its only real rival in size, perhaps, is the **Les Encants** secondhand market next to **Pl. Glòries** (M: Glòries, L3, in **l'Eixample;** M, W, and F-Sa 9am-7pm). **Antiques** are on sale every Thursday in front of the cathedral (9am-7pm). Christmastime brings a number of specialized fairs like the **Santa Llúcia market** in **Plaça Nova** (M: Liceu, L3, in **Barri Gòtic**) and the **toy market,** which takes place on the Gran Via. As always, particularly with the secondhand flea markets, watch your personal belongings in the shopping crowds. For more up-to-date info, check with www.firabcn.es.

Mercat de Sant Antoni. M: Sant Antoni, L2, in **El Raval.** Barcelona's biggest flea market, with everything from antiques to anchovies. Visit M, W, F, or Sa for the best stuff. Sift through a mountain of *libros* at the book market, Su mornings.

Farcells, C. Banys Vells, 9 (☎93 310 56 35). M: Jaume I, L4, in **La Ribera.** Secondhand bazaar with low prices for everything from dishes to furniture to record albums to clothing. Sift through the mountains of junk and you'll find some real treasures. Open M-F 10am-8pm, Sa 10am-2am.

MUSIC

For music shopping in **El Raval,** the area around **C. Tallers** offers a good selection of new and used CDs and records.

Casa Beethoven, Las Ramblas, 97 (☎93 301 48 26; www.casabeethoven.com). M: Catalunya, L1/3/4 on **Las Ramblas.** Casa Beethoven has been around since 1880, not offering music but the notes behind it; this unique music shop specializes in written not recorded music. Books of sheet music fill the shelves, featuring greats such as Bach, Beethoven, the Beatles, and the B-52's. An impressive collection of scores spanning centuries. Open M-F 9am-8pm, Sa 9am-1:30pm and 5-8pm, closed Su.

FNAC, Pl. de Catalunya, 4 (☎93 344 18 00). M: Catalunya, L1/3 in **Pl. de Catalunya.** Multi-level one-stop book, electronics, and music shop. Well-stocked English books, CD and video section. Has listening stations and a cafe. Credit card user requires a passport as ID. Open M-Sa 10am-10pm. **Branch** at Av. Diagonal, 549 (M: Maria Cristina, L3).

Overstocks, C. Tallers, 9 (☎93 412 72 85) in **El Raval.** From M: Catalunya, L1/3 right on C. Tallers. Has the area's widest and most eclectic collection of CDs, from Spanish, English, and Catalan pop to trip-hop to jazz-funk. T-shirts, records, books, and music videos make this a one-stop music-lover's dream. Ticket office for BBVA tickets to most major club shows. Open M-Sa 10am-8:30pm. MC/V.

Revolver, C. Tallers, 11 (☎93 412 73 58) M: Catalunya, L1/3, in **El Raval.** Specializes in used CDs and vinyl. There is some pop, but the emphasis here is on punk and metal, with a nod to 60s psychedelica. Ticket office for ServiCaixa, Ipllogic, Radiaction, and Iguana and major club shows. Open M-Sa 10am-9pm. MC/V accepted for purchases other than tickets.

SPORTS EQUIPMENT

Cap Problema Bicicletes, Pl. Traginers, 3 (☎93 310 00 82; www.capproblema.com). M: Jaume I, L4, in the **Barri Gòtic.** Follow Via Laietana south and make a right onto C. d'Angel Baixeras, and then a right on either C. Sots or C. l'Hostal d'en Sol to get to Pl. Traginers; it's next to the 4th century Roman tower (see **Southern Roman Walls,** p. 68). This bike shop offers a great deal for long-term visitors to Barcelona. You can buy a new bike with insurance and a padlock starting at €200; after 1 month they'll buy it back for 40% of the price, after 2 months for 35%, and after 3 months for 30%. They also offer the select line of Brompton folding bicycles. Best of all, if you bring a cut padlock to prove the theft of your bike, they'll replace your wheels for free. Repair work €25 per hour. Open Tu-Sa noon-2pm and 5-8pm. Closed Su-M. MC/V.

Decathlon, Pl. Villa de Madrid, 1-3 (☎ 93 342 61 61). M: Catalunya, L3, in **Barri Gòtic.** Walk down Las Ramblas and take the 1st left and then bear right onto C. Canuda; it's on the left in *plaça.* This sports megastore takes "one-stop shopping" to a whole new level. Whether you're looking for a tennis racket, basketball, windbreaker, or just a new pair of socks, they have it. Bicycle rental €5 per hr., €12 per day, €18 per weekend, €55 per week. Open M-F 10am-9pm, Sa 10am-9:30pm. AmEx/MC/V.

TATTOOS, ETC.

Tattoo Dolar, C. Boqueria, 11 (☎93 268 08 29). M: Liceu, L3, in the **Barri Gòtic.** A left off Las Ramblas. An extremely hygienic, sleek tattoo and piercing parlor. Tattoos €48-300, depending on design. Piercing €42-150, depending on location. Open in winter M-Sa 10:30am-2pm and 4:30pm-9pm, in summer 10:30am-9pm. AmEx/MC/V.

L'Embruix, C. Boqueria, 18 (☎93 301 11 63; www.lembruix.com). M: Liceu, L3 in the **Barri Gòtic.** A left off Las Ramblas coming from the metro. Extremely popular among rebellious kids trying to sneak in a tongue ring while away from home; the waiting area is almost a self-contained social scene. Must be sober to be tattooed or pierced. Tattoos €40-240. Henna tattoos €12 and up. Normal piercing flat-rate €36 plus pendant; genitalia €60 plus pendant. Walk-in piercing; reservations required for tattoos. They also offer specialized piercing courses. Open M-Sa 9:30am-9:30pm. MC/V.

Accommodations

While accommodations in Barcelona are easy to spot, finding a room in one can be more difficult. If it is one of the busier travel months (June-September or December), just wandering up and down Las Ramblas looking for a place to stay can quickly turn into a frustrating experience. If you want to stay in the touristy areas—Barri Gòtic or Las Ramblas—you should make reservations weeks, or even months, in advance. Consider staying outside the tourist hub of the Ciutat Vella; there are plenty of great hostels in the Zona Alta, like Gràcia (see p. 199), that will have more vacancies.

Hostels in Spain are generally not of the dorm variety, but rather a private, basic room, with or without a private bathroom. Because heat and electricity are expensive in Spain, travelers should not assume that rooms have A/C, TV, or phone in the rooms unless specified; most come with fans only in the summer and some places do not have heat in the winter. Hotel accommodations, while more expensive, almost always include amenities.

Many establishments demand credit cards over the phone, some ask for a cash deposit upon arrival, while others want complete payment up front; be sure you know the policy where you are staying so you can cover your bill. The IVA tax is not necessarily included in these quotes. The following accommodations are listed by neighborhood and ranked within neighborhood by decreasing value; for a list of **accommodations by price**, see p. 186.

ACCOMMODATIONS BY PRICE

€15 AND UNDER ❶

Casa de Huespedes Mari-Luz (189)	BG
Pensión Bienestar (189)	BG
Casa de Huespedes Mari-Luz (189)	BG
Hostal Malda (191)	BG
⊠ Ideal Youth Hostel (194)	ER
Albergue Mare de Déu de Mont. (HI) (199)	G

€16-25 ❷

Hostal Benidorm (187)	LR
Pension Noya (187)	LR
Hostal Marítima (187)	LR
⊠ Hostal Levante (189)	BG
⊠ Pensión Fernando (189)	BG
Hostal Avinyó (189)	BG
Hostal Marmo (191)	BG
Pensión Canadiense (191)	BG
⊠ Hostal-Residencia Rembrandt (191)	BG
⊠ Hostal Campi (191)	BG
Hostal-Residencia Lausanne (191)	BG
Hostal Paris (191)	BG
Pensión Dalí (192)	BG
Hostal Layetana (192)	BG
Pensión Aris (192)	BG
Pensión Santa Anna (192)	BG
Pensión Arosa (192)	BG
⊠ Hostal de Ribagorza (192)	RB
Pensión Lourdes (193)	RB
Pensión Rondas (193)	RB
Gothic Point Youth Hostel (193)	RB
⊠ Pensión L'Isard (194)	ER
Pensión 45 (194)	ER
Barcelona Mar Youth Hostel (194)	ER
Hostal La Terrassa (194)	ER
⊠ Hostal Residencia Oliva (196)	EIX
Hostal Felipe II (197)	EIX
Pensión Puebla de Arenoso (198)	EIX
Pensión Iniesta (198)	M
Hostal Residencial Sants (200)	ST
Hostal Bejar (200)	ST

€26-40 ❸

Hotel Toledano/Hostal Res. Cap. (187)	LR
Hostal Parisien (187)	LR

€26-40 ❸, CONT.

Hostal Fontanella (192)	BG
Residencia Victoria (192)	BG
Hostal Palermo (192)	BG
Pensión Ciutadella (193)	RB
Hostal Orleans (193)	RB
Hostal Nuevo Colón (193)	RB
Pensión Port-bou (193)	RB
Hostal Opera (194)	ER
Hotel Peninsular (194)	ER
Hostal La Palmera (194)	ER
Hostal Residencia Windsor (196)	EIX
Hostal Girona (196)	EIX
Hostal Residencia Neutral (197)	EIX
Hostal San Remo (197)	EIX
Hostal Hill (197)	EIX
⊠ Hostal Eden (197)	EIX
⊠ Pension Francia (198)	BAR
Hostal del Mar (198)	BAR
Hostal-Residencia Barcelona (198)	M
⊠ Hostal Lesseps (199)	G
Pensión San Medín (199)	G
Pensión Norma (199)	G
Hostal Valls (199)	G
⊠ Hostal Sofia (200)	ST

€41-50 ❹

Hotel Lloret (187)	LR
Mare Nostrum (187)	LR
Hostal Campi (192)	BG
Hotel Triunfo (194)	RB
Hotel Universal (196)	EIX
Hostal Rio de Castro (198)	M
Hotel Transit (200)	ST

€51 AND UP ❺

⊠ Hostal Plaza (191)	LR
Hotel Internacional (187)	LR
California Hotel (189)	BG
Hostal Ciudad Condal (196)	EIX
Hotel Paseo de Gràcia (196)	EIX
Hotel Everest (197)	EIX
Aparthotel Silver (199)	G
Hotel Roma (200)	ST

NEIGHBORHOOD ABBREVIATIONS: LR Las Ramblas **BG** Barri Gòtic **RB** La Ribera **ER** El Raval **EIX** l'Eixample **BAR** Barceloneta **M** Montjuïc **G** Gràcia **ST** Sants

BARRI GÒTIC & LAS RAMBLAS

The Barri Gòtic and Las Ramblas are the most sought-after destination for tourists. Consequently, reservations are always recommended and are usually necessary at least two weeks in advance. The neighborhood also has more dorm-style hostels than other areas.

see map pp. 334-335

LAS RAMBLAS

Hostal Benidorm, Las Ramblas, 37 (☎/fax 93 302 20 54). M: Drassanes, L3. With phones and complete baths in each of the 45 clean rooms, balconies overlooking Las Ramblas, and excellent prices, this is a great value. Singles €30; doubles €45-53; triples €65; quads €75; quints €85-90. MC/V. ❷

Hotel Lloret, Las Ramblas, 125 (☎93 317 33 66). M: Catalunya, L1/3. At the head of La Rambla. After undergoing serious renovations, the new rooms of Hotel Lloret include large bathrooms, high-quality tiled floors, tasteful furniture, A/C, heat, TV, and phone. All these amenities plus its location next to Pl. Catalunya make it worth the extra cost. Breakfast (€4) served in a gorgeous marble-laden dining room overlooking Las Ramblas. Singles €45-48 depending on season; doubles €75-81; triples €89-95; quads €105. AmEx/MC/V. ❹

Mare Nostrum, Las Ramblas, 67 (☎93 318 53 40; fax 93 412 30 69). M: Liceu, L3. Somewhere in the realm between hostel and hotel. Its 30 rooms are about the same size as ordinary hostel rooms (some with shared bath), but all of them feature A/C, telephone, a view of Las Ramblas (with double-crystal windows to keep out the noise), and satellite TV with English CNN and BBC. This is definitely the swankiest hostel on the strip. High-season prices include breakfast in the pretty dining room overlooking the Miró Mosaic on Las Ramblas. Prices vary by season, but in the high season (summer and holidays) singles €57; with bath €72; doubles €66/76; triples €88/100; quads €99/114. MC/V. ❹

Hotel Toledano/Hostal Residencia Capitol, Las Ramblas, 138 (☎93 301 08 72; www.hoteltoledano.com). M: Catalunya, L1/3. Just off Pl. de Catalunya. This family-owned, split-level hotel/hostel has been making tourists happy since 1914, and new additions like wood floors and free wireless Internet make it anything but old-fashioned. Rooms come with cable TV, phones, and some balconies. Hotel rooms include full bath, hostel rooms do not. Book early. 4th-floor Hotel Toledano: singles €30, with bath €35; doubles with bath €57; triples with bath €72; quads with bath €81; small room for a couple with bath €46. 5th-floor Hostel Residencia Capitol: singles €28; doubles €39, with shower €44; triples €51/56; quads €58/64. Wheelchair accessible. AmEx/MC/V. ❸

Hostal Parisien, Las Ramblas, 114 (☎93 301 62 83). M: Liceu, L3. Smack in the middle of the excitement (and noise) of Las Ramblas, 13 well-kept rooms with heat keep young guests happy. Balconies provide front-row seats to the street's daily pedestrian spectacle. Friendly owner speaks a bit of English, German, Dutch, and Italian. TV lounge with vending machine. Quiet hours after midnight. Prices vary, but generally singles €30; doubles with bath €54; triples with bath €57. Cash only. ❸

Hotel Internacional, Las Ramblas, 78-80 (☎93 302 25 66; hinternacional@husa.es). M: Liceu, L3. 59 standard rooms, all with private bath, safe, and telephone. Nothing extraordinary, but you can't beat the location. Full breakfast included. High season singles €56; doubles €102; triples €134; quads €167; quints €197. AmEx/MC/V. ❺

Pensión Noya, Las Ramblas, 133 (☎93 301 48 31). M: Catalunya, L1/3. Above the Núria restaurant. If you don't have a lot of money to spend but still want to be in the center of all the action, this is the place for you. This 10-room hostel has time-warped back to the colors and styles of the 1950s. Bathrooms and hallways are somewhat cramped. No heat in winter. Singles €20; doubles €33-35; extra person €10. Cash only. ❷

Hostal Marítima, Las Ramblas, 4 (☎93 302 31 52). M: Drassanes, down a tiny alley off the port end of Las Ramblas. Follow the signs to Museu de Cera (see p. 56), which is next door. The location is convenient, the rooms are cozy, and the prices are dirt cheap for Las Ramblas. No reservations. Singles €20; doubles €30, with bath €35; triples with bath €45. ❷

LOWER BARRI GÒTIC

The following hostels are all located in the southern half of the Barri Gòtic, between C. Ferran and the waterfront. This is the best place to stay if you're willing to sacrifice a few extra euros for an unbeatable location in the beating heart of Barcelona. When choosing a hostel, check out the places off Las Ramblas (to

the east) as they are generally a better value. The area is fairly safe, but as always, remember to guard your wallet, especially at night.

Hostal Levante, Baixada de San Miguel, 2 (☎93 317 95 65; fax 93 317 05 26; www.hostallevante.com). M: Liceu, L3. Walk down C. Ferran, turn right onto C. Avinyó, and take the 1st left onto Baixada de San Miguel (you'll see the sign from C. Avinyó). Possibly the best deal in lower Barri Gòtic: 50 large, tastefully decorated rooms with light wood interiors and balconies or fans, and a relaxing TV lounge. Ask for one of the newly renovated rooms. Singles €30; doubles €50, with bath €60. Six very chic apartments also available each for 4 to 8 people (kitchen, living room, wood floor, and laundry machine), €30 per person per night. MC/V. ❷

Pensión Fernando, C. Ferran, 31 (☎ 93 301 79 93; www.barcelona-on-line.es/fernando). M: Liceu, L3. On the left on C. Ferran coming from Las Ramblas. This clean hostel is so well located it fills its 20 rooms almost entirely from walk-in requests. Beds come with free lockers in the spacious dorms, some with balconies overlooking Església de Sant Jaume (see **El Call,** p. 69). Fans in every room. Guests get keys. Common TV/dining room. High season: dorms €19, with bath €20; doubles €44/€58; triples with bath €68. MC/V. Dorms cash only. ❷

Casa de Huespedes Mari-Luz, C. Palau, 4 (☎/fax 93 317 34 63; pensionmariluz@menta.net). M: Liceu, L3. From Las Ramblas, follow C. Ferran, go right on C. Avinyó, left on C. Cervantes, and then right on tiny C. Palau. With over 25 years under their belt, Mari-Luz and husband Fernando (the same owners as Pensión Fernando) know how to run a clean and efficient hostel. Narrow hallways flanked by tidy dorm rooms for 4-6 people and a few comfortable doubles. Kitchen available June-Aug. (open only 8-10:30am). Each dorm bed comes with a locker. Laundry €5.50. Reservations require a credit card number. In summer dorms €16, doubles €41. MC/V. ❶

Hostal Avinyó, C. Avinyó, 42 (☎93 318 79 45; fax 93 318 68 93; www.hostalavinyo.com). M: Drassanes, L3. Just a stone's throw from Plaça "Trippy," this hostel puts you near the center of the action (which may also mean noise at night). 28 bedrooms with couches, high ceilings, in-room safes, and stained-glass windows. Singles €22; doubles €34, with bath €47; triples €48/€66. Cash only. ❷

California Hotel, C. Rauric, 14 (☎93 317 77 66; www.seker.es/hotel_california). M: Liceu, L3. Enjoy the 31 clean, sparkling rooms, all with TV, phone, full bath, and A/C. Take the price plunge, and you'll feel the comfort added to the convenience of the Barri Gòtic. Breakfast included. Singles €52; doubles €82; triples €102. AmEx/MC/V. ❺

Pensión Bienestar, C. Quintana, 3 (☎93 318 72 83). M: Liceu, L3. A left off C. Ferrán, coming from Las Ramblas. Located on a less-traveled sidestreet, the building

the hidden deal

Youth Hostels in the Barri Gòtic

Albergue Juvenil Palau (HI), C. Palau, 6 (☎93 412 50 80; fax 93 319 53 25; albergpalau@champinet.com). M: Liceu, L3. A tranquil refuge in the heart of the Barri Gòtic for the budget set. Kitchen (open 7-10pm), dining room, and 45 clean dorm rooms with lockers (3-8 people each). Breakfast included. Curfew 3am. No reservations. Dorms €19. 3am curfew. Cash only. ❶

Albergue de Juventud Kabul, Pl. Reial, 17 (☎93 318 51 90; www.kabul-hostel.com). M: Liceu, L3. Head to the port on Las Ramblas, pass C. Ferrán, and turn left onto C. Colon Pl. Reial; Kabul is on the near right corner of the *plaça*. Listed as one of Europe's "Famous Five Hostels," this place is legendary among backpackers; the cramped co-ed dormitory rooms can pack in up to 220 travellers. The tavern-like common area includes a satellite TV, a small restaurant/snack bar, free Internet, a pool table, and even beer and french-fry vending machines. Key deposit €15. Breakfast included, served 9am-noon. No reservations. Dorms €20. Sheets €2. No curfew. Frequent pub crawls, boat excursions, and beach parties for around €15 (alcohol included). Cash only. ❷

looks somewhat less inviting than other hostels, however the friendly owners, larger, high quality rooms, and good location make this a good pick (plus it probably won't fill up as fast as the others). Prices vary by season, singles €16-18; doubles €30-33; triples €45-48. Cash only. ❶

Hostal Marmo, C. Gignàs, 25 (☎93 310 59 70). M: Jaume I, L4. A right off Via Laietana from the Metro. Rooms in an old house still bedecked with plenty of plants, lacy curtains, and tiled floors. All rooms have balconies. No reservations. Singles €19; doubles €35. Cash only. ❷

Pensión Canadiense, Bajada de San Miguel, 1 (☎93 301 74 61). M: Liceu, L3. Across the street from Hostal Levante. This small hostel of 9 rooms has dark hallways, but the friendly owner and the clean, quiet rooms with showers and balconies make this a good choice. Prices vary by season, but generally singles €30; doubles with shower €58. Cash only. ❷

UPPER BARRI GÒTIC

The upper Barri Gòtic is a bit more spread out and less labyrinthine than its southern brother. It encompasses the area south of Pl. de Catalunya, bounded by C. Fontanella to the north and C. Ferrán to the south. **Portal de l'Angel,** which is often less hectic and easier to navigate than Las Ramblas, is a broad pedestrian thoroughfare that is more of an extension of Pl. Catalunya than anything else. As with the lower Barri Gòtic, early reservations are practically obligatory in the summer months. The nearest Metro stop is M: Catalunya, L3 unless otherwise specified. As always, the prices listed are subject to seasonal changes.

Hostal-Residencia Rembrandt, C. Portaferrissa, 23 (☎/fax 93 318 10 11; hostrembrandt@yahoo.es). M: Liceu, L3. Make the 2nd left off of Las Ramblas coming from Pl. Catalunya; the hostel is on the left. This fantastic hostel drips with quality, space, and an overall attention to detail. The 28 rooms are much nicer than any other hostel in the area; all *habitaciones* are unique in their own way, some with large baths, patios, TVs, and/or sitting areas. Make sure to take advantage of the restaurant-quality dining area for breakfast (served 9:30-10:30am, €5). Ask for a room with a balcony or a patio. Cold drinks €2. Fans €2 per night. Singles €25, with bath €35; doubles €42, with bath €50; triples €60, with bath €65. One suite with 2 balconies, a marble tub, and a sitting area €75. MC/V. ❷

Hostal Plaza, C. Fontanella, 18 (☎/fax 93 301 01 39; www.plazahostal.com). One of the best hostels in the city. Super-friendly Texan owners and brightly painted rooms on top of a great location make this place worth every penny. The common room boasts black leather couches, a drink/coffee/breakfast bar, TV, phone, and Internet access (1€ per 15min.). Laundry €9. 24hr. reception. Singles €60, with bath €75; doubles with shower only €65, with bath €75; triples €86/€96. €10 discount Nov. and Feb. AmEx/MC/V. ❺

Hostal Campi, C. Canuda, 4 (☎/fax 93 301 35 45; hcampi@terra.es). The first left off Las Ramblas (bearing right at the fork) coming from M: Catalunya, L3. A great bargain for the quality and location. All rooms are spacious, with light, comfortable furniture and large balconies overlooking C. Canuda. No kitchen, but they have a nice lounge with dining table and TV. Reservations accepted 9am-8pm. Prices tend to vary by season and availability; in high season doubles €42, with shower €49; triples €58/€68. Cash only. ❷

Hostal Malda, C. Pi, 5 (☎93 317 30 02). M: Liceu, L3. Go down C. Casañas from Las Ramblas, walk through Pl. del Pi, and make a left on C. Pi; the stairwell up to the hostel is inside a shopping center. With an antique motif, Hostal Malda keeps its rooms occupied year round by offering the same quality as other Barri Gòtic hostels at an unbeatable price. Reservations recommended. Singles €13; doubles €26; triples with shower €36. Cash only. ❶

Hostal Residencia Lausanne, Av. Portal de l'Angel, 24 (☎93 302 11 39 or 93 302 16 30). M: Catalunya, L1/3/4. Main entrance next to a Zara display window; walk left past the grand marble staircase in front to the smaller stairs in back by the elevator. A single-hallway hostel with 17 nice rooms and a posh lounge with TV and vending machines overlooking one of Barcelona's most popular shopping streets. Doubles €48, with bath €65. Cash only. ❷

Hostal Paris, Cardenal Casañas, 4 (☎93 301 37 85; fax 93 412 70 96). M: Liceu, L3. The bright yellow sign is visible from Las Ramblas, right across from the Metro. About 50 slightly aged rooms and a common area overlooking the street. All rooms facing the inside patio have A/C, all exterior ones have fans, and all with bath have TVs. No reservations. Singles €23, with shower €26; doubles €46, with shower €48, with bath €60. MC/V. ❷

Pensión Dalí, C. Boqueria, 12 (☎93 318 55 90; fax 93 318 55 80; pensiondali@wana-doo.es). M: Liceu, L3. Designed with religious purpose in mind by the architect of the Palau de la Música Catalana Domènech i Montaner and originally run by a friend of Dalí's, the rooms are past their prime, but all have TVs, telephones, and windows onto the street. Huge, couch-filled common room and great location in the center of all the action. In the high season, doubles €46.50, with bath €53; triples with bath €75; quads with bath €85. MC/V. ❷

Hostal Fontanella, Via Laietana, 71 (☎/fax 93 317 59 43). M: Urquinaona, L4. Tastefully decorated and clean, with a floral waiting room, wood furniture, and fans in each of the 11 rooms. Safe for valuables available, as well as information on planning excursions. Singles €29, with shower €35; doubles €45, with shower €50, with bath €58; triples €63, with shower €70, with bath €81; quads €79, with shower €88. AmEx/MC/V. ❸

Hostal Layetana, Pl. Ramón Berenguer el Gran, 2 (☎/fax 93 319 20 12; hostallayet-ana@hotmail.com). M: Jaume I, L4. A short walk from the Metro going north Via Laietana. Look for the multinational flags on the third-floor balcony in the *plaça*. A sophisticated, hostel with clean bathrooms and spacious rooms. Rooms with bath have fans; for others they cost €1.20. In the high season singles €25; doubles €43, with bath €55. MC/V. ❷

Pensión Aris, C. Fontanella, 14 (☎93 318 10 17 or 93 318 46 59). M: Catalunya, L1/3. About 100m from Pl. Catalunya. 7 huge, clean, sparse rooms with fans, balconies, and white washed walls. Basic hostel but with good prices for the proximity to Pl. Catalunya. Laundry €2 (no dryer). Singles €20; doubles €40, with bath €50; triple €50. Cash only. ❷

Residencia Victoria, C. Comtal, 9 (☎93 317 45 97 or 93 318 07 60; victoria@atriumho-tels.com). From Pl. Catalunya, walk down Av. Portal de l'Angel and take a left on C. Comtal. Cafeteria-style lounge/dining room (open until midnight) with outdoor terrace (open until 1am), large and fully equipped kitchen (open 7am-midnight), TV, and small library. The 30 rooms are basic but more spacious than usual for this part of town. Laundry €2.50 (no dryer). Singles €29-32; doubles €44; triples €55; quads €66; quints €69. Cash only. ❸

Pensión Santa Anna, C. Santa Anna, 23 (☎/fax 93 301 22 46). M: Catalunya, L3. From Pl. Catalunya, walk down Las Ramblas and turn left on to C. Santa Anna; it's on the left. Tight quarters, but the floors and bathrooms are clean and the rooms are cheap. Most rooms have fans. Guests get keys. Singles €20; doubles €45, with bath €60; triples €55. Cash only. ❷

Hostal Palermo, C. Boqueria, 21 (☎/fax 93 302 40 02). M: Liceu, L3. Watch your head on the way up the stairs. 36 large, party-conducive rooms with green plaid bedspreads. Small, plastic-chaired turquoise TV room and white-washed walls. This place is a little bit more expensive than other comparable hostels in the area. Laundry €2.50, safe €1.50 per day. Reservations require a credit card number. Singles €36, with bath €39; doubles €59/€70; triples with bath €109; quads with bath €113. MC/V. ❸

Pensión Arosa, Av. Portal de l'Angel, 14 (☎93 317 36 87; fax 93 301 30 38; harosa@eres-mas.net). A decidedly unmarked shared entrance with Andrew's Tie Shop. 7 bright and airy rooms in a homey private flat, some of them overlooking Av. Portal de l'Angel. Guests get keys. Singles €21; doubles €40, with shower €50; triples with shower €60. MC/V. ❷

Hostal Campi, C. Canuda, 4 (☎/fax 93 301 35 45, hcampi@terra.es). The first left off Las Ramblas (bearing right at the fork) coming from M: Catalunya, L1/3. A great bargain for the quality and location. The rooms are spacious, with light, comfortable furniture and lacy curtains. Reservations accepted 9am-8pm. Prices tend to vary by season and avail-ability, but generally doubles €40, with bath €48; triples €60. ❹

LA RIBERA

see map p. 337

❇ **Hostal de Ribagorza,** C. Trafalgar, 39 (☎93 319 19 68; fax 93 319 19 68). M: Urquinaona, L1. With your back to Pl. Urquinaona, walk down Ronda Sant Pere and turn right on C. Méndez Núñez. Hostal is 1 block down on the corner. Rooms in an ornate Modernist building com-plete with marble staircase and tile floors. TVs, fans, and homey deco-rations. Doubles only during high season (Mar.-Sept.).€38/€50. Prices decrease a bit the rest of the year, and sometimes single rooms are available (€30). ❷

Pensión Ciutadella, C. Comerç, 33 (☎93 319 62 03). M: Barceloneta, L4, follow Pg. Joan de Borbó, turn right on Av. Marqués de l'Argentera, and make the 6th left onto C. Comerç. Small hostel with 6 spacious rooms, each with fan, TV, and balcony. Family feel. A/C in the works. Doubles only. Nov.-Feb. €36, with bath €40; June-Sept. €36-40, with bath €50. Each additional person (up to 4) €9. ❸

Hostal Nuevo Colón, Av. Marqués de l'Argentera, 19 (☎93 319 50 77; www.hostalnuevocolon.com). M: Barceloneta, L4. Follow Pg. Joan de Borbó and turn right on Av. Marqués de l'Argentera. Newly renovated hostel with very clean, modern rooms and a large common area with TV and balcony. Singles €35; doubles €48, with bath €62. 6-person apartments with kitchens €150/day. ❸

Pensión Lourdes, C. Princesa, 14 (☎93 319 33 72). M: Jaume I, L4. Cross Via Laietana and follow C. Princesa. Popular backpacker destination in the heart of La Ribera. 27 adequate, no-frills rooms with telephones. Common area with TV. Singles €23; doubles €33, with bath €42. Cash only. ❷

Pension Dalí

Pensión Rondas, C. Girona, 4 (☎93 232 51 02; fax 93 232 12 25). M: Urquinaona, L4. With your back to Pl. Urquinaona, walk down Ronda Sant Pere and turn left on C. Girona, hostel is on the right. Ten Clean, basic rooms, some with balconies. English-speaking owner. Singles €32; doubles €43 (low season €32), with shower €50 (low season 638). Cash only. ❷

Pensión Port-bou, C. Comerç, 29 (☎93 319 23 67). From M: Barceloneta, L4, follow Pg. Joan de Borbó, turn right on Av. Marqués de l'Argentera, and make the 6th left onto C. Comerç. Small hostel in 150-year-old building with high ceilings and balconies. Simple rooms with eclectic, mismatched furniture. Sept.-June Singles €26-29; doubles €33-35, with bath €44-46. July-Aug. singles €33; doubles €38, with bath €52. Extra person in double room €10. Reservations suggested. Cash only. ❸

Inside a Hotel Room

Gothic Point Youth Hostel, C. Vigatans, 5 (☎93 268 78 08; badia@intercom.es). M: Jaume I, L4. Walk down C. de l'Argentera; C. Vigatans is the 1st street on your left. Large Modernist building with orange and black lobby area boasting picnic tables, free Internet access, art posters, and large TV. A/C dorm-style rooms (housing 150 beds) have individual curtained-off bed compartments, each with its own table and light. Rooftop terrace. Breakfast included. Sheet rental, towel rental €1.80. Lockers €1.20/day. Beds €19.50 high season, €17 low. AmEx/MC/V. ❷

Hostal Orleans, Av. Marqués de l'Argentera, 13 (☎93 319 73 82; www.hostalorleans.com). From M: Barceloneta, L4, follow Pg. Joan de Borbó and turn right on Av. Marqués de l'Argentera. Spotless,

Balcony

newly renovated hostel with comfortable common area. Singles with TV €31, with bath €45; doubles in high/low seasons €45/39 with shower, €55/51 with bath, and €60 A/C; triples €60-68; quads €80. ❸

Hotel Triunfo, Pg. de Picasso, 22 (☎93 315 08 60). M: Barceloneta, L4. Walk up Pg. Joan de Borbó, turn right on Av. Marqués de l'Argentera, and left on Pg. Picasso. Hotel is across from the Parc de la Ciutadella. Budget hotel with whitewashed, clean walls and heavy floral curtains. All rooms have full bath, TV, and A/C. Singles high/low season, €45/€41; doubles U€70/€65. MC/V. ❹

see map p. 336

EL RAVAL

Hostels in El Raval, the area west of Las Ramblas, are hard to come by and less touristed; staying here will give you a better feel for the Catalan lifestyle. Be careful in the area at night, particularly near the port and farther from Las Ramblas.

▨ **Pensión L'Isard,** C. Tallers, 82 (☎/fax 93 302 51 83) M: Universitat, L1/2. Take the C. Pelai exit, turn left at the end of the block, and then left again at the pharmacy. A simple, elegant, and unbelievably clean find. Bright rooms have enough closet space for even the worst over-packer. Ask for a room with a balcony. Singles €20; doubles €36, with bath €52; triples €52. AmEx/MC/V. ❷

▨ **Ideal Youth Hostel,** C. la Unió, 12 (☎93 342 61 77; www.idealhostel.com). M: Liceu, L3. Off Las Ramblas, on the street next to the Gran Teatre Liceu. Located just a block off of Las Ramblas, this hostel offers one of the best deals in the city. Breakfast included. Free Internet access in the swanky lobby area. Sheets €2.50, laundry €4. Dorms €16. ❶

Hostal Opera, C. de Sant Pau, 20 (☎93 318 82 01; info@hostalopera.com). M: Liceu, L3. Turn left before the Liceu Opera House on Las Ramblas. Hostal Opera has been recently renovated, making its sunny rooms feel like new. All rooms come with bath, telephone, and the coveted A/C. Internet access available in the common room on ground floor. Singles €35; doubles €55; triples €80. MC/V. ❸

Hotel Peninsular, C. de Sant Pau, 34 (☎93 302 31 38). M: Liceu, L3. Off Las Ramblas. This venerable building, now one of the 50 sights on the Ruta del Modernisme (see **Sights & Museums,** p. 51), served as the monastery for the Augustine order of priests in the mid-1800s. The rooms still have a certain austerity about them, although they are located off a bright inner patio. All 60 rooms come with telephones and A/C. Breakfast included. Singles €30, with bath €50; doubles €50/€70; triples with bath €85. MC/V. ❸

Pensión 45, C. Tallers, 45 (☎93 302 70 61). M: Catalunya, L1/3. From Pl. de Catalunya, take the first right off Las Ramblas onto Tallers. What "45" lacks in name-choice originality, it makes up for in charm. Old paintings and photographs decorate its 25 small rooms. All the coffee you want, all day. Singles €20; doubles €35, with bath €45. Cash only. ❷

Barcelona Mar Youth Hostel, C. de Sant Pau, 80 (☎93 324 85 30; www.youthostel.com). M: Parallel, L2/3. Situated in a peaceful area far from the late-night noise, this new hostel crams 120 dorm-style beds into non-smoking rooms with A/C. All beds come with a safe for personal belongings. Laundry service. Internet €1 per 30min. Breakfast included. Dorms €21-23 in summer, €14-18 the rest of the year. Online reservations recommended. ❷

Hostal La Terrassa, C. Junta de Comerç, 11 (☎93 302 51 74; fax 93 301 21 88). M: Liceu, L3. Take C. Hospital and turn left after Teatre Romea. 50 small, aging, but clean rooms. The social courtyard is rare for a non-youth hostel. Singles €18; doubles €28, with bath €34; triples €36/€45. MC/V. ❷

Hostal La Palmera, C. Jerusalén, 30 (☎93 317 09 97; fax 93 342 41 36). M: Liceu, L3. From Las Ramblas, just behind and to the right of the Boqueria market (see **Sights & Museums,** p. 54). Somewhat spartan rooms feature new wood paneling, decent beds, and clean bathrooms. Breakfast included. Singles €30; doubles €45, with bath €50. MC/V ❸

The Expansion of the Old City into l'Eixample

Barcelona radiates style. Everyone is stylish: the elderly couples promenading the Passeig de Gràcia in shades of distinguished gray and beige, the hipsters slinking by in engineered Levi's in the Barri Gòtic, the slow circle of people dancing the *sardanas* in front of the *Catedral* on Sunday afternoons, the young businessmen in their tailored suits crowding the metro. But style in Barcelona is hardly limited to the people; it encompasses almost everything from the mundane to the actual layout of the city.

Barcelona is a city of, by, and for designers. In many ways what most enabled Barcelona to become a city of architectural gems was the planning of the new city, l'Eixample, or the Extension (*Ensanche* in Castilian). The first stone was laid in the Eixample in 1860, but the historical groundwork for this radical creation of a city began much earlier.

In the early 1800s, Barcelona hardly resembled the ample city that tourists gush over today. Barcelona proper was cramped within the walled-in Barri Gòtic. As Robert Hughes wrote in his seminal work, *Barcelona*, "mid-century Barcelona made Dickensian London look almost tolerable." The city walls had stood for over 100 years, since the Bourbons conquered the city in the early 1700s, and despite the promising construction of the new Passeig de Gràcia in 1927 connecting Barcelona from the towns of Gràcia, Sants, and Sant Gervasi across open fields, nothing was built.

After much political wrangling between civil and military authorities, in 1854 the go-ahead for demolition was given. Now faced with the necessity to build a city beyond the Barri Gòtic, some crucial decisions were made that ultimately created the long avenues that help make beloved Barcelona so stylish today. The Ajuntament of Barcelona held a competition for a new city plan in 1859. While cities were being redesigned throughout Europe (most notably Paris beginning in 1848), Barcelona was particularly unique in that there was no old city to demolish to make space for the new. Barcelona was a blank slate for the architect, an expanse of fields dotted only by a few scattered buildings.

Two plans came forward. One was by Antoni Rovira i Trias, the Ajuntament's resident architect. He proposed a plan similar to that of the new Paris, a fan-like radial layout extending out from what presumably would remain the heart of the new city, the Barri Gòtic. The other plan was by Ildefons Cerdà. Cerdà was an ideological socialist. He had researched worker conditions within the old city and had a vision of a new egalitarian city. His plan covered nine square kilometers with a carefully calculated grid with planned services. Among its specifications were that every 400 blocks would have a hospital and park, every 100 blocks would have a market, and every 25 blocks would have a school. Only a third of the area of each block would be covered by buildings. The rest would be trees and gardens in the interior of the block. Some blocks were to be undeveloped park space. Buildings were to be 57 feet high, or around three stories.

Conservative Catalans were not interested in Cerdà's radical idealized city, and Rovira i Trais's plan was selected in late 1859. But inexplicably, Madrid reversed the decision eight months later and awarded the commission to Cerdà. Many Catalans were adamantly against the plan, but gradually the Eixample was built. As anyone who visits Barcelona knows, Cerdà's plan was hardly followed to the letter. There is a grid and angled corners, but buildings tower above the three-story limit and there is limited green space. Developers ignored the details of Cerdà's plan and the Ajuntament turned a blind eye.

But Cerdà's plan left a legacy for the Modernisme architects who have left such a deep imprint on the fabric of Barcelona's style. The rigid street plan let the fantastical and colorful designs of the *modernistas* truly flourish. Passeig de Gràcia is lined with Modernista buildings. The glorious buildings of Lluís Domènech i Montaner, Josep Puig i Cadaflach, and Antoni Gaudí, just to mention the superstars, shine in l'Eixample. Gems are nestled in the side streets of l'Eixample—great *modernista* details rising above the tree-lined streets that Cerdà envisioned—creating the glamorous background for the stylish folks of Barcelona.

Sarah Jacoby was a Let's Go *Managing Editor, a Researcher-Writer for* India & Nepal 2001 *and* Spain & Portugal 1999, *and an associate editor for* Europe 2000. *While living in Barcelona she worked for an Internet consulting company.*

see map pp. 340-341

L'EIXAMPLE

Barcelona's most beautiful accommodations lie along l'Eixample's wide, safe avenues—style is of the essence in this famously bourgeois neighborhood. Many hostels have colorfully tiled, carpeted interiors and Modernist elevators styled with wood and steel; most rooms have high ceilings and lots of light. L'Eixample is one of the more expensive places to stay in the city; as a newer neighborhood full of Modernist sights, classy restaurants, and fancy shops, it's a popular destination for tourists with a comfortable budget. L'Eixample is divided by Passeig de Gràcia into left and right sections: *l'Eixample Esquerra* and *l'Eixample Dreta*.

AROUND PASSEIG DE GRÀCIA

Hostal Residencia Oliva, Pg. de Gràcia, 32, 4th floor, (☎93 488 01 62 or 93 488 17 89; fax 93 487 04 97; www.lasguias.com/hostaloliva). M: Pg. de Gràcia, L2/3/4. At the intersection with C. Diputació. Elegant wood-worked bureaus, mirrors, ceilings, and a light marble floor give this hostel a classy ambiance. All 16 rooms have color TVs, and a few come with fans. Some overlook the Manzana de la Discòrdia. Reservations a must. Singles €26; doubles €48, with bath €55; triple with bath €78. Wheelchair accessible. Cash only. ❷

Pensión Fani, C. València, 278 (☎93 215 36 45). M: Catalunya, L1/3. Just off Pg. de Gràcia on the left (facing Pl. de Catalunya). This long-term pension is dirt cheap and oozing with character and quirky charm, from colorful floor tiles and rows of hanging plants to a huge cage of birds in the sunroom. Rooms are generally rented by the month but can be used for a single night as well. Three shared bathrooms, full kitchen with refrigerator, pots, pans, and utensils, dining room/TV room, laundry room (handwash and air-dry), and pay phone. Bring your own towel. Singles €276 per month; doubles €490 per month; triples €760 per month. One-night stay €20 per person. Payments due the 1st of each month. Cash only. ❶

Hostal Residencia Windsor, Rambla de Catalunya, 84 (☎93 215 11 98). M: Pg. de Gràcia, L2/3/4. On the corner with C. Mallorca. With carpeted hallways, gilded mirrors, and a plush TV room, this hostel lives up to its royal name. Rooms come equipped with comfy sleep sofas and heat in winter (no A/C). Singles €25, with bath €42; doubles €52, with sink and shower €55, with bath €60; extra beds €10 each. Wheelchair accesible. Cash only. ❸

Hostal Girona, C. Girona, 24 (☎93 265 02 59; fax 93 265 85 32; www.hostalgirona.com). M: Urquinaona, L1/4. Between C. Casp and C. d'Ausiàs Marc. A medieval twist on royal decor, with a cavernous stone entry foyer and dark carpeted and tiled hallways. All of the 16 beautifully decorated, spacious rooms have TVs. Some have bath, others have balconies. Singles €25, with bath €35; doubles €46-60. MC/V. ❸

Hostal Ciudad Condal, C. Mallorca, 255 (☎93 215 10 40; fax 93 487 04 59). M: Diagonal, L3/5. Just off Pg. de Gràcia, 2 blocks from La Pedrera. Prices reflect the generous amenities and prime location. All rooms have full bath, heat, TVs, and phones. 24hr. reception. Must reserve with a credit card for late arrivals. Singles €70; doubles €95. Prices often drop in winter and vary according to room size. Wheelchair accessible. AmEx/MC/V. ❺

Hotel Paseo de Gràcia, Pg. de Gràcia, 102 2nd floor, (☎93 215 58 24; fax 93 215 37 24). M: Diagonal, L3/5. On the corner with C. Rosselló. Though a single is a little steep, double rooms here are a good deal for a 3-star hotel on the same block as La Pedrera. The decor is a step up from any hostel, especially the plush, old-fashioned waiting area. Try to get a room with a balcony on Pg. de Gràcia, at no extra charge. Breakfast €3.25. Singles €58; doubles €68. Wheelchair accessible. AmEx/MC/V. ❺

Hotel Universal, C. Aragó, 281 (☎93 487 97 62; fax 93 487 41 28). M: Pg. de Gràcia, L2/3/4. 1 block to the left of Pg. de Gràcia when facing Pl. de Catalunya. This relaxing, tiny, one-star hotel offers better bang for your buck than many hostels. All 18 rooms have bath, heat, fans, TVs, phones, and free safes; most have windows overlooking the street. Reservations are highly recommended. Singles €47; doubles €55; triples €65. Wheelchair accessible. MC/V. ❹

Hostal Residencia Neutral, Rambla de Catalunya, 42 (☎93 487 63 90; fax 93 487 68 48). M: Pg. de Gràcia, L2/3/4. On the corner of C. Consell de Cent. Feels more like an old house than a hostel. TV room with overstuffed old couches and a classy breakfast area. All 28 rooms have fans, heating, and TVs. Continental breakfast €5. Reserve with a credit card. Two singles €28; doubles €42, with bath €48; triples €50/€57. ❸

L'EIXAMPLE DRETA

Hostal San Remo, C. Bruc, 20 (☎93 302 19 89; www.hostalsanremo.com), on the corner with C. Ausiàs Marc. M: Urquinaona, L1/4. This tiny hostel fills up quickly. Each room is decked out with TV, A/C, and soundproof windows. Reserve a month ahead of time. Singles €30; doubles €42, with bath €55. Nov. and Jan.-Feb. prices slightly lower. MC/V. ❸

Hostal Hill, C. Provença, 323 (☎93 457 88 14; http://kamirura.com), between C. Girona and C. Bailen. M: Verdaguer, L4/5. A great deal for the location, with funky, modern furniture and fans in the rooms. Welcoming hosts, guests get keys. Reservations with a credit card number. Singles €28, with bath €38; doubles €45/€54. V. ❸

Hostal Felipe II, C. Mallorca, 329 (☎93 458 77 58), between C. Girona and C. Bailèn. M: Verdaguer, L4/5. 11 well-kept rooms with lace curtains, new furniture, fans, TVs, and extremely clean bathrooms. Singles €28, with bath €40; doubles €46/€52-57; triples with bath €60. Cash only. ❷

Hotel Everest, Trav. de Gràcia, 441 (☎93 436 98 00), to the left of the main entrance to the Hospital de St. Pau. M: Hospital de St. Pau, L5. This simple, recently redecorated hotel feels slightly more clinical than Domènech's lush Modernist creation next door, but the price isn't bad for the hotel amenities: TVs, A/C, phones, heat, and even some balconies. Singles €48; doubles €72; triples €90. Cash only. ❺

L'EIXAMPLE ESQUERRA

🏩 **Hostal Eden,** C. Balmes, 55 (☎93 452 66 20; http://hostaleden.net). M: Pg. de Gràcia, L2/3/4. From the Metro, walk down C. Aragó past Rambla de Catalunya to C. Balmes and turn left. Modern, well-kept rooms are equipped with TVs, lockboxes, and fans; most have big, brand-new bathrooms and A/C. Airy, bright sitting area to make coffee and relax in. Free Internet available in 2nd floor lounge. Reservations suggested. May-Oct. singles €29, with bath €39; doubles €39/€60. Nov.-Apr. singles €23/€32; doubles €29/€45. AmEx/MC/V. ❸

LGB ▼
BARCELONA

How *You* Doin'?

Hostal Qué Tal (which translates to What's up Hostel) is an extremely high-quality gay and lesbian accommodation. Located close to some of the best shopping and nightlife in the city in the trendy "Gayxiample," the hostel is usually packed. The interior is one of the best of all hostels in Barcelona, with landscape-painted walls and gorgeous antique mirrors.

The fourteen carefully decorated rooms are characterized by creative motifs, and each has its own distinct personality. Ask for a room with balcony at no extra cost. The spacious baths are covered in colorful tiles and are always spotless. Guests get keys. An inner patio is filled with plants and is perfect for enjoying an afternoon coffee and a good book, or the company of fellow hostelers. Reservations at least one month in advance are recommended, morning tea and coffee included.

C. Mallorca, 290, near C. Bruc in **l'Eixample Dreta.** *☎/ fax 93 459 23 66; www.quetalbarcelona.com. M: Pg. de Gràcia, L2/3/4 or Verdaguer, L4/5. Singles €39; doubles €58, with bath €74. Cash only.* ❹

Pensión Aribau, C. Aribau, 37 (☎/fax 93 453 11 06). M: Pg. de Gràcia, L2/3/4. From the Metro, walk down C. Aragó past La Rambla de Catalunya to C. Aribau and turn left. Basic rooms have all the necessities plus TVs, and most have A/C. Friendly owner speaks English. Reservations highly recommended. June-Sept. 20 singles €36; doubles €45, with bath €60; triples with bath €70; Sept. 21-May singles €30; doubles €40, with bath €55; triples with bath €60. AmEx/MC/V. ❸

Pensión Puebla de Arenoso, C. Aribau, 29 (☎93 453 31 38). M: Pg. de Gràcia, L2/3/4. Walk down C. Aragó past La Rambla de Catalunya to C. Aribau and turn left. This family-run *pensión* has adequate rooms and clean bathrooms. Singles €20; doubles €35. Cash only. ❷

see map p. 348

BARCELONETA

Lodging is not Barceloneta's forte, and rooms here are few and far between. A couple places can be found in the area around M: Barceloneta, L4, but not in the neighborhood itself, which is purely residential.

🏠 **Pensión Francia,** C. Rera Palau, 4 (☎93 319 03 76). M: Barceloneta, L4. Head right toward Pl. Palau, cross Pl. Palau, and turn right onto Av. Marqués de l'Argentera; C. Rera Palau is the 2nd left. A young crowd fills the 14 rooms of this out-of-the-way gem. Excellent amenities include balconies and satellite TV (20 channels) in every room, gleaming furniture, and a friendly owner. The location allows for easy access to Barceloneta, La Ribera, and the Estació de França train station. Singles €35; doubles with shower €40, with complete bath €50-55; triples with shower €55-65. AmEx/MC/V. ❸

Hostal del Mar, Pl. del Palau, 19 (☎ 90 222 22 70; www.gargallo-hotels.com). M: Barceloneta, L4. From the station, head up the street away from the water toward Pl. de Palau, turn left and cross the plaza in front of the palace; it will be on the other side of the plaza (look for a sign). A busy yet comfortable hostel. Singles €24; doubles €43, with shower €48, with complete bath €58; triples €55/65/72; quads €71/85/85. MC/V. ❸

see map p. 346

MONTJUÏC

The neighborhood of **Poble Sec,** at the foot of Montjuïc, is a diverse, working class community crammed with theaters and other nightlife options. The hostels listed here are close to the attractions on Las Ramblas and Montjuïc, but far enough away from the tourist hot spots to still be good deals.

Hostal-Residencia Barcelona, C. Roser, 40 (☎93 443 27 06; hostalbarcelona@terra.es). M: Parallel, L2/L3. C. Roser is one block up Parallel in the direction of Pl. Espanya; the hostel is one block ahead on the right. Verging on hotel-like in quality and size, the Hostal Residencia has 63 rooms, all with TV and bath, most with A/C. Large, comfortable breakfast area with extensive buffet (€4). Friendly, English-speaking staff. Reservations suggested. Doubles €54; triples €70; quads €90. AmEx/MC/V. ❸

Pensión Iniesta, C. d'En Fontrodona, 1 (☎93 329 10 15). M: Parallel, L2/L3. Look for the hostel sign across from the Metro on the corner of Fontrodona and Parallel; enter on Fontrodona. Slightly cramped hallways give way to spacious rooms with TV and fans. Singles €20; doubles €35, with bath €45; triples €45. Cash only. ❷

Hostal Rio de Castro, Av. Parallel, 119 (☎93 441 30 46; hrcastro@teleline.es). Across from M: Poble Sec, L3. Quiet, 15-room hostel offers doubles only. All rooms have TVs and sinks, and are nicely furnished. Owner speaks English. Doubles €47, with bath €53. MC/V. ❹

ZONA ALTA

GRÀCIA

Locals outnumber travelers in Gràcia, Barcelona's deceptively quiet "undiscovered" quarter. Native 20-somethings have definitely discovered, and subsequently taken over, Gràcia's lively weekend nightlife. The accommodations listed here are small and well kept. When making a reservation, be sure to ask for a room away from the noisy streets. During the winter, prices are usually 10% less than as listed. Last-minute arrivals might have luck finding vacancies here during high season.

see map p. 342-345

Hostal Lesseps, C. Gran de Gràcia, 239 (☎93 218 44 34). M: Lesseps, L3. This hostel, conveniently located a few blocks from the metro on bustling C. Gran de Gràcia, offers spacious, classy rooms sporting red velvet wallpaper. All 16 rooms have a TV and bath, 4 have A/C (€5.50 extra per day). Singles €38; doubles €60-52; triples €75; quads €90. MC/V. ❸

Pensión San Medín, C. Gran de Gràcia, 125 (☎93 217 30 68; sanmedin@telefonica.net). M: Fontana, L3. Embroidered curtains and ornate tiling adorn this family-run pension; 12 newly renovated rooms have nice furniture, sinks, phones, and TV. Owner speaks English. Singles €30, with bath €39; doubles €48/€60. MC/V. ❸

Pensión Norma, C. Gran de Gràcia, 87 (☎93 237 44 78). M: Fontana, L3. Clean, simple rooms on third floor of building in great location. Convenient for those who want to take advantage of the area's lively bar scene. Singles €27; doubles €42-45, with bath €50. 10% cheaper for stays of four days or more. Cash only. ❸

Albergue Mare de Déu de Montserrat (HI), Pg. Mare de Déu del Coll, 41-51 (☎93 210 51 51; www.tujuca.com), beyond Parc Güell. Buses #28, 92, 15 and Nitbus N4 stop across the street from the hostel. From M: Vallcarca, L3, walk up Av. República d'Argentina and cross the bridge at C. Viaducte de Vallcarca; signs point the way up the hill. This 220-bed government-sponsored hostel is gorgeous, complete with stained-glass windows and intricate tile work. Its fatal flaw is its location, but the silver lining of being in the boonies is private woods and a hilltop view of Barcelona. Restaurant, Internet access, vending machines, and multiple common spaces. Great way to meet backpackers from all over the world. **HI members only.** Breakfast included. Sheets €2. Flexible 3-day max. stay. Check-in 10am-3pm and 4:30-11pm. Check-out 9:30am. Midnight curfew, but doors open every 30min. Reservations suggested. Dorms €13.50, over 25 €18. Safe available. AmEx/MC/V. ❶

Hostal Valls, C. Laforja, 82 (☎93 209 69 97). FGC: Muntaner. Walk downhill on C. Muntaner for 4 blocks and turn left on C. Laforja. Remote location is a drawback, but the building is beautiful. Has several large common spaces with marble floors and Modernist details. TV lounge. Singles €33; doubles €52. Cash only. ❸

Aparthotel Silver, C. Bretón de los Herreros, 26 (☎93 218 91 00; fax: 93 416 14 47; www.hotelsilver.com). From M: Fontana, L3, walk downhill on C. Gran de Gràcia for 1 block, and turn right on C. Bretón de los Herreros. Aparthotel is on your right at the end of the block. Catering to short-term tourists and longer-term residents, Aparthotel Silver has 49 rooms, each with A/C, bath, TV, phone, and cleverly concealed mini-kitchens. Extra bed can be added in a double for €18 (adults) or €9 (12 and under). Continental breakfast €6. Parking €9. Singles €62-82; doubles €65-100. Wheelchair accessible. AmEx/MC/V. ❺

SANTS

The neighborhood around the Sants-Estació train station is not Barcelona's most exciting, but there is plenty of safe and convenient lodging for late-night arrivals, and it is well connected by Metro to Pl. de Catalunya and Las Ramblas.

Hostal Sofia, Av. Roma, 1-3 (☎93 419 50 40; fax 93 430 69 43). M: Sants Estació, L3/ 5. Directly across from the front of the train station; cross C. Numància on the left and look up for the blue sign. This small hostel provides young traveling students with 17 sun-lit, breezy rooms heated in winter. Excellent value for price. TVs and safes available. Prices vary by season. In summer, singles €30-35, with bath €42; doubles €40/€50; triples €51/€60. Wheelchair accessible. MC/V. ❸

Hostal Residencial Sants, C. Antoni de Campany, 82 (☎93 331 37 00; fax 93 421 68 64). Leave the station from the back and follow C. Antoni through Pl. Sants, across C. Sants; look for the large vertical yellow sign on the left as you cross the *plaça*. A huge, clean, and inexpensive hostel in a convenient location. All 74 rooms have heat and A/C. Singles €25, with bath €31; doubles €32/€39. Wheelchair accessible. MC/V. ❷

Hostal Béjar, C. Béjar, 36-38 (☎93 325 59 53). Take a right onto C. Rector Triado from the station, go immediately left onto C. Mallorca, and then right on C. Béjar. In an unassuming brick building with a cool, plant-lined interior stairwell. Clean, cheap rooms relatively close to the train station. All 22 rooms have desks and heaters, and most have fans. Singles €24; doubles with bath €48. Wheelchair accessible. MC/V. ❷

Hotel Transit, C. Rector Triadó, 82 (☎93 424 60 13), on the street immediately to the right out of the front of the station. 27 rooms with heat, bath, phones, and TVs. Some have A/C. Close to the train station. Singles €62-66; doubles €75-80; triples €77. AmEx/MC/V. ❹

Hotel Roma, Av. de Roma, 31 (☎93 410 66 33; fax 93 410 13 52; www.hoteles-catalonia.es). M: Sants Estació, L3/5. Same directions as Hostal Sofia (see above), but farther down Av. de Roma (on the same side). If you have the money to spend and feel like staying somewhere a bit more luxurious but still near the train station, this is the place to go. A 3-star hotel with bright, clean rooms. Prices vary by season. In summer, singles with bath €118; doubles with bath €136. AmEx/MC/V. ❺

CAMPING

Although there are no campsites within the city, intercity buses (€1.50) run to all the following locations in 20-45min. For more info, contact the **Associació de Càmpings de Barcelona,** Gran Via de les Corts Catalanes, 608 (☎93 412 59 55; www.campingsbcn.com).

El Toro Bravo, Autovía de Castelldefells, km 11 (☎93 637 34 62; www.eltorobravo.com). Take bus L95 (€1.50) from Pl. de Catalunya to the campsite, 11km south. Offers beach access, laundry facilities, currency exchange, 3 pools, 2 bars, a restaurant, and a supermarket. Possibility for long-term stays. Reception 8am-7pm. June 15-Aug. €5.20 per person, €5.50 per site, €5.20 per car, €4 electricity charge. Sept.-June 14 €5 per person, €5 per site, €5 per car, €4 electricity charge. AmEx/MC/V. ❶

Filipinas, Autovía de Castelldefells, km 12 (☎93 65 828 95; fax 93 658 17 91), 1km down the road from El Toro Bravo (see above), accessible by bus L95. Same prices and services as El Toro Bravo. AmEx/MC/V. ❶

LONG-TERM ACCOMMODATIONS

Care to stay a while? With a little leg-work, a person can find a comfortable and cheap place to live in Barcelona. Securing a *habitación* (room) or *piso* (apartment) from outside the city can be difficult, however, so it's best to book a hostel for the first week of hunting. The easiest route is to check the many **bulletin boards** to look for possible sublets. Many rooms are available to sublet year-round. Those seeking a private apartment for only a few months will have a more arduous time. In general, the shorter the stay, the harder it is to rent, with the summer months being particularly difficult. The city's **accommodation agencies** are helpful, as are the city **newspapers**. Depending on the location and the apartment, good prices range from €200 to €350 per person per month. There are plenty of short-term establishments that also cater to long-term guests, such as Aparthotel Silver (p. 199), El Toro Bravo (p. 200), and ⬛Pensión Fani (p. 196). In addition to rent, expect to pay an agency or contract fee (where applicable), which can increase actual prices substantially, as well as monthly utilities. For convenience to public transportation and services, reasonable rents, and neighborhood safety, ◩l'Eixample is a good all-around choice.

BULLETIN BOARDS

Many restaurants, hostels, and cafes have mini bulletin boards. Also, universities and libraries also tend to have listings posted. When checking out the city sights, keep your eyes peeled for sub-let advertisments.

International House, C. Trafalgar, 14 (☎93 268 45 11, 93 268 02 39). M: Urquinaona. Open daily 8am-9:30pm.

Centre d'Informació Assesorament per a Joves (CIAJ), C. Ferrán, 32 (☎93 402 78 00; www.bcn.es/ciaj), off Las Ramblas. M: Liceu, L3. Open M-F 10am-2pm and 4-8pm.

RENTAL AGENCIES

Habit Servei, C. Muntaner, 206 (☎93 209 50 45; habitservei@habitservei.com), between Londres and Paris. M: Hospital Clìnic, L5. From the Metro, walk north on Villarroel for 2 blocks, take a right on Paris, and take a left on Muntaner after 2 blocks. The helpful, patient staff speaks English, and understands if you know nothing about renting an apartment in Spain. Wide range of prices and lengths of stay (including homestays and shared apartments), according to the client's needs. Open M-F 10am-2pm and 4-7:30pm.

Barcelona Allotjament, C. Pelai, 12 (☎93 268 43 57; www.barcelona-allotjament.com), off Pl. de Catalunya. M: Catalunya, L1/3. Reasonably priced apartments throughout the city. Open M-F 10am-2pm.

Habitatge Jove, C. Calàbria, 147 (☎93 483 83 92; www.habitatgejove.com). M: Rocafort. The multilingual web site can locate an apartment, room, or host family before you even visit the office, often at an excellent price. However, the minimum length of rental for an apartment is one year. Open M-F 9am-2pm and 3-5:30pm.

Daytripping

COSTA BRAVA

Tracing the Mediterranean Sea from Barcelona to the French border, the Costa Brava's jagged cliffs and pristine beaches draw throngs of European visitors, especially in July and August. Early June and late September can be remarkably peaceful; the water is still warm but the beaches are less crowded. In the winter fierce winds sweep the coast, leaving behind boarded-up and almost empty coastal towns. Unlike its counterparts, Costa Blanca and Costa del Sol, Costa Brava offers more than just high-rises and touristy beaches. The rocky shores have traditionally attracted romantics and artists like Marc Chagall and Salvador Dalí, a Costa Brava native. Dalí's house in Cadaqués and his museum in Figueres display the largest collections of his work in Europe.

GETTING AROUND THE COSTA BRAVA

Transportation to the Costa Brava from Barcelona is seasonal, with frequent service during July and August, sporadic service May-June and September-October, and little to no service from November to April. However, bus service between the towns remains fairly regular throughout the year. Be aware of possible scheduling differences and availability between weekday and weekend service. **RENFE trains** (☎ 902 24 02 02; www.renfe.es) stop at Blanes, Figueres, and then farther north at Llançà and Portbou (near the French border) and are preferable to buses because they are less expensive and faster. **Buses** are the only mode of inter-city transportation along the coast, however, and as they often run along beautiful winding roads, they are an enjoyable option. **Sarfa** (☎97 230 02 62; www.sarfa.com), **Pujol i Pujol** (☎97 236 42 36), and **Teisa** (☎97 220 48 68) are Costa Brava's principal carriers.

FIGUERES

In 1974, the mayor of Figueres (pop. 35,000) asked native Salvador Dalí to donate a painting to an art museum the town was planning. Dalí refused to donate a painting. Instead, he was so flattered by his hometown's recognition that he donated an entire museum. With the construction of the Teatre-Museu Dalí, Figueres was catapulted to international fame. Ever since, a multilingual parade of Surrealism fans has been awed and entranced by Dalí's bizarre perspectives and erotic visions.

TRANSPORTATION

Trains: Pl. de Estació. ☎90 224 02 02. To: **Barcelona** (2hr.; M-F 25 per day, Sa-Su 15 per day; €8.05); **Girona** (30min.; M-F 25 per day, Sa-Su 15 per day; €2.50); **Portbou** (30min.; 11 per day; €1.85).

Buses: All buses leave from the **Estació Autobuses** (☎97 267 33 54), in Pl. Estació. **Sarfa** (☎97 267 42 98; www.sarfa.com) runs to: **Cadaqués** (1hr.; July-Aug. 5 per day, Sept.-June 3-4 per day; €3.55); **Palafrugell** (1½ hr.; M-F 4 per day, Sa-Su 3 per day; €5.80); **Llançà** (25min.; July-Aug. 4 per day, Sept.-June 2 per day; €2.20). **Barcelona Bus** (☎97 250 50 29) runs to: **Barcelona** (2¼hr., 2-6 per day, €12.50) and **Girona** (1hr.; M-F 5 per day, Sa-Su 2-3

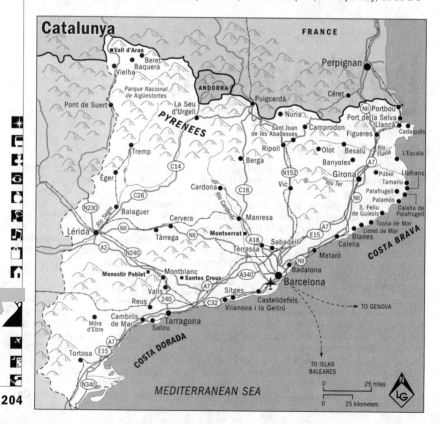

per day; €3.60). **Teisa** (☎97 250 31 75) goes to **Olot** (1hr., 3 per day, €4.35). **Eurolines** (☎97 250 63 00) ticket office is open M-F 9am-1:30pm and 3:30-9pm, Sa 10am-1pm and 6-9pm. MC/V.

Taxis: Taxis line the Rambla (☎97 250 00 08) and the train station (☎97 250 50 43).

Car Rental: Hertz, Pl. Estació, 9 (☎97 267 28 01 or 90 240 24 05). All-inclusive rental from €59 per day. 23+, valid driver's license of 2 years. Open M-F 8am-1pm and 4-8pm, Sa 9am-1pm. AmEx/D/MC/V. **Avis,** Pl. Estació, **RENFE** train station (☎97 251 31 82) rental includes taxes, insurance, unlimited kilometers. €63 per day. 23+, valid driver's license of 1 year, and credit card. Open M-Sa 9am-1pm and 4-7pm. AmEx/MC/V.

ORIENTATION & PRACTICAL INFORMATION

Modernist Architecture in Figueres

Trains and buses arrive at **Pl. de Estació** on the edge of town. Cross the plaza and bear left on C. Sant Llàtzer, walk several blocks to Carrer Nou, and take a right to get to Figueres's tree-lined Rambla. To reach the **tourist office,** walk up the Rambla and continue on C. Lasauca straight out from the left corner. The blue, all-knowing **"i"** beckons across the rather treacherous intersection with Ronda Frial.

Tourist Office: Main office, Pl. Sol (☎97 250 31 55; www.figueresciutat.com). Good map and free list of accommodations; pick up *la Guía,* revised annually, for hotel, food, culture, and shopping recommendations. Open Nov.-Mar. M-F 9am-3pm; Apr.-June and Oct. M-F 9am-3pm and 4:30-8pm, Sa 9:30am-1:30pm and 3:30-6:30pm; July-Aug. M-Sa 9am-8pm, Su 9am-3pm; Sept. M-Sa 9am-8pm. Free guided walking tours of the city Sa 11am. Two **branch offices** in summer, one at Pl. Estació (open July-Sept. 15 M-Sa 10am-2pm and 4-6pm), and the other in a yellow mobile home in front of the Dalí museum.

Dalí Museum's Mae West Installation

Currency Exchange: Banco Santander Central Hispano, Rambla, 21. **ATM.** Open Apr.-Sept. M-F 8:30am-2pm; Oct.-Mar. M-F 8:30am-2pm, Sa 8:30am-1pm. Cashes **traveler's checks.** MC/V.

Luggage Storage: At the train station, large lockers €3; open daily 6am-11pm. At the bus station €2; open daily 6am-10pm.

Bookstore: Llibreria J. Mallart, C. Besalu, 12 (☎97 250 01 33) sells regional, Spanish and European travel guides in English, Catlan, Spanish, and French. Open M-F 9am-1pm and 4-8pm, Sa 9:30am-1pm and 4:30-8pm.

Emergency: ☎112. **Police:** Ronda Final, 4 (☎97 251 01 11; local police emergency ☎092). **National police** (☎091) should be contacted regarding theft or loss of important document (passports) but not for emergencies.

Architecture outside Figueres

in recent news

Education Discrimination

Immigration in Spain has recently been on the rise; between 1993 and 2001, the percentage of foreign children in Spanish public schools quadrupled in size to 2.22% (according to data collected by the Public Defender and UNICEF) and Spanish schools are facing the challenge of adjusting to this new population. After 40 years of a closed society, immigration is new concern. Catalunya has experienced a particularly high influx with the second largest population of foreign students at 2.46% (behind Madrid at 5%). Changing the education system—one originally designed for Spanish natives—is a task in itself, is even harder to manage in Barcelona where all students are required to take Catalan.

Another problem is a backlash of discrimination. Many Spaniards blame immigrants for the faltering economy and rising crime rates. The responsibility for educating this quickly growing number of foreign students has fallen mainly upon public schools. Critics cite this as evidence of discrimination and are suggesting increased regulation of the admissions process in schools subsidized by government funds.

Internet Access: Tele Haddi, C. Joan Reglá, 1 (☎97 251 30 99). €1 per 15min., €1.50 per 30min., €2.50 per 1hr. Open daily 9:30am-10pm. **Oh!net** Internet kiosk at the bus station €0.50 per 4min., €1 per 8min., and €2 per 20min. **Hotel Rambla,** Rambla, 33 (☎97 267 60 20; fax 97 267 60 19; www.hotelrambla.net). €1 per 15min. Open 24hr.

Post Office: C. Santa Llogaia, 60-62 (☎97 250 54 31). Open M-F 8am-1pm.

Postal Code: 17600.

ACCOMMODATIONS

Most visitors to Figueres make the journey a daytrip from Barcelona, but affordable accommodations in Figueres are easy to find. Most tend to be on the upper floors of small bars or restaurants. Some cluster on C. Jonquera, around the Dalí museum; others are located closer to La Rambla and C. Pep Ventura.

Hostal La Barretina, C. Lasauca, 13 (☎97 267 64 12 or 97 267 34 25). From the train station, walk up the left side of La Rambla to its end and look for C. Lasauca directly ahead. A luxury experience—each room has TV, A/C, heat, and private bath. Reception is downstairs in the jointly owned restaurant. Reservations recommended. Singles €23; doubles €39. July-Aug. prices tend to increase slightly. AmEx/MC/V. ❷

Hostal San Mar, C. Rec Arnau, 31 (☎97 250 98 13). Follow C. Girona off La Rambla and continue as it turns into C. Jonquera. Take the 5th right onto C. Isabel II and then take the 2nd left. It is down the street on the right. Enter through the bar. If you make it all the way out here, you will be rewarded with a clean, modern room that has a bath and TV. Ask for a room with a view of the countryside. Singles €14; doubles €28. Cash only. ❶

Pensión Mallol, C. Pep Ventura, 9 (☎97 250 22 83). Follow the Rambla toward the tourist office, turn right on Castell at its end, and take the 2nd left. Look for the "Habitaciones-Chambres" sign. Clean and simply decorated rooms with shared bath and firm mattresses. Excellent value. Singles €15.50; doubles €26.50. Cash only. ❶

FOOD

Comida típica (classic Catalan cuisine) seems to be the most popular food theme in Figueres. However, with the growing Latino population, alternatives are springing up, making for an occasional break from the staple fish and meat. Look out for the Culinary Forum, every other February, when the city hosts a cooking convention for respected chefs. The **market** is at Pl. Gra and Pl. de Cat-

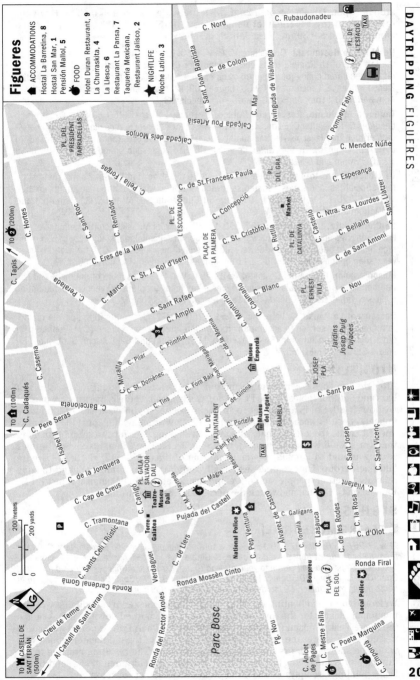

Figueres

▲ **ACCOMMODATIONS**
Hostal La Barretina, **8**
Hostal San Mar, **1**
Pensión Mallol, **5**

● **FOOD**
Hotel Duran Restaurant, **9**
La Churraskita, **4**
La Llesca, **6**
Restaurant La Pansa, **7**
Taqueria Mexicana, Restaurant Jalisco, **2**

★ **NIGHTLIFE**
Noche Latina, **3**

alunya (open Tu, Th, Sa 5am-2pm, with the widest selection on Th). Buy your own food at the **supermarket Bonpreu,** Pl. Sol, 5. (☎97 251 00 19. Open M-Th 9am-2pm and 5-9:30pm, F-Sa 9am-9pm. MC/V.)

Hotel Duran Restaurant, C. Lasauca, 5 (☎97 250 12 50). From the train station, walk up the left side of La Rambla to its end and look for C. Lasauca directly ahead. Relax in the regally decorated dining room and enjoy carefully prepared Catalan cuisine with a distinctive French influence. Lunch menú €9.50. Entrees €9-42, most between €16-20. Open daily 1-4pm and 8:30-11pm. AmEx/MC/V, traveler's checks. ❹

Taquería Mexicana, Restaurant Jalisco, C. Tapis, 21 (☎97 250 53 52). C. Peralada becomes C. Tapis after C. Hortes, then walk half a block more. For those looking for a change in their diet, this Jalisco-styled restaurant serves Mexican classics (entrees €4-14, mainly in the €4.50-7 range). Try the *Fajitas de Pollo* (€6.50). Vegetarian options. Open M-Tu, Th-Su 12:30-3:30pm and 8-11:30pm. MC/V. ❷

La Llesca, C. Mestre Falla, 15 (☎97 267 58 26), just beyond Pl. Sol. Family-run restaurant specializes in *llesques,* toasted sandwiches topped with just about anything (€4-11). Menús €7.20-12; salads €3-4.50. Open Su 6pm-midnight, M and W-Sa 9am-4pm and 7:30pm-midnight. AmEx/MC/V. ❷

La Churraskita, C. Magre, 5 (☎97 250 15 52; www.lachuraskita.com). Hammocks and hand-weavings adorn the colorful walls of this popular Argentinian restaurant. A romantic terrace hides out back. Offers a wide selection of grilled meats (€5-14, €19 for two). Plenty of vegetarian options. Open Su, Tu-Sa 11am-4pm and 8pm-midnight. AmEx/MC/V. ❷

Mesón Asador, Pujada del Castell, 4 (☎97 251 01 04). Serves more of the meat and fish traditionally a part of Catalan cuisine. Figueres has recognized this 30 year old restaurant as a classic. Tapas €3-15. Open M-Sa 11am-4pm and 7:30-11pm. MC/V. ❸

Restaurant La Pansa, C. Emporda, 8 (☎97 250 10 72). A comfortable, upscale restaurant has speedy service to accompany its Catalan fare. 4-course menú (€9). Popular with older locals. Open July-Aug. Su 8-11:30pm, M-Sa 1-4pm and 8-11:30pm; Sept.-June. Su also 1-3:30pm. AmEx/MC/V. ❷

NIGHTLIFE

After the sun goes down, a young and fun, light-hearted crowd fills up the string of bars and outdoor tables on the Pl. del Sol. Occasionally there is live music, but even without it, Pl. Sol is a safe bet for a social scene. If you want something more upbeat, consider **Noche Latina,** C. Ample, 17, (www.nochelatina.org) the recently-opened Latino discoteque that will have you shaking your hips to salsa beats in no time (or should we say 3/2 time?). Open Su, Th-Sa 11pm-5am, no cover. Outdoor seating around La Rambla, especially in front of the old Hotel Paris, draws a more laid-back group. On evenings, especially Sundays when families spend the day relaxing together, people sip coffee and drinks at the **Pl. l'Ajuntament,** just off La Rambla on C. Girona, and watch the occasional street performer.

SIGHTS

▨ TEATRE-MUSEU DALÍ

🚩 ☎97 267 75 00; fax 97 250 16 66; www.salvador-dali.org. From the Rambla, take C. Girona from the end farthest from the tourist office. C. Girona goes past Pl. Ajuntament and becomes C. Jonquera. Steps by a Dalí statue to your left lead to the maroon and white, egg-covered museum. Open Oct.-June daily 10:30am-5:15pm; July-Sept. daily 9am-7:15pm. Call ahead about night hours during the summer. €9, students and seniors €6.50. Cash only.

Welcome to the enchanting world of the Surrealist master. This building was the municipal theater for the town of Figueres before it burned down in 1939—hence the name Teatre-Museu ("theater-museum") Dalí. When Dalí decided to donate a museum to Figueres, he insisted on using the ruins of the old theater, which was where he showed his first exposition as a teenager. The resulting homage to his first gallery is the reconstructed theater, covered in sculptures of eggs and full of Dalí's paintings, sculptures, and other creations—even his own tomb.

Dalí was infamous for being an unabashed self-promoter, and his personally designed mausoleum/museum/monument to himself dramatically lives up that reputation. It's all here: Dalí's naughty cartoons, his dramatically simple tomb, and many paintings of Gala, his wife and muse, one of which, when viewed through a telescope (€0.20), transforms into a portrait of American president Abraham Lincoln. The treasure-trove of paintings includes, among others, the remarkable *Self Portrait with a Slice of Bacon*, *Poetry of America*, *Galarina*, and *Galatea of the Spheres*. Don't miss the spectacular *Sala de Mae West*, created by Dalí for the museum; when viewed from the lookout in the plastic camel, the furnished room resembles the face of actress Mae West. Other works include the surreal appearance of his own Cadillac in the middle of the museum. There is also a small offering of works by other artists selected by Dalí himself, including pieces by El Greco, Marcel Duchamp, and the architect Peres Piñero. While the museum is full of interesting art, not all the works are on the walls; be sure to look up as well.

MUSEU DEL JOGUET (TOY MUSEUM)

🚩 *Sant Pere, 1, off La Rambla. ☎ 97 250 45 85; www.mjc-figueres.net. Open June-Sept. M-Sa 10am-1pm and 4-7pm, Su 11am-1:30pm and 5-7:30pm; Oct.-May Tu-Sa 10am-1pm and 4-7pm, Su 11am-1:30pm. €4.70, students and children under 12 €3.80.*

Delight in the wonders of your favorite childhood toys at this small toy museum, the winner of Spain's prestigious National Prize of Popular Culture in 1999. The collection includes antique dolls, blocks, board games, comics, rocking horses, and toys for the blind, as well as toys donated by famous Catalans such as Joan Miró and Salvador Dalí. Don't miss the impressive selection of Christmas-time *caganers* (shitters), a Catalan favorite (see **Waste with Taste**, p. 132).

CASTELL DE SANT FERRÁN

🚩 *Av. Castell de Sant Ferrán, follow Pujada del Castell from the Teatre-Museu Dalí. ☎ 97 250 60 94; http://ww2.grn.es/santferran. Open July-Sept. 15 daily 10:30am-8pm; Nov.-Feb. daily 10:30am-2pm; Mar.-July and Sept. 16-Oct. daily 10:30am-2pm and 4-6pm. €2.*

A 10min. walk from the Museu Dalí, this massive 18th-century castle/fortress, built to defend against the French during boundary disputes, commands a spectacular view of the surrounding countryside and at 555,000sq. m, is the largest fortress of its kind in Europe. Ask about the guided tour (€12) which takes you through the moat and into one of the water deposits in tunnels under the castle.

MUSEU EMPORDÀ

🚩 *Rambla, 2. ☎ 97 250 23 05. Open Su 11am-2pm Tu-Sa 11am-7pm. €2, students and seniors €1. Free entrance with presentation of Teatre-Museu Dalí ticket (see above).*

Though small, this museum's permanent exhibition manages to offer a satisfying taste of over 2000 years of the Alt Empordà region's (the northern section of the Costa Brava) art, from Neolithic to modern. On display are ancient Roman artifacts, 16th-century frescoes, Baroque paintings, and works by Casas, Tàpies, Dalí, and Miró, among others. Although most pieces have descriptions only in Catalan, art-lovers may enjoy a short visit.

FESTIVALS

2004 has been designated the "Dalí Year", so next year many exhibits and celebrations in honor of the town's patron artist will come to Figueres—call the tourist office for more information on specific dates. In September, classical and jazz music come to Figueres during the **Festival Internacional de Música de l'Empordà.** (Tickets available at Caixa de Catalunya. Call ☎ 97 210 12 12 or get a brochure at the tourist office.) From September 10-14, the **Mostra del Vi de L'Alt Empordà,** a tribute to regional wines, brings a taste of the local vineyards to Figueres. Around May 3, the **Fires i Festes de la Santa Creu** sponsors cultural events and art exhibitions. General merrymaking can be

Castell de Sant Ferran

After the Festival

Grounds of Sant Ferran

expected at the **Festa de Sant Pere,** held June 28-29, which honors the town's patron saint. Look for the **Culinary Forum**, which brings renowned chefs every other February, transforming Figueres into the culinary capital of Catalunya.

GIRONA

Girona (pop. 75,000) seems to be a city of counter-balancing contradictions: it manages to maintain the safe and communal feel of a small city while also supporting numerous quality museums, variety in food, fun night-life, and strong fashion consciousness. It presents the interesting juxtaposition of hip and stylish—and young, thanks to the large university in town—people living against the stone backdrop of medieval city steeped in history. First a Roman settlement and then an important medieval cultural center, Girona was one of the few Spanish cities where Christians, Arabs, and Jews were, at times, able to coexist peacefully. From artifacts dating all the way back to the prehistoric Paleolithic Period, to the founding of the renowned *cabalistas de Girona* (see **The Jewish Sepharad**, p. 214), Girona is the perfect option for those who don't want to confine the past to glass cases and stuffy museums.

TRANSPORTATION

Flights: the airport, **Aeropuerto de Girona-Costa Brava,** Termino Municipal de Vilobi d'Onyar (☎97 218 66 00), is small and services few regular flights on **Iberia** (☎97 247 41 92; www.iberia.com) and **Ryanair** (www.ryanair.com). Charter flights also come through the airport. Airport tourist office (☎97 218 67 08) has more complete information. €15 from the airport to the Old City by taxi (12km).

Trains: RENFE (☎97 224 02 02; www.renfe.es), in Pl. de Espanya. Info open daily 5:45am-10pm. To: **Barcelona** (1½hr., M-F 24 per day 6am-9:30pm, Sa and Su starting 9:48am; €5); **Figueres** (30-40min., 23 per day 6:15am-10:44pm, €2.10); **Madrid** (10½hr., 1 per day, €35); **Portbou** (1hr., 10 per day 6:15am-10:44pm, €3.25); **Flaca** (30min., 11-15 per day 7:45am-10:30pm, €1.35); **Paris** (11hr.; 1 per day at 10:17pm; €109, under 26 €85).

Buses: Next to the train station. **Sarfa** (☎97 220 17 96; open daily 7:30am-8:30pm) runs to: **Celra** (€1.10); **Cadaques** (€6.85); **Palafrugell** (1hr., 17 per day, €5), for connections to Begur, Llafranc, Calella, and Tamariu and **Tossa de Mar** (40min.; July-Aug. 2 per day, Sept.-June 1 per day). **Teisa** (☎97 220 02 75; open M-F 9am-1pm and 3:30-7:15pm, Sa-Su 9am-1pm, Su 4:30-5:30pm; cash only) runs to: **Lerida** (3½hr.; 2 per day; €15.80, students €14.20);

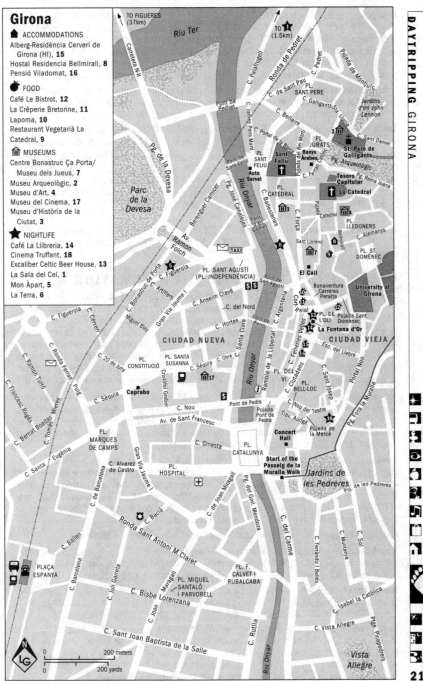

Girona

♦ ACCOMMODATIONS

Alberg-Residència Cerverí de
 Girona (HI), **15**
Hostal Residència Bellmirall, **8**
Pensió Viladomat, **16**

🍴 FOOD

Café Le Bistrot, **12**
La Crêperie Bretonne, **11**
Lapoma, **10**
Restaurant Vegetarià La
 Catedral, **9**

🏛 MUSEUMS

Centre Bonastruc Ça Porta/
 Museu dels Jueus, **7**
Museu Arqueològic, **2**
Museu d'Art, **4**
Museu del Cinema, **17**
Museu d'Història de la
 Ciutat, **3**

★ NIGHTLIFE

Café La Llibreria, **14**
Cinema Truffant, **18**
Excaliber Celtic Beer House, **13**
La Sala del Cel, **1**
Mon Àpart, **5**
La Terra, **6**

Olot (1hr., 9 per day, €4.30); **Ripoll** (2hr., M-F 3 per day, Sa-Su 2 per day; €9.35); **St. Feliu** (1hr., 9-14 per day, M-F €3.25, Sa-Su €3.70). **Barcelona Bus** (☎97 220 24 32; www.barcelonabus.com; open M-F 6:30-10:10am, 10:40am-2:25pm, and 4:30-7:10pm; MC/V) sends express buses to **Barcelona** (1¼hr.; M-F 5 per day, Sa-Su 3 per day; €11.45) and **Figueres** (50min.; M-F 6 per day, Sa 2 per day, Su 3 per day; €4.55). International travel by bus is also available through **Eurolines** buses to destinations throughout Europe and Morocco.

Public transportation: City buses (☎97 220 1540) run throughout the city, although most everything is within walking distance. Schedules and route maps available at the tourist office. All service stops when the University of Girona closes for the summer. (mid-June to mid-Sept.)

Taxis: Taxi Girona (☎97 220 33 77) or **Girotaxi** (☎97 222 10 20; 6am-11pm). Stands at Pl. Independència or Pont de Pedra. Taxis cannot be hailed; go to one of the two taxi stands or call for one.

Car Rental: Europcar (☎65 045 31 46; www.europcar.es) is inside the train station. Open M-F 9am-1:30pm and 4:30-7pm, Sa 9am-2pm. Must be 21+ and have had a license for 1 year. MC/V. **Avis** (☎97 222 46 64; reservations 90 213 55 31; www.avis.es) is across from Europcar inside the train station. Open M-F 9am-1pm and 4-7pm, Sa 9am-1pm. Must be 23+ and must have had a valid licence for at least 1 year. Costs start at €17 per day. Extra charge of €10 per day for those under 25. AmEx/MC/V.

Bike rental: Bicicletes TRAFACH (☎97 223 49 43) in Salt, 2km from Girona. Open Th-F 1:30-8:30pm. €14 per day. **Centre BTT** (☎97 246 82 42), in Quart, 3km from Girona, open Sa-Su 8am-3pm.

ORIENTATION & PRACTICAL INFORMATION

The **Riu Onyar** separates the New City from the Old. The **Pont de Pedra** is the primary bridge among the many that connect the two banks and lead into the old quarter by way of C. Ciutadans and C. Força, which lead towards the cathedral and El Call, the historic Jewish neighborhood. The **RENFE** and **bus terminals** are situated off C. de Barcelona, in the modern neighborhood. To get to the Old City from the stations, head straight out through the parking lot, turn left on C. Barcelona and continue to follow C. Barcelona for two blocks until it forks at the traffic island. Take the right fork via C. Santa Eugenia to Gran Via de Jaume I, across the Gran Via to C. Nou, which leads to the Pont de Pedra.

Tourist Office: Rambla Llibertat, 1 (☎97 222 65 75; www.ajuntament.gi), in a yellow, one-story neo-classical building directly on the left as you cross Pont de Pedra from the new town. Tons of free info on the city and region. English, French, Portuguese, and German spoken. Pick up a free map and the free bi-weekly *La Guía*, in Catalan but with easy-to-follow listings. Open M-F 8am-8pm, Sa 8am-2pm and 4-8pm, Su 9am-2pm.

Bank: All banks have more or less the same hours: M-F 8:30am-2:15pm, Sa 8:30am-1pm. **BBVA** (Banco Bilbao Vizcaya Argentaria; 24hr. hotline ☎90 222 44 66; www.bbva.es) and **Caixa de Girona** (24hr. hotline ☎97 218 22 47; www.caixagirona.es) are next to each other at Pl. Independència, 18, and both have 24 hr. **ATMs.** AmEx/MC/V. **La Caixa,** at the corner of C. Santa Clara and C. Nou (immediately across the Pont de Pedra in the Ciudad Nueva on the right-hand corner) will cash MC/V **traveler's checks.**

Luggage Storage: Lockers in train station €4.50 per 24hr. Open M-F 6:30am-10pm.

Travel Bookstore: Ulyssus, C. Ballesteries, 29 (☎/fax 97 221 17 73; ulyssus@ulyssus.com), on the left as you walk up Ballesteries toward the Pl. Cathedral. Offers guides to Girona and Spain, some in English (€18-27). Open M-Sa 10am-2pm and 4:30-8:30pm. MC/V.

Travel Agency: Halcon, C. Nou, 37 (☎97 220 0055), offers discount student prices and group prices for everything from Eurorail passes to car, bus, and boat rental and flight reservations. Open M-F 9:30am-1:30pm and 4:30-8pm, Sa 10am-1:30pm. AmEx/MC/V.

Supermarket: Caprabo, C. Sequia, 10 (☎97 221 45 16), a block from C. Nou off the Gran Via toward the river in the New City. Open M-Sa 9am-9pm. For those staying in the Old City, try **Auto Servei,** C. Calderers, 1 (☎97 220 33 16), on the left immediately after C. Ballesteries leads into Pl. St. Feliu. Small yet conveniently located, this neighborhood grocery store covers basic food and hygiene needs. Open M-F 8am-8pm, Sa 8am-3pm.

Laundry: Albergue-Residencia Cerveri de Girona, C. Ciutadans, 9 (☎97 221 80 03). Wash €2, dry €1. Open 24hr.; call ahead to find out when laundry service is available. **Laso (lavandería)**, C. Balmes, 6 (☎97 220 51 25). Open M-F 8am-8pm, Sa 8am-1pm.

Emergency: ☎112 for medical emergency. **Police: Policía Municipal**, C. Bacià, 4 (☎092). From Banco Central Hispano, turn right on the Gran Via, then right on Bacià. They handle traveler-specific problems such as lost or stolen documents or luggage.

Hospital: Hospital Municipal de Santa Caterina, Pl. Hospital, 5 (☎97 218 26 00).

Internet Access: Corado Telephone, C. Barcelona, 31 (☎97 222 28 75), across from the train station. €2 per hr. Open M-Sa 9am-2pm and 5-9pm. **Café la Llibreria**, C. Ciutadans, 15 (☎96 220 48 18). €1 per 20min. **Cafeteria Nimhs**, C. Sequia, 5 (☎97 222 03 86; www.nimhs.net), on C. Sequia across from Pl. Constitucio about 1/2 block past the Museu del Cinema if walking away from the river. Open M-F 8am-10pm.

Post Office: Av. Ramón Folch, 2 (☎97 222 21 11), at the start of Gran Via de Jaume I. Turn right on Gran Via when coming from the old city. **Western Union** in same office. Open M-F 8:30am-8:30pm, Sa 9:30am-2pm. **Second office**, Ronda Ferrán Puig, 17 (☎97 222 34 75). Only for sending things out. Open M-F 8:30am-2:30pm, Sa 9:30am-1pm.

Postal Code: 17070.

ACCOMMODATIONS

Reservations are highly recommende~~d~~ ~~at~~ least four weeks in advance for the months of June, July, and August, as we~~ll a~~s for festivals. Budget accommodations in the old quarter are reasonably pric~~ed~~ ~~a~~nd centrally located near restaurants, cultural centers, and museums.

Pensió Viladomat, C. Ciutadans, 5 (☎97 220 31 76; fa~~x 9~~7 220 31 76). From the New City, cross Pont de Pedra, take a left on Ciutadans; it's about ~~a~~ ~~b~~lock up on your left. Sparkling clean and well-furnished rooms in an old apartment buildin~~g i~~n the historic neighborhood. Rooms with bath have TVs. Singles €16; doubles €32, with ba~~th~~ €55; triple with bath €75. Long-term options, apartments, and family-size rooms available. ~~Cas~~h only. ❷

Hostal Residencia Bellmirall, C. Bellmirall, 3 (☎97 220 40 09). W~~ith~~ the cathedral directly behind you, C. Bellmirall is straight ahead to the left; look for the blue ~~ho~~tel sign. Expensive but worth the splurge. Features delightful rooms, all with private bath, in a ~~14~~th-century stone house. Breakfast included and served by the warm hostess in the cozy din~~ing~~ area or plant-filled garden patio. The perfect, romantic environment from which to enjoy ~~Giro~~na. Closed Jan.-Feb. Singles €32; doubles €56; triples €75; quads €96. Cash only. ❸

Albergue-Residència Cerverí de Girona (HI), C. Ciutadans, 9 (☎97 221 ~~80~~ 03; alberg_girona@tujuca.com). Next to the Pensió Viladomat. The sterile, whitewashed wa~~lls a~~nd blue metal bunks in this college dorm building may cause flashbacks to sleep-away ca~~mp~~, but the price and location make it worthwhile. A good place to meet other travelers as well ~~as~~ students from the university who live here during the academic year. 90 beds available Oct.-June; 100 beds July-Sept. Sleek sitting rooms with TV/VCR, video library, and ping-pong; rooms of 2, 3, and 8 beds with lockers. Breakfast €2.70; other meals €5. Sheets €2; towel rental €2; combined sheets and towel rental €3. Wash €2, dry €1. Internet €1 per 30 min. **Members only,** but HI cards for sale. Make reservations at the Barcelona office (☎93 483 83 63). Dorms for under 25 years of age €13.50, for over 25 €18; for groups €12; all prices increase by €2 on the weekend. 24hr. check-in. MC/V. ❶

FOOD

Considered home to some of the best cuisine in Catalunya, Girona's specialties are *botifarra dolça* (sweet sausage with pork, lemon, cinnamon, and sugar) and *xuxo* (sugar-sprinkled croissants filled with cream) which can be found at *carnicerias* and *pastellerias*, respectively. Popular throughout Spain, *xuxo* originated in here in Girona. By far the best concentration of good, cheap food is on C. Cort Reial, at the top of C. Argenteria. Health food and vegetarian options also abound on both sides of the river. Year-round, an open **market** can be found near the Polideportivo in Parc de la Deversa, open Tuesday and Saturday 8am-3pm.

The Jewish Sepharad

Though Girona has a reputation for tolerance, the Jews of Girona were still victims of discrimination, ostracism, and eventual expulsion. Despite it all, they contributed ineradicably to the city's culture. The *aljama* (Jewish quarter) in Girona, once populated by 300 people, became a leading center for the study of the **Kabbala**, a mystical reading of the Torah in which number values are assigned to each Hebrew letter and numerical sums are interpreted to reveal spiritual meaning. Operating like a tiny, independent country within the city (inhabitants answered to their King, not the city government), El Call (see p. 214) was protected by the crown of Catalunya in return for financial tribute.

Until the 11th century, Christians and Jews coexisted peacefully, occasionally even intermarrying. Unfortunately, this did not last. Historical sources cite attacks and looting of the Jewish quarter in eight separate years, the first in 1276 and the last in 1418. Eventually, almost every entrance to El Call was blocked off. The reopening of the streets of El Call began only after Franco's death in 1975. In recent years, eight Spanish mayors have created a network called *Caminos de Sepharad*, an organization aimed at restoring Spain's Jewish quarters and fostering a broader understanding of the Sephardic legacy. For more on Jews in Catalunya, see **Catalan Jews**, p. 62.

La Crêperie Bretonne, C. Cort Reial, 14 (☎97 221 81 20). Potent proof of Girona's proximity to France, this popular crêpe joint combines a funky atmosphere with great food and cheap prices. Old French posters decorate the stone walls, and your food is cooked inside a small bus bound for "Cerbère." Menú €8.45. Crêpes €2.35-7. Unusual salads €6.50-7.45. Open Su 8pm-midnight, Tu-Sa 1-4pm and 8pm-midnight. IVA not included. MC/V. ❷

Lapoma, C. Cort Reial, 16 (☎ 97 221 29 09). The helpful service, friendly prices, and delicious dishes entice many to this recently revamped restaurant. Entrees are a contemporary French twist on Catalan fare (€2.35-11.80). Wine tasting also available. Open M, W-Su 8pm-midnight year-round, and June-Sept. noon-3:30pm as well. Closed in Aug. AmEx/MC/V. ❷

Café Le Bistrot, Pujada Sant Domènec, 4 (☎97 221 88 03), a right off C. Ciutadans toward the Cathedral. An elegant, turn-of-the-century atmosphere, with a great view overlooking one of the old city's slanting streets. Excellent food. Fresh specialty pizzas €4.50-5.30. Crêpes €3.50-5. Lunch menú begins at €9.50. Terrace costs 10% extra. Open M-Th 1-4pm and 8pm-1am, F-Sa 1-4pm and 7pm-2am, Su 1-4pm and 8pm-midnight. AmEx/MC/V. ❷

Restaurant Vegetarià La Catedral, C. Claveria, 4 (☎97 221 83 88). Walk straight out the side exit to the Cathedral (Pl. des Apóstols), down Claveria; the restaurant is on the left. If you're looking to escape the more touristy area of the city, check out this out-of-the-way vegetarian restaurant serving creative vegetable, rice, and tofu dishes. Lunch menú €9.50, dinner *menú* €11.50, €1 extra for terrace. Open daily 1-4pm, F-Sa 8:30-11pm. AmEx/MC/V. ❷

SIGHTS

The narrow, winding streets of the medieval city, interspersed with steep stairways and low arches, are ideal for wanderers, but a bit much for those not used to climbing stairs. Start your self-guided historical tour at the **Pont de Pedra** and turn left at the tourist office down tree-lined **Rambla de la Llibertat.** Continue on C. Argenteria, bearing right across C. Cort Reial. Up the flight of stairs, C. Força begins on the left.

🖾 EL CALL

🖪 *The entrance to the center is 23 C. Força, about halfway up the hill. ☎97 221 67 61; callgirona@ajgirona.org. Center and museum open May-Oct. M-Sa 10am-8pm, Su 10am-3pm; Nov.-Apr. M-Sa 10am-6pm, Su 10am-3pm. Museum €2, students and over 65 €1, under 16 free. Holidays follow Su schedule.*

C. Força and C. Sant Llorenç were once the center of Girona's medieval Jewish community ("call" comes from *kahal*, "community" in

Hebrew), a city within a city where Jews lived as an independent community for at least 600 years, experiencing alternating periods of peace and persecution by their Christian neighbors. During this time they also created and distributed important theological works and brought the city of Girona into the world religious spotlight. The site of the last synagogue in Girona now serves as the **Centre Bonastruc Ca Porta,** named for Rabbi Moshe Ben-Nahman (Nahmanides), a scholar of Jewish mysticism and the oral tradition known as the *Kabbala* (see **The Jewish Sepharad,** p. 214). The center includes the **Museu d'Història dels Jueus Girona,** notable for its detailed wooden model of the original Call and its collection of Hebrew-inscribed tombstones.

CATHEDRAL COMPLEX

🔲 *Tesoro ☎ 97 221 44 26; www.lacatedraldegirona.com. Cathedral and Tesoro open Mar.-June Tu-Sa 10am-2pm and 4-7pm; July-Sept. Tu-Sa 10am-8pm; Oct.-Feb. Tu-Sa 10am-2pm and 4-6pm; open year-round Su and holidays 10am-2pm. Tesoro and cloister €3.*

Farther uphill on C. Forçà and around the corner to the right, Girona's imposing Gothic **cathedral** rises a record-breaking 90 steps (its Baroque stairway is the largest in Europe) from the *plaça*. The **Torre de Charlemany** (bell tower) and **cloister** are the only structures left from the 11th and 12th centuries; the rest of the building dates from the 14th-17th centuries. The most unique feature of the cathedral is its interior, where the three naves, customary in Gothic architecture, have been compressed into one. The Cathedral contains the world's widest Gothic **nave** (22m) and is surpassed in sheer size only by St. Peter's in Rome. A door on the left leads to the trapezoidal cloister and the **Tesoro Capitular (treasury),** home to some of Girona's most precious possessions, including an 11th-century tapestry, **Tapis de la Creació,** which depicts the creation story and is the only one of its kind in the world.

MUSEUMS

MUSEU DEL CINEMA

🔲 *C. Sèquia, 1, one block north of C. Nou off C. Santa Clara. ☎ 97 241 27 77. Open May-Sept. daily 10am-8pm, Oct.-Apr. M-F 10am-6pm, Sa 10am-8pm, Su 11am-3pm. Museum entrance €3, students and over 65 €1.50, under 16 free. MC/V.*

This unusual collection, the best of its kind in Europe, documents the rise of cinema from the mid-17th to the 20th century, with a few pieces from as early as the 11th century (Chinese shadow theater). It walks you through the chronological development of the *camera obscura* (9th-12th century), magic lantern (1659), panorama (1788), diorama (1822), Thomas Edison's kinetoscope (1891), and more. The hands-on visual displays will get you in touch with your early modern childhood, as you play with trick-of-the-eye technologies from yesteryear and watch early cartoons.

OTHER MUSEUMS

The remarkably well-done **Museu d'Història de la Ciutat,** C. Forçà 27, showcases 2000 years of Girona's history, from the first settlers in Catalunya to the present day. Check out the festival giants and the room dedicated to the Napoleonic War. (☎97 222 22 29. Open Su, Tu-Sa 10am-2pm and 5-7pm, Su 10am-2pm. Some descriptions in English. €2, €1 for students, under 16 and over 65 free.) To get to the **Banys Arabs** from the cathedral, with your back to the stairs, take a right on C. Ferrán Catòlic. Inspired by Muslim bath houses, the graceful 12th-century structure once contained saunas and baths of varying temperatures; now they occasionally host outdoor art exhibits. (☎97 221 32 62; www.ddgi.es/ccgirones. Open Apr.-Sept. M-Sa 10am-7pm, Su 10am-2pm; Oct.-Mar. daily 10am-2pm. €1.50; students, under 16, and over 65 €0.75.) The **Museu d'Art,** Pujada de la Catedral, 12 (☎97 220 38 34; www.museuart.com), next to the cathedral holds medieval through modern art, including themed rooms on glass, ceramics, and liturgical art. Open Mar.-Sept. Tu-Sa 10am-7pm; Oct.-Feb. Tu-Sa 10am-6pm; Su and holidays 10am-2pm. €1.80, students, HI members €1.50, under 16 and 65+ free.) The **Museu Arqueològic,** (☎97 220

26 32; mac@mac.es) is located past the Banys Arabs through Pl. Jurants, on the right, in the Monastery of Sant Pere de Galligants. As one of the oldest museums in Catalunya, the Museu Arqueològic complements its prehistoric displays with detailed booklets on the history of the area (available in English). (Open June-Sept. Tu-F 10:30am-1:30pm and 4-7pm, Sa-Su 10am-2pm; Oct.-May Tu-F 10am-2pm and 4-6pm, Sa-Su 10am-2pm. €1.80, students €1.35, under 16 and over 65 free.)

WALKS & TOURS

Girona's renowned ▓**Passeig de la Muralla** begins at the bottom of La Rambla in Pl. de la Marvà, and, though the initial stair climb may be a bit physically challenging, once you're at the top, a pleasant walk awaits. In the 20-30min. it takes to descend again behind the Cathedral (don't worry, there are places to climb down along the way if you get tired), some breathtaking views of Girona, as well as a newfound appreciation of the city's architecture, are yours to savor. Take the steps up to the guard's rampart atop the old Roman defense walls and follow them around the entire eastern side of the old town. The walk ends behind the Cathedral, where the equally beautiful **Pg. Arqueològic** begins, featuring well-preserved medieval gardens and buildings. Partly lined with cypresses and flower beds, this path skirts the northeastern medieval wall and also overlooks the city. After 10-20min., you'll find yourself at C. Pedret in the northeastern part of town. For the less athletically inclined, a small trolley, "Girona en tren," gives a 30min. guided tour of the main sights of the old town, including the town hall, the Cathedral, St. Feliu church, El Call, and the walls. (In summer, it leaves daily every 20-25min. from the Pont de Pedra, 10am-8pm or so. In winter, it runs less frequently, sometimes only weekends; check at the tourist office. Available in English. €3. ☎97 235 20 64; fax 97 235 06 82).

NIGHTLIFE

The concentrated nightlife locales in Girona are the **Pl. de l'Oli** (and nearby streets), the old quarter, and in summer, the expansive, impeccably designed **Parc de la Devesa**, which explodes with *carpas*, temporary outdoor bars. (Across the river from the old town, several blocks to the left. Open June-Sept. 15 Su-Th 10pm-3am and F-Sa 10pm-4:30am, though people tend to congregate only after midnight. Drinks €4.20-5.40. Cash only.) The bars and cafes in the old quarter are particularly mellow and relaxing, a good way to start the evening. Also, try the movie theater, **Cinema Truffaut**, C. Portal Nou, 7, to catch the weekly foreign movie. (From C. Nou, go right on C. Subida de la Merced, and then left immediately after the stairs. ☎97 222 50 44; www.cinematruffaut.com. Open daily 6pm-12:30am. €4.50, under 23 €3.80, over 65 €1.80. Cash only.)

▓ **Mon Àpart,** Figuerola, 12. Wear what you want to wear, dance how you want to dance, act how you want to act against the Kieth-Harring-esque colorful mural of this University of Girona favorite. The people are kind and friendly, the music is good and bumping, the atmosphere is warm and inviting–and best of all, you can decide whether to partake or just watch. Beer €2-4, cocktails €5-6. Open Su, Th-Sa 11pm-5am.

Excalibur Celtic Beer House, Pl. de l'Oli, 1 (☎97 220 82 53), at the top of C. Ciutadans. The only authentic place in Girona to go for a pint of Guinness (€4) and English-speaking expat company. Irish rock and American pop from the speakers, lots of European sports on the TV, and a chalkboard outside advertising what games will be showing. Cocktails €5, Beer €3.30-4. Open Su 4pm-2:30am, M-F 6pm-3am, Sa 4pm-3am. MC/V.

Café la Llibreria, C. Ciutadans, 15 (☎97 220 10 82). Behind the bookstore; enter on C. Ferreires Vellas, parallel to C. Ciutadans. Cocktails (€3-4), beer (€0.80), tea (€1.40-1.80), and tapas (€0.80-2.50) served to older intellectual types and those who will eventually follow in their footsteps. Live music (usually guitar) W and F after 11pm. Internet €1 per 20min., €3 per hr. Open M-Th 8:30am-midnight and F-Su 8:30pm-1am. AmEx/MC/V.

La Sala del Cel, Ronda Pedret, 118 (☎97 221 46 64; www.salacel.com). A 15min. walk upriver from the Pont de St. Feliu, on the old town side, brings you to the alien-topped building. More than a mere club, with 2 techno thumping dance floors, a huge hangout area with black leather couches and pool tables. Play Station computers and free massage room. €12 cover includes 1 drink. Open F-Sa midnight-5:30am. Must be 16 to enter, 18 to drink; bring identification. V.

La Terra, C. Ballesteries, 23 (☎97 221 92 54). Serious women dressed in all black serve fresh-squeezed juices at this understated hang-out decorated with mismatched ceramics. Try their fruit juices or a hamburger. Everything on the menu €3 or less. Free ticket to Cinema Truffaut with a purchase of €7 or more. Open M-Th 5pm-1:30am, F-Su 5pm-2am. Cash only.

FESTIVALS

For one week during the second half of May, government-sponsored **flower exhibitions** spring up in the city. Local monuments and pedestrian streets swim in blossoms, and the courtyards of Girona's fine old buildings open to the public. Summer evenings often inspire spontaneous *sardana* dancing in the city *plaças* (see **May I Have This Dance,** p. 72). Like the rest of Catalunya, Girona also lights up on June 24 for the **Focs de Sant Joan,** an outdoor party featuring fireworks and campfires. In July, Girona celebrates the Festival of Religious Music of the World. September finds the city busy with the Festivals of Jazz, Film, and Amateur Theater. Check www.ajuntament.gi for updated listings and festival dates.

NEAR GIRONA: PÚBOL

🚊 *From Girona, take the train or bus to Flaça and pick up a taxi to Púbol, 3km away (approx. €7); taxis will usually arrange to bring you back to the station at your designated time.* **Sarfa** *(☎97 220 17 96 or 97 264 09 64) runs* **buses** *from Girona to Flaça (30min.; every 30min. M-F 7:45am-8:15pm, every hr. Sa-Su 9am-8:30pm; €2).* **RENFE** *(☎902 24 02 02) trains go from Barcelona Estació-Sants to* **Flaça** *(1¾hr., every 30min.-1hr. 5:50am-9:20pm, €6) and from Girona to* **Flaça** *(15min., several per hr. 7:15am-8:36pm, €1-1.40). To* **Figueres,** *continue on the same train.* **Taxi:** *At the train station in Flaça, or call and reserve one.* **Taxi Sagué** *(☎97 2488 105).*

In the late 1960s, the adoring Salvador Dalí bought a crumbling 14th-century castle in the tiny village of Púbol for his beloved muse, Gala. The Surrealist master set about restoring the castle to its former glory, while insuring that it maintained a slightly time-worn appearance which he and his wife prized. When Gala moved into her Púbol mansion, Dalí declared he would never visit without her written request. Rumors suggest that in Dalí's absence, Gala entertained her fair share of male visitors. The **Casa-Museu Castell Gala Dalí,** Púbol's major—and only—attraction,

Hanguing out on the Street

Devilish Puppet at the Toy Museum

Afternoon Snack

217

GET sm**art**

DALÍ OR NOT DALÍ

When Spanish police busted into the Centre d'Art Perrot-Moore in Cadaqués in April 1999, they arrested Captain Peter Moore and his wife Catherine Perrot on charges of art forgery. Moore, a British Army captain, was a friend and assistant to Salvador Dalí for 20 years until the artist passed away in 1989. The private collection of Captain Moore was on display at the Centre d'Art Perrot-Moore, which was quietly shut down following the couple's arrest and subsequent release on bail.

Police, aided by a team of art historians, are still collaborating in their efforts to discover whether over 10,000 prints ready for sale at the Centre d'Art Perrot-Moore are fakes. Authorities believe that Moore pressured an ailing Dalí into signing thousands of blank pieces of paper which were then printed with "limited edition" lithographs and sold as Dalí originals. Dalí thus continues to be the scandal-monger of the art world, even in death.

has been open to visitors since 1996. Besides Gala's tomb, tastefully sandwiched between the garage and gardens, the castle contains several of Dalí's works, including a colorful ceiling painting (painted by Dalí so that Gala could always see him in her heaven, a chess set whose pieces resemble thumbs, and an elaborate gold and blue throne constructed for Gala. The artist lived in the castle in 1982 after Gala's death, and was almost killed when he accidently set fire to his bedroom two years later. One of his last works, a refined painting with strong, contrasting colors, sits on an easel in the castle's dining room. (☎97 248 86 55. Open Mar. 15-June 14 and Sept. 16-Nov. 1 Su, Tu-Sa 10:30am-5:15pm; Jun. 15-Sept. 15 daily 10:30am-7:15pm. €5.50, students and seniors €4. Free guided tours at noon in Catalan and at 5pm in Spanish. Wheelchair accessible.) There is little else to see in tiny Púbol, but if you get hungry before or after visiting the castle, **Can Bosch ❷**, on C. Fera Muralia next to the castle, offers solid Catalan fare and is about the only option. (☎97 248 83 57; www.salvador-dali.org. Open July 15-Aug. 31 daily 9am-11pm, kitchen open 1-4pm and 8-11pm; Sept.-June M-W 9:30am-6pm, Th-Su 9:30am-8pm, kitchen open 1-4pm.)

CADAQUÉS & PORT LLIGAT

The whitewashed houses and small bay of Cadaqués (pop. 2000) have attracted artists, writers, and musicians ever since Dalí built his summer home in neighboring Port Lligat in the 1930s. Cadaqués is the bigger of the two towns (Port Lligat is basically just Dalí's house), which are so close to each other that they are virtually super-imposed. To preserve the towns' authentic Mediterranean flavor, an affluent crowd of property owners and renters have kept at bay the commercial influx of sprawling condos, big hotels, and trains. Cadaqués has not been immune, however, to the trendy influence of the hordes of French tourists and Barcelona daytrippers who flock there in the summer to see Dalí's house; chic galleries and shops have cropped up to suit the cosmopolitan crowd. The rocky beaches and dreamy landscape attract their share of tourists, but Cadaqués preserves a pleasantly laid-back atmosphere. Be forewarned: if you're traveling to Cadaqués between September and May, most food and entertainment options will be shut down. It is best to make it a daytrip only, though the bus schedule may make it difficult to do so (see below).

TRANSPORTATION

Buses: Sarfa buses (☎97 225 87 13) run to: **Barcelona** (2½hr., daily 7:15am and 4:15pm, €15.60); **Figueres** (1hr., 2-3 per day, €3.55); **Girona** (2hr., M-F 1 per day, €6.85).

Bike and Boat Rental: Escola de Vela Ones for boat rental and **Rent@bit** for bike rental, see **Entertainment** below.

Taxi: No taxi stands; call ☎97 225 82 68.

ORIENTATION & PRACTICAL INFORMATION

The bus to Cadaqués halts to the right of the Sarfa office. With your back to the Sarfa office, walk right and downhill on Av. Caritat Serinyana to the waterfront square, **Pl. Frederic Rahola,** where a signboard map with indexed services and accommodations can help to orient you.

Tourist Office, C. Cotxe, 2 (☎97 225 83 15; fax 97 215 94 42), off Pl. Frederic Rahola, has a helpful map of Cadaqués and the surrounding beaches; friendly, multi-lingual help. Open June-Aug. M-Sa 9am-2pm and 4-9pm, Su 10:30am-1pm; Sept.-June M-Sa 9am-1pm and 4-7pm. Call ☎93 317 42 89 for information regarding festivals.

Currency Exchange: Banco Central Hispano, C. Caritat Serinyana, 4 (☎97 225 83 62; 24hr., ☎90 224 24 24). Open Oct.-Mar. M-F 8:30am-2:30pm, Sa 8:30am-1pm; Apr.-Sept. M-F 9am-2pm, Sa 9am-1pm. There are many **ATMs** along the waterfront promenade. MC/V.

Police: C. Carles Rahola, 9 (☎97 215 93 43).

Medical Assistance: C. Nou, 6 (☎97 225 88 07).

Internet Access: on@, C. Miquel Rosset, 3 (☎97 225 10 42; www.onacadqques.com), just off Av. Caritat Serinyana. €0.60 per 10min., €1.20 per 30min., €3.60 per hr. Open Su-Th 11am-2pm and 4-7pm, F-Sa 11am-2pm and 5pm-midnight or 1am. **Rent@bit,** Av. Caritat Serinyana, 9 (☎97 225 10 23; www.rentabit.net). €2 per 30min., €4 per hr. Also rents bikes (€4.50 per hr., €16 per day) and scooters (€20 per 2hr., €35 per day). Open daily 10am-1pm and 3-10pm.

Post Office, Av. Rierassa, 1 (☎97 225 87 98), off Av. Caritat Serinyana. Open June-Aug. M-F 9am-2pm, Sa 9:30am-1pm; Sept.-May M-F 9-11am, Sa 9:30am-1pm.

Postal code: 17488.

ACCOMMODATIONS & CAMPING

As Cadaqués is a beach town, many accommodations are open only during the summer; however, during the month of August they close in order to enjoy their own vacations, so plan accordingly. Though room prices soar in these summer months, you still find high quality accommodations for relatively reasonable prices.

Hostal Cristina, C. Riera, 1 (☎97 225 81 38). Right on the water, to the right of Av. Caritat Serinyana. Bright, colorful, newly renovated rooms with sink; rooftop terrace overlooks the water. Ask for a terrace for no extra charge. July-Sept. singles €29; doubles €39, with bath €49. Oct.-June singles €25; doubles €35, with bath €45. MC/V. ❸

Pensión Ranxo, Av. Caritat Serinyana, 13 (☎97 225 80 05), on the right as you walk down from the bus stop. Potted plants and whitewashed hallways lead to clean and comfortable rooms. All rooms come with bath. July-Sept. singles €22; doubles €45; Oct.-June singles €18-20, doubles €35. Breakfast €4. MC/V. ❷

Hostal Marina, C. Riera, 3 (☎97 225 81 99), boasts clean rooms with modern furniture. Some rooms have balconies. Open Apr.-Dec. Singles €21, with bath €30; doubles €40/€55. MC/V. ❷

Camping Cadaqués, Ctra. Portlligat, 17 (☎97 225 81 26), about a 15min. walk from the bus station, turn with your back to the station and walk to the left, uphill Av. Caritat and then take the right fork; located on the left on the way to Dalí's house; follow the signs for Hotel Port Lligat. 100m from the beach. Popular and crowded campsite. Amenities include pool and bungalows (€28-40). Open Apr.-Sept.; reception open 9am-1pm and 3-7pm; €4.75 per person, €5.85 per tent, €4.75 per car; IVA not included. MC/V. ❶

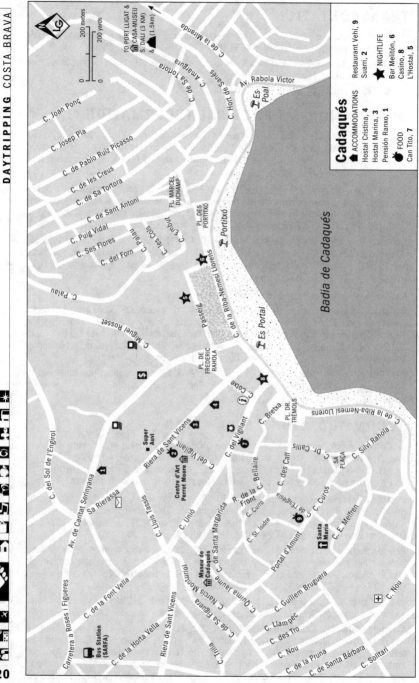

Cadaqués

♦ ACCOMMODATIONS
Hostal Cristina, 4
Hostal Marina, 3
Pensión Ranxo, 1

● FOOD
Can Tito, 7

Restaurant Vehi, 9
Suarri, 2

★ NIGHTLIFE
Bar Melitón, 6
Casino, 8
L'Hostal, 5

Badia de Cadaqués

TO PORT LLIGAT &
CASA-MUSEU
S. DALÍ (3 KM)
& (1.5km)

C. de la Miranda
Av. Rabola Victor
C. Hort des Sanés
C. de Sa Tortora
C. Amargura
C. Joan Ponç
C. Josep Pla
C. de Pablo Ruiz Picasso
C. de les Creus
C. de Sa Tortora
C. de Sant Antoni
C. Puig Vidal
C. Ses Flores
C. del Forn
C. Palau
C. Enput
C. les Cois
C. del Palau
PL. MARCEL DUCHAMP
PL. DES PORTITXÓ
Portitxó
Es Poal
Es Portal
passeig
C. de la Riba-Nemesi Llorens
C. Miquel Rosset
C. Palau
C. del Sol de l'Engirol
PL. DE FREDERIC RAHOLA
C. Coixe
C. del Vigilant
C. Breta
PL. DR. TREMOLS
Av. de Caritat Serinyana
Super Auvi
Riera de Sant Vicens
C. del Vigilant
Centre d'Art Perrot Moore
C. del Vigilant
C. de Santa Margarida
Sa Rierassa
C. Lluís Tassis
C. Unió
C. Bellaire
R. de la Front.
C. des Call
C. Caills
C. de la Riba-Nemesi Llorens
C. Silvi Rahola
C. Curro
C. de l'Església
SA PLAÇA
C. St. Isidre
C. Curos
C. E. Mefren
Santa Maria
Portal d'Amunt
C. Guillem Bruguera
C. Nou
C. Llampec
C. des Tro
C. Nou
C. de la Pruna
C. de Santa Bàrbara
C. Solitari
Museu de Cadaqués
C. de Sa Figuera Montjuïu
C. Narcís Montjuïu
C. Quima Jaume
Carretera a Roses i Figueres
Bus Station (SARFA)
C. de la Font Vella
C. de la Horta Vella
Riera de Sant Vicens
C. Tinia

0   200 meters
0   200 yards

FOOD

Cadaqués harbors the usual slew of overpriced, unexciting tourist restaurants on the waterfront. Try wandering into the back alleys for options that make the winding-street hikes more than worthwhile. **Groceries** can be purchased at **Super Auvi,** C. Riera on the right if facing away from the water. (☎97 225 86 33. Open July-Aug. M-Sa 8am-2pm and 4:30-9pm, Su 8am-2pm; Sept.-June M-Sa 8:30am-1:30pm and 4:30-8pm.)

☒ Can Tito, C. Vigilant, 8 (☎97 225 90 70). An exceptional historic and culinary experience. The stone archway at the entrance to this elegant restaurant is 1 of 5 portals from the original town walls dating back to AD 1100, when Cadaqués was still a fortified village at the mercy of roving pirates. Try the house specialty, *pastel de escalivada,* a soufflé of onions, peppers, eggplant, and pepperoni (€7.85). Lunch menú €12. Fish and meat entrees €5-18, mostly €5-7. Open Mar.-Jan. daily 1:30-3pm and 8-10:30pm. Closes at 10pm in winter. MC/V. ❷

Suarri, C. Vigilant, 3. An elegant, spacious place to escape from the heat of the sun and enjoy a wide range of Catalan and Italian dishes. Tasty spinach and cheese ravioli with nut sauce (€11) can sooth tummies tired of typical Spanish cuisine. Entrees €8.50-24. Open M-Tu and Th-Su 12:15-3:30pm and 7:15-10:30pm. Open Mar.-Oct. ❹

Restaurant Vehí, C. de l'Església, 6 (☎97 225 84 70). After walking up small, winding stone streets, bask in the striking views from at this 2nd-floor restaurant. Feast on traditional Catalan grub that goes far beyond *jamón.* With an emphasis on seafood, Restuarant Vehí satifies hungry locals and tourists with large portions. Split a 2-person dish (€19-21) with that special someone. Menú (€11.50-13) includes wine. Entrees €4-20. Open Mar.-Oct. ❸

SIGHTS & ENTERTAINMENT

The local church, **Església de Santa Maria,** is a 16th-century gothic building with a Baroque altarpiece. Unfortunately, the church is only open for services, M and W-F 7pm, Sa 8pm, Su 11am. Down the hill, the **Museu de Cadaqués,** C. Narcis Monturiol, 15, has changing exhibits, often with a Dalí theme. (☎97 225 88 77. Open late June-Sept. daily 10:30am-1:30pm and 4-8pm. €5, students €3.)

From the museum, take a pleasant walk (30min.) to ☒**Casa-Museu Salvador Dalí,** in Port Lligat, the home where Dalí and his wife Gala lived until her death in 1982. With your back to the Sarfa station, looking uphill, walk up Av. Caritat and then take the right fork and continue on this road, following the signs to Port Lligat and heading past Camping Cadaques; eventually Casa de Dalí signs appear. At C. President Lluís Companys, where signs point to the house in two different directions, follow the one to the right—the other road is the auto route. Originally a modest fisherman's abode, the house was transformed to meet the aesthetic and eccentric lifestyle led by Dalí and his treasured wife. The roof is covered in egg sculptures and the building houses Dalí's favorite lip-shaped sofa as well as more stuffed snakes and swans than you bargained for. Though only two (unfinished) Dalí originals remain in the house, the excellent conservation effort has helped in understanding how this genius worked. The decorating style is a masterpiece in itself. (☎97 225 10 15; www.salvador-dali.org; Open June 15-Sept. 15 daily 10am-8:10pm; Sept. 16-Jan. 6. and Mar. 15-June 14 Su, Tu-Sa 10am-5:10pm. Tours are the only way to see the house; make reservations 1-2 days in advance. Ticket office closes 45min. before closing. €8. MC/V with passport.) If you still haven't gotten enough Dalí, **boat rides** in Dalí's boat Gala leave in front of the house on the hour for a 55min. trip to Cap de Creus, the eastern most point in Spain. (☎61 746 57 57. Open daily 11am-8pm. €10.)

The **Centre d'Art Perrot-Moore,** on C. Vigilante, 1, a small pedestrian street off of C. Riera to the left, which has been closed because of a huge art fraud scandal (see **Dalí or not Dalí?,** p. 218), might be reopening to the public; however, dates have not been set. Check with the tourist office for developments. Outdoor activities in Cadaqués are popular, and in addition to **water sports** and **biking,** a map of various 2-8km **hikes** is available at the tourist office.

Bike and Boat Rental: Escola de Vela Ones (☎972 259 029; info@bluerentcadaques.com), on the beach directly in front of the tourist office, rents kayaks, sailboats, and windsurfing gear. Choose from 3, 4, or 6hr. guided kayak excursions (€30-55), or head out on your own in a single kayak (€9 per hr., €22 half-day, €35 full day) or a double kayak (€13 per hr., €35 half-day, €55 full day). Windsurfing gear (€10 per hr.) and sailboats (€22 per 1 hr., €60 per 4hr., €105 per 8hr.) also available. Open July-Sept. 15 daily 10am-7pm depending on weather conditions. Bike rental also available at **Rent@bit.**

Trolley tours are available to those who want to sit back and relax but still get a chance to see the beautiful coastline. **Tren Turistic Cultural Roses Expres** (☎97 225 66 25; www.tren-rosesexpres.com) travels to Port Lligat, Casa Dalí, and Cap de Creus among other destinations; stand can be found in front of Hostal Cristina in Pl. Frederic Rahola. Open 11am-8pm in the summer; closes at 5pm in the winter. €5 per hr. for adult, €4 per hr. for children.

Beaches: If you can't get enough of the Cadaques beaches and want to explore beyond them for an even more private viewing, Platja d'el Ros, 0.5km away eastward toward Port Lligat, and Sa Conca, 1km westward, can be reached by foot (as well as by car). For a longer walk, another 1km from Port Lligat will reward you with S'Alqueria.

NIGHTLIFE

When the sun sets, head to one of Cadaqués's beachfront bars for drinks and music. **Bar Melitón** (☎97 225 82 01) on the *passeig* has a popular terrace with plenty of tables. **L'Hostal,** Pg. 8 (☎97 225 8000) is a rock and jazz club housed in a dark and ambiance-inducing turn-of-the-20th-century building. Listen to occasional live music inside or watch the water from the outside wicker chairs. Open daily 11pm-5am. The oldest bar in town, **Casino** (☎97 225 81 37), on Pl. Doctor Tremols facing the water and next to Hostal Cristina, has high ceilings, big windows, and a stream of drink-sippers all day and into the night. Cocktails €1.20-4.65. Wine up to €12.

PALAFRUGELL

In the year AD 988, inhabitants of the beach town of Llafranc founded inland Palafrugell (pop. 10,000), seeking refuge from the constant plundering of Mediterranean pirates. Today, budget travelers come here to flee the wallet-plundering of seaside hotels and restaurants. Forty km. east of Girona, Palafrugell serves as a base for trips to the picturesque nearby beach towns of **Calella, Llafranc,** and **Tamariu,** which cater to wealthy Europeans whose idea of a budget accommodation is any hotel that doesn't leave mints on the pillow. To save some euros, stay in admittedly bland (and beachless) Palafrugell and daytrip to the beaches. The small beaches are connected by the **Camino de Ronda,** a series of stone footpaths allowing exploration of the rocky, wooded coast.

TRANSPORTATION

Buses: Sarfa, C. Torres Jonama, 73-79 (☎97 230 06 23). Prices rise on weekends. To: **Barcelona** (2hr.; 12 per day, last bus 7:30pm; €11.40); **Calella** and **Llafranc** (15-20min.; 12-24 per day, in winter months 4-5 per day; €1.05); **Figueres** (1½hr., 3-4 per day, €5.65); **Girona** (1hr., 18 per day, €3.75).

Taxis: Radio Taxi (☎97 261 00 00). 24hr. service throughout the area. **Taxi Costa Brava,** C. Lluís Companys, 4 (☎97 261 22 22 daytime, 65 930 61 57 nighttime.) Stands in Palafrugell located on the corner of C. Torres Jonama and C. de Girona, and on the corner of C. de la Lluna and C. Sant Sebastià, by the Pl. Camp d'en Prats.

ORIENTATION & PRACTICAL INFORMATION

To get from the bus station to the center of town, turn right and walk down C. Torres Jonama to C. de Pi i Maragall. Then turn right and walk past the Guardia Civil and the market until you hit **Pl. Nova,** the main square of the town, off of which are C. San Sebastià and C. Cavallers. On your way you'll pass the **Pl. l'Església** on the right. To

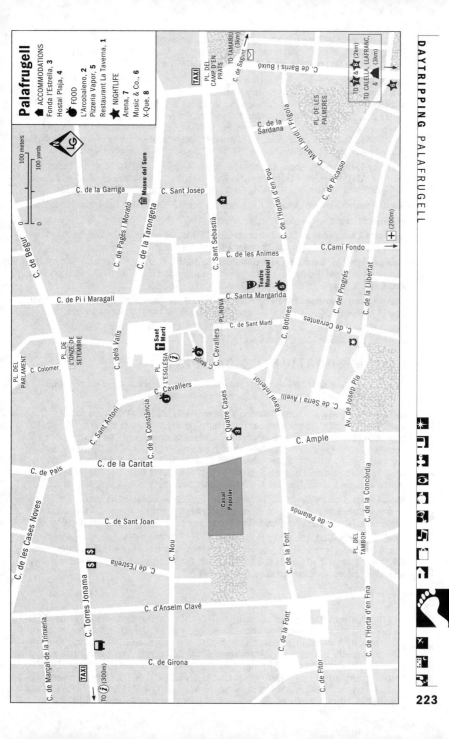

Palafrugell

⌂ ACCOMMODATIONS
Fonda l'Estrella, **3**
Hostal Plaja, **4**

🍴 FOOD
L'Arcobaleno, **2**
Pizzeria Vapor, **5**
Restaurant La Taverna, **1**

★ NIGHTLIFE
Arena, **7**
Music & Co., **6**
X-Que, **8**

100 meters
100 yards

C. de la Garriga
🏛 Museu del Suro
C. Sant Josep
C. de Pagés i Morotó
C. de la Tarongeta
C. Sant Sebastià
C. de Begur
C. de Pi i Maragall
C. de les Animes
C.Camí Fondo
➕ (200m)
PL. DEL PARLAMENT
C. Colomer
PL. DE L'ONZE DE SETEMBRE
C. dels Valls
Sant Martí
🛈 PL. L'ESGLÉSIA
C. Major
2
PL.NOVA
C. Cavallers
Teatre Municipal 🎭
C. Santa Margarida
5
C. de Cervantes
C. del Progrés
C. de la Llibertat
C. Sant Antoni
C. de la Constància
C. Cavallers
1
C. de Sant Martí
C. Botines
✚
C. Quatre Cases
3
Raval Inferior
C. de Serra i Avelli
Av. de Josep Pla
C. de Pais
C. de la Caritat
C. Ample
C. de les Cases Noves
C. de Sant Joan
Casal Popular
C. de Palamós
PL DEL TAMBOR
C. de la Concòrdia
C. de l'Estrella
C. Nou
$
$
C. de la Font
C. Torres Jonama
C. de Marçal de la Trinxeria
🚌
C. d'Anselm Clavé
C. de Girona
C. de la Font
C. de Fitor
C. de l'Horta d'en Fina
TAXI
TO 🛈 (300m)

PL. DEL CAMP D'EN PRATS
TAXI
C. de Barris i Buixó
C. de Sagunt
TO TAMARIU (3km)
C. de la Sardana
C. Martí Jordi i Frigola
PL. DE LES PALMERES
C. de Picasso
C. de l'Hortal d'en Pou
TO 🚩 & 🚩 (2km)
TO CALELLA, LLAFRANC, & ▲ (3km)

223

get to the nearby beach towns of Calella, Llafranc, and Tamariu, take a bus (see **Transportation,** above), spin away on a moped or mountain bike, or take a pleasant, if lengthy, walk through the countryside (about 1hr. to each town).

Tourist Office: Can Rosés, Pl. l'Església (☎97 261 18 20; www.palafrugell.net). First right off C. Cavallers walking away from Pl. Nova. Ask for the indispensable *Guía Municipal,* updated monthly and with relevant night information. A **branch** is at C. Carrilet, 2 (☎97 230 02 28; fax 97 261 12 61). From the bus station, go left on C. Torres Jonama, left again at the traffic circle, and walk about 200m. An inconvenient location, but loaded with info. Both open May-Sept. M-Sa 10am-1pm and 5-8pm, Su 10am-1pm; Oct.-Apr. M-Sa 10am-1pm and 4-7pm, Su 10am-1pm; Carrilet branch also open July-Aug. M-Sa 9am-9pm, Su 10am-1pm.

Currency Exchange: Banesto, C. Torres Jonama, 43 (☎97 230 18 22), at the corner of C. l'Estrella. **ATM.** Open M-F 8:30am-2pm, Sa 8:30am-1pm. **Caja Madrid,** C. Torres Jonama, 45 (☎97 230 60 22), across from Banesto, cashes **traveler's checks. ATM.** Open daily 8:15am-2pm.

Money transfer: Western Union, C. Torres Jonama, 2 (☎92 230 11 03). Open daily 10am-10pm.

Luggage Storage: Sarfa bus station, the attendant will hold your bag for €1.30.

Roadside Emergency: ☎112. **Police:** ☎092. **Municipal police:** ☎97 261 31 01, at Av. Josep Pla and C. Cervantes. Call them for **24hr. pharmacy** info.

Medical Services: Centro de Atención Primaria (CAP), C. d'Angel Guimerà, 6 (clinic and non-emergencies☎97 261 06 07; emergencies and ambulance 97 230 00 23). Open 24hr. **Red Cross,** C. Ample, 130 (☎97 230 09 92).

Internet Access: Internet Papereria Palé, C. Cavallers, 16 (☎97 230 12 48). €1 per 30min. Open July-Sept. Su 10am-1:30pm, M-F 9am-1pm and 4:30-8:30pm, Sa 9am-1pm and 5-9pm.

Post Office: C. Barris i Buixó, 23 (☎97 230 06 07). **Lista de Correos.** Open M-F 8:30am-2:30pm, Sa 9:30am-1pm. **Postal Code:** 17200.

ACCOMMODATIONS & CAMPING

Though options are few, accommodation prices are reasonable and room quality high in Palafrugell. Be sure to call ahead on summer weekends.

▨ **Fonda l'Estrella,** C. Quatre Cases, 13-17 (☎/fax 97 230 00 05), at the corner of C. La Caritat, a right off C. Torres Jonama. This building, from the turn of the 17th century, has high-ceilinged, well-lit rooms with sinks off a Moorish courtyard bursting with plant life. Common baths, but even the bathrooms of this carefully preserved 1605 historic building are gorgeous. Renovations are scheduled; 5 rooms will have private baths. Breakfast served in high season, €4. June-Sept. singles €26; doubles €35; July-Aug. doubles €39; triples and quads available. Call ahead for dates and prices in April and May. ❸

Hostal Plaja, C. Sant Sebastià, 34 (☎97 230 05 26; www.hostalplaja.com), off Pl. Nova. Frescoed foyer gives way to a courtyard surrounded by spotless rooms, all with balconies, bathrooms, TVs, bottled water, clotheslines, and new beds. Singles €26; doubles €46. ❷

Camping: Moby Dick, Av. Costa Verda, 16-28 (☎97 261 43 07). Take the Sarfa bus to Calella and ask the driver to let you off. No white whale in sight, but it is close to the water. €4.35 per adult, €2.50 per child, €4.35 per tent, €4.35 per car during July and Aug. Open May-Sept.; prices decrease Apr.-June and Sept. ❶

FOOD

Restaurants near the beach are predictably expensive, making meals in Palafrugell proper a wiser option. For some reason, the town has a disproportionately high number of pizzerias and Italian restaurants. Shrugs one local, "We just really like pizza." **L'Arcobaleno** ❷, C. Mayor, 3, brings a touch of Tuscany to Catalan classics. The delicious all-inclusive lunchtime menú (€7.50) has everything from *gnocci* to roast chicken. (☎97 261 06 95. Open Apr.-Sept. 14 daily 1-4pm and 6:30pm-midnight; Sept. 15-Mar. closed M. AmEx/MC/V.) **Pizzeria Vapor** ❷, C. de les Botines, 21, is a popular restaurant with, in addition to the requisite pizza (€4.50-5.50), a fresh menú for €7. (☎97 230 57 03. Entrees €4.50-10. Open June-Aug. daily noon-4:30pm and 7pm-midnight; Sept.-May Su, Tu-Sa noon-4:30pm and 7pm-midnight.) For a respite from pizza and a return to Catalan classics, **Restaurant La Taverna ❷,** C. Giralt i Subiros, 3 (☎97 230 04 30), across from the Església de Sant Marti, serves the traditional fare; the rotisserie chicken is delicious. Entrees €3-11, but it's possible to have a filling meal for €5. Lunch menu €9. Open daily 1-4pm and 7:30-11:30pm. Ice cream shops and restaurants with terraces dominate the **Pl. Nova.**

SIGHTS & ENTERTAINMENT

In addition to its nearby beaches, Palafrugell boasts one of the world's few cork museums. The **Museu del Suro,** C. Tarongeta, 31, has everything you ever (never?) wanted to know about cork. (☎97 230 78 25. Open June 15-Sept. 15 daily 10am-2pm and 4-9pm; Sept.16-June 14 Su 10:30am-1:30pm, Tu-Sa 5-8pm. €1.20, students and seniors €0.60. English explanations available.) The **Teatre Municipal (TMP),** C. de Sta. Margarida, 1 (☎97 261 11 72), has weekly film showings and theater productions as well as occasional dance and music.

A Palafrugell Friday evening stroll ends up at Pl. Nova, where young and old often dance the traditional Catalan *sardana* (see **May I Have This Dance**, p. 72) around 10:30pm in July and August; some nights also offer live music. The tourist office prints a monthly bulletin of upcoming events; also check the *Guía Municipal*. The town's biggest party takes place July 19-21, when the dance-intensive **Festa Major** bursts into the streets. Calella honors **Sant Pere** on June 29 with lots of *sardana* dancing, and Tamariu celebrates on August 15, coinciding with the Assumption of the Blessed Mother. The **Festivals of the Hanaveras** (Spanish-Cuban sea songs) come to town the first Saturday of every July.

BEACH TOWNS

Take a Sarfa bus from Palafrugell to ***Calella*** *(15min., 12-24 per day, €1.05), which continues on to Llafranc and then back to Palafrugell. You can also follow the Camino de Ronda from Calella (see below) and walk 20min. to* ***Llafranc.*** *From Llafranc,* ***Tamariu*** *is a 2hr. walk farther along the path. To get to Tamariu by bus, take one directly from Palafrugell.*

CALELLA

Calella is the liveliest of the three beach towns near Palafrugell, with lots of small restaurants and shops in the streets around the beach. The town is also a great starting point for a trip to Llafranc. The bus stops in town, and the small beach at **Port Bo** is only a short walk downhill. From there, take a left to get to the bigger **Canadell** beach, at the far end of which begins the Camino de Ronda path to Llafranc. Port Pelegri, another local favorite beach, is located further south along the coast. Calella's **tourist office,** C. Voltes, 4, provides maps of paths that criss-cross the area, including the **Camino de Ronda,** which climbs the coast from Calella to Llafranc. (☎97 261 44 75. Open July-Aug. daily 10am-1pm and 5-9pm; Apr.-June and Sept.-Oct. 12 M-Sa 10am-1pm and 5-8pm, Su 10am-1pm.)

The **Jardí Botànic de Cap Roig,** the botanical garden in front of Hotel Garbí, has an excellent view of the coast. (☎97 261 45 82. Open daily June-Aug. 9am-8pm; Sept.-May 9am-6pm. €2) To get to the garden, take a right at Port Bo and follow the road as far as Hotel St. Roc. There the Camino de Ronda starts up again—look for signs, and when in doubt, look for the small red and white parallel stripes painted along the path as markers. The hike ends in a steep climb up a set of steps (45min. in all after arriving in Calella). The castle also hosts regular concerts and the **Festival de Jazz de la Costa Brava** in July and August. For tickets and info, contact the tourist office or call ☎90 244 77 55. You can also get information from Caixa de Girona, the bank which sponsors this festival (☎97 220 98 36; www.caixagirona.es).

The nightlife here is more active, as bars and clubs stay open later. Try **X-Que,** (☎97 230 58 32), playing techno and house, seems to be everyone's favorite club, on the road from Palafrugell to Llafranc. Although it is possible to walk, 20-30min. southeast on Av. del Mar, a taxi might be the best option. **Arena,** another oft-frequented club, is located in the same complex. **Music & Co.** is a bit closer, on the corner of C. Picasso and C. Barris i Buixo.

LLAFRANC

The largest of the beaches, Llafranc and its coarse sand are usually covered with French and German tourists. To get there from Calella, take a pleasant 15-20min. hike from Calella along the Camino de Ronda or take the municipal bus (see above). The bus stops in two different locations—if coming from Palafrugell, get off at the first one after Calella on C. de la Sirena. Walk to your left (against traffic), make the first left onto C. Juli Garreta; at the fork at the pharmacy, follow the right fork all the way down to the waterfront, continuing on until the Pl. del Promontori. There is a tourist office branch in Llafranc, C. Roger de Llúria. (☎97 230 50 08. Open July-Aug. daily 10am-1pm and 5-9pm; Apr.-June and Sept.-Oct. 12 M-Sa 10am-1pm and 5-8pm, Su 10am-1pm.) An emergency medical center is located right next door. Although prices for rooms in resorty Llafranc tend to reach for the sky, ☒**Hostal Celimar ❸,** C. Carudo, 12-14, is the one exception, offering clean, florally decorated rooms with balconies and bathrooms only two blocks from the beach. To get there from the tourist office, go down Pg. de Cípsela along the beach. Take the first left at Pl. del Promontori, and continue down for two blocks; it will be on your right. (☎/fax 97 230 13 74. Singles July and Aug. €30; doubles €48; June and Sept. €27/€45; Mar.-May and Oct. €24/€42.) **La Barraca ❷,** C. de Santa Rosa, 9 (☎97 230 04 08; www.labarraca@ya.com), has small, clean rooms and is a great value: singles €20; doubles €40. Open July-Sept.

For a quick peek into Llafranc social history, slip into **Hotel Llafranch,** Pg. Cypsele, 16 (☎97 230 02 08; www.hllafranch.com). While on the expensive side (entrees €12-23, with €8 the exception), the bar is worth a visit and a drink. This hotel, made famous during the 60s when one of the three brother owners, Manel Bisbe, was proclaimed the "Gypsy of the Costa Brava" by famed flamenco dancer Carmen Amaya. It continues to live off of its reputation.

On the port side of the beach, **Barracuda Diving Center,** Alberto Munoz Cypsele, 40, (☎97 261 15 48; albort_llafranc@wanadoo.es) offers scuba diving courses (5 days, €330) and rents equipment. Their main office is located at Font del Xecu, 12 (☎60 787 12 13). Every two hours from 11am onward, they also take two-hour boat excursions to caves and inlets along the coast, with snorkeling and swimming (€15, children €13). For an outdoor adventure, take a 30min. walk (or a quick drive) from Llafranc to the ☒**Ermita de San Sebastià.** Crowning the mountain of the same name (next to the lighthouse), the hermitage offers views of the entire Palafrugell valley, beaches, and sea. Ask about guided tours at the tourist office, as they are seasonal. From the far end of the Llafranc beach, hop onto the good old Camino and head up. At the paved road, wind up and up (and up) 30min. to the lighthouse (unfortunately not open to visitors) and to lookout points. After the climb up and a nice rest at the peak, the remaining 1¼hr. hike to Tamariu will be a relative cinch. **Bike rental** is available from the **Tourist Service** (☎69 602 72 03), across from the Llafranc tourist office. (€12 for one day, €75 for one week.)

TAMARIU

The beaches get quieter the farther you walk from Calella; Tamariu is the most peaceful, a reward for anyone who makes the challenging two-hour hike. From the far end of the Llafranc beach, take the Camino de Ronda and then the paved road up the mountain to the Ermita de San Sebastià. From there, the remaining 1¼hr. along the wooded Camino de Ronda to Tamariu, are easier. Be sure to follow the red and white parallel stripes along the way, especially when in doubt. For all the tranquility but none of the blisters, take the **bus,** which loops to Tamariu and back four times a day from Palafrugell (15min.; 8:20, 10am, 5:20, 7:45pm; last bus leaves Tamariu at 8pm) from the town bus stop. Tamariu's **tourist office** is on C. Riera. (☎97 262 01 93. Open June-Sept. M-Sa 10am-1pm and 5-8pm, Su 10am-1pm.)

TOSSA DE MAR

Falling in love in (or in love with) Tossa de Mar (pop. 5000) is easy. In 1934, French artist Marc Chagall commenced a 40-year love affair with this seaside village, deeming it "Blue Paradise." When *The Flying Dutchman* was filmed here in 1951, Ava Gardner fell hard for Spanish bullfighter-turned-actor Mario Cabrera, much to the chagrin of Frank Sinatra, her husband at the time. (A statue of the actress at the top of Tossa's old city commemorates her visit.) Like many coastal cities, Tossa suffers from the usual tourist industry blemishes: souvenir shops, inflated prices, and crowded beaches. That said, it resists a generic beach town ambiance, drawing from its ancient historical setting, artistic-hippy roots, and cliff-studded landscape to preserve a unique and friendly small-town feel. Built in the 12th century as a fortified medieval village, the sun-baked walls of Vila Vella continue to overlook Tossa's blue Mediterranean water and beautiful vacationers.

TRANSPORTATION

Buses: (☎97 234 09 03) on Av. Pelegrí at Pl. de les Nacions Sense Estat. Ticket booth open daily 7am-12:40pm and 2:20-8:10pm. **Pujol i Pujol** (☎61 050 58 84) goes to **Lloret del Mar** (20min.; June-Aug. every 30min., Sept.-May every hr. 8am-8:10pm; €1.10). **Sarfa** (☎97 234 09 03) goes to **Barcelona** (2hr.; 18 per day 7:40am-7:40pm, with a break from noon-3pm; €7.80) and **Girona** (1hr.; 1 per day at 7:30am; €4).

Boats go to various towns along the coast, including Lloret and St. Feliu. **Viajes Maritimos,** (☎61 690 91 00 or 97 236 90 95; www.viajesmaritimos.com) departs at various times and with varying numbers of trips 9:25am-6:45pm; tickets €5-16. Buy tickets on Pg. de Mar in front of the First Aid/Emergency stand.

Car Rental: Viajes Tramontana, Av. Costa Brava, 23 (☎97 234 28 29 or 97 234 27 53). **Avis** (☎90 213 55 31), their affiliates **Olimpia** (☎97 234 02 41), and **SACAR** (☎97 234 10 73) operate from the same storefront. 21+; if under 25, Avis charges an additional €6 per day. Expect to be asked for a major credit card, driver's license (international driver's license required for longer rentals), and passport. One-day rentals €39-60. Open daily July-Aug. 9am-9pm; Apr.-June and Sept.-Nov. 9am-3pm and 4-8pm.

Bike and Moped Rentals: Jimbo Bikes, La Rambla Pau Casals, 12 (☎97 234 30 44; jimbotossa@logicontrol.es). Staff gives bike route information; bring license for moped rental. Mountain bikes €3.50-4.50 per hr., €17-21 per day. Open M-Sa 10am-8pm, Su 9:30am-2pm and 4-8pm. AmEx/MC/V.

Boat rentals: Kayaks Nicolau (☎97 234 26 46), on the beach at Mar Menuda, offers 1½hr. kayak excursions to Cala Bona (10am, noon, and 4pm; €10.30), but deals vary so check at the beach. Kayak and paddle boat rental €6 per hr. Open Apr.15-Oct.15 daily 9am-7pm.

Taxis: ☎97 234 05 49. Stand outside the bus station.

ORIENTATION & PRACTICAL INFORMATION

Buses arrive at **Pl. de les Nacions Sense Estat** where **Av. del Pelegrí** and **Av. Ferrán Agulló** meet at a giant Modernist sculpture that resembles a ball of people holding hands; the town slopes gently down from there to the waterfront. Walk away from the station on Av. Ferrán Agulló and turn right on Av. Costa Brava; as Av. Costa Brava turns into Pou de la Vila, take a right on any side street and continue until your feet get wet (10min. total). **Pg. del Mar,** to the right at the end of Av. Costa Brava, curves along the **Platja Gran** (Tossa's main beach) to the old quarter, **Vila Vella.**

Tourist Office: Av. Pelegrí, 25 (☎97 234 01 08; fax 97 234 07 12; www.infotossa.com), in the bus terminal at Av. Ferrán Agulló and Av. Pelegrí. Grab a handy, thoroughly indexed (and free!) map. English, French, and Spanish, to begin with, are spoken. Offers advice on hiking trails and tourist sights, and a posted schedule of upcoming events. They also lead guided hikes and walks June-Aug. on weekends in the mountains (€6-9). Maps have different paths marked out for you if you want to go without a guide. Open June 15-Sept. 15 Su 10am-2pm and 5-8pm, M-Sa 9am-9pm; Apr.-June 15 and Oct. Su 10:30am-1:30pm, M-Sa 10am-2pm and 4-8pm; Nov.-Mar. M-Sa 10am-1pm and 4-7pm.

Currency Exchange: Santander Central Hispano, Av. Ferrán Agulló, 2 (☎97 234 10 65). Open M-F 8:30am-2pm. MC/V.

Police: Municipal Police, Av. Pelegrí, 14 (☎97 234 01 35), down the street from the tourist office. English spoken. They'll escort you to a **24hr. pharmacy** at night if you need.

Pharmacy: Farmàcia Castelló, Av. Ferrán Agulló, 12, is open daily 9:30am-1:30pm and 4:30pm-9pm; 8pm close in winter.

Medical Services: Casa del Mar (☎97 234 18 28 or 97 234 01 54), Av. de Catalunya. Primary health care and immediate attention. The nearest hospital is in Blanes, 30min. south.

Internet Access: Tossa Bar Playa, C. Socors, 6, off the main beach; €1 per 15min., €2 per 30min. Open May-Oct. daily 10am-10pm. **Tossa Locutorio,** C. Sant Telm, 20 (☎66 012 60 29). Internet and long-distance phone calls. Internet €0.75 per 15min. Open daily Apr.-Sept. 10:30am-midnight, Oct.-Nov. and Mar. daily 10:30am-11pm. Dec.-Feb. open Su and Sa 4-9:30pm.

Post Office: C. Maria Auxiliadora, 4 (☎97 234 04 57), down Av. Pelegrí from tourist office. Open M-F 8:30am-2:30pm, Sa 9:30am-1pm. **Postal Code:** 17320.

ACCOMMODATIONS & CAMPING

Tossa is a seasonal town, and therefore many hostels, restaurants, and bars are open only from May to October. During July, August, and festivals, Tossa fills quickly, sometimes growing nearly tenfold to a massive 40,000 people. Make reservations in advance. The **old quarter** hotels are the only ones really worth considering, given steep prices and especially if you are avoiding massive hotels. The tourist office website (www.infotossa.com) offers rooms.

Fonda/Can Lluna, C. Roqueta, 20 (☎97 234 03 65; fax 97 234 07 57). From Pg. del Mar, turn right onto C. Peixeteras, veer left onto C. Estalt, walk up the hill until the dead-end, go left, and then head straight. Delightful family offers immaculate single, double, and triple rooms, all with private baths. Breakfast included—eat on the rooftop terrace and enjoy a breathtaking view of the water. Washing machine €6. A popular choice with Spanish tourists; rooms are booked months in advance in summer. Sept.-June €15 per person. July-Aug. €17. Cash only. ❶

Pensión Carmen Pepi, C. Sant Miguel, 10 (☎97 234 05 26). Turn left off Av. de Pelegrí onto Maria Auxiliadora and veer to your immediate right through the Pl. de l'Antic Hospital and onto C. Sant Miguel. This old, traditional house with its small, greenery-covered courtyard has an authentic feel and good location. The high-ceilinged rooms, each with private bath, are somewhat beyond their prime, but are spacious and comfy. Breakfast €3. July-Aug. singles €20; doubles €40. May-June €17/€30; Sept.-Apr. €15/€30. Cash only. ❷

L'Hostalet de Tossa, Pl. de l'Església, 3 (☎97 234 18 53; fax 97 234 29 69; www.hostelet-tossa.com), in front of the Sant Vicenç church. Clean and annually renovated with hotel-quality rooms. Many of L'Hostalet's 32 double rooms with baths overlook its orange tree terrace and face the church. Common areas boast foosball, pool table, and TV. In room TV or balcony extra €4 per day. Doubles Apr.-May and Oct. €18, June-July 14 and Sept. €21, *Semana Santa* (week before Easter) and July-Aug. €28. MC/V. ❷

Pensión Moré, C. Sant Telmo, 9 (☎97 234 03 39). Downstairs sits a dim, cozy sitting room with TV. Upstairs, large doubles and triples with views of the old quarter. Common bath. July-Aug. doubles €24; triples €36, Sept.-June €20/€30. Cash only. ❶

Can Tort, C. Pescadors, 1 (☎97 234 11 85). Friendly owner maintains 14 very clean double rooms in her pottery-filled restaurant-hostel on the corner of C. Pescadors and C. Portal. All rooms have bathrooms, homey furnishings, and views of Tossa's old quarter. Breakfast included. Apr.-Oct. doubles €34, July €39, Aug. €48. No singles. Cash only. ❸

Camping: Can Martí (☎97 234 08 51; fax 97 234 24 61), at the end of La Rambla Pau Casals, off Av. Ferrán Agulló, 15min. from the bus station, is the closest site. Popular, tree-lined campsite on fringes of a wildlife reserve. Hot-water showers, telephones, swimming pool, and restaurant. Minutes from the municipal sports area. June 20–Aug. €5.50 per person, €6 per tent, €3.50 per car; May 12-June 19 and Sept. 1-16 €4.50 per person, €5 per tent, €2.70 per car. Traveler's checks or cash. ❶

Caganer

FOOD

Restaurants catering to tourists serve up menús at reasonable prices in the old quarter. Dining on **Pg. del Mar** offers the best people watching; **Mar Menuda** has the same ocean views with a quieter, less touristy feel. If it's food quality and diversity you're after, the old quarter hides some secrets; otherwise you'll have to sojourn into town. If you need groceries, especially fresh produce, head to **Supermercats Proxim,** C. La Guardia, 1, in the old quarter on the corner of C. Socors and La Guardia. **Magatzems Palou,** C. Enric Granados, 4. sells other necessary items, and has store locations throughout the city. (☎97 234 08 58. Open daily June-Sept. 9am-9pm.)

Catalan Flag

Restaurant Santa Marta, C. Francesc Aromi, 2 (☎97 234 04 72), just inside entrance to old fortress off C. Portal. Housed in one of the medieval dwellings long ago inhabited by the city's elite, log-cut tables and chairs spill out of the stone-walled, romantically dimmed interior and onto an elegant patio covered by soft, shady leaves. The contemporary cuisine proves a delectable contrast to the historic building, with such winners as salmon with raspberry and kiwi sauce (€12.95). Entrees €9.85-27.95. Open daily 12:30-4pm and 7:30-11pm from *Semana Santa* to Oct. 15. AmEx/MC/V. ❸

La Taberna de Tossa, C. Sant Telm, 26 (☎97 234 19 39). In the heart of the old quarter, right off La Guardia. Serves up inexpensive house wine (€3.60 per L), traditional tapas (€1.75-4.30), and provincial specialities in a large old-world style dining room. Popular among Spanish tourists. Entrees €4.10-10.95. Open Apr.-Sept. daily 1-4pm and 7pm-1am; Oct.-Mar. Su, F-Sa 1-4pm and 7pm-1am. V. ❷

Country Scene

Giant Figures at a procession

Rolled Hay in the Countryside

Fish

Restaurant Marina, C. Tarull, 6 (☎97 234 07 57). Faces the Església de Sant Vincenç and has outdoor seating for prime people-watching. A nice family restaurant with benches bedecked with green checkered tablecloths. Multilingual menu features pizza, meat, fish dishes, and lots of *paella,* including a vegetarian option. Entrees €3.50-12.30. Menús €8.50 and €10.50. Open daily 10am-midnight. MC/V. ❷

Pizzeria Anna, Pont Vell, 13 (☎97 234 28 51). Turn right on Pont Vell from Pg. Mar; it's the small restaurant on the left-hand corner with C. Portal. Though homesick Italians might be a bit disappointed, the seafood-sick traveler will be in heaven. Pasta €4.25-5.50; pizza €5.25-6.70. Open Mar.-Nov. daily noon-4pm and 7-midnight. AmEx/MC/V. ❶

Dino's, Sant Telm, 28 (☎972 34 07 30). Italian fare with German flare. Open for late afternoon dining when everything else is closed. Pizzas €5.50-7. Open daily 1pm-midnight. ❷

SIGHTS

The prime destination in Tossa (besides the beach) is the **Vila Vella,** a medieval fortress that wraps around the base of the town. Built in the 12th century, then restored in 1387, the fortress defended the Spanish elite from Moorish attack in the 16th century. Inside, a spiral of medieval alleys leads to Pl. Pintor J. Roig y Soler, where the first contemporary art museum in Spain, the ◪**Museu Municipal,** Pl. Pintor Roig i Soler, 1 (☎97 234 07 09; museu.tossa@ddgi.es) has a rather large collection of 1920s and 1930s art in an open and airy space, including—because the artist had a house here—one of the few Chagall paintings still in Spain. In addition, Tossa's Roman mosaics, dating from the 4th to the first century BC, and other artifacts from the nearby Vila Romana are displayed in the museum, originally a 12th-century palace. (Open June 1-15 and Sept. 16-30 M-F 11am-1pm and 3-5pm, Sa-Su 11am-6pm; June 16-Sept. 15 M-Sa 10am-8pm; Oct.-May M-F 11am-1pm and 3-5pm, Sa-Su 11am-5pm. €3, students and seniors €1.80.)

BEACHES

Tossa's main beach, **La Platja Gran,** is surrounded by cliffs and the dreamy Vila Vella, and draws the majority of beach-goers. To escape the crowds, visit some of the neighboring *calas* (small coves), accessible by foot. The tiny ◪**Es Codolar** sits just under the tower of the Vila Vella palace, hugged by precipices cloaked in foliage, and lacks the throngs of swimmers and sunbathers on the main beach. To get there, follow C. Portal to its end. On the opposite side of the shore is Mar Menudo, with natural pools created among the rocks and nice kiosk bars serving excellent *calamari a la plancha* (grilled calamari). This is a fairly social, yet not over-populated, stretch of beach. Snorkeling and diving are popular sports; pick up gear at **Andrea's Diving Center,** Av. Sant Raimon de Penyafort, 11 (☎97 234 20 26; www.andreas-diving.com). Well-marked hiking and mountain-biking paths also criss-cross the **Massif of Cadiretes** wildlife reserve and offer impressive views of the coastline as the mountain, at 518m, is the tallest in Tossa. For less strenuous activity, several companies, like **Fonda Cristal,** send glass-bottomed boats to nearby beaches and caves, where you can jump in for a swim at the beach stops. Tickets are available at booths on the Platja Gran. (☎97 234 22 29. 1hr. Apr.-June, excursions daily every hr. 10am-5pm. July-Sept. daily every 30min. 10am-6pm; €7.50 per person, ages 5-12 €5.) **Club Aire Libre,** on the highway to Lloret (ask the bus driver to stop), organizes various excursions and rents equipment for water sports. (☎97 234 12 77; www.clubairelibre.com. Canoeing and kayaking €13, water skiing €26 for 2 lessons, scuba diving €264 for 5-day certification course; sailing €11 per hr., windsurfing €10.30 per hr.)

NIGHTLIFE

Bars line the streets of the old quarter and have live music from time to time. At ▓**Bar Trinquet,** C. Sant Josep, 9, flirt over drippy candles and under romantic chandeliers or enjoy the stars in the flower- and ivy-drenched interior courtyard, where young people relax and meet and greet one another to the lounge, jazz, and minimal techno music spun by DJs. Open June-Sept. daily 10pm-3am, Sept.-Oct. 24 Su and Th-Sa 10pm-3am. Cash only. **Bar El Pirata,** C. Portal, 32, and its companion bar **Piratín,** C. Portal, 30, have outdoor tables overlooking the sea at Es Codolar. DJs spin acid jazz and house on weekend nights. (☎61 638 55 87. Open year-round 10pm-2:30am. Cash only). The **Sant Antoni Disco-Pub,** C. Portal, 9 (☎97 234 17 33) keeps the beers flowing late-night as the crowds come, to sing along with the pumping music. Perfect for all your late-night drunken yelling conversations. For live music try **Don Pepe,** C. Estolt, 6, a small bar which hosts a flamenco guitarist every night. €10 per 0.5L sangria. (☎97 234 22 66. Open Apr.-Oct. daily 10pm-4am. Cash only.)

MATARÓ

Extremely close to Barcelona, Mataró (pop. 100,000) has beaches that are nearly comparable to the better-known Sitges but with a far more low-key, family-friendly setting. This wonderfully easy daytrip from Barcelona will have you out of the train station and onto the beach minutes after arrival.

TRANSPORTATION

RENFE Trains (☎93 490 02 02) **Line #3** runs to Mataró frequently from Barcelona-Sants and Pl. de Catalunya (40min., every 10-20min. from Barcelona-Sants 6:12am-11:55pm, €2.20). The last train from Mataró back to Barcelona leaves at 10:18pm. **Mataró Bus,** C. Francesc Layret, 72 (☎93 757 53 94), has an extensive network of buses that hits almost all points of the town. Lines #1-5 all originate at the train station, with Line #0 running across town. €0.90 per ride. Buses run 6am-10pm daily. For a **taxi,** call ☎93 798 60 60 or 93 799 14 14, or hail one in front of the train station.

ORIENTATION & PRACTICAL INFORMATION

The **RENFE train station** is conveniently located right on the coast, just a few m. from the town beaches. Upon exiting the station, turn right, descend the ramp at the end of the block, and cross under the train tracks to get to the beach. However, to get to other beaches, the town center, or food, expect a hefty walk;

big beaches don't come without a price. To get to the town center, cross Av. Maresme, the street in front of the train station, head right, and take the second left onto C. Lepanto. This street leads to La Rambla (5min.), the main street that circles around the commercial district. A right onto La Rambla cuts through Pl. Santa Anna to C. La Riera, the home of the **Ajuntament,** La Riera, 48. (a left off Pl. Santa Anna, the town hall of Mataró.) Come here for basic **tourist information.** They are not well-stocked with printed info, but there is a huge map posted at the back of the foyer. (www.infomataro.net. Open M-F 9am-7pm). The nearby cultural center, **Patronat Municipal de Cultura de Mataró,** C. Sant Josep, 9, also has information on upcoming events and festivals, usually in Catalan. (☎93 758 23 61. Open M-F 9am-2pm and 6-8pm.) Services include **Police:** ☎092 and **Emergencies:** ☎112, ☎061 for ambulances. **Internet access** is available on two coin-fed machines at **Flin's Burger Restaurant,** La Rambla, 22, in Pl. Santa Anna. (☎93 790 49 84. €1 per 17min. Open daily 10am-midnight). The **post office** is at C. Lepanto, 31. (☎90 219 71 97; www.correos.es. Open M-F 8:30am-8:30pm, Sa 9:30am-2pm.) **Western Union** office inside. **Postal code:** 08302.

ACCOMMODATIONS

Most people travelling to Mataró make it a daytrip because of its proximity to the big city. There are a few cheap options and most are far from the sandy shores. **Hostal Cerdanyola ❸,** Pl. Isla Cristina, 1, is relatively inexpensive and tidy, but a 30min. walk from the beach. To get there, walk down St. Josep, turn right onto C. Ronda Prim, then left on Puid i Cadafalch until Pl. Isla Cristina; or take bus #1 or 2 from the train station, the latter of which drops you off directly in front of the hotel, just ask the driver to stop. (☎93 798 20 45. June-Sept. singles €24; doubles €40. Oct.-May singles €18; doubles €33.) **Castell de Mata ❺,** Ctra. N-II, km. 649, lies on a highway that leads away from town, and it is only reachable by taxi, but is the only hotel right on the water. Amenities include a pool, a terrace, and a restaurant; 52 rooms with satellite TV, and phones. (☎93 790 10 44. Singles €51; doubles €61.)

FOOD

Both on the beach and in town, quick-service cafes and tapas restaurants thrive by getting the crowds fed and back on the sand where they belong. **Racó d'en Margarit ❷,** Pg. Callao, 15, on the beach at the beginning of Platja del Callao (about 20min. away from the station after exiting to your right, past the Centre Natacio Mataró), has a standard tapas selection (€2.75-6) as well as a variety of *paella* (€7.25-8.50), with fast-food service and crowded beachside seating. (☎93 790 66 78. Open in summer daily 9am-midnight; in the winter closes at 6pm. MC/V). The slightly fancier **Al Punt de Sal: Cuina Mediterranea ❷,** C. Lepanto, 25, located just blocks from the train station, serves mediterranean-style fish and meat for reasonable prices. Entrees €6.20-13.20. (☎93 796 24 54. Open Su-M and Th-Sa 1-5pm and 8:30-11pm. MC/V.)

BEACHES

Mataró's beaches are the town's biggest draw, with soft sand, refreshing waves, and plenty of room to spread out, but they do tend to fill up on weekends and steamy afternoons. The first, **Platja del Varador,** is the widest, with enough room for three full beach-soccer fields behind its sunbathers. An outcropping of rocks, easily circumvented, separate it from the town's other two beaches, **Platja del Callao** and **Platja de St. Simó,** the first about 20min. from the train station. Outdoor showers are everywhere, and Red Cross stations (open June 14-Sept. 14 daily 10am-7pm) are found on Varador and Callao beaches.

FESTIVALS

On the last weekend in July, Mataró pulls out all the stops in celebrating **Les Santes** (The Saints), its *Festa Major* in honor of patroness saints Juliana and Semproniana. Nearly a week of activities includes parades, concerts, fireworks, and all-night beach dance parties. The Saturday afternoon parade is worth catching, with regal giants, spinning bulls with fireworks for horns, and the 400-year-old tradition of the Mataró eagle performing a jig in front of the Ajuntament.

COSTA DORADA

SITGES

Forty kilometers south of Barcelona, the beach town of Sitges merits its self-ordained title, "jewel of the Mediterranean," with its prime tanning grounds baked by 300 sunny days a year. First prominent in the late 19th century as one of the principal centers of the *Modernisme* art movement, today Sitges is swarmed by tourists from around the world who have heard the tales of its thriving gay community and vibrant nightlife. Whereas this flood of daytripping Spaniards, tourist families, and twenty-something partiers tends to drown many towns in the banalities of commercial tourism, in Sitges it only seems to supply exhilarating flavor. So close it's in the same area code as Barcelona, Sitges is the ideal daytrip and well worth a couple of nights' stay.

TRANSPORTATION

Cercanías Trains (RENFE; ☎93 490 02 02) run from Estació Barcelona-Sants to Sitges (40min., every 15-30min. 5:27am-11:52pm, €2.20) and continue on to **Vilanova** (7min.; every 15-30min., last train from Sitges at 12:44am; €1.05). To get to the beaches in between the two cities, rent a car in Barcelona (see **Service Directory,** p. 310) or in Sitges at **Europcar** (☎93 811 19 96), on the 1st fl. of the Mercat next to the train station. For a **taxi,** call ☎93 894 13 29. A taxi between Barcelona and Sitges costs €45-50.

ORIENTATION & PRACTICAL INFORMATION

Most everyone coming into Sitges starts out at the RENFE train station, on **C. Carbonell,** in the northern section of town. From here, the town center is 5min. by foot, the beach about 10min. To get to either, take a right as you leave the station, and then your third left onto **C. Sant Francesc.** This will lead straight to the old town, and intersect with **C. Parellades,** the main path of stores and restaurants, which runs parallel to the ocean. Any street off of Parellades will lead you to the waterfront. **Pg. Ribera** runs along the central and most crowded beaches.

For a good free map and info on accommodations, stop by the **tourist office,** Sínia Morera 1. From the station, turn right onto C. Carbonell and take a right a block later. The office is across the street, a block to the left—look for the sign with the big "i". (☎93 894 50 04. Open July-Aug. daily 9am-9pm; Sept.-June Su-M and W-Sa 9am-3pm and 4-6:30pm.) In summer, a smaller branch opens by the museums on C. Fonollar. (☎93 894 42 51. Open Su 11am-2pm, W-F 10:30am-1:30pm, Sa 11am-2pm and 4-7pm.) **Super Avui,** C. Carbonell, 24, is a **supermarket** across from the train station. (Open M-Sa 9am-9pm.) Other town services include **medical assistance** (☎93 894 64 26) and **emergency assistance** (☎93 894 39 49). The local **police** (☎90 410 10 92) are in the Pl. Ajuntament. To get there from C. Parellades, take C. Major south; the station is on the right. **Internet access** and **fax** service are available at **Café Art,** C. Sant Frances, 42 (☎93 811 00 52. €1 per 30min., €1.50 per hr. Open daily 11am-1am) and **Sitges Internet Access,** C.

Espanya, 7. (☎ 93 811 40 03. non-members pay €4.50 per hr., €1.20 per 15min. Open daily 11am-1am.) The **post office** is in Pl. Espanya. (☎ 93 894 12 47. Open M-F 8:30am-2:30pm, Sa 9:30am-1pm. No packages Sa.) The **postal code** is 08870.

ACCOMMODATIONS

Accommodations are expensive and difficult to find on summer weekends, so consider daytripping to Sitges from Barcelona and reserve early if you plan to stay. Also, Sitges nightlife is crazy and you may not actually end up needing a bed of your own, anyway. In the listings below, price range includes both low season and high season, with lower prices corresponding to low season.

Hostal Parellades, C. Parellades, 11 (☎ 93 894 08 01), one block from the beach. Offers clean rooms and an airy terrace. Dirt cheap for Sitges. Singles €24; doubles €40, with bath €45; triples with bath €50. Cash only. ❷

Hotel El Cid, C. Sant Josep, 39 (☎ 93 894 18 42; fax 93 894 63 35). From the train station, take the 4th left off C. Carbonell. One of the best deals in town. All 77 of the colorful and comfortable rooms come with bathrooms, safety deposit box, and A/C. Small pool, bar and garden in back. Breakfast included. Doubles €37-63. MC/V. ❸

Hostal Internacional, C. Sant Francesc, 52 (☎ 93 894 26 90; www.sitges.tv), off C. Carbonell. Bright rooms not far from the train station. Doubles €31-37, with bath €37-43. MC/V. ❷

Pensión Maricel, C. Tacó, 13 (☎ 93 894 36 27; www.milisa.com), 1min. from the beach and close to the museums. Big double rooms all come with phones, radios, and fans, much needed on the occasional sticky summer night. Bar and laundry service available. Doubles with bath €39-54. AmEx/MC/V. ❹

Hostal Bonaire, C. Bonaire, 31 (☎ 93 894 53 26), off Parellades, toward the beach. Though the 9 rooms are somewhat cramped, the ceiling fans and TVs in every room make amends. Singles €31, with bath €37; doubles with bath €38-46. Cash only. ❸

FOOD

Izarra, C. Mayor, 24 (☎ 93 894 73 70), behind the museum area. This Basque tapas bar can be either a quick food fix before a long night of club-hopping or a more substantial and leisurely meal before a short night with the family. Ask for a *plato* and grab whatever tapas look tastiest, from Basque fish tapas to more traditional Spanish *croquetas* to chicken wings (€0.75 each). Big entrees (€5-11.50) and Basque *sidra* (cider; €2) are also available. Open daily 1:30-4pm and 8:30-11pm. MC/V. ❷

Restaurante La Oca, C. Parellades, 41 (☎ 93 894 79 36). Chickens roasting on an open fire attract long lines of hungry tourists. Try the succulent *pollo al ast* (roasted chicken) for €5.10 or cover one with sauce for €5.75. The chicken *croquetas* (€2.60) are outstanding. Open Su-F 1pm-midnight, Sa 1pm-1am. MC/V. ❷

Restaurante El Pozo, C. Sant Pau, 3 (☎ 93 894 11 04), off C. Parellades, is a throwback to the town's days as a quiet fishing village. Paintings depicting rustic Spanish landscapes dot the walls inside this tiny tavern. Fresh fish tastes as if someone caught it just for you. Seafood-heavy menu, with plenty of wine and beer to fill your stomach to the brim. Entrees (€7-13) include lobster soup, sole, shrimp, and squid. Open M-W and F-Su 1:30-4pm and 7-11pm. MC/V. ❷

SIGHTS

The pedestrian walkway **C. Parellades,** which features shopping, eating, and drinking galore, is the central attraction. Cultural activities may seem as undesirable as rain to some beachgoers, but Sitges has some can't-miss sights, including Morell's whimsical **Modernist clock tower,** Pl. Cap de la Vila, 2, above Optica at the intersection of Parellades and Sant Francesc. Behind it, on C. Fonollar, the **Museu Cau Ferrat** (☎ 93 894 03 64) hangs over the water's edge. Once home to Catalan Modernist Santiago Rusiñol and a meeting point for

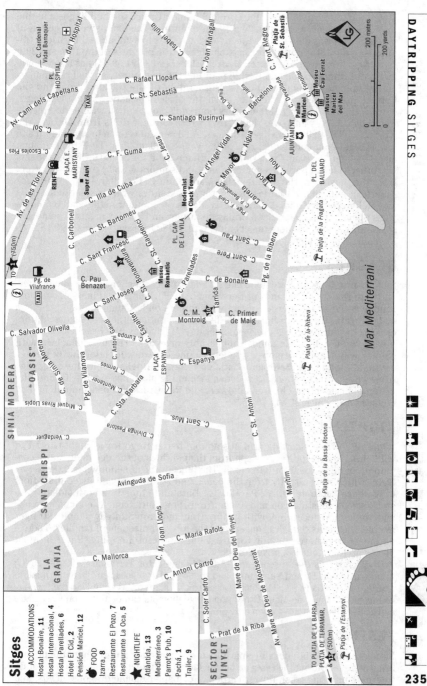

Sitges

ACCOMMODATIONS
Hostal Bonaire, **11**
Hostal Internacional, **4**
Hostal Parellades, **6**
Hotel El Cid, **2**
Pensión Maricel, **12**

FOOD
Izarra, **8**
Restaurante El Pozo, **7**
Restaurante La Oca, **5**

NIGHTLIFE
Atlántida, **13**
Mediterráneo, **3**
Parrot's Pub, **10**
Pachá, **1**
Trailer, **9**

SINIA MORERA

"OASIS"

SANT CRISPI

LA GRANJA

SECTOR VINYET

Mar Mediterrani

young Catalan artists Pablo Picasso and Ramon Casas, the building is a shrine to Modernist iron work, glass work, and painting. The extensive collection of wrought iron was amassed by Rusinyol in an effort to symbolize the various traditions of the 18th century lost in exchange for the progress of the 19th and 20th centuries. Next door, the **Museu Maricel del Mar** (☎ 93 894 03 64) has a select collection of Romanesque and Gothic painting and sculptures, as well as an interesting marine collection showcasing models of the Catalan navy and the Catalan fishing fleet. Farther into town, the **Museu Romàntic,** C. Sant Gaudenci, 1, off C. Parellades, is a 19th-century bourgeois house filled with period pieces like music boxes and over 400 17th- to 19th-century dolls from all over the world. (☎ 93 894 29 69; m.sitges@diba.es. All 3 museums open in summer Su and Tu-Sa 10am-2pm and 5-9pm; rest of the year Su 10am-3pm, Tu-F 10am-1:30pm and 3-6:30pm, Sa 10am-7pm. Combo entrance good for 30 days €5.40, students €3; otherwise €3 per museum, students and seniors €1.50.) Across the street from the museums, the stately **Palau Maricel**, on C. Fonollar, built in 1910 for American millionaire Charles Deering, wows visitors with its sumptuous halls and rich gardens. Guided tours are available on summer nights and include a glass of cava (champagne); on Friday, Saturday, and Sunday nights, a piano and soprano concert complete the evening. Call ahead for reservations. (☎ 93 811 33 11. Tours €6; F-Su concert and tour €8.)

BEACHES

Sitges's proximity to Barcelona and its beautiful beaches make it a viable alternative to the crowded sands of Barceloneta or Port Olímpic. Plenty of soothing sand accommodates hordes of sun worshippers on hot summer days. At **Platja de la Fragata,** the beach farthest to the left as you face the sea, sand sculptors create new masterpieces every summer day. By midday, the beaches closest to downtown can become almost unbearably crowded. The best beaches, with calmer water and more open space, are one or two kilometers walk farther down, at **Platja de la Barra** and **Platja de Terramar.** Rocks shield these beaches from waves, creating a shallow ocean swimming pool that extends far into the water and is ideal for children. Showers and Red Cross stations abound. In case of **emergency,** call ☎ 93 811 76 25.

NIGHTLIFE

While Sitges is an easy daytrip, it's almost better to go for a "night-trip." The wild clubs are the perfect escape from the confines of the decidedly more cosmopolitan night scene of Barcelona. The place to be at sundown is **C. Primer de Maig** (which runs directly from the beach and Pg. Ribera) and its continuation, **C. Marquès Montroig,** off C. Parellades. Bars and clubs line both sides of the small street, blasting pop and house from 10pm until 3am. The clubs here are wide-open and accepting, with a vibrant mixed crowd of gay people, straight people, the occasional drag queen, and the most wholesome of families. There's no cover anywhere, making for great bar- and club-hopping. Beers at most places go for about €3, mixed drinks €6.

Even crazier is the "disco-beach" **Atlàntida,** in Sector Terramar (☎ 93 894 26 77; foam parties on Th and Su nights), and the legendary **Pachá,** on Pg. Sant Didac in nearby Vallpineda (☎ 93 894 22 98). Buses run all night on weekends to the two discos from C. Primer de Maig. Other popular nightspots can be found on C. Bonaire and C. Sant Pau, but most open only on weekends.

FESTIVALS

Sitges celebrates holidays by sparing no extravagance and pushing the boundaries of style. During the **Festa de Corpus Christi** in June, townspeople collaborate to create intricate fresh-flower carpets. For papier-mâché dragons, devils, and giants dancing in the streets, visit during the **Festa Major,** held August 22-27 in honor of the town's patron saint Bartolomé. Nothing compares to the **Carnaval,** a preparation for Catholic fasting during the first week of Lent (Feb. 27-Mar. 5). Spaniards crash the town for a frenzy of parades, dancing, outrageous costumes, and vats of alcohol. The last night is the wildest, as hundreds of dragqueens parade through the streets. On the first Sunday in March, a pistol shot starts the **Rally de Coches de Epoca,** an antique car race from Barcelona to Sitges. June brings the **International Theater Festival** (€10-22 per show), and July and August the **International Jazz Festival** (€10.50 per concert). From September 12-14, competitors trod on fresh grapes on the beach for the annual **Grape Harvest.** October 1-12 brings the famous **Festival Internacional de Cinema de Catalunya.**

NEAR SITGES: VILANOVA I LA GELTRÙ

🚆 *Cercanías trains (RENFE) run from Vilanova to Sitges (7min., every 15-30min., €1.05), and continue to Barcelona (50min., €2.65). Mon Bus (☎ 93 893 70 60) connects Vilanova to Sitges (€1.25), Vilafranca (€1.60), and Barcelona (€3). The bus station is in the plaza in front of the train station. A taxi (☎ 93 893 32 41) from Vilanova to Sitges costs about €9-12.*

One of Catalunya's most important ports, **Vilanova i la Geltrù,** actually turns out to be two cities in one: an industrial hub and a well-groomed beach town. There is little in the dusty uptown area, save old churches and stone facades; most visitors spend the day on the beach (10min. from the train station). In the evening, Vilanovans generally forgo late-night madness for beach volleyball or soccer at Parc de Ribes.

To get to the **beaches,** exit the station, turn left on C. Forn de Vidre, and take the third left onto the thoroughfare Rambla de la Pau. You'll know you're going the right way on Rambla de la Pau when you head under a pedestrian overpass; after that follow the rambla all the way to the port and onto **Pg. del Carme.** The **tourist office,** about 100m to the right, off Pg. del Carme in a small park called **Parc de Ribes Roges,** offers excellent **maps.** (☎ 93 815 45 17. Open July-Aug. M-Sa 10am-8pm, Su 10am-2pm; Sept.-June M-Sa 10am-2pm.) The wide **Platja de Ribes Roges** is past the tourist office; to the left is the smaller **Platja del Far.** Expect fine sand, sun, and a bit of company. The beaches are refreshingly calm, like a giant swimming pool but with the added bonus of topless women. If you decide to stay in town, the popular **Can Gatell ❸,** C. Puigcerdà 6-16, has clean rooms and full baths. With your back to the station, head down C. Victor Balaguer and at the end, turn right onto La Rambla and then take the first left. (☎ 93 893 01 17. Singles €30; doubles €47, with A/C €53. Extra bed €10.) The hostel's menú (€8, served M-F, includes wine) is popular with locals. (Open daily 7-10:30am, 1-5pm, and 8:30-10pm.) Numerous restaurants serving fresh seafood line Pg. del Carme, but they can be quite pricey. An inexpensive alternative is **Supermarket Orangutan,** Rambla de la Pau 36, on the way to the beach. (Open M-Sa 9:30am-2pm and 5:30-9pm.)

TARRAGONA

Before Barcelona was even a twinkle in anyone's eye, Tarragona was a bustling city, key to Rome's colonization of Iberia (see **Life & Times,** p. 38). In 218 BC, the Carthaginian general **Hannibal** and his troops were tearing through Spain on a march toward Rome. The Romans, led by the **Scipio brothers** Gnaeus and Publius, set out (successfully) to cut them off and turn them back to North Africa. They set up headquarters and began building giant, impenetrable stone walls in a small coastal port, then called Tarraco, and a provincial capital was born. Tarragona's strategic position made the city a thriving provincial power in ancient times; today, an amphitheater and numerous other ruins pay homage to the city's imperial glory days. These vestiges of Tarragona's Roman past are the city's most compelling attractions, but plenty of visitors are satisfied with lolling on the beaches in one of Catalunya's most important port cities.

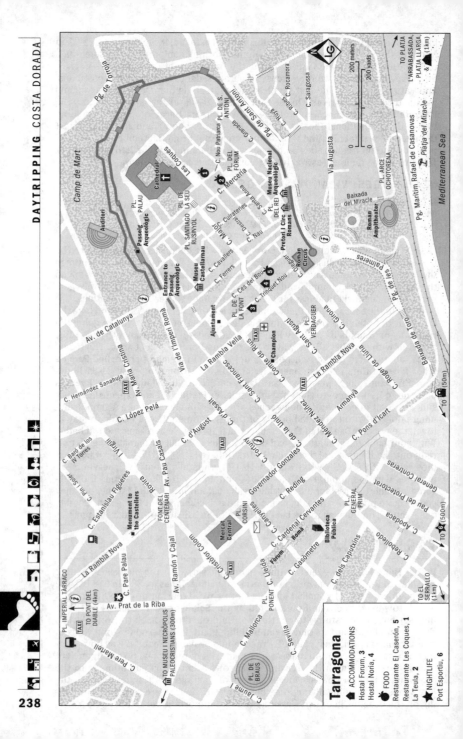

Tarragona

♦ ACCOMMODATIONS
Hostal Forum, 3
Hostal Noria, 4

● FOOD
Restaurante El Caserón, 5
Restaurante Les Coques, 1
La Teula, 2

NIGHTLIFE
Port Esportiu, 6

TRANSPORTATION

Trains: ☎90 224 02 02. On Pl. Pedrera by the water. Info open daily 6am-9pm. The best transportation option. To: **Alicante (Alacant)** (4hr., 10 per day, €34.50); **Barcelona** (1¼hr., 30 per day, €4.25); **Madrid** (6½-8hr., 4 per day, €40.50); **Sitges** (45min., 20 per day, €2.60); **Valencia** (2-3hr., 15 per day, €13.35); **Zaragoza** (4hr., 10 per day, €14.40).

Buses: ☎97 722 91 26. Pl. Imperial Tarraco. **Alsa Enatcar** (☎90 242 22 42) serves most destinations. To: **Barcelona** (1½hr., 8 per day, €8) and **Valencia** (4hr., 6 per day, €15.20).

Public Transportation: EMT Buses ☎97 754 94 80 run daily 6am-11pm. €1, 10-ride *abono* ticket valid only 20 days €4.40.

Taxi: Radio Taxi ☎97 722 14 14.

ORIENTATION & PRACTICAL INFORMATION

Most sights are clustered on a hill, surrounded by remnants of Roman walls. At the foot of the hill, **La Rambla Vella** and **La Rambla Nova** (parallel to one another and perpendicular to the sea) are the main thoroughfares of the new city. La Rambla Nova runs from **Pg. de les Palmeres** (which overlooks the sea) to **Pl. Imperial Tarraco**, the monstrous rotunda and home of the bus station. To reach the old quarter from the train station, turn right and walk 150m to the killer stairs parallel to the shore. Keep going on Pg. les Palmeres until you get to a large circle drive with an info booth; this is the southwestern corner of the old quarter. From there, take some more intermittent stairs up Pg. de Sant Antoni, take your first left, and you'll find yourself on the other side of the fortress walls that surrounded the city of Tarraco.

Tourist Office: C. Major, 39 (☎97 725 07 95; fax 97 724 55 07; www.tarragonanaturisme.com), below the cathedral steps. Crucial **free map**, accommodation listings, museum info, and a guide to Tarragona's Roman ruins. Open M-F 9am-9pm, Sa 9am-2pm and 4-9pm, Su and holidays 10am-2pm.

Regional Tourist Office: C. Fortuny, 4 (☎97 723 34 15), off of La Rambla Nova on C. Fortuny. Regional map, and extensive information about tourism in the immediate areas outside of Tarragona. Open M-F 9am-2pm and 4-6:30pm, Sa 9am-2pm.

Tourist Information Booths: Pl. Imperial Tarraco, at the bottom of La Rambla Vella, just outside the bus station; another at the intersection of Av. Catalunya and Via de l'Impera Romi; a 3rd at the corner of Via Augusta and Pg. Sant Antoni. Open July-Sept. daily 10am-1:30pm and 4:30-8pm; Nov.-June Sa-Su 10am-1:30pm and 5:30-8:30pm.

Luggage Storage: At the train station 4:30am-midnight; €4.50.

Emergency: ☎092 **Police: Comisaria de Policía** (☎97 724 98 44), on Pl. d'Orleans. From Pl. Imperial Tarraco, walk northwest along Av. Pres. Lluís Companys, and take the 3rd left on C. J. Irla to the station.

Medical Emergency: ☎061. **Medical Assistance: Hospital de Sant Pau i Santa Tecla,** La Rambla Vella, 14 (☎97 725 99 00). **Hospital Joan XXIII** (☎97 729 58 00), on C. Dr. Mallafré Guasch.

Internet Access: Ciberspai.net, C. Estanislau Figueras, 58 (☎97 724 57 64), off the Imperial Tarraco rotunda. €0.75 per 15min. Open M-F 9am-midnight, Sa-Su 10am-midnight. **Biblioteca Pública,** C. Fortuny, 30 (☎97 724 05 44). Public library; free 30min. use of the Internet with passport. Open M-F 10am-8pm, Sa 10am-2pm.

Post Office: Pl. Corsini, 12 (☎97 724 01 49), below La Rambla Nova off C. Canyelles. Open M-F 8:30am-8:30pm, Sa 9:30am-1pm.

Postal Code: 43001.

ACCOMMODATIONS & CAMPING

Tarragona is not known for its abundance of cheap beds, as most of the city's accommodations are two- to four-star hotels near the center. Still, a few good deals can be had in the old quarter in Pl. Font (parallel to La Rambla Vella). Low- and high-season prices are provided, high-season being June-September.

Hostal Noria, Pl. de la Font, 53 (☎97 723 87 17), in the heart of the historic town. Enter through the restaurant. 24 clean and bright rooms with pretty-in-pink bathrooms. Singles with bath €21-28, doubles with bath €34-45. Cash only. ❷

Hostal Forum, Pl. de la Font, 37 (☎97 723 17 18), upstairs from the restaurant. Clean rooms and bathrooms don't leave much space for spreading out, but Forum is a decent place to sleep for the night. Singles with bath €16-19; doubles with bath €32-38. MC/V. ❷

Camping: Several campsites line the road toward Barcelona (Via Augusta or CN-340) along the northern beaches, especially around km 1.17. Take bus #9 (every 20min., €1) from Pl. Imperial Tarraco. **Tarraco** (☎97 729 02 89 and 97 722 48 59; fax 97 729 02 89) is the closest campsite, at Platja de l'Arrabassada. Well-kept facilities near the beach. €2.75-3.75 per person, per car, or per tent, and €2-2.50 per child. Open Apr.-Sept. MC/V. ❶

FOOD

Pl. Font and Las Ramblas Nova and Vella are full of cheap menús (€5-8) and greasy *platos combinados*. Tarragona's indoor **Mercat Central** (market) is located in Pl. Corsini next to the post office. (☎97 723 15 51. Open M-W and Sa 8am-2pm, Th-F 7am-2pm and 5:30-8:30pm. Flea market Tu and Th.) Tarragona also has several markets that only open once or twice a week, see the tourist office for details. For **groceries**, head to **Champion,** C. Augusta at Comte de Rius, between Las Ramblas Nova and Vella. (Open M-Sa 9am-9:15pm.) **El Serrallo,** the fisherman's quarter right next to the harbor, has the best seafood. Try your food with Tarragona's typical 🔲*romesco* sauce, simmered from red peppers, toasted almonds, and hazelnuts.

Restaurant Les Coques, Nou Patriarca, 2 (☎97 722 83 00), off Pl. La Seu near the cathedral. Roman walls, chandeliers, paintings, antiques, and wine bottles create an eclectic interior. The ambience is relaxing and waiters provide first class service. Try the cod filet with garlic sauce (€17.20), grilled baby goat (€12), or fresh Tarragonan *cigalitas* (a native shellfish related to shrimp) sauteed in a garlic sauce (€16). Entrees €10-32. Open M-Sa 1:15-3:45pm and 9-10:45pm. AmEx/MC/V. ❹

La Teula, C. Mercería, 16 (☎97 723 99 89), in the old city near Pl. del Fórum. Great for salads (€4-6) and toasted sandwiches with interesting Catalan veggie and meat combos (€7-12). Lunch menú €7.90. Open daily noon-4pm and 8pm-midnight. MC/V. ❷

Restaurant El Caserón, C. Ces Del Bou, 9, or Trinquet Nou, 4 (☎97 723 93 28), parallel to La Rambla Vella (off Pl. Font). This popular local diner serves homestyle food. Entrees €4.25-13. Menú €7.50. Open Sa-M 8:30-11pm, Tu-F 1-4pm and 8:30-10:30pm. MC/V. ❷

SIGHTS

Tarragona's status as provincial capital transformed the small military enclosure into a glorious imperial port. Countless Roman ruins stand silently amid 20th-century hustle and bustle, all just minutes from the beach.

▨ ROMAN RUINS

🛈 *All ruins open May-Sept. Su 9am-3pm, Tu-Sa 9am-9pm; Oct.-Apr. Su and Tu-Sa 9am-7pm. Admission to each €2, students €0.65.*

Below Pg. de las Palmeres and set amid gardens above Platja del Miracle beach is the **Roman Amphitheater** (☎97 744 25 79), where gladiators once killed wild animals and each other; this barbaric but popular activity dates back to the founding of the city. Built at the beginning of the 2nd century, the *amfiteatre* became a place of Christian significance when in AD 259, the Christian bishop Fructuosus and his two deacons were burned alive here; in the sixth century, these martyrs were honored with a basilica built in the arena.

Next to the Museu Nacional Arqueològic in Pl. del Rei is the entrance to the **Pretori I Circ Romans** (☎97 724 19 52), which gives access to both the **Praetorium Tower,** the former administrative center of the region, and the **Roman Circus,** the site of chariot races and other spectacles: picture Ben Hur. Visitors descend into the long, dark tunnels that led fans to their seats, and see a model reconstruction of what the complex looked like. The Praetorium was the governor's palace in the first century BC, and was later used as the King's castle during medieval times. Rumor has it that the infamous hand-washer Pontius Pilate was born here. Ascend to the top of the tower for a view of the entire city.

The scattered **Fórum Romà,** with reconstructed Corinthian columns, lies near the post office on C. Lleida. All Roman cities had a forum, which the center of political, economic, and social life. The placement of this particular forum demonstrates the extent of the ancient city of Tarraco. To see what remains of the 2nd-century BC walls, stroll through the **Pg. Arqueològic.** The walls originally stretched to the sea and fortified the entire city.

OTHER SIGHTS

The **Pont del Diable (Devil's Bridge),** a Roman aqueduct 10min. outside of the city, is visible on the way in and out of town by bus. Take municipal bus #5 (every 20min., €1) from the corner of C. Christòfer Colom and Av. Prat de la Riba or from Pl. Imperial Tarraco. Lit by octagonal rose windows is the gigantic Romanesque-Gothic **cathedral,** founded in 1331 and one of the most magnificent cathedrals in Catalunya. The Cathedral's interior, fully restored in 1999, is filled with lavishly decorated altars, paintings, sculptures, and 16th-century tapestries, not to mention the tomb of Joan d'Aragó. The adjoining **Museu Diocesà** showcases religious relics from the last 700 years. (Entrance to both on C. Claustre, near Pl. La Seu. Open June to mid-Oct. M-Sa 10am-7pm; mid-Oct. to mid-Nov. M-Sa 10am-5pm; mid-Mar. to May M-Sa 10am-1pm and 4-7pm; mid-Nov. to mid-Mar. M-Sa 10am-2pm. €2.40, students €1.50.)

MUSEUMS

The worthwhile **Museu Nacional Arqueològic,** across Pl. Rei from the Praetorium, displays ancient architecture, utensils, statues, and mosaics, along with informative descriptions of daily life during the reign of the Roman Empire. (☎97 723 62 09. €2.40, students €1.20; includes admission to the Necropolis. Open June-Sept. Su and Tu-Sa 10am-8pm; Oct.-May Su and Tu-Sa 10am-1:30pm and 4-7pm.) The huge Christian burial site at the **Museu i Necròpolis Paleocristians,** Av. Ramón y Cajal, 78, has yielded a rich variety of urns, tombs, and sarcophagi, the best of which are in this relatively small museum. (☎97 721 11 75. €2.40, students €1.20; Tu free; includes admission to Museu Arqueològic. Open June-Sept. Su 10am-2pm, Tu-Sa 10am-8pm; Oct.-May Su 10am-2pm, Tu-Sa 10am-1:30pm and 4-7pm.) If you've had too much Roman roamin', descend the steps in front of the cathedral and take the third right onto C. Cavellares to visit the **Casa-Museu Castellarnau.** This Gothic-style house has belonged to some of the wealthiest families of Tarragona since the 15th century, including the Viscounts of Castellarnau in the 18th century. Don't miss the breathtaking ceiling painting in the main room. (☎97 724 22 20. €2, students €0.65. Open May-Sept. Su 9am-3pm, Tu-Sa 9am-9pm; Oct.-Apr. Su-Tu and Sa 9am-7pm.)

BEACHES

The hidden access to **Platja del Miracle,** the town's main beach, is along Baixada del Miracle, starting off Pl. Arce Ochotorena, beyond the Roman theater. Walk away from the theater until you reach the underpass, continue under the train tracks to the beach. The beach isn't quite as large or peaceful as other Costa Dorada stops, nor even the beaches of Barcelona—but it's as good as any for a few hours of sun and relaxation. About 1km farther are the larger beaches, **Platja l'Arrabassada,** with dirt-like sand, and the windy **Platja Llarga** (either walk or take bus #1 or #9 from Pl. Imperial Tarraco or any of the other stops, €1).

I'VE GOT THE TOWER

Imagine the last time you tried to lift a friend onto your shoulders. Now, imagine that person standing on your shoulders instead of sitting. But wait, somebody else is climbing on top of you, and another, and another...Shoulders hurt yet? With this in mind, consider in wonder Catalunya's *castellers*—the castle makers. The sport of creating *castells*—human towers (literally, "castles") is a popular competition in the province of Tarragona, usually performed at the most important town festivals in the main *plaça*.

Castell-making teams, called *colles*, wear a colorful traditional costume called the *xiquet*, consisting of white pants, a shirt of the team color, and a cloth belt, which serves as a foothold for teammates. Hundreds of people crowd together to form the foundation of the "castle," and the *colle* begins its grueling work. *Castells* vary in height, width, and degree of difficulty; the best teams can create up to nine stories of three to four people each, clinging tightly to each other's arms. The tower is topped off by a small girl or boy, called the *anxaneta* (weather vane), who fearlessly scrambles to the top, waves upon completion, and scrambles back down just as fast. Even trickier, the *castell* must then disassemble without collapsing into a jumble of tangled limbs.

NIGHTLIFE & ENTERTAINMENT

Weekend nightlife in Tarragona is on a much smaller scale than that of its northern neighbors, Sitges and Barcelona. Between 5 and 9pm, Las Ramblas Nova and Vella (and the area in between) are packed with strolling families. After 9pm, the bars start to liven up; around 10pm on Saturdays in summer, fireworks brighten the skies. The most popular place to be is **Port Esportiu,** a port-side plaza full of restaurant-bars and mini-discos. Heading up La Rambla Nova away from the beach, take a left onto C. Unió; bear left at Pl. General Prim and follow C. Apodaca to its end and cross the tracks.

From the middle of June to the middle of August, the **Festival de Verano** showcases a variety of theatre, music, and dance (☎97 724 47 95; 24hr. tickets 902 33 22 11). Pyromaniacs shouldn't miss the first week of July, when six major firework producers compete on the beach, each attempting to outshine its competitors in **El Concursi Internacional de Fuegos Artificiales.** In even-numbered years, the first Sunday in October brings the **Concurs de Castells,** an important regional competition featuring tall human towers, as high as seven to nine "stories," called *castells* (see **I've got the Tower,** p. 242). *Castells* also appear amid beasts and fireworks during the annual **Fiesta de Santa Tecla** on September 23, when people come from all over Spain to see nearly 300 musical, theatrical, traditional, and athletic street shows. If you're unable to catch the *castellers* in person, don't miss the impressive life-size bronze monument to the *castellers* on La Rambla Nova.

INLAND: MONTSERRAT

With its 1236m peak protruding from the flat Río Llobregat Valley and its colorful interplay of limestone, quartz, and slate stone, Montserrat (Sawed Mountain) has long inspired poets, artists, and travelers. The unique mountain formations of Montserrat are neither volcanic nor tectonic in origin. Instead, they are the result of millions of years of sedimentary deposits from ancient rivers that ran from the Mediterranean coast towards Montserrat. Montserrat's anthropological history, however, is a bit more ambiguous. As the story goes, in AD 888, a shepherd wandering the crags of Montserrat had a blinding vision of the Virgin Mary. His story spread, attracting pilgrims to the mountain in droves. In 1025 an opportunistic bishop-abbot named Oliba founded a monastery to worship the Virgin, who had become the spiritual patroness of Catalunya (see p. 244). Today, 80 Benedictine monks tend the building, most of which dates from the 19th century (although two wings of the original Gothic cloister survive). During the Catalan *Renaixença* of the early 20th century (see p. 40), politicians and artists like poets Joan Maragall and Jacint Verdaguer turned to Montserrat as a source of Catalan legend and tradition. In the Franco era the monastery became a center for Catalan resistance—Bibles were printed here in Catalan, and nationalist demonstrations were held on the mountain. Today, the site attracts devout worshipers and tourists who come to see the Virgin of Montserrat, her ornate basilica, the accompanying art museum, and last but certainly not least, the panoramic views of the mountain's awesome rock formations.

TRANSPORTATION

The R5 (Manesa-bound) line of the **FGC trains** (☎ 93 205 15 15) connects to Montserrat from M: Espanya in Barcelona (1hr., 1 per hr. 8:36am-5:36pm, round-trip including cremallera €11.80); get off the train at Montserrat Monistrol, not Montserrat Aeri or Montserrat Olesa. The last train for Barcelona leaves at 6:36pm. From Monistrol catch the **Cremallera de Montserrat,** a recently opened rack railway that offers spectacular views all the way up to the monastery. (☎ 90 231 20 20; www.cremalleradeMontserrat.com. Daily every 15min. 7:22am-9pm; round-trip including FGC train and cremallera €11.80; only round-trip cremallera €6, students and 65+ €5.40, ages 4-13 €3.30.) You can also take the **Aeri cable car** from Montserrat Aeri, although when you're purchasing tickets through the FGC you have to choose "Other Ticket Options" on the ticket machine for the Aeri combos. (☎ 93 877 77 01. March-Oct. daily every 15min. 9:25am-1:45pm and 2:20-6:45pm; round-trip including train ride and cable car €11.80; only round-trip Aeri cable car adult €4, children €2.10, groups over 20 €3.) Both cable car schedules change frequently; call the respective numbers for current times. **Autocars Julià** runs a daily bus to the monastery, from right near the Estació Sants train station in Barcelona. (Leaves daily 9:15am, June 25-Sept. 14 returns 6pm, rest of the year returns 5pm. Call ☎ 93 317 64 54 for reservations. €10. MC/V.) If you plan to use the funiculars at Montserrat to reach hiking paths, the **Tot Montserrat** is a good investment: available at tourist offices or in M: Espanya, it gets you round-trip tickets for the FGC train, the Cremallera or Aeri cable car, both mountaintop funiculars, entrance to the Museu de Montserrat and audiovisual display (see p. 245), and a meal at the *cafetería*, all for €34.50 (€20.50 if you buy it at Montserrat without the train fare included, or €20 without audiovisual, museum entrance, or lunch). If you miss the last cable car or bus down the mountain, call ☎ 93 835 03 84 or 60 732 99 46 for a **taxi,** open 24 hr.

PRACTICAL INFORMATION

Montserrat is not a town; it is a monastery with adjacent housing and food for pilgrims, both of the religious and camera-toting varieties. Most visitor services are in **Pl. Creu,** the area straight ahead from the cremallera station. The **info booth** in Pl. Creu provides free maps, schedules of daily religious services, accommodation listings, and advice on mountain navigation. (☎ 93 877 77 01; www.abadiaMontserrat.net. Open July-Sept. daily 8:50am-7:35pm; Oct.-June M-F 8:50am-5pm, Sa-Su 8:50am-7:35pm.) For more detailed information, buy the *Official Guide to Montserrat* (€7) or the official guide to the museum (€6.30). Other services in Pl. Creu include **currency exchange** with poor rates (open June-Sept. M-F 9:15am-2pm, Oct.-May Sa 9:15am-1:30pm), **ATMs, parking,** (located outside the Basilica; €3 per day, €4 for 3 days) and a **post office** (open M-F 10am-1:30pm, Sa 10am-noon). For an **ambulance** or the **mountain rescue team,** call ☎ 90 410 55 55.

Mary and Montserrat

The origins of the monastery of Montserrat are clouded in myth and mystery. Legend has it that toward the end of the 9th century a handful of shepherds witnessed what they could only describe as a miracle; a strange light and an equally inexplicable melody flooded the Montserrat area. When the same course of events took place a week later, area residents sent word to the local Bishop. When the Bishop arrived to legitimize the miracle, he discovered a small grotto with a wooden sculpture of the Virgin Mary. He ordered that the figure be removed and transported down into the valley. When his subordinates attempted to remove the relic, however, it became too heavy to lift. The Bishop quickly recognized Mary's sudden weight gain as a sign of God's will. He repealed his former orders and declared that the object be left in its God-given place. Subsequently, a Benedictine community sprang up and established a monastery on top of Montserrat.

Despite further research into this myth which proved it historically false, the figure, known as la Moreneta, still resides in the monastery and each year receives thousands of kisses and good-luck rubs from visitors.

ACCOMMODATIONS

For those who choose to spend the night at Montserrat, there aren't many options: choose from camping, an apartment in one of two different buildings, or a room in the three-star hotel. All but the campsite are wheelchair-accessible, and all prices listed include the IVA. For reservations (a must) for the apartments or hotel, contact the **Central de Reserves i Informació** (☎93 877 77 01; www.abadiaMontserrat.net). The apartment administration office, **Administració de les Celles,** is located in the corner of the *plaça.* (Open daily 9am-1pm and 2-6pm; after 6pm at the Hotel Abat Cisneros reception. 2-day min. stay, 7-day in July and Aug.)

Abat Marcet ❷, the newest building, has 94 apartments for one to four people, all with full bath, phone, TV, heat, a dining room, and a kitchen with microwave. (Singles €13-32; doubles €25-41, students €21-34.) **Abat Oliba ❶,** which is much older than Marcet, has rooms for two to seven people. (Doubles €24-27; quads €37-40; quints €46-51; sixers €56-60; sevens €62-67.) The **Hotel Abat Cisneros ❸,** next to the basilica, offers 56 spacious rooms that are more comfortable than the apartments. They also have a restaurant downstairs (Singles €27-75; doubles €45-138. Breakfast included.) The **campsite ❶** is a 5min. walk up the hill from the monastery level of the Sta. Cova funicular. (☎93 835 02 51. Open Apr.-Oct. Office open daily 10am-8:30pm. €2.70 per person, under 12 €2; €2.30 per tent. No fires allowed.)

FOOD

Food options on Montserrat remain limited and are all marked clearly on the free map available from the info counters. If you want to take food hiking with you, the tiny 2-aisle **Queviures supermarket** in Pl. Creu (open daily 9am-5:45pm), which is more of a convenience store than a supermarket, offers the best available selection of grocery goods, including fruit, utensils, yogurt, and cookies. Meat, cheese, candy, pastries, and souvenirs are available at **la Botiga.** (Open M-F 9am-7:40pm, Sa-Su 8:30am-8:15pm.) For quick, informal food, try the **Bar de la Pl. ❶,** next to the supermarket (bocadillos and hamburgers €2.75-3:30; open M-F 9:30am-5pm, Sa 9:30am-4:40pm), or the main **cafeteria ❶** right in front of the cremallera stop, with ample seating and a large selection of sandwiches and hot foods (most under €3.50; ice cream €2; open Apr.-Nov. M-F 9am-7:30pm, Sa-Su 9am-8pm; Dec.-

Mar. daily 9am-5pm; MC/V). For a larger lunch with a gorgeous panoramic view of the valley, the **self-service cafeteria ❷** (the included meal for *Tot Montserrat* card-holders but open to anyone for €9.50) is up the hill to the right of the cremallera stop. (Open Mar. 15-Nov. 15 M-F 9am-5pm, Sa-Su 9am-6pm. Wheelchair accessible. AmEx/MC/V.) Nearby is the scenic **Restaurant de Montserrat ❷**. (Menú €12.60, kids €5.75. Open Mar. 15-Nov. 15 M-F 9am-5pm, Sa-Su 9am-6pm. Wheelchair accessible. AmEx/MC/V.) Despite the price difference you'll get the same view from both, because they are in the same building. The **Restaurant Hotel Abat Cisneros ❺** has the most expensive menú (€23.60) in the nicest setting; an arched brick ceiling shelters the stone-walled, brightly lit dining room. (Entrees €13-23. Open daily 1-4pm and 8-10pm. Wheelchair accessible. AmEx/MC/V.)

SIGHTS

The **monastery** is the defining characteristic of Montserrat, and most other sights are somehow related to the monastery and/or the history of Catholicism. Above Pl. Creu, the entrance to the **basilica** (open daily 7:30am-9pm, office hours 9:30am-1pm and 4-6pm) looks out onto Pl. Santa Noría. Austere and somber in its dark, ornate glory, the basilica was consecrated in 1592. To the right of the main chapel, a route through the side chapels leads to the Romanesque **Cambril de la Mare de Déu** (the shrine of the Virgin) which encapsulates **La Moreneta** (the black Virgin Mary), Montserrat's venerated icon of Mary, the mother of Jesus. (Walkway open Nov.-June M-F 8-10:30am, noon-6:30pm, and 7:30-8:15pm, Sa-Su 8-10:30am and noon-6:30pm; July-Sept. daily 8-10:30am and noon-6:30pm.) Montserrat was built in order to give this miracle its proper home (see **Mary and Montserrat,** p. 244). However, the story of the Virgin Mary seems as "hole-y" as Spanish lace, as it was indeed removed from Montserrat; twice, as a matter of fact: once after the Napoleonic Wars and again during the Spanish Civil War. Moreover, carbon dating has revealed that la Moreneta was sculpted in the 12th century, not the 7th. But faith defies reason and the statue is now showcased in an elaborate silver case. If you can, schedule your visit so that you can hear the renowned **Escalonia Boys' Choir** sing *Salve Regina* in the basilica. (Su noon, M-Sa 1pm and 7pm; except July.)

Also in Pl. Santa María, the **Museu de Montserrat** exhibits a wide enough variety of art, including archaeology from the Biblical East, gold and silver work, and art by Dalí, El Greco, Monet, Renoir, and Picasso, including his *Sardana of Peace*, painted just for Montserrat, and *Old Fisherman*. The museum's Impressionist paintings deservedly steal the spotlight; Ramon Casas's famous *Madeline Absinthe* is one of many evocative portraits, and may make you think twice about indulging in the little green fairy. (informacio@larsa-Montserrat.com. Open July-Sept. M-F 10am-7:35pm, Sa-Su 9:30am-7:35pm; Nov.-June M-F 10am-6pm, Sa-Su 9:30am-6:30pm. €5.30, students and 65+ €4.50, ages 10-14 €3.50; combo ticket with Espai Audiovisual €6.50, students and 65+ €5.50, ages 10-14 €4.50.) The **Espai Audiovisual,** across from the Cremallera stop offers a brief CD-ROM and video summary of the life and organization of the Benedictine community of Montserrat, though the presentation is somewhat disorganized. (€2, students and 65+ €1.50. Same timetable as Museu de Montserrat.)

WALKS

A visit to Montserrat is not complete without a walk along the "mountain of a hundred peaks." Some of the most beautiful areas of the mountain are accessible only on foot. The **Santa Cova funicular** descends from Pl. Creu to paths that wind along the sides of the mountain to ancient hermitages. Take a walk to the **Santa Cova monastery,** an 18th-century chapel that used to house la Moreneta. (Apr.-Oct. daily every 20min. 10am-1pm and 2-5:45pm; Nov.-Mar. Sa-Su 10am-5pm. Round-trip €2.50, students and 65+ €2.30.) Take the **St. Joan funicular** for more inspirational views of Montserrat. (Apr.-Oct. daily every 20min. 10am-7:15pm; Nov.-Mar.

M-F 11am-6pm, Sa-Su 10am-6pm. Round-trip €6.10, students and 65+ €5.50; joint round-trip ticket with the Sta. Cova funicular €6.90, students and 65+ €6.20, ages 10-14 €3.50.) The dilapidated **St. Joan monastery** and **shrine** are only a 20min. walk from the highest station. But be forewarned; the "monastery" appears to have become the stomping grounds for late-night boozing and garbage dumping. The real prize is **Sant Jeróni** (the area's highest peak at 1236m), with its mystical views of Montserrat's rock formations. The enormous domes and serrated outcroppings resemble a variety of human forms, including "The Bewitched Friars" and "The Mummy." The hike is about 2½hr. from Pl. Creu or a 1hr. trek from the final stop of the St. Joan funicular. The paths are long and winding but not all that difficult—after all, they were made for guys wearing long robes. En route, make sure you take a sharp left after about 45min., when you come to the little old chapel—otherwise, you're headed straight for a helicopter pad. On a clear day the hike offers spectacular views of Barcelona and surrounding areas.

For **guided visits** and hikes, call ☎93 877 77 01 at least two weeks in advance. (Hiking tour in English €4, museum tour €4.50, joint tour €8. In Spanish, hiking and museum tour €4 each, joint tour €7.) For rock climbing and more athletic hiking in the area, call Marcel Millet at ☎93 835 02 51 or stop by his hiking/climbing office next to the Montserrat campsite.

CATALAN PYRENEES

RIPOLL

In the heart of Catalunya sits sleepy Ripoll (pop. 11,000), the region's strongest link to its proud history. Ripoll houses the 9th-century monastery started by Guifré el Pilós (Wilfred the Hairy; see p. 38), the founding father of Catalunya, as well as his tomb. The Monasterio de Santa Maria attracts visitors in search of Spain's Romanesque architectural legacy; its elaborately carved portal is one of the most famous in all of Spain. Ripoll also has convenient access to the convent in the nearby town of Sant Joan de las Abadesses.

TRANSPORTATION AND PRACTICAL INFO

Ripoll is more industrial than the other villages in Catalunya. When you first arrive, you might notice that the streets close to the train and bus stations are filled with large, intimidating trucks. The lack of official crosswalks can make the trek to the center of Ripoll a little nerve-racking, enough to make you wonder whether trucks or pedestrians have the right of way (officially it's pedestrians). Once you make it to Pl. Ajuntament, however, the traffic eases up. Watch out for cars, though, as drivers tend to speed through the narrow streets.

RENFE trains, Pl. Mova, 1 (☎97 270 06 44), run to Barcelona (1¾hr., 9-12 per day 6:32am-8:04pm, €5) and Puigcerdà (1hr., 6 per day 8:56am-8:54pm, €2.65). The bus station (separated from the train station by a small park) sends **TEISA buses** (☎97 220 48 68) to: Barcelona (4hr., 1 per day, €7.70, all bus fairs increase on weekends and holidays); Girona (2hr., 1 per day, €4.75); Sant Joan de las Abadesses (15min., 8-10 per day, €1.10). The **tourist office** gives out a free map of the city; look for the information symbol in the right corner of the open area next to the monastery on Pl. Abat Oliba (☎97 270 23 51. Open Su 10am-2pm and 4-7pm, M-Sa 9:30am-1:30pm and 4-7pm. Connect to the **Internet** at **Xarxtel,** Pl. d'Espanya, 10, a computer-electronics store. The **public library,** C. de les Vinyes, 6, offers free use of their computers. (Open M-Tu and Th-F 4-8:30pm, W 9am-1:30pm, Sa 10am-1:30pm.) In an **emergency** call ☎112 or the **police** at Pl. Ajuntament, 3 (☎97 271 44 14). The **post office,** C. d'Estació, faces the tree-lined park. (☎97 270 07 60. Open M-F 8:30am-2:30pm, Sa 9:30am-1pm.) **Postal code:** 17500.

ACCOMMODATIONS AND FOOD

Ripoll is an ambitious daytrip, and there are enough budget-friendly accommodations to warrant an overnight stay. The luxurious and friendly ■**Fonda La Paula ❷**, C. Berenguer, 4, on Pl. Abat Oliba, is alongside the tourist office. Cream-colored rooms combine with comfortable beds, TVs, and tiled bathrooms. (☎97 270 00 11. Singles €22; doubles €37; triples €51; quads €65. V.) Slightly more pricey is the **Hostal del Ripollès ❸**, Pl. Nova, 11. From the monastery's plaza, follow C. Sant Pere for two blocks. The hostal provides small but well-furnished rooms with TV, phone, and full bath. (☎97 270 02 15; www.elripolles.com/hostaldelripolles. Breakfast €3.65. Singles €30; doubles €48; triples €72. MC/V.) **La Trobada Hotel ❸**, Pg. de Honorat, 4, offers similar rooms in a convenient location, on the right as your approach the Pont d'Olot, the bridge between the train/bus stations and the center of town. (☎97 270 23 53. Singles €29; doubles €51; triples €58.)

Restaurants surround Pl. Gran. Follow C. Bisbe Morgades and take a right before the river on C. Mossen; the *plaça* is to the left. If you are looking for fancy Catalan fare, try ■**Reccapolis ❸**, Ctra. Sant Joan, 68, about a 15min. walk down Ctra. Sant Joan from Pl. Ajuntament. (☎97 270 21 06. Entrees €10-18. Open Su-Tu 1-4pm and 8:30-10:30pm, W 1-4pm, Th-Sa 1-4pm and 8:30-10:30pm. AmEx/MC/V.) At **La Piazzetta ❷**, Pl. Nova, 11 the ambience may be Catalan, but the food is Italian. The restaurant has same owners and location as the Hostal del Ripollès. (☎97 270 02 15. Pizzas €5-9, pasta €5.50-8. Open M-Sa 1-3:15pm and 8:15-11:30pm, Su 8:15-11:30pm. MC/V.) Stock up on **groceries** at the supermarket across from the bus station, **Champion,** C. Progress, 33-37. (☎97 270 26 32. Open M-Th 9am-9pm, F-Sa 9am-9:30pm, Su 10am-2pm. AmEx/MC/V.)

SIGHTS

Almost everyone who visits Ripoll comes to see the incredibly intricate 11th-century portal of the ■**Monasterio de Santa María.** To reach the monastery, take a left on C. Progrés from the train and bus stations, and follow it until it merges with C. Estació. Take the first left after the colorful modern statues onto Pont d'Olot, cross the river, and continue straight on C. Bisbe Morgades to the Pl. Ajuntament and Pl. Abat Oliba. (Church open daily 10am-1pm and 3-7pm; €2, with student ID€0.50, groups over 20 €1 per person. English brochure €1.)

Founded in AD 879 by Count Guifré el Pilós (Wilfred the Hairy), the Santa María monastery was once the most powerful in all of Catalunya. The arched doorway, nicknamed the "Stone Bible," is considered perhaps the finest piece of Romanesque architecture in all of Spain. It depicts scenes from the Old and New Testaments, as well as a hierarchy of the cosmos and a 12-month calendar. The panels around the door are representations of the 12 months, and the panels next to the arch depict the Exodus. After centuries of battering from the elements, the worn portal is now sheltered in a state-of-the-art climate-controlled glass enclosure.

Inside, you'll find the Romanesque basilica, which is very different from its original form due to extensive renovations. A number of tombs line the interior, the most famous of which lies to the left of the altar: Guifré el Pilós, Catalunya's beloved first count (see p. 38). He was killed in battle in AD 897, and his bones were regathered and honored here in the early 1980s.

Adjoining the church is a beautiful two-story Romanesque and Gothic **cloister**, with artifacts from the monastery dating back hundreds of years. The cloister sometimes hosts temporary exhibits. Next door to Santa Maria is the **Museu Etnogràfic de Ripoll,** which is undergoing extensive renovations but will reopen soon as a gallery for temporary cultural exhibits.

NEAR RIPOLL: SANT JOAN DE LAS ABADESSES

🔢 *TEISA buses in Ripoll or Sant Joan (☎97 274 02 95) connect Sant Joan to Ripoll (15min., 8-10 per day, €1.10), stopping next to the church. The helpful **tourist office**, Pl. l'Abadia, 9 (☎97 272 05 99), is next door to the monastery alongside a 15th-century cloister. Office open M-F 10am-2pm and 4-7pm.*

A visit to Sant Joan leaves you with a greater appreciation for a two aspects of modern existence that you might otherwise look down upon: both overpopulation and hedonism would have served the Catalans well at the end of the 19th century. After a costly but successful campaign to reconquer Catalunya from the Arabs, Wilfred the Hairy was faced with the problem that nobody was left alive in Central Catalunya. In a stroke of brilliance, Wilfred founded a convent at Sant Joan de las Abadesses (pop. 3700) in AD887. He made his daughter, Emma, head abbess. Wait, how is a celibate convent going to lead to repopulation? Good question. The answer came two hundred years later, when Augustines took the convent over and converted it to a monastery. Needless to say, the new inhabitants of San Joan proved to be much more capable of facilitating the miracle of life. Today the monastery contains a Romanesque **church** and adjoining **museum**, which proudly display religious art and artifacts from throughout Catalunya. (☎97 272 23 53. Open July-Aug. daily 10am-7pm; May-June and Sept. M-Sa 10am-2pm and 4-7pm; Mar.-Apr. and Oct. M-Sa 10am-2pm and 4-6pm; Nov.-Feb. M-F 10am-2pm, Sa 10am-2pm and 4-6pm. Museum and church €2.) The highlight of the candlelit church may be the haunting **Santíssim Misteri**, a 13th-century wooden sculpture depicting Christ's removal from the cross. On Christ's forehead is a piece of the Host that has been preserved for over 700 years. In addition to the 12th-century Romanesque church and the 15th-century Gothic cloister, the complex also includes an 18th-century Baroque **Chapel of the Virgin of Sorrow.**

PUIGCERDÀ

A challenging name for foreigners, Puigcerdà (pop.7000; Poo-chair-DAH) has become a popular town by virtue of its location in the picturesque mountains of the Cerdanya region. Puigcerdà's view of the valley is beautiful, and the town serves as a cheap base for hiking, biking, or skiing the surrounding hillsides. The town is perhaps best known for appearing in the 1993 *Guinness Book of World Records* for the world's longest *butifarra* (sausage), a Freudian nightmare measuring 5200m.

TRANSPORTATION

RENFE trains (☎97 288 01 65) run to: Barcelona (3hr., 6 per day, €7) and Ripoll (1¼hr., 6 per day, €2.60). **Alsina Graells buses** (☎97 335 00 20) run to Barcelona (3¼hr., 2-4 per day, €12) and La Seu d'Urgell (1hr., 6-7 per day, €4). Buses depart in front of the train station and from Pl. Barcelona. Purchase tickets on board. See the schedule in Bar Estació, to the right as soon as you walk into the train station. Taxis (☎97 288 00 11) wait on Pl. Cabrinetty. For **bike rental**, try **Sports Iris**, Av. de França, 16. (☎97 288 23 98. Bikes €9 per half day, €15 per day. MC/V.)

ORIENTATION & PRACTICAL INFORMATION

Puigcerdà's center is at the top of a hill. **Pl. Ajuntament,** located off the main *plaça,* is nicknamed *el balcón de Cerdanya* for its view of the valley and the less picturesque **train station** at the foot of the slope. It's best to get off buses at Pl. Barcelona, not at the train station. To reach Pl. Ajuntament from the train station, walk straight out of the station about 100 ft. and ascend the first set of stairs you see. In front of you you'll see a small building, which is the entrance to a small inclined elevator (free) that goes up and down the side of the hill every few minutes. At the top, walk out and you can either take one of the stairways in front of you up to Pl. Ajuntament or take another elevator located underneath a rock enclosure to your left. Once at Pl. Ajuntament, walk one block on C. Alfons I to **C. Major,** the principal commercial street. Turn left on C. Major to Pl. Santa Maria. From Pl. Santa Maria, with your back to the bell tower, walk diagonally to the left to Pl. Barcelona.

The **tourist office,** C. Querol, 1, has a helpful town map. To get there, take a right off Pl. Ajuntament with your back to the view. They have an English-proficient staff that gives out various maps, skiing info, and lodging listings. (☎97 288 05 42; www.puigcerda.com. Open M 9am-1pm, Tu-F 10am-1pm and 4-7pm, Sa 10am-1:30pm and 4:30-8pm, holidays 10am-2pm). **Banco Central Hispano** is on

Pl. Cabrinetty. (Open Oct.-Mar. M-F 8:30am-2pm, Sa 8:30am-1pm; closed Sa Apr.-Sept.) Other services include: **emergency** (☎091 or 092); **municipal police,** Pl. Ajuntament, 1 (☎97 288 19 72); and the **Centre Hospitalari** (☎97 288 01 50 or 97 288 01 54), in Pl. Santa Mar. You can get on the **Internet** at the **library,** Biblioteca Comtat de Cerdanya on Pg. 10 d'Abril (☎97 288 03 04. €1.20 per hr. Open M, W, and F 3:30-8:30pm, T, Th and Sa 10am-1:30pm). You can also log on at **Punt com,** C. Espanya, 10. (☎97 288 31 55. €1.20 per 30min. Open daily 10am-1pm and 4-8pm.) The **post office,** Av. Coronel Molera, 11, is off Pl. Barcelona on the left after a block and a half. (☎97 288 08 14. Open M-F 8:30am-2:30pm, Sa 9:30am-1pm.) **Postal code:** 17520.

ACCOMMODATIONS, CAMPING & FOOD

Rooms in Puigcerdà come easily, if not relatively cheaply. Most less-expensive pensiones are off Pl. Santa María in the old town. Try the inexpensive **Hostal Muntanya ❷,** C. Coronel Molera, 1. Muntanya offers basic, well-kept rooms and a friendly, helpful staff. From Pl. Barcelona head down C. Coronel Molera; it's on the left. (☎97 288 02 02. Singles €19; doubles €38; triples €57. Breakfast €3.) **Alfonso Habitaciones ❷,** C. Espanya, 5, offers decent, dimly-lit rooms with TVs, bathrooms, and colorful bedspreads. Heading away from the church, take a left off C. Alfons I (☎97 288 02 46. Singles €30; doubles €42. Cash only). If you're looking for something a bit nicer, try the three-star **Avet Blau Hotel ❺,** Pl. Santa Maria, 14 (right next to the bell tower) which has six spacious and comfortable doubles. You can even bring your dog, provided you don't leave it alone in the room. (☎97 288 25 52; fax 97 288 12 12. Rates vary by season, from €71 to €97. Reservations recommended.) If you're planning to ski in La Molina, try **Mare de Déu de les Neus (HI) ❶,** on Ctra. Font Canaleta, which has modern facilities and an excellent location just 500m from the La Molina RENFE station and 4km from the slopes. In winter a bus goes up to the slopes every 30min. (☎97 289 20 12; reservations ☎93 483 83 63. Breakfast included. Sheets €2. Reserve in high season. Jan.-Nov. dorms €15, over 25 €20. Dec. dorms €17/€22. Doubles and triples available, same price per person. MC/V.) **Camping Stel ❷,** 1km from Puigcerdà on the road to Llivia, offers full-ser-

Kerresetcaps

Do you believe in monsters? A trip to Puigcerdà may make you change your mind. In the middle of the 18th century, a father and son ventured into the forest to chop firewood. Leaving the boy alone to search for timber, the father suddenly heard screams and giggles. He ran back only to catch a glimpse of his son disappearing into the forest in the arms of a hideous seven-headed monster. Surprisingly, the boy returned home a few hours later completely unscathed, claiming the beast was very friendly. But the father ignored the son's story and gathered villagers to hunt the monster. After its capture, the beast snarled and resisted all the way back to town, where he was caged in the Pl. Mayor.

Those who dared approach the beast, dubbed *Kerresetcaps* (seven heads), were met with growls, making the boy's story of his kindness difficult to swallow. However, during the next festival, the boy went to visit his monstrous friend, amazing the villagers as all seven heads smiled in welcome. Other children soon followed suit, becoming friends with the beast. Eventually, they broke the cage lock in the dead of night and set their beloved monster free. The story is told today to remind adults to respect the innocence of youth.

vice camping with the benefits of a chalet-style restaurant, bar, and lounge. (☎97 288 23 61. Site with tent and car €20, plus €5 per person. 220V electricity for €3. Open Sa-Su only June-Sept. and Oct. 27-May 1).

The neighborhood off C. Alfons I is has many food options. For fresh produce, try the weekly **market** at Pl. 10 d'Abril. (Su 6am-2pm.) Get **groceries** at **Bonpreu,** C. Colonel Molera, 12, the small supermarket diagonally across from the post office. (Open Su 10am-2pm, M-Th 9am-1:30pm and 5-9pm, F-Sa 9am-9pm. MC/V.) At **◼Cantina Restaurant Mexicà ❷**, Pl. Cabrinetty, 9, you can kick back with a margarita and take in some excellent and relatively authentic Mexican tacos, fajitas, and quesadillas. (☎97 288 16 58. Entrees €4-15. Open Su-W and F-Sa 1:30-3:30pm and 8:30-11:30pm.) **El Pati de la Tieta ❷**, C. dels Ferrers, 20, serves large portions of pasta and pizzas (€6-10) and heavenly desserts on an ivy-covered patio. (☎97 288 01 56. Fish and meat entrees €11.50-17. Open daily 1-3:30pm and 8-11:30pm. MC/V.)

SIGHTS & OUTDOOR ACTIVITIES

Between ski runs and cycling, dash over to the **campanario,** the octagonal bell tower in Pl. Santa Maria. This 35m high 14th-century bell tower is all that remains of the **Església de Santa María,** an eerie reminder of the destruction wreaked by the Civil War. Climb to the top for a 360-degree view of Puigcerdà and the Pyrenees. (Open July-Aug. M-F noon-2pm and 5-8pm, Sa-Su 11am-noon and 5-8pm. Free.) The 13th-century **Església de Sant Domènec,** on Pg. 10 d'Abril, contains diaphragmatic arches and several Gothic paintings considered to be among the best of their genre. (Open 9:30am-8pm. Free.) Puigcerdà's picturesque **Lake Estany,** a 2min. walk up C. Pons i Gasch from Pl. Barcelona, was created in 1380 for irrigation purposes. It now serves the town well as a lovely place to rent a boat. (€2 per person per 30min.; inquire at the cafe.)

Puigcerdà calls itself the "capital of snow." **Ski** in your country of choice (Spain, France, or Andorra) at one of 19 ski areas within a 50km radius. The closest and cheapest one on the Spanish side is **La Molina.** (☎97 289 20 31; www.lamolina.com.) Nearby **Masella** (☎97 214 40 00; www.masella.com) offers the longest run (7km) in the Pyrenees. For cross-country (nordic) skiing, the closest site is **Guils-Fontanera** (☎97 219 70 87). A little farther out, try **Lles** (☎97 329 30 49) or **Aranser** (☎97 329 30 51). For ski rentals, check out **Esports Tubosa,** Av. Del Segre, 2 (☎97 288 03 93), **Neosurf Cerdanya,** Av. Catalunya, 35 (☎60 843 17 64), **Top-Bikes,** Carrer de l'Estacio (☎97 288 20 42), or **Sports Iris,** Av. De Franca (☎97 288 23 98). The Puigcerdà area is also popular for **biking;** the tourist office has a brochure with 17 potential routes mapped out. You can rent a bike at both Top-Bikes and Sports Iris. La Molina opens trails up for biking in the summer months, and provides rentals for €12.62 per day. You can also navigate the trails on horseback for €12 per hr. For indoor sports, the **Club Poliesportiu Puigcerdà,** on Av. del Poliesportiu, has a pool, tennis courts, basketball courts, and a skating rink. (☎97 288 02 43. Open M-F 11am-10pm, Sa 11am-9:30pm, Su 11am-8pm. €6 per day.)

NIGHTLIFE & FESTIVALS

While Puigcerdà is not known for its nightlife, cafes and bars crowd the *plaças*, particularly the adjacent Pl. Santa María and Pl. Herois. **Bar Miami** (☎97 288 00 13) and **Kennedy** (☎97 288 11 91) sit next to each other on Pl. Herois and have popular outdoor patios perfect for people-watching both day and night. **Central,** Pl. Santa Maria, 6 (☎62 749 23 15), is a hip bar with eclectic and cozy furniture.

Puigcerdà hosts several festivals throughout the year, including the popular **Festival de Música Clásica** during the last two weeks of July, the **Festa de L'Estany** (Festival of the Lake), with grand fireworks displays at the end of August, and at Easter, the **Antic Puigcerdà,** the town's biggest market and fair.

ISLAS BALEARES MALLORCA, MENORCA & IBIZA

GETTING THERE

Flying to the islands is cheaper and faster than a ferry. Those under 26 can receive discounts from **Iberia/Aviaco Airlines** (☎ 90 240 05 00 in Barcelona). **SOM** (Servicios de Ocio Marítimo; ☎ 97 131 03 99) lines up bus companies, ferry lines, and *discotecas* for packages designed for disco fiends who seek an all-night party but have no use for lodging. Book through a travel agency in Barcelona or on any of the islands.

Beachbums

BY PLANE

Scheduled flights are the easiest to book, and flights from Spain to any of the islands won't break the bank. Frequent flights soar from cities throughout Spain and Europe (including Frankfurt, London, and Paris). Many daily **Iberia** flights (☎ 90 240 05 00) connect Palma and Ibiza to Barcelona, Madrid, and Valencia. Service from Alicante and Bilbao also exists, but is less frequent. Iberia offers **student fares** (with an ISIC) on flights from Barcelona (40min., €60-120) and Madrid (1hr., €150-180). **Air Europa** (☎ 90 224 00 42) and **Spanair** (☎ 90 213 14 15) also offer inexpensive flights to the islands. Schedules and prices are subject to change.

BY BOAT

Ferry service is considerably less expensive than flights, but longer in duration. On-board discos and small swimming pools on some boats ease the longer ride. Ferries run from Barcelona and Valencia to Palma (on Mallorca) and Ibiza City (Eivissa, on Ibiza); ferries also run from Dénia (in Alicante) to Ibiza. Seats may be available up to an hour before departure, but it's best to reserve tickets a few days in advance.

Summertime Frollicking

Buquebus (☎ 90 241 42 42 or 93 481 73 60) has super-fast catamaran service between **Barcelona** and **Palma** (4hr.; 2 per day; €49, cars €112).

Trasmediterránea (☎ 90 245 46 45; www.trasmediterranea.com) boats depart daily from Barcelona's Estació Marítima Moll and Valencia's Estació Marítima to **Mallorca, Menorca,** and **Ibiza.** Fares from the mainland to the islands are €43 slowpoke, €58 fast boat. Fares between the islands range from €23 slow to €37 fast.

Bikini Watcher

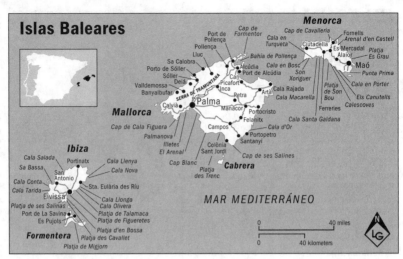

Islas Baleares

Umafisa Lines (☎ 90 219 10 68 or 97 131 02 01) has service between **Barcelona** and **Ibiza** 3 times per week. €47.10, some economy tickets available for €38.

TRANSPORTATION

INTER-ISLAND TRANSPORT

Iberia flies between Palma and Ibiza (45min., 5 per day, €54-80) and between Palma and Mahón, Menorca (35min., 4 per day, from €54). **Air Europa** (☎ 90 224 00 42) and **Spanair** (☎ 90 213 14 15) connect the islands at similar prices. However, flying isn't necessarily the best way to go.

A cheaper option is to take the **ferry.** Prices and times change with the wind; consult the tourist office or a travel agent. **Trasmediterránea** (☎ 90 245 46 45) sails between Palma and Mahón (6½hr., Su only, €23) and between Palma and Ibiza. (Fast 2½hr.; 1 per day at 7am from Palma, 7:45am from Ibiza; €37. Slow 4½hr., 3 per week, €23.) There is no direct Mahón-Ibiza connection. **Trasmapi** (☎ 97 131 20 71) links Ibiza and Formentera (fast ferry 25min., 12 per day). **Umafisa Lines** (☎ 97 131 45 13) runs car ferries on the same route. **Iscomar Ferries** (☎ 90 211 91 28) run between Menorca's Port de Ciutadella and Mallorca's Port d'Alcúdia for daytrips.

INTRA-ISLAND TRANSPORT

The three major islands have extensive **bus** systems, although transportation nearly comes to a halt Sundays in most locations, so check schedules. Mallorca has two narrow-gauge **train** systems that are more of a tourist attraction than a major mode of transportation. Intra-island travel is reasonably priced—bus fares between cities range €1.20-6 each way. While it's possible to visit any of the islands without renting a vehicle, a car or moped is a great way (if you can afford to rent one) to explore remote areas not accessible by bus. On Formentera, bicycles are a great way to get around. A tiny, standard transmission **car** costs around €36 per day including insurance. **Mopeds** are around €18, and **bicycles** a mere €6-10. Prices drop in low season and for long-term rentals.

MALLORCA

Mallorca has long attracted the rich and famous. The site of the scandalous honeymoon of Polish pianist Frédéric Chopin and French novelist George Sand, Mallorca is also the choice vacation spot for Spain's royal family. Although the coastline has been sacrificed to developers, even the most jaded travelers sigh at the sprawling expanses of sea, sand, and rock.

PALMA

A stroll along the streets of Palma (pop. 323,000) can be a dizzying, but at the same time thoroughly satisfying, experience. Wander through the expansive maze of twisting lanes in the old quarter and you seem to forget that you are on an island. After a visit to the various department and designer stores near Pl. d'Espanya, it becomes hard to imagine that the city was once a devotional retreat for Fernando and Isabel. Nevertheless, despite the fairly recent foreign invasion and growth as a major urban center, Palma still retains a genuinely local flavor. In its many cafes and traditional *tapas* bars, where the native dialect of *mallorquí* is the only language heard, it becomes quite clear why Palma reigns as the cultural capital of the Balearics.

TRANSPORTATION

Flights: Aeroport Son San Juan (☎97 178 90 00), 8km from downtown Palma. Bus #1 runs between the airport and the port, stopping along the way in Pl. d'Espanya (every 15min. 6am-2:30am, €1.80). **Iberia** (☎90 240 05 00), **Air Europa** (☎90 224 00 42), foreign carriers, and a host of charter operators all offer service to Palma. See **By Plane,** p. 251, or **Inter-Island Transport,** p. 252.

Ferries: Trasmediterránea, Estació Marítima, 2 (☎902 45 46 45). Ferries dock at Moll Pelaires south of the city. Bus #1 goes along Pg. Marítim/Av. Gabriel Roca. Tickets sold M-F 9am-1pm and 5-7pm, Sa 9am-noon. Tickets and info also available at travel agencies. Daily ferries to Barcelona, Ibiza, and Valencia. **Balearia** (☎902 16 01 80) sends ferries to Dénia. See **By Boat,** p. 251, or **Transportation,** p. 252.

Trains: Ferrocarril de Sóller (☎97 175 20 51), Pl. d'Espanya. Runs to **Sóller** (1hr., 5 per day 8am-7pm, €2.40). Avoid the 10:40am "tourist train," when prices inflate to €4.80. **Servicios Ferroviarios de Mallorca (SFM),** Pl. d'Espanya, 6 (☎97 175 22 45), departs to **Inca** (35min., 22 per day 5:45am-10pm, €1.80).

Buses: Bus travel to and from Palma is not too difficult, but travel between most other areas is inefficient and restrictive. Nearly all buses stop at the main stop on C. Eusebi Estada, several blocks down from Pl. d'Espanya; buy tickets on the bus. The tourist office has a detailed schedule of all buses. Some of the more popular destinations include: **Alcúdia** and **Port d'Alcúdia** (1hr.; M-F 16 per day 8am-9pm, Sa-Su 5 per day 9:30am-9pm; €4); **Covetes/Es Trenc** (M-F 3 per day 10am-5pm, Sa-Su 1 per day 10:30am; €3.84); **Coves del Drac** (1hr., M-F 4 per day 10am-1:30pm, Sa-Su 1 per day 10am; €6.35); **Port Pollenca** (1hr.; M-F 5 per day 9am-7:15pm, Sa 3 per day 11:30am-6pm, Su 2 per day 10am, 8:30pm; €4.60); **Sóller** and **Port de Sóller** (45min.; M-F every hr. 8:30am-8:30pm, Sa 3 per day 10:30am-7:30pm, Su 3 per day 9am-5:30pm; €2.20); **Valldemossa** (30min.; M-F every 2hr. 7:30am-7pm; Sa 2 per day 11:30am, 3:30pm; Su 2 per day 10:30am, 12:30pm; €1.10-2.20).

Public Transportation: Empresa Municipal de Transportes (EMT; ☎971 75 22 45). Pl. d'Espanya is the hub. Stops around town and as far as Palma Nova and Arenal. €1, 10 tickets €9. Buy tickets on board. Buses run approx. 6am-10pm. The airport bus, #1, runs until 2am (€1.80).

Taxis: (☎97 175 54 40). Airport fare from center of town approx. €15. From the old town to Estació Marítima, €8-10.

Car Rental: Mascaro Crespi, Av. Joan Miró, 9 (☎97 173 61 03). €30 per day with insurance. Open M-Sa 8am-1pm and 3-7pm, Su 9am-1pm and 5-7pm.

Hiking in the Countryside

Fountain

Topless Women Smoking Cigarettes

ORIENTATION & PRACTICAL INFORMATION

To get to town from the airport, take bus #1 to **Pl. d'Espanya** (15min., every 20min., €1.80). From the dock, take Pg. Marítim/Av. Gabriel Roca, or bus #1 to Av. d'Antoni Maura, which leads to **Pl. Reina** and **Pg. des Born.** From the sea, Pg. des Born leads to **Pl. Rei Joan Carles I,** the center of the old town, and **Av. Rei Jaume III,** the business artery. To the right, C. de la Unió leads (after some stairs) to **Pl. Major,** the center of Palma's pedestrian shopping district.

Tourist Offices: Palma branch, C. Sant Dominic, 11 (☎97 172 40 90). The office is at the bottom of a stairway, below street level. Open M-F 9am-8pm, Sa 9am-1:30pm. **Info booth** in Pl. d'Espanya. **Island tourist office,** Pl. Reina, 2 (☎97 171 22 16). Open M-F 9am-8pm, Sa 10am-2pm.

Budget Travel: TIVE, C. Jeróni Antic, 5 (☎97 171 17 85). ISIC cards, HI cards, Interrail tickets, and mainland flights. Not for inter-island travel or charters. Open M-F 9am-2pm and 5-7:30pm.

Currency Exchange: Santander Central Hispano, Pg. des Born, 17 (☎97 172 51 46). Open May-Sept. M-F 8:30am-2:30pm; Oct.-Apr. M-F 8:30am-2:30pm, Sa 8:30am-1pm.

El Corte Inglés: Av. Rei Jaume III, 15 (☎97 177 01 77) and Av. Alexandre Roselló, 12-16. Both open M-Sa 9:30am-9:30pm.

Laundromat: Coronet Lavandería, corner of C. Annibal and C. Argentina. A block from Hostal Cuba. €9 for 5kg. Open M-Sa 8am-1pm.

Bike Rental: Rent a Bike Palma, C. del Mar, 10 (☎97 171 81 58). Bicycles €3 for first hr., €1.10 per subsequent hr., €9 per day. Inline skates €2.50/€1/€8. Open M-F 10am-10:30pm, Sa 10am-10pm, Su noon-10pm.

Emergency: ☎112. **Police:** Av. Sant Ferrà (☎091 or 092).

Medical Services: Clínica Juaneda, C. Son Espanyolet, 55 (☎97 173 16 47), and **Femenía,** Av. Camilo José Cela, 20 (☎97 145 23 23). **Clínica Rotger,** C. Santiago Rusiñol, 9 (☎97 144 85 00), is more centrally located. All open 24hr.

Internet Access: Xpace, C. Sant Gaieta, 4D (☎97 172 92 19). €2.50 per hr., €6 for 4 hr. Sign up a friend and get 1 free hr. Open M-Sa 9am-1am, Su 2pm-1am. **Cyber Central,** C. Soletat, 4 (☎97 171 29 27). €2.50 per hr., €1 for 20min. Open M-F 9:30am-10:30pm, Sa 10am-10pm, Su noon-10pm.

Post Office: C. de la Constitució, 5 (☎90 219 71 97). Parcels upstairs. **Fax** service. Open M-F 8:30am-8:30pm, Sa 9:30am-2pm.

Postal Code: 07080.

ACCOMMODATIONS

This resort town has few hostels or bargains. Call in advance for summer stays.

Hostal Cuba, C. Sant Magí, 1 (☎97 173 81 59), at C. Argentina. From Pl. Rei Joan Carles I, turn left and walk down Av. Jaume III, cross the river, and turn left on C. Argentina. Spotless rooms with high ceilings, modern baths, and pretty wood furniture. Second-floor rooms are cushier than first-floor rooms. Singles €20; doubles €36. ❷

Hostal Ritzi, C. Apuntadors, 6 (☎97 171 46 10), conveniently situated above "Big Byte" cybercafe. Centrally located *hostal* with rooms overlooking an interior patio that can get noisy at night. Rooms have a funky, old-fashioned feel with nifty metal light fixtures and lace curtains. Laundry €7. Singles €25; doubles €35, with bath €38-49. ❷

Alberg Platja de Palma (HI), C. Costa Brava, 13 (☎971 26 08 92), in El Arenal. Take bus #15 from Pl. d'Espanya or Pl. Reina (every 8min., €1) and get off at C. Costa Brava, about 45min. from city center. Four-person dorms with shower. HI card required. Breakfast included. Sheets €2.50. Laundry €6. 24hr. reception. Dorms €9-12, 27+ €10.20-14. ❶

Hostal Bonany, C. Almirante Cervera, 5 (☎97 173 79 24), in a wealthy residential area 3km from the town center. Take bus #3, 20, 21, or 22 from Pl. d'Espanya to Av. Joan Miró and walk up C. Camilo José Cela. Take the first right, then the first left. Feels more like a hotel than a hostel: large swimming pool, comfy sitting room, and clean, spacious rooms with bath and balcony. Breakfast €3. Singles €26; doubles €40. ❸

FOOD

Palma's multi-ethnic restaurants are paradise for those sick of *tapas*. Pricey but popular outdoor restaurants fill **Pl. Mayor** and **Pl. Llotja,** but budget eaters head to the side streets off **Pg. del Born,** to the cheap digs along **Av. Joan Miró,** or to the pizzerias along **Pg. Marítim.** Make sure to try the *ensaimadas* (pastries smothered in powdered sugar) and the *sopa mallorquina* (a pizza-like snack of stewed vegetables over brown bread). Two **markets** vie for customers: one, Mercat de l'Olivar, is in Pl. Olivar off C. Padre Atanasio, and the other, Mercat Santa Catalina, is across town at the corner of C. Pou and C. Dameto. For **groceries,** try **Servicio y Precios** on C. Felip Bauza, near C. Apuntadors and Pl. Reina (☎90 070 30 70; open M-F 8:30am-8:30pm, Sa 9am-2pm), or the supermarket downstairs in either **El Corte Inglés** (see **Orientation & Practical Information**).

Strolling in the Park

Residences

Waiting for the Bus

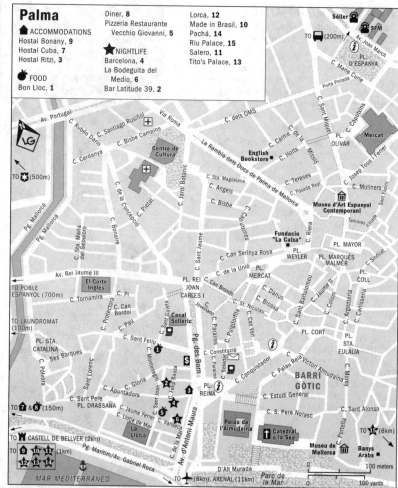

Palma

🏠 ACCOMMODATIONS
Hostal Bonany, **9**
Hostal Cuba, **7**
Hostal Ritzi, **3**

🍴 FOOD
Bon Lloc, **1**

Diner, **8**
Pizzeria Restaurante
Vecchio Giovanni, **5**

⭐ NIGHTLIFE
Barcelona, **4**
La Bodeguita del
Medio, **6**
Bar Latitude 39, **2**

Lorca, **12**
Made in Brasil, **10**
Pachá, **14**
Riu Palace, **15**
Salero, **11**
Tito's Palace, **13**

Diner, C. Sant Magí, 23 (☎97 173 62 20), down the street from Hostal Cuba. American-style favorites served in a fun, kitschy, classic diner setting. Delicious, affordable menu includes burgers (€3-5), hot dogs and grilled cheese sandwiches (€3.50), tuna melt (€5), ribs (€6.50), and more. Open 24hr. ❶

Bon Lloc, C. Sant Feliu, 7 (☎97 171 86 17). Ultra-hip vegetarian restaurant. Menu features salads (€5.70), falafel (€7.20), and dishes like basmati rice with Chinese-style sauteed vegetables (€9.60). Midday menú €10. Open M-Th 1-4pm, F-Sa 1-4pm and 8:30-11:30pm. MC/V. ❷

Pizzeria Restaurante Vecchio Giovanni, C. Sant Joan, 3 (☎97 172 28 79). Lively family restaurant with excellent pizzas (€7-9) and pastas (€6-12). Don't be fooled by the touristy facade; the food is great. Gets crowded for dinner, especially on weekends. Open daily noon-3:30pm and 6:30pm-midnight. ❷

SIGHTS & MUSEUMS

Palma's architecture is a medley of Arabic, Christian, and Modernist styles: a reflection of the island's multicultural past and present. Many of its landmarks are nestled amidst the narrow streets of the *Barri Gòtic* (Gothic quarter).

■ CATEDRAL (LA SEU)

∄ *C. Palau Reial, 29. ☎ 97 172 31 30. Cathedral and museum open Apr.-Oct. M-F 10am-6pm, Sa 10am-2pm; Nov.-Mar. M-F 10am-3pm. €3.50.*

This Gothic giant towers over Palma and the bay. The cathedral, dedicated to Palma's patron saint San Sebastián, was begun in the 1300s, finished in 1601, and then modified by Gaudí in Modernista fashion in 1909. Now the interior and the ceiling ornamentation blend smoothly with the stately exterior. Its southern facade, perhaps the most impressive, overlooks a reflective pool and the ocean.

■ PALAU DE L'ALMUDAINA

∄ *C. Palau Reial, just off Pl. Reina. ☎ 97 121 41 34. Open Apr.-Sept. M-F 10am-6:30pm; Oct.-Mar. M-F 10am-2pm and 4-6pm, Sa 10am-2pm. Guided visits €4, unguided €3.20. Students and children €2.25. EU citizens free on W.*

Built by the Moors, this imposing austere palace was at one point a stronghold of los Reyes Católicos, Fernando and Isabel. Guided tours, which pass through the museum, are given in numerous languages, including English, French, and German. The pleasant garden off Pl. Reina directly in front of the palace also merits a visit.

CASTELL DE BELLVER

∄ *Bus #3, 21, or 22 from Pl. d'Espanya. ☎ 97 173 06 57. Open Apr.-Sept. M-Sa 8am-8:30pm, Su 10am-5pm; Oct.-Mar. M-Sa 8am-7:15pm, Su 10am-5pm. €1.75.*

Overlooking the city and bay, Castell de Bellver was a summer residence for 14th-century royalty; it also housed Mallorca's most distinguished prisoners. The castle contains a slightly-boring municipal museum which houses models of archaeological sites.

MUSEU D'ART ESPANYOL CONTEMPORANI

∄ *C. Sant Miquel, 11. ☎ 97 171 35 15. Open M-F 10am-6:30pm, Sa 10am-1:30pm. €3.*

Now part of the Fundació Joan March, this mansion-turned-museum displays works of the 20th century's most iconic Spanish artists—Picasso, Dalí, Miró, Juan Gris, and Antoni Tápies.

OTHER MUSEUMS

Inaugurated in December 1992, the **Fundació Pilar i Joan Miró** displays the works from Miró's Palma studio at the time of his death. (C. Saridakis, 29. From Pl. d'Espanya, take bus #3, 21, or 22 to Av. Joan Miró. ☎ 97 170 14 20. Open May 16-Sept. 14 Tu-Sa 10am-7pm, Su 10am-3pm; Sept. 15-May 15 Tu-Sa 10am-6pm, Su 10am-3pm. €4.40.) **Fundació "la Caixa"** hosts a collection of Modernist paintings in Domènech i Muntaner's Modernist Gran Hotel. (Pl. Weyler, 3. ☎ 97 117 85 00. Open Tu-Sa 10am-9pm, Su 10am-2pm. Free.) The **Casal Solleric** houses modern art. (Pg. del Born, 27. ☎ 97 172 20 92. Open Tu-Sa 10:30am-1:45pm, Su 10am-1:45pm. Free.) **Centre de Cultura "Sa Nostra"** features rotating exhibits and cultural events such as lectures, concerts, and movies. Swing by for a schedule of upcoming events. (C. de la Concepció, 12. ☎ 97 172 52 10. Open Tu-F 10:30am-9pm, Sa 10am-1:30pm.) The **Museu de Mallorca** is ideal for travelers interested in archaeology or medieval painting. (C. Portella, 5. ☎ 97 171 75 40. Open Tu-Sa 10am-7pm, Su 10am-2pm. €2.40.) For those fed up with being inside, there's the **Poble Espanyol,** a small village with replicas of famous Spanish architecture and traditional handicrafts. (C. Poble Espanyol, 39. Buses #4 and 5 pass on Av. Andrea Doria. ☎ 971 73 70 75. Open daily Apr.-Nov. 9am-8pm; Dec.-Mar. 9am-6pm. Shops closed Sa afternoon and Su. €5.)

BEACHES

Mallorca is a huge island, and many of the best beaches are a haul from Palma. Still, several picturesque (though touristy) stretches of sand are accessible by city bus. The beach at **El Arenal** (Platja de Palma, bus #15), 11km to the southeast (toward the airport), is the prime stomping ground of Mallorca's most sunburnt German tourists. The waterfront area is full of German signs for restaurants, bars, and hotels—think *Frankfurt am Mediterranean*. Other beaches close to Palma include **Palma Nova** (bus #21), 15km southwest, and **Illetes** (bus #3), 9km southwest, which are smaller than El Arenal, but equally popular. The tourist office distributes a list of 40 nearby beaches—take your pick and remember to say *danke*.

NIGHTLIFE & ENTERTAINMENT

In the past, Pl. Reina and Pl. Llotja were the place for bar-hoppers, but a recent law requiring downtown bars to close by 3am has shifted the action to the waterfront. Nevertheless, many partiers still start in the *casco viejo*. **La Bodeguita del Medio,** C. Vallseca, 18, plays Cuban rhythms and serves tasty *mojitos*. (Mixed drinks €5. Open Th-Sa 8pm-3am, Su-W 8pm-1am.) Follow the Aussies to **Bar Latitude 39,** C. Felip Bauza, 8, a "yachtie" bar. (Beer €1.50. "Twofer nights"—2 for the price of 1—Tu, Th, and Sa 9-10pm. Open M-Sa 7pm-3am.) **Barcelona,** C. Apuntadors, 5, a small, dark bar with lots of atmosphere, jams with live music from midnight to 3am. (Cover €1.80 for live concerts. Open Su-Th 8:30pm-1am, F-Sa 8:30pm-3am.)

Palma's clubbers start the night in the *bares-musicales* on the **Pg. Marítim/Av. Gabriel Roca** strip which runs along the water from Av. d'Antoni Maura to the ferry station. Each mini-disco plays different tunes, but Spanish pop dominates. Come 2am, disco-goers head to the salsa-happy **Made in Brasil,** Pg. Marítim, 27 (mixed drinks €3.60-4.80; open daily 8pm-4am) or dance-crazy **Salero,** Pg. Marítim, 31 (open daily 8pm-6am). These bars are about a 20min. walk from Pl. Reina, or you can hop on bus #1 from Pl. d'Espanya. (Bus service stops at 2:30am.) Nearby, several clubs and bars are centered on Pl. Gomila and along Av. Joan Miró—but exercise caution here at night, as there have been a number of reported instances of petty crime. One great spot in the area for gay nightlife is **Lorca,** C. Federico García Lorca, 21. Blue and yellow walls pay homage to the Andalusian poet himself while the mostly gay crowd moves to a mix of pop, rock, and flamenco. (Mixed drinks €4. Open daily 11am-3am.) The bars and clubs around **El Arenal** (aka Berlin) are German-owned, German-filled, and German-centric. But if you don't mind partying with Deutschland, quite possibly the best deal for entertainment in Palma is here at ⚑**Riu Palace,** one block in from the beach. Two huge rooms, one playing techno and the other spinning hip-hop, fill nightly with hip, young, fashion-conscious German disco fiends. All guests receive free t-shirts, "Rapper caps," necklaces, and coupons for free food at a nearby beer garden. Themed parties every weekend. (Cover €15; open bar, all you can drink. Open daily 10pm-6:30am.) When the bar scene fades at 3am, partiers migrate to Palma's *discotecas*, which attract more locals than tourists. **Tito's Palace,** Pg. Marítim, is Palma's hippest disco, with two floors of house in an indoor colosseum of mirrors and lights. (Cover €15-18. Open daily 11pm-6am.) A couple of blocks further down, **Pachá,** Av. Gabriel Roca, is a toned-down version of the Ibiza landmark, but this little sibling has a massive dance floor, tropical terrace, and enthusiastic patrons. (Cover €12-18. Open daily 11pm-6:30am.)

Mallorcans use any and every occasion as an excuse to party. One of the more colorful bashes, **Día de Sant Joan** (June 24), brings singing, dancing, and drinking to Parc del Mar. The celebration begins the night before with a fireworks display.

AROUND MALLORCA

The west coast of Mallorca is one of the most beautiful landscapes in the Mediterranean. The small town of **Sóller** basks in a fertile valley lined with orange groves. The town, with a backdrop of spectacular mountains, is a pleasant change from Las Palmas's more touristed beaches. From Sóller, a 30min. walk down the valley will bring you to **Puerto de Sóller,** a pebble and sand beach where windsurfers zip back and forth. Old-fashioned trolleys also connect the two (every 30min. 7am-9pm, €0.75). On the southeast coast, scalloped fringes of bays and caves are investors' most recent discovery. The ■**Cuevas Drach,** near Porto Cristo in the southeast, are among the most dramatic natural wonders in Mallorca. The caves amaze with their droopy, finger-like rock formations, illuminating the cave in a spectrum of red and pink color. A 30min. walk into the depths of the cave leads to one of the largest **underground lakes** in the world. The performances given by classical musicians boating across the lake can be classified somewhere between absurd and bizarre; audience members can take free boat rides at the concert's end. A bus runs from Palma to the caves, leaving from the main station by Pl. Espanya (M-Sa 4 per day 10am-1:30pm, Su 10am; €5.40).

MENORCA

Menorca's beaches, rustic landscapes, and picturesque towns draw ecologists, sun worshippers, and photographers. In 1993, UNESCO declared the island a biosphere reserve; since then, administrators have emphasized preservation of the island while encouraging the protection, excavation, and study of Menorca's stone homestead complexes, remnants of a mysterious Talayotic stone-age culture dating from 1400 BC. Quieter and more upscale than the other Balearics, Menorca (pop. 71,617) attracts wealthy young families in search of a peaceful beach vacation and has less to offer budget travelers than its larger neighbors. Menorca's main city, Mahón, serves as the gateways to the island's attractions.

MAHÓN

Atop a steep bluff, Mahón (pop. 25,000) overlooks a well-trafficked harbor. The British occupied the city for most of the 18th century, leaving Georgian doors, brass knockers, and wooden shutters in their wake. Two centuries later, the predominance of British tourists testifies to continuing influence. Most people clear out during the day, using the town as a jumping-off point for the numerous beaches nearby.

TRANSPORTATION

Flights: Airport (☎97 115 70 00), 7km out of town. **Iberia/Aviaco** (☎97 136 90 15); **Air Europa** (☎97 124 00 42); **SpanAir** (☎97 115 70 98). In summer early booking necessary. See **By Plane,** p. 251, or **Inter-Island Transport,** p. 252. City center accessible only by taxi.

Ferries: Estació Marítima, Moll de Ponent (☎97 136 60 50). Open M-F 8am-1pm and 5-7pm, Sa 8am-noon, Su 8-10:30am and 3:30-5:15pm. **Trasmediterránea** (☎97 136 29 50) sends ferries daily to **Barcelona** and weekly to **Palma** and **Valencia. Balearia** sends ferries to **Alcúdia, Mallorca.** For more info, see **By Boat,** p. 251, or **Inter-Island Transport,** p. 252.

Buses: Check the tourist office or the newspapers *Menorca Diario Insular* and *Menorca* for schedules. There is no central bus station; buses stop around Pl. de s'Esplanada. **Transportes Menorca (TMSA)** (☎97 136 03 61), a right on Av. J.A. Clavé, off Pl. de s'Esplanada. To: **Ciutadella** via **Ferreries** and **Es Mercadal** (1hr., 6 per day 8am-7pm, €3.51); **Es Castell** (20min., every 30min. 7:45am-8:45pm, €1); **Platja Punta Prima** (20min., 9 per day 8:30am-7:30pm, €1.10); **Son Bou** (30min., 6 per day 8:30am-7pm, €1.75). All depart from the depot near Pl. de s'Esplanada, up Av. J.A. Clavé and on your right. Tickets available when boarding the bus or at office on Av. Josep M. Quadrado. **Autobuses Fornells Roca Triay** (☎971 37 66 21) depart from C. Vassallo, the same depot as TMSA, but around a corner. To: **Arenal d'en Castell** (30min.; 5 per day 10:40am-7pm, Su 3 per day 11am-7pm; €1.70); **Es Grau** (20min., 3 per day 10:30am-6pm, €1.10); **Fornells** (40min., 5 per day 10:40am-7pm, €2.50); **Son Parc** (30 min., 5 per day 11am-7pm, €1.70). Buy tickets on board.

Taxis: Main stand at Pl. de s'Esplanada (☎97 136 12 83), or **Radio Taxi** from anywhere on the island (☎971 36 71 11). To: **airport** (€8); **Cala Mesquida** (€8); **Cala'n Porter** (€11.75); **Es Castell** (€5).

ON THE MENU

Patatas Bravas

Whilst perusing your way through a tapas bar's menu, you're bound to notice *las patatas bravas*. The appearance and/or ingredients of this seemingly odd take on French fries may discourage you; after all, you wouldn't think that fried potatoes, olive oil, seasoning, alcohol, and a fair amount of garlic would yield anything better than carnival food. Ignore your intuition, however, and order a plateful; these spuds pack a punch that you don't want to miss.

Most establishments have their own way of making *patatas bravas*. Some adhere to the list of aforementioned ingredients, others serve the potato wedges with garlic mayonnaise *aioli*, while others still serve them with a spicy tomato-based sauce of pimento and cayenne. Whatever the recipe, you'll undoubtedly appreciate the subtle simplicity of the palate-pleasing flavor in every batch.

Some Spaniards manifest their love for *patatas bravas* outside of the restaurant. In 1997, mainland Spain's first Ultimate Frisbee team was created with the name, you guessed it, Patatas Bravas. The team competes internationally; for more information visit http://barnadisc.tripod.com/html/inicioe.html.

Car Rental: Autos Menorsur, C. Luna, 23 (☎97 136 56 66), off C. Hannóver. Aug. €40 per day, €210 per week; July €36/€180; substantial discounts in low season. English spoken. Open M-F 10am-1:30pm and 5-8pm, Sa-Su 9am-2pm.

Bike and Scooter Rental: Autos Menorca, Moll de Llevant, 35-36 (☎97 135 47 86), Puerto de Mahón. Bicycles €10 per day, €37-42 per week. Scooters €21-27/€93-150. Open Apr.-Sept. daily 9:30am-1:30pm and 5-7:30pm.

ORIENTATION & PRACTICAL INFORMATION

Take a taxi (€8) between the **airport** and Mahón. To get to the heart of the city from the **ferry station,** go left (with your back to the water) about 150m, then turn right at the steps that cut through the serpentine **Costa de ses Voltes.** The steps end between Pl. de la Conquesta and Pl. d'Espanya. To reach **Pl. de s'Esplanada,** take Portal de Mar to Costa de Sa, which becomes C. Hannóver and C. de ses Moreres, and continue to the *plaça.* To reach **Pl. de la Miranda,** walk through Pl. d'Espanya and Pl. Carme; at Pl. Príncep, turn left. Pl. de la Miranda is 100m ahead.

Tourist Office: C. de Sa Rovellada de Dalt, 24 (☎97 136 37 90). English spoken. Open M-F 9am-1:30pm and 5-7pm, Sa 9am-1pm. Summer office at the airport (☎97 115 71 15) provides similar materials. Open Mar.-Oct. daily 8am-11pm.

Currency Exchange: Banks with 24hr. **ATMs** line C. Hannóver and C. Nou.

Emergency: ☎112. **Police: Municipal,** Pl. de la Constitució (☎97 136 39 61).

Medical Assistance: Hospital Verge del Toro, C. Barcelona, 3 (☎97 115 77 00; emergency 36 77 26). English spoken. **Ambulance:** ☎061.

Internet Access: Comunicate, C. Vassallo, 22 (☎97 136 55 11). €3 per hr., students €1.50 per hr. Open M-Sa 10am-11pm, Su 6-11pm. More centrally located, and with more computers (though sometimes more expensive), is **Ciber Principal,** C. Nou, 25 (☎971 36 26 89). €1.20 up to 20min., €2.40 for up to 40min., €3.50 up to 1hr. Open M-F 9:30am-10pm, Sa 11am-2pm and 6-10pm.

Post Office: C. del Bon Aire, 11-13 (☎97 135 66 34), at C. de l'Església. Open M-F 8:30am-8:30pm, Sa 9:30am-2pm.

Postal Code: 07703.

ACCOMMODATIONS

It's easier to find a room in Menorca than on the other islands, but it's still a good idea to call ahead, especially in July and August.

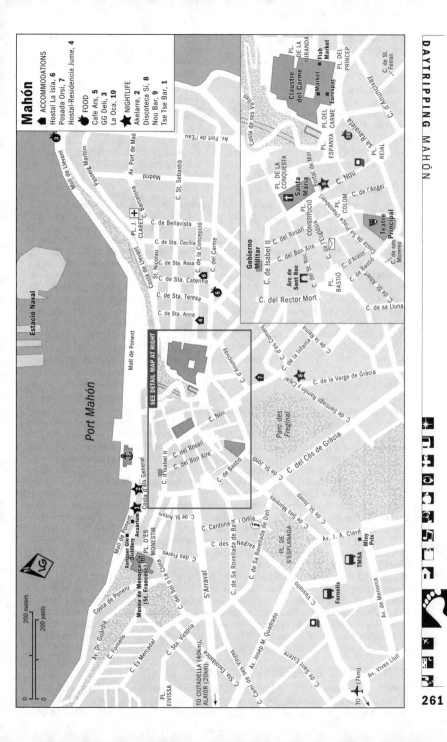

Mahón

▲ ACCOMMODATIONS
Hostal La Isla, **6**
Posada Orsi, **7**
Hostal-Residencia Jume, **4**

● FOOD
Cafe Ars, **5**
GG Deli, **3**
La Oca, **10**

★ NIGHTLIFE
Akelarre, **2**
Discoteca Sí, **8**
Nou Bar, **9**
Tse Tse Bar, **1**

Port Mahón

Estació Naval

SEE DETAIL MAP AT RIGHT

Parc des Freginal

200 meters
200 yards

TO CIUTADELLA (40km),
ALAIOR (20km)

TO (7km)

Posada Orsi, C. de la Infanta, 19 (☎97 136 47 51). Renovated in 2003, rooms are beautiful, modern, and attract a fun crowd with unbeatable prices for the quality. Brightly colored walls and linens. Comfy TV room and sitting room. Breakfast €5. Call before arriving. Singles €15-21; doubles €26-35, with shower €30-42. MC/V. ❷

Hostal-Residencia Jume, C. de la Concepció, 6 (☎97 136 32 66; fax 36 48 78). Standard rooms, all with full bath. Large windows and efficient fans cool things down nicely in summer. Breakfast included for €4 extra; make sure to specify if you don't want it. Lots of services available at reception—car rental, books, snacks, etc. June-Aug. singles €20; doubles €40. Sept.-May €18-36. Closed Dec. 15-Jan. 5. ❷

Hostal La Isla, C. de Santa Catalina, 4 (☎/fax 97 136 64 92). Immaculate rooms all come with private bath. Restaurant downstairs serves a typical menú. Singles €24.50; doubles €40. MC/V. ❷

FOOD

There is a produce **market** in the large Claustre del Carme, which extends from Pl. d'Espanya to Pl. de la Miranda, with entrances at all four corners. (Open M-Sa 9am-2pm). **Groceries** are sold below the produce market at **Eurospar** (☎97 136 93 80; open M-Sa 8am-8pm) and at **Miny Prix,** on the corner of Av. J. A. Clavé and Av. de Menorca. (Open M-Sa 8am-2pm and 5-8:30pm.) **Grand General Delicatessen ❶,** Moll de Llevant, 319, has fresh vegetarian dishes, fish and meat entrees, Italian sandwiches, and an excellent variety of salads. The 20min. walk from the port is well worth it. (Sandwiches €1.50-2.10, entrees €3.90-6. Open M-Sa noon-midnight. ☎97 135 28 05.) In town, **La Oca ❷,** C. s'Arravaleta, 27, off Pl. del Carme, serves reasonably priced pizzas (€6.45-8.10) and pastas (€7.50-10). (☎97 135 37 45. Open daily noon-4pm and 7:30-11pm.) For lighter fare in a bohemian setting, try **Cafe Ars ❷,** C. del Carme, 13. Their salads (€5-9), pastas (€5-7), and sandwiches (€2.50-3.50) are tasty and affordable. Dim lights and jazz are a nice way to relax, and large windows frame the outside world. (☎97 136 80 41. Three-course menú €11. Open M-Sa 10am-midnight.)

SIGHTS

The most awe-inspiring sights in Menorca lie outside of its cities, although Mahón does have a few attractions. The **Museo de Menorca,** Av. Dr. Guàrdia, an old Franciscan monastery closed in 1835, displays excavated items and exhibits on Menorcan history dating back to Talayotic times. (☎97 135 09 55. Open Tu-Su 10am-2pm and 6-8:30pm. €2.) Founded in 1287 and rebuilt in 1772, the **Església de Santa María La Major,** in Pl. de la Constitution, trembles from the 51 stops, four keyboards, and 3210 pipes of its über-organ, built by the Swiss Juan Kilburz in 1810. (Free organ concerts M-Sa 11am. Open for visits 8am-1pm and 6-8:30pm.) The **Arc de Sant Roc,** up C. Sant Roc from Pl. de la Constitució, the last fragment of the medieval wall built to defend the city from Catalan pirates, straddles the streets of Mahón. Get sauced off free liquor samples at the **Xoriguer Gin Distillery** on the port. Through glass windows at the back of the store, visitors watch their drinks bubble and froth in large copper vats. (☎97 136 21 97. Open M-F 8am-7pm, Sa 9am-1pm.) Mahón is close to numerous **archaeological sites,** including prehistoric caves, settlements, and monuments, but they are accessible only by car; see the tourist office for info on a self-guided driving tour. Perhaps the most famous of these monuments is **Torre d'en Galmes,** off the road to Platges de Son Bou from Alaior. Atop a hill overlooking the island's interior, this Talayotic city dates from 1400 BC and served as both a religious and commercial center for Menorca's original inhabitants. Though many of the monuments have yet to be fully excavated and seem to be nothing more than piles of disorganized rubble, of special interest is the eerie **Sala Hipostila,** a prehistoric house whose roof is suspended by columns that are narrower at their bases than at their crowns. (Open daily 10am-8pm. €1.80.)

NIGHTLIFE & FESTIVALS

Mahón is not known for its nightlife. Weekdays are quiet except in August. A string of *bares-musicales* line the **Costa d'els General,** near the water. The colorful, lively **Tse Tse Bar,** Moll de Ponent, 14, fills nightly with energetic 18-20 year-olds eager to take advantage of the ample dance floor. (Beer €2.40; mixed drinks €5. Open daily 10pm-4am, in winter Th-Sa 10pm-4am.) One of the more fashionable places on the strip is **Akelarre,** Moll de Ponent, 41-43, a spacious, trendy bar and dance club. Occasional free jazz concerts start earlier. A mixed straight-gay crowd fills the dance floors upstairs around midnight. (Open daily June-Oct. 8am-5am; Nov.-May 7:30pm-4am. ☎971 36 85 20.) Away from the port, **Discoteca Sí,** C. Verge de Gràcia, 16, turns on the strobe light after midnight, while **Nou Bar,** C. Nou, 1, 2nd fl., serves drinks (€4-6) to a calm, older crowd. (Open daily noon-3pm and 7:30pm-3am.)

Film lovers should check out **cine a la fresca,** held every night except Friday in the Claustre del Carme at 10pm. A different film is shown each week in the outdoor courtyard of the cloister. Look for the posters around town advertising the current movie. (Enter from Pl. de la Miranda. €5.)

From May to September, merchants sell shoes, clothes, and souvenirs in **mercadillos** held daily in various town squares (Es Castell M and W; Ferrerias Tu and F; Mahón Tu and Sa; Alaior Th; Ciutadella F-Sa; Mercadal Su). In mid-July, Mahón's **Verge del Carme** celebration brings a colorfully trimmed armada into the harbor. Mahón's **Festival de Música de Maó** in July and August showcases Santa María's Swiss organ. (Pl. de la Constitució. Festival concerts start at 9:30pm; see tourist office for upcoming events. Seat "donation" €3.)

AROUND MENORCA

The coves and beaches near Mahón are best explored with a rental car and the *Let's Go to the Beach* (no relation) brochure and map available at the tourist office. Though the highway from Mahón to Ciutadella is straight and well-maintained, the local roads are curvy, pot-holed, and oftentimes unpaved. Exercise caution if driving here at night.

THE NORTH SHORE

ALBUFERA ES GRAU. A large natural reserve, Albufera Es Grau entices visitors with lagoons, pine woods, and farmland, as well as diverse flora and fauna. Some of the best swimming areas are across from the main lagoon and uphill from town, along a series of bluffs that form secluded coves. **Viajes Isla Colom** sends boats from the marina on the lagoon in Es Grau to **Illa d'en Colom,** a tiny island with more beaches. (☎971 35 98 67; 4 boats per day 10:30am-5pm, last boat returns at 7pm. Autocares Fornells leave from C. Vassallo in Mahón. 20min., 3 per day 10:30am-6pm, €1.10.)

ARENAL D'EN CASTELL. Breathtaking views, calm water, and packed sands make this tiny cove a popular destination for daytrippers from Mahón. (Autocares Fornells leave from C. Vassallo in Mahón. 30min.; M-Sa 5 per day 10:40am-7pm, Su 3 per day 11am, 1:30, 7pm; €1.70.)

FORNELLS. A small fishing village known for its lobster farms, Fornells has only recently begun to attract tourists. Windsurfers zip around Fornells's long, shallow port, while beach gurus make excursions to **Cala Tirant** and **Binimella,** both only a few kilometers to the west. (Autobuses Roca Triay run to Fornells from C. Vassallo in Mahón. 30min., 5 per day 10am-7pm, €2.50.)

SOUTH SHORE

PUNTA PRIMA. While this beach may not be as secluded or expansive as some, it draws a crowd on account of its proximity to Mahón. A lighthouse on a strip of land across from the beach overlooks the coastline. (TMSA buses run to and from Pl. de s'Esplanada in Mahón. 20min., 8 per day 8:30am-7:30pm, €1.10.)

ES CANUTELLS. Situated off the road from Mahón to Cala'n Porter (a 15min. drive from Mahón), Es Canutells is a pleasant and secluded cove with calm, turquoise waters good for swimming and snorkeling. (TMSA buses run to and from Av. Josep M. Quadrado in Mahón. 20 min., 4 per day 8:45am-7pm, €1.10.)

CALASCOVES. Past Es Canutells and off the road from Mahón to Cala'n Porter (a 20min. drive from Mahón) is this pristine serpentine cove with rocky cliffs and a small beach perfect for a refreshing swim. Equally refreshing is this area's lack of tourists. Since Calascoves cannot be reached by public transportation, leave your car at the top of the hill and continue down the dirt path for about 20min. until you reach the rocky part of the cove. The beach is over the cliffs to your right.

CALA'N PORTER. Expansive and touristy, Cala'n Porter greets thousands of visitors each summer with its whitewashed houses, orange stucco roofs, and red sidewalks. Its small but well-used beach lies at the bottom of a steep, bouldered hillside, but pedestrian access is easy via the main road and a marked staircase. (TMSA buses run to and from Av. Josep M. Quadrado in Mahón. 7 per day 9:30am-7:30pm, €1.10.) A 10min. walk away, at the end of Av. Central, the **Covas d'en Xoroi** dominate cliffs high above the sea. The caves are inhabited by a network of bars by day and a popular disco (which attracts a largely young British crowd) by night. (☎97 137 72 36. Bars open Apr.-Oct. daily 10:30am-9pm, disco open nightly at 11pm. Foam parties every Th. Cover for bars €4.90, includes 1 drink. Cover for disco €15.)

PLATGES DE SON BOU. The longest beach on the island, Son Bou offers 4km of sand on the southern shore, covered with throngs of sunburned tourists. As the most popular of Menorca's beaches, it's also the most visitor-friendly. Be aware, though, that part of the beach is also for nudists, and the farther away from the commercial center you walk, the more naked it gets. (TMSA buses to the beachesleave from Av. Josep M. Quadrado in Mahón. 30min., 7 per day 8:45am-7pm, €1.65.)

CALA MITJANA & CALA MITJANETA. On the main highway from Mahón to Ciutadella, head toward Ferreries, and then take the road to Santa Galdana. Directly on your left before reaching the roundabout above the town is the dirt road that leads to **Cala Mitjana** (a 30min. drive from Mahón). Park your car in the small dirt lot and continue on foot to the small beach overlooking a dramatic cove bordered by white limestone cliffs that plunge into the turquoise sea. Though this beach is not totally secluded, if you climb the staircase on your right upon entering the cove and head down the dirt path for about 5min., you get to **Cala Mitjaneta,** a smaller cove which affords even more dramatic views of the limestone cliffs and the wide expanse of the Mediterranean beyond the inlet. While some wade into the water here, others prove their bravery (or recklessness) by diving from the rocks.

IBIZA

Nowhere on Earth does style rule over substance (or do substances rule over style) more than on Ibiza (pop. 84,000). Once a 1960s hippie enclave, Ibiza has forgotten her roots in favor of a new age of decadence. Disco fiends, high-fashion gurus, movie stars, and party-hungry backpackers arrive in droves to debauch in the island's outrageous, sex- and substance-driven culture. Surprisingly, there is more to Ibiza than spectacular nightlife; its beaches and mountains are some of the most spectacular in all the Balearics.

EIVISSA (IBIZA CITY)

Eivissa (Ibiza City; pop. 35,000) is the world's biggest 24-hour party. The town itself is like Dr. Jekyll and Mr. Hyde. During the day, families sightsee through the walled D'alt Vila, and the city streets remain tranquil while the majority of visitors sleep off hangovers while tanning at nearby beaches. During the day, Eivissa could easily be mistaken for any other seaside village in Spain. At night, however, there's no mistaking this town for any other. Flashy bars appear seemingly out of nowhere, filling street after street with neon lights, blasting music, and fast-talking club promoters; grab a front-row seat at the outdoor tables to enjoy the prime people-watching action. Come 3am, the scene migrates to the clubs, where parties last until dawn (and often well into the next day)—then it all begins again.

TRANSPORTATION

Flights: Airport (☎971 80 90 00), 7km south of the city. Bus #10 runs between the airport and Av. Isidor Macabich, 20, in town (30min., every hr. 7am-11.10pm, €1). Info booth open 24hr. **Iberia,** Pg. Vara de Rey, 15 (☎902 40 05 00 or 971 30 03 00), flies to Alicante, Barcelona, Madrid, Palma, and Valencia. **Air Europa** and **Spanair** offer similar options.

Ferries: Estació Marítima, directly across the street from the tourist office. To get to the city center and bus stop from the waterfront, take Av. Bartolomé Roselló, which becomes Av. Isidor Macabich. **Trasmediterránea** (☎971 31 51 00 or 902 45 46 45) sells tickets at Estació Marítima and sends ferries to **Barcelona, Palma,** and **Valencia.** Office open M-F 9am-1pm, 4:30-7:30pm, and 2hr. before ferry departures. **Trasmapi-Balearia** (☎971 31 40 05 or 902 16 01 80) runs daily to and from **Dénia,** near Alicante; a connection in Eivissa continues to and from **Palma.** Office open M-F 9am-2:15pm, 4:30-8pm, and midnight-1:15am; Sa 9am-2:15pm and 6-8pm; Su 9am-2:15pm and midnight-1:15am. **Umafisa Lines** (☎97 121 02 01) sends ferries to and from **Barcelona** 3-4 times per week.

Buses: The main bus stop is on Av. Isidor Macabich, past Pl. Enrique Fajarines y Tur when walking away from the port. For an exact schedule, check the tourist office or *El Diario.* Intercity buses €1.80; leave from Av. Isidor Macabich, 42 (☎97 131 21 17) to **Sant Antoni** (M-Sa every 15min., Su every 30min. 7am-11:30pm) and **Santa Eulàlia del Riu** (M-F every 30min., Sa-Su every hr. 7:30am-11:30pm). Buses (☎97 134 03 82) to the beaches cost €1.15 and leave from Av. Isidor Macabich, 20, and Av. d'Espanya to: **Cala Tarida** (5 per day 10:10am-6:45pm); **Cap Martinet** (M-Sa 11 per day 8:15am-8pm); **Platja d'en Bossa** (every 30min. 8:30am-11pm); **Salinas** (every hr. 9:30am-7:30pm).

Taxis: ☎97 130 70 00 or 97 130 66 02.

Car and Moped Rental: Casa Valentín, Av. B.V. Ramón, 19 (☎97 131 08 22). Mopeds €25-30 per day. Cars from €39. Open daily 9am-1pm and 3:30-8:30pm.

ORIENTATION & PRACTICAL INFORMATION

Three distinct sections make up the city. **Sa Penya,** in front of Estació Marítima, is crammed with bars and boutiques. Atop the hill behind Sa Penya, high walls circle **D'alt Vila,** the old city. **Sa Marina** and the commercial district occupy the gridded streets to the far right (with your back to the water) of the Estació. **Av.d'Espanya,** continuing from Pg. Vara de Rey, heads toward the airport and local beaches.

Tourist Office: Pl. de Antoni Riquer, 2 (☎97 130 19 00). Open M-F 9:30am-1:30pm and 5-7:30pm, Sa 10:30am-1pm. **Booth** at the airport (☎97 180 91 18; fax 97 180 91 32). Open May-Oct. M-Sa 9am-2pm and 3-8pm, Su 9am-2pm.

Currency Exchange: Exchanges are all over town, but banks and ATMs offer better rates. **La Caixa,** Av. Isidor Macabich, has good exchange rates for cash and traveler's checks.

Laundromat: Wash and Dry, Av. d'Espanya, 53 (☎97 139 48 22). Wash and dry €4.20 each. **Internet** access €5.40 per hr. Open M-F 10am-3pm and 5-10pm, Sa 10am-5pm.

Emergency: ☎ 112. **Police:** C. Vicent Serra (☎97 131 58 61).

Medical Assistance: Hospital, Barrio Can Misses (☎97 139 70 00), west of town. **Ambulance:** ☎971 39 32 32. **Hospital Nuestra Senora** (☎97 139 70 21).

Internet Access: Centro Internet Eivissa, Av. Ignacio Wallis, 39 (☎97 131 81 61). €1.20 per 15min., €1.50 per 30min., €3 per hr. Open M-Sa 10am-midnight, Su 5pm-midnight. **Ciber Matic,** C. Cayetano Soler, 3 (☎97 130 33 82). €1.80 per 30min., €3 per hr. Open Sept.-June M-Sa 10am-11pm; July-Aug. 1pm-2am.

Post Office: (☎97 131 43 23). At the very end of Av. Isidor Macabich heading away from the port. **Lista de Correos.** Open M-F 8:30am-8:30pm, Sa 9:30am-2pm.

Postal Code: 07800.

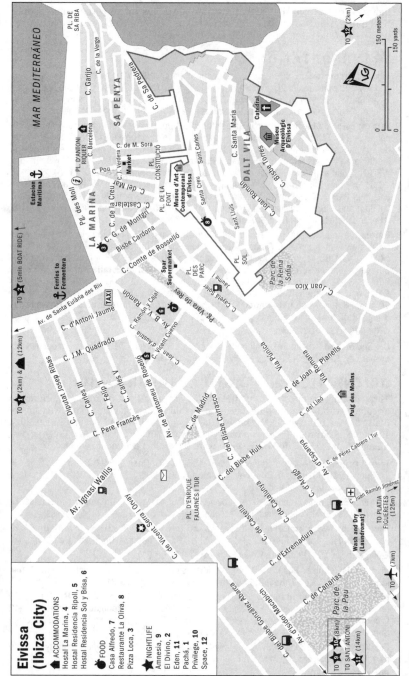

Eivissa (Ibiza City)

▲ ACCOMMODATIONS
Hostal La Marina, **4**
Hostal Residencia Ripoll, **5**
Hostal Residencia Sol y Brisa, **6**

● FOOD
Casa Alfredo, **7**
Restaurante La Oliva, **8**
Pizza Loca, **3**

★ NIGHTLIFE
Amnesia, **9**
El Divino, **2**
Eden, **11**
Pachá, **1**
Privilege, **10**
Space, **12**

MAR MEDITERRÁNEO

PL. DE SA RIBA

SA PENYA

LA MARINA

DALT VILA

Catedral

Museu Arqueològic D'Eivissa

Estación Marítima

Ferries to Formentera

TO **2** (5min BOAT RIDE)

Market

PL. DE LA FONT

Museu d'Art Contemporani d'Eivissa

Spar Supermarket

PL. DES PARC

Parc de la Reina Sofia

Parc de la Pau

Puig des Molins

Wash and Dry (Laundromat)

TO PLATJA FIGUERETES (125m)

TO **9** TO SANT ANTONI
(8km)
(14km)

TO (7km)

0   150 meters
0   150 yards

TO (2km)

C. Garijo
C. de la Verge
C. Barcelona
C. de M. Sora
C. de Sa Pedrera
C. Santa Maria
C. Santa Carles
C. Pou
C. del Mar
C. J. Verdera
C. Castelar
C. de la Creu
C. G. C. de Montgrí
Bisbe Cardona
C. Comte de Rosselló
C. d'Antoni Jaume
Av. de Santa Eulária des Riu
C. Ramón y Cajal
Av. B. V. Ramón
C. d'Austria
C. Vicent Cuervo
C. Joan d'Austria
C. de Bartomeu de Rosselló
C. J.M. Quadrado
C. Diputat Josep Ribas
C. Carles III
C. Felip II
C. Carles V
C. Pere Francès
Av. d'Ignasi Wallis
Av. de Vicent Serra i Orvay
C. de Madrid
C. del Bisbe Carrasco
PL. D'ENRIQUE FAJARNÉS I TUR
C. de Catalunya
C. del Bisbe Huix
C. de Castella
C. d'Extremadura
C. de Canárias
C. del Bisbe González Abarca
Av. d'Isidor Macabich
C. Joan Ramón Jiménez
C. de Pérez Cabrero i Tur
Av. d'Espanya
C. d'Aragó
Via Púnica
C. del Lleó
C. de Joan Planells
Via Romana
C. Joan Roman
C. Bisbe Torres
Santa Creu
Sant Carles
Santa Maria
Sant Lluís
PL. SOL
C. Caietà Soler
Pg. Vara de Rey
TAXI
PL. D'ANTONI RIQUER
Pg. des Moll
PL. CONSTITUCIÓ

TO (2km) & (12km)

ACCOMMODATIONS

Decent, cheap hostels in town are rare, especially in the summer—but then again, who actually *sleeps* here anyway? Call several weeks in advance for summer stays, when prices climb and hostels fill fast. All prices listed below are for high season and can drop by as much as €12 in the off-season.

Hostal Residencia Sol y Brisa, Av. B. V. Ramón, 15 (☎97 131 08 18). Upstairs from Pizzeria da Franco. Clean and centrally located. Social atmosphere. Singles €24; doubles €42. ❷

Hostal La Marina, C. Barceloneta, 7 (☎97 131 01 72), amid the raucous bar scene. Rooms have sophisticated, vaguely ocean-related decor. Four buildings offer lodging ranging from stark to lavish. The best (and most expensive) have TV, A/C, private bath, carpet, and balcony. Singles €30-62; doubles €41-150. ❸

Hostal Residencia Ripoll, C. Vicente Cuervo, 14 (☎97 131 42 75). Fastidiously clean hallways and bathrooms and unusually large, fan-cooled rooms with pretty bedspreads are among the best in town, though the singles are a bit pricey. Apartments more spacious and fun. July-Sept. singles €30; doubles €42; 3-person apartments with TV, patio, and kitchen €78. ❸

Camping: Es Cana (☎97 133 21 17). €5.95 per person, €1.80 per site, €5.60-9.95 per tent (depending on the number of people). Bungalow €45-65, cabin €15-25. Reserve via fax. **Cala Nova** (☎97 133 17 74). €4.70 per person, €4.10 per tent. Both sites close to Sta. Eulàlia del Riu. Take bus #13 or 15 from Eivissa to Sta. Eulària del Riu, and then bus #18 from Sta. Eulàlia d'alt to Es Cana. Both sites a 10min. walk from the bus stop; follow signs. ❶

FOOD

Inexpensive cuisine is hard to find; it's not uncommon to see budget travelers stocking up at grocery stores or chowing down at fast food joints to save their euros for the discos. Ibizan dishes include *sofrit pagès,* a deep-fried lamb and chicken dish; *flao,* a lush lemon- and mint-tinged cheesecake; and *graxonera,* cinnamon-dusted pudding made from eggs and bits of *ensaimada* (candied bread). The **market,** at C. Extremadura and C. Canarias, sells meat, fruits, and vegetables (open M-Sa 7am-1pm). For **groceries,** try **Spar,** on the corner of C. d'Avicenna and Pl. des Parc. (Open M-Sa 9am-9pm.)

Pizza Loca, C. de Luis Tur i Palau, 15 (☎97 131 45 68), about 2 blocks from the corner of Av. Bartolomé Roselló. Delicious rectangular pizzas with a variety of toppings including veggies, tuna, and salami. Eat outside at the wooden tables or get it to go and chow down on the beach. Slices €2-3. Open daily noon-5am. ❶

Restaurante La Oliva, C. Sa Creu, 2 (☎97 130 57 52). Pricey but scrumptious Italian fare. Get a candlelit outdoor table and people-watch. Pasta €8-11; meat and fish entrees €9-18. Open daily 8pm-1am. ❸

Casa Alfredo, Pg. Vara de Rey, 16. Fish, meat, and heavenly desserts fill the menú (€6-9) that locals deem the best in town. Open M-Sa 1-4pm and 8pm-midnight. ❷

SIGHTS

Wrapped in 16th-century walls, the **D'alt Vila** (High Town) rises above the town. Its twisting streets lead to the 14th-century **cathedral,** built in several phases and styles. (Open daily 10:30am-1pm.) Next to the cathedral is the **Museu Arqueològic D'Eivissa,** home to a variety of regional artifacts. (Open Tu-Sa 10am-2pm and 6-8pm, Su 10am-2pm. €2, students €1.) Amid stone walls, the small **Museu D'Art Contemporani D'Eivissa** displays a range of art exhibitions. (C. Sa Carrosa, on the left when entering through D'alt Vila's main entrance. ☎97 130 27 23. Open M-F 10am-1pm and 6:30-10pm, Sa 10am-1:30pm. €1.20, students free.) The archaeological museum, **Puig des Molins,** Via Romana, displays Punic, Roman, and Iberian artifacts. (☎97 130 17 71. Open M-Sa 10am-2pm and 5-8pm, Su 10am-2pm. €1.20.)

BEACHES

The power of the rising sun draws thousands of topless solar zombies to nearby tanning grounds. **Platja Figueretes,** a thin stretch of sand in the shadow of large hotels, is the best foot-accessible beach from Eivissa. To get there, walk down Av. Espanya for about 10min. and take a left on C. Juan Ramón Jiménez. Farther down, **Platja d'en Bossa** is the liveliest of Ibiza's beaches, home to numerous beach bars, as well as throngs of sun-seeking tourists. **Platja des Duros** is tucked across the bay from Sa Penya and Sa Marina, just before the lighthouse. At **Platja de Talamanca,** the water—more an enclosed bay than open sea—is accessible on foot by following the road to the new port and continuing on to the beach (20min.). **Platja de ses Salinas** is one of Ibiza's most popular and famous beaches, although others are actually more scenic. Bask among the beautiful people and groove to chilled-out house pulsating from **Sa Trincha** bar at the end of the beach. Neighboring **Platja des Cavallet** is decidedly clothing-optional and attracts a beautiful, largely gay crowd. To get to both, take the bus from Eivissa to Salinas; for Es Cavallet, get off at the stop before Salinas (look for the T-intersection to the left or just ask the bus driver) and walk to the beach (10min.) or walk from Salinas (20min.).

More private coastal stretches lie in the northern part of the island and are accessible by car or moped. Among these, the German enclave at **Cala de Sant Vicent** (past Santa Eulàlia on the road to St. Carles de Peralta) offers white sands and breathtaking views that are far from secluded, but peaceful nonetheless. The small coves in the rocky northernmost point of the island (between Portinatx and St. Agnes de Corona) are worth visiting if you seek serenity or the company of modern-day flower children. **Cala Xarraca** is a beautiful EU *bandera azul* cove popular with families, who fight for spots on its small beach. The views from **Cap de Rubió** are among the most dramatic on the island. On the road from Sant Miquel to Sant Mateu, take the left fork up a semi-paved road; the road rises and then drops suddenly to a rocky path, which leads to impressive limestone cliffs. Hike down to any of the coves at the bottom of the paths next to the abandoned mine shafts, and you'll be rewarded with your own private swimming hole.

NIGHTLIFE

The island's discos (virtually all have a mixed gay/straight crowd) are world-famous—veterans claim that you will never experience anything half as wild or fun. The best sources of information are disco-goers and the zillions of posters that plaster the stores and restaurants of Sa Marina and Sa Penya. There is something different each day of the week, and each club is known for a particular theme party—be sure to hit up a club on a popular night, or you'll end up shelling out a lot of money for a not-so-happening party. For listings, check out *Ministry in Ibiza* or *DJ* magazines, free at many hostels, bars, and restaurants. The **Discobus** runs to all the major hotspots (leaves Eivissa from Av. Isidoro Macabich every hr. 12:30am-6:30am, schedule for other stops available at tourist office and hotels, €1.50).

Privilege (☎971 19 80 86; www.privilege-ibiza.com), on the Discobus to San Antonio or a €9 taxi. The world's largest club, according to the Guinness Book of World Records. This enormous complex packs in up to 10,000 with bars in the double digits and a pool. *The* place to be on Monday for its infamous "Manumission" parties. Cover €40 and up. Open June-Sept. daily midnight-7am. V.

Pachá (☎971 31 36 00; www.pacha.com), 15min. walk from the port, 2min. in a cab. The most famous club chain in Spain, and the most elegant of Ibiza's discos. Locals and tourists alike get their groove on in a dim but beautiful setting. "Ministry of Sound" on Th brings the biggest crowd, and "Made in Italy" on F is, not surprisingly, very popular with Italian clubbers. The only club in Ibiza open year-round. Cover €50. Open daily midnight-7:30am.

Amnesia (☎971 19 80 41; www.amnesiaibiza.com), on the road to San Antonio; take the Discobus. Converted warehouse with psychedelic lights and movie screens has 2 gigantic rooms; a largely gay crowd congregates in the one to the left. Foam parties Su and W. Best known for "Cream" on Th, when London DJs play hard house or trance. Cover €40 and up. Open daily midnight-7am.

Space, Platja d'en Bossa (☎971 39 67 93; www.space-ibiza.com). Starts hopping around 8am, peaks mid-afternoon, and doesn't wind down until after 5pm. Known for its Su morning show, Sa-Tu mornings are popular too. Hosts the official after-parties for "Ministry of Sound" at Pachá, "Manumission" at Privilege, and "La Troya Asesina" (the infamous drag queen party) at Amnesia. Cover €30-40.

Eden, C. Salvador Espíritu (☎971 34 25 51), across from the beach in Sant Antoni. Gaining in popularity, Eden pulls out all the stops for "Judgement Sunday," when DJ Judge Jules attracts huge crowds. Popular among British visitors. Retro nights on Tu feature house from the past decade. Cover €37-45. Open daily midnight-7am.

El Divino, Puerto Ibiza Nueva (☎971 19 01 76; www.eldivino-ibiza.com). Head to the waterfront terrace for a break from the techno insanity. El Divino fliers serve as free passes for the disco shuttle boat—otherwise, it costs €1.50 each way. Cover €40. Open mid-June to mid-Sept. daily midnight-6am.

NEAR EIVISSA: FORMENTERA

The tiny island of Formentera provides a quiet (but pricey) getaway from more hectic Ibiza. Despite the recent invasions by bourgeois, beach-hungry Germans and Italians, the island's beaches maintain a sense of hypnotic calm. Join Formentera's "save our island" spirit by hiking or renting a bike—the tourist office offers a comprehensive list of Green Tours for hikers and cyclists, and bike paths are plentiful.

TRANSPORTATION, ORIENTATION & PRACTICAL INFORMATION

Ferries at Estació Marítima in Eivissa offer transportation. **Pitra** car ferries (☎97 119 10 88), **Trasmapi-Balearia** (☎97 131 20 70), and **Umafisa** car ferries (☎971 31 45 13) all run to and from Formentera. If you're in a hurry, choose **Línea Jet's** speedy ride (25min., 16 per day 7:45am-8:30pm, €14) or ride with the trucks on the cheaper, slower mothership (1hr.; M-Sa 9 per day 6:45am-8pm, Su 5 per day 9am-8pm; €9.50). Trasmapi-Balearia also offers a 35min. version for €10, probably the best deal of the three (6 per day, 9:30am-5:45pm).

You will arrive at the main port, **La Savina,** on the northern side of the island. The main artery runs from the port (km0) to the eastern tip, **Punta D'Esfar** (km20). The island's "capital," **San Francisco,** at km 3.1, has the basics but little else. **Es Pujols,** km 4, is the island's liveliest town. **Buses** run from La Savina to: **Platja de ses Illetes** (10:30am and 5pm, €1); **Platja Migjorn** (8 per day 8:30am-7:15pm, €1.40); **San Francisco** (12 per day 8:30am-7:15pm, €1). For a **taxi,** call ☎97 132 80 16. Car, scooter, and bike **rental booths** line the dock in La Savina. (Cars €30-36 per day. Scooters €18-21. Bikes €3-6.) **Autos Ca María** offers friendly service and advice on routes. (☎97 132 81 91. Cars €36. Scooters €20. Bikes €3-6. Open daily 9am-9pm. MC/V.) The **tourist office,** Edificio Servicios La Savina, is at the port. (☎97 132 20 57. Open M-F 10am-2pm and 5-9pm, Sa 10am-2pm.) Services include **police** (☎97 132 20 87), **medical center** (☎97 132 23 69), and **emergency** line (☎092). **Postal Code:** 07870.

BEACHES

To bask on Formentera's best beaches, take Av. Mediterránea from the port, turn left at the sign pointing toward Es Pujols, and take another left onto the dirt road at the sign marking Verede de Ses Salines. Paths to the right lead to **Platja de Llevant,** a long strip of fine sand. Farther up the peninsula, roads to the left lead to **🏖Platja de Ses Illetes,** with its more popular, but rocky, swimming holes. **Platja de Mitjorn,** the longest beach on the island, is less crowded than the others. A tourist boat runs to Ses Illetes and Espalmador from La Savina (leaves La Savina 10:15, 11:45am, 1:15pm; returns 4:15, 5:30, 6:45pm; round-trip €9). For sailing, windsurfing, and canoe rental, try **Wet 4 Fun** on Es Pujols beach. (☎97 132 18 09. Sailboats €35.60 per hr., €98 per day. Windsurfing €13 per hr. Canoes €5.40 per hr., €12 per half-day.) For stunning sightseeing, those with mopeds should drive through the mountainous regions of **La Mola** to the lighthouse at **Far de la Mola** and **Punta de Sa Ruda** on the easternmost extreme of the island, or cruise by the groves of olive trees to Cap de Barbaria just south of La Savina. Those seeking a less touristed beach should head to **Cala Saona,** a pleasant cove on the western part of the island.

SAN ANTONIO

Every summer, masses of young Brits migrate to Sant Antoni. The rowdy nightlife and down-to-earth atmosphere combined with proximity to some of the island's best beaches turn the town into a twenty-something enclave. With two clubs, plenty of bars, and cheaper food and accommodations than Eivissa, Sant Antoni is the perfect budget alternative to its sister city's high prices and lifestyle.

TRANSPORTATION & PRACTICAL INFORMATION

Buses run from Pg. del Mar in Sant Antoni to: **Cala Bassa** (20min., 8 per day 9:30am-6:30pm, €1.15); **Cala Conta** (15min., 7 per day 9:10am-6pm, €1.15); **Cala Tarida** (10min., 8 per day 9:30am-7:05pm, €1.15); **Eivissa** (25min.; every 30min. M-Sa 7-9:30am and 10-11:30pm, every 15min. 9:45am-9:30pm, Su every 30min. 7:30am-10:30pm; €1.45); **Santa Eulária** (35min., M-Sa 4 per day 9:30am-6pm, €1.05). **Ferries** leave Sant Antoni for **Dénia** (see **Transportation,** p. 252). Smaller companies run daily **boats** to nearby beaches. Signs posted daily along the port have schedules. For a **taxi,** call ☎97 134 07 79. Sant Antoni is very easy to get around, as major streets lie on something of a grid. For **car** and **moped rental,** try **Motos Luis,** Av. Portmany, 5. (☎97 134 05 21. Mopeds €22 and up. Cars €39 and up. Open M-Sa 9am-2pm and 4-8pm, Su 9am-2pm.) The **tourist office** is a stone building in the middle of the pedestrian thoroughfare by Pg. des Fonts. (☎97 134 33 63. Open M-F 9:30am-2:30pm and 3-8:30pm, Sa 9am-1pm, Su 9:30am-1:30pm.) In an **emergency,** call ☎112 or the **police,** Av. Portmany, km 14 (☎97 134 08 30). The **Centro de Salud** is on C. Alicant (☎ 97 134 51 21).

ACCOMMODATIONS & FOOD

Hostels in Sant Antoni are numerous, cheap, and full of Brits. Call well in advance for any summer stay; in the low season, prices drop. ▓**Hostal Residencia Roig ❸,** C. Progreso, 44, has gorgeous, clean rooms all with private bath, comfortable couches in the lobby, and access to a nearby hotel's pool. (☎97 134 04 83. Singles €27; doubles €48.) The large bedrooms, huge TV lounge, and great location make **Hostal Salada ❷,** C. Soletat, 34, one of the best bargains in town. Walk up C. Bartolomé Vicente Ramón from the port and turn left on to C. Soletat. (☎97 134 11 30. Singles €18.50; doubles €30.50-33.50; triples €36.50.) Another option is clean, spacious **Hostal Rita ❷,** C. Bartolomé Vicente Ramón, 17B. Doubles and triples have private baths; singles share common baths. (☎97 134 63 32. Singles €18; doubles €32; triples €45.) **Restaurants** are everywhere in San Antonio. A variety of choices are available at the outdoor cafes along Pg. del Mar or on its sidestreets leading uphill. Of the more trendy beachfront establishments, ▓**The Orange Corner ❶,** Av. Doctor Fleming, 2-4, stands out. The orange building right on the water serves cheap sandwiches, salads, fruit drinks, milkshakes, and alcoholic favorites. (Entrees €5-8. Alcoholic milkshakes €6, non-alcoholic shakes and smoothies €4. Open daily 10am-4am.) For cheap eats with an ocean view in a slightly less hectic setting, try **Manilla ❶,** C. Balanzat, 19, just down the beach from Café del Mar and its companions. Pastas (€4-5), Mexican entrees (€8-12), and crêpes (€6-8.50) served by candlelight on an ample terrace with a bubbling fountain. (☎97 134 55 24. Open daily noon-midnight.)

BEACHES & NIGHTLIFE

The town itself is situated on a long, narrow strip of sand, but better beaches are only a stone's throw away. Check out **Cala Bassa,** one of the more popular tanning spots, for a gorgeous (and sometimes nude) beach that's accessible by bus. **Cala Gració,** 1.5km from Sant Antoni, is easily reached by foot. **Santa Eulària** is more built up, but it's substantially larger than some of the other beaches nearby. Hoof it or bike to the small coves of **Es Povet** and **Caló d'es Moro.** If you have a car or moped, head to **Cala Salada,** just a few kilometers north of town, for calm, beautiful waters and a picturesque hippie community. Sant Antoni's **nightlife** revolves largely around three main areas. The area on the far end of town, near the littered beach of Es Ganguil, has several waterfront bars. Crowds gather on the small beach to watch the ✦sunset and chill to mellow house. **Café del Mar,** "the original sunset bar," serves overpriced drinks, the chic **Café Mambo** is a popular pre-party bar, and, much farther down toward Caló d'es Moro, **Kanya** offers a lively scene. The crowded streets of town are packed with low-key watering holes and drunk pre-partiers. The clubs **Eden** and **Es Paradis Terrenal,** beach bars (including the popular and upscale **M Bar**), and mini-discos facing the main beach round out the options.

Planning Your Trip

WHEN TO GO

The tourist season officially runs from mid-June through late August, when the city is filled to capacity with travelers and the weather is at its most beachy. Be aware that July and especially August are also vacation months for native Barcelonese, and many take advantage of their month off from work to vacation outside the city, leaving many restaurants and services closed. Cheaper tickets and comparably good weather prevail throughout the spring and in early fall. Traveling to Barcelona around Christmas can get expensive, as travel companies know that Europeans will pay exorbitant amounts of money to celebrate the holidays with their families. See the **Seasonal Highlights** (p. 18) for detailed festival information.

DOCUMENTS & FORMALITIES

EMBASSIES & CONSULATES

For a list of embassies and consulates in Barcelona, see the **Service Directory,** p. 310.

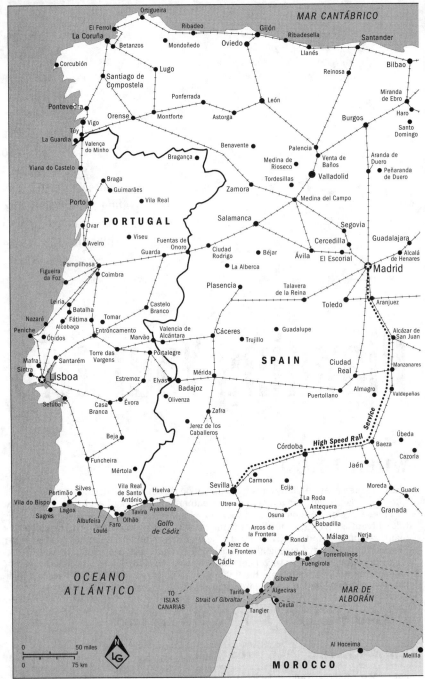

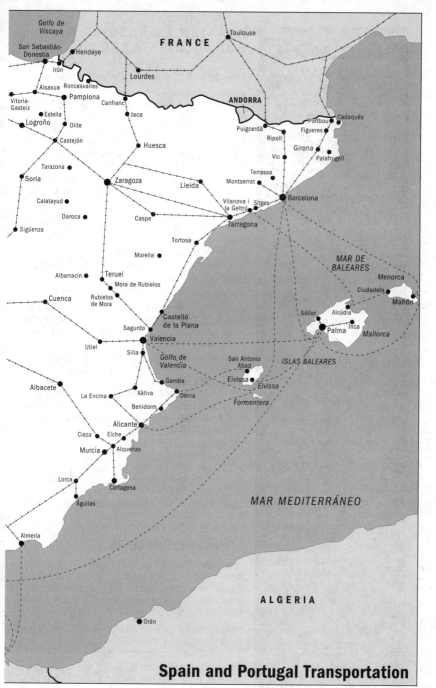

Spain and Portugal Transportation

ONE EUROPE

The idea of European unity has come a long way since 1958, when the European Economic Community (EEC) was created to promote solidarity and cooperation between its six founding states. Since then, the EEC has become the European Union (EU), with political, legal, and economic institutions spanning 15 member states: Austria, Belgium, Denmark, Finland, France, Germany, Greece, Ireland, Italy, Luxembourg, The Netherlands, Portugal, Spain, Sweden, and the UK.

So what does this mean for the average non-EU tourist? In 1999 the EU established **freedom of movement** across 15 European countries—the entire EU minus Ireland and the UK, plus Iceland and Norway. This means that border controls between participating countries have been abolished and visa policies harmonized. While you're still required to carry a passport (or government-issued ID card for EU citizens) when crossing an internal border, once you've been admitted into one country, you're free to travel to all participating states. Britain and Ireland have also formed a common travel area, abolishing passport controls between the UK and the Republic of Ireland. This means that the only place you'll see a border guard within the EU is traveling between the British Isles and the Continent.

SPANISH EMBASSIES & CONSULATES ABROAD

Questions concerning visas and passports go to consulates. Embassies handle weightier matters.

Australia: Embassy: 15 Arkana St., **Yarralumla,** P.O. Box 9076, Deakin ACT 2600 (☎2 62 73 35 55; fax 73 39 18; www.embaspain.com). **Consulates:** Level 24, St. Martin's Tower, 31 Market St., **Sydney,** NSW 2000 (☎2 92 61 24 33; fax 83 16 95); 146 Elgin St., Carlton, **Melbourne,** VIC 3053 (☎3 93 47 19 66; fax 47 35 80).

Canada: Embassy: 74 Stanley Ave., **Ottawa,** ON K1M 1P4 (☎613-747-2252; fax 744-1224). **Consulates:** 1 Westmount Sq., Suite 1456, Ave. Wood, **Montreal,** QC H3Z 2P9 (☎514-935-5235; fax 935-4655; www.docuweb.ca/spainincanada); Simcoe Place, 200 Front St., Suite 2401 **Toronto,** ON M5V 3K2 (☎416-977-1661; fax 593-4949).

Ireland: Embassy: 17a Merlyn Park, Ballsbridge, **Dublin** 4 (☎1 35 3269 1640; fax 269 1854).

New Zealand: Contact the embassy in Australia.

South Africa: Embassy: 169 Pine St., Arcadia, P.O. Box 1633, **Pretoria** 0083 (☎12 344 3875; fax 343 4891). **Consulate:** 37 Shortmarket St., **Cape Town** 8001 (☎021 22 2415; fax 22 2328).

UK: Embassy: 39 Chesham Pl., **London** SW1X 8SB (☎20 7235 5555; fax 7259 5392). **Consulates:** 20 Draycott Pl., **London** SW3 2RZ (☎20 7589 8989; fax 581 7888); Suite 1A, Brookhouse, 70, Spring Gardens, **Manchester** M2 2BQ (☎16 1236 1262; fax 228 7467); 63 North Castle Street, **Edinburgh** EH2 3LJ (☎220 1843; fax 226 4568).

US: Embassy: 2375 Pennsylvania Ave., NW, **Washington, D.C.** 20037 (☎202-728-2330; fax 728-2302; www.spainemb.org). **Consulates:** 150 E. 58th St., 30th fl., **New York,** NY 10155 (☎212-355-4080 or 355-4081; fax 644-3751); **others** in Boston, Chicago, Houston, Los Angeles, Miami, New Orleans, San Juan (PR), and San Francisco.

TOURIST OFFICES

Spain's official tourist board operates an extensive website at www.tourspain.es and offers Barcelona specifics at www.barcelonaturisme.com. The board also has offices abroad in Canada, the US, and the UK.

Canada: Tourist Office of Spain, 2 Bloor St., W., Suite 3402, Toronto, ON M4W 3E2 (☎416-961-3131; fax 961-1992; www.tourspain.toronto.on.ca).

UK: Spanish Tourist Office, 22-23 Manchester Sq., London W1M 5AP (☎207 486 8077; fax 486 8034; www.tourspain.co.uk).

US: Tourist Office of Spain (www.okspain.org), 666 Fifth Ave., 35th fl., New York, NY 10103 (☎212-265-8822; fax 265-8864). Additional offices in Chicago, IL (☎312-642-1992), Los Angeles, CA (☎323-658-7188), and Miami, FL (☎305-358-1992).

PASSPORTS

REQUIREMENTS. Citizens of Australia, Canada, New Zealand, South Africa, and the US need valid passports to enter Spain. For citizens of some countries, Spain does not allow entrance if the holder's passport expires in under six months; check with the appropriate consulate to see if this applies to you. Returning home with an expired passport is illegal. European Union citizens do not have to travel with a passport; a National Identification Card is sufficient for entry.

PASSPORT MAINTENANCE. Be sure to photocopy the page of your passport that contains your photo, as well as your visas, traveler's check serial numbers and any other important documents. Carry one set of copies in a safe place, apart from the originals, and leave another set at home. Consulates recommend carrying an expired passport or an official copy of your birth certificate in a part of your baggage separate from other documents.

If you lose your passport, immediately notify the local police and the nearest embassy or consulate of your home government. To expedite its replacement, you will need to know all information previously recorded and show ID and proof of citizenship. In some cases, a replacement may take weeks to process, and it may be valid only for a limited time. Any visas stamped in your old passport will be irretrievably lost. In an emergency, ask for immediate temporary traveling papers that will permit you to re-enter your home country. Lost passports may be replaced in a matter of days and the process is always faster with a copy of the lost document. The consulate in Barcelona can issue emergency papers and passports within three days.

VISAS & WORK PERMITS

VISAS

As of August 2000, citizens of South Africa need a visa—a stamp, sticker, or insert in your passport specifying the purpose of your travel and the permitted duration of your stay—in addition to a valid passport for entrance to Spain; citizens of Australia, Canada, the Republic of Ireland, the UK, and the US do not need visas for brief stays. **All tourists need a visa for any stay of 90 days or longer in Spain.** Double-check entrance requirements at the nearest embassy or consulate of Spain (see **Embassies & Consulates**, p. 273) for up-to-date info before your departure.

WORK PERMITS

Admission to Spain as a visitor does not include the right to work, which is authorized only by a work permit. For more information, see **Alternatives to Tourism**, p. 304.

IDENTIFICATION

When you travel, always carry two or more forms of identification on your person, including at least one photo ID; a passport combined with a driver's license or birth certificate is usually adequate. Many establishments, especially banks, may require several IDs in order to cash traveler's checks; some stores in Spain require a passport if you want to use a credit card. Never carry all your forms of ID together, and keep photocopies of them in your luggage and at home.

TEACHER & STUDENT IDENTIFICATION. The **International Student Identity Card (ISIC),** the most widely accepted form of student ID, provides discounts on sights, accommodations, food, and transport; ISIC in Barcelona will cut admission to many museums and sights in half. All cardholders have access to a 24hr. emergency helpline (☎+44 20 8762 8110; in the US call collect ☎1-715-345-0505) and receive insurance benefits (see **Insurance,** p. 282). Applicants must be degree-seeking students of a secondary or post-secondary school and must be at least 12 years of age; these requirements make ISIC a good identification choice for those too young for a driver's license. The **International Teacher Identity Card (ITIC)** offers teachers the same insurance coverage as the ISIC, but with limited discounts. For travelers who are 25 years old or under but are not students, the **International Youth Travel Card** (**IYTC;** formerly the **GO 25** Card) also offers many of the same benefits as the ISIC. Each of these identity cards costs US$22. ISIC and ITIC are valid until the end of the year issued; IYTC cards are valid for one year from the date of issue.

CUSTOMS

Upon entering Spain, you must declare certain items from abroad and pay a duty on the value of those articles if it exceeds the allowance established by Spain's customs service. Goods and gifts purchased at duty-free shops abroad are not exempt from duty or sales tax at your point of return and thus must be declared as well; "duty-free" merely means that you need not pay a tax in the country of purchase. Duty-free allowances were abolished for travel between EU member states on July 1, 1999, but still exist for those arriving from outside the EU.

Upon returning home, you must similarly declare all articles acquired abroad and pay a duty on the value of articles in excess of your home country's allowance. In order to expedite your return, make a list of any valuables brought from home and register them with customs before traveling abroad. Also be sure to keep receipts for all major purchases abroad.

MONEY

CURRENCY & EXCHANGE

The currency chart below is based on August 2003 exchange rates between the Euro and Australian dollars (AUS$), Canadian dollars (CDN$), New Zealand dollars (NZ$), South African rand (ZAR), British pounds (UK£), and US dollars (US$). Check the currency converter on financial websites such as www.bloomburg.com and www.xe.com, or a large newspaper, for the latest exchange rates.

As a general rule, it's cheaper to convert money in Spain than at home. However, you should bring enough euros to last for the first 24-72hr. of a trip should you arrive after bank hours or on a holiday. When changing money, go to banks or *casas de cambio* that have at most a 5% margin between their buy and sell prices. Since you lose money with every transaction, **convert large sums, but no more than you'll need.**

If you use traveler's checks or cash, carry some in small denominations (the equivalent of US$50 or less) for times when you are forced to exchange money at disadvantageous rates, but bring a range of denominations since charges may be levied per check cashed. Store your money in a variety of forms; ideally, at any given time you will be carrying some cash, some traveler's checks, and an ATM and/or credit card.

EUROS (EUR€)		
AUS$1 = EUR€0.58	EUR€1 = AUS$1.73
CDN$1 = EUR€0.64	EUR€1 = CDN$1.57
NZ$1 = EUR€0.52	EUR€1 = NZ$1.93
ZAR1 = EUR€0.12	EUR€1 = ZAR8.36
UK£1 = EUR€1.41	EUR€1 = UK£0.71
US$1 = EUR€0.89	EUR€1 = US$1.16

TRAVELER'S CHECKS

Traveler's checks, one of the safest and least troublesome means of carrying funds, are readily accepted in Barcelona. American Express and Visa are the most widely recognized brands. Check issuers provide refunds if the checks are lost or stolen, and many provide additional services, such as toll-free refund hotlines abroad, emergency message services, and stolen credit card assistance.

American Express: Checks available with commission at select banks and all AmEx offices. US residents can also purchase checks by phone (☎888-887-8986) or online (www.aexp.com). Checks available in American, Australian, British, Canadian, euro, and Japanese currencies. For more information, contact AmEx's service centers: in Barcelona ☎93 301 1166; in Australia ☎800 25 19 02; in New Zealand 0800 441 068; in the UK ☎0800 521 313; in the US and Canada ☎800-221-7282; elsewhere US collect ☎801-964-6665.

Visa: Checks available (generally with commission) at banks worldwide. For the location of the nearest office: in the US ☎800-227-6811; in the UK ☎0800 89 50 78; elsewhere UK collect ☎020 7937 8091. Checks available in American, British, Canadian, Japanese, and euro currencies. To report lost or stolen checks in Spain, or to find the location of their nearest office, call ☎90 097 44 14.

CREDIT, DEBIT, AND ATM CARDS

Credit cards are widely accepted in Barcelona, and often offer superior exchange rates—up to 5% better than the retail rate used by banks and other currency exchange establishments. Credit cards may also offer services such as insurance or emergency help. While credit cards are sometimes necessary to reserve hotel rooms or rental cars, cash is often required at budget establishments. **MasterCard** (a.k.a. EuroCard or Access in Europe) and **Visa** (a.k.a. Carte Bleue or Barclaycard) are the most welcomed; **American Express** cards work at some ATMs, AmEx offices, and at major airports. The AmEx national number in Spain is ☎900 994 426.

ATMs are widespread in Spain and everywhere in Barcelona. Depending on the system that your home bank uses, you can most likely access your personal bank account from abroad. ATM cards get the same wholesale exchange rate as credit cards, but there is often a limit on the amount of money you can withdraw per day (around US$500), and unfortunately, computer networks sometimes fail. There is typically also a surcharge of US$1-5 per withdrawal.

Debit cards are a relatively new form of purchasing power and are as convenient as credit cards but have a more immediate impact on your funds. A debit card can be used wherever its associated credit card company (usually Mastercard or Visa) is accepted, yet the money is withdrawn directly from the holder's checking account. Debit cards often also function as ATM cards and can be used to withdraw cash from associated banks and ATMs throughout

i **ESSENTIAL** INFORMATION

PINS

To use a cash or credit card to withdraw money from a cash machine (ATM) in Europe, you must have a four-digit **Personal Identification Number (PIN).** If your PIN is longer than four digits ask your bank if you can just use the first four, or whether you'll need a new one. **Credit cards** don't usually come with PINs, so if you intend to hit up ATMs in Europe with a credit card to get cash advances, call your credit card company to request one before you leave.

People with alphabetic, rather than numerical, PINs may also be thrown off by the lack of letters on most European cash machines (In Barcelona, most ServiCaixa machines list letters; other companies do not). The following handy chart gives the corresponding numbers to use: 2=ABC; 3=DEF; 4=GHI; 5=JKL; 6=MNO; 7=PQRS; 8=TUV; and 9=WXYZ. Note that if you mistakenly punch the wrong code into the machine three times, it will swallow your card.

Floquet

Seafood

Pony Ride

Spain. Ask your local bank about obtaining one. The two major international money networks are **Cirrus** (to locate ATMs, contact US ☎ 800-424-7787 or visit www.mastercard.com) and **Visa/PLUS** (to locate ATMs US call ☎ 800-843-7587 or www.visa.com).

COSTS

STAYING ON A BUDGET

Before you go, calculate a reasonable per-day budget that will meet your needs. To give you a general idea, a bare-bones day in Barcelona (camping or sleeping in hostels/guest houses, buying food at supermarkets) would cost about US$35/€37; a slightly more comfortable day (sleeping in hostels/guest houses and the occasional budget hotel, eating one meal a day at a restaurant, going out at night) would run US$50/€53; and for a day of luxury, the sky's the limit. Don't underestimate the cost of partying in Barcelona; while some clubs may charge no cover, drink prices can get out of hand. Also, don't forget to factor in emergency reserve funds (at least US$200) when planning how much money you'll need.

TAXES

Spain has a 7% **Value Added Tax,** known as IVA, at all restaurants and accommodations. The prices listed in *Let's Go* include IVA unless otherwise mentioned. Retail goods bear a much higher IVA (16%), although, again, listed prices usually include the tax. Non-EU citizens who have stayed in the EU for fewer than 180 days can claim back at the airport the tax paid on purchases. Ask the shop where you have made the purchase to supply you with a tax return form.

HEALTH

In your **passport,** write the names of any people you wish contacted in case of a medical emergency, and also list any allergies or medical conditions a doctor would need to know about. Matching a prescription to a foreign equivalent is not always easy, safe, or possible; not only are drug names different, not all the substances that are legal in your home country will be legal in Europe. Carry up-to-date, legible prescriptions or a statement from your doctor stating the medication's trade name, manufacturer, chemical name, and dosage. While traveling, be sure to keep all medication with you in your carry-on luggage.

IMMUNIZATIONS

Travelers over two years old should be sure that the following vaccines are up to date: MMR (for measles, mumps, and rubella); DTaP or Td (for diptheria, tetanus, and pertussis), OPV (for polio), HbCV (for haemophilus influenza B), and HBV (for hepatitis B). For recommendations on immunizations and prophylaxis, consult the CDC (see below) in the US or the equivalent in your home country.

USEFUL ORGANIZATIONS & PUBLICATIONS

The US **Centers for Disease Control and Prevention** (**CDC;** ☎877-394-8747; www.cdc.gov/travel) maintains an international travelers' hotline and an informative website. The CDC's comprehensive booklet, *Health Information for International Travel*, an annual rundown of disease, immunization, and general health advice, is free online or US$25 via the Public Health Foundation (☎877-252-1200). Consult the appropriate government agency of your home country for consular information sheets on health, entry requirements, and other issues (see the box on **Travel Advisories**, p. 282). For quick information on health and other travel warnings, call the **Overseas Citizens Services** (☎202-647-5225, after-hours 647-4000), or contact a passport agency, embassy, or consulate abroad. US citizens can send a self-addressed, stamped envelope to the Overseas Citizens Services, Bureau of Consular Affairs, #4811, US Department of State, Washington, D.C. 20520. For information on medical evacuation services and travel insurance firms, see the US government's website at http://travel.state.gov/medical.html or the **British Foreign and Commonwealth Office's** website at www.fco.gov.uk.

MEDICAL ASSISTANCE

There are no particular health risks associated with traveling in Spain. The public health care system is very reliable; in an emergency, seek out the *urgencia* (emergency) section of the nearest hospital. For more information about medical services in the city, see **Once In** (p. 27).

If you are concerned about obtaining medical assistance while traveling, you may wish to employ special support services. The *MedPass* from **GlobalCare, Inc.**, 2001 Westside

Balancing an Egg on a Fountain

Barça Fans

Shopper with Mobile Phone

TRAVEL ADVISORIES

The following government offices provide travel information and advisories by telephone, by fax, or via the Internet. Remember to check the advisories while on the road during long stints of travel; governments constantly update warnings:

Australian Department of Foreign Affairs and Trade: ☎1300 555135; fax back service 02 6261 1299; www.dfat.gov.au.

Canadian Department of Foreign Affairs and International Trade (DFAIT): In Canada and the US ☎800-267-6788, elsewhere +1 613-944-6788; www.dfait-maeci.gc.ca. Call for the free booklet, *Bon Voyage...But*.

New Zealand Ministry of Foreign Affairs: ☎04 494 8500; fax 494 8506; www.mft.govt.nz/trav.html.

South African Department of Foreign Affais: ☎09 27 12 351 1000; fax 351 1306; www.dfa.gov.za.

United Kingdom Foreign and Commonwealth Office: ☎020 7008 0232; fax 7008 0155; www.fco.gov.uk.

US Department of State: ☎202-647-5225; fax back service 647-3000; http://travel.state.gov. For *A Safe Trip Abroad*, call ☎202-512-1800.

Pkwy., #120, Alpharetta, GA 30004, USA (☎800-860-1111; www.globalems.com), provides 24hr. international medical assistance, support, and medical evacuation resources. The **International Association for Medical Assistance to Travelers** (**IAMAT;** US ☎716-754-4883, Canada ☎416-652-0137, New Zealand ☎03 352 20 53; www.sentex.net/~iamat) has free membership, lists English-speaking doctors worldwide, and offers detailed info on immunization requirements and sanitation. Those with medical conditions (such as diabetes, allergies to antibiotics, epilepsy, or a heart condition) may want to obtain a **MedicAlert** membership (first year US$35, annually thereafter US$20), which includes a stainless steel ID tag, a 24hr. collect-call number, and other benefits. Contact the MedicAlert Foundation, 2323 Colorado Ave., Turlock, CA 95382, USA (US ☎888-633-4298, elsewhere ☎209-668-3333; www.medicalert.org).

AIDS, HIV & STDS

For detailed information on **Acquired Immune Deficiency Syndrome** (**AIDS,** or **SIDA** in Spanish) in Spain and Barcelona, call the **US Centers for Disease Control's** 24hr. hotline at ☎800-342-2437, or contact the **Joint United Nations Programme on HIV/AIDS (UNAIDS),** 20, ave. Appia, CH-1211 Geneva 27, Switzerland (☎41 22 791 3666; fax 22 791 4187). Travelers should be aware that Spain has the highest AIDS rate in all of Western Europe, due mainly to its proximity to Africa and high immigration rates from the region.

Sexually transmitted diseases (STDs) such as gonorrhea, chlamydia, genital warts, syphilis, and herpes are easier to catch than HIV and can be just as deadly. **Hepatitis** B and C can also be transmitted sexually. Though condoms may protect you from some STDs, oral or even tactile contact can lead to transmission. If you think you may have contracted an STD, see a doctor immediately.

INSURANCE

Travel insurance generally covers four basic areas: medical/health problems, property loss, trip cancellation/interruption, and emergency evacuation. Although your regular insurance policies may extend to travel-related accidents, you may consider purchasing travel insurance if the cost of potential trip cancellation/interruption is greater than you can absorb. Travel insurance generally runs about US$50 per week for full coverage, while trip cancellation/interruption may be purchased separately at a rate of about US$5.50 per US$100 of coverage.

Medical insurance often covers costs incurred abroad; check with your provider. **US Medicare** does not cover foreign travel. **Canadians** are protected by their home province's health insurance plan for 90 days abroad; check with the provincial Ministry of Health or Health Plan Headquarters for details. **Homeowner's insurance** often covers theft during travel and loss of travel documents up to US$500.

ISIC and **ITIC** (see p. 277) provide basic insurance benefits; card holders have access to a 24hr. helpline (run by the insurance provider **TravelGuard**) for medical, legal, and financial emergencies overseas (US and Canada ☎ 877-370-4742, elsewhere US collect ☎ 715-345-0505). **American Express** (US ☎ 800-528-4800) grants most cardholders automatic car rental insurance (collision and theft, but not liability), and ground travel accident coverage of US$100,000 on flight purchases made with the card.

Insurance Providers **Council** and **STA** (see p. 284) offer a range of plans that can supplement your basic coverage and often include substantial emergency evacuation costs. Other private insurance providers in the US and Canada include: **Access America** (☎ 800-284-8300), **Berkely Group/Carefree Travel Insurance** (☎ 800-323-3149; www.berkely.com), **Globalcare Travel Insurance** (☎ 800-821-2488; www.globalcare-cocco.com), and **Travel Assistance International** (☎ 800-821-2828; www.europ-assistance.com). For a provider in the **UK**, contact **Columbus Direct** (☎ 020 7375 0011). In **Australia**, try **AFTA** (☎ 02 9375 4955).

ESSENTIAL INFORMATION

CURRENTS & ADAPTERS

In Barcelona, electric current is 220 volts AC, enough to fry any 120V North American appliance. Americans and Canadians should buy an adapter (which changes the shape of the plug) and a converter (which changes the voltage; US$20). Don't make the mistake of using only an adapter (unless appliance instructions explicitly state otherwise). New Zealanders and South Africans (who both use 220V at home), as well as Australians (who use 240/250V), won't need a converter, but will need a set of adapters to use anything electrical.

PACKING

Barcelona is a stylish city; if you will be staying for an extended period of time, be sure to bring a pair of dress shoes and slacks. Otherwise, when travelling continuously on the road, pack lightly: lay out only what you absolutely need, then take half the clothes and twice the money.

LUGGAGE. If you plan to cover most of your itinerary by foot, a sturdy **frame backpack** is unbeatable. Toting a **suitcase** or **trunk** is fine if you plan to live in the city and explore from there, but not a great idea if you plan to move around. A **daypack** (a small backpack or courier bag) will be useful.

SLEEPSACK. Some hostels require that you either provide your own linen or rent sheets. Save cash by making your own sleepsack: fold a full-size sheet in half, then sew the long side and one of the short sides.

FIRST-AID KIT. A basic first-aid kit includes: bandages, pain reliever, antibiotic cream, a thermometer, a Swiss Army knife, tweezers, moleskin, decongestant, motion-sickness remedy, diarrhea or upset-stomach medication, an antihistamine, sunscreen, insect repellent, burn ointment, and a syringe for emergencies.

OTHER USEFUL ITEMS. For safety purposes, you should bring a **money belt** and small **padlock**. Consider bringing **electrical tape** for patching tears, and a **needle and thread** for sewing holes. If you want to do laundry by hand, bring detergent, a small rubber ball to stop up the sink, and string for a makeshift clothes line.

Other things you're liable to forget are **plastic bags** (for damp clothes, soap, food, shampoo, and other spillables), an **alarm clock,** safety pins, matches or a lighter, earplugs, garbage bags, and a small **calculator.**

IMPORTANT DOCUMENTS. Don't forget your passport, traveler's checks, ATM and/or credit cards, adequate ID, and photocopies of all of the aforementioned in case these documents are lost or stolen (see p. 277). Also check that you have any of the following that might apply to you: driver's license (see p. 277), travel insurance forms, and/or rail or bus pass (see p. 288).

CONTACTING SPAIN

BY MAIL

Spain's postal service is good, although it may not be quite as fast as other Western European countries'. A letter should take about 7-8 working days to reach Spain from North America, 3-4 days from Europe, or 9 days from anywhere else with a decent postal system. Packages should hypothetically take the same amount of time but are much more susceptible to enigmatic delays.

BY PHONE

Barcelona is one hour ahead of Greenwich Mean Time, two hours ahead during Daylight Savings Time. To place an international call: first, dial the international dialing prefix of the country you are calling from (from Australia, dial 0011; Canada or the US, 011; the Republic of Ireland, New Zealand, or the UK, 00; South Africa, 09); second, dial Spain's country code (34); third, dial the city code (for Barcelona, 93) and the local number. All numbers in listings include the city code. For more info on phones in Barcelona, see **Once In Barcelona,** p. 30.

GETTING TO BARCELONA

BY PLANE

AIRFARES

Airfares to Barcelona peak between June and August; major Catholic holidays are also expensive. The cheapest time to travel is winter, November to February. Midweek (M-Th morning) round-trip flights run US$40-50 cheaper than weekend flights, but they are generally more crowded and less likely to permit frequent-flyer upgrades. Not fixing a return date ("open return") or arriving in and departing from different cities ("open-jaw") is pricier than purchasing a round-trip ticket. Patching one-way flights together is the most expensive way to travel. **Fares** for round-trip flights to Barcelona from the US or Canadian east coast may cost US$700 or more in peak months or US$350-500 in winter months; from the US or Canadian west coast US$800 to well over US$1000; from the UK £100-450; from Australia AUS$1800-2500.

BUDGET & STUDENT TRAVEL AGENCIES

While knowledgeable agents specializing in flights to Spain can make your life easier and help you save money, they may not spend the time to find the lowest possible fare—they get paid on commission. Travelers with student cards, such as **ISIC and IYTC** (see p. 277) qualify for big discounts from travel agencies. Most flights from budget agencies are on major airlines, but in peak season some may sell seats on less reliable chartered aircraft.

CTS Travel, 30 Rathbone Pl., **London** W1T 1QG, UK (☎0207 290 00630; www.ctstravel.co.uk).

STA Travel, 7890 S. Hardy Dr., Suite 110, Tempe, AZ 85284, USA (☎800-781-4040; www.sta-travel.com). A student and youth travel organization with over 150 offices worldwide (check the website for a listing of all their offices), including US offices in Boston, Chicago, L.A., New York, San Francisco, Seattle, and Washington, D.C. Ticket booking, travel insurance, rail passes, and more. In the UK, walk-in office at 11 Goodge St., **London** W1T 2PF (☎0207 436 7779), in New Zealand, Shop 2B, 182 Queen St., **Auckland** (☎09 309 0458), in Australia, 366 Lygon St., **Carlton** VIC 3053 (☎03 9349 4344).

Travel CUTS (Canadian Universities Travel Services, Limited), 187 College St., **Toronto,** ON M5T 1P7 (☎416-979-2406; www.travelcuts.com). 60 offices across Canada and a few in the US, including Boston, New York, San Francisco, and Seattle. Also in the UK, 295-A Regent St., **London** W1B 2H9 (☎0207 255 1944).

Usit World, 19-21 Aston Quay, **Dublin** 2 (☎01 602 1600; www.usitworld.com) Ireland's leading student/ budget travel agency has 22 offices throughout Northern Ireland and the Republic of Ireland. Offers programs to work in North America. Offices all over the world, including a gateway office in Barcelona; see **Service Directory,** p. 313.

Wasteels, Skoubogade 6, 1158 **Copenhagen** (☎3314 4633; fax 7630 0865; www.wasteels.dk/ uk). A huge chain with 165 locations across Europe. Sells Wasteels BIJ tickets discounted 30-45% off regular fare, 2nd-class international point-to-point train tickets with unlimited stopovers for those under 26 (sold only in Europe).

COMMERCIAL & DISCOUNT AIRLINES

The commercial airlines' lowest regular offer is the **APEX** (Advance Purchase Excursion) fare, which provides confirmed reservations and allows "open-jaw" tickets. Generally, reservations must be made seven to 21 days ahead of departure, with a seven- to 14-day minimum-stay and up to 90-day maximum-stay restrictions. These fares carry hefty cancellation and change penalties. Book peak-season APEX fares early; by May you will have a hard time getting your desired departure date. The Air Travel Advisory Bureau, in London (☎020 7636 5000; www.atab.co.uk), provides referrals to travel agencies and consolidators that offer discounted airfares out of the UK. All major international airlines offer service to Barcelona; popular carriers are listed here.

Birdcage in Window

Museu del Perfum

Miro Mosaic

Air France: US ☎800-237-2747; www.airfrance.com. Connections to Barcelona from Paris.

British Airways: US ☎800-247-9297, UK ☎84 5779 9977; www.british-airways.com. Flights through the UK from Europe and the east coast of North America.

British Midland Airways: UK ☎87 0607 0555; www.flybmi.com. Departures from throughout the UK.

EasyJet: UK ☎0870 600 00 00; www.easyjet.com. London to Barcelona UK£47-136.

Iberia: US and Canada ☎800-772-4642, UK ☎020 7830 0011, Spain ☎902 400 500, South Africa ☎11 884 92 55, Ireland ☎1 407 30 17; www.iberia.com. Serves all domestic locations and major international cities.**Aviaco,** a subsidiary of Iberia, covers only domestic routes. Ask about youth and other discounts—ages 12 and under often get a 25% discount, and Iberia usually offers a range of ticket types with different restrictions and prices. Some fares purchased in the US require a 21-day minimum advance purchase.

SpanAir: US ☎888-545-5757, Spain ☎971 745 020; www.spanair.com. Offers international and domestic flights.

COURIER FLIGHTS

Those who travel light should consider courier flights. Couriers help transport cargo on international flights by using their checked luggage space for freight. Generally, couriers must travel with carry-ons only and must deal with complex flight restrictions. Most flights are round-trip only, with short fixed-length stays (usually one week) and a limit of one ticket per issue. Generally, you must be over 21 (in some cases 18). In summer, the most popular destinations usually necessitate a reservation booked two weeks in advance (you may book up to two months ahead). Super-discounted fares are common for "last-minute" flights (three to 14 days ahead).

FROM NORTH AMERICA

Round-trip courier fares from the US to Barcelona run about US$200-500. Most flights leave from New York, Los Angeles, Miami, or San Francisco in the US; and from Montreal, Toronto, or Vancouver in Canada. The organizations below provide members with lists of opportunities and courier brokers for an annual fee. Prices quoted below are round-trip.

Air Courier Association, 350 Indiana St., #300, Golden, CO 80401, USA (US☎800-282-1202; www.aircourier.org). Ten departure cities throughout the US and Canada (high-season US$150-360). One-year membership US$49.

International Association of Air Travel Couriers (IAATC), P.O. Box 980, Keystone Heights, FL 32656, USA (US☎352-475-1584; www.courier.org). From 9 North American cities. One-year membership US$45.

Global Courier Travel, P.O. Box 3051, Nederland, CO 80466, USA (www.globalcourier-travel.com). Searchable online database. Six departure points in the US and Canada to Madrid. Lifetime membership US$40, 2 people US$55.

NOW Voyager, 315 W. 49th St., New York, NY 10019, USA (☎212-459-1616). Flights to Madrid US$500-700. Usually one-week max. stay. One-year membership US$50. Non-courier discount fares also available.

FROM THE UK AND IRELAND

The minimum age for couriers from the **UK** is usually 18. **Brave New World Enterprises,** P.O. Box 22212, London SE5 8WB (www.courierflights.com) publishes a directory of all the companies offering courier flights in the UK (UK£10, in electronic form UK£8). **Global Courier Travel** (see above) also offers flights from London and Dublin to Madrid. **British Airways Travel Shop** (☎0870 240 0747; www.batravelshops.com) arranges some flights from London to destinations in continental Europe (specials may be as low as UK£60; no registration fee).

TICKET CONSOLIDATORS

Ticket consolidators, or **"bucket shops,"** buy unsold tickets in bulk from commercial airlines and sell them at discounted rates. The best place to look is in the Sunday travel section of any major newspaper (such as the *New York Times*), where many bucket shops place tiny ads. Call quickly, as availability is typically extremely limited. Not all bucket shops are reliable, so insist on a receipt that gives full details of restrictions, refunds, and tickets, and pay by credit card (2-5% fee) so you can stop payment if you never receive tickets. For more information, see www.travel-library.com/air-travel/consolidators.html.

FROM THE US & CANADA

Travel Avenue (☎800-333-3335; www.travelavenue.com) searches for best available published fares and then uses several consolidators to attempt to beat that fare. **NOW Voyager,** 74 Varick St., Suite 307, New York, NY 10013 (☎212-431-1616; fax 219-1793; www.nowvoyagertravel.com) arranges discounted flights from New York to Barcelona. Other consolidators worth trying are **Rebel** (☎800-227-3235; www.rebeltours.com), **Travel Information Services** (www.tiss.com), **TravelHUB** (www.travelhub.com), and **The Travel Site** (www.thetravelsite.com). Keep in mind these are just suggestions to get you started in your research; *Let's Go* does not endorse any of these agencies.

FROM THE UK, AUSTRALIA & NEW ZEALAND

In London, the **Air Travel Advisory Bureau** (☎0207 636 5000; www.atab.co.uk) can provide names of reliable consolidators and discount flight specialists. For flights from Australia and New Zealand, look for consolidator ads in the travel section of the *Sydney Morning Herald* and other papers.

STANDBY FLIGHTS

Traveling standby requires considerable flexibility in arrival and departure dates and cities. Companies dealing in standby flights sell vouchers rather than tickets, along with the promise to get you to your destination (or near your destination) within a certain window of time (typically 1-5 days). Carefully read agreements with any company offering standby flights, as fine print can leave you in the lurch. To check on a company's service record in the US, call the Better Business Bureau (☎212-533-6200). One established standby company in the US is **Whole Earth Travel,** 325 W. 38th St., New York, NY 10018, USA (☎800-326-2009; www.4standby.com). Offers one-way flights to Europe from the Northeast (US$169), West Coast (US$249), Midwest (US$219), and Southeast (US$199). Intracontinental connecting flights within the US or Europe cost US$79-139.

CHARTER FLIGHTS

Charters are flights a tour operator contracts with an airline to fly extra loads of passengers during peak season. Charter flights fly less frequently than major airlines, making refunds particularly difficult, and are almost always fully booked. Schedules and itineraries may also change or be canceled at the last moment (as late as 48hr. before the trip, and without a full refund), and check-in, boarding, and baggage claim are often much slower. However, they can also be cheaper.

Discount clubs and **fare brokers** offer members savings on last-minute charter and tour deals. Study contracts closely; you don't want to end up with an unwanted overnight layover. **Travelers Advantage** specializes in European travel and tour packages. (US ☎203-365-2000; www.travelersadvantage.com. A US$60 annual fee includes discounts and cheap flight directories.)

Portraits on Las Ramblas

Cambios

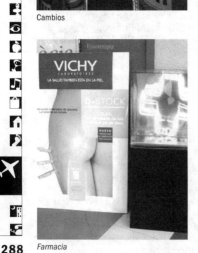

Farmacia

BY TRAIN

Spanish trains are clean, relatively punctual, and reasonably priced. Spain's national railway is **RENFE** (☎ 90 224 02 02, international 93 490 11 22; www.renfe.es). RENFE offers extensive service in Spain and all of Europe, on a variety of trains. (Open daily 7am-10pm.) *Tranvía*, *semidirecto*, and *correo* trains are very slow. The Euromed has the fewest stops, while the Estrella, Talgo, Arco, Diurno and the Regional usually take much longer. The prices listed below are for the sitting *turista* class only (*preferente* and beds cost more). Non-smokers (or even non-chain-smokers) should consider buying a *no-fumador* (non-smoking) seat a few days in advance, as they are apt to sell out. For more details on prices and routes, ask at an information window for an *horario* (schedule). Some of the most popular connections to and from Barcelona include: **Alicante** (4-5hr., 8 per day, €30-41); **Bilbao** (8-9hr., 5 per day, €30-32); **Granada** (11-12hr., 4 per day, €46-47); **Madrid** (7-8hr., 7 per day, €31-42); **Pamplona** (6-7hr., 2 per day, €27.50); **Salamanca** (10-12hr., 5 per day, €37.50); **San Sebastian** (8-9hr., 5 per day, €29.50-31); **Sevilla** (11-12hr., 6 per day, €47-51); **Valencia** (3-5hr., 15 per day 7am-9pm, €27.50-32). International destination include **Milan** (through **Figueres** and **Nice**) and **Montpellier** with connections to **Geneva, Paris**, and various stops along the French Riviera. There is a 20% discount on round-trip tickets.

There is absolutely no reason to buy a Eurail pass if you are planning on traveling just within Spain. Trains are cheap, so a pass saves little money, and may actually be more expensive than buying individual tickets. Ages 4-11 are half-price; children under four are free. You must purchase rail passes at least 15 days before departure. Call ☎ 1-800-438-7245 in the US or go to www.raileurope.com.

Spain Flexipass offers 3 days of unlimited travel in a 2-month period. 1st-class US$200; 2nd-class US$155. Each additional rail-day (up to 10) US$35 1st-class, US$30 2nd-class.

Iberic Railpass is good for 3 days of unlimited 1st-class travel in Spain and Portugal for US$205. Each additional rail-day (up to 10) US$45.

Spain Rail n' Drive Pass is good for 3 days of unlimited 1st-class train travel and 2 days of unlimited mileage in a rental car within a 2-month period. US$239-325, depending on how many people are traveling and the type of car. Up to 2 additional rail-days and extra car days are also available, and a 3rd and 4th person can join in the car using only a Flexipass.

BY CAR

For more information on traveling by car once you get to Spain, check out **Once in Barcelona,** p. 21.

INTERNATIONAL DRIVING PERMIT (IDP).

You must be at least 18 to drive a car in Barcelona. An International Driving Permit (IDP) is recommended, though Spain allows travelers to drive with a valid American or Canadian license for a limited number of months. Some rental agencies may require an IDP. Furthermore, an IDP will be useful if you're in a situation (involved in an accident or stranded in a small town) in which the police do not know English; information on the IDP is printed in ten languages, including Spanish. AAA members and non-members alike can call US ☎ 800-AAA-HELP (800-222-4357) or visit www.aaa.com for info. Your IDP, valid for one year, must be issued in your own country before you depart. An application usually needs to include one or two photos, a current local license, and an additional form of identification. Fees vary depending on your country.

Information at Casa Robert

CAR INSURANCE. Most credit cards cover standard insurance, though you should always ask before renting a car. If you rent, lease, or borrow a car, you will need a **green card,** or **International Insurance Certificate,** to certify that you have liability insurance and that it applies abroad. Green cards can be obtained at car rental agencies, car dealers (for those leasing cars), some travel agents, and some border crossings. Rental agencies may require you to purchase theft insurance in countries that they consider to have a high risk of auto theft.

Carriage Ride

RENTING. You can rent a car from a US-based firm with European offices, from a European-based company with local representatives, or from a tour operator that will arrange a rental for you from a European company but at its own rates. Multinationals offer greater flexibility, but tour operators often strike better deals. Most available cars will have standard transmission—cars with automatic transmission are difficult to find and much more expensive. Reserve well before leaving for the region and pay in advance if at all possible. The minimum age in Spain is usually 25 with the larger agencies (Hertz, Avis) and 21 at small, local businesses. At most agencies, all that's needed to rent a car is a US license, and possibly an international driver's license (see above). Rental agencies in Barcelona include:

Store Display

289

Hotel on Las Ramblas

Pension Dali

Ducklings for sale on Las Ramblas

Avis/Auto Europe, Casanova, 209 (☎93 209 95 33). Will rent to ages 21-25 for an additional fee of about US$5 a day.

Budget, Av. Josep Tarradellas, 35 (☎93 410 25 08). Must be 25. **Branch** in El Prat de Llobregat airport (see p. 21).

Docar, C. Montnegre, 18 (24hr. ☎93 439 81 19). M: Les Corts. Free delivery and pickup. From €14 per day, plus €9 insurance and €0.15 per km. Open M-F 8:30am-2pm and 3:30-8pm, Sa 9am-2pm.

Hertz, C. Tuset, 10 (☎93 217 80 76; www.hertz.es). M: Diagonal or FCG: Gràcia. Open M-F 9am-2pm and 4-7pm, Sa 9am-2pm. **Branch** in El Prat de Llobregat airport (☎93 298 36 37; see p. 21).

Tot Car, C. Berlín, 97 (☎93 430 01 98). Free delivery and pickup. From €27 per day, plus €0.13 per km. Insurance included. Open M-F 8am-2pm and 3-8pm, Sa 9am-1pm.

SPECIFIC CONCERNS

FEMALE TRAVELERS

Women exploring on their own inevitably face some additional safety concerns, but it's easy to be adventurous without taking undue risks. If you are concerned, consider staying in hostels that offer single rooms that lock from the inside, or in religious organizations with rooms for women only. Stick to centrally located accommodations in well-lit areas. Avoid solitary late-night walks or bus rides, and if you're carrying a purse, make sure it has a zipper or other secure closure and wear it across your body, as purse snatchings are not a rarity in Barcelona.

Always carry extra money for a phone call, bus fare, or taxi. **Hitchhiking** is never safe for a lone woman, or even for two women traveling together. Choose train compartments occupied by women or couples. Look as if you know where you're going and approach older women or couples for directions if you're lost or uncomfortable.

Your best answer to verbal harassment is no answer; the perpetrators generally lose interest quickly if you do not respond at all. The extremely persistent can sometimes be dissuaded by a firm, loud, and very public "*Vete*"—"Go away" in Spanish. However, don't hesitate to seek out a police officer or a passerby if you feel uncomfortable. Memorize the relevant emergency numbers, and consider carrying a whistle on your keychain. Also, think about taking a self-defense course; it will not only prepare you for a potential attack, but will also raise your level of awareness of your surroundings as well as your confidence.

SOLO TRAVELERS

There are many benefits to traveling alone, including independence and greater interaction with locals. On the other hand, any solo traveler is a more vulnerable target of harassment and street theft. Lone travelers need to be well organized and look confident at all times. Try not to stand out as a tourist, and be especially careful in deserted or very crowded areas. If questioned, never admit that you are traveling alone. Maintain regular contact with someone at home who knows the number of your hostel and what you'll be doing from day to day. For more tips, pick up *Traveling Solo* by Eleanor Berman (Globe Pequot Press, US$17), or subscribe to **Connecting: Solo Travel Network,** 689 Park Road, Unit 6, Gibsons, BC, V0N 1V7 Canada (☎604-886-9099; www.cstn.org; membership US$35). **Travel Companion Exchange,** P.O. Box 833, Amityville, NY 11701, USA (☎800-392-1256; www.whytravelalone.com; US$48), links solo travelers with companions with similar travel habits and interests.

OLDER TRAVELERS

Senior citizens are eligible for a wide range of discounts. If you don't see a senior citizen price listed, ask, and you may be delightfully surprised, as they are almost as frequent as student discounts. Throughout the book we note sights and museums which proivde discounts for seniors, usually 60 or 65 years of age and older. The books *No Problem! Worldwise Tips for Mature Adventurers* by Janice Kenyon (Orca Book Publishers; US$16) and *Unbelievably Good Deals and Great Adventures That You Absolutely Can't Get Unless You're Over 50* by Joan Rattner Heilman (NTC/Contemporary Publishing; US$13) are both excellent resources. For more information, contact one of the following organizations:

Elderhostel, 11 Ave. de Lafayette, Boston, MA 02111 USA (☎877-426-8056; www.elderhostel.org). Organizes 1- to 4-week "educational adventures" in Barcelona for those 55+.

The Mature Traveler, P.O. Box 15791, Sacramento, CA 95852 USA (☎800-460-6676). Deals, discounts, and travel packages for the 50+ traveler. Subscription $30.

BISEXUAL, GAY & LESBIAN TRAVELERS

As a predominantly Catholic country with a recent history of fascism, Spain leans toward the conservative side when it comes to recognizing the sexuality spectrum. However, Barcelona is perhaps the most accepting, most comfortable, and most exciting city in Spain for LGB travelers; it's proximity to gay-friendly **Sitges** is another plus (see **Daytripping**, p. 233). The Mediterranean coast is an LGB nightlife mecca. No special precautions should be necessary for gay travel in Barcelona.

For the inside scoop on all things gay and lesbian in Barcelona—from gay-friendly hostels to the best gay nightlife—check out the **LGB** sidebars scattered throughout this guide. The *plano gay* is a map with listings in both Sitges and Barcelona and is available at many gay-friendly listings. Below are contact organizations, mail-order bookstores, and publishers that offer materials addressing some specific concerns. **Out and About** (www.planetout.com) offers a bi-weekly newsletter and a comprehensive site addressing gay travel concerns.

Gay in Spain: www.gayinspain.com. A webpage that offers comprehensive coverage of LGB resources and establishments in Spanish and English in Barcelona, Sitges, and Girona.

Gay's the Word, 66 Marchmont St., London WC1N 1AB (☎20 7278 7654; www.gaystheword.co.uk). The largest gay and lesbian bookshop in the UK, with both fiction and non-fiction titles. Mail-order service available.

Giovanni's Room, 1145 Pine St., Philadelphia, PA 19107, USA (☎215-923-2960; www.queerbooks.com). An international lesbian/feminist and gay bookstore with mail-order service carries many of the publications listed below.

International Lesbian and Gay Association (ILGA), 81 rue Marché-au-Charbon, B-1000 Brussels, Belgium (☎2 502 2471; www.ilga.org). Provides political information, such as homosexuality laws of individual countries.

> **FURTHER READING: BISEXUAL, GAY & LESBIAN.**
> *Spartacus International Gay Guide 2001-2002.* Bruno Gmunder Verlag (US$33).
> *Damron Men's Guide, Damron's Accommodations,* and *The Women's Traveller.* Damron Travel Guides (US$14-19). For more info, call ☎800-462-6654 or visit www.damron.com.
> *Ferrari Guides' Gay Travel A to Z, Ferrari Guides' Men's Travel in Your Pocket,* and *Ferrari Guides' Inn Places.* Ferrari Publications (US$16-20). Purchase the guides online at www.ferrariguides.com.
> *The Gay Vacation Guide: The Best Trips and How to Plan Them,* Mark Chesnut. Citadel Press (US$15).

TRAVELERS WITH DISABILITIES

Because sections of Barcelona are so old, it can be difficult to get around in certain neighborhoods, specifically the Ciutat Vella, which includes the Barri Gòtic, La Ribera, and El Raval. Hostels, mostly in aging buildings, tend to have narrow doorways, and only a few boast elevators. Restaurants and shops, particularly in the Ciutat Vella, also tend to have unmanageable entrances. In this medieval area, the sidewalks are narrow and the streets are cobblestone. Spain has made huge improvements over the last ten years, but wheelchair accessibility does not mean the same thing in Spain as in the US. Those with disabilities should inform airlines, hotels, and hostels of their disabilities when making reservations; some time may be needed to make the necessary preparations. Call ahead to restaurants, museums, and other facilities to find out about the existence of ramps, the widths of doors, the dimensions of elevators, etc. *Let's Go* has investigated the accessibility of the sights and establishments we list; be advised, however, that when something is labeled "wheelchair-accessible," that term may only denote an adequate width of doors and absence of steps, and not necessarily an accessible bathroom.

The **train** is probably the most convenient form of travel for disabled travelers in Europe; many (but not all) stations have ramps, and some trains have wheelchair lifts, special seating areas, and specially equipped toilets. Usually **bus** companies say that all their vehicles are wheelchair accessible, however, the validity of this claim is debatable; be sure to call ahead and double check. For those who wish to rent cars, some major **car rental** agencies (Avis, Hertz, and National) offer hand-controlled vehicles. For wheelchair accessibility, major museums and sites tend to be the most reliable. The **Institut Municipal de Disminuits,** C. Llacuna, 171 (☎93 291 84 00), provides specific information on accessibility. The Ajuntament information office has a map of wheelchair-accessible routes, available at Pl. Sant Miquel or the TMB office in the Universitat Metro stop. For information about wheelchair access points and adapted bus routes, call the **transport information phoneline** (☎93 486 07 52). **Guide dog owners** will not need to quarantine their dogs, but they will need to provide certificates of immunization, and those coming from the US must have their health certificates stamped by the USDA.

USEFUL ORGANIZATIONS

Directions Unlimited, 123 Green Ln., Bedford Hills, NY 10507, USA (☎800-533-5343). Books individual and group vacations for the physically disabled; not an info service.

Mobility International USA (MIUSA), P.O. Box 10767, Eugene, OR 97440 USA (voice and TTD ☎541-343-1284; www.miusa.org). Sells *A World of Options: A Guide to International Educational Exchange, Community Service, and Travel for Persons with Disabilities* (US$35).

Society for the Advancement of Travel for the Handicapped (SATH), 347 Fifth Ave., #610, New York, NY 10016, USA (☎212-447-7284; www.sath.org). An advocacy group that publishes free online travel information and the travel magazine *Open World* (US$18, free for members). Annual membership US$45, students and seniors US$30.

MINORITY TRAVELERS

The Spanish suffer from little interaction with different ethnicities due to closed borders under Franco (see **Life and Times,** p. 42). Barcelona is perhaps the most cosmopolitan city in Spain because of its relative proximity to most of Europe. Despite a growing immigrant community and increasing diversity, however, minority travelers may encounter a certain degree of curiosity with respect to their skin color. In general, comments or reactions that minority travelers perceive as offensive are not meant to be hostile.

TRAVELERS WITH CHILDREN

Family vacations often require that you slow your pace and always require that you plan ahead. When deciding where to stay, remember the special needs of young children; if you pick a small hotel, call ahead and make sure it's child-friendly. **Be sure that your child carries some sort of ID** in case of an emergency or in case he or she gets lost.

Museums and tourist attractions in Barcelona frequently offer discounts for children. Children under two generally fly for 10% of the adult airfare on international flights (this does not necessarily include a seat). International fares are usually discounted 25% for ages two to 11. Barcelona is full of children and full of activities for families to do together; *Let's Go: Barcelona* features a special **Kids in the City** sidebar with suggestions for family- and kid-oriented activities. For more information, consult one of the following books or check with a local library:

How to take Great Trips with Your Kids, Sanford and Jane Portnoy. Harvard Common Press (US$10).

On the Go With Baby: A Stress Free Guide to Getting Across Town or Around the World, Ericka Lutz. Sourcebooks Trade (US$15).

The Penny Whistle Traveling-with-Kids Book, Meredith Brokaw. Fireside (US$14).

Trouble-Free Travel with Children, Vicki Lansky. Book Peddlers (US$9).

DIETARY CONCERNS

Spain can be a difficult place to visit as a strict vegetarian; meat or fish is featured in the vast majority of popular dishes. Most restaurants serve salads, and there are also many egg-, rice-, and bean-based dishes that can be requested without meat. Be careful, though, as some servers may interpret a "vegetarian" order to mean "with tuna instead of ham." While you have to be careful to avoid miscommunications in non-vegetarian restaurants, Barcelona has a respectable number of vegetarian and vegan establishments to choose from, especially in Gràcia. Check the table of **Restaurants by Type,** p. 113, for more info.

The travel section of the Vegetarian Resource Group's website, at www.vrg.org/travel, has a comprehensive list of organizations and websites that are geared toward helping vegetarians and vegans traveling abroad. The website www.vegdining.com has an excellent database of vegetarian and vegan restaurants worldwide. For more information, visit your local bookstore or health food store, and consult *The Vegetarian Traveler: Where to Stay if You're Vegetarian,* by Jed and Susan Civic (Larson Publications; US$16).

Travelers who keep kosher should contact synagogues in Barcelona for information on kosher restaurants. Your own synagogue or college Hillel should have access to lists of Jewish institutions around the world. If you are strict in your observance, you may have to prepare your own food on the road; a good resource is the *Jewish*

Travel Guide, edited by Michael Zaidner (Vallentine Mitchell; US$17). For information on Jewish life in Barcelona, contact the Communidad Israelita de Barcelona, C. Porvenir, 24 (☎93 200 85 13), which also houses a community center.

OTHER RESOURCES

Let's Go tries to cover all aspects of budget travel, but we can't put *everything* in our guides. Listed below are books and websites that can serve as jumping-off points for your own research.

TRAVEL PUBLISHERS & BOOKSTORES

Hippocrene Books, Inc., 171 Madison Ave., New York, NY 10016, USA (☎718-454-2366; www.hippocrenebooks.com). Publishes language dictionaries and language learning guides.

Hunter Publishing, 470 W. Broadway, 2nd fl., South Boston, MA 02127, USA (☎617-269-0700; www.hunterpublishing.com). Has an extensive catalog of travel guides and diving and adventure travel books.

Rand McNally, P.O. Box 7600, Chicago, IL 60680, USA (☎847-329-8100; www.randmcnally.com). Publishes road atlases.

Adventurous Traveler Bookstore, P.O. Box 2221, Williston, VT 05495, USA (☎800-282-3963; www.adventuroustraveler.com).

Bon Voyage!, 2069 W. Bullard Ave., Fresno, CA 93711, USA (☎800-995-9716, from abroad 559-447-8441; www.bon-voyage-travel.com). Specializes in travel. Free newsletter.

Travel Books & Language Center, Inc., 4437 Wisconsin Ave., NW, Washington, D.C. 20016, USA (☎800-220-2665; www.bookweb.org/bookstore/travelbks). Over 60,000 titles from around the world.

WORLD WIDE WEB

Almost every aspect of budget travel is accessible via the web. With ten minutes at the keyboard, you can make a reservation at a hostel, get advice on must-see Modernist sights, and get the latest soccer scores from the FCB website.

Listed here are some sites to start off your surfing; many other relevant websites are listed throughout this book.

THE ART OF BUDGET TRAVEL

How to See the World: www.artoftravel.com. A compendium of great travel tips, from cheap flights to self-defense to interacting with local culture.

Recreational Travel Library: www.travel-library.com. A fantastic set of links for general information and personal travelogues.

Backpacker's Ultimate Guide: www.bugeurope.com. Tips on packing, transportation, and where to go. Also tons of country-specific travel information.

Backpack Europe: www.backpackeurope.com. Helpful tips, a bulletin board, and links.

INFORMATION ON BARCELONA

The City of Barcelona Online: www.bcn.es/english/ihome.htm. The city's official webpage, covering everything from shopping and beaches to current events.

Tourist Office of Spain: www.okspain.org. The tourist office's official American webpage, full of links to everything from media to gastronomy.

Tourist Office of Barcelona: www.barcelonaturisme.com. Barcelona's own tourist office webpage offers basic information about the city and its culture, as well as a hotel booking service and virtual tours of the city's main sights.

Barcelona On Line: www.barcelona-on-line.es. This new travel agency provides a useful online guide about Barcelona.

Fútbol Club Barcelona: www.fcbarcelona.com. For those soccer enthusiasts among us, El Barça's official webpage is your guide to Catalunya's favorite team.

Spanish Cheese: www.cheesefromspain.com. Complete with photos of some of Spain's most succulent dairy products. Lactose-intolerants beware.

Foreign Language for Travelers: www.travlang.com. Provides free online translating dictionaries and lists of phrases in both Spanish and Catalan.

PlanetRider: www.planetrider.com. A subjective list of links to the "best" websites covering the culture and tourist attractions of Spain.

AND OUR PERSONAL FAVORITE...

WWW.LETSGO.COM Our website, www.letsgo.com, now includes introductory chapters from all our guides and a wealth of information on a monthly featured destination. As always, our website also has info about our books, a travel forum buzzing with stories and tips, and additional links that will hlp you make the most of a trip to Barcelona. In addition, all nine Let's Go City Guides are available for download on Palm OS PDAs.

Alternatives to Tourism

When we started out in 1961, about 1.7 million people in the world were traveling internationally each year; in 2002, nearly 700 million trips were made, and that number is projected to rise to a billion by 2010. The dramatic rise in tourism has created an interdependence between the economy, environment, and culture of many destinations and the tourists they host. Each year, Barcelona alone attracts around ten million visitors.

Later in this section, we recommend organizations that can help you find the opportunities that best suit your interests, whether you're looking to pitch in for a day or a year. Those looking to **volunteer** in the efforts to resolve these issues have many options. You can participate in projects from helping fight AIDS to teaching at-risk kids, either on an infrequent basis or as the main component of your trip. Most organizations welcome volunteers, though a degree of Spanish or Catalan proficiency is sometimes required. In the fight against AIDs, groups are looking to promote awareness in this historically conservative (and Catholic) population.

Other volunteer opportunities exist for assisting the marginalized populations in the city. Like the rest of Spain, Barcelona and Catalunya have seen an increase in immigration in the last quarter-century. Because of closed borders during Franco's dictatorship, the native Spanish were not prepared for this influx of population. Due to an increase in the number of northern Africans crossing the Mediterranean and the recent deterioration of the Latin American economy, Spain is working to integrate this immigrant population on economical and political fronts, and simultaneously foster social acceptance. Barcelona, as a cosmopolitan city close to the French border, has not dealt with the same issues as more central cities on the Iberian peninsula. However, the make-up of smaller communities in Catalunya has changed significantly. One problem specific to Catalunya has been educating immigrants not only in Spanish, but also Catalan. However, educating the incoming population is not the only problem. Educating the native population on immigrant acceptance is just as important in light of the persistence of xenophobia. In this line of volunteering, travelers with language skills beyond Spanish, Catalan, or English are often in greater demand; for example, many immigrants from northern Africa speak French.

Though AIDS and immigration are two of the primary concerns facing Barcelona and Spain today, other social problems do exist. With a little leg work, it is probably possible to do any sort of volunteer work in the city, from animal rights advocacy and political interning to peace activism and promoting labor rights. In terms of interning, as a general rule, if you are willing to work for free, many non-profit and non-government organizations welcome extra help. On the Balearic Islands (Islas Baleares; see **Daytripping,** p. 251) there are both ecological reserves and ongoing archeological projects. These islands may afford opportunities for volunteering and interning which are unavailable in the city. Many international groups have opportunities all over the region; in addition to checking the listings below for suggestions, try organizations based in your home country which may have branches or projects in Barcelona or Catalunya.

There are any number of other ways in which you can integrate yourself with the communities you visit. Studying at a college or language program is one option. Barcelona has many schools to choose from, with options to learn in either Catalan or Spanish. Many travelers also structure their trips through work that can finance their stay—either odd jobs as they go, or full-time stints if they plan to stay for some time. The best bet for finding long-term work in Barcelona is teaching English, working as an au pair, or finding an internship (internships are most easily found through placement programs); be sure to make long-term plans before departure, as you'll have to contend with extensive visa requirements (see p. 305). Short-term work, however, is most easily found while in Barcelona rather than arranged prior to your trip; for example, bars and restaurants, especially those which cater to tourists, often look for extra (and English-speaking) help in the high season. Check bulletin boards and local newspapers for job listings.

For those who seek more active involvement, Earthwatch International, Operation Crossroads Africa, and Habitat for Humanity offer fulfilling volunteer opportunities all over the world. For more on volunteering, studying , and working in Barcelona and beyond, consult Let's Go's alternatives to tourism site, www.beyond tourism.com.

Before handing your money over to any volunteer or study abroad program, make sure you know exactly what you're getting into. It's a good idea to get the name of **previous participants** and ask them about their experience, as some programs sound much better on paper than in reality. The **questions** below are a good place to start:

-Will you be the only person in the program? If not, what are the other participants like? How old are they? How much will you be expected to interact with them?

-Is room and board included? If so, what is the arrangement? Will you be expected to share a room? A bathroom? What are the meals like? Do they accommodate any dietary restrictions?

-Is transportation included? Are there any additional expenses?

-How much free time will you have? Will you be able to travel around the island?

-What kind of safety network is set up? Will you still be covered by your home insurance? Does the program have an emergency plan?

A NEW PHILOSOPHY OF TRAVEL

We at *Let's Go* have watched the growth of the 'ignorant tourist' stereotype with dismay, knowing that the majority of travelers care passionately about the state of the communities and environments they explore—but also knowing that even conscientious tourists can inadvertently damage natural wonders, rich cultures, and impoverished communities. We believe the philosophy of **sustainable travel** is among the most important travel tips we could impart to our readers, to help guide fellow backpackers and on-the-road philanthropists. By staying aware of the needs and troubles of local communities, today's travelers can be a powerful force in preserving and restoring this fragile world.

Working against the negative consequences of irresponsible tourism is much simpler than it might seem; it is often self-awareness, rather than self-sacrifice, that makes the biggest difference. Simply by trying to spend responsibly and conserve local resources, all travelers can positively impact the places they visit. Let's Go has partnered with **BEST** (**Business Enterprises for Sustainable Travel,** an affiliate of the Conference Board; see www.sustainabletravel.org), which recognizes businesses that operate based on the principles of sustainable travel. Below, they provide advice on how ordinary visitors can practice this philosophy in their daily travels, no matter where they are.

TIPS FOR CIVIC TRAVEL: HOW TO MAKE A DIFFERENCE

Travel by train when feasible. Rail travel requires only half the energy per passenger mile that planes do. On average, each of the 40,000 daily domestic air flights releases more than 1700 pounds of greenhouse gas emissions.

Use public mass transportation whenever possible; outside of cities, take advantage of group taxis or vans. Bicycles are an attractive way of seeing a community first-hand. And enjoy walking—purchase good maps of your destination and ask about on-foot touring opportunities.

When renting a car, ask whether fuel-efficient vehicles are available. Honda and Toyota produce cars that use hybrid engines powered by electricity and gasoline, thus reducing emissions of carbon dioxide. Ford Motor Company plans to introduce a hybrid fuel model by the end of 2004.

Reduce, reuse, recycle—use electronic tickets, recycle papers and bottles wherever possible, and avoid using containers made of styrofoam. Refillable water bottles and rechargable batteries both efficiently conserve expendable resources.

Be thoughtful in your purchases. Take care not to buy souvenir objects made from trees in old-growth or endangered forests, such as teak, or items made from endangered species, like ivory or tortoise jewelry. Ask whether products are made from renewable resources.

Buy from local enterprises, such as casual street vendors. In developing countries and low-income neighborhoods, many people depend on the "informal economy" to make a living.

Be on-the-road-philanthropists. If you are inspired by the natural environment of a destination or enriched by its culture, join in preserving their integrity by making a charitable contribution to a local organization.

Spread the word. Upon your return home, tell friends and colleagues about places to visit that will benefit greatly from their tourist dollars, and reward sustainable enterprises by recommending their services. Travelers can not only introduce friends to particular vendors but also to local causes and charities that they might choose to support when they travel.

VOLUNTEERING

Though Barcelona is considered wealthy relative to the rest of the world, there is no shortage of aid organizations to benefit the very real issues the region faces. Volunteer jobs are readily available in Barcelona, and many provide room and board in exchange for labor. Volunteering can be one of the most fulfilling experiences you have in life, especially if you combine it with the thrill of traveling in a new place.

Shopping for Eggs

Most people who volunteer in Barcelona do so on a short-term basis, at organizations that make use of drop-in or once-a-week volunteers. These can be found in virtually every city, and are referenced both in this section and in our town and city write-ups themselves. The best way to find opportunities that match up with your interests and schedule may be to check with the ☒**Centre d'Informació i Assessorament per a Joves (CIAJ)**, C. Ferran 32 (☎ 93 319 23 00; www.bcn.es/ciaj). It is the best place to look for volunteering opportunities once in Barcelona. Other options include **AmeriSpan, COINED,** or **Volunteer Abroad** (see below). Placement options range from tutoring impoverished children to participating in work camps or aiding immigrants.

More intensive volunteer services may charge you a fee to participate. These costs can be surprisingly hefty (although they frequently cover airfare and most, if not all, living expenses). You can sometimes avoid high application fees by contacting the individual work camps directly. Most people choose to go through a parent organization that takes care of logistical details and frequently provides a group environment and a support system. There are two main types of organizations—religious and non-sectarian—although there are rarely restrictions on participation for either.

Dancing

HIV AND AIDS

Spain has one of the highest AIDS infection rates in Western Europe. As a result, organizations are always looking for volunteers to assist in promoting awareness, especially in adolescents.

Stop SIDA, C. Finlandià 45, 08014 Barcelona, Spain (☎ 90 006 01 60; www.stopsida.org). Helps combat the spread of AIDS by providing info on AIDS prevention, offering support services, and promoting understanding. Much of Stop SIDA's activities are made possible by volunteers.

Associació Ciutadana Antisida de Catalunya, C. Junta de Comerç 23, 08001 Barcelona, Spain (☎ 93 317 05 05; www.lanzadera.com/acasc).

Souvenir Shop

IMMIGRATION

Volunteering with organizations focusing on immigration can include educating both the native and immigrant populations, as well as lobbying for political and legal changes.

Comisión Espanola de Ayuda al Refugio (CEAR), Fonthonrada 10-2, 08015 Barcelona, Spain (☎93 424 27 09; fax 93 426 56 52; www.cear.es). This fundamental aim of this non-profit non-governmental organization is to protect the right to asylum, especially in Spain. Volunteer opportunities in outreach, legal assistance, translation, or human rights research.

POVERTY

Like any large city, poverty does exist in Barcelona and many tourists see it manifested in the "gypsies" who beg for money on the streets. There are many more lasting ways to help financially distressed populations.

Tapas

Art Solidari, La Lluna, 22, 08001 Barcelona, Spain (☎93 441 04 33; perso.wanadoo.es/artsolidari). Helps integrate children from marginalized backgrounds by developing their self-esteem, creativity, and academic interest through programs in artistic expression. Volunteers can make short- or long-term commitments.

Fundació COMTAL, Amadeu Vives, 6, 08003 Barcelona, Spain (☎93-319-98-55; www.comtal.org). Provides education and support programs for impoverished and/or at-risk children and adolescents in Barcelona.

OTHER OPTIONS

Shopping for Shoes

AmeriSpan, PO Box 58129, Philadelphia, PA, 19102-8129, (In US and Canada ☎1-800-879-6640, elsewhere 215-751-1986; www.amerispan.com). Provides listings of volunteer and internship opportunities in Barcelona and beyond.

Comisión de Intercambio Educativo (COINED), Avenida Mistral, 36, Entl. 2a, 08015 Barcelona, Spain (☎54 351 4299402; www.coinedspain.org). Offers cultural immersion programs in Barcelona that include volunteer placement in public service organizations. Also offers internship and study opportunities.

Elderhostel, Inc., 11 Avenue de Lafayette, Boston, MA 92111-1746, USA (☎877-426-8056; fax 877-426-2166; www.elderhostel.org). Sends volunteers age 55 and over around the world to work in construction, research, teaching, and many other projects. Costs an average of $100 per day plus airfare.

Fries for Sale

Service Civil International Voluntary Service (SCI-IVS), SCI USA, 3213 W. Wheeler St., Seattle, WA 98199, USA (☎/fax 206-350-6585; www.sci-ivs.org). Arranges placement in work camps in Barcelona and throughout Spain for those 18+. Registration fee US$65-125.

Volunteers for Peace, 1034 Tiffany Rd., Belmont, VT 05730, USA (☎802-259-2759; www.vfp.org). Arranges placement in work camps in Barcelona. Membership required for registration. Annual *International Workcamp Directory* US$20. Programs average US$200-500 for 2-3 weeks.

Volunteer Abroad (www.volunteerabroad.com). Posts and searches listings of volunteer opportunities worldwide. In Barcelona these opportunities usually involve teaching English.

STUDYING ABROAD

Study abroad programs range from basic language and culture courses to college-level classes, often for credit. In order to choose a program that best fits your needs, you will want to research all you can before making your decision—determine costs and duration, as well as what kind of students participate in the program and what sort of accommodations are provided.

Many options are available for study abroad in Barcelona. For students with strong Spanish or Catalan skills, enrolling directly in a Spanish university in Barcelona may be the cheapest and best option. The instructional language is a controversial point at public universities in regions like Catalunya that have their own languages. Despite what they might prefer, professors at public universities in Catalunya are required to offer classes in Spanish—not Catalan—if even one student is uncomfortable with Catalan. Consequently, the choice between enrolling in a public or a private university may depend on whether a student wants to study Spanish or Catalan.

Barcelona is also a fantastic place to study art; most study abroad programs offer an art component, and students with a stronger interest can enroll directly in an art school.

STUDY VISAS

To obtain a study visa for Spain, you must be enrolled in a program. Most study abroad programs are accustomed to dealing with foreign students, and will send everything you need for your visa when you sign up for the program; if you are enrolling directly in a Spanish university, getting a visa may require a little more initiative. At the very least, be prepared to present a visa application form (best filled out in advance), your passport, passport photos, a medical letter, two letters from an institution verifying your full-time enrollment, and copious numbers of copies of these documents. In the interest of saving time, it is imperative to discuss visa requirements with both your program and your resident Spanish consulate. Be forewarned that most consulates are only open in the morning and some may require you to file for a visa in person.

UNIVERSITIES

Some American schools still require students to pay them for credits obtained elsewhere. Most university-level study-abroad programs are meant as language and culture enrichment opportunities, and therefore are conducted in Spanish. Still, many programs do offer classes in English and beginner- and lower-level language courses. Those relatively fluent in Spanish, on the other hand, may find it cheaper to enroll directly in a university abroad, although getting college credit may be more difficult. A good resource for finding programs that cater to your particular interests is **www.studyabroad.com,** which has links to various semester abroad programs based on a variety of criteria, including desired location and focus of study. The following is a list of organizations that can help place students in university programs abroad, or have a branch in Barcelona.

AMERICAN PROGRAMS

American Institute for Foreign Study, College Division, River Plaza, 9 West Broad St., Stamford, CT 06902, USA (☎800-727-2437, ext. 5163; www.aifs-abroad.com). Organizes programs for high school and college study in universities in Barcelona.

Arcadia University for Education Abroad, 450 S. Easton Rd., Glenside, PA 19038, USA (☎866-927-2234; www.arcadia.edu/cea). Operates programs in Barcelona. Costs range from $2200 (summer) to $29,000 (full-year).

Central College Abroad, Office of International Education, 812 University, Pella, IA 50219, USA (☎800-831-3629 or 641-628-5284; www.central.edu/abroad). Offers internships, as well as summer-, semester-, and year-long programs in Barcelona. US$25 application fee.

Fishmonger

Council on International Educational Exchange (CIEE), 633 3rd Ave., 20th floor, New York, NY 10017-6706 (☎800-407-8839; www.ciee.org/study). Sponsors work, volunteer, academic, and internship programs in Barcelona.

International Association for the Exchange of Students for Technical Experience (IAESTE), 10400 Little Patuxent Pkwy. Suite 250, Columbia, MD 21044-3519, USA (☎410-997-2200; www.aipt.org). 8- to 12-week programs in Barcelona for college students who have completed 2 years of technical study. US$25 application fee.

Institute for the International Education of Students (IES), 33 N. LaSalle St., 15th fl., Chicago, IL 60602, USA (☎800-995-2300; www.IESabroad.org). Offers year-long, semester, and summer programs in Barcelona for college students. Internships offered. US $50 application fee. Scholarships available.

Café con Leche

International Studies Abroad, 901 W. 24th, Austin, TX 78705, USA (☎800-580-8826; www.studiesabroad.com). Programs at the University of Barcelona in Hispanic Studies or Spanish Language and Culture. Costs range from $3300 (summer) to $13,750 (full-year).

School for International Training, College Semester Abroad, Admissions, Kipling Rd., P.O. Box 676, Brattleboro, VT 05302, USA (☎800-336-1616 or 802-257-7751; www.sit.edu). Semester- and year-long programs in Barcelona run US$10,600-13,700. Also runs the **Experiment in International Living** (☎800-345-2929; fax 802-258-3428; www.usexperiment.org), a group of 3- to 5-week summer programs that offer high school students cross-cultural homestays, community service, ecological adventure, and language training in Barcelona. US$1900-5000.

Out at Night

PROGRAMS IN BARCELONA

University of Barcelona (☎93 403 53 79; fax 93 403 53 87; www.ub.es). For academic exchange programs within the EU, contact ☎93 403 53 86; fax 93 403 53 87; bec-soc@pu.ges.ub.es. For academic exchange programs outside of the EU, ☎93 403 55 81; fax 93 403 53 87; elo@pu.ges.ub.es. Foreign students looking for information about enrolling in the University of Barcelona and the procedure for obtaining a student visa, ☎93 403 55 62; fax 93 403 53 87; gema@pu.ges.ub.es.

LANGUAGE SCHOOLS

Unlike American universities, language schools are frequently independently run international or local organizations or divisions of foreign universities that rarely offer college credit. Language schools are a good alternative to university study for those who desire a deeper focus on the language or a slightly less rigorous course-load. These programs are also good for younger high school students who may not feel comfortable in a university program. Some good programs include:

BCN Languages, Av. Diagonal, 407 ent. 2a, 08008 Barcelona, Spain (☎93 218 21 77; www.bcnlanguages.com). Organizes a variety of courses, from standard to super-intensive. Choose host family accommodations or student residence.

El Casal, Balmes, 163, 3, 08008 Barcelona, Spain (☎34 932 179 038). A program for high school students that offers seminars in Spanish and Catalan, and contemporary Spanish culture and politics. Also places students in volunteer programs, internships, and offers guided excursions in Barcelona. Costs (including room, board, and tuition) range $7500-8700.

Consorci per a la Normalització Lingüística, C. Mallorca 272, 8a planta, 08037 Barcelona, Spain (☎93 272 31 00; www.cpnl.org/presentacio/welcome.htm). Organizes programs for adults learning Catalan.

Eurocentres, 101 N. Union St. Suite 300, Alexandria, VA 22314, USA (☎703 684 1494; www.eurocentres.com) or in Europe, Head Office, Seestr. 247, CH-8038 Zurich, Switzerland (☎41 1 485 50 40; fax 481 61 24). Language programs for beginning to advanced students with homestays in Barcelona.

Language Immersion Institute, 75 South Manheim Blvd., SUNY-New Paltz, New Paltz, NY 12561-2499, USA (☎845-257-3500; www.newpaltz.edu/lii). 2-week summer language courses and some overseas courses in Spanish. Program fees are around US$1000 for a 2-week course.

S.O.L. Barcelona, Entenza, 320, ent. 1a, 08029 Barcelona, Spain (☎93 405 12 00; www.solbarcelona.com). Classes in business Spanish and preparation for the D.E.L.E. exam for Spanish proficiency. Program fee US$500

WORKING

As with volunteering, work opportunities tend to fall into two categories. Some travelers want long-term jobs that allow them to get to know another part of the world as a member of the community, while other travelers seek out short-term jobs to finance the next leg of their travels. In Barcelona, popular temporary jobs for foreigners include being an au pair, teaching English, or waiting tables. Irish pubs are almost always staffed with English-speaking expats, and the demand for English tutors is high. A good way to line up a more permanent job from home is to get a job with an international corporation with offices in Barcelona; large consulting and investment banking firms generally have offices abroad.

It is much easier to line up a job in Spain when you are already there; invaluable resources like "help wanted" signs just aren't visible from other countries, and the Internet can only get you so far. Get your hands on a copy of Catalunya's leading newspaper, *La Vanguardia*, to look at job ads; other publications in Spanish are *El Periódico* and the English-language *Barcelona Metropolitan*.

VISA INFORMATION American, Canadian, South African, and Australian citizens need a work visa to work in Spain. Those desiring such a visa should contact the Spanish consulate in their country for the exact requirements, which usually include: a passport valid for at least six months, a job offer in Spain filed at the Ministry of Labor in Spain, a letter of good conduct from the police department in the city of original residence, a letter from a physician affirming good health and freedom from addiction, four passport photos, and approximately US$45. These visas may take four months or more to process, although certain cases may be rushed; if necessary, call the consulate multiple times to make sure you have the necessary paperwork, or you will have to wait, and wait, and wait. European Union citizens can work in Spain, and if your parents were born abroad in an EU country, you may be able to claim the right to a work permit. Any stay of over 90 days in Spain requires a visa; what you are doing with your time in Spain will dictate what sort of a visa you will get. It is always better to get these papers in advance; making arrangements for a longer stay while you are already in Spain will involve a lot of long lines and angry, intimidating visa personnel. Spain has good border control, and travelers crossing back and forth from Spain in a period of over 90 days will not be permitted to re-enter without the appropriate visas. Getting a visa is straight-forward, but also a hassle. To avoid having to make multiple trips, call to inquire about the necessary documents before going to the consulate. It is difficult to get an appointment during the study abroad crunch months of September and January; if you'll need a visa then, call at least one month in advance.

Upon arrival in Spain, all long-term visitors must register at the **comisaria** (police station) immigration authority for an alien residency identification card. All persons staying in Spain for more than 90 days must complete this process **in addition to** having a visa. Your job/program/school will have to file papers with the comisaria, and will be able to direct you to the comisaria in question. At the station you will provide fingerprints, a photo, and a signature; in return you will get an ID. Be prepared to wait in line.

For US college students, recent graduates, and young adults, the simplest way to get legal permission to work abroad is through **Council Exchanges Work Abroad Programs.** For a US$300-425 fee, Council Exchanges can help you obtain a three- to six-month work permit/visa and provide assistance finding jobs and housing.

LONG-TERM WORK

If you're planning on spending a substantial amount of time (more than three months) working in Barcelona, search for a job well in advance. International placement agencies are often the easiest way to find employment abroad, especially for teaching English. **Internships,** usually for college students, are a good way to segue into working abroad, although they are often unpaid or poorly paid (many people say the experience, however, is well worth it). Be wary of advertisements or companies that claim the ability to get you a job abroad for a fee—often the same listings are available online (check out www.internabroad.com) or in newspapers. Some good resources include:

Adelante, 601 Taper Drive, Seal Beach, CA 90740, USA (☎562-799-9133; www.adelanteabroad.com). Program includes a two-week language course followed by a **305**

work assignment in one of two hotels in Barcelona. Participants can intern for anywhere between one and six months. Costs start at $1750 (lodging is included).

American College in Barcelona, Via Augusta, 123, 08006 Barcelona, Spain (☎34 93 240 5115; college.ien@nexo.es). Places participants in internship programs in various Barcelona companies in addition to offering language courses and advising.

BEST Programs, Calle Solano 11, 3-C, Pozuelo de Alarcón, Madrid, 28223, Spain (☎011 34 91 518- 7110; www.bestprograms.org). Combines a two-week Spanish language course with an internship in Barcelona. The language course can be taken in Madrid or Barcelona. Participants much be at least 18 years old.

www.internabroad.com. Provides listings of internship opportunities in Barcelona and around the world.

www.barcelonaconnect.com. A website supplying practical information about living and traveling in Barcelona; includes a classifieds section with local job listings.

TEACHING ENGLISH

Teaching jobs abroad are rarely well-paid, although some elite private American schools can pay somewhat competitive salaries. Volunteering as a teacher in lieu of getting paid is also a popular option; even in those cases, teachers often get some sort of a daily stipend to help with living expenses. In almost all cases, you must have at least a bachelor's degree to be a full-fledged teacher, although college undergraduates can often get summer positions teaching or tutoring.

Many schools require teachers to have a **Teaching English as a Foreign Language (TEFL)** certificate. This does not necessarily exclude you from finding a teaching job, but certified teachers often find higher-paying jobs. Native English speakers working in private schools are most often hired for English-immersion classrooms where no Spanish is spoken. Those volunteering or teaching in public, poorer schools, are more likely to be working in both English and Spanish. Placement agencies or university fellowship programs are the best resources for finding teaching jobs in Barcelona. The alternative is to make contacts directly with schools or just to try your luck once you get there. If you are going to try the latter, the best time of the year is several weeks before the start of the school year. The following organizations are extremely helpful in placing teachers in Barcelona.

International Schools Services (ISS), 15 Roszel Rd., Box 5910, Princeton, NJ 08543-5910, USA (☎609-452-0990; fax 609-452-2690; www.iss.edu). Hires teachers for more than 200 overseas schools including Barcelona; candidates should have experience teaching or with international affairs; 2-year commitment expected.

Office of Overseas Schools, US Department of State, Room H328, SA-1, Washington, D.C. 20522, USA (☎202-261-8200; fax 261-8224; www.state.gov/m/a/os/). Keeps a comprehensive list of schools abroad (including several in Barcelona) and agencies that arrange placement for Americans to teach abroad.

Teach Abroad (www.teachabroad.com). Posts listings of positions for English-speaking instructors and offers courses to prepare participants to be English language teachers.

AU PAIR WORK

Au pairs are typically women, aged 18-27, who work as live-in nannies, caring for children and doing light housework in exchange for room, board, and a small spending allowance or stipend. Most former au pairs speak favorably of their experience, and of how it allowed them to really get to know the country without incurring the high expenses of traveling. Drawbacks, however, often include long hours of constantly being on-duty and the somewhat mediocre pay. The average weekly pay for au pairs in Barcelona is between 50 and 60 euros. Much of the au pair experience really does depend on the family you're placed with. The agencies below are a good starting point for looking for employment as an au pair.

InterExchange, 161 Sixth Ave., New York, NY 10013, USA (☎212-924-0446; fax 924-0575; www.interexchange.org).

The World Au Pair, 7 de la Commune West Bureau 204, Montreal (Quebec) Canada, H2Y 265 (☎514-281-3045; toll-free from U.S./Canada ☎1-888-281-3045; www.generation.net/~aupair).

SHORT-TERM WORK

Traveling for long periods of time can get expensive; therefore, many travelers try their hand at odd jobs for a few weeks at a time to make some extra cash to carry them through another month or two of touring around. Unemployment is high in Spain, so it may be difficult for someone just passing through to get a job in any Spanish city. An added impediment in Barcelona is that many employers require that their workers speak Catalan as well as Spanish and English. A better bet would be to travel to the beach towns that cater specifically to sun-loving tourists but whose employees take their month off in August. Most often, these short-term jobs are found by word-of-mouth, or simply by talking to the owner of a hostel or restaurant. Another popular option is to work several hours a day at a hostel in exchange for free or discounted room and/or board. Most often, these short-term jobs are found by word of mouth, or simply by talking to the owner of a hostel or restaurant. Many places, especially due to the high turnover in the tourism industry, are eager for help, even if only temporarily. *Let's Go* tries to list temporary jobs like these whenever possible; check out the list below for some of the available short-term jobs in popular destinations.

FOR FURTHER EADING ON ALTERNATIVES TO TOURISM

Alternatives to the Peace Corps: A directory of third world and U.S. Volunteer Opportunities, by Joan Powell. Food First Books, 2000 (US$10).

How to Get a Job in Europe, by Sanborn and Matherly. Surrey Books, 1999 ($US22).

How to Live Your Dream of Volunteering Oversees, by Collins, DeZerega, and Heckscher. Penguin Books, 2002 (US$17).

International Directory of Voluntary Work, by Whetter and Pybus. Peterson's Guides and Vacation Work, 2000 (US$16).

International Jobs, by Kocher and Segal. Perseus Books, 1999 (US$18).

Overseas Summer Jobs 2002, by Collier and Woodworth. Peterson's Guides and Vacation Work, 2002 (US$18).

Work Abroad: The Complete Guide to Finding a Job Overseas, by Hubbs, Griffith, and Nolting. Transitions Abroad Publishing, 2000 ($16).

Work Your Way Around the World, by Susan Griffith. Worldview Publishing Services, 2001 (US$18).

Invest Yourself: The Catalogue of Volunteer Opportunities, published by the Commission on Voluntary Service and Action (☎718-638-8487).

Service Directory

ACCOMMODATIONS

For information on **rental agencies, home exchanges,** and how to acquire **long-term accommodations** in Barcelona, see p. 200.

AIRLINES

See also **Transportation Services,** p. 313.

Air Europa, 24hr. reservation and info ☎90 240 15 01; www.air-europa.com.

British Airways, El Prat de Llobregat Airport (☎93 298 34 55, 24hr. reservation and info 90 211 13 33). Open 6am-7pm. **Branch** at Pg. de Gràcia, 16.

Delta, 24hr. reservation and info ☎90 111 69 46; www.delta-air.com.

Easy Jet, 24hr. reservation and info ☎90 229 99 92; www.easyjet.com.

Iberia/Aviaco, Diputació, 258 (24hr. reservation and info ☎90 240 05 00). Student discounts.

Spanair, Pg. de Gràcia, 57 (24hr. reservation and info ☎90 213 14 15). Offers fares that are often cheaper than Iberia.

BANKS

Banco de Espanya, Pl. de Catalunya, 17 (☎93 482 47 00). Charges no commission on traveler's checks.

Caixa de Catalunya, Pl. Espanya, 6-8 (☎93 426 08 73). The most helpful with cash advances from credit cards without PINs.

La Caixa (☎90 222 30 40). Practically an office on every corner. Phone lines open M-F 10am-8pm; call for hours of specific branches.

BICYCLE AND MOPED RENTAL

Vanguard Rent a Car, C. Viladomat, 297, between Londres and Paris (☎93 439 38 80). Mopeds start at €37 per day, if renting for 3 days or less, €35 per day for 3-7 days, €33 per day for more than 7 days. More expensive 2-person motos also available. Insurance, helmet, and IVA included. Must be 19 with ID to rent. Open M-F 8am-1:30pm and 4-7:30pm, Sa-Su 9am-1pm.

BUSES

See also **Transportation Services**, p. 313.

Alsa Enatcar (☎90 242 22 42; www.alsa.es), Estació Nord.

Eurolines (☎90 240 50 40; www.eurolines.es), Estació Nord.

Linebús (☎93 265 07 00), Estació Nord. Discounts for travelers under 26 and over 60. Open M-F 8am-8pm, Sa 8:30am-1pm and 5-8pm.

Sarfa (☎90 230 20 25; www.sarfa.com), Estació Nord. Open daily 8am-9pm.

CAR RENTAL

See **Planning Your Trip**, p. 289.

CLINICS

See also **Hospitals**, p. 311.

Barcelona Centro Médico (BCM), Av. Diagonal, 437, #14 (☎93 414 06 43). M: Maria Cristina, L3. Coordinates referrals, for Spaniards and foreigners.

CRISIS LINES

Oficina Permanente de Atención Social, 24hr. toll-free ☎90 070 30 30.

DISABILITY RESOURCES

Ajuntament, Pl. Sant Miquel. Information office has a map of wheelchair-accessible routes and establishments. (Also available at TMB office in the Universitat Metro.)

Centre d'Aterncró a Dismïnuits, Badal, 102 (☎93 331 21 62). General information on help for disabilities.

Institut Municipal de Disminuits, C. Llacuna, 171 (☎ 93 291 84 00). Provides specific information on accessibility of sites, restaurants, etc.

Taxi: ☎93 420 80 88.

EMBASSIES AND CONSULATES

American Consulate, Pg. Reina Elisenda de Montcada, 23 (☎93 280 22 27; fax 93 280 61 75; www.embusa.es). FCG: Reina Elisenda. Building open M-F 9am-1pm; by telephone M-F 3-5pm.

Australian Consulate, Gran Via Carlos III, 98, 9th fl. (☎93 490 90 13; fax 93 411 0494; www.embaustralia.es/hours.htm). M: Maria Cristina, L3.

British Consulate, Edificio Torre de Barcelona, Av. Diagonal, 477 (☎93 366 62 00; fax 93 366 62 21; www.ukinspain.com). M: Hospital Clìnic, L5.

Canadian Consulate, Elisenda de Pinós, 10 (☎93 204 27 00; fax 93 204 27 01; www.canada-es.org). FCG: Reina Elisenda.

Irish Consulate, Gran Via Carlos III, 94 (☎93 451 90 21; fax 93 411 29 21; www.goireland.com/low/visitorsguide/irembassies.html). M: Maria Cristina, L3.

New Zealand Consulate, Trav. de Gràcia, 64 (☎93 209 03 99; fax 93 201 08 90).

South African Consulate, C. Teodora Lamadrid, 7 (☎93 418 64 45; fax 93 418 05 38; www.sudafrica.com).

EMERGENCY SERVICES

See also **Clinics** (p. 310), **Crisis Lines** (p. 310), and **Hospitals** (p. 311).

Emergency: ☎112

Local Police: ☎092

National Police: ☎091

Medical: ☎061

Police: Las Ramblas, 43 (☎93 344 13 00), across from Pl. Reial and next to C. Nou de La Rambla. M: Liceu, L3. Tourists in need of assistance should visit the department labeled "Tourist Attention," where they will find helpful multilingual officers. Open 24hr., tourist assistance open daily 8am-2am. Branches beneath the Pl. de Catalunya on the side facing the Banco Nacional, and at the Barcelona-Nord bus station.

GAY AND LESBIAN SERVICES

Antinous, C. J. Anselm Clavé, 6 (☎93 301 90 70; www.antinouslibros.com). M: Drassanes. On the right as you walk down C. Clavé from Las Ramblas. A large bookstore and cafe specializing in gay and lesbian books, including several guide books. Decent selection of books in English. Open M-F 10:30am-2pm and 5-9pm, Sa noon-2pm and 5-9pm.

Cómplices, C. Cervantes, 2 (☎93 412 72 83; complices@retemail.es). M: Liceu, L3. From C. Ferrán, take a left onto C. Avinyó and then the 2nd left onto C. Cervantes. A small gay and lesbian bookstore with publications in English and Spanish, as well as a decent selection of gay and lesbian films. Also provides an informative **map** of Barcelona's gay and lesbian bars and discos. Open M-F 10:30am-8:30pm, Sa noon-8:30pm. AmEx/MC/V.

HOSPITALS

Hospital Clìnic, Villarroel, 170 (☎93 227 54 00). M: Hospital Clìnic, L5. Main entrance at the intersection of C. Roselló and C. Casanova.

Hospital de la Santa Creu i Sant Pau (☎93 291 90 00; emergency ☎93 291 91 91), at the intersection of C. Cartagena and C. Sant Antoni Moria Claret. M: Hospital de Sant Pau, L5.

Hospital Vall d'Hebron (☎93 274 61 00). M: Vall d'Hebron, L3.

INTERNET ACCESS

bcnet (Internet Gallery Café), Barra de Ferro, 3 (☎93 268 15 07; bcnetcafe@bcnetcafe.com), right down the street from the Picasso museum. M: Jaume I, L4. €3 per hr.; €1 if you pay ahead; 10hr. ticket with 1 additional free hr. €20. Open M-F 10am-10pm, Sa noon-8pm.

Café Interlight, Av. Pau Claris, 106 (☎93 301 11 80; interlight@bcn.servicom.es). M: Urquinaona, L1/4. €0.60 per 15min., €1.50 per hr. Open daily 9am-3pm.

CiberOpción, Gran Via, 602 (☎93 412 73 08), across from the Universitat building. M: Universitat, L1/2. €0.60 per 30min. Open M-F 9am-1am, Sa-Su 11am-1am.

Conèctate, C. Aragó, 283 (☎93 467 04 43). M: Pg. de Gràcia, L2/3/4. One block to the right of the Metro, when you're facing away from Pl. de Catalunya. Internet €0.60 per hr. Most other services an additional €0.60. Open 24hr. Wheelchair accessible.

Cybermundo Internet Centre, Bergara, 3, and Balmes, 8 (☎93 317 71 42). M: Catalunya, L1/3. Just off the Pl. de Catalunya, behind the Triangle shopping mall. Allows uploading of disks. €1 per hr. at Balmes, €1.20 per hr. at Bergara. Open daily 9am-1am.

🖾 **Easy Everything,** Las Ramblas, 31 (www.easyeverything.com). M: Liceu, L3. €1.20 for about 40min.—price fluctuates according to the number of computers in use. Open 24hr. Also on Ronda Universitat, 35, right next to Pl. de Catalunya, at the same prices.

El Pati d'Internet, C. Astúries, 78 (☎93 292 02 45). M: Fontana, L3, or Joanic, L4. €0.90 per hr. Open M-F 4-10pm.

h@ppy world, C. Muntaner, 122 (☎93 454 91 69). M: Hospital Clìnic. €1.20 for 30min., €2.40 per hr., €9 for 5 hr., €17.45 for 10hr., €39.10 for 25hr. Open M-Sa 10am-10pm, Su 5-10pm. Closed Su in Aug.

Idea, Pl. Comercial, 2 (☎93 268 87 87; www.ideaborn.com). From M: Jaume I, L4, follow C. Princesa almost to its end and turn right on C. Comerç; the plaça is ahead on the right. €3 per hr. Open M-F 9am-11pm, Sa-Su 9am-2pm.

Intergame, Pl. Rius i Taulet, 8 (☎93 416 01 71). M: Fontana, L3. €1.20 per hr. Open daily 10am-midnight.

Internet Exchange, Las Ramblas, 130 (☎93 317 73 27). M: Catalunya, L1/3. €0.06 per minute; €12 for 5hr., €27 for 20hr.; students €15 for 10hr., €30 for 30hr.

Locutorio, Gran Via, 820 (☎93 246 36 07), right near the Monumental bullring, en route to Pl. Glòries, in **l'Eixample.** M: Monumental, L2. Internet 3pm-11pm €2 per hr.; noon-3pm €1 per hr. Black-and-white printing €0.60 per page. Color printing €1 per page. Open daily noon-11pm. Cash only.

Music Center-Internet, C. Córsega, 171. M: Hospital Clìnic, L5. €1.20 per 30min. Open M-Th 8am-10pm, F-Sa 8am-3am.

Travel Bar, C. Boqueria, 27 (☎93 342 52 52; www.barcelonatravelbar.com). M: Liceu, L3. Just off Las Ramblas. €1 per 15min. Open daily 9am-2am.

Workcenter, Av. Diagonal, 441 (☎90 211 50 11; www.workcenter.net). M: Hospital Clìnic, L5, or Diagonal, L3/5. Another **branch** at C. Roger de Lluria, 2. M: Urquinaona, L1/4. €0.52 per 10min. Large range of printing and computer services. Open 24hr.

LAUNDROMATS

Lavanderia Roca, Joaquín Costa, 14 (☎93 442 59 82). Full-service €8.42, available in 2-4hr. Open M-F 8:30am-7:30pm, Sa 8:30am-2pm.

Tintorería Ferran, C. Ferran, 11. M: Liceu, L3. Ferran runs off Las Ramblas, just below Liceu. Open M-F 9am-8pm.

Tintorería San Pablo, C. San Pau, 105 (☎93 329 42 49). M: Parallel, L2. Wash, dry, and fold €10; do-it-yourself €7.25.

Open July-Sept. M-F 9am-2pm; Oct.-June M-F 9am-2pm and 4-8pm.

LIBRARIES

Biblioteca Sant Pau, Carrer de l'Hospital, 56 (☎93 302 07 97). M: Liceu, L3. Take C. Hospital off Las Ramblas and walk a few blocks to a castle on your right; enter the courtyard and walk to its far end; the library is on the left. Open M, W, and F 3:30-8:30pm; Tu, Th, and Sa 10am-2pm and 3:30-8:30pm.

Institut Nord-americà, Via Augusta, 123 (☎93 240 51 10). Open Sept.-July M-F 9am-2pm and 4-7pm.

MEDICAL SERVICES

See also **Clinics** (p. 310), **Hospitals** (p. 311), and **Emergency Services** (p. 310).

Association Ciutadana Anti-SIDA de Catalunya, C. Junta de Comerç, 23 (☎93 317 05 05). AIDS information. Open M-F 10am-2pm and 4-7pm.

MOTO RENTAL

See **Bike and Moped Rental,** p. 309.

PHARMACIES

Pharmacies are open 24hr. on a rotating basis; look for the green and red neon crosses to find one. Check pharmacy windows for current listings or call ☎93 481 00 60 and ask for the closest *farmacia de guardia*.

POST OFFICES

Lista de Correos (general info on Barcelona post offices ☎902 19 71 97, for this specific office ☎93 486 80 50; www.correos.es), Pl. de Antoni López, at the corner of Pg. Colom (the street that runs along the port from the Columbus Monument) and Via Laietana. Across the street from the port. M: Jaume I, L4, or Barceloneta, L4. Fax and *lista de correos.* Open M-F 8:30am-9:30pm. A little shop in the back of the post office building, across the street, wraps packages for mailing (about €1.80). Shop open M-Sa 9am-2pm and 5-8pm. **Postal code:** 08003.

Lista de Correos, C. Aragó, 282, across from the Amena cell phone store, near Gaudí's Casa Batlló. M: Pg. de Gràcia, L2/3/4. Fax and *lista de correos.* Open M-F 8:30am-8:30pm, Sa 8:30am-1pm. **Postal code:** 08007.

Lista de Correos, Ronda Universitat, 23, off Pl. de Catalunya. M: Catalunya, L1/3. Open M-F 8:30am-8:30pm, Sa 9:30am-1pm.

RELIGIOUS RESOURCES

Comunidad Israelita de Barcelona (Jewish services), C. Avenir, 29 (☎93 200 61 48).

Comunidad Musulmana (Muslim services), Mosque Toarek Ben Ziad, C. Hospital, 91 (☎93 441 91 49). Services daily at prayer times.

Església Catedral de la Santa Creu, in Pl. Seu, up C. Bisbe from Pl. St. Jaume. M: Jaume I, L4. Cathedral open daily 8am-1:30pm and 4-7:30pm. Cloister open 9am-1:15pm and 4-7pm.

Església Santa Maria del Mar (☎93 310 23 90), on Pl. Santa Maria del Mar. M: Jaume I, L4. Services in Spanish Su and Holy days noon and 7:30pm. Open M-Sa 9am-1:30pm and 4:30-8pm, Su 9am-2pm and 5-8:30pm.

Església Sant Pau de Camp, at the intersection of C. Sant Pau and C. Carretes, 2 blocks off Av. Parallel. M: Parallel, L2. Open Su-M and W-Sa 5-8pm.

SUPERMARKETS

Champion Supermarket, Las Ramblas, 113 (☎93 302 48 24). M: Liceu, L3. From Liceu, walk up Las Ramblas and look to the left. All the essentials, as well as an inexpensive menu of ready-to-eat foods (meats €6 per kg and up) and a salad bar. Open M-Sa 9:15am-10pm.

Condis, Junta de Comerç, 19, in **El Raval,** off C. Hospital. Open M-Th 9am-2pm and 5pm-9pm, F-Sa 9am-9pm.

El Corte Inglés, Pl. de Catalunya, 14 (☎93 306 38 00). M: Catalunya, L1/3. The Spanish superstore has a sizable supermarket on its basement level, with a more exotic variety of items than most local places.

TAXIS

RadioTaxi (☎93 225 00 00).

Servi Taxi (☎93 330 03 00; www.servitaxi.com).

Taxi Barcelona (☎93 090 09 08; www.taxibarcelona.com).

Taxigroc (☎93 490 22 22; www.taxigroc.com).

Taxi 033 (☎93 303 30 33; www.taxi033.com).

Disabled travelers should call ☎93 420 80 88.

TELEPHONE INTERNATIONAL ACCESS NUMBERS
See **Once In,** p. 30.

TICKETS
See also theater venues in **Entertainment,** p. 167.

Tel Entrada (☎902 10 12 12). Call for information, listings, and reservations to theatrical and musical performances.

TOURS
Bus Turístic: The easiest place to hop on the Bus Turístic is Pl. de Catalunya, in front of El Corte Inglés. Buses run daily (except Dec. 25 and Jan. 1) every 10-30min. 9am-9:30pm. Purchase tickets on the bus, at the Pl. de Catalunya tourist office, or at Estació Barcelona-Sants. 1-day pass €14, ages 4-12 €8; 2-day pass €18.

Ruta del Modernisme: Passes (€3; students, over 65, and groups over 10 people €2 per person) are good for a month and give holders a 25-30% discount on entrance fees to major Modernist attractions. Purchase passes at Casa Amatller, Pg. de Gràcia, 41, near the intersection with C. Consell de Cent (☎93 488 01 39). For information on which sights the pass offers discounts to, see p. 51.

Walking Tours of the Barri Gòtic (☎906 301 282). Sa-Su at 10am in English and noon in Catalan and Spanish. Group size is limited; buy tickets in advance. €6.60, ages 4-12 €3.

TOURIST OFFICES
Tourist Info Line: ☎90 730 12 82, from abroad ☎93 368 97 31 30.

Aeroport El Prat de Llobregat (☎93 478 05 65), in the international terminal. English-speaking agents offer information on Catalunya and Barcelona, maps, and hotel reservations. Open daily 9am-9pm.

Informació Turística Plaça Catalunya, Pl. Catalunya, 17S, below Pl. de Catalunya. M: Catalunya, L1/3. Open daily 9am-9pm.

Informació Turística Plaça Sant Jaume, Pl. Sant Jaume, 1, off C. Ciutat. M: Jaume I, L4. Open M-Sa 10am-8pm, Su 10am-2pm.

Oficina de Turisme de Catalunya, Palau Robert, Pg. de Gràcia, 107 (☎93 238 40 00; fax 93 292 12 70; www.gencat.es/probert). M: Diagonal, L3/5. Open M-Sa 10am-7pm, Su 10am-2pm.

TRANSPORTATION SERVICES
See also **Airlines** (p. 309), **Bike and Moped Rental** (p. 309), **Buses** (p. 310), **Car Rental** (p. 310), and **Taxis** (p. 312).

Airport: El Prat de Llobregat (☎93 298 38 38; www.aena.es/ae/bcn/homepage), 12km (8 mi.) southwest of Barcelona; see **Once in Barcelona,** p. 21.

Buses: Barcelona Nord Estació d'Autobuses, C. Ali-bei, 80 (☎90 230 32 22). M: Arc de Triomf, exit to Nàpols. Info office open daily 7am-9pm.

Trains: Estació Barcelona-Sants, in Pl. Països Catalans. M: Sants-Estació, L3/5. Buses to the station include #30 from Pl. de Espanya 44, through l'Eixample (stops at La Sagrada Família), and N2. Station open M-F 4:30am-midnight, Sa-Su 5am-midnight. See **Once In Barcelona,** p. 22.

Estació França (☎902 24 02 02), Av. Marqués de l'Argentera. M: Barceloneta. Buses include #17 from Pl. de Catalunya and N6. Open daily 7am-10pm.

RENFE, 24hr. info ☎902 24 02 02; www.renfe.es.

TRAVEL AGENTS
See **Budget and Student Travel Agencies,** p. 313.

WESTERN UNION
Most *correos y telégrafos* (post offices) offer Western Union services. Check www.westernunion.com for exact locations.

Admon Manuel Martín, Las Ramblas, 41. Open daily 9am-midnight.

YOUTH SERVICES
Centre d'Informació Assesorament per a Joves, C. Ferrán, 32 (☎93 402 78 00; www.bcn.es/ciaj). M: Liceu, L3. 1 block off Las Ramblas. More of a student assistance office than a travel agency. No tickets for sale, but plenty of free advice and a bulletin board with youth events and opportunities. Excellent library of travel guides for browsing. Open M-F 10am-2pm and 4-8pm.

Appendix

SPANISH & CATALAN PHRASEBOOK

THE BASICS

ENGLISH	CATALAN	SPANISH
Hello	Hola	Hola
Good morning	Bon dia	Buenos días
Good afternoon	Bona tarde	Buenas tardes
Good night	Bona nit	Buenas noches
Goodbye	Adéu	Adiós
Please	Si us plau	Por favor
Thank you	Gràcies	Gracias
You're welcome	De res	De nada
Excuse me	Perdoni	Perdón
I don't understand Catalan/Spanish	No entenc català/castellà	No entiendo catalán/castellaño
Do you speak English?	Parleu anglès?	¿Habla inglés?
Can you repeat that?	Pot repetir-lo?	¿Puede repetirlo?

DIRECTIONS

ENGLISH	CATALAN	SPANISH
Where is/are...?	On està/esten...?	¿Dónde está/están...?
...the bathroom	...els lavabos	...los aseos/servicios
...the train station	...estació de trenes	...la estación de trenes
...the church/the mueum	...l'església/el museu	...la iglesia/el museo
...the hostel	...l'hostal	...el hostal
...the store/the market	...magatzem/el mercat	...la tienda/el mercado
...the pharmacy/the hospital	...la farmàcia/l'hospital	...la farmacia/el hospital
Turn right/left	Giri al dret/esquerre	Doble a la derecha/izquierda
Is it near/far from here?	Es prop/lluny?	¿Está cerca/lejos de aquí?
street/corner/block	carre/cantonada/illa	calle/esquina/cuadra

ACCOMMODATIONS & TRANSPORTATION

ENGLISH	CATALAN	SPANISH
Do you have...?	Té...?	¿Tiene...?
...a single room/double room?	...una habitació individual/doble?	...una habitación individual/doble?
...for two people	...per dues persones	...para dos personas
I need another key/towel/pillow	Necesito altra llave/tovallola/coixí	Necesito otra llave/toalla/almohada
bath/shower/water	bany/dutxa/agua	baño/ducha/agua
I am going to stay for (three) days	Em poso (tres) dias	Me voy a quedar (tres) días
Could I see a room?	Pue veure una habitació?	¿Podría ver una habitación?

I would like to reserve a room	Vull reservar una habitació	Quisiera reservar una habitación
There are cockroaches in my room	Hi ha escarabat en la meva habitació	Hay cucarachas en mi habitación
How much does it cost?	Quan és?	¿Cuánto cuesta?
I would like a train ticket	Voldria un bitllet	Quisiera un billete
a round-trip ticket	un bitllet d'anar i tornar	un billete de ida y vuelta
At what time does it leave/arrive?	A quina hora va/llega?	¿A qué hora sale/llega?
Which bus goes to...?	Quin autobús va a...?	¿Cuál autobús tiene servicio a...?

NUMBERS

ENGLISH	CATALAN	SPANISH
1	un/una	uno
2	dos/dues	dos
3	tres	tres
4	quatre	cuatro
5	cinc	cinco
6	sis	seis
7	set	siete
8	vuit	ocho
9	nou	nueve
10	deu	diez
11	onze	once
12	dotze	doce
13	tretze	trece
14	catorze	catorce
15	quinze	quince
16	setze	dieciseis
17	disset	diecisiete
18	divuit	dieciocho
19	dinou	diecinueve
20	vint	veinte
21	vint-i-un	veintiuno
22	vint-i-dos	veintidos
23	vint-i-tres	veintitres
30	trenta	treinta
40	quaranta	cuarenta
50	cinquant	cincuenta
60	seixanta	sesenta
70	setanta	setenta
80	vuitanta	ochenta
90	nouranta	noventa
100	cent	cien

METRIC CONVERSIONS

1 foot (ft.) = 0.30 meter (m)	1m = 3.28 ft.
1 mile (mi.) = 1.61 kilometers (km)	1km = 0.62 mi.
1 pound (lb.) = 0.45 kilogram (kg)	1kg = 2.2 lb.
1 gallon (gal.) = 4 quarts (qt.) = 3.78 liters (L)	1L = 1.06 qt.= 0.264 gal.

DAYS

ENGLISH	CATALAN	SPANISH
Monday	dilluns	lunes
Tuesday	dimarts	martes
Wednesday	dimecres	miércoles
Thursday	dijous	jueves
Friday	divendres	viernes
Saturday	dissabte	sábado
Sunday	diumenge	domingo
today	avui	hoy
tomorrow	demà	mañana
yesterday	ahir	ayer
week	setmana	semana
weekend	cap de setmana	fin de semana

AVERAGE TEMPERATURES

AVG. TEMP	JANUARY	APRIL	JULY	OCTOBER
F°	40-55	50-64	69-79	54-70
C°	4-13	10-18	22-26	12-21

SIZE CONVERSIONS

WOMEN'S CLOTHING

US SIZE	4	6	8	10	12	14	16
UK SIZE	6	8	10	12	14	16	18
EUROPE SIZE	36	38	40	42	44	46	48

WOMEN'S SHOES

US SIZE	5	6	7	8	9	10	11
UK SIZE	3	4	5	6	7	8.5	10
EUROPE SIZE	36	37	38	39	40	41	42

MEN'S SUITS/JACKETS

US/UK SIZE	32	34	36	38	40	42	44
EUROPE SIZE	42	44	46	48	50	52	54

MEN'S SHIRTS

US/UK SIZE	14	14.5	15	15.5	16	16.5	17
EUROPE SIZE	36	37	38	39	40	41	42

MEN'S SHOES

US SIZE	6	7	8	9	10	11	12
UK SIZE	5.5	6.5	7.5	8.5	9.5	10.5	11.5
EUROPE SIZE	38.5	39.5	40.5	41.5	42.5	43.5	44.5

Index

T

Wilfred the Hairy. See Guifré
  el Pilós
windsurfing
    Formentera 269
    Tossa de Mar 231
Wok & Bol 128
women travelers 290
work permits 277
working 304
World Trade Center 95

X

Xaloc 119
Xampanyet 122

Xavi Petit 135

Y

youth hostels
    Alberg Platja de Palma (HI)
      255
    Albergue de Juventud Kabul
      189
    Albergue Juvenil Palau (HI)
      189
    Albergue Mare de Déu de
      Montserrat (HI) 199
    Albergue-Residència Cerverí
      de Girona (HI) 213

youth services 313

Z

Zahara 133
Zara 177
Zeus 180
Zona Alta
    accommodations 199
    food 134
    nightlife 156
    orientation 15
    sights & museums 100
zoo 74

Let's Go Phonecard
your global phonecard with more!

LET'S GO

JOIN NOW & receive
$5
BONUS talk time!*

www.letsgo.ekit.com

- Save up to 70% on calls from over 55 countries
- Family & friends can leave you voicemail messages for FREE
- Choose your own Account Number and PIN
- Recharge your account anywhere, anytime - over the phone or the web

TO JOIN OVER THE PHONE: In the US dial 1-800-706-1333
then press **0** **#** to speak with a Customer Service Consultant.
Visit **www.letsgo.ekit.com** for Access Numbers in over 55 countries.

TO JOIN OVER THE WEB: Visit www.letsgo.ekit.com and click 'Join eKit.'

Quote reference code **LGBAR2004** when joining to receive
your $5 BONUS.*

Download a full list of Access Numbers and Instructions for your Let's Go
Phonecard - **visit www.letsgo.ekit.com** and click on 'User Guide.'

LGO031 Aug03

For assistance and information about additional features
contact 24-hour Customer Service
or visit **www.letsgo.ekit.com**

Powered by
ekit

*$5 bonus on initial charge of $20. All amounts in US$. All information correct at time of printing Aug 2003.

Map Appendix

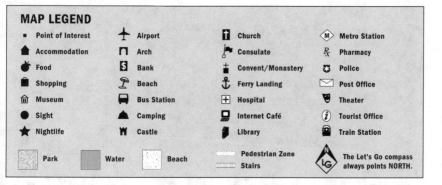

MAP LEGEND

■ Point of Interest	✈ Airport	⛪ Church	Ⓜ Metro Station
🏠 Accommodation	⊓ Arch	⚑ Consulate	℞ Pharmacy
🍴 Food	🟦 Bank	✝ Convent/Monastery	✚ Police
🛍 Shopping	🏖 Beach	⚓ Ferry Landing	✉ Post Office
🏛 Museum	🚌 Bus Station	✚ Hospital	🎭 Theater
● Sight	▲ Camping	💻 Internet Café	ⓘ Tourist Office
★ Nightlife	🏰 Castle	📖 Library	🚆 Train Station

Park	Water	Beach	▨ Pedestrian Zone	The Let's Go compass
			▨ Stairs	always points NORTH.

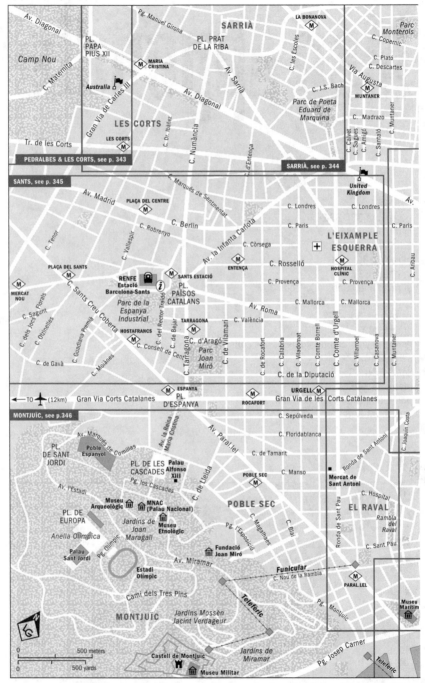

Av. Diagonal

Pg. Manuel Girona

SARRIÀ

LA BONANOVA Ⓜ

Parc Monterols

C. Copernic

Camp Nou

PL. PAPA PIUS XII

PL. PRAT DE LA RIBA

C. les Escoles

C. Plató

C. Descartes

Via Augusta

Ⓜ MARIA CRISTINA

Av. Sarrià

C. J.S. Bach

Ⓜ MUNTANER

Australia 🚩

Gran Via de Carles III

Av. Diagonal

Parc de Poeta Eduard de Marquina

C. Madrazo

C. Maternita

C. Calvet

C. Sagués

C. Amigó

C. Santaló

C. Muntaner

LES CORTS

C. Dr. Ibáñez

C. Numància

d'Entença

Tr. de les Corts

LES CORTS Ⓜ

PEDRALBES & LES CORTS, see p. 343

SARRIÀ, see p. 344

United Kingdom

SANTS, see p. 345

Av. Madrid

C. Marquès de Sentmenat

Av.

PLAÇA DEL CENTRE Ⓜ

C. Berlín

C. Londres

C. Londres

C. Arbau

C. Tenor

C. Robrenyo

C. Paris

C. Paris

Av. la Infanta Carlota

C. Vallespir

C. Còrsega

L'EIXAMPLE ESQUERRA ✚

PLAÇA DEL SANTS Ⓜ

ENTENÇA Ⓜ

C. Rosselló

HOSPITAL CLÍNIC

MERCAT NOU Ⓜ

RENFE Estació Barcelona-Sants ℹ

Ⓜ SANTS ESTACIÓ

C. Provença

C. Provença

C. Sants Creu Coberta

PL. PAÏSOS CATALANS

Parc de la Espanya Industrial

C. del Rector Triadó

C. Mallorca

C. Mallorca

C. dels Jocs Florals

C. Obrineles

C. Sagunt

C. Guadiana Pemià

TARRAGONA

Av. Roma

HOSTAFRANCS Ⓜ

Ⓜ TARRAGONA

C. de Béjar

C. Tarragona

C. de Vilamarí

C. València

C. d'Aragó

C. de Rocafort

C. Calàbria

C. Viladomat

C. Comte Borrell

C. Comte d'Urgell

C. Villarroel

C. Casanova

C. Muntaner

C. de Gavà

C. de Moianes

C. Consell de Cent

Parc Joan Miró

C. de la Diputació

Ⓜ ESPANYA

URGELL Ⓜ

⬅ TO ✈ (12km) Gran Via Corts Catalanes

PL. D'ESPANYA

Ⓜ ROCAFORT

Gran Via de les Corts Catalanes

C. Joaquim Costa

MONTJUÏC, see p.346

C. Sepúlveda

C. Floridablanca

Av. Marquès de Comillas

Av. la Reina Maria Cristina

Av. Paral·lel

Ronda de Sant Antoni

PL. DE SANT JORDI

Poble Espanyol

C. de Tamarit

PL. DE LES CASCADES

Palau Alfonso XIII

C. de Lleida

POBLE SEC Ⓜ

C. Manso

Mercat de Sant Antoni

Av. l'Estadi

Pg. los Cascades

POBLE SEC

C. Hospital

EL RAVAL

Museu Arqueològic 🏛

🏛 MNAC (Palau Nacional)

Ronda de Sant Pau

Rambla del Raval

PL. DE EUROPA

Jardins de Joan Maragall

🏛 Museu Etnològic

Pg. l'Exposició

C. Magalhaes

C. Blai

C. Sant Pau

Anella Olímpica

🏛 Fundació Joan Miró

Palau Sant Jordi

Pg. Olímpic

Av. Miramar

Funicular

C. Nou de la Rambla

Museu Marítim 🏛

Estadi Olímpic

Ⓜ PARAL·LEL

Camí dels Tres Pins

Teleféric

Pg. Monjuic

MONTJUÏC

Jardins Mossèn Jacint Verdaguer

Jardins de Miramar

Pg. Josep Carner

Teleféric

0 ___ 500 meters

0 ___ 500 yards

Castell de Montjuïc 🏰

🏛 Museu Militar

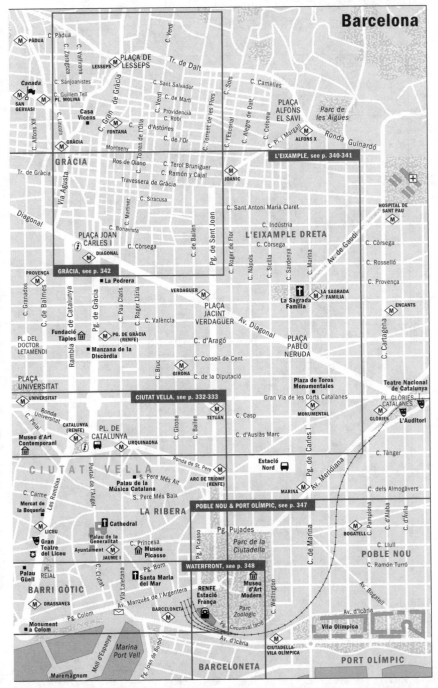

Barcelona

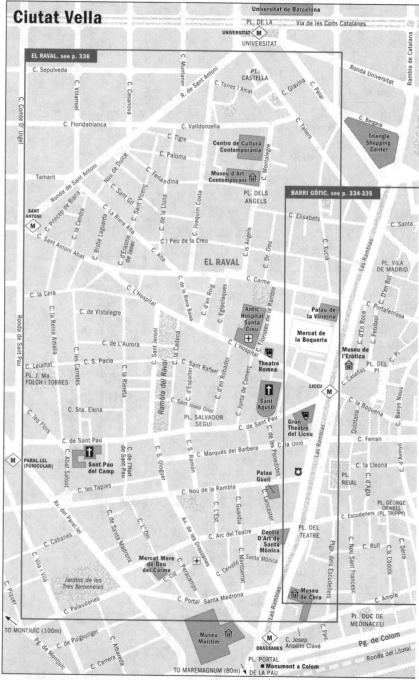

Ciutat Vella

Universitat de Barcelona
PL. DE LA
UNIVERSITAT M
UNIVERSITAT
Via de les Corts Catalanes

EL RAVAL, see p. 336

EL RAVAL, see p. 336

C. Sepulveda
C. Villaroel
C. Comte D' Urgel
C. Muntaner
R. de Sant Antoni
C. Torres I Amat
PL. CASTELLA
C. Gravina
C. Pelai
Ronda Universitat
Rambla de Catalana

C. Casanova
C. Floridablanca
C. Valldonzella
C. Fallers
C. Bergara

C. Tigre
C. Paloma
Centro de Cultura Contemporània
Triangle Shopping Center

Tamarit
Ronda de Sant Antoni
Nou de Dulce
C. Ferlandina
Museu d'Art Contemporani
C. Montalegre
PL. DELS ANGELS

SANT ANTONI M
C. Princep de Biana
C. Sant Gil
C. Sant Vicenç
C. de la Lluna
C. Joaquim Costa
C.ls Angels
BARRI GÒTIC, see p. 334-335

BARRI GÒTIC, see p. 334-335

C. la Cendra
C. La Riera Alta
C. Bisbe Laguarda
C. d'Erasme de Janer
C. Alta
C.l Peu de la Creu
C. Elisabets
C. Santa

C. Sant Antoni Abat
C. Dr. Dou
C. Xuclà
PL. VILA DE MADRID

C. la Cera
C. L'Hospital
C. de la Riera Baixa
C. en Roig
C. Egipciaques
EL RAVAL
C. Carme
Palau de la Virreina
C. D'En Bot
C. D'En Roca
C. Portaferrissa
C. Petritxol

C. de Vistalegre
C. Sant Jeroni
C. de la Cadena
Antic Hospital Santa Creu
Mercat de la Boqueria
C. Casanas
Museu de l'Eròtica
PL. DEL PI

C. de L'Aurora
C. S. Pacia
C. d'Espalter
C. Sant Rafael
C. Floristes de la Rambla
C. L'Hospital
Theatre Romea
C. la Boqueria
C. Banys Nous

C. les Carretes
C. la Riereta
C. Junta de Comerç
C. d'en Robador
Sant Agustí
LICEU M
C. Ferran

C. Leialtat
PL. J. Ma. FOLCH i TORRES
Rambla del Raval
C. Sant Josep Oriol
PL. SALVADOR SEGUÍ
C. de Sant Pau
Gran Theatre del Liceu
C. la Lleona
C. d'Aviñó

C. Sta. Elena
C. les Flors
C. de Sant Pau
Sant Pau del Camp
C. de l'Hort de Sant Pau
C. Marqués del Barbera
C. la Unió
PL. REIAL
C. d'Agla

PARAL.LEL (FUNICULAR) M
C. Abat Sàfont
C. S. Ologuer
C. S. Ramón
Palau Güell
PL. GEORGE ORWELL (PL. TRIPPY)
C. Escudellers
C. Nou Sant Francesc
C. Serra

C. les Tapies
C. de l'Est
C. Guarda
C. Nou de la Rambla
C. Lancaster
PL. DEL TEATRE
C. Rull
C. ls Còdols

Av. del Paral.lel
C. Cabanes
C. de Santa Madrona
C. L'Om
Arc del Teatre
Centre D'Art de Santa Mònica
Pge. dels Escudellers
C. Ample

C. Vila i Vilá
Jardins de les Tres Xemeneies
Mercat Mere de Deu del Carme
C. Peracamps
C. Cid
C. Cerveró
C. Montserrat
Santa Mònica
Museu de Cera
PL. DUC DE MEDINACELI

C. Piquer
C. Palaudàries
Las Ramblas
Pge. dels
Pg. de Colom

TO MONTJUÏC (100m)
C. de Puigxuriger
Museu Marítim
DRASSANES M
C. Josep Anselm Clavé
Ronda del Litoral

C. Albareda
C. Carrera
PL. PORTAL DE LA PAU
Monument a Colom
Pg. de Montjuïc

TO MAREMAGNUM (80m)

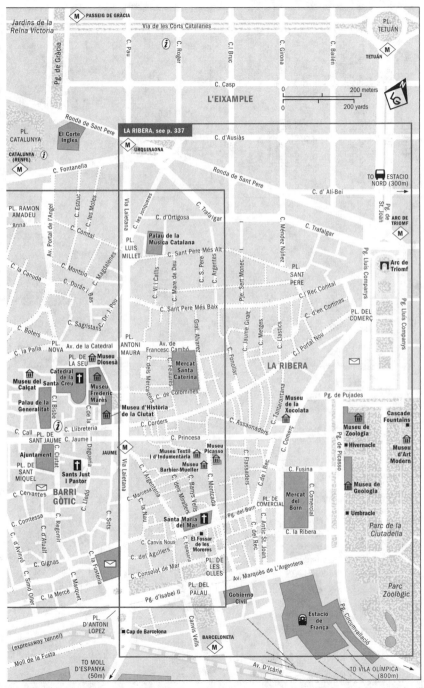

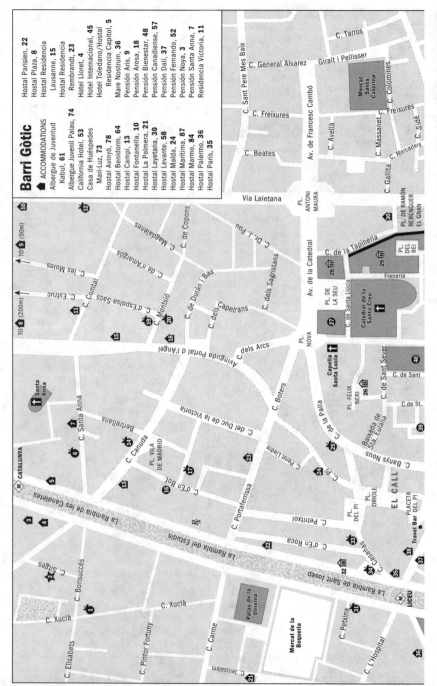

Barri Gòtic

♦ ACCOMMODATIONS

Albergue de Juventud
  Kabul, **61**
Albergue Juvenil Palau, **74**
California Hotel, **53**
Casa de Huéspedes
  Mari-Luz, **73**
Hostal Avinyó, **78**
Hostal Benidorm, **64**
Hostal Campi, **13**
Hostal Fontanella, **10**
Hostal La Palmera, **21**
Hostal Layetana, **30**
Hostal Levante, **58**
Hostal Malda, **24**
Hostal Marítima, **87**
Hostal Marmo, **84**
Hostal Palermo, **36**
Hostal Paris, **35**

Hostal Parisien, **22**
Hostal Plaza, **8**
Hostal Residencia
  Lausanne, **15**
Hostal Residencia
  Rembrandt, **23**
Hotel Lloret, **4**
Hotel Internacional, **45**
Hotel Toledano/Hostal
  Residencia Capitol, **5**
Mare Nostrum, **36**
Pensión Arís, **9**
Pensión Arosa, **18**
Pensión Bienestar, **48**
Pensión Canadiense, **57**
Pensión Dalí, **37**
Pensión Fernando, **52**
Pensión Noya, **3**
Pensión Santa Anna, **7**
Residencia Victoria, **11**

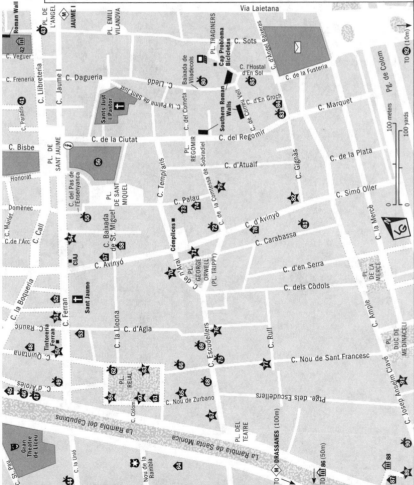

● FOOD
L'Antic Bocoi del Gòtic, **80**
Arc Café, **81**
The Bagel Shop, **14**
Bar Ra, **44**
Betawi, **20**
Buenas Migas, **1**
Buen Bocado, **68**
Café de l'Opera, **47**
Los Caracoles, **75**
La Colmena, **43**
Escribà, **31**
Govinda, **17**
Irati, **33**
Italiano's, **46**
Juicy Jones, **34**
Kamasawa, **69**
Il Mercante Di Venezia, **90**
Maoz Falafel, **49**
Mi Burrito y Yo, **55**
Oolong, **83**
Els Quatre Gats, **19**
Les Quinze Nits, **62**
Restaurante Self
  Naturista, **6**
El Salón, **85**
Terrablava, **12**
Thiossan, **66**
Venus Delicatessen, **72**
Xaloc, **25**

Museu de Cera, **88**
Museu de l'Eròtica, **32**
Museu d'Història de la
  Ciutat, **42**
Museu Diocesà, **28**
Museu Frederic Marès, **29**

● SIGHTS
Ajuntament, **56**
Cap de Barcelona, **92**
Casa de l'Ardiaca, **27**
Hebrew Plaque, **39**
Palau de la Generalitat, **40**
Roman Tombs, **16**
Temple of Augustus, **41**

★ NIGHTLIFE
Barcelona Pipa Club, **59**
El Bosq de les Fades, **89**
Café Royale, **65**
Casa El Agüelo, **82**
Dot Light Club, **77**
Fonfone, **76**
Glaciar Bar, **63**
Harlem Jazz Club, **79**
Jamboree, **60**
Bar Ovisos, **70**
Margarita Blue, **91**
Molly's Fair City, **50**
New York, **67**
La Oveja Negra, **2**
Schilling, **51**
La Verónica, **71**
Vildsvin, **54**

🏛 MUSEUMS
Centre d'Art de Santa
  Monica, **86**
Museu del Calçat, **26**

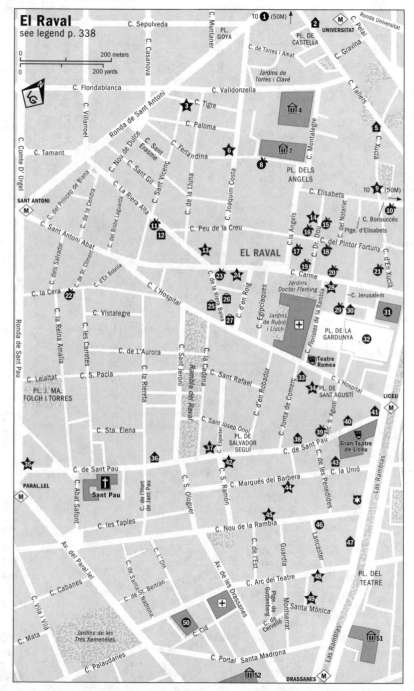

El Raval
see legend p. 338

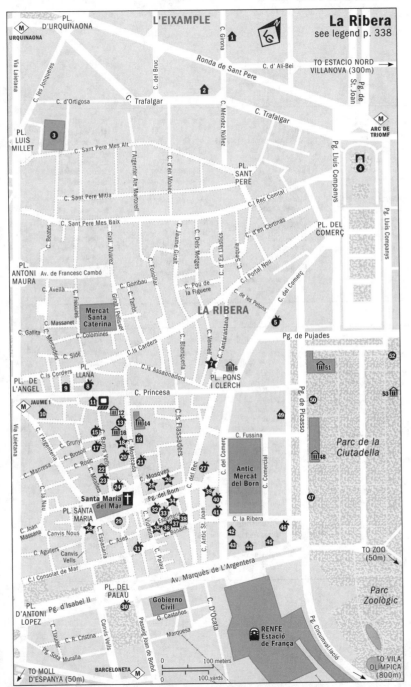

El Raval
see map p. 336

🏠 ACCOMMODATIONS
Barcelona Mar
  Youth Hostel, **36**
Hostal Benidorm, **47**
Hostal Opera, **40**
Hostal La Palmera, **30**
Hostal La Terrassa, **33**
Hotel Peninsular, **38**
Ideal Youth Hostel, **43**
Mare Nostrum, **41**
Pensión 45, **5**
Pensión L'Isard, **2**

🍎 FOOD
Bar Ra, **29**

Bar Restaurante Los
  Toreros, **21**
Bar Restaurante Romesco, **39**
Buenas Migas, **10**
Carmelitas, **19**
Colibri, **11**
Dos Trece, **20**
L'Hortet, **16**
Mamacafé, **15**
Pla dels Angels, **8**
Restaurante Biocenter, **18**
Restaurante Can Lluís, **22**
Shalimar, **23**
Silenus, **17**

🛍 SHOPPING
Discos Edison's, **26**
GI Joes Surplus, **27**

Mies & Felj, **25**
Zeus, **12**

🏛 MUSEUMS
Centre de Cultura
  Contemporània, **4**
Museu d'Art Contemporani, **7**
Museu de Cera, **51**
Museu Marítim, **52**

⬤ SIGHTS
Mercat de la Boqueria, **32**
Mercat de Deu del Carme, **50**
Palau Güell, **46**
Palau de la Virreina, **31**
Universitat de Barcelona, **1**

⭐ NIGHTLIFE
El Cafe que pone
  Muebles Navarro, **13**
Casa Almirall, **6**
La Confiteria, **35**
London Bar, **45**
Lupino, **28**
Marsella Bar, **42**
Moog, **48**
Muy Buenas, **24**
La Paloma, **3**
Pastis, **49**
La Oveja Negra, **9**
The Quiet Man, **44**
Raval-Bar, **14**
Rita Blue, **34**
Sant Pau 68, **37**

La Ribera
see map p. 337

🏠 ACCOMMODATIONS
Gothic Point Youth Hostal, **10**
Hostal de Ribagorza, **2**
Hostal Nuevo Colón, **45**
Hostal Orleans, **44**
Hotel Triunfo, **49**
Pensión Ciutadella, **43**
Pensión Lourdes, **11**
Pensión Port-bou, **42**
Pensión Rondas, **1**

🍎 FOOD
Barcelónia, **41**
Bodega la Tinaja, **33**
Café del Born, **40**
Cal Pep, **31**
La Cocotte, **32**
Euskal Etxea, **21**
Gades, **36**
La Habana Vieja, **15**

El Pebre Blau, **24**
Restaurant 7 Portes, **30**
Sandwich and Friends, **27**
Suborn, **46**
Taira, **5**
Tèxtil Café, **13**
Tomate, **24**
Txirimiri, **8**
Va de Vi, **17**
Xampanyet, **20**

🛍 SHOPPING
0,925 Argenters, **19**
Arlequí Máscares, **9**
Farcells, **22**
Las 40 Ladronas, **38**
Outlet del Born, **37**

🏛 MUSEUMS
Museu Barbier-Mueller, **16**
Museu d'Art Modern, **53**
Museu de Geologia, **48**
Museu de la Xocolata, **6**

Museu de Zoologia, **51**
Museu Picasso, **14**
Museu Textil i d'Indumentària, **12**

⬤ SIGHTS
Arc de Triomf, **4**
Cascade Fountains, **52**
El Fossar de les Moreres, **29**
Hivernacle, **50**
Palau de la Música Catalana, **3**
Umbracle, **47**

⭐ NIGHTLIFE
El Born, **34**
El Copetin, **26**
Mudanzas, **35**
Palau Dalmase, **18**
Pitin Bar, **39**
Plàstic Café, **26**
Upiaywasi, **7**
La Vinya del Senyor, **28**

L'Eixample
see map pp. 340-341

L'Eixample

see key p. 339

Travessera de Gràcia

C. Granada del Penedès

C. Lluis Atúnez

C. Buenos Aires

TO 3 (300m) & 4 (500m)

TO 5 (100m)

C. Londres

Av. Diagonal

TO 8 (30m)

C. Paris

L'EIXAMPLE ESQUERRA

C. Còrsega

Riera San Miquel

Gran de Gràcia

C. St. Pere Màrtir

C. Maspons

C. Penedès

C. Puigmarti

C. Goya

C. Diluvi

C. Siracusa

Via Augusta

Casablanca

C. Sèneca

C. Mozart

C. F. Giner

C. M. de la Rosa

C. de Progrés

C. de Tordera

C. Torres

C. de la Libertat

C. Bonavista

C. del Torrent de l'Olla

C. del Perill

PL. JOAN CARLES I

C. Rosselló

DIAGONAL

C. Muntaner

C. Aribau

C. Enrique Granados

C. Balmes

Rambla de Catalunya

Pg. de Gràcia

Av. Diagonal

C. Provença

C. Mallorca

C. València

PL. DOCTOR LETAMENDI

PASSEIG DE GRÀCIA

C. de Roger de Llúria

C. Bruc

C. Diputació

Universitat de Barcelona

TO 68 (300m), 69 & 70 (800m)

PL. DE LA UNIVERSITAT

UNIVERSITAT

C. de Pau Claris

GIRONA

Ronda Universitat

Av. Gran Via de les Corts Catalanes

PASSEIG DE GRÀCIA

TO 84 (100m)

Ronda de Sant Antoni

C. Tallers

PL. DE CASTELLA

C. Valldonzella

C. de Casp

Bus Stop for Airport & Bus Turistic

El Corte Inglés

PL. URQUINAONA

C. Trafalgar

Ronda St. Pere

CATALUNYA

PL. DE CATALUNYA

C. Fontanella

URQUINAONA

Barcelona Allotjament

Ronda Universitat

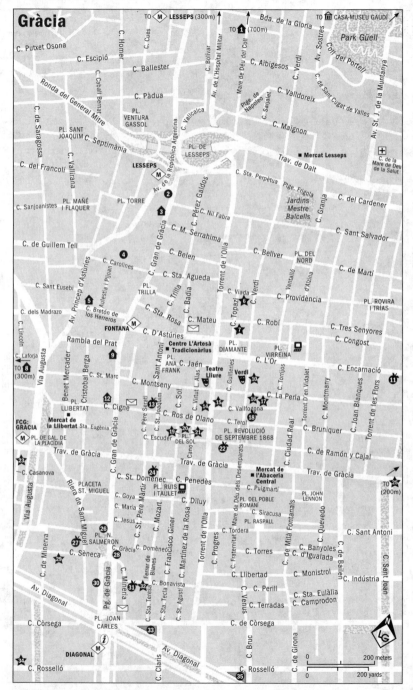

Gràcia

TO Ⓜ **LESSEPS** (300m)

Bda. de la Gloria

TO 🏛 **CASA-MUSEU GAUDÍ**

TO 🏢 (700m)

Park Güell

C. Putxet Osona

C. Escipió

C. Homer

C. Cues

C. Ballester

C. Bolívar

Av. de L'Hospital Militar

Mare de Déu del Coll

C. de Déu, Aïbigesos

C. Verdí

Av. Sostres

Coll del Portell

C. de Sant Cugat de Valles

Ronda del General Mitre

C. Caball Bernat

C. Pàdua

PL. VENTURA GASSOL

C. Vallcalca

Ptge. de Napoleo

C. Sanjalet

C. Valldoreix

C. Maignon

Av. St. J. de la Muntanya

C. de Saragossa

PL. SANT JOAQUIM

C. Septimània

PL. DE LESSEPS

Trav. de Dalt

■ Mercat Lesseps

C. de la Mare de Déu de la Salut

C. del Francolí

C. Vallirana

LESSEPS

Ⓜ

Av. de la República Argentina

C. Sta. Perpètua

Ptge. Frigola

Jardins Mestre Balcells

C. Granja

C. del Cardener

C. Sanjoanistes

PL. MAÑÉ I FLAQUER

PL. TORRE

②

C. Pérez Galdós

C. Nil Fabra

C. Sant Salvador

C. de Guillem Tell

③

C. Gran de Gràcia

C. M. Serrahima

C. Belen

Torrent de l'Olla

C. Bellver

PL. DEL NORD

C. de Martí

④

C. Carolines

C. Sta. Agueda

C. Viada

C. Verdí

C. Ventalló

C. d'Alzina

C. Providència

PL. ROVIRA I TRÍAS

C. Sant Eusebi

C. Príncep d'Astúries

C. Iglesia i Pijoan

PL. TRILLA

C. Trilla

C. Badia

C. Topazi

⑥

C. dels Madrazo

⑤

C. Bretón de los Herreros

C. Sta. Rosa

C. Mateu

C. Robí

C. Tres Senyores

C. Lincoln

FONTANA

Ⓜ ✉

C. D'Astúries

C. Congost

C. Laforja

TO **⑧** (300m)

Via Augusta

Rambla del Prat

Centre L'Artesà ■ Tradicionàrius

PL. DIAMANTE

PL. VIRREINA

C. L'Or

C. Encarnació

⑪

⑨

C. Sant Antoni

PL. ANA L. Alas FRANK

C. Verdí

⑩

Torrent d'En Vidalet

Benet Mercader

Cristobal Berga

C. St. Marc

PL. ANA L. Jaén

Teatre Lliure

C. Guilleries

C. Torrijos

C. La Perla

C. Montmany

C. Joan Blanques

Torrent de les Flors

PL. LLIBERTAT

⑫

C. Cigne

C. Montseny

C. Sol

C. Virtut

⑯

⑰

C. Vallfogona

FCG: GRÀCIA

Mercat de la Llibertat ■

Sta. Eugènia

C. Père Serafí

C. St. Joaquim

⑮

C. Terol

⑱

C. Bruniquer

Ⓜ PL. DE GAL. DE LA PLACÍDIA

C. Ros de Olano

⑲

PL. DEL SOL

C. Cano

PL. REVOLUCIÓ DE SEPTEMBRE 1868

C. Ciudad Real

C. de Ramón y Cajal

㉓

Trav. de Gràcia

C. Escuder

㉒

Trav. de Gràcia

C. Casanova

Riera de Sant Miquel

C. St. Doménec

C. Penedès

Mercat de ■ l'Abaceria Central

Trav. de Gràcia

TO **㉕** (200m)

㉔

PL. RUIS I TAULET

C. Puigmartí

PL. JOHN LENNON

PLACETA ST. MIGUEL

C. Goya

C. Diluy

PL. DEL POBLE ROMANÍ

C. Mila i Fontanals

C. Minerva

C. Gran de Gràcia

C. María

C. Mozart

C. St. Pere Màrtir

Torrent de l'Olla

C. Siracusa

C. Quevedo

C. Sant Antoni

C. Jesús

C. Francisco Giner

PL. RASPALL

C. Sant Joan

㉖

㉗

PL. N. SALMERON

C. Gràcia

C. Doménech

C. Martínez de la Rosa

C. Tordera

C. Torres

C. Banyoles

C. d'Igualada

C. Sèneca

㉘

C. Bonavista

C. Progrés

C. Llibertat

C. Monistrol

C. Indústria

㉚

Pg. de Gràcia

㉛

C. Minería

C. Sta. Teresa

C. Ferrer de Blanes

C. Sta. Tecla

C. St. Agustí

Venus

C. Perill

C. Sta. Eulàlia

C. Camprodon

Av. Diagonal

✉

PL. JOAN CARLES

C. Terradas

C. Còrsega

㉝

C. de Còrsega

C. Bruc

C. de Girona

0   200 meters

㉞

ℹ

DIAGONAL

Ⓜ

C. Claris

Av. Diagonal

㉟

C. Rosselló

C. Rosselló

0   200 yards

Gràcia

🏠 ACCOMMODATIONS
Albergue Mare de Déu de
  Montserrat, **1**
Aparthotel Silver, **5**
Pensión Norma, **12**
Hostal Lesseps, **3**
Hostal Valls, **8**
Pensión San Medín, **9**

🍎 FOOD
Casa Regina, **27**
OvUm, **11**
La Gavina, **13**
Nut, **18**
Restaurant Illa de
  Gràcia, **24**
El Tastavins, **22**
Xavi Petit, **31**

🔴 SIGHTS
Casa Cama, **26**

Casa Comalat, **33**
Casa de les Punxes, **35**
Casa Fuster, **28**
Casa Ramos, **2**
Casa Bonaventura
  Ferrer, **30**
Casa Vicens, **4**

⭐ NIGHTLIFE
Bahía, **29**
Bamboleo, **6**
Blues Café, **16**

Buda, **15**
Cafe del Sol, **20**
Casablanca, **32**
Flann O'Brien's, **23**
Gasterea, **10**
Ikastola, **17**
I qué?, **7**
KGB, **25**
Nick Havanna, **34**
St. Germain, **14**
Sol de Nit, **21**
Sol Soler, **19**

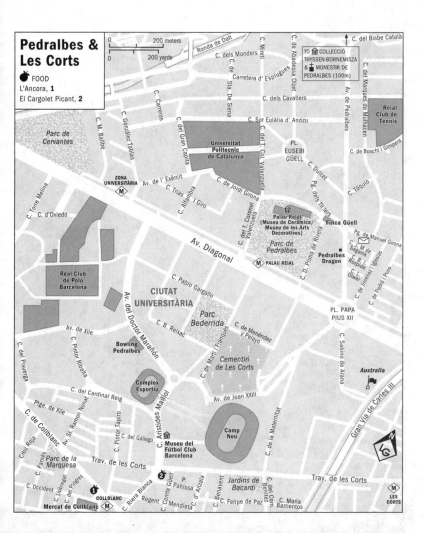

Pedralbes & Les Corts

🍎 FOOD
L'Ancora, **1**
El Cargolet Picant, **2**

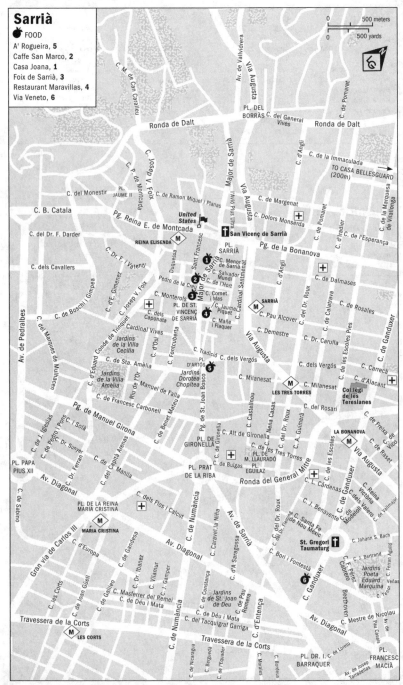

Sarrià
🍎 FOOD

A' Rogueira, **5**
Caffe San Marco, **2**
Casa Joana, **1**
Foix de Sarrià, **3**
Restaurant Maravillas, **4**
Via Veneto, **6**

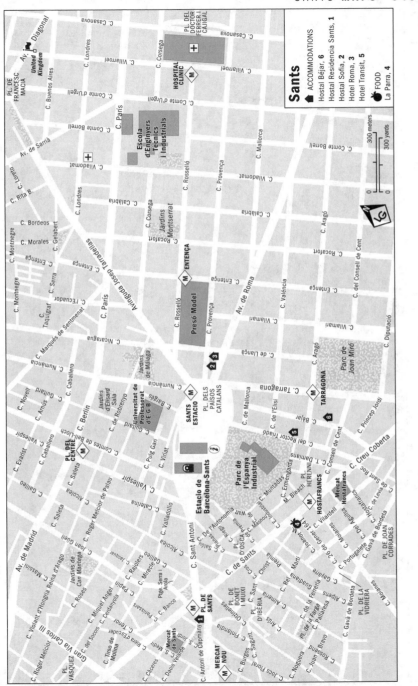

Sants

ACCOMMODATIONS
Hostal Béjar, **6**
Hostal Residencia Sants, **1**
Hostal Sofía, **2**
Hotel Roma, **3**
Hotel Transit, **5**

FOOD
La Parra, **4**

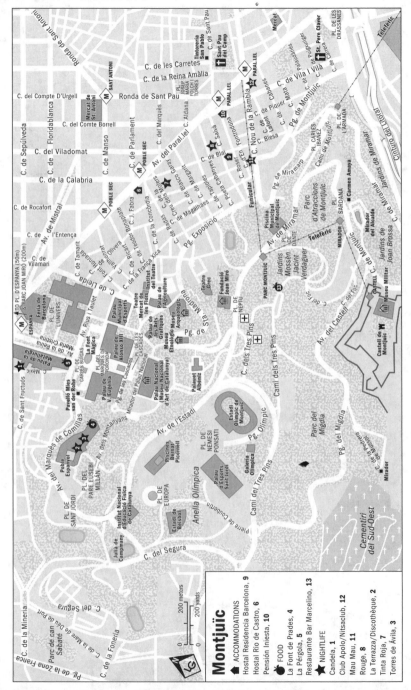

Montjuïc

ACCOMMODATIONS
Hostal Residencia Barcelona, **9**
Hostal Rio de Castro, **6**
Pensión Iniesta, **10**

FOOD
La Font de Prades, **4**
La Pérgola, **5**
Restaurante Bar Marcelino, **13**

NIGHTLIFE
Candela, **1**
Club Apolo/Nitsaclub, **12**
Mau Mau, **11**
Rouge, **8**
La Terrazza/Discothèque, **2**
Tinta Roja, **7**
Torres de Ávila, **3**

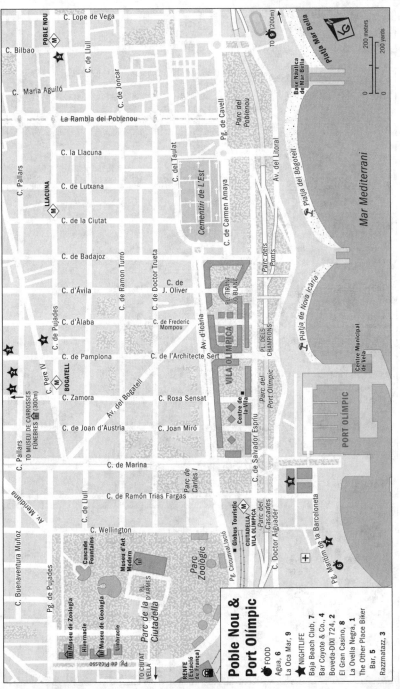

Poble Nou & Port Olímpic

🍴 **FOOD**
Agua, 6
La Oca Mar, 9

⭐ **NIGHTLIFE**
Baja Beach Club, 7
Bar Coyote & Co., 4
Boveda-DiXi 724, 2
El Gran Casino, 8
La Ovella Negra, 1
The Other Place Biker Bar, 5
Razzmatazz, 3

C. Lope de Vega
POBLE NOU Ⓜ
C. Bilbao
C. de Llull
C. Maria Aguiló
C. de Joncar
La Rambla del Poblenou
Pg. de Cavell
C. la Llacuna
C. del Taulat
LLACUNA Ⓜ
C. de Lutxana
Parc del Poblenou
C. de la Ciutat
Cementiri de L'Est
C. Pallars
C. de Badajoz
C. de Carmen Amaya
Av. del Litoral
C. de Ramon Turró
C. d'Àvila
C. de Doctor Trueta
C. de J. Oliver
Parc dels Ports
C. d'Àlaba
C. de Frederic Mompou
PG. TIRANT LO BLANC
C. de Pujades
BOGATELL Ⓜ
C. Pere IV
C. de Pamplona
C. de l'Architecte Sert
Av. d'Icària
VILA OLÍMPICA
PL. DELS CHAMPIONS
C. Zamora
C. Rosa Sensat
Av. del Bogatell
Parc del Port Olímpic
Centre de la Vila
C. de Joan d'Austria
C. de Joan Miró
C. de Salvador Espriu
C. de Marina
Parc de Carles I
PORT OLÍMPIC
Centre Municipal de Vela
C. de Ramón Trias Fargas
Av. Meridiana
C. de Llull
C. Wellington
Pg. del Cascades
CIUTADELLA/ VILA OLÍMPICA Ⓜ
Globus Touristic
Pg. Circumval·lació
C. Doctor Aiguader
Pg. Marítim de la Barceloneta
C. Buenaventura Muñoz
Cascade Fountains
Museu d'Art Modern
Parc Zoològic
PL. D'ARMES
Pg. de Pujades
Museu de Zoologia
Museu de Geologia
Hivernacle
Umbracle
Parc de la Ciutadella
Pg. de Picasso
RENFE (Estació de França)
TO CIUTAT VELLA

TO MUSEU DE CARROSSES FÚNEBRES 🏛 (300m)
C. Pallars

TO ⑨ (200m)
Platja Mar Bella
Base Nàutica de Mar Bella
Mar Mediterrani
Platja del Bogatell
Platja de Nova Icària

0   200 meters
0   200 yards

POBLE NOU

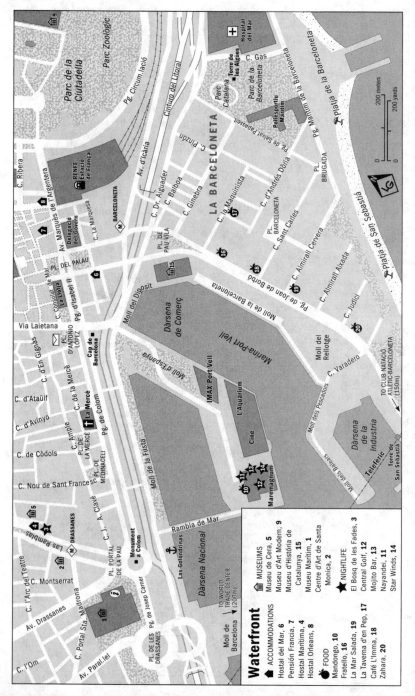

Waterfront

ACCOMMODATIONS
Hostal del Mar, **6**
Pensión Francia, **7**
Hostal Marítima, **4**
Hostal Orleans, **8**

FOOD
Mandongo, **10**
Fratello, **16**
La Mar Salada, **19**
La Taverna d'en Pep, **17**
Café L'Imma, **18**
Zahara, **20**

MUSEUMS
Museu de Cera, **5**
Museu d'Art Modern, **9**
Museu d'Història de
    Catalunya, **15**
Museu Marítim, **1**
Centre d'Art de Santa
    Monica, **2**

NIGHTLIFE
El Bosq de les Fades, **3**
Central Golf, **12**
Mojito Bar, **13**
Nayandei, **11**
Star Winds, **14**

ABOUT LET'S GO

FORTY-THREE YEARS OF WISDOM

For over four decades, travelers have relied on *Let's Go* for inside information on undiscovered backstreet cafes, secluded beaches, and the best routes from border to border. All that is still in there, but this year is different: we've revamped the series to bring you not only the hard facts you need to get around, but also the information you need to make sense of the place you're in. With new features focused on current events, culture, and politics, this year's *Let's Go* series provides depth you won't find in any other guidebook. For the last 20 years, our rugged researchers have stretched the frontiers of backpacking and expanded our series into Australia, Asia, Africa, and the Americas. This year we've beefed up our coverage of Latin America with *Let's Go: Costa Rica* and *Let's Go: Chile*. On the other side of the globe we've added *Let's Go: Thailand* and *Let's Go: Hawaii*. Some say you can't go to Hawaii without breaking the bank, but we beg to differ.

It all started in 1960 when a handful of well-traveled students at Harvard University handed out a 20-page mimeographed pamphlet offering a collection of their tips on budget travel to passengers on student charter flights to Europe. The following year, in response to the popularity of the first volume, students researched the first full-fledged edition of *Let's Go: Europe*. Throughout the 60s and 70s, our guides reflected the times—in 1969, for example, we taught you how to get from Paris to Prague on "no dollars a day" by singing in the street. In the 90s we focused on producing guides that showed how to get off the beaten path and experience destinations without hordes of tourists in the way. Now in its 43rd edition and translated into seven languages, *Let's Go: Europe* reigns as the world's bestselling travel guide. Our new guides bring the total number of titles to 61, each infused with the spirit of adventure that travelers around the world have come to count on. But some things never change: our guides are still researched, written, and produced entirely by students who know first-hand how to see the world on the cheap.

WHY WE DO IT

We don't think of budget travel as the last recourse of the destitute; we believe that it's the only way to travel. Our books will ease your anxieties and answer your questions about the basics, so you can get off the beaten track and explore. Once you learn the ropes, we encourage you to put *Let's Go* down and strike out on your own. You know as well as we that the best discoveries are often those you make yourself. When you find something worth sharing, please drop us a line. We're Let's Go Publications, 67 Mount Auburn St., Cambridge, MA 02138, USA (feedback@letsgo.com). For more information visit our new website, feauring our full text, online at www.letsgo.com.

HOW WE DO IT

Every spring, we recruit over 300 well-traveled students to overhaul the series. After several months of training, researcher-writers hit the road for seven weeks of exploration, from Anchorage to Adelaide, Iceland to Indonesia. Hired for their rare combination of travel savvy, writing ability, stamina, and courage, these adventurous travelers know that train strikes, stolen luggage, food poisoning, and marriage proposals are all part of a day's work. Back at our offices, the editors work from spring to fall, massaging copy written on Himalayan bus rides into witty, informative prose. A student staff of typesetters, cartographers, publicists, and managers keeps our lively team together. In September, the collected efforts of the summer are delivered to our printer, turned into books in record time, and delivered to stores so you have the most up-to-date information available for your trip. Even as you read this, work on next year's editions is well underway.